The Dear-Bought Heritage

Landing of De Soto with Francisca Hinestrosa. (From the Collections of the Library of Congress)

The Dear-Bought Heritage

by Eugenie Andruss Leonard

Foreword by Margaret Chase Smith

Philadelphia

University of Pennsylvania Press

7436
Printed in the United States of America

Foreword

The purpose of the author has been to show what the American colonial women brought with them from the seventeen lands of their origins; what they found when they arrived in the new land; and what they did to help in building a nation out of the primeval forests, rolling plains, and snow-capped mountains from ocean to ocean.

She traces the struggle of colonial women in helping their menfolks to build mansions from shanties and dugouts, feeding their families from ghastly want to adequate diets, clothing their families in warmth and comfort, and defending their homes from Indian outbursts of resentment. The list of their accomplishments, in spite of their legal disabilities, is impressive. They are the roots of our present rights and privileges. How women under legal bondage bent the laws to accommodate their contribution to survival necessities is sheer drama. It is not only that they were blacksmiths, doctors, or barbers, but that they augmented the strength and power of the cry for freedom that swept the colonies from Maine to Florida.

All this they did because they believed in themselves as co-tenants in the new land, responsible for adding their contribution to the maintenance and improvement of community living. Their contribution was the prologue to ours today. Only the machinery has changed. They sought to improve social living by the gifts of their abilities and aspirations to the solution of the problems of their day as we, today, seek to use our talents in aiding in the solution of our problems.

MARGARET CHASE SMITH

Preface

The more one delves into the history of the American colonies, the more one is impressed with the magnificent courage of the men and women who came to the strange new land. For it was not the meek and the mild who braved the ocean and came to our shores but the daredevils, the staunch and the courageous. This was equally true for men and women. Hundreds of books have been written about the bravery of the men, which was, indeed, impressive, but one must look long and read many books to gather together even a thin patchwork on the bravery and inventiveness of the women. Sometimes, as I have read volume after volume on colonial life, I have had the strange feeling that women existed only as a kind of ectoplasm that materialized occasionally in some unusual act of heroism. For the most part they fade into the background so effectively that only now and then can you discern the outline of their stature.

Of course, women have always been on the stage of each civilization, but the parts they have played have often been dimly lighted, perhaps only by the glow of the red embers of the cook-fire while the coarse bread baked. This, I think, is natural. The spotlight goes to the returning hero. It is his right, and generally he has recorded it in the histories we read.

If the hearth-fire, where the women huddle, does not burn as brightly, there are many compensations. And if one looks long enough one can find a hero, now and then, who will share the spotlight with the woman he loves.

All this talk about the changing functions of women in society used to disturb me very much, until I was forced by "hidden persuaders" to look painstakingly into the history of their functions. I found that in the six thousand years of recorded history women have had one basic function, namely, the perpetuation of the race. No one has seriously questioned this point. It is rather on the peripheral responsibilities of the maternal function that men and women have clashed.

It has seemed to me that, next to actually conceiving and bearing children, woman's insistent urge through the centuries has been to improve the conditions surrounding their children. First, just to keep the child alive longer, she wrapped it in fur or bark, fed it cooked food, and bathed it in the river. In each succeeding civilization there is evidence that she sought to improve the environment of her children in many ways, but this has meant the expansion of her sphere of work from the small circle of the campfire to the life of the community, the nation, and of the world.

Seventeenth century Europe was just emerging from feudalism when the first colonists boarded their leaky, stinking vessels and sailed westward. They possessed the heritage of fifteen centuries of Christian culture when they faced the primeval forests and the native tribes that inhabited them. Little wonder, looking back, that they changed the face of the land in two brief centuries. And the women—what share had they in this wondrous work? Did they do what women did before them—seek to lengthen and enrich the life of their children? And in what ways?

This is the question I have sought to answer, and all that follows is a part of my learning of the height, and depth, and breadth of the women who dared to venture and share in the building of a nation.

Many People have assisted me in assembling the historical data, especially the staff of librarians in the Thomas Jefferson Room in the Library of Congress, without whose aid I should frequently have been lost. Inspiration and many helpful suggestions have been given me by Sophie Hutchison Drinker, Mary Settle, Regina Reitmeier Rush, and my daughter,; Eugenie Leonard Mitchell.

Contents

DEDICATED TO THE WOMEN OF TODAY

Let it not be greiveous unto you that you have
been instruments to breake the ise for others
who come after with less difficulty, the honour
shall be yours to the world's end.

—William Bradford

Give us a little more time to clean up the
house and fill the lamps. Help us to outlaw
war, prostitution, drunkeness, illness, poverty,
dirt, crime, slums. You'll see!

—Kathleen Norris

List of Illustrations

The Dear-Bought Heritage

1

From Whence They Came

The women of Europe came to the new land bound and free, at the side of their husbands, alone, or leading a company. Wave on wave they came, undeterred by the blood on the ground beneath their feet—some toddling at their mothers' side, some straight and tall, some heavy with child, some bent with labor. None came without fear, none without courage, though for some it was the courage of desperation. These were the women who gave us our "dear-bought" heritage of freedom.

Some came on the arms of their husbands, beloved and respected, the rustle of their silk petticoats soft on the air. Some were dragged from the gutters, the prisons, and slave markets of Europe and Africa with the clank of chains still in their ears. Some were shanghaied or enticed aboard a vessel and sold as wives or bondswomen or slaves at the first convenient landing place. Some were among the boat-loads of shivering children that were shipped to the new world as workers in the fields and nascent factories. They came from many diverse nations and from many divergent cultural patterns.

The first of this long line of women pioneers was a young Spanish woman, Francisca Hinestrosa, wife of Fernando Baustista, who was one of De Soto's soldiers. It was a limpid spring day toward the end of May in 1539 that Francisca Hinestrosa and her companions set foot on the new land and trudged up the shining beaches of what is now Tampa Bay, Florida. What they saw must have been breathtakingly beautiful. The weather was warm, food plentiful, and life in De Soto's elaborate army emcampment not too difficult in the first few months. But as the expeditionary forces moved north and west they met with increasing opposition from the native tribes. The gay tents became tattered and mud drenched, the harnesses mildewed, the glittering armor crusted with rust, and the food scarce and often tainted. Safe sites for the encampment of his men became a crucial problem for De Soto. Whenever possible he took over a deserted native village so that Fancisca and her companions could live in grass or skin huts and cook over the open fires.

By March of 1541, De Soto and his expeditionary forces reached the land of the Chickasaw Indians in what is now northern Mississippi. De Soto's men routed the Chickasaws and took possession of one of the villages for their encampment. In reprisal, the Indians set fire to the village. Francisca, who was expecting her baby in a few days, went back into her hut to save some pearls which represented the family fortune. She was caught in the flames and perished before help could reach her. However, there is some evidence that another woman who accompanied the expedition survived the hardships and returned to Havana, Cuba, with the remnants of De Soto's expeditionary forces.[1]

Twenty years after De Soto's expedition (1559), Don Luis de Velasco, then viceroy of New Spain, started out for the new world from Vera Cruz with thirteen vessels, carrying 1,500 soldiers and a number of women, priests, and other settlers.; These adventurers landed at Pensacola, Florida, but life was so difficult that after two years the few still alive abandoned the colony.[2]

But Spain was not disconcerted by the failure, for the nation was at the height of its glory. Spain's armies had conquered Algeria,; Tripoli, the Netherlands, Milan and Sicily. Her conquistadores had occupied Mexico and the Philippines. Velazques was painting her aristocrats, Cervantes was writing about Don Quixote, and Ignatius Loyola was founding the militant Jesuit order.

Four years later (1563), Pedro Menendez headed a fleet of twenty vessels carrying 2,646 persons from the different ports of Spain.; He had spent fourteen months and more than a million ducats in preparation for the venture. By the time he reached Puerto Rico, two-thirds of his fleet had been lost, but he continued on to St. Augustine, Florida, where he established the first permanent settlement within the present United States.

The women came as members of family groups from various parts of Spain, Portugal, and the Azores. They were daring and resourceful, and though many died from sickness and Indian raids, others took their places, and in doing so they left us a heritage of dauntlessness and vitality which was characteristic of Spain in her glory.[3]

More than a thousand miles to the west other women of Spanish and Mexican descent joined a group of colonizers in 1598 under the leadership of Don Juan de Onate. He collected an expedition in Mexico of four hundred men, of which 130 were members of family groups, and started north to conquer in the name of the Spanish king, Philip III, what is now New Mexico and Arizona.

The women in the expedition came from all walks of life; a few were women of distinction whose names and deeds have been recorded. Onate's wife was Dona Isabel, great-granddaughter of Montezuma and granddaughter of Hernando Cortez. She is said to have been a woman of surpassing beauty and high courage. Dona Maria de Galarca, a sister of Onate's, was a woman of great wealth and influence. Dona Ana de Mendoze, wife of Juan Guerra de Rosa, was also a woman of great wealth. Jointly, she and her brother equipped 80 soldiers and paid other expenses requisite to the success of the expedition. Dona Eufemia,; wife of Francisco de Sosa Penalosa, royal ensign, was a women of "singular courage and wisdom."

The journey north into the new territory was arduous as well as dangerous, for the settlers traveled with 7,000 live stock and 83 solid-wood, two-wheel carts of ammunition and household goods. The records state that "when all was in readiness, the march began mid a deafening screeching of the cart wheels and the applause of all. It was a noble sight indeed to see this caravan go forth. The wagons led the way, and in the wheel tracks they left across the plain followed the oxen, of which there were a great number; then the goats, sheep, lambs, mares, mules and last a great herd of horses." The expedition moved north slowly. The land was hot and dry and water was often scarce.

When the soldiers became discouraged by the long delays and the irksome duties of camp life and began to desert the expedition, it was Dona Eufemia who addressed them in words of fiery courage:

Tell me, O noble soldiers, where is that courage which you so professed when you enlisted in this noble cause? Why give you then to understand that nothing could resist the might of your arms if now you turn your back and ignobly desert? What explanation have you for such conduct if you hold yourself men? For shame! Such are not the actions of Spaniards. Even though everything else might be lost, there is yet land on the banks of some mighty river where may raise a mighty city and thus immortalize our names. To such a place we can go, and it were better that we halted right here and rested than to retrace our steps and leave upon ourselves and our posterity a stigma which can never be erased.[4]

Two years later, when the Araucanian Indians were imperiling the expeditionary encampment, Dona Eufemia "gathered all the women together on the housetops to aid in the defense. Dona Eufemia had stated that they would come down if the general so ordered, but that it was their desire to be permitted to aid their husbands in the defense of the capital. Don Juan Onate was highly pleased at this display of valor coming from feminine breasts, and he delegated Dona Eufemia to defend the housetops with the women. They joyfully held their posts and walked up and down the housetops with proud and martial steps."

Later in the same year, the first permanent settlment in New Mexico was finally made in the Chama River Valley and called San Juan de los Caballeros. From the first valley settlement the colony prospered and expanded. The women took up the tasks of homemaking in a barren land, but they had brought with them an audacious, joyous mode of life and left us a heritage in art and the dance, developed in their isolation, that is unique and beautiful.;

The first women from England to brave the ocean trip came with John White on one of Raleigh's expeditions and landed at Roanoke Island, North Carolina, in 1587. Among the seventeen courageous women was John White's own daughter, Eleanor,[5] who had married Ananias Dare. Their child, Virginia, was the first English baby to be born in the new world. John White was enthusiastic over the new land and soon had the 121 coloninsts settled in rude shelters. He then returned to England for supplies and more colonists. But when he arrived home he found Raleigh and all England preparing for war. The invincible Spanish Armada was forming for an attack on England and Holland. Every vessel was needed for national defense. Accordingly it was not until 1590 that John White was able to return to the Roanoke colony. On landing he found the little colony had vanished, the houses had been torn down, "the chests rifled and his own armour almost eaten through with rust."

English men and women were not deterred by the tragedy. In 1607 the first permanent settlement was made at Jamestown, Virginia, and in the fall of 1608 Mrs. Thomas Forrest came to join her husband and brought with her Anne Burras, her maid.[6] Captain John Smith mentions them in his history as "the first gentlewoman and woman-servant that arrived in our colony." The following year Anne Burras married John Laydon. This was the first marriage service held in the colony.

Although many of the women died during the "starving time" of 1609, twenty other women came during the year, and still others followed year after year to venture, to struggle, and to gain property for themselves and a foothold for England in the new land. These were also adventurous women who spent themselves and their fortunes, their arts and industries, to help in molding a primeval land into one of comfort and culture.

They came from the England of William Shaksspeare, Ben Johnson, John Milton, and John Bunyan, the England of Francis Bacon, Isaac Newton, Edmund Halley, and William Harvey, the England that witnessed the translation of

the Bible into the venacular in 1526 and that heard the
voices of John Calvin, George Fox, and John Wesley, the
England that saw in one century (1600–1700) five wars
with her enemies and thirty years of civil strife, four monarchs and one Lord Protector, the great fire of London,
and a series of devastating epidemics.

From the imbroglio of the seventeenth century, the Pilgrim and the Puritan women sought refuge in a strange
land. They were the vanguard of many women who fled
from religious persecution in England and Europe. Twenty-six of them came to the New World on the Mayflower.[7]
By the end of the first year only eleven remained in the
"howling desert," but the seed of religious freedom had
been sown and no amount of hardship halted its progress.

Many of the English women who came to the New
World were members of one or the other of the dissenter
churches, such as the Puritans, Anabaptists and Quakers.
A few Catholic women came to Maryland with Lord Baltimore. But of whatever faith, the common purpose of these
valiant women was to escape from persecution and to find
freedom to believe and worship as they chose. No more
courageous women ever suffered and died for a religious
idea than the women who pioneered for religious freedom
from Maine to Georgia in the period of American colonization.; Most of them came with the men of their families,
but a few independent spirits came as leaders or missionaries to save the souls of all who would join their
bands of worshippers.

Other English women came in bondage and left us a
heritage of courage and endurance that has seldom been
equaled. Whether they came willingly, to be sold for passage money at the first convenient port, or as bondswomen
who worked for their chance of freedom or were brought

by force from the crowded jails, orphanages, almshouses, and streets of England, they brought with them the skills to produce the commodities needed by the colonists.

The French women who came to the New World also came from a homeland torn by constant political and religious strife.[8] Religious persecution was the driving force that sent hundreds of the Huguenot women out of their homeland and onto the ships that sailed westward across the tumultous ocean. Ribaut's two efforts to use Huguenots in his colonizing plans both failed. Thousands of other Huguenot women fled for their lives. Some shipped in English vessels and settled in New England. Others came in Dutch trading vessels that brought them at last to the quiet waters of the Hudson River. Still others settled in Pennsylvania, Virginia, and the Carolinas. Some were highly educated and gifted in the arts, while others were skilled in the household industries. But they had a common heritage in the art of Eustache Lesseur and Charles Lebrun and in the writings of Pierre Corneille, Jean Racine, Jean Poquelin Moliere, Rene Descartes, and Francois Fenelon and, very significantly, with such women as Catherine de Rambouillet and Madame de Sevigne. Wherever they settled from Maine to Louisiana, the colony prospered, for they brought with them besides their knowledge and skills a kind of gaiety that eased the tensions of fear and want and made their endurance of hardships truly gallant.

In 1755, when the English took over Nova Scotia, more than 1,200 destitute French Acadians were landed in Boston and dispersed among the towns of New England.[9] The women among these displaced persons also enriched our heritage by their courage and industry.

The first four groups of French women who were shipped to the Crown colony of Louis XIV in Louisiana were pathetic derelicts from the prisons, hospitals, and houses of correction in the French cities.[10] Between 1717 and 1720, 7,000 persons came to the Crown colony. Of these 2,462 were indentured servants, 1,278 were classed as criminals or exiles; 1,500 were slaves, and 119 were managers or heads of concessions granted by the Crown. Their convivial life in the colony led to protests to Governor D'Bienville. In 1727, he requested that a number of girls from worthy families be brought over as possible brides for the settlers. In 1728, twenty-three "Cassette girls" were carefully selected and sent to the colony under the care of two nuns. They were immediately taken to the newly opened Ursuline Convent in New Orleans, where they were married to local swains on payment of passage monies. Only one girl declined to marry. Ten Ursuline nuns, under the leadership of Mother Marie Tranchepain of Rouen, France, had already opened a convent and a hospital, set up a school for girls, and gathered orphans into a comfortable home. They were the first nuns to come to the new land, the first professional nurses to establish a hospital, the first social workers to erect an orphanage, and among the first professional teachers to come to the United States. Many other worthy and cultured French women came in the years that followed, leaving us a legacy of the skills of gracious living.

Probably the best prepared of all the groups of pioneer women who came to America were the Dutch women colonists. They were, from the beginning, an active part of a great mercantile and colonizing enterprise. With gusto and amazing speed, they transplanted their homes, their business interests, their church, and their community customs to the "place of safe landing" on the tip of Manhattan Island and along the banks of the Hudson River.

Their former life in Holland had fitted them well for the adventure. In the homeland they had been educated with the boys and had carried on many types of industries and mercantile ventures as independent owners. As Howell wrote in 1622: "Nor are the men only expert therein but the women and maids also in their common Hostries; in Holland the wives are so well versed in bargaining, cyphering and writing, that in the absence of their husbands in long sea voyages they beat the trade at home and their words will pass in equal credit. These women are wonderfully sober." [11]

The Dutch East India Company had been formed in 1602 and their vessels had sailed to the Indian Archipelago. Headquarters had been set up at Batavia in Java, and trade relations had been developed at Ceylon, Malacca, and Sumatra. By 1669 the company had 150 trading ships, 40 ships of war, 10,000 soldiers on their payroll and still paid a 40 percent dividend to the stockholders.

When the Dutch West India Company was formed in 1621, the promoters had considerable knowledge of the needs of the colonists. They stocked their ships with sufficient supplies so that the colony in America never suffered a "starving time" as did many of the other settlements.

The disorganized, untidy wilderness was a challenge to the Dutch women, and the seemingly unlimited resources was an enticing opportunity for commercial gain. They are said to have laughed and set to work with a hearty good will. They brought with them an appreciation of the writings of Jacob Cats, Joost van den Vondel, and Constantijn Huygens and the art of Michiel Mierivelt, Frans Hals, and Rembrandt van Ryn. Thus, they left us a heritage of independent enterprises, great resourcefulness, high courage, and beautiful homes and gardens.

The German women who came to the American colonies were members of several Protestant groups who had been forced to leave their homes during the religious persecutions. Like the Puritan and the Huguenot women, many had wandered about Europe for years before they were able finally to come and live in the New World. They had learned how to live with fear in a foreign land and how to adapt themselves to new and frightening conditions. The first group of Germans came with Pastorius of Krefeld, in 1683, and founded Germantown, Pennsylvania.[12] The Pietists from Westphalia settled at Ephrata, Pennsylvania, in 1732. A group of Moravians settled at Bethlehem, Pennsylvania, and another group, the Walloons, emigrated from their hideouts along the Rhine and were brought by Governor Robert Hunter of New York and finally settled in the Mohawk Valley. Other refugees from the Austrian Alps and the German Palatinate settled in Georgia, Alabama, the Carolinas, and Louisiana.

The German immigrants left behind a homeland torn with religious and political upheavals, but some could remember the art of Albercht Durer and the two Hans Holbein, the writing of Gottfried Leibnitz, and the hymns of Paul Gerhardt. The German women were deeply religious, sober, and industrious, and they brought with them the tools and utensils of the farm and home industries. They rapidly became producing units in their communities. While all of the religious groups of settlers urged the rudimentary education of the young girls, it was the Moravian and Pietists women who brought with them an intense desire for more advanced education for women and for extensive musical training.

Other European nations were represented in the colonial migration of women, though in smaller numbers. A few

Portuguese women accompanied the Spanish colonizers to Florida. Some Belgian women, often referred to as Walloons, came with the Dutch traders to New Amsterdam and other settlements. Some Swiss women joined the religious groups of German and French colonists. Scotch and Irish colonists, both Protestant and Catholic, were shipped over as children or as servants or they came as dissenters settling in the colonies from New Hampshire to the Carolinas. An Englishman, John Mason, sent over a small group of Danes to work on his plantation in New Hampshire. Swedish and Finnish women were among the immigrants sponsored by Queen Christiana. They settled at Wilmington, Delaware, and were noted for their industry and frugality.

Women were in the group of Jewish refugees from Brazil who landed in New Amsterdam in 1654.[13] Others came in small groups, settling in most of the English colonies along the Atlantic seaboard. In 1722 a group came with the French and German refugees from Europe and settled in Louisiana. The first negro women to come to the colonies were sold as slaves to the settlers in Jamestown. Hundreds of others followed them into the tobacco, rice, and cotton fields of the southern plantations, where they left us a wealth of deeply moving spirituals and throbbing rhythmic dances.

In 1763, when Florida became an English colony, Dr. Andrew Turnbull, a Scotch physician, formed a colony of 1,500 people from Greece, Italy, and the Minorcan Islands.[14] They planned to produce silk, cotton, and indigo at "New Smyrna," but were finally driven by Indian raids and sickness to seek shelter in St. Augustine, where they contributed their knowledge concerning cultivation of orange, fig, and olive trees to the colony.

Each group of women colonists brought with them, besides courage and fortitude, their special abilities and cultural backgrounds. With these they wrought out their cotenancy in a new nation. And in so doing—whether for religious freedom, patriotic expansion, material gain, or sheer adventure; whether with hoe, or spindle, or business acumen or the flame of faith—they gave all the women who followed them a birthright beyond that of any other women, then or now.

The American colonial women possessed three inspiring and sustaining advantages or gifts from their heritage which were greater and more enduring than those of other women in other ages who had worked out their destinies under primitive living conditions. These are their lasting gifts to us, the core from which all their other gifts emanate.

First, and most deeply motivating, they brought with them the Christian concept of the equality of all people before God, which is still in sharp contrast to the concepts of Asian religions. The concept found expression in the universality of the "inner light" of the Quakers, the belief in the equality of the sexes maintained by the Moravians and the Mennonites of Ephrata, and the matriarchal rights and customs of the Catholic settlements in New Mexico and Arizona. Even in the Calvinistic strongholds the voices of such women as Anne Hutchison, Deborah Moody, and Mary Dyer were heard through the curtain of imposed silence. In a very vital and remarkable way these women believed in themselves and in their right to live, work, and contribute to the common social good.

The dynamic potential of the idea of the equality of the sexes, which is still a major problem for women today, can be seen in the limited number and kinds of church and civic rights that were accorded the women in the colonies in defiance of the common laws of England which they brought with them. In New England, where Calvinism flourished and Old Testament concepts were dominant, very few rights were given to women either married or single, in spite of the great need for women and the elimination of the obedience clause in their civil marriages.

In other Protestant settlements the limitations on women's rights bore a direct relation to the extent and fervor with which Calvinistic philosophy was accepted. For instance, in New Netherlands the Calvinistic Dutch Reform Church was not the motivating factor in the colonization and did not dominate civil affairs, and it was here that women were among the most active participants in the commercial and other productive enterprises of the early colonies.

The Quakers and several of the Pietistic groups which repudiated Calvin's belief of the inferiority of women came to the new land because of their religious beliefs. Wherever they settled, women were given equal rights in the church, and, since it is difficult to maintain equal rights on Sunday and unequal rights the rest of the week, the women were given a considerable share in community life as well.

In the Catholic settlements in Florida, New Mexico, and Louisiana, the women were given extensive proprietory rights. In the Spanish settlements the women retained their own family names in marriage and had the rights of personal ownership of their own property. In the colonies adhering to the Church of England, there was no pressure of persecution and no great concern for a change in the status quo of civic life during seventeenth century. Women's rights remained largely those of the common law of England until other factors in pioneer life forced their modification. For religious motivations, however strong,

were only one of several potent influences that, acting upon
each other, released the mollusk colonies from their distant
moorings and set them free to shap a "new nation under
God."

Secondly, the women as well as the men brought with
them a very considerable amount of the knowledge and
skill that was necessary for survival in the wilderness. Over
and above the value of women as wives and mothers, which
all of the colonies recognized, was their economic value.
They could produce the items needed for the survival of
the settlers and the development of the colonies. As the
Journal of the Virginia House of Burgesses records in 1619,
the colonists provided "shares [of land] for their wives as
for themselves, because that in a new plantation it is not
knowen whether man or woman be the most necessary." [15]

All of the colonies offered inducements for women settlers "whereby the planter's minds may be the faster tyed...
by the bonds of wyves and children, care hath been taken
to provide them younge hansome and honestly educated
mayds...." [16] But the promoters expected far more of the
women than merely to have them tie their husbands to the
land. They expected the women to establish orderly, producing households and help in meeting the problems of
the communities. To this expectation the colonial women
brought a wealth of knowledge, skill, and experience. They
knew how to heat, light, care for, and protect their homes.
They knew how to plant, harvest, prepare, and preserve
the available food. They had for centuries been the chief
producers of thread, cloth, and clothing of all kinds. They
knew the healing arts from ancient times. As nurse and
"chirurgien" they had made splints and soothing ointments,
lanced swollen wounds, and brewed healing herbs. As midwives they had attended the births of the nations. As mem-

bers of the guilds of artizans they had knowledge and skill in butchering, brewing, innkeeping, shoemaking, black-smithing, iron mongering, chandling, carpentering, print-ing, salesmanship, and many other crafts. Thus the valiant women of the great migration to the new shores did not come empty-handed. Rather, they brought the priceless gifts of knowledge and skill that were vital to survival and progress.

This need and respect for the contributions of women showed most clearly the inconsistency with which woman's disabilities under the common law of England were treated. There is, perhaps, no better illustration of this than in the laws of the Massachusetts Bay Colony, 1692–1693, which required that every single person under twenty-one years of age be "under some orderly family government," but further stipulated that "this act shall not be construed to extend to hinder any single woman of good repute from the exercise of any lawful trade or employment for a live-lihood, whereunto she shall have the allowance and ap-probation of the selectmen... any law, usage, or custom to the contrary notwithstanding." [17]

Relentlessly the economic need for the products of wom-en's work bent the old Mosaic concept of the inferiority of women into an honest, if grudging, respect for her as an intelligent, hard-working partner in the great adventure.

The third great advantage, or gift, which the American colonial women had (excepting those in New Mexico) over the women of past civilizations was the amazing hetero-geneity of their backgrounds. Each woman had available both the learnings and skills of her own cultural back-ground and the very different learnings and skills of her neighbors, who frequently came not only from a different social strata of society but from one of the fifteen other widely different national backgrounds. The French traveler De Crevecoeur in his *Letters of an American Farmer* says, "I could point out to you a family whose grandfather was an Englishman, whose wife was Dutch, whose son married a French woman, and whose present four sons have now four wives of different nations." [18]

This was true of each of the colonial settlements. For instance, the English colony at Jamestown, Virginia, included Dutch and French settlers, Poles, Swedes, Germans, Jews, and Scotch and Irish craftsmen. The Dutch settlement of New Netherlands included Belgians, Germans, Frenchmen, Jews, Swedes, and Finns. Even the religiously segregated New England colonies included settlers from Ireland, Scotland, France, Belgium, Denmark, Germany, and other European countries.

The women from these diverse background, working together in moments of danger, or high adventure, or at routine tasks, broadened the cultural pattern of the colonies immeasurably, enriched the language from many tongues, encouraged a tolerance of race and religion, and expanded their productive capacity a hundredfold.

The letters, diaries, and other documents of the colonial days give us glimpses of how the pioneer women used their three priceless advantages or gifts, which were belief in themselves as individuals, ability and training in many fields, and the heterogeneous quality of their backgrounds. Each glimpse into their lives gives us a new panorama of their accomplishments. No one can learn of them and not marvel at the greatness of their courage and inventiveness, for they possessed a zest for living that has become characteristic of the whole western world. In them it reached superlative expression. Through bitter cold and nauseous heat, through bloody warfare, starvation times, sickness, and disaster, they bent their backs to labor along with the men of the colonies. They lived by faith and survived by sharing their ingenuity and by adapting their knowledge and skills to new and strange conditions. Out of faith they helped to build a nation—faith in themselves, in their abilities, and in the worth of their contribution to the common good of the new society.

2

Ah Wilderness, We Learned Thy Ways

The first "way" of the wilderness that the colonial women learned was its murderous power of death. Each of the colonial groups succeeded or failed according to their ability to meet and conquer the elements of man and nature which they faced. Their desperate struggles to survive are not only heart-sickening in the reading but actually are the foundation of our nation. In each instance, it was the faith, courage, and resourcefulness of the men and women of many different national backgrounds that through failures and successes finally made possible the achievement of permanent settlements in the vast expanse of an unknown world.

The women of the first Spanish settlement at Pensacola, Florida, the first French settlement at Fort Caroline, Florida, and the first English Settlement on Roanoke Island, North Carolina, all were killed, died of sickness, met an unknown death, or were sold into bondage within a few years after landing. As Peter Martyr of Anghiere wrote earlier in the century in summing up the tradgedies of earlier expeditions:

But the resydewe consumed by famen breather out theyr wery sowles, openynge a waye to the newe landes for such as shall coome after them, appeasinge the fury of the barbarous nations, with the price of theyr bludde. Consyderinge therefore after these stormies, with what ease other men shall ouerrunne and inhabite these landes . . .[1]

One such colonizing expedition under the leadership of Pedro Menendez de Aviles came to America in 1565 and established the first permanent colony at St. Augustine, Florida, but the settlers found no "ease" in their settlement of the land. The women who survived the tempestuous ocean voyage, during which over half of the colonists were lost, came ashore on a sandy spit of land on September 7. Fortunately, the natives of the immediate vicinity were hospitable. Chief Seloy gave the colonists his own large communal hut as temporary shelter.[2] The men set to work at once to build a triangular entrenchment around the hut and mount their bronze guns. When this was done, they strengthened timbers of the hut and brought their ammunition and supplies from the ships.

The women colonists meanwhile exchanged information and various articles with the Indian women. Cloth, beads, and other trinkets were bartered for woven mats, corn, fish, and fresh meat. The Indian women taught the colonists how to crush corn in stone mortar, how to find and cook shellfish, where to look for berries and herbs of many kinds, and how to dry and weave the local grasses.

As soon as the fort was completed, the men built temporary huts nearby for the individual families. These were made of rough hewn timber, palmetto branches, and dried grass which protected not only the members of the family from the weather but also the swine, goats, horses, and cattle. It was in these overcrowded huts that the Spanish women set up their first housekeeping ventures in the new land. They had only an open fire in the center of the hut, crude pallets of straw, and a very limited number of cooking utensils with which to build homes for their families.

Though Menendez had started from Spain with a goodly number of cattle, sheep, swine, goats, and poultry, most of them had been eaten or lost en route. A month after landing Menendez wrote in a letter to Spain:

"with the burning of the fort we are suffering very greatly from hunger because the meal was burnt up and the biscuit I landed here is spoiling and being consumed, and unless we are succoured very shortly we will be in suffering and many will depart this world from starvation." [3]

He sailed for Cuba to obtain supplies. Before he returned, the colonists reached the "point of no return." In their extremity, they moved twenty leagues down the lagoon where they had found friendly Indians who showed them where they could gather fresh berries and find other kinds of fish. Over one hundred of the colonists died before the end of the first year. All of the survivors were nearly naked, and during the last weeks before the relief ship returned they lived on palmettos, berries, grasses, and water.

Despite the roster of deaths, 1,500 new colonists were brought by Sancho de Arminiego in 1566, and with them several other settlements were made near St. Augustine.[4] However, the places chosen for the settlements were primarily selected as forts and did not have good farm land near enough for extensive cultivation. Small gardens of vegetables were planted near the houses, and orchards of citrus fruits, peaches, and figs were started near the forts. But the colony continued to be dependent on Cuba, which had been settled since 1515, for the necessities of life.

Hence, there were many periods of near starvation in the first ten years of the colony. In 1570, De La Alas, who was later governor of the colony, reported to the king in Spain that there were only 150 persons in the three existing forts of the colony and only twenty-one married men and soldiers at St. Augustine.[5] The rest of the colonists had died of sickness, been killed by the Indians, starved to death, or returned in terror to the West Indies.

Menendez, who had been made Governor of Cuba, continued to assist the struggling Floridian colony. In 1573, he included prisoners, deserters, and galley convicts to increase the number of laborers among the colonizers of Florida. At the same time he induced fifty Asturian men and their families, one hundred men and their families from the Azores, fifty others from Seville, and one hundred Portuguese laborers to settle in the colony. The result was a gradual development of colonial life. In 1580 he wrote to the king in Spain that St. Augustine had more than sixty houses made from the lime of oyster shells and sand with flat roofs and about thirty houses made of wood and mud covered with lime inside and out.[6] When Sir Francis Drake sacked the town in 1586 he reported that the colony had homes, gardens, a public building, and a church.

The inhabitants, who had retreated to San Matheo on the approach of Drake, returned and rebuilt the town, this time using chiefly homemade brick and stone. The houses were the first permanent homes of the women who came to colonize America. Menendez, having lost his only son at sea, bequeathed all of his Florida interests to his daughter, Dona Catalina, along with his title of Adelantado of Florida. But the colony grew very slowly; by 1649 there were only 300 families in the several settlements.

The Spanish and Mexican women who settled in the

Chama River Valley of New Mexico (1598) were in some ways the most fortunate of all the women colonists who settled in what is now the United States. They suffered from no long and debilitating ocean voyage. Instead, they travelled slowly over territory that was not unlike their homeland in Mexico. (One young bride counted the journey her honeymoon).[7] While the journey was long, laborous, and often dangerous, the women were able to bring with them abundant food, clothing, household equipment, and servants and slaves. (There were 83 carts in the entourage, of which only a few were reserved for ammunition and other military supplies.)

Though the members of the expedition had to defend themselves against attacks from a number of hostile tribes along the journey, the Pueblo natives of the Chama River Valley "came forth and gladly shared their homes" with the colonists. Adobe houses were soon erected, and such were the resources and industry of the colonists that each rancho, or hacienda, soon became an almost completely self-sustaining pueblo. Some of the women colonists, such as Dona Isabel de Bohorques, who owned a hacienda near the San Felipe pueblo, or Dona Ana Baco, who lived in her "estancia de Alamo," operated their own ranchos.[8] Others superintended the household industries that supplied the food, clothing, and other articles necessary to the life of the pueblo.

The land was not rich enough to support the Indians and the colonists in comfort. In 1608 Onate decided to return to Mexico, but the priests urged the settlers to "tighten their belts" and work harder to meet their needs.[9] They did so, and the colony expanded until there were 64 pueblos and a number of smaller stations along the Rio Grande River with a small capital at Santa Fe. But death stalked their homes through starvation and the galling hatred of a few of the Indian tribes who made repeated raids upon the settlements. Then, in 1680, El Pope, a Tejua Indian who had been working for 14 years to arouse the Indians against the colonists, succeeded in leading a massive attack.[10] Three hundred and eighty men, women, and children were slaughtered; the rest of the colonists escaped as far south as El Paso. Twelve years later Diego de Vargas was appointed governor and led an expedition of forty families north to reconquer and resettle the colony. The families, the carts laden with supplies, and the herds of cattle, sheep and goats, all moved north slowly, camping frequently amid the ruins of former haciendas. Some of the settlers were to reclaim lost ranchos, while others were to venture for the first time into the perilous land of opportunity where the odds for gaining a fortune, or even for survival, were fifty to one against them. These were truly adventurous women who knew something of the hazards they would have to face but who nonetheless stoutly supported their leader in his conquest of a new land for Spain.

The English women who came to America during the first half of the seventeenth century faced very different situations. To begin with, many of them were seriously ill when they arrived, and all of them had been weakened by the long enervating ocean voyage to America. They suffered from scurvey, dysentery, and recurring fevers.

When Mrs. Thomas Forrest and her maid, Anne Burras, arrived at Jamestown, Virginia, in the fall of 1608, they found themselves in "a verie noysome and unholsome place . . . by reason that it is in a marish ground . . . and hath no water springs . . . but what we draw from a well six or seven fathoms deepe fed by brackish River owzing into it"[11]

The fort and huts of the first encampment had been burned to the ground the year before, and sickness had caused so many deaths that there were very few of the men who could work. In January of 1608, when the first supply ship arrived, the colony was "utterly destitute of howses, not one as yet built so that they lodged in cabbins and holes in the ground . . . after this first supplie there were some few poore howses built."

Mrs. Forrest's first view of her new home included a palisade wall of uneven, rotting poles set in the ground, three crude block houses for the garrison, some twenty shabbily built shacks, and a church, all of which were crowded irregularly within the small enclosure. The shacks were made of rough-hewn, green timber frames filled in with plaster or brick nogging and covered with weatherboarding and thatched roofs that rotted rapidly in the damp atmosphere. The floors were of beaten earth, the beds were narrow straw pallets, and the open fireplaces were made of green logs, sometimes covered with mud or plaster to prevent rapid burning. Perhaps Mrs. Forrest brought an iron or copper pot to hang over the fire and a pan in which to bake her bread. A well of sweet water had recently been dug, and beyond the palisade thirty or forty acres of ground had been cultivated and sown with seed which had been brought from England.

But the crop failed and rats and mould devastated the supplies in the storehouse. Mrs. Forrest, Anne Burras, and the twenty women who arrived on the *Blessing* the following year were faced with the frightening problem of finding enough food to prevent starvation. The supplies from the ship had proved totally inadequate, and the Indians refused to barter their own limited supply of corn or allow the colonists to hunt over their land. By the fall of 1609, all of the hogs, fowls, and even the horses had been eaten.

According to John Smith, "So great was our famine that a savage slew and buried, the poorer sort tooke him up againe and eat him and so did diverse one another boyled and stewed with roots and herbs: And one amongst the rest did kill is wife, powered (salted) her and had eaten part of her before it was known, for which he was executed, as he well deserved." [12]

By the spring of 1610 only sixty of the original 500 men and women colonists still survived. Temperance Flowerdieu was among the survivors. She was twenty years old at the time and lived to marry Sir George Yeardley and to bear him three children. In June of that year the few who remained alive decided to abandon the settlement and return to England. When they were ready to sail out of the harbor, they were met by Lord De la Warre with a shipload of supplies and a new group of colonists. Strachey, the secretary of the colony, reported that with the impetus of the newcomers the church was renovated and better houses built with "wide and large country chimnies . . . (and covered) with bark of trees." They were built "in no great uniformity either for fashion or beauty of the street. A delicate wrought kind of mat the Indians make, with which . . . our people do dress their chambers and inward rooms, which make their houses much more handsome." [13]

Life in the crowded palisade was very difficult for the women, and particularly for the unmarried women who were serving the men of the company in return for their allowances from the common storehouse. They were expected to cook, wash clothes, clean the houses, and care for the sick. Simple sanitation was a serious problem in the crowded encampment. Much of the sickness and death undoubtedly was due to the unsanitary conditions of the settlement. In 1610 Sir Thomas Gates drew up a series of laws concerning murder, theft, impiety, sacrilege, etc., and sanitation. One of the laws required that "every man shall have an especiall and due care to keepe his house sweete and cleane, as also so much of the streete as lieth before his door, and especially he shall provide, and set his bedstead whereon he lieth, that it may stand three foote at least from the ground. . . ." [14] Another forbade the women to wash their "fowle clothes" on the streets or clean their cooking utensils within twenty feet of the "old well or new pumpe."

The following year the little town had "three streets of well framed houses, a handsome church . . . besides storehouses, watch houses and such like . . . on the verge of the river five faire Block houses . . . [for] continual sentinell. . . . On the other side of the river an area of 2 miles was impaled . . . five forts among them 'Mount Malady,' a guest house for sicke people." [15]

Each area had to be carefully guarded, for even as John Smith sought the friendship of Chief Powhatan, at Jamestown the Indians "came creeping upon all four from the hills like bears . . . [carrying] bows in their mouths charged us very desperately in the faces." John Smith achieved only an uneasy peace. After the marriage of John Rolfe to Chief Powhatan's daughter, Pocahontas, the settlers thought they were safe.

It should be remembered that the colonists were not independent adventurers but part of a closely controlled English company. The colonists were required to work for the benefit of the company in England and, in return, received rations from the common storehouse. The land was held by the company and not divided for the first seven years. Then in 1611 Governor Sir Thomas Dale, seeing the evident dissatisfaction of the men and women, encouraged individual initiative by authorizing the right of every man with a family to have a four-roomed house, sufficient provisions for a year, twelve acres of fenced-in land, a cow, some goats, swine and poultry, and such tools as were available for the maintenance of their homes.[16] The results were most gratifying. New and better homes were built, the individual plots of ground flourished under the care given them, and even the common ground was better cared for, though it was owned by the company.

The individual ownership of land was confirmed by Governor Sir George Yeardley in 1619 when he began the systematic subdivision of the land of the company. Many of the settlers moved out of the crowded palisade and built shelters for themselves and their families in the rich "valley of Virginia." The massacre of 1622 was a direct result of this expansion of the colony into Indian territory.[17] It is estimated that about 400 persons (one-third of the total population of the colony) were killed along a 140-mile front though not a single negro was harmed, possibly because their black faces frightened the Indians.

The following year the General Assembly ordered "that every dwelling house shall be palisaded for defense against Indians" and "that no man go or send abroad without a sufficient party, well armed." In 1644 the Indians struck again, killing about 300 colonists, laying waste most of the year's crops, and destroying many of the homes of the settlers.

It was while the problems of land tenure were being debated that the members of the House of Burgesses petitioned for shares of land for their wives (1619). The petition was granted, and in 1621 Lady Elizabeth Dale (widow) received the patent for 3,000 acres of land along the Eastern Shore.[18] In 1624, Mary Holland received a patent for twelve acres, Elizabeth Lupo for fifty acres, and Elizabeth Dunthorne (Old Planter) and Mary Bouldin (Ancient Planter) for one hundred acres each. This was from fifteen to seventeen years after the first settlement at Jamestown.

The number of land patents granted to women colonists increased with the growing number of immigrant families and the importation of 140 maids for wives in 1620–1622. The records show that most of these women received land patents as wives of settlers, in which case the title passed into the hands of their husband. Widows and single women received permanent title to their property provided they did not marry again, thus establishing the precedent of the property rights of women in the English colonies of America.

The twenty-six women who came to the New World in the Mayflower (1620) faced even more difficult hardships than the women who had helped in the settlement of Jamestown, Virginia.[19] After sixty-three days on the ocean, many of them were scarcely able to disembark in the foot of snow that covered the beaches of Boston Harbor on the bleak December day of their landing. Governor William Bradford has described the scene that the women faced as they looked out on their new homeland. Little wonder that Bradford's own wife, exhausted by sickness, was unable to face the scene. He wrote: "We sought out in foule winter a place of habitation . . . and there saw nothing but a naked and barren place . . . a hideous and desolate wilderness, full of wild beasts and wild men? and what multituds ther might be of them they knew not . . . all things stand upon them with a wetherbeaten face; and the whole countrie, full of woods and thickets, represented a wild and savage heiw."

Landing of the Pilgrims at Plymouth, 1620. (From the Collections of the Library of Congress)

As soon as Plymouth was chosen as the most desirable site for the settlement, the men set to work to build a "first house for common use to receive them and their goods." [20] But, before they could complete the transfer of supplies, the structure was burned to the ground. The men set out at once to rebuild the common house. The work progressed slowly for "that which was most sadd and lamentable was, that in 2, or 3, months time halfe of their company dyed espetialy in Jan. and February, being in the depth of winter, and wanting houses and other comforts; being infected with scurvie and other diseases, which thing long vioage and their inacomodate condition had brought upon them; so as ther dyed sometimes 2, or 3, of a day. . . ."

Edward Johnson writing of the conditions in the Massachusetts Bay Colony nearby described the first homes of both settlements in his *Wonder Working Providence*. "After they had found out a place of aboad, they burrow themselves in the earth for their first shelter, under some hillside, casting the earth aloft upon timber; they made a smoky fire against the earth at the highest side, and thus these poor servants of Christ provide shelter for themselves, their wives and little ones, keeping off the short showers from their lodgings, but long rains penetrate through to their grate disturbance in the night season." [21]

Little wonder that Governor Bradford records that "it pleased God to vissite us then with death dayly and with so generall a disease that the living were scarce able to burie the dead; and the well not in any measure sufficiente to tend the sick."

Great as the malady was, it was only one of the problems that the men and women had to face. Years later Bradford recalled that "all this while the Indians came skulking about them, and would sometimes show themselves aloofe

... but would run away ... But about the 16. of March a certain Indian came boldly among them and spoke to them in broken English ... His name was Samaset ... another Indian whos name was Squanto, ..."[22] With these two Indians as interpreters, the Pilgrims were able to talk to Chief Massoit and to explain their peaceful purpose. After some discussion and exchange of gifts, they were able to make a peaceful agreement which was adhered to for nearly a quarter of a century. This was, probably, the most fortunate achievement of the early years of the colony, for it not only prevented warfare but made it possible for the colonists to learn from the Indians how and where to get fresh food, sweet water, timber, and other necessities for living in the wilderness.

During the first winter, most of the food came from the ship's supplies, which were very poor and scarce. In the spring of 1621, the men and some of the women planted corn under the guidance of the Indians, who also taught them how to catch cod and bass and salt them for winter use. Bradford tells us that "all the sommer ther was no wante," for water fowl, wild turkeys, venison, and other wild animals were had in such abundance that little thought was given to future supplies.[23] But by the following spring he wrote, "Now in a manner their provisions were wholy spent and they looked hard for supply; but none came." The summer and fall crops were very poor, and food became so scarce that only a quarter of a pound of bread per person per day could be allowed during the winter that followed. When it came time to plant the corn in the spring of 1623, "all ther victuals were spente and they were only to rest on God's Providence; at night not many times knowing wher to have a bitt of anything the next day."
Conditions became so serious that Governor Bradford

The Distribution of five kernels of corn per person at Plymouth, 1623.
(From the Collections of the Library of Congress)

and his counselors decided to abandon their communal ownership of the land and to give every head of family from one to seven acres of land, according to the size of the family, to use for seven years.[24] The result was to greatly heighten individual initiative and pride in personal ownership. Years later he reported that "this had very good success; for it made all hands very industrious. . . . The women now wente willingly into the feild, and tooke their litle-ones with them to set corne, which before would aledg weaknes, and inabilitie; whom to have compelled would have bene thought great tiranie and oppression."

Until the corn ripened, the settlers lived on acorns and ground nuts from the forest, the shell fish which the women collected at low tide, the cod and bass the men caught, and the occasional wild fowl or deer that they were able to kill. It is said that each person was rationed five kernels of corn a day.

Toward the end of July two supply ships arrived from England with sixty new colonists, of which ten were women. The newcomers were "much danted and dismayed . . . in a word, all were filled with sadness" when they saw the "low and poore condition" of the earlier settlers. . . ." The best dish they could present their friends with, was a lobster, or piece of fish, without bread or anything els but a cupp of fair spring water."[25] This to a middle class English woman must have been a very shocking kind of poverty because any kind of fish was thought contemptible by them. It is little wonder that some of them returned to England. Most of them stayed, however, and helped to harvest the goodly crop of corn which provided them with food for a full year. So that, as Bradford wrote, "any general wante, or famine hath not been amongst them since to this day."

The little colony at Plymouth, depleted by sickness and death, had not been able to construct substantial homes until after the coming of the supply ships in 1623. The new houses were built of green timber with thatched roofs and wooden fireplaces and chimneys which were generally lined with clay or mortar. They had batten doors and floors of beaten earth, a few windows covered with oiled paper, and, in some instances, attic spaces under the low, sloping roofs. By 1624 the colony was firmly established with thirty two houses occupying a palisaded site about a half-mile in circumference, surrounded by well-cultivated land and pastures for the cattle.

Reports of the success of the colony led to greatly increased immigration in the area. One such group, led by Governor John Endicott, arrived at Salem, Massachusetts, in September 1628. Other groups settled as far north as Maine and as far south as Connecticut.[26] Women were a part of each venture. At Salem "maid lotts" were to be granted unmarried women according to the original plan for the division of land, through which ten lots were granted to each family (1634). An Turland was granted a two-acre lot in 1635, but in 1636 "Deborah Holmes [was] refused land being a maid (but hath four bushels of corn granted her, one by Mr. Endicott, one by Mr. Stileman, one by John Woodbury and one by Mr. Verrin) and would be a president to keep hous alone."

The following year nine widows were granted from ten to 150 acres each. Widows and single women are listed among the original proprietors of most of the settlements in Massachusetts and in some instances as founders of towns, as in the case of Elizabeth Poole, the "ancient Maid" of forty-eight years who founded Taunton, Massachusetts, in 1638. Widows and single women were also among the original proprietors of land in Maine, Vermont, New Hampshire, and Connecticut.

A few hundred miles to the south another experiment

in colonization was under way so different in intent and management as to bear little resemblance to the earlier experiments in colonization along the Atlantic Coast.[27] When the *New Netherland* sailed into New York Harbor in May of 1624 with 30 families of employee-colonists of the Dutch West India Company, a plan for several settlements had already been determined. The ship was to land eight men and one woman, Catelina de Trico, a nurse, at the trading station on Manhattan Island, to send six men and two families to a trading post in Connecticut, a small party to Long Island, and another to Fort Nassau (Hoboken, New Jersey) and to carry the remaining eighteen families to Fort Orange (Albany, New York), which was then the chief trading post of the company in the New World.

The scattered outposts had been carefully chosen by the Dutch trading masters who had carried on a lucrative trade, mostly in furs, with the Indians of the area since 1609. The Dutch were experienced in handling colonization projects as mercantile enterprises and had built snug trading stations and storehouses at convenient landing places. Each settlement was prepared to live comfortably on the provisions and equipment supplied them by the company. The women were securely housed and well clothed and had no serious difficulties in obtaining fresh food from the Indians, with whom they were very friendly. Most of them were Walloons, refugees from religious persecution in France and Belgium who had escaped to Holland a few years earlier. They were inured to danger and suffering and grateful for the well-paid jobs in the Dutch West India Company.

As they settled into the land-locked harbor, their first impressions of the New World were exhilarating. They saw a land of tall trees and vivid spring verdure. In its primeval forests they envisioned unfathomed riches, not in gold or power but in richness of soil and opportunity. Here they could seek their destiny far from the haunting fears of persecution. Here they could explore with free hearts the welcoming land and its simple people. Little wonder their accounts of the beauty, fertility, and resources of the new land quickened the interest of the men and women of Holland and started the flow of emigrants westward across the ocean.

In the following year (1625), Peter Eversen Huft of Amsterdam sent over three vessels with forty-five colonists, and other groups of colonists followed soon after.[28] With each shipload came cattle, hogs, and sheep as well as agricultural tools, seeds for gardens, young trees for orchards, bricks for chimneys, mechanical tools, mill hoppers, grindstones and wheels, and, in Mr. Huft's vessels, also several houses, shipped in sections all ready to assemble into comfortable homes.

In 1626, Peter Minuit, recently appointed governor of the colony, purchased Manhattan from the Indians and proceeded to erect a blockhouse surrounding a palisade of red cedar poles which was extended across the tip of the Island and "faced outside entirely with stone." By 1628 there were 270 settlers living in or close to the fort.[29] For those "who have no means to build farm houses at first according to their wishes, dig a square pit in the ground, cellar fashion, six or seven feet deep, as long and as broad as they think proper, case the earth inside all around the wall with timber, which they line with the bark of trees or something else to prevent the caving in of the earth; floor this cellar with plank and wainscot it overhead for a ceiling, raise a roof of spars clear up and cover spars with bark or green sods, so they can live dry and warm in these houses with their entire families for two, three or four years. . . ."

The first permanent homes of New Amsterdam were substantial dwellings of wood or stone.[30] Many of the wide chimneys were built with bricks which had been shipped from Holland or made locally in the brick-kiln. The small glass windows were soon adorned with bright curtains and the open cupboards, made of rough timber, were polished and filled with gleaming dishes and copper utensils. The benches against the walls, which had been used for beds at first, were broadened, made more comfortable, and draped about with homespun. Before the settlement was ten years old it had a church, a bake house, a grist mill, a saw mill, a brick-kiln, a lime-kiln, and houses for the midwife and the minister.

The women settlers did more than cook and scour. They planted lombard poplars before their stoeps, flower gardens in front of their houses, and herb and vegetable gardens in every convenient place. They traded extensively with the Indians, set up a market place for the exchange of produce and took an active part in community affairs.

When the land of the colony was thrown open to any purchaser, many women became landowners.[31] Sarah Joresey was given land as a widow, perhaps because she was the mother of the first Christian child to be born in the colony. Catheryna Brett had her home along the upper Hudson and as a widow owned and operated a grist mill for the convenience of herself and her neighbors. Madame Kierstede was given a track of land on the Hackensack River by the Indians in appreciation of her help to them, and Lady Deborah Moody, who was a widow, bought a large tract of land on Long Island in 1643.

Because of their extensive trade relations with the Indians and their friendly attitude of helpfulness, which was greatly fostered by the women, the colony suffered no sweeping massacre. However, Indian raids occurred in all the outlying areas, largely as reprisal for real or imagined injuries.

The Swedish and Finnish women who came with Peter Minuit's settlers in 1638 to Delaware and New Jersey were also employee-colonists of the Dutch West India Company, and they were joined in 1643 by other permanent settlers from their homelands.[32] They had much the same experience as the Dutch women of New Amsterdam. Though they were not as well supplied with food and equipment, they lived in sturdy log cabins and effected peaceful negotiations with the Indians. The women cared for the livestock, cultivated the fields, spun, wove, and knitted the clothing of their families. They were noted for their thrift and loyalty.

One other group of women were in the advance guard of all those who came to colonize the land that is now the United States. They were the women who sloshed through the swamps of the Gulf of Mexico.[33] In 1699, Pierre Le Moyne, Sieur D'Iberville, and his brother Jean Baptiste Le Moyne, Sieur D'Bienville, brought with them 200 men and women to settle Louisiana under the direct patronage of Louis XIV, King of France. The ships arrived at Biloxi, Mississippi, late in January and were warmly received by the Indian chiefs of the area. Peace songs were sung by the natives, and after the exchange of many gifts a pact of mutual helpfulness was agreed upon. The gifts from the settlers included beads, mirrors, combs, kettles, clothing, knives, pick axes, and hatchets. From the Indians the settlers received furs, corn, fruits, and other native products.

D'Iberville selected a spot on the first high ground and

superintended the building of a fort with four bastions and twelve cannons, a palisade, and a few rude huts of cypress board, roofed with slabs of cypress bark. The women were brought ashore with the provisions and household equipment.

Since D'Iberville's intent was to keep Biloxi as a fort and eventually to move the main colony to the banks of the Mississippi, no town was laid out and no gardens cultivated. D'Iberville left for France almost immediately to obtain new colonists and provisions. His brother, D'Bienville, and a small group of men set out to explore the mouth of the Mississippi River. The women in the little colony were left at Biloxi with a few men in the fort to struggle with yellow fever, scanty provisions, and the hot, humid climate to which they were not accustomed. Many died before repeated floods and famine had forced the removal of the colony to Fort Louis (Mobile) in 1702. Here a larger fort was erected, streets were laid out, and land was allotted to the colonists. The houses were still thatch roofed cabins of cypress, but the colony began to take on the apperance of a permanent settlement.

Two years later the supply ships brought livestock, food, and merchandise as well as missionaries, soldiers, artizans, and twenty-three young women in the care of two nuns.[34] The young women were reported to be modest, obedient, and virtuous. All but one married within a month. However, when they found that they were expected to eat corn bread instead of white bread, they rebelled. They locked their husbands out of their cabins and refused to open the doors until the men proved themselves good providers by bringing them white flour with which to make their bread. The men were at a loss until a supply ship arrived with sufficient grain to make white flour and satisfy the women.

The colony grew slowly, largely because of the problems of the government at home, upon which it was wholly dependent. In 1712, the whole colonizing project was leased to Antoine Crozart. When it continued to fail as a mercantile venture, the colony was transferred to John Law's Company in 1717. In 1718 Bienville laid out the city of New Orleans, which soon thereafter was made the capital of the colony. It had about 100 huts of cypress boards. One witness described it as of "no better aspect than of a vast sink or sewer." It was surrounded by a wide ditch and fenced in with willow copses wedged close together. A ditch ran along the four sides of every lot in every square, and every ditch swarmed with reptiles and deadly insects. Tall weeds and coarse grasses grew in every street, presenting an unkempt appearance.

In 1721 the directors of the company, finding it difficult to persuade either middle class Frenchmen or aristocrats to immigrate to the new colony, had eighty women selected from the public institutions of Paris and sent to New Orleans.[35] They were accompanied by three nuns, and each woman had with her a well-filled hope chest. One nun left a description of the scene that greeted them: "The aspect of the whole place was wretched. The frail huts were half hidden by reeds and tall grasses; the swamp had its miniature isles and stagnant lakes; snakes and alligators wriggled in the ditches, the frogs croaked forever in the slime of the palisaded moat, in the cane brakes, and wet jungles. . . ."

This was the fourth group of young women who had been sent to the colony. Most of the women married soon after their arrival, but there were serious complaints from the better families in New Orleans regarding the conduct of the women from the prisons of France. Accordingly, the "filles a la cassette" sent over thereafter were very carefully chosen for their good characters. The first group of these young women numbering twenty-three, arrived with two Ursuline nuns in 1728 and were warmly welcomed. Others followed, the last group arriving in New Orleans in 1751.

Both D'Iberville and D'Bienville had made special efforts to form strong alliances with the Indian tribes of the area. They assisted the Indians in their warfare against the English and Spanish settlers and other tribes of Indians. There was also considerable intermarriage with the Indians so that there were no massacres of the French settlers during the early years of the colony. In 1729 the colonists at Natchez were massacred, but few such incidents occurred.

The pioneer women who came after the six original groups of permanent settlers found the wilderness scarcely less hazardous. Some of these women came from the original settlements, as in the case of the group of Virginia colonists who pushed through the forests of North Carolina and settled at Albemarle on the Chowan River and along the Pamlico and Neuse Rivers (1659–1690). Some of these women were Huguenots who were dissatisfied with the life at Jamestown; others sought adventure or greater gains.[36] In the next two decades they were joined by settlers from Pennsylvania, mostly German, Irish, and Scotch Protestants who had trekked many weary miles through the primeval forests.

Other women came in the groups of adventurers who were given land in the new "Carolana" under the charter granted by Charles II (1663) to eight of his court friends. The adventurers, both men and women if they were unmarried, widows, or heads of families, were granted fifty acres for each person in the family group. The bond servants were promised land to be given them at the expiration of their term of service. Settlements were made at several places along the coast of North and South Carolina. A number of women's names appear among the original grantees at Charlestown, South Carolina. Among these were such single women and widows as Mary Crosse, Priscilla Burke, and Susan Varran. They were followed by many others. Lady Berkeley, who was the wife of three governors, acquired considerable land during her widowhood, as did Madame Blake, who owned large tracts of land and was very influential in the development of the colony. Judith Manigault was a Huguenot refugee who helped her husband and sons carve a family fortune out of the primeval forest.

The women who settled in the Carolinas knew all of the hardships and dangers of pioneer life, and many of them died in Indian raids, but they did not suffer the extreme agony of complete isolation or prolonged "starving periods" that came so near to breaking the hearts and minds of the original women settlers.

This was true also for the women who shared in the settlement of the land to the north and south of the original Massachusetts Bay communities. Some of these women came with independent ventures from England, others were inspired to escape the intolerant theocracy of the Puritans of Massachusetts. The first attempt to settle Maine was made as a commercial venture in August, 1607.[37] One hundred and twenty persons (no women are mentioned) arrived to make the settlement, but by the following spring more than half of the group had died from the cold and starvation. The remainder abandoned the colony as soon as the ice melted. In 1613, Madame de Guercheville, a lady of Maria de Medici's Court in France, having obtained

a charter granted by Henry IV to all the land in the new
world between the 40th and 46th degrees north latitude,
outfitted a colonizing expedition with the help of a few
court friends.[38] The territory included in the charter com-
prised all of the land between Philadelphia and Newfound-
land. The emigrants started in fair weather but met treach-
erous winds which finally landed them at Mt. Desert,
Maine, where they attempted to form a permanent settlement. Other groups of French emigres followed, sparsely
settling the land as far west as Lake Champlain.

In the meantime a grant of the "Province of Maine"
was made by James I of England to Sir Ferdinands Gorges
and John Mason in 1622, but no extensive English settlements were made during the first decade.[39] In 1639 Gorges
received a royal charter from Charles I to his share of the
former grant with provisions similar to those granted Lord
Baltimore. Hardy individuals in small groups of colonists
trekked north into what is now Maine and New Hampshire, despite the confusion in land grants from England
and France and the belligerent attitude of the Indians who
lived in the mighty forests of the north land. Women com-
prised a part of each group, sharing the rigors with their
husbands or as widows or independent proprietors of grants
of land. Considerable impetus was given to the movement
of colonists northward by the Antinomian controversy and
other bitter religious disputes that arose in the Massachusetts Bay communities. Some dissenters moved north voluntarily, others were exiled forcibly from the Puritan settlements.

The northern settlements grew slowly not only because
of the difficulties involved in maintaining community life
during the long bitterly cold winters, but also because of
the disagreements with the settlers who were brought in

by Gorges, who were members of the Church of England, and the French Catholics, who considered Maine a part of Acadia.

As the English communities grew stronger and more numerous, the Indians were forced further north into French Acadia and Canada, where their growing hatred of the English settlers was reenforced by the French settlers' desires to hold the land for France. The women as well as the men were caught up in the desperate struggle of two great nations. Among the French women, for instance, Mrs. Pentry defended her home and children from the Indians who attacked her homestead at Moosehead Lake. Madame La Tour and her husband built a fort to defend their homestead. She fought with all of her resources to hold her land against the English but eventually failed.[40]

Many of the Indians of the territory made ready allies with the French and raided the English settlement. Sarah Gerish, Isabella McCoy, and Jemina Howe were among the many women who were taken captive and sold to the French in Canada. Ursula Butts, widow of the president of the province, was killed, as were scores of other women who dared to venture into the northland.

The first permanent English settlement in Vermont was not made until 1724 when Fort Dummer was built at Brattleboro, Vermont.[41] The settlers were chiefly from Massachusetts and Connecticut. Later in the same year Dutch squatters from upper New York made a settlement at Pownal in the south-western corner of the state. Women were members of each group and fought the French, the Indians, and the wild animals alongside the men of the settlements.

To the south of the Massachusetts Bay communities, trading posts were set up by Dutch and English settlers in

1633 in what is now Connecticut.[42] In the next ten years
other trading posts were established, and many dissenting
groups of settlers moved south to gain religious freedom.
Rhode Island was also settled by religious refugees from
the Puritan communities of Massachusetts Bay. Roger Williams, Anne Hutchinson, and many others became involved
in the Antinomian and other religious disputes and were
expelled from the Puritan Church and colony. Anne Hutchinson had made the further error of speaking up in
church, holding meetings in her home, and even instructing ministers in the interpretation of the Bible, which was
highly irregular. Other discontents joined the Rhode Island and Connecticut settlements, and gradually new colonies were formed out of the faith, work, and sufferings of
the pioneer men and women. Roger Williams lived to establish his colony by an English grant in 1644, but Anne
Hutchinson left Rhode Island four years after her husband's
death and settled near New Rochelle, New York, where
she was killed in an Indian raid.

Maryland was the first English-born colony to be established in the New World for the avowed purpose of religious freedom for all faiths.[43] George Calvert, the first
Lord Baltimore, conceived the plan of establishing a haven
for the persecuted Catholics of England. He received some
encouragement from the king but died before a colony
which would be "an asylum for conscience" could be
formed. His eldest son Cecilius carried the project forward,
promising religious freedom to all who wished to join the
expedition. In March 1634 his two younger brothers, Leonard and George Calvert, sailed up the Chesapeake Bay in
the *Ark* and the *Dove* with 220 persons. The *Ark* was a
350-ton ship and the *Dove* a 50-ton ship. From the old
records we learn: "At the first appearance of the ship on

the river, we found (as was foretold us) all the country in arms. The King of the Paschattowayes had drawn together 1500 bowmen, which we ourselves saw, the woods were fired in manner of beacons the night after; and for that our vessel was the greatest that even those Indians saw, the scouts reported we came in a canoe, as big as an island, and had as many men as there be trees in the woods."

When the Calverts reached the town of Yoacomoco (rechristened St. Mary's), they worked out an alliance-treaty with the Indians. For "some 30 miles of land" and other immediate assistance the Calvert brothers agreed to assist the Paschattowaye Indians in the warfare against the mighty Susquehannocks. ". . . Seeing we came so well prepared with arms, their fear was much less, and they could be content to dwell by us: Yet do they daily relinquish their houses, lands, and cornfields, and leave them to us." The colonists, of which only a few were women, moved into one half of the Indian village and lived in the native "withotts," or huts, which they "dressed up something better than when the Indians had them." The Indian women taught the newcomers how to make beds of animal skins that had been well dressed and "set on boards and four stakes in the ground" and how to utilize many native products.

Food appears to have been no immediate problem for the women. The Indians supplied them with corn, wild game, fruits and nuts. Calvert had purchased one hundred hogs, thirty cows, some goats and some hens from Virgina plantations that they had passed in the lower Chesapeake Bay.

Soon after the first settlement was made the government was established at St. Mary's and the land was apportioned to the settlers soon thereafter. The first entry of land apportioned to a woman is dated July 30, 1638. "To Mistress Winifred Seaborne 100 acres. Miss Trovghton to grant her as much land as any of the first adventurers had in respect of the transporting of five persons and the rest mentioned in the first conditions.[44] . . . (Aug. 2). To Mistress Mary and Margaret Brent the same with Miss Trovghton."

Each male adventurer was offered one hundred acres of land for himself, one hundred acres for his wife, fifty acres for each child, one hundred acres for each man servant and sixty acres for each woman servant. Independent single women and widows were counted as the men. Margaret and Mary Brent brought four women and five men with them and were granted the rights of Courts—baron on their estates which are the only instances of such judicial privileges being granted to individual settlers in any colony.

The colonial women of Maryland suffered chiefly from Indian raids, primitive living conditions and occasional droughts, but help from neighboring colonies was always available, and the richness of the land soon made it possible for them to export some of their produce in exchange for English goods.

The women who came to the new world as members of William Penn's "Holy Experiment" (1681–1682) were a robust group of Quakers who had already endured ignominy and hardships on account of their religious beliefs.[45] Many of them had been members of trade guilds and very active in the productive life of England. Two attributes make them outstanding among colonial women. They not only believed in the equality of men and women as a tenet of their religion, but they acted upon their belief and became aggressive missionaries to the Indians and the other colonists. Women like Mary Austin, Mary

Dyer and Rebecca Hubbs left an indelible imprint on the life of the colonists.

The first large group of Quakers came to New Jersey in 1677, and others followed, settling on the land near the Dutch, Swedish and Finnish communities. In 1681 William Penn received a charter from Charles II for the land now known as Pennsylvania. By autumn of the same year he had outfitted the *John and Sarah* and the *Bristol Factor* and sent them forth laden with colonists and supplies to lay out a new colony. The *John and Sarah* made the voyage safely to Philadelphia by early December. Conditions were difficult at the landing. Mrs. Chandler, for instance, "having lost her husband on shipboard and who was left with eight or nine children" was destitute. "Her companions prepared her the usual settlement in a cave on the riverbank." The *Bristol Factor* got caught in the ice at Chester, Delaware on December 11 and the colonists spent the winter in improvised caves along the banks.

William Penn, who came the following year, had warned the colonists that conditions in the new colony would not be easy. He wrote, "I would have them [the colonists] understand that they must look for a winter before a summer comes, and they must be willing to be two or three years without some of the conveniences they enjoy at home; and yet I must need say that America is another thing than it was at the first plantation of Virginia and New England, for their is better accommodation [now] . . ."

While this was true, for land had been cleared and settlements established, the housing conditions along the Chesapeake Bay and the Delaware River were still very primitive. Proud informs us that some of the settlers actually lodged in the trees. Most of the immigrants spent their first months, or years, in the caves along the river bank. William Penn arrived in "The Welcome," a 300 ton vessel, in October 1682 after three months at sea during which time he lost a third of his 100 colonists from small pox. Sick and weary, the adventurers struggled up the banks of the river and took shelter for the winter wherever they could find it. Elizabeth Hard and her husband, William, were fortunate enough to find a temporary home in the cave dwelling of her sister Alice Guest. A niece of Elizabeth Hard's records:

All that came wanted a dwelling and hastened to provide one. As they lovingly helped each other, the women even set themselves to work that they had not been used to before ... [Elizabeth Hard] thought it expedient to help her husband at the saw, and to fetch all such water to make such kind of mortar, as they then had to build their chimney. At one time being overwearied therewith, her husband desired her to forbear, saying "Thou had better, my dear, think of dinner," on which, poor woman, she walked away, weeping as she went —and then knew not where to get a dinner, for their provision was all spent, except a small quantity of biscuit and cheese— but thought she would try which of her friends had any to spare.... When she ... was going ... her cat came into the tent and had caught a fine large rabbit which she thankfully received and dressed as an English hare.[46]

Penn's optimism, however, was unflagging for late in 1683 he wrote, "We are daily in hopes of shipping to add to our number; for blessed be God, here is both room and accommodation for them."[47] Earlier he had written that the colony actually was producing hides, tallow, staves, beef, port, sheep, wheat, barley and furs, but that he thought it could also produce silk, flax, hemp, wine, cider, wood madder, liquorice, tobacco, potash and iron. To these ends he granted lands freely to his co-religionists. In the

1682 lists of grantees included fifteen widowed women, among whom were Mary Penington, 1,250 acres, Margaret Martindel, 1,000 acres, and Pricilla Sheppard, Sarah Barsnet and Elizabeth Sims, 500 acres each.

In 1683 a large group of Mennonites from Germany bought 8,000 acres of land and founded Germantown.[48] A few years later (1700) Catherine Elizabeth Schutz gave 4,000 acres to the pietists, known as Dunkers, on which they built the Ephrata community. Penn personally aided Mary Warenbuer Ferree, a French Huguenot widow with six children, to obtain 2,000 acres of land from Queen Ann in 1711 and organize a colonizing expedition of religious refugees who settled in Lancaster County, Pennsylvania. Other religious refugees poured into the colony, which soon became a center of productive activity.

Besides the appeal William Penn made to the religious refugees of Europe was the remarkable treaty he made with the local Indians, which freed the colonists from the danger of Indian raids during his lifetime. About the treaty he wrote (1683) "when the purchase was agreed, great promises passed between us of kindness and good neighborhood, and that the Indians and English must live in love, as long as the sun gave light."

William Penn died in 1718 after a lingering illness. His second wife, Hannah Callowhill Penn,[49] had handled the problems of the colony during his illness and continued to do so until her death in 1726.[49] Much of the comfortable prosperity of the colony was due to her wise leadership. After the first ten years, food, clothing and warm houses were available to practically all of the families except those on the western frontier. Women's work was still exhausting, but actual privation of basic needs was no longer asked of them.

Georgia was not settled until 1733, when James Edward

Oglethorpe and some of his philanthropic friends, having obtained a charter from George II of England and 10,000 pounds from the English Parliament collected thirty five families (130 persons) and settled near the mouth of the Savannah River.[50] The first settlers were indigent persons from the prisons of England and religious refugees of English, German, Scotch, Swiss, Portuguese and Jewish ancestry.

Oglethorpe stated, "The trustees intend to relieve such unfortunate persons as cannot subsist here, and establish them in an orderly manner so as to form a well regulated town. As far as the fund goes, they will defray the charge of their passage to Georgia; give them necessaries, cattle, land and subsistence, till such time as they can build their houses and clear some of their land."

Women came with each of the groups of settlers, but they were granted no land and deprived of all rights of inheritance. This caused considerable dissention and was later modified to permit limited inheritance rights to the women of the colony as daughters or widows. Oglethorpe was deeply concerned with the problem of the conciliation of the Indians in the area. Through the services and friendship of Mary Musgrove Bosomworth, "Queen of the Creeks" he was able to procure the land for the settlers without warfare. She acted as a liaison person between the Indian tribes and Oglethorpe and his colonists so that there were fewer Indian raids in Georgia than in some other colonies. The women of the colony still had to meet the problems of pioneer life, but these were not as severe as those that had harrassed the women of the earlier settlements.

Soon after Florida became an English colony in 1763, Dr. Andrew Turnbull and his wife Maria Gracia formed a group of 1,500 prospective colonists from the countries bordering on the Mediterranean Sea and brought them to "New Smyrna" in Florida.[51] The colonists were indentured for their passage money and required to work for a number of years as payment. Some were set to work long hours in the production of silk, cotton and indigo. Others worked in the fields and orchards of oranges, figs and olives. The clothing given them was of the coarest variety and the housing accommodations shockingly poor and crowded. Three times as many colonists arrived as were expected, but no effort was made to alleviate their suffering. Further, they were required to eat in common dining rooms where the food was rationed at one quart of corn per day and two ounces of pork per week. Even fishing was forbidden. The work was very arduous and the task masters gallingly harsh. Riots broke out, and finally, after nearly a thousand had died, the 600 remaining colonists were allowed to go to St. Augustine where they were given small plots of land. Little is known concerning the women of the colony, except that they slaved and died alongside of the men who sought freedom and found greed and suffering instead.

Far to the west another settlement was being made by the Spanish. It was the last large colonial settlement to be made in the United States prior to the Revolutionary War. The first colonizing expedition to California was made by sixty-two persons in a vessel in 1768.[52] The first land expedition to include women was Anza's expedition of 1774 which brought twenty soldiers and thirty-four other persons to Monterey, California from Tubac, Mexico. The women were, undoubtedly, part Mexican and Indian and used to the work of the pioneer. The following year Anza brought two hundred and forty colonists of whom twenty-nine were wives of soldiers and 136 were members of other family groups. They traveled from Sinaloa, Mexico, with 1,050 domestic animals of which 340 were horses and 302 were cattle. Women were granted land along with the men. Maria Rita Valdez was one of the first settlers in what is now Beverly Hills. Fermina Espinoza's rancho was near the present Soloville. At the Sal si Puedes rancho the women of the family roamed the mountains guarding the cattle and felling the trees. They drove the wooden-wheeled oxcarts over the rough roads, made woolen blankets, and fed their families cheese and other delicacies made by their own efforts.

The first "lady of pretension" to come to California was Dona Eulalia Callis, wife of the Governor Pedro Fages. She arrived at the governor's headquarters in Monterey in 1783 and liked almost nothing about her new home, including her irascible husband. She made headlines in the local history books by quarreling publicly with him. He was a poor governor and was soon recalled, but others followed and established a prosperous colony on the shores of the Pacific Ocean, thus completing the sweep of colonization even to the "rim of Christendom."

3

From Shanties to Mansions

Probably the most amazing accomplishment of the intrepid colonial women was the way they transformed their first dwellings of grass, mud and green-wood slats into gracious homes of comfort and culture. While the men fought and formed a government, the women turned the "dug-outs," the mud-sealed shanties or the clumsy log cabins into opulent homes from Portland, Maine, to Charleston, South Carolina.

How they accomplished this wonder of achievement in a primeval land without the resources of an established culture of skilled artisans, requisite tools and resourceful tradesmen reads like a modern thriller. It comprehends adventure that makes Dick Tracy sound like a bedtime story, terror that never eased, labor beyond pain, love and child-bearing in lonely outposts, loyalty to a faith in God that spelled freedom to each sect, intellectual surgings that would not be stilled and, most often, death. (There is evidence in the history of every group of settlers that women stood the physical tests of pioneer life better than the colonial men.)

Because she and the work of her hands were so greatly needed, the colonial woman held an important position in the home. While her status was not legally equal to that of the men in any of the colonies, in matter-of-fact living she often operated on an equal basis. Where she owned the land and dwelling, as widow or single person, she acted as head of the household with all the privileges (and problems) pertaining thereto. Where married she acted as second in command, taking on all the responsibilities of the homestead during her husband's frequent absences or illnesses.

Her limited legal rights in the estate of matrimony were due in part, at least, to her immaturity as a bride.[1] Some colonial girls married at 13 or 14 years of age and most of them before they were 16. If they had not married by the time they were 20 years old they were considered "a stale maid" or "a curse as nothing can exceed it." This universal pressure for early marriages stemmed from several causes, not least of which was the ratio of 200 to 600 men to every 100 women. In the expanding population the ratio gradually changed until in 1790 there were slightly more women than men in the new nation. However, the custom of early marriages still pertained and "old maids" remained anathema.

In spite of public opinion, a few very talented spinsters such as Margaret Brent, Mary Morgan, Elizabeth Poole and Mary Carpenter, sister-in-law of Governor Bradford, braved the storms of ridicule and suspicion and were eventually highly respected in their communities, but they were each unique exceptions in their settlements rather than the rule.

Such early marriages implied parental authority in the courtship and marriage of the girls. Thus at Lynn, Massachusetts, in 1647, an order was passed "that if any young man should address a young woman without consent of her parents, or in their absence, of the county court, he shall be fined 5 pounds." And Stanley Matthew was so fined later in the year.[2]

Capital and other material resources were almost as much in demand as brides. They, too, were essential in the struggle for existence. Romantic love had little place in the consideration of the basic needs of survival in a wilderness. Parents quite naturally gave first consideration to the capabilities and resources of the suitors for their daughters' hands, and young men asked most often whether the brides-to-be were skilled and industrious in household production and management, rather than about the fairness of their skins or the color of their eyes. Widows seem to have had a great advantage over the young girls since they frequently owned property and were generally experienced in hoeing the garden, tending the cattle and making the soap for the household and hence were more desirable than the giggling teenagers.

Courtships were short and carried on under the eyes of the elders. The custom of bundling,[3] brought over from England and Holland, survived in New England and Middle Atlantic colonies until near the end of the 18th century when it was replaced by "tarrying." Such customs were due in large part to the one-roomed houses, the lack of firewood and other conveniences for the entertaining of guests, especially in the humbler homes.

The practical bent of the Puritan mind is seen in the marriage ceremony itself. William Bradford records that on May 12, 1621, was "the first marriage in this place . . . (it) was thought most requisite to be performed by the magistrate, as being a civill thing upon which many questions about inheritance doe depende with other things most proper to their cognizance, and most consonante to the scriptures."[4] The Pilgrims, by repudiating the religious ceremony and thus emphasizing the material aspects of marriage, had no intention of weakening the bonds of matrimony. They considered the magistrate a representative of both church and state. However, since the civil ceremony was the only legal form of marriage it opened the way for many abuses among the extremist religious groups which permitted couples to perform and dissolve the marriage contract themselves as in the case of the Brownists.

To lift the ceremony from the purely mercenary basis of the law, Cotton Mather recorded that "there was maintained a solemnity called contraction a little before the consummation of a marriage was allowed of. A pastor was usually employed and a sermon also preached on the occasion." But in spite of the "contractions," "shift" marriages in which the shivering brides were married in nothing but thin "shifts," or chemises, and the bridegroom's sheet continued to emphasize the economic aspects of colonial marriages in New England and in New Jersey.[5] Nor were the settlers in the southern colonies less mercenary, as is shown by the following notice, one of many convincing bits of evidence, that appeared in the March 15, 1771, issue of the Virginia *Gazette*. "Yesterday was married in Henrico, Mr. William Carter, aged 23 to Mrs. Sarah Ellyson, Relict of Mr. Gerard Ellyson, deceased, aged 85, a sprightly old tit, with three thousand pounds fortune."[6]

Opposition to religious marriage ceremonies existed as late as 1685 in Massachusetts when a Huguenot clergyman was hailed into court for performing a marriage ceremony in Boston. But three years later Judge Sewall records in his diary, "Thorsday, October 4, 1688. About 5 p.m. Mr. Williard (the pastor) married Mr. Samuel Danforth and Mrs. Hannah Allen."[7] Six years later the Connecticut Court ruled that "for the satisfaction of such as are conscientiously desireous to be marryed by a minister of their plantations do grant the ordayned ministers . . . liberty to joyne in marriage such persons as are qualified for the same according to law."

Thus in New England civil authority rather than religious authority was retained as the basic right of government in the contraction of marriage, even when the ceremony itself was performed by an ordained minister. In time this concept was incorporated into the constitution of every state in the Union.

In the middle Atlantic and southern colonies, the religious marriage ceremony was preceeded by the publishing of banns of the young couple in the churches. This was required by the Church of England in the southern colonies, the Catholics in Maryland, the Quakers in Pennsylvania and the Lutherans in New York.

Strangely enough, marriage was recognized as a transitory state of life, not as a result of recourse to a divorce court as is so frequent today, but because life itself was transitory. Colonial men and women married three, four or five times during their lives, not so much for love as for help in the ever desperate struggle against wilderness conditions.[8] Widows remained unmarried only days, weeks or months, depending on their immediate resources for meeting life's problems. Calhoun cites the instance of Peter Sargent, "a rich Boston merchant (who) had three wives. His second had had two previous husbands. His third wife has lost one husband, and she survived Peter, and also her third husband, who had three wives. His father had four, the last three of whom were widows." Spruill states that the women having the most husbands to her credit was one Elizabeth whose maiden name is long since forgotten but who married successively six husbands, all of whom were prominent in the colony. But the *London Daily Advertiser* of Saturday, July 13, 1765, appeared the following: "One Margaret Gray died lately in Philadelphia aged sixty years remarkable for her having had nine husbands."

Mary Stanard has drawn a delightful illustration from the early records of the Virginia courts.[9] It seems that Cicily Jordan's husband died early in 1623 and Rev. Grevell Pooley sought to propose marriage to her a few days later. Cicily said she would "as willingly have Mr. Pooley as any other" but she did not wish to marry at present. Rev. Pooley tried to trick her into a promise of engagement and then boasted of his achievement at the town inn, whereupon Cicily engaged herself to William Farrar. Rev. Pooley, highly incensed, brought suit against Cicily for breach of promise (the first such suit in the colonies), but he did not win his suit, and Cicily became Mrs. Farrar a few days later.

The numerous marriages of the colonial women tended to lengthen their childbearing years and increase the number of children they bore. Frequently the first child was born before the 16th birthday of the young mother and in one instance the mother of a new-born child is reported in the newspaper as 69 years old and in another instance 76 years old. Mothers and daughters were often recorded as bearing children at the same time. Nelly Custis Lewis, who had several children of her own, wrote to a friend, "My Dear Mother has just recovered from her confinement with her twentieth child, it is a very fine girl, large and healthy. Mamma has suffered extremely, and is still weak."[10]

Twenty children was not an uncommon record for a colonial woman. Sir William Phips was one of twenty-six children, all with the same mother. Jonas Green, the famous printer, had thirty children. Benjamin Franklin was one of seventeen children but he had only three children. Cotton Mather mentions women friends in his diary who had from twenty to twenty-seven children. Elizabeth Thatcher of New Jersey had seventeen children, 118 grandchildren, 133 great-grandchildren and one great-great-grandchild when she died at eighty-seven years (1771). In the south, Robert "King" Carter had five children by his first wife and ten by his second. Robert Carter of "Nomini Hall" had seventeen children, and Charles Carter had twenty-three by his two wives. All of this reads like "population explosion," but it was not. The sober fact is that in spite of the pain of the colonial women in frequent childbearing, the average size of the family in New England including children, servants and all other dependents is estimated at only 9.2 persons per family (1633–1690). The cause of the discrepancy between the birthrate and the size of the average family is found in the very high death rate of infants and women's total lack of authority over their persons.

The unequal rights of married women in the American colonies had more than one unfortunate effect on family and community life. For instance, divorces were made virtually impossible for women (and very few were granted to men). The only recourse for women under intolerable conditions in her home, which she had not the authority to correct, was to disrupt her home and community by "eloping" either with or without a companion-lover.

The newspapers and court records of the periods abound in notices of these elopements. The following notice which appeared on October 4, 1770, is typical of many:

Whereas Hannah, the wife of Daniel Hand, Esq; hath behaved herself in a very unbecoming manner and eloped from her husband, on Thursday night last, without any provocation (supposed to have gone away with a certain Nathan Hand and Ezekiel Hand.) These are to forewarn all persons not to trust her on his account, as he will pay no debts of her contracting from the date hereof. Daniel Hand, Cape May County, New Jersey.[11]

Sometimes the elopement of a wife became a community problem as in the case of Mrs. Daniels of Boundbrook, New York, in 1771. The notice reads:

William Daniels, . . . having beat his wife sometime last week which he had frequently done before, she left him, and went to reside with a Daughter she had at some distance and on Monday night last a number of persons who are termed there Regulators went to Daniels and taking out of bed whipped him.[12]

The next day he was found dead but no one was prosecuted for the act. In the *Pennsylvania Chronical* of April 15–22, 1771, there appeared the following notice of a reward offered:

Ran away, from the subscriber, living in Northampton County, New Jersey, between Mount Holly and Burlington, one John

Alcut, a flatman, about 5 feet 10 inches high, a very likely, portly looking man. Had on a grey bearskin surtout coat, a pair of leather breeches, and a good beaver hat. Went off with him, one Margaret Elton the wife of Thomas Elton, a very likely round-favoured woman. She had on a black crape gown —they are supposed to be gone to Baltimore in Maryland. Whoever will apprehend and secure the said Alcut in any of his Majesty's goals, so that I may obtain justice shall have the above reward payd by Ruel Elton.[13]

Two weeks later, on May 2, Thomas Elton, the injured husband, published the following notice offering more than double the original reward to protect his rights in the situation:

Whereas Margaret, the wife of the subscriber, hath eloped from her husband, with one John Allcott, a flatman, and carried off sundry household goods, of a very considerable value, and the said John Allcott being also greatly in debt to the said subscriber: these are therefore to caution all persons from crediting the said Margaret as her husband will pay no debts of her contracting from this date: and any person who will secure the said John Allcott, and the said Margaret, in anyone of his Majesty's goals upon the continent, so that the subscriber may have an opportunity of getting his money and good again, shall have the above reward, and all reasonable charges, paid by Thomas Elton. . . . The said Margaret answers the following description; she is a short thick body, has a round likely face, black hiar, a little flat nose, her eyes stand at a greater distance from each other than commonly women's eyes do, her cheeks very rosy, she has a small scar under her right nostril, something resembling a cross, she has lost two of her fore teeth, talkative and very fond of singing, about 22 years of age. The said John Allcott answers the following description; he is a well set fellow, about 5 feet 10 inches high, sandy complexion, with grey eyes, has a down look, large hooked nose, wears his hair tied.

Then in the August 30 issue of the same newspaper we learn that:

Whereas, Margaret the wife of Thomas Elton . . . eloped from her husband the first time in company with one John Allcott, and took with her goods to a considerable value, leaving her husband with one child not a year old, and by virtue of an advertisement with a reward of five pounds, it is supposed they parted, and she returned without goods or her cloaths, save what she had on, and still continues in a state of not being reconciled to her husband; these are therefore to forwarn all persons not to harbour her, either by night or day, nor trust nor have any dealings whatsoever with her, at their peril, as I am resolved to prosecute whoever shall be found so doing; and any person or persons who have received the goods which are my property, and her cloaths, which I bought for her, are desired to return them to me at Mountholly, or Burlington, where I will receive them, and gratefully reward them and will pay any debt that she has contracted· upon them. And whereas the said John Alcott is not yet apprehended . . . five pounds reward.[14]

Only a few women dared to publicly refute the accusations brought against them by their husbands as did Hannah Gardiner of Elizabethtown, New Jersey. Levy, her husband, advertised on April 5, 1779:

Whereas the subscriber has great reason to believe that his wife Hannah is determined to run him in debt, as she has been guilty of many lewd practises, and has bedded with another woman's husband for a considerable time: this is to forwarn all persons from trusting her on my account, as I am deter-

mined to pay no debts of her contracting from this date. Levy
Gardner.

Hannah replied in the same newspaper:

Whereas a most malicious and infamous advertisement, signed
Levy Gardner, hath been published, greatly to the prejudice of
his wife Hannah Gardner: this is therefore to inform the public, that said Gardner eloped from his bed and board, left his
wife with five small children, and cohabited with other women;
and as he is a man addicted to all kinds of vice, she forewarns
all persons bedding or boarding with him—any person that will
take up said Gardner, and secure him in any goal, so that his
wife may have restitution made her, shall have thirty dollars
reward, and all reasonable charges paid by Hannah Gardner.

A few colonial women advertised that they would no
longer live with their husbands nor pay their debts. Mary
Quackinbush's notice is a case in point. She advertised:

Whereas John Quackinbush, late of the city of New Brunswick, Cooper, hath eloped from his wife, and left his bed and
board, and contrary to all reason and Christianity, hath contrary to the laws of nature and justice, to stroll about, keeping bad company, stripped her of her goods and bedding, that
she has nothing left to subsist upon: therefore these are to
inform the publick, that the said Mary forewarns any person,
or persons whatever trusting him, for she will pay no debts
he shall contract from the day of the date hereof as witness my
hand the 31st day of August 1762. Mary Quackinbush.[15]

Other Colonial women are reported as handling their
marital problems by physical combat. The wife of John
Davis was hailed into court at Lynn, Massachusetts, in

1680 for "breaking her husband's head with a quart pot."[16] and another turned on the constable who sought to restrain her and pounded him vigorously with a large Bible. Sarah Morgan in July, 1671, was convicted of "striking her husband. . . . The delinquent to stand with a gagg in her mouth half an hour at kittery at a publick town meeting and the cause of her offence writ and put upon her forehead or pay 50 (the price of ten gallons of rum) to the treasurer."

There is no way of knowing how many of these heartbreaking experiences were later adjusted. We can only hope that many like William Carter and his wife eventually came to understand and appreciate each other but did not advertise their reunion as William Carter did in the *Pennsylvania Journal*, November 25, 1762:

Whereas I· William Carter, of Trenton Hunterdon County, some time since advertised my wife Phebe Carter in this paper; this is to inform the publick that as we are upon good terms again, and have agreed to live together, our dealings will be the same as heretofore.[17]

While the number of elopements and the evidences of violence used by the colonial women in their attempts ot solve their marital difficulties may have been due in large part to their legal status of "servant and slave" of their husbands, there remains considerable evidence that many of the colonial women had the same adventurous, freedomloving and lawless attitudes that characterized so many of the brave colonial men.

Fortunately, the majority of the emigrés in each of the colonies were law abiding people and most of the women were loving wives. In spite of their immaturity as brides, the mercenary and unequal aspects of their marriages, their continuous childbearing and the endless hardships of life in the wilderness, most of the colonial women succeeded in making their homes glow with the warmth of love and respect. For the records of the lives of these women one must be content with the slim file of letters and other writings of the relatively few women of the times who had had the great good fortune of having been taught to read and write.

Such a one was Ann Dudley, the first American poet. She was born in 1612 in an English home of education and culture. She was married when she was 16 years old to Simon Bradstreet and at 18 years she emigrated to Massachusetts in company with her husband and others, among whom was her friend Lady Arabella Johnson. Both women were frail and found the pioneer life very difficult;. Lady Arabella died the following spring and Ann Bradstreet was so ill that she wrote:

> Twice ten years old not fully told
> since nature gave me breath,
> My race is run, my thread is spun,
> lo! here is fatal Death.

She recovered, however, and lived another thirty years in the wilderness. Through all the years of struggle her husband was her "magazine of earthly store." She wrote of her love:

> If ever two were one, then surely we!
> If ever man were loved by wife, then thee;
> If ever wife was happy in a man,
> Compare with me, ye women, if you can.

> I prize thy love more than whole mines of gold,
> Or all the riches that the East doth hold,

My love is such that rivers cannot quench,
Nor ought but love from thee give recompense.

My head, my heart, mine eyes my life, my more,
My joy, my magazine of earthly store.
If two be one as surely as thou and I,
How stayest thou there, whilst I at Ipswich lye? [18]

Ann Bradstreet did not live to see her husband become
governor of the colony, or share in his later financial successes. But his love for her deterred him from remarrying
for three years, which was a considerable time for a widower to maintain a home alone in those days.

Mercy Otis was born at Barnstable on Cape Cod in
1728 of a family of "decent elegance" and thirteen children. She was the oldest daughter and studied at home
while her older brothers went to college. At twenty-six she
married James Warren, a merchant at Plymouth, and had
five sons between 1757 and 1766. She died at eighty years
of age after fifty-four years of married life. Besides her
many duties concerning her home and family, she carried
on an extensive correspondence with outstanding people
of her day, wrote a volume of poems, two tragedies and a
three-volume history of the American Revolution. To her
husband she wrote in 1775: "I had contemplated to spend
a day or two with my good father but as you talk of returning so soon I shall give up that and every other pleasure
this world can give for the superior pleasure of your company. I thank you for the many expressions in yours which
bespeak the most affectionate soul. . . . My heart has just
leaped in my bosom and I ran to the stairs imagining I
heard both your voice and your footsteps in the entry.
Though disappointed I have no doubt this pleasure will

be realized as soon as possible by your affectionate M. Warren." Two years later while he was away on patriotic duty she wrote: "Oh! these painful absences. Ten thousand anxieties invade my bosom on your account and sometimes hold my lids waking many hours of the cold and lonely night." And again she to her husband: "It is a matter of equal indifference with me whether I am in the city or the villa provided I have the company of that man whose friendship I have had more than twenty years experience and without whom life has few charms for more." [19]

Abigail Smith was a close friend of Mercy Warren and in frequent correspondence with her. Abigail was born at Weymouth, Massachusetts, in 1744 and was such a frail child that she never went to school nor apparently was greatly encouraged to develop her intellectual life. However, her correspondence covering the last quarter of the 18th century reveals a woman of great intellectual ability and broad social insight. She married John Adams, a lawyer in Boston, in 1764 and had a daughter and three sons during the first ten years of their fifty-four years of married life. Of that life she wrote on May 18, 1778: "...Beneath my humble roof, blessed with the society and tenderest affection of my dear partner, I have enjoyed as much felicity and as exquisite happiness, as falls to the share of mortals. . . ." [20] At another time she wrote: "To be the strength, the inmost joy, of a man who within the conditions of his life seems to you a hero at every turn—there is no happiness more penetrating for a wife than this."

Eliza Lucas was born in 1722 and educated in Mrs. Bodicott's very proper school in England until her father, Lieutenant-Colonel George Lucas, went to South Carolina in 1737 where he bought three large plantations. Two years later he was sent to the West Indies as governor of

Abigail Smith Adams, by C. Schessele. (From the Collections of the Library of Congress)

Antigua. He left Eliza, then seventeen years old, in charge of the plantations as well as his ailing wife and three younger children.

Eliza wrote to her father by every boat, and it is from these letters that we learn of her marriage, in 1744, to Charles Pinckney, a lawyer of Charlestown. He was forty-five years old and recently made a widower by the death of his first wife. Eliza was nineteen years old, in spite of which it was a very happy marriage. Eliza had two sons and a daughter all of whom survived her. On the occasion of one of his numerous trips away from home, Eliza wrote to him: "I can indeed tell you I have the greatest esteem and affection imaginable for you; that next to Him that form'd it, my heart is intirely at your disposal, but this you knew the day I gave you my hand;...." After his death in 1758 she wrote to her mother who was in Antigua: "I was for more than 14 years the happiest mortal upon earth! Heaven had blessed me beyond the lott of mortals & left me nothing to wish for.... I had not a desire beyond him." [21] Though she lived to be 80 years old, she did not remarry. She managed the plantations of her husband, educated her children, and saw them marry and become valuable citizens in the new Republic.

The love and fidelity of Ann, Abigail and Eliza were not unique, or even uncommon in their times. As the attics and cellars of olden days give way to modern structures, old bundles of letters and journals, yellowed with age, tumble out of odd corners and cob-webbed niches and give us new glimpses into the hearts of the women who gave us our dear-bought heritage.

For, happily or unhappily, the colonial homes had to be maintained if life was to be sustained under the primitive conditions. In the early years of each settlement, the women had very little with which to create homes of love and comfort. The flimsy plank shanties or dank "dug-outs," even when replaced by sturdier log houses, were small and dark within for lack of windows. Also they were herded together in cramped palisades, or were themselves palisaded against the ever-present foe of man or beast.[22]

For instance, in 1664, at Dedham, Massachusetts, there were 95 log houses (18 feet by 16 feet) built close together on a small plot of ground that offered some natural protection. At Waterbury, Connecticut, there were 40 such houses by 1678, "sit down close together" for mutual protection.

The poorer houses in time were torn down and replaced by larger houses, or were left to the newcomers or poorer elements in the communities. The later houses were built of brick, stone and seasoned timber. By 1675 there were a considerable number of such well-built homes in the larger settlements but in the "back country" the houses were still crude shelters. Chester, New Hampshire, did not have a frame house until 1732; Hallowell, Maine, settlers lived in log huts until after 1784, and at Ryegate, Vermont, there were log houses still occupied in 1865.

The later houses were one and one-half or two stories in height, having two to four rooms on the ground floor and two lofts or bedrooms on the second floor. By the end of the century there were a few substantial mansions in each of the colonies. In Virginia, the first great mansion was built by Governor William Berkeley in 1642. During the 18th century the number of substantial homes and elaborate mansions increased greatly. The thriving cities of New England and the Middle Atlantic colonies could boast of many two and three storied homes of elegance with stables, barns and storehouses. In the Southern colo-

The David Field House, Madison, Connecticut, 1719. (From the Collections of the Library of Congress)

Mount Vernon and the Powell Coach, similar to the one used by Martha Washington. (Courtesy of the Mount Vernon Ladies Association)

nies the wealthy landowners expanded their houses and built onto, or nearby, them a number of special work houses such as washhouses, bakehouses, dairyhouses, storehouses, smokehouses, kitchenhouses, stables, barns, henhouses, and schoolhouses. Farther away were the dwellings for the slaves. These workhouses kept the main house "more cool and sweet" and free from the "smell of hot victuals offensive in hot weather."

About the French colony in New Orleans Madeleine Hachard wrote of "well-built houses, with pillars of whitewashed masonry, wainscotted and laticed, covered with shingles, that is thin boards cut to resemble slates and having all the beauty and appearance of slates."

Women's work in these colonial homes, whether they were stately mansions or a one-roomed cabin, included five major funtions. These were: (1) the maintenance of the house and workhouses; (2) the procuring, processing and preserving of most of the food for the household; (3) the clothing of the members of the family, apprentices, servants, slaves and other dependents; (4) the caring for the very young, the very old and the sick of the household, and (5) sharing in the social and religious life of the home.

Generally, the colonial homemaker shared each of these functions, to a greater or lesser extent, with her husband and other male members of the household, but in an astounding number of instances the colonial women had to carry the full burden of responsibility alone through months and years of struggle.

For instance, Frank Noble died in a snow storm near Dover, New Hampshire, in 1664. Mrs. Noble was left with four small, starving children.[23] She not only killed a moose that was caught in a thicket during the snow storm but dragged the carcass, which she had quartered, to her cabin and thus saved the children's lives. She stayed on and continued to redeem the homestead land from the wilderness until she had 200 acres of ground under cultivation and her children had grown to maturity.

Mrs. Storey was in Connecticut with her ten children when she received word that her husband had been killed by a falling tree on their new homestead at Salisbury, Vermont.[24] She gathered up her children and went at once to the site of her husband's death. Because of the danger from Indians and wild animals, she built a cave-like room behind a dense thicket that grew by a stream. Here she and her children lived for a number of years while she was clearing the land and turning the forest, acre by acre, into a profitable farm. For food she killed wild animals, fished in the streams and gathered greens, berries and herbs in the forest until her land produced enough to feed them all and she could turn over the heavy burdens of work to her grown children.

Mrs. Williamson of Pennsylvania saw both her father and her husband killed by the Indians, yet she remained to improve the homestead until her sons were mature enough to shoulder the load.[25] Later she was taken captive in an Indian raid but escaped and returned safely to her home. Mary Slocumb of North Carolina took entire charge of her husband's large plantation during his protracted absences even splitting the rails and killing the wild animals for food. The heroism of other women who survived similar circumstances can be found in the records of each of the colonies.

The maintenance of the home itself included keeping the house warm, lighted at eventide, clean and defended against all types of marauders. Today that would mean turning up the thermostat, turning on the electric lights, guiding the vacuum cleaner about the house, stuffing the washer-dryer and checking on the door locks, all of which rarely consumes two hours of work in the day of an average homemaker.

In contrast, merely keeping the colonial house warm meant constantly feeding the ever-hungry flames in the enormous open fireplace.[26] Many of the fireplaces were from ten to twelve feet square with brick ovens that measured two and a half feet wide by one and a half feet high. It took from thirty to forty cords of great logs to keep the fire burning through one year. This would have made a pile of logs from two to four times the size of the early houses each year. Generally, the men of the family hauled the logs from the forests, stacked them near the house, chopped or sawed them into usable lengths and brought them into the fireplaces. But when the men were away or sick or dead, the women had to replenish the fire or freeze or starve, for it was also her only heat for cooking.

But keeping the flames bright was not just a back-breaking haul. It also involved the careful selection of the right logs. Green, slow-burning wood was needed for the back log and the lug-pole. Pitch wood was used for quick heat, just enough to warm the house or boil the stew and still not burn the chimney itself or the thatched roof above it. In the early years so many houses caught fire from the wood and clay chimneys that laws were passed in 1631 forbidding the building of wooden chimneys or the thatching of the roofs.

Although wood and clay chimneys continued to be built in the open country, most of the houses in the settled communities had chimneys of brick and stone. By 1653 many of the fireplaces had iron back-pieces wrought in handsome designs. These helped to control the fire and led to the invention of other improvements. Mantel pieces of carved wood, tiling, and stone came into use among the Dutch. One writer tells us "the chimney-places are very droll-like: they have no jambs nor lintell as we have, but a flat grate, and there projects over it a lum in the form of the cat-and-clay lum, and commonly a muslin or ruffled pawn around it."

The fire was rarely allowed to die as the crude flint and steel devices for sparking a fire were very scarce and not improved greatly before the Revolution. Live coals of peat or slow burning wood were buried deep in the ashes each night and brought back to flames by heavy blowing upon them the next morning.; Bellows for this purpose were available to some colonial women by 1633.

Because the houses were very drafty, the heat from the fireplaces rarely reached across the room or into the sleeping quarters. Circular metal warming pans of brass and copper four or five inches in diameter with two or three foot handles were partly filled with hot coals and moved about between sheets or blankets to warm the beds before retiring. Foot stoves were also used not only at church and on sleigh rides, but also in the homes. At first hot stones were put in a metal box, or stove, but later the boxes were lined with perforated tin, and live coals were used to keep the people warm.

It was not until well into the 18th century that the colonial women saw any real improvements in the methods of heating their homes. Coal was used in grates placed in the fireplaces in New England by 1724, but as the coal had to be shipped from Scotland and Nova Scotia, few housewives could afford to use it. Coal mines were opened on the James River in Virginia in 1750 and in Pennsylvania in 1766 but were not greatly developed until after 1800.

The German settlers in Pennsylvania had the first real stoves in the new country. They consisted of sheetmetal square or oblong shaped boxes, three sides of which were within the house. The fourth side, with a door, was outside the house. The fire was thus built and replenished from outside the house, which was very inconvenient in cold weather. Their "jamb stove" consisted of five iron stove plates clamped together at the back of the fireplace and extending into the adjoining room. They also developed hot air drums for heating the second floor rooms above the fireplace.

Then in 1742 Benjamin Franklin brought the whole fireplace out from the wall and into the room by extending the chimney, or stove pipe, from the wall, thus greatly improving the heat-potential of the stove and reducing the labor of maintaining the fire. Henry Stiegel improved and elaborated on the Franklin stove so that by the end of the century some of the rooms in the homes could be heated with comparative ease. But this was true for only a very few homes, since the new-fangled stoves did not come into common use until after 1800 and, even then, only in the larger communities along the eastern seaboard.

Lighting the small rooms in the early colonial homes would seem to have been an easy and simple operation, but it was not.[27] Candle-wood tapers and torches made from roots or knots of resinous pine first supplemented the fitful light from the open fireplaces. The torches were fragrant, sooty and gave an uneven light. Worst of all, they dripped black, gluey tar continuously so that most often they were placed at the side of the fireplace over a flat stone which could be replaced when it became heavily coated with tar. As late as 1662 Governor Winthrop wrote to the Royal Society in England that candlewood was much used for house light in Virginia, New York and New England.

Mr. Higginson wrote in 1630 that "though New England has no tallow to make candles of, yet by abundance of fish thereof it can afford oil for lamps." The "Betty Lamps" and "Phoebe Lamps" of the period were at first shaped like old Roman lamps with one or two cotton rags used for wicks. These were improved upon by shielding the flame from drafts with variously shaped glass chimneys and placing bright pieces of metal back of the light to reflect its brilliance. A number of fatty substances were used as fuel. The lamps were made of iron, brass, copper, pewter and glass continued to be used in the city homes throughout the periods, though they gave only a smoky, dull light and were exceedingly hard to keep free of soot.

Candles were very precious even when tallow and wax were available because they represented weeks or months of hard labor. But as they were vastly cleaner than candle wood or oil lamps, they soon became the most popular method of lighting the house. Tallow candles were made from the grease rendered from deer, moose, bear and beet fat which had been collected through months of labor. Tallow and water were placed in large kettles (often two feet in diameter) over a fire and heated. Impurities were skimmed off the tallow, and when fairly clear the great kettles were lifted off the trammels and placed ready for the wicks to be dipped into them. The wicks were made of twisted hemp, cotton, tow and milkweek silk and tied to rods at regular intervals. The average candle was dipped many times and a long days hard work might produce as many as 200 candles if multiple dipping was possible. Later, tallow candles were also formed by pouring the melted tallow into moulds in which the wicks had been

Interior, showing the fireplace moved away from the wall, Painter
House, West Haven, Connecicut, 1695. (From the Collections of the
Library of Congress)

carefully set. Rush lights were made from the pith of rush plants dipped repeatedly into kettles of tallow or grease and the adhering layers allowed to harden.

Wax candles were made by pressing bits of heated wax around a wick and smoothing the surface. The wax used was of three kinds: beeswax from honey combs which was never very plentiful, the wax from bay berries and myrtle berries which were gathered in the autumn and boiled until all of the dark green wax had been skimmed off and made ready to form the fragrant candles, and spermaceti, a fatty substance from the head of a species of whale. The spermaceti candles came into use along the Atlantic seaboard about 1750 and soon proved to burn longer and brighter than any other candle. By the end of the century they became the most popular method of lighting in the homes of those who could afford to buy them.

If heating and lighting her home were burdensome travail for the colonial homemaker, keeping her house reasonably clean must have been a back-breaking job. As a matter of fact, it was so difficult a task that the women joined forces and helped each other "speed the hours and misery." This cooperative work was called a "whang" in some areas, and rightly so, for the women beat and "whanged" every article of furniture that they did not wash or scour.

Consider what the colonial homemaker had to do before she could invite her neighbor to help her in a "whang." [28] First, she had to obtain the water needed. Bucket by bucket it had to be carried from the nearby well or spring, the town pump, or a water cart. Boston had a 12 by 12 foot reservoir by 1652, and every town in New England had a public pump by 1776. The Moravians at Bethlehem, Pennsylvania had wooden pipes from a spring, through which they pumped water into the town in 1755. Tradition has it that John Headley of Newport, Rhode Island, had the first home with running water in it. He had piped the water from an underground spring into the kitchen of his home which was a wonder to all who saw it. Water piped to a consumer did not come until the 19th century. The colonial homemaker carried her water as best she could and perforce used it sparingly.;

Soap was the colonial homemaker's next cleaning requirement, but soap took a long time to make, so the process had to be started long before the "whangs" began. First, the ashes from hard wood burned in the fireplace were collected in elevated "leach" tubs, covered with water and allowed to leak lye into tubs below. Animal grease which had also been collected through the preceding months was put in huge kettles over a blazing fire and the tubs of lye added. When the saponified grease had jellied, it was considered usable and called soft soap. Tubs of it were stored and lasted for several months. One old recipe for soap states: "The Great Difficulty in making Soap come is the want of Judgment of the Strength of the Lye. If your Lye will bear up an Egg or a Potato so you can see a piece of the Surface as big as a Ninepence it is just strong enough." [29]

For scouring the colonial homemaker brought sand from the beaches or river banks.[30] Brooms were made from slim branches of birch, ash or hickory trees bound together with twisted lengths of hemp, tow or cotton. In later years, Benjamin Franklin planted the seeds found on an imported broom, and by the end of the century brooms made from "broom-corn" and "guinea wheat straw" came into common use in the cities. Brushes were made of corn husks and tough-stemmed weeds and feather dusters from barnyard fowl, but these did not come into use until late in the period, when elaborate furniture required delicate dusting.

Cleanliness in the home as we know it today was impossible. Not only was moderate cleanliness extremely difficult to attain, but as late as 1774 one diarist reports. "The spirit of cleanliness has not yet in the least troubled the major part of the inhabitants; for in general, they are very great sluts and slovens. When they clean their houses, which by the bye, is very seldom, they are unwilling to remove the filth from themselves, for they place it close to their doors, which in summertime, breeds an innumerable quantity of bugs, fleas and vermin." [31]

To get any real idea of what a "whang" really meant in terms of work, you need to close your eyes and imagine yourself in the doorway of a one-roomed shack. First, look at the floor. In the earliest years it was of hard-packed earth that could be swept of trash but was always either dusty or damp or both. Soon it became a rough puncheon floor of slats of wood hewed flat with axe or adze that defied your best efforts to keep it clean.; Later, the floor was made of wide smooth boards that could be scoured and delicately traced with designs of sprinkled blue and white sand. Toward the end of the eighteenth century carpets replaced the bearskin rug before the fireplace, the one room was increased to several, but by that time the "whangs" had moved westward with the pioneers, and slaves or servants had taken over the work of cleaning in the city homes.

The walls, at first, were shaggy with bark and bits of mud and plaster and were impossible to keep clean.[32] But need for greater insulation from the cold winter snows, rather than the desire for cleanliness, led to the improve-

ment of the inner walls of the colonial homes. Paneling
and wainscotting the walls of the principle rooms of the
homes became fairly common by 1632 in the New England
and Middle Atlantic colonies. Paneled walls with secret
closets were common in the South by 1700. Some walls
were "white-limed" with crushed clam any oyster shells
mixed to make them bright. Some women mixed clay with
linseed oil and dyes and decorated the walls of their homes.
The Dutch women hung their walls with skins and decorated leather, other wealthy homes had tapestries. Wall-
paper was brought to the colonies in 1735 and was manufactured in Pennsylvania in 1785, but it was so expensive
that it did not come into common use until long after 1800.
The ceilings of the colonial homes remained unfinished for
most of the periods as the crossbeams were handy storage
places for filches of pork, beef, venison and bundles of
corn, beans, and herbs of all kinds.

One thing is fairly certain—the colonial homemakers
had no window-washing problem until very late in the period and then it was the problem of only the well-to-do
women in the towns.[33] During the early years, and always
in the out-post homes, the windows were mere loop-holes
in the walls often covered by heavy, split logs, or bark
shutters for protection. At first greased paper was used to
cover the opening and give a little light. By 1700 some of
the homes in the south and in the New England villages
had small leaded glass windows, though outlying settlements such as Kennebec, Maine, did not have a square of
glass as late in 1745. In New Orleans the French settlers
had many windows in their houses, but instead of glass,
the sashes were covered with a thin linen cloth which let
in almost as much light as glass and much more air.

The colonial homemakers of the earlier decades also

had no dish washing problem because they had few if any dishes. Few colonial homemakers before 1750 had any chinaware, glassware or silverware and very few pieces of pewter. Wooden trenchers were used to hold the food for one or more persons and often the whole family. Their problem was the cleaning of the great iron or copper kettles and pans that hung in the fireplace. As early as 1610 [34] they were forbidden to "rench and make cleane, any kettle, pot or pan or such vessel within twenty foote of the old well or new pumpe" at Jamestown, Virginia. So they were forced to drag the kettles and pans down to the river bank or carry water to some secluded spot for the cleaning.

Their tables were one or two great slabs of wood, fastened together for greater breadth, and laid on trestles. These could be picked up and carried out of doors to scour clean, or give room for the extra beds when needful. Stools and benches were used with chests and trunks for storage purposes. The ever-present cradle was at first a log hewn out sufficiently to hold the baby. Later they were made of hand-hewn boards with rockers. These also could be moved out of doors and cleaned in the sunshine.

Not so easily moved were the principle articles of furniture, the beds. Beds seem to have been one of the colonial homemaker's most nagging problems. She seems never to have had enough sleeping space for the guests who came to her door. In 1733 William Byrd wrote in his diary "We were obliged to lodge very sociably in the same apartment with the family, where, reckoning men, women and children, we mustered no less than nine persons who all pigged very lovingly together." [35] In 1748, when George Washington was surveying Shenandoah Valley, he wrote that he lived with "a parcel of barbarians" and usually "lay down before the fire upon a little hay, straw, fodder or bearskin . . . with man, wife and children like a parcel of dogs and cats." As late as 1780–1782 Chastellux wrote of the better class homes, "Their houses are spacious and ornamented, but their apartments are not commodious. They· make no ceremony of putting three or four persons in the same room; nor do these make any objection to their being heaped together; . . . they want nothing in the whole house but a bed, a dining room, and a drawing room for company." [36]

The first beds were often straw pallets in the corners of the rooms or bear skins arranged close to the fireplace. These were replaced by wooden slabs laid across poles supported by forked posts and by rude, cord-laced wooden bedsteads with trundle or "truckle" beds for the children pushed underneath when not in use. These appeared in every room and still were not enough in the earlier decades. In the better homes some of the beds were heavily draped for privacy and to prevent the entrance of a breath of night air which they feared greatly. The Dutch women had alcove beds with drapes and beds on hinges that could be turned up against the walls in the daytime. Both kinds were a real task to keep clean.

Blankets, mostly homespun, were used extensively and were washed infrequently.[37] Sheets and pillow slips were used sparingly in the better homes. When the women had gathered enough soft goose feathers, they made their famous feather beds and bolsters, which were also very difficult to keep fresh and clean. "Flock" beds and bolsters were similar to the feather beds but were stuffed with bits of wool, cotton or other rags and so were not as light and fluffy as those of goose down. Coverlets of oznaburg and other homespun fabrics were used in the better homes, but they were so heavy and hard to wash that they were cleaned infrequently, perhaps once every several years. Other pieces of furniture such as spinning wheels and looms were added as it became possible for the women to produce the clothing and other necessary articles.

While home furnishings remained rude and simple in the out-lying homes, with the growing wealth of the communities, there was a marked change in the furnishing of the city homes during the 18th century. The first chair mentioned in colonial documents is the one Lord Delaware sat in at church in Virginia in 1623.[38] The inventories of the settlers show very few chairs before 1650. In general, chairs were seats for the patriarchal heads of the government or the home. They were used only by governors, presiding chairmen, and in the families by the fathers or eldest male member of the family. The wife and children sat on stools and benches until much later, when side-chairs or "Lady chairs" came into vogue. The benches by the fireplace were given high-board backs to protect the occupant from the cold drafts by 1640. Toward the end of the 18th century the furniture became elaborate in proportion to the accumulated wealth of the family. Mahogany replaced pine and maple. Leather and woven tapestry upholstery took the place of split willow and corded chairs seats and lovely imports from the far-off countries embellished the tables and mantles of the well-to-do homes.

Washing the family laundry has been a hardy perennial problem for women from earliest times. It appears in the records of every generation of homemakers throughout history. Today it is a matter of moments of work, since the beating and scrubbing is done by machines and detergents, and ironing is almost eliminated. Not so in Jamestown in 1610. Then "no launderesse, dare to wash any unclean linnen, drive bucks, or throw out the water or suds of fowle cloathes in the open streete, within the palizadoes or within 40 foote of the same. . . ." [39]

Thus, the earliest colonial homemakers, for good sanitary reasons, were forced to do their washing by the side of the nearest stream until the colony had outgrown the cramped quarters of the palisades.

Rev. White, in his report of the landing of the settlers in Maryland (1634) gives a picture of the hazards of such laundry work. "We took land first in Saint Clement's which is compassed about with a shallow water, and admits no access without wading; here by the overturning of the shallop the maids which had been washing at the land were almost drowned, beside the loss of much linen, and among the rest, I lost the best part of mine. . . ." [40]

"Bucking tubs" and "cowles" were available to the colonial homemaker within 50 years of their first landing at Jamestown. The tubs were made either by burning and gouging out sections of tree trunks, or later, made of wooden staves. By then she also had grooved wooden washboards and soon after hempen clotheslines and headless wooden clothespins. In an inventory of one large plantation in Virginia in 1728 there was listed under "In the wash house: 7 box irons, 12 heaters, 8 wash tubs, 2 old chests, 1 pot rack, 1 andiron and parcell new feather in bag." [41]

Washings were done less frequently than now, sometimes once a year, once in three months, or once a month in good drying weather. Ironing of the linens in New England and some of the Middle Atlantic colonies was done with cold blocks of hard wood by which the linen was slowly brought to a shining texture. Later, box iron heaters and sad irons came into use. These were heated on the hearth, or, in the Southern colonies, in brick-lined holes in the ground, or sunken ovens located near the cooking house for convenience.[42]

Soon after 1725, advertisements of experts in the field of laundry work began to appear in the newspapers. Fine laundering, clear-starching, scouring, dyeing and dry cleaning were all done "after the best manner" according to the advertisements. But, the services of such experts were too expensive for all but the very well-to-do homemaker.

Overshadowing the gayest moments or the dullest hours was the ever-present terror of attack from Indians. Few colonial women were entirely free from this terror even in the well established cities. On the westward moving frontier, the danger was imminent at all times. Day and night, winter and summer, no one could foretell when the fury of the tribesmen would fall upon them, their children and their homes and fields.

Yet in each of the original settlements, the Indians had made gestures of friendship, particularly to the women colonists. At St. Augustine Chief Seloy gave the Spanish settlers his own council house and the Indian women showed the newcomers how to cook and preserve many of the indigenous foods and herbs. Later, the news of the massacre of the French at Fort Caroline and subsequent attacks destroyed the friendly relations and left terror in their wake. Yet the women of the Indian tribes continued to exchange goods with the women settlers, often in secrecy.

The Jamestown settlers inherited the bitterness and tragedy of Roanoke Island, where in 1585 Grenville and his party were warmly received by the Indians. Later, when an Indian boy stole a silver cup belonging to Grenville, he ordered a whole Indian village and its corn fields destroyed by fire. Thus, he made bitter enemies for the white settlers who followed.

The Jamestown settlement was repeatedly attacked by the Indians, in spite of the efforts of John Smith and other leaders to work out peaceful relations. The women as well as the men had to be constantly on the alert.[43] In the massacre of 1622, Mrs. John Baldwin, though wounded, held a number of Indians at bay by shooting at them from within her cabin until a rescue party arrived from a nearby plantation. Mrs. Proctor fought the Indians again and again. Mrs. Boys, who was taken prisoner by the Indians, managed to assuage the anger of her captors and was returned to the colony unharmed, but she was "sent back naked and in Manner and Fashion like one of the Indian Queens."

When the Pilgrims came to Massachusetts, they had already learned of the earlier Indian attacks on the Spanish and English settlements. They landed in fear and sought at once to establish friendly relations with the local tribes. In 1621, Governor Winslow wrote "We have found the Indians very faithful in their convenant of peace to us, very loving, and ready to pleasure us. We often go to them, and they come to us."[44]

The women settlers helped in maintaining the friendly relations in many ways, especially by their willingness to learn from the Indian women and to share their own knowledge of cooking and caring for the sick and wounded. However, the friendly relations did not last long. Inter-tribal rivalry led to raid after raid upon isolated settlements. Later, the French and Indian War added fuel to the enmity and took the lives of hundreds of settlers. Men and women alike were forced to fight for their lives and the lives of their loved ones. To illustrate, Mrs. Pentry was returning home in a canoe when she saw an unusual movement in the water nearby.[45] She hastily shot the Indian as he rose from the water, hit another and then fled to her house. She found her husband gone, followed his trail and shot the Indian who was about to kill her husband, then turned just in time to drive a hunting knife into the Indian who was attacking her. When she was sure there were no other Indians about, she carried her husband to their cabin and eventually nursed him back to health.

Mrs. Hendee was another such woman.[46] While Mr. Hendee was away on military duty and Mrs. Hendee was working in the field, a party of Indians captured her children. She swam the river and marched into the middle of the Indian encampment and there demanded the return of her children. Astonished at her bravery the Indians took her to the commanding officer who not only released her children but later, when she returned, gave her, also, the children of her distressed neighbor.

Mrs. Bradley was making soap when a party of Indians came, whereupon she poured the boiling soap on one of them.[47] Later, she was taken prisoner, gave birth to a child who was killed during her captivity and was eventually sold to a Frenchman for eighty livres. Mrs. Bradley's harrassing experience was not unlike that of many other colonial women who were taken captive. Mary White Rowlandson is perhaps the best-known illustration, since she was not only returned to her home, but also wrote a clear account of her harrowing experiences for us to read.

Since the captive women had a market value either in ransom money or as the result of sales to the French in Canada, the women taken captive in New England were not ravaged. Rev. Thury in 1689 stated that the Indians ". . . offered no insult to the Englishwomen and girls; and I can attest as an eyewitness now, that these same Englishwomen are as tranquil and secure for their honor as if they

Return of the Captives. (From the Collections of the Library of Congress)

were in their own homes." [48] They were made drudgery slaves to their owners and killed or left to die when they were made unequal to the tasks assigned them. A few of the captive women escaped or were ransomed from the Indians or the French people who had purchased them.

A few of the captive women accepted Indian husbands and seem to have lived happy and productive lives. Eunice Williams of Deerfield, Massachusetts, and Frances Slocumb, who was captured during the Wyoming Valley massacre in Pennsylvania, both married Indian chiefs and were reported to have lived long and happy lives. Mary Jemison was twelve years old when she was captured in 1755. [49] She was adopted by the Seneca tribe; married to a Delaware warrior, had one son before her husband died; married again and had six more children by her second husband; and wrote the story of her life before she died in 1833 at ninety years of age.

The Dutch settlers were unusually successful in making friendly alliances with the Indians. They admitted the Indians freely within the palisadoes and in their homes. The women had a large share in these peaceful negotiations. Though the Indians did not make good servants, the Dutch women hired them to lift heavy kettles and split the firewood. When the Indians were in need they often gave them food and shelter. Many of the Dutch women learned the Algonquin language and talked freely with the Indian women.

In 1656, when the Dutch women planned their market place, they invited the "wilden" women to join them. Several women were especially interested in the "wilden" women. Madame Sarah Kierstede had a large shed erected in her back yard for their accommodation. [50] She spoke their language fluently and helped them so many times that they gave her a tract of land along the Hackensack River. Mrs. Polly Alexander's home overlooked the market place. She frequently visited with the Indian women. As she spoke their language she soon learned of many of their problems and was able to help them in various ways. One such helpful act was the gift of a spinning wheel which she taught them to use. The "wilden" women were so grateful that they offered to adopt her into their tribe. Mrs. Caty Van Cortlandt Phillipse provided a school for the Indian children and built and endowed a church for their use at Rensselaerswyck.

There is no doubt but that the friendly activities of the Dutch women materially assisted the Dutch men in the defense of the homes of the early settlers. But as the population of the colony grew, and white settlers penetrated deeper and deeper into Indian territory, so did the fear within the Indian tribes grow and their sense of grievance mount. Treaties were signed and peace temporarily restored after each violent attack, but hate and a deep-seated desire for retaliation remained in the hearts of the Indians to torment the colonists throughout the period.

Mrs. Mack, for instance, left her cabin-fortress to get some corn to cook. She heard a slight noise nearby and nearly panicked.[51] She took a deep breath and walked stiffly back to her cabin, put her hungry children to bed with promises, loaded her gun, put it to a loophole in the cabin and waited, tense and white with terror, through the long hours of the night. Toward dawn, an Indian dropped down through the chimney and started to attack her with his tomahawk. She shot and killed him and three others who were outside the cabin. Fearing more and larger attacks, she started with her children for the nearest fort some miles away. The Indians captured her and the children en route, but she contrived to kill her attackers and, eventually, brought her children safely to the English fort where her husband was stationed. Another woman, Nancy Van Alstine, fought the Indians successfully so many times that she became known as the "Patriot Mother" of the Mohawk Valley in upper New York.

Similar agonizing experiences were the fate of the women settlers in each of the colonies, in spite of the best efforts of peaceful men and women, such as William Penn, Madame Montour and Mary Musgrove. The basic facts of land forfeiture, fear, and the desire for vengeance rancored in the minds of the Indians. The chief of the Delaware summarized their attitude succinctly to Governor William Denny at Easton, Pennsylvania, in 1756 when he stamped his foot and said, "This ground that is under me is mine and has been taken from me by fraud and forgery." [52] No amount of talks or gifts could change his attitude, nor that of the other tribes of Indians who had for centuries roamed along the shores of the Atlantic.

While wild animals did not have the skill or cunning of the Indians, they were a very serious problem to all the pioneer colonists. Wolves, bears (black and brown), cougars or mountain lions, and other wild animals were an ever-present danger from Maine to Florida. One of the experiences of Mrs. Vredenberg will illustrate the immediacy of this kind of danger.

In the absence of her husband, Mrs. Vredenbergh attended to the evening chores, put her three children to bed and laid down herself to rest until her husband's return. [53] She did not bolt the window, or cover the fire since she expected her husband to return by midnight. She had scarcely composed herself when she saw a mountain lion, his mouth dripping blood, leap through the window and saunter to the hearth where he laid down and presently went to sleep. She laid utterly still through several hours of paralyzing torture until she heard her husband's returning footsteps. The mountain lion stirred and she shrieked to warn her husband. The lion, now as terrified as she, leaped over the man in the doorway and fled into the darkness, while Mrs. Vredenbergh collapsed sobbing in her husband's arms.

Besides the physical hazards of maintaining a home in a wild and untamed land, the colonial homemaker had to face the dangers inherent in the colonies themselves. Women as well as men had to defend their property rights when there was any change in government, or government policy, that affected their homes. For instance, when the Dutch took over the English settlements in Connecticut, or when the English took over the Dutch settlements along the Hudson River and the Swedish and Finnish settlements along the Delaware River, property ownership had to be reestablished under the new government. Each change in government, or overlord, as in the case of Maryland or the Carolinas, meant the adjustment of the vaguely drawn boundary lines. Since few of the colonists could read or write, the problems of the ajudication of property rights were often unfair and discriminatory against women. The colonial court records abound in claims and suits brought by women widowed or single for the ownership of their homes and farmlands.

Because the boundary lines were very inaccurately drawn, newcomers often encroached on land already allotted. A case in point is that of 527 families of Palatines who were brought to New York in 1711 by Governor Robert Hunter. They were first detained on Governor's Island while a dispute regarding the land assigned them was fought in the Governor's home. Then they were promised land along the west bank of the Hudson River. This decision was contested, and finally the majority of the Palatinates took squatter's rights on land along Schoharie River in 1712–1713 and settled in seven "dorfs" or compact villages. When in 1715 Sheriff Adams arrived and tried to arrest the leaders, he found himself facing a mob of angry women led by the superb Magdalena Zeh.[54] He was overpowered by brooms, rakes, and hoes and dragged through the barnyards. Then he was put on a rail and ridden "skimington" through the several settlements and dumped on a far bridge en route to Albany and left to die. Sometime later Sheriff Adams and a posse returned and arrested a few of the squatters. The land grants, however, were not clearly established until 1725.

The unequal legal rights of married women in the colonies presented the most subtle and difficult danger to the colonial homemaker in the safe-guarding of her family. In Masachusetts, for example, if her husband was a "poor provider," the local court could, and did, take her children away from her, and she could do nothing about it.[55] The records of Dorchester, Massachusetts, 1679, contain references to a certain Francis Bale who was interviewed "concerning his outward estate" at the town meeting. His answers were found unsatisfactory so that they ". . . advised him to dispose of two of his children," and when "his answer was that his wife was not willing, the Selectment p'swaded him to p'swad his wife to it" since it must be done by their order whether the mother agreed to the loss of the little children or not.

But, in New England poverty was not the only hazard which the colonial homemaker faced in endeavoring to hold her family together. If she and her husband were illiterate and so could not teach their children to read the alphabet and catechism, the town council could and did take the children out of the home and apprentice or bind them to whomever they determined could teach the children. The mother was impotent to protect the sanctity of her family life. In the New England colonies the universal education laws were enforced on all the families whether rich or poor, but in the southern colonies the laws affected only the poor families.

Religious bigotry also contributed to the hazardous life of the colonial homemaker. In each of the colonies some women were forced out of the settlements and into the wilderness because of their religious beliefs. Such women as Ann Hutchinson, Deborah Moody, and many Quaker women were persecuted and their homes destroyed because their faith in a God of love and mercy did not coincide with the faith of the men in authority in some of the colonies.

Looking back over two centuries one can see how slowly, through infinite patience and pain and dogged persistence, the colonial homemakers, with or without the aid of their husbands, changed the dank, dark hillside caves, the flimsy shacks and log chabins, into homes of beauty and comfort along the eastern seaboard, while her sisters in the westward flow of the colonists still fought to win and enrich their family hearthstones in the wilderness.

4

She Rose up While it is yet Night
and Gave Meat to her Household

Of the five primordial functions of the colonial homemaker mentioned in the preceding chapter, the work involved in feeding her family was undoubtedly the most
strenuous and time consuming. From the day the first
colonial women set foot on American soil until long after
the Revolutionary War, the fierce struggle for food continued unabated with only brief period of affluence for the
great majority of colonial homemakers. In each colony
there were a few wealthy settlers who soon acquired a surplus of foods and were lavish in their table service, but all
around them were struggling, half-starved pioneers who
had yet to gain the luxury of abundance.

Supplies from Spain, France, England, Holland and the
West Indies were often delayed, spoiled, or lost at sea,
sometimes by storms and sometimes by plundering pirates.
Whatever the cause, the supplies were at first generally
inadequate to the needs of the colonists, so that there was
more than one "starving time" in most of the settlements.

118

At St. Augustine starvation periods recurred many times during the Spanish occupation of Florida. The basic causes lay in four facts: that the men of the colony were mostly soldiers where farmers were needed, that the sites selected for the settlements were chosen for their military advantage rather than for farming use, that the Indians were conquered rather than treated as equals, and that the help from Spain was totally inadequate. Pedro Menendez reported to the Spanish King in October 1577: "As for farmers there is nothing to say for they do not dare cultivate the ground two hundred paces away and starve to death, themselves and their wives and children. Accordingly they beg him to give them food or send them out of the country . . . . he has enough flour for three months and wine for one month. . . . It would be necessary to send immediately . . . wine, flour, and other small things . . . for provisioning the men." [1]

In the same year the king received two other reports on the food conditions in the colony. Bartolome Martinez reported that he was raising a garden within the fort. He wrote, "I planted with my own hands grape vines, pomegranate trees, orange and fig trees; wheat, barley, onions and garlic." [2]

Gastillo Y Ahedo reported that the soldiers were receiving the 2½ "reals" or pieces of eight, worth a few English pennies, for each person for their daily ration, but so much of the supplies were spoiled when they arrived that the ration only bought them a pint of wine and a pound and a half of bread, so "that they suffered the greatest need from hunger." [3]

The following year the governor of Cuba refused to send farmers or food to St. Augustine because of their own local shortage of food stuffs. Menendez reported on conditions in the Florida settlements again in 1579 ". . . when I cam from Spain two years ago I found all the people in revolt, for if they had had the opportunity, they would have abandoned the country . . . and last year I made them sow much maize, for at this fort alone, over one thousand fanegas [1600 bushels] were gathered, and this season they will gather many more. There are beginning to be many of the fruits of Spain, such as figs, pomegranates, oranges, grapes in great quantity; there are many mulberries, vegetables and greens in large quantities such as beans, kidney beans, melon, pumpkins, lettuce, cardoons [artichokes], onions and garlic." [4]

Later the same year he requested two ship loads of wine, flour and oil as their food supply was exhausted. The king ordered a relief ship sent in May of the following year (1600) and in June granted permission for cattle to be sent to the colony as "there is no fresh meat to eat in those forts." [5]

Twenty years later Villegas wrote the king that he had cultivated many acres of land and that some of the soldiers had followed his example.[6] But the results were discouraging, for in 1627 the colonists were again begging for food in Havana, and in 1675 the colonists reported that their food was so low that they were forced to live on wild roots to prevent starvation.

In August of 1696 Jonathan Dickenson of London was shipwrecked along the Florida coast. He, his wife, and his child were washed ashore and eventually reached the governor's home in St. Augustine. Dickenson explained his destitute condition and the governor gave him some "Indian corn, pease, stringed beef, salt and earthen pots. . . . But cloathing was not to be had, except as much staff as made a suit for my wife and child, and a few skins. . . . I got also seven Blankets. . . . We had five Roves of Ammunition Bread, so full of Weavel that corn was far better; twenty Roves of strung Beef; sixty Rove of salt, jars of water and earthenware pots to boil our victuals in." [7]

The following year the colonists reported that three years had elapsed since they had received any supplies of food or clothing from Spain. In 1712 they were reduced to eating their horses, dogs, and even their cats. Famine came again in 1722 and 1741, at which times they applied to the English colonies in Georgia and Carolina for enough food to prevent further starvation. Thus, for nearly two hundred years the Spanish women colonists in the fertile land of Florida saw death stalk their homes and could only fend it off with empty hands. [8]

The English women at Jamestown had equally difficult problems in feeding their families in the early years. After the terrible famine of 1609–1610, Lord Delaware left enough food in the common storehouse to feed 200 people for ten months and seed for the next year's crop. But in 1613 Diego de Molina reported that ". . . thus they have suffered much want with only a miserable supply of wheat or maiz and dressing wretchedly, . . . last year there were seven hundred people here and only 350 remain because the hard work and scanty food on public works kills them and increases the discontent . . ." [9]

Three years later Rolfe stated that "they had Indian corn, English wheat, peas, beans, barley, turnips, cabbages, pumpkins, parsnips, etc., so good, so fruitful, so pleasant and profitable as the best made ground in England can yield." [10] But in 1618 there was a serious drought and such severe storms at sea that they were again in a desperate situation. John Smith states that they pounded the dried sturgeon and mixed caviare, sorell and other herbs to make their bread.

Two hundred and forty new settlers arrived with prac-

tically no food supplies.[11] The colonists asked help from
the Indians and most of them survived until the corn crop
was harvested and cattle arrived the following year. In the
great massacre of 1622 the Indians not only killed many
of the settlers but also burned and ravaged the cultivated
fields so that the colonial women again faced the horror of
the starvation of their families. The Virginia Assembly in
1623 ordered all the land owners to plant corn instead of
tobacco, but there were serious shortages in food supplies
three years later and again in 1628. It was not until about
1650 that the homemakers of Virginia found any real
surcease from the frightening problem of food shortages,
and even then there was no real security from droughts,
Indian raids and other disasters to the food crops.

The women of the Plymouth colony lived for the first
three years on near starvation diets. When each boat returned to England they urged that all new settlers bring
with them enough food to last at least a year. Governor
Bradford recorded that "the grim and grizzled face of
starvation" stared at them each day.

In 1630, ten years after the first landing, Prince wrote
of the Massachusetts settlers, "It goes harder with this poor
people in their beginnings because of the scarcity of all
sorts of grain this year [1630] in England. . . . We found
some English at Salem and some at Charlestown who were
very destitute. . . . Bread was with many a very scarce thing
and the hunger that many suffered and saw no hope . . .
but with fish, clams and mussels." [12]

The following year Thomas Dudley, Deputy Governor
of the colony, wrote to the Countess of Lincoln, mother
of Lady Arbella Johnson, "we found the colony in a sad
and unexpected condition, above eighty of them being dead
the winter before and many of those alive weak and sick;

all the corn and bread amongst them all hardly sufficient
to feed them for a fortnight, insomuch that the remainder
of a hundred and eighty servants we had the two years before sent over, coming to us for vituals to sustain them,
we found ourselves wholly unable to sustain them, . . .
where upon necessity forced us, to our extreme loss, to
give them all liberty who had cost us about sixteen pounds
or twenty pounds a person, furnishing and sending over." [13]

In 1637 the scarcity of grain forced the colony to pass
the first food law in the new land. It stated that, "No person shall sell any cakes or buns either in the market or
victualling houses or elsewhere upon pain of then shillings
fine [the price of two bushels of corn] except . . . for any
burial or marriage or such like special occasion." [14]

Three years later the general court of the colony forbade
the bakers to bake bread "finer than to afford at twelve
ounces the two-penny loaf," [15] and tried to regulate the
value of corn to meet the lowering prices.

In the twenty years (1640–1660) following the concerted efforts of Charles I and the English Parliament to
ease the political and religious life of the people of England, more colonists returned to England than emigrated.
This resulted in serious food shortages in New England
because the colonists had not yet become self supporting.
They had depended on imports from England, particularly
of wheat, rye, barley, peas and other staple foods that did
not grow well in New England. Thus they were forced to
use corn as a basic food because it was generally available.[16] But corn crops in spite of their best efforts were
often a failure. In 1640, 1643, and 1646 there were serious
shortages. In 1648 a survey was made by the court, and it
was found that there was not enough corn to last the colony
two months. In 1652 a fine was placed on all imports of

malts, wheat, barley, biscuit meal and flour in an effort to protect and encourage local production. In 1660 it was reported that the colonies in New England had shipped "biscott, flower, peas, beife, porke, butter and other provisions to the supply of the Barbadoes." But in 1675 corn was again so scarce that the general court ordered the militia and selectment to remove all cereals to the garrisons for protection against marauding Indians.

In Connecticut five years later Governor William Leete wrote to the Lords in England: "We are but a poore people . . . lost and spint much of or estates in the last Indian War . . . . the holy Providence of God hath smitten us year after year, with blastings and mildews, wrby we have lost a great part of or wheat every year; and these 3 or 4 last years there is a worme breeds in or pease, which doth much damnify them." [17]

The harvest of 1695 was a disastrous failure causing suffering on all sides. To prevent further shortage an act was passed forbidding the export of any grain from the colony since there was not enough to last to the next harvest. In 1713 Dr. Sewall records that the shortage of bread stuffs caused the first and only bread riot in colonial Boston.[18] Throughout the New England settlements women were forced many times to gather and bake, or boil, acorns from the red and white oak trees, chestnuts and any other nuts they could find in the nearby forests. When cooked thoroughly and ground to a coarse flour they made a fair substitute for corn in the daily diet.

The Swedish women settlers along the Delaware River also suffered from food shortages.[19] Hunting was their chief source of food, but powder and shot were so scarce that they were forced to live on such fish and other sea food as they could catch. Governor Printz reported that many of the colonists died in 1643 for lack of food, and Van Tien-hoven in 1650 wrote to warn all new settlers to bring with them enough food to keep them alive for 2 or 3 years at least.

By the time the Quaker women arrived in Pennsylvania in 1683, Penn could write with some truth "the stories of our necessity being either the fear of our friends, or the scare-crows of our enemies for the greatest hardship we have suffered hath been salt-meat, which by fowl in winter, and fish in summer together with some poultery, lamb, mutton, veal and plenty of venison the best part of the year, hath been made passable." [20]

Ten years later the colonists in and about Philadelphia were exporting grain, horses, beef and pork to the West Indies, but on the western frontier there was no abatement in the struggle for enough food for the families.

The French women who settled in Louisiana were almost wholly dependent on external sources for their food supplies. Very few of the men or women knew anything about raising crops or caring for animals. [21] The homeland was involved in a desperate struggle with England (1702–1713) and paid little attention to the needs of her colonists. Such food stuffs as were sent to the colony were sold at outrageous prices, sometimes with six hundred per cent profit, or were unfit for human consumption on arrival. During 1709–1710 the women of the colony were forced to forage for food in the swamps and forests, gathering acorns, nuts, berries and edible roots. By 1716 the conditions in the colony became so serious that the government made arrangements with the neighboring Indian tribes to quarter soldiers and colonists in the Indian villages. This was also done in 1718 and 1720 as food stuffs still remained wholly inadequate. The French women were thus forced to live and work with the Indian women to pay for the food for their families. The governor of the colony reported that "the men in the colony began through habit to use corn as an article of food; but the women, who are mostly Parisians, have for this food a dogged aversion, which has not been subdued. They inveigh against [it constantly]."

Relief came in the form of a group of German settlers (1719), who knew how to farm and were willing to work the rich loam of the land, and a ship load of three hundred galley slaves who were promptly put to work. Gradually swamps were drained and fields cultivated so that there was enough not only for the colonists but for export to the homeland.

To the west in the arid lands of New Mexico and Arizona, the homemaker lived, or died, through the periods of drought and disaster. But with each generation they renewed and enriched the lands they had chosen for their homes.

When Dona Maria Menendez left the "San Pelayo" and stepped onto the sandy beach at St. Augustine, she, like the other women in the colony, faced the hungry men and children of her family. They had only the remains of the ships' mouldy supplies to feed them. The friendly Indians offered to share their food with the newcomers, and while the food was strange it did prevent their starving at least for a time. At Jamestown Mrs. Forrest and Ann Burras had no friendly Indians to offer them even unpalatable food. However, the settlers who had been there over a year had a small supply of corn and beans (local products) which added to the very limited supplies from the ships but lasted only for a few brief weeks. Katherine Carver and Elizabeth Winslow at Plymouth had neither offerings

Cooking at Plymouth, 1620. (From the Collections of the Library of Congress)

from friendly Indians nor salvage from former settlers when they stepped on to Plymouth Rock. Furthermore, it was bitterly cold with ten inches of snow on the ground where they and the other women bent over the open fires to cook whatever food they could badger from the ship's purser. All of the settlers along the Atlantic seaboard were in great need of fresh meat, vegetables and fruits to offset the scurvy diet of their long ocean voyages. Fish was readily available, and while not as acceptable as meat to the colonists, their empty stomachs more than once drove them to relish the rich food from the sea. John Josselyn, writing in 1672, enumerated two hundred varieties of sea food in the New England waters, and other records tell us of oysters a foot long, lobsters six feet long weighing twenty-five pounds and crabs a foot and a half in breadth and sufficient food for four hungry men.[22] Today these foods are sold as delicacies at relatively high prices, but in the 1600's they composed the daily diet that meant the difference between comfort and the agony of starvation for the homemaker and her family. They were the first stable food resource of the colonial homemaker.

The wild animal meats available to the colonial home-maker along the Atlantic seaboard consisted chiefly of venison, bear meat, rabbits, squirrels and other small animals. She also had several kinds of wild fowl available such as, pigeons, pheasant, partridges, quail, plover, snipe, curlew, woodcocks and turkeys that weighed forty to sixty pounds and were new to the colonists. Venison and wild fowl soon became scarce and were thought of as real delicacies, but the colonial homemaker seems to have had bear meat available throughout the period. She roasted and stewed it and even made mince pies of it.

The French women colonists of Louisiana who so vigorously resented corn bread were fortunate in having wild pork, beef, and buffalo meat available to them as the colony became self supporting.[23] The meat may have been tough and highly flavored, since it was from wild herds, but the Indian women taught them to make it palatable. It will be remembered that De Soto and Coronado had brought swine, cattle and sheep with them, many of which went wild so that when d'Bienville and his colonists arrived they found great herds of wild cattle and swine. Buffalo meat was new to the French women but acceptable either fresh, dried or salted.

The women colonists along the eastern seaboard had no such good fortune.[24] There were no wild herds of cattle and the Indians along the Atlantic seaboard had few if any domestic animals because the forage was not adequate. The wild rye and broomstraw that grew profusely along the coast did not contain enough nutriment for winter feeding. The domestic animals brought over by the colonists did not do well until blue grass, white clover and timothy were introduced by the English probably between 1633–1635. In the early years the cattle had to be fed during the winters and drought periods on "browse" which consisted chiefly of dried buds of hemlock and birch. Years later the colonists in Georgia (1735) and notably Eliza Lucas in South Carolina (1739–1740) experimented successfully with lucerne (alfalfa) which made excellent forage.

The year after Mrs. Forrest arrived the supply ships from England brought over about 500 hogs, 500 chickens, goats and sheep and six mares.[25] By the following year the colonists and Indians had eaten all but one sow. In 1611 Lord Delaware brought in a few cattle which he reported were prospering. He wrote that the milk was "a great nourishment and refreshing to our people, serving also in (occasion) as well for physicke as for food." In the same year Lord Dale also shipped in a few cattle. He ordered that no live stock, not even chicken, be killed, without his consent on pain of death. So effective was this order that by 1614 the colony had "200 neat cattell, as many goats, hogges, mares, horses, poultry, tame turkeis, peacockes and pigeons."

But the fodder was poor and appetites were great so that two years later there were only 144 cattle, six horses and 216 goats. However, the swine prospered and became the homemakers' chief supply of meat from domesticated animals. By 1649 the colony was shipping very superior bacon to England.

Katherine Carver had to wait three years for the arrival of three heifers and a bull, which were shipped from Devon, England to Plymouth, Massachusetts, and more than seven years before any sheep or horses arrived.[26] It was well over thirty years before the colony had even a small herd of cattle. Mrs. Endicott and Ann Bradstreet in the Massachusetts Bay colony were a little better off as the colony received thirty cows, twelve mares and a number of goats and swine during their first year in the new land. Between 1630 and 1633 nearly every ship brought a few more livestock to the colony. Farther north at Mason's Plantation on the Piscataqua River and Trelawny's Plantation at Portland, Maine, the women had very limited supplies of cattle, goats, hogs and sheep to augment the available meat from wild animals.

Annekje Jans and Margaret Hardenbroeck in New Netherlands had no problem regarding the availability of fresh meat from domestic animals, as about 300 meat cattle, sheep and swine were brought into the colony with the first settlers. The Swedish and Finnish women who settled along the Delaware River were less fortunate. Governor Printz reported in 1647 that the colony had only twenty-five cattle, most of which had been purchased from other colonies.[27] However, by the last years of the 17th century, the colonial women along the Atlantic seaboard had a supply, if limited, of fresh meat from domesticated animals to augment the rapidly diminishing amount of meat from wild animals. Out in Louisiana the women did not have an ample quantity of domesticated cattle for over forty years after the first settlement was made. But in New Mexico and California fresh meat from domesticated animals was never a serious problem except in times of great drought.

To supplement the meat in their diet the colonial homemakers found four chief varieties of products which were new to them and which the Indian women helped them to utilize in a number of ways. These were corn, beans, sweet potatoes and the whole cucurbit family of pumpkins, cucumbers, gourds and squashes. Columbus had found corn in the West Indies and introduced it into Spain and Southern Europe. Corn was used by the Spanish at St. Augustine, although it was not well liked. The Jamestown colonists had not heard of it, and Chief Powhatan sent some of his people to teach the English how to sow the grain and prepare it for eating.[28] John Smith reported in 1629 that very soon the colonists found "the Indian corne so much better than ours, they beginne to leave [off] sowing it," so that corn never became a principle crop of the colony.

A scouting party from the Mayflower discovered a denuded cornfield with half the stalks rattling and swaying in the wind. Nearby they came upon mounds of sand which, "digging up, found in them diverce faire Indian baskets filled with corne, and some in eares, faire and good, of diverce collours, which seemed to them a very goodly sight, (havening never seen any shuch before)." [29] In the spring Squanto, an Indian friend who spoke some English, taught them to plant the corn which they called "gunney wheat" or "turkey wheat." The Indian women taught the "yangees" or English women how to prepare the corn in many ways.

The women in the Dutch and Swedish colonies had similar experiences. The "wilden" women were most helpful in showing them how to grow and cook the native corn. In Father White's report on the Calvert colony in Maryland, he states that "the Indian women seeing their servants to bee inacquainted the the manner of dressing it [corn] would make bread therof for them and teach them how to doe the like. They found also the country well stored with corne (which they brought with truck such as there is desired, the Natives having no knowledge of the use of money) whereof they sold them such a plenty as that they sent 1000 bushells of it to New England to provide them some salt fish and other commodities which they wanted." [30]

The great variety of indigenous beans were also very valuable to the colonial homemaker. Some of them were the kidney bean, lima beans, scarlet-owners and tepary beans. It was the Indian women who taught our foremothers to bake the beans in earthenware crocks buried in pits of hot ashes and stones.

It was the Huguenot women, perhaps Judith Manigault, who discovered the dietary pleasure of sweet potatoes which grew wild in the Carolinas. The women baked them in the hot ashes, boiled them, and used them to make bread, puddings and pan cakes.

Varieties of pumpkins, squashes and other cucurbit vegetables were found in all the colonies. Added to these were tomatoes, or love apples, Jerusalem artichokes, garden peppers, sunflowers and wild rice, all of which were indigenous to the land and new and exciting to the colonial homemakers.

The "yangeese" women brought with them seeds of barley wheat, cabbages, turnips, carrots, onions, parsnips, peas, french beans and herbs.[31] The Dutch women brought seeds of beets, spinach, endive, leeks, melons and many herbs. The German women added asparagus, cauliflower and potatoes to the colonial diet. Potatoes which came originally from South America were planted at Jamestown in the spring of 1607 and again in 1612 but did not grow well. The Calvert colonists mentioned growing them in 1634 and 1640 and the Dutch in 1650. There are also references to potatoes in the early Carolina and Pennsylvania records, and one of the items on the Harvard University commencement dinner menu of 1708 was potatoes. However, they were not commonly used until the Scotch and Irish settlers started to cultivate them in New Hampshire in 1719.

The colonial homemakers in all of the colonies found many fruits and berries growing wild in their new homeland such as huckleberries, blackberries, raspberries and wild grapes in abundance. Josselyn reported an abundance of apple, pear, quince, cherry, plum, and barberry trees in New England. Many of these were mentioned in the records as far south as Georgia.

The Spanish settlers in Florida planted orange, lemon, lime, pomegranate, fig and peach trees and most of the other settlers from England and the continent brought seeds and young plants from their homelands.[32] Many of the imported plants survived and became the nucleus of later orchards in the colonies from Maine to Georgia.

In each of the early colonial settlements, the men generally supplied the meat for the household, and the women cared for the meats, vegetables, and other produce. As early as 1610 Strachey reported that "the women [at Jamestown] sow their corne well and cleane same as neat as we doe our garden beddes in England.[33] And Bradford reported that the women "went willingly into the fields" at the Plymouth colony. Nor were the Spanish, Dutch, German, or French homemakers less energetic in the care of their gardens and orchards. Oldmixon, writing about 1704, reported that "This country is in a very flourishing condition; the Families are very large, in some are 10 or 12 children; . . . The children are set to Work at 8 Years old, the ordinary Women take care of Cows, Hogs and other small Cattle, make butter and cheese, spin Cotton and Flax, help to sow and reap corn, wind Silk from the Worms, gather Fruit and look after the House."

While the single women and widows in all of the colonies were eligible for the acquisition of land, there were a number of extraordinary women in each of the settlements who became large land owners and producers of extensive crops. Besides the pioneer women already mentioned such as Dona Maria Menendez of Florida, Lady Berkeley and Judith Manigault, and Elizabeth Dale, who owned over 3,000 acres of land, there were in Virginia Ann Toft, who acquired 19,250 acres of good land as a single woman, Elizabeth and Ann Makemie, also single women who owned 5,000 acres between them, and a long list of other homemaker-landowners who produced the food for their household. For instance, Mrs. Pearce of Jamestown reported that she produced one hundred bushels of

figs per acre (about 1629); Mrs. Mary Naylor leased her
succulent orchards for 10 pounds sterling per year, which
was worth more than a hundred weight of cotton in 1697;
and Elizabeth Digges became, as reports say, the wealthiest
woman landowner in all the colonies. William Byrd wrote
in 1710 of a "Mrs. Jones from whose house we came that
she is a very civil woman and shews nothing of rugged-
ness or Immodesty in her Carriage, yett she will carry a
Gunn in the woods and kill deer, turkeys etc., shoot down
wild cattle, catch and tye ye hoggs, knock down beeves
with an ax and perform the most manfull Exercises as well
as most men in those parts." [34]

In the Carolinas many single women and widows owned
large tracts of land and a number of married women operated large plantations for their husbands. To name only a
few, there was Affra Coming, Eliza Lucas Pinckney, Ann
Partridge, Margaret Haslen and Rebecca Mendez Da Costa
who owned 20,000 acres of profitable land. In Georgia
Mary Musgrove, who was half Indian, owned large sections of land, and other women acquired land as single
women or widows. Abigail Minis, Elizabeth Anderson,
Martha Ricketson and Mary Powell, who willed 1,000
acres to her daughter-in-law as well as a large tract of
land to her son, were among many women who produced
food.

Besides the Brent sisters in Maryland there were a number of single women and widows who owned large estates
of over 1,000 acres, such as Frances White, Lady Diane
Egerton, Jane Ellenhead and Mary and Eleanor Carroll,
who with their brother owned over 10,000 acres, as well
as Mary Trenton and a host of other homemakers who
acquired small farms. Just how much land in the southern
colonies was owned or operated by the homemakers is not

known, but the records indicate that a good portion of the land was owned by single women and widows and that they actually produced a large share of the food that sustained their families, thereby shouldering their share of the food problems of the family.

The same conclusions can be drawn from the records of the Middle Atlantic and New England colonies. Besides Mary Ferree and Deborah Moody, who were virtually explorers of the new land, there were many single women and widows who were homemaker-landowners. Mary Penington and Hannah Dubre of Pennsylvania and Mary Spratt Provoost Alexander, Margaret Hardenbroeck de Vries Phillipse and the intrepid Sarah Wells Bull who took up 160,000 acres of wilderness in upper New York were outstanding examples. In New England the land holdings were generally smaller than in the more southern colonies. However, Elizabeth Poole, a single woman, purchased the land and became proprietor of Taunton, Massachusetts, and Mrs. John Winthrop, as a widow, was granted 3,000 acres in 1640. In each of the new settlements in New England, women were allotted farm land as widows or independent heads of households. Among these were Martha Sergeant and Bridget Usher of Worcester, Massachusetts, who were given 150 acres apiece, or Widows Mason and Skarlett of Salem, Massachusetts, who were assigned 30 acres each.

In New Mexico Ana Lujan and Ana de Archuleta among others received grants of land from de Vargas in 1696, and Isabel Jorge de Bera and Josefa Duran, widow of Faustin Griego, each received deeds for half a "famega" in the city of Santa Fe where they established their homes. The archives of the colony are filled with records of the participation of the women landowners in the life and productivity of the growing settlements. In California Fermina Espinoza, who owned the Santa Reta, had a large family and did all the work of the rancho such as breaking the colts and branding her cattle. The four daughters of V. Avila of Sal si Puedes Rancho shared all the work of the ranch and fed their families well.

Most of the land owning homemakers of the colonies experimented with the seeds and young plants that they brought from their homeland or acquired en route in the West Indies or other settlements. A few became famous for their skill—Lady Alice Fenwick for her healing herbs, Mrs. Carter for her successful grafting of fruit trees and her productive orchards, Jane Colden and Martha Logan for their extensive botanical knowledge, and Eliza Lucas Pinckney for her large estates and her considerable experimentation with ginger, cotton, cassada, figs, and, most of all, indigo.

But experimenting and producing food products were only the first steps for the colonial homemaker in the feeding of her family. There were no supermarkets with pre-cooked, canned or frozen dinners that merely needed re-heating. Preparing any of the basic foods required much time, energy and forethought. Since all of the cooking was done at an open fire, three general means of cooking were possible—boiling in the great kettles, baking in the hot coals, or roasting on the spits. None of these methods was easy or speedy.[35]

The kettles of brass, iron or copper often weighed forty to seventy pounds and held up to fifteen gallons of liquid. They were hung over the fire on the "lug pole" by means of adjustable pot hooks, or trammels. Later iron cranes were used in place of the dangerous "lug poles." Some of the kettles had short legs which permitted the raking of hot coals under them, others were set on trivets.

The first ovens were heavy, covered kettles on short

Fireplace, Block House, Naaman's on Delaware, New Castle County, Delaware, 1654. (From the Collections of the Library of Congress)

legs that were virtually buried in hot stones, coals and ashes. In time ovens were built into the side of the fireplace and heated by hot stones and coals. Later saucepans, baking pans, frying pans, turning spits for roasts and iron dripping pans to catch the juices and ornate trivets and iron "peeles" or shovels were acquired by the well-to-do homemaker. In Mrs. Digges kitchen there were "one still, a warming-pan, and a small quantity of old brass, two gridirons, seven spits, four iron pots and pothooks, two pair of old tongs, a fire-shovel, a nutmeg grater, three brass stands, two kettles, one brass skillet with an iron frame, a small skillet, one large and one small copper, and an old chest."

Since the colonial homemakers had no refrigerators or deep freezers, the preparation of the various meats, grains, vegetables, and fruits was of necessity seasonal. But one season nudged the preceding one in rapid succession. Hardly had the fall crops been harvested before it was butchering time, which was, perhaps, the busiest time of the year, for it was then that the oxen, cows and swine which had been fattened all fall were slaughtered. This was done early in the morning so that the meat might be hard, cold and ready for further processing. Maple sugar time came next and spring planting time was followed by the need to care for the early fruits and vegetables. Barley crops came in May, wheat in June, and corn in the summer.

The colonial homemakers came to depend on corn as a basic food for several reasons. First, it was indigenous and grew well in every settlement from Florida to Maine and from the Atlantic to the Pacific coast. Then it was easier for women to raise and process than wheat, barley or rye. The roots of corn remain close to the surface of the ground and need only light hoeing and weeding. The

ears of corn could be readily gathered, husked and ground
in wooden or stone mortars, or samp mills, in the home,
whereas wheat had to be cut, threshed and milled, which
was a much more difficult process.

While it is evident that practical reasons determined the
use of corn as a basic food, the rites of an ancient Indian
ritual linked the homemakers very closely to it.[36] According to tribal custom, in the spring, after the corn had been
planted, the wife of the planter chose the first dark night,
slipped silently out of her wigwam, disrobed and dragged
her principal garment, a "matchecota", around the field to
create a charmed line that would keep out all harm from
her field. Then she slipped back into her wigwam, feeling
that in some mysterious way she had assured the safety
of her family's food supply for another year. The colonial
homemakers understood the anxiety of the Indian women
for they too sought help from the supernatural with fasting
and prayers.

Corn—red, blue, yellow, green and white—was prepared
by the colonial homemakers in a hundred ways. It was
roasted, steamed and boiled while still on the ear. As whole
grains it was popped, or as Governor Winthrop put it,
"parched corn which turned inside out and was white and
flowry within." [37] It was boiled while green with other
vegetables as in succatach, crushed to "mawsamp" and
mixed with berries in a kind of cake, or it was parboiled
and treated to make hominy.

Most of the corn, however, was ground. In the early
years it was ground by hand in querns of wood, stone or
iron. Governor George Yeardley set up the first windmill
in Virginia in 1616 and a water mill was constructed in
1621.[38] By 1649 the Virginia homemakers had four windmills and five water mills on which they could depend for

grinding their grain crops. Later, some homemakers had their own mills. Dorothy Jordan and Ann Michael owned both horse and hand mills. In the Carolinas, according to De Graffenried in 1711, there was "only one wretched water mill: the wealthiest use hand mills and the poorer class are obliged to pound their grain in mortars made of oak, or rather tree stocks, which are dug out and instead of sifting it in a sieve they shake it barely in a kind of basket."

In Maryland a water mill for grinding the corn was set up a year after the first landing and others were built on the large estates soon after the land was apportioned. In the middle Atlantic colonies Catheryna Brett had a grist mill on the upper Hudson River, Grace Reynolds and Elizabeth Hatkinson had grist mills in New Jersey, and in Pennsylvania Ann West Gibson, Katherine Griffith and Sybille Masters were concerned with their operation. Sybille Masters became so interested in the process that she invented a machine for cleaning and curing corn and a method of making hominy called "Tuscarora rice," for which she received an English patent, one of the first to be had by any person in the American colonies.[39]

In New England, progress moved more slowly. The first wind mill was built in 1632, twelve years after the first settlement. An inventory, dated 1633, like many others listed "13 great iron morter and pestle" and one "mustard-quarne." Mills were so few that in 1635 a law was passed forbidding any miller to "take above the sixteenth part of the corn he grinds. . . ."[40] Widow Tuthill owned a windmill in 1624, but windmills were found unsatisfactory, so that a number of water mills were built between 1641 and 1643. Some of these were powered by the streams of the area and others by the tide. A few homemakers also had bolting mills for sifting the impurities out of their ground grain.

The corn was conveyed to the mills in wheelbarrows in summer, on hand sleds in the winter, or on the shoulders of the planter if he or she had no other way. The dangers involved are illustrated by an excerpt from Governor Winthrop's diary of 1646. He recorded that "A woman of Charlestown having two daughters aged under 14 years, sent them to the tide mill nearby with a little corn. They delivered their corn at the mill, and returning back (they dwelt towards Cambridge) they were not seen till three months after, supposed to be carried away by the tide, which was then above the marsh." [41]

Once ground, the corn meal was either boiled into a thick porridge called "suppawn" or "hasty pudding" or baked into a form of bread or cake. Roger Williams said that a spoonful of the meal of parched corn and water, called "nokake," made many a good meal for him on his journeys.

"Journey cake" or "Johnnycake" was a kind of corn meal griddle cake,[42] or "corn pone," which was firm enough for the children of New England to put in their hats or coat pockets. Three or four of these would keep them warm for some time and also formed their lunch. Thus they became known as "Journey cakes." Sometimes they were made of a buck-wheat and corn mixture but always baked on a soap stone griddle over an open fire. "He-we" was another kind of corn bread made in New Mexico. It consisted of finely ground corn meal mixed with water to form a very thin paste. This was smeared quickly on very hot stone slabs which cooked the thin cakes almost immediately. The thin sheets of corn cake tinted blue, pink, green and yellow from the color of the corn, were piled on one another and eaten dry or dipped in mutton broth. But perhaps the most famous corn bread of the period was the Boston brown bread made by Mr. Latly Gee and Mrs. Bennet. The records state that "they were allowed to bake and sell household bread of wheat, Indian [corn] or Rye Indian [corn] or both." Their bread became popular almost at once and is still a favorite with many homemakers.

One of the reasons for the popularity of Boston brown bread was the difficulty the colonial homemakers had in making bread of wheat; white bread was a real delicacy in all the colonies because wheat was difficult to produce and therefore scarce. Yeast was not only hard to obtain but also difficult to keep alive, and the available ovens were very poor. Some white bread, such as seinnels, craknels, jannocks, cheat-loaves, cocket-bread, wastrel-bread, manchet and buns, were brought from England. But after two or three months at sea they were not very appetizing.

It is interesting to note, that largely due to the inadequacies of the colonial kitchens, baking was one of the first so-called "home industries" to leave the colonial homes. There was a definite limit to the number and kind of bread stuffs that could be baked over an open fire or in a brick oven at the side of a fireplace. One of the first references to bakers in New England was an admonition of the General Court of the Massachusetts Bay colony in 1639 to a man and his wife to "make bigger bread." [43] In 1646 the same court ordered that each of the bakers devise and use distinct markings on their loaves and buns, so that each baker could be held acountable for the adequacy of his or her products. Eight years later President Dunster of Harvard University petitioned the court on behalf of Sister Bradish that "she be encouraged and countenanced in her present calling for baking of bread and brewing and selling of beer without which she cannot continue to bake."

In 1707 Susana Stoddard started to build a baker's

oven on her property but was stopped by the objections of her neighbors. In 1715 Madam Tudor came with her 6 year old son from London and set up a bakery on "White Bread Alley" where she baked penny rolls. Other bakers, both men and woman, came in the years that followed, so that "choice ship, white and milk bread" were available in limited quantities for those who could afford to buy them.

Home baking continued, however, throughout the periods in most of the homes since bakery bread was not only expensive but to many unavailable, especially in times of emergency. For instance, after the Battle of Lexington in 1775, there were many hungry soldiers passing through Dedham, Massachusetts, and no bread. Mary Draper and her daughter started baking dozens and dozens of loaves of brown bread. They kept two large ovens going for thirty-six hours, which was quite a feat for any baker, and greatly appreciated by the tired soldiers.

In New York a law was passed in 1656 requiring all bakers to bake coarse, eight-pound loaves and white bread for Christians and Indians alike, suggesting that even then discrimination was a problem. Perhaps the law was the result of a "sit-down" strike on the part of the Indians. In contrast at Ephrata, Pennsylvania, no charge was made either for the baking or for the bread itself.[44] The first industry set up by the pious women of the community-colony was the building of a bake-house where all the homemakers of the vicinity might bake their bread, or were given bread if they were in need. In Georgia Elizabeth Anderson advertised good bread at reasonable prices in 1764. The French homemakers in New Orleans continued to dislike corn bread. They frequently mixed the corn meal with rice flour, and in 1723 two women who sold bread were fined because the mixture used was not acceptable. Later in the century, wheat was shipped down the Mississippi River from the French settlers in Illinois and largely supplanted the supply of wheat from France.

To supplement the meat in their diet, the colonial homemaekrs had eggs plus milk from cows and goats that were shipped to the colonies. The milk was used to some extent as a beverage but more often n the form of cheese, which had better keeping qualities. Earle points out that making cheese was an unending care for the homemaker "from the time the milk was set over the fire to warm and then to curdle; through breaking the curds in the cheese-basket; through shaping into cheeses and pressing in the cheese-press, placing them on the cheese-ladders, and constantly turning and rubbing them." [45]

Butter was, at first, made by shaking the cream in a bottle, or whipping it in a bowl with a spoon. This was a slow, tiring process, so butter was very scarce in the early years. In a listing of six estates of Lynn, Massachusetts, in 1650 only one churn was mentioned. Hannah Gallup of Connecticut had butter at her wedding breakfast, but her mother recorded "I made some very goode buttere althbough it seemed almost wicket to soe yuse milk yt is so sore needet for ye littell ownes." [46]

In the listing of Lord Fairfax's large estate in Virginia two churns are mentioned, and by the middle of the 18th century most of the colonial homemakers had simple wooden churns and butter became a commodity that she could exchange for necessities. It was still considered a delicacy in 1800, appearing mostly on the tables of the rich. George Washington had the first ice cream freezer on record (1784) but Martha Washington did not include a recipe for ice cream in her cook book.[47]

One of the major problems that every colonial homemaker had was the preservation of the fresh food. Their ingenuity in devising methods for keeping the seasonal food from spoiling is quite remarkable. They used at least eight methods—freezing, cooking and keeping from the air, salting, parching or drying, smoking, pickling or "sousing," spicing, and fermenting and preserving in sugar and molasses.

The colonial homemakers froze turkeys and other fowl and beef, pork, and milk for indefinite periods. They not only packed the food in ice but they also stuffed snow into the fowl and other small animals to keep them cold longer.

Food caches in cellars and pits were very common in all the colonies. The homemakers thus kept potatoes, turnips, beets, parsnips and other root vegetables as well as apples and some other fruits for several months. Oysters and clams were brought in, put in beds of sand and corn meal and watered twice a week, thus being made available all winter.

Salting, or "powdering," was a very common method by which the colonial homemaker preserved beef, pork and several varieties of fish such as cod, mackerel, salmon and shad. Most of their cellars held barrels of "powdering tubs" of corned beef, salt pork, etc., for winter use.

Drying, "parching" or "scorching" was a method of hanging the "flitches" of meat or fish, vegetables, herbs or fruits in the sun to dry. Or they were hung from the rafters near the fireplace. It was not uncommon to see a whole salmon "hooked by the mouth in a dusty rafter" along side of bunches of herbs, corn or strings of sliced apples and apricots.

The colonial homemaker smoked beef, pork, venison and some varieties of fish. The process consisted of hanging the meat over a slow burning fire made of especially chosen wood to give a particular flavor to the meat. Sometimes aromatic herbs were added in the smoking of certain kinds of fish. The whole process was at first done over an open fire near the house, but later "smoke houses" were built by the well-to-do homemakers, which greatly facilitated the work involved, as the fire had to be kept at an even temperature for several days or weeks depending on the weight of the pieces of meat.

Pickling or "sousing," was used as a method of preserving a wide variety of foods from pig's feet and head cheese to barberries and nasturtium seeds.[49] Fish and oysters were also "soused," and among the vegetables that were pickled were samphire, asparagus, fennel, mushrooms, purple cabbage, radish pods, parsley and elder buds. Lemons and green walnuts were also "soused," and Martha Laurnes Ramsay discovered a way to pickle olives as well as the Spanish had done. Spices were used in the preserving of both meat and fruits as well as to give variety to the flavor. Fermentation was used in the making of vinegar, cider, ale, beer, wines and cordials.

Lastly, the colonial homemakers preserved some foods in sugar, molasses and honey, not as it is done today by sterilizing heat and hermetically sealed jars and cans, or by quick, deep freezing. The colonial homemaker preserved her fruits and nuts by cooking them slowly with equal part of sugar or molasses so that there was no need for sterilizing the jars or rushing the quiddonies to a nonexistent ice box. They made sure that the toothsome delicacies could not ferment, sour or mould even when exposed to the open air. Their candied fruits, nuts, marmalades, macaroons, marchpanes, jellies and preserves could and did stand the test of summer's heat and winter's cold to add zest to the often limited diets of their families.

Wild honey was available to the first settlers but was soon replaced by the products of carefully tended bee hives. Maple sugar was first noted by Governor Berkeley of Virginia in 1706.[50] He wrote "The sugar-tree yields a kind of sap or juice which by boiling is made into sugar. This juice is drawn out, by wounding the Trunk of the Tree, and placing a receiver in the Wound. It is said that the Indians make one pound of sugar out of eight pounds of the liquor. It is bright and moist with a full large grain, the Sweetness of it being like that of a good Muscovada."

Sugar maples were also found in the northern colonies and were one of the chief sources of this much appreciated commodity. White sugar from sugar cane was imported from the West Indies and was therefore very expensive. It came in the shape of large cones weighing about ten pounds each, which with care could last a family a whole year, since it was rarely used for anything but a sweetener for tea and other drinks.

Sugar cane was cultivated in Louisiana as early as 1725[51] but without much success until 1751 when two priests from San Domingo brought in not only some young plants but some skilled Negroes to cultivate them. By 1762 there were several sugar mills and enough sugar to export considerable quantities.

Tea, coffee, chocolate, and certain spices were also imported commodities through this period. Chocolate appeared in New England about 1670 and tea about twenty years later. They were, at first, considered medicinal beverages. Dr. Lemery of Paris, for instance, recommended coffee because it "comforts brain and drives up crudities in the stomach . . . good for pains in the head, vertigo, lethargy, coughs, melancholy, vapours, and hot brains, consumptions, swooning, fits, fevers, sores, etc."[52] Tea was also considered to be good for practically every ailment. Coffee mills and pots, and tea kettles and cannisters began to appear in the household inventories of the well-to-do people in most of the colonies by the first quarter of the 18th century and coffee and tea houses were licensed in the colonies by the middle of the century. Advertisements appeared in the newspaper of Genteel Coffee and Tea Houses run by both men and women, and several became famous as political rendevous for restless elements in the colonies. Spices such as pepper, nutmeg and cinnamon were always scarce and expensive. Small amounts were brought in and sparingly used. Mention is made in many of the letters of the period of the need for spices.

The basic reason why the imported beverages and spices were so expensive was that the colonial homemaker had so little to offer in exchange. During the first one hundred and fifty years the great concern of the colonists was to acquire enough of the bare necessities of life to feel secure and comfortable in their new homes.

Prosperity came first to the southern colonies. In 1634 a visitor at Jamestown reported that in the better homes the tables were "fournished with porke, kidd, chickens, turkeys, young geese, caponetts, and such other fouls ... besides plentie of milk cheese butter and corne." [53] And in 1700 Beverly wrote that the colonists had a great variety of food stuffs and that the gentry had "their victuals drest and served as nicely as if they were in London."

At about the same time in New England the colonists had for their breakfast and supper "rye-an-injun" bread and milk. In winter they had beef broth with brown bread or porridge. On Sundays they had baked beans and pork with "injun" pudding and butter. The poorest people lived on a "hog-hominy" diet and often even John Winthrop's diet consisted of "pease, pudding and fish." Pies were a common dish at any meal.[54] Meat, vegetables and fruit were used as filling. Acrelius, writing in 1758, reported, "Applepie is used through the whole year, and when fresh apples are no longer to be had, dried ones are used. It is the evening meal of children. House pie, in country places, is made of apples neither peeled nor freed from their cores, and its crust is not broken if a wagon wheel goes over it."

By 1725 the provisions of the well-to-do colonist included meat, fowl or fish, bread, butter, cheese and milk, loaf sugar, white salt and seasonal vegetables and fruits, most of which were produced on the farm. In 1787 an old farmer stated of his earlier years, "At this time my farm gave me and my whole family a good living on the produce of it, and left me one year with another one hundred and fifty silver dollars, for I never spent more than ten dollars a year which was for salt, nails, and the like. Nothing to eat, drink or wear was bought, as my farm provided all." [55]

An example of the self sufficiency of a southern household is found in William Byrd's letter of 1726 in which he stated, "I have a large Family of my own, and my Doors are open to Every Body, yet I have no Bills to pay, and half-a-crown will rest undisturbed in my Pocket for many Moons together. Like one of the Patriarchs, I have my Flocks and my Herbs, my Bond-men and Bond-women, and every Soart of Trade amongst my own Servants, so that I live in a Kind of Independence on everyone but Providence." [56]

At "Nomini Hall" in Virginia, Mrs. Carter informed Philip Fithiam, the tutor of her children, that her household consumed in one year 27,000 pounds of pork, 20 beeves, 550 bushels of wheat besides corn, 4 hogs-head of rum, and 150 gallons of brandy. One hundred pounds of flour were used weekly by the immediate household; white laborers and Negroes ate corn meal.[57]

Perhaps the best illustration of the affluence of the well-to-do homemaker of the second half of the 18th century was the appearance of one of the earliest known American cookbooks in 1761 by Mrs. E. Smith entitled *The Complete Housewife; or, Accomplished Gentlewoman's Companion; Being a Collection of Several Hundred of the most Approved Receipts in Cookery, Pastry, etc.* Most of the colonial homemakers had hand written collections of recipes which they had brought with them or inherited. The original English and European recipes gradually gave place to new recipes which they acquired from each other through the bitter school of experience with new food products. Martha Washington's *Book of Cookery* is a good example. It contains 550 recipes, one of which is dated 1706. It includes such items as how "to Boil Green pease," how "to make ginger bread," and how to wash silk stockings and "keape the teeth clean and white and to fasten them." Her recipe for "Humble pie" reads: "Take ye humbles of a deer, or a calves heart or pluck or a sheeps heart, perboyle it and when it is colde shread it small with beefe suet & season it with cloves, mace, nutmeg & ginger beaten small, & mingle with currans verges & salt, put all into ye pie & set in the oven an houre, then take it out cut it up & put in some clarret wine melted butter & sugar beat together then cover it a little & serve it up." [58]

The Revolutionary War cut deeply into the food supply of both home-grown and imported commodities. The homemakers were forced again to make do with what they could themselves produce. As one homemaker stated in

and was given by her to Mrs. Martha Peter

THE
ART of COOKERY,
H MADE *Glasse*
PLAIN and EASY.

CHAP. I.

Of ROASTING, BOILING, &c.

THAT profeffed cooks will find fault with touching upon a branch of cookery which they never thought worth their notice, is what I expect: however, this I know, it is the moft neceffary part of it; and few fervants there are, that know how to roaft and boil to perfection.

I don't pretend to teach profeffed cooks, but my defign is to inftruct the ignorant and unlearned (which will likewife be of great ufe in all private families) and in fo plain and full a manner, that the moft illiterate and ignorant perfon, who can but read, will know how to do every thing in cookery well.

I fhall firft begin with roaft and boil'd of all forts, and muft defire the cook to order her fire according to what fhe is to drefs; if any thing very little or thin, then a pretty little brifk fire, that it may be done quick and nice; if a very large joint, then be fure a good fire be laid to cake. Let it be clear at the bottom; and when your meat is half done, move the dripping-pan and fpit a little from the fire, and ftir up a good brifk fire;

B for

1779, "Of course we could have no roast Beef. None of us have tasted beef this three years back as it all must go to the Army and too little they get, poor fellows." [59] And in Maine the settlers at Augusta nearly starved for lack of enough corn to survive the winter of 1781.

It was suggested in the previous chapter that the colonial homemaker did not need an electric dish washer. The reason is quite obvious. She had practically no dishes until late in the 18th century. She served her ragouts, stews, hashes, roasts and porridge in wooden trenchers, and pewter plates and occasionally her liquor in silver tankards. The trenchers were generally made of poplar wood or the roots of yellow ash. Often they were only a block of wood, about ten or twelve inches square which had been hollowed out three or four inches deep to form a bowl. Into one of these she placed the family's food and everyone helped himself with knives, fingers and hunks of bread. She generally served the children separately in small trenches, or pewter bowls. As soon as time permitted, additional trenchers, bowls, and mugs were made of wood, and she was able to serve her guests in separate containers.

Nearly every homemaker had at least one or two pieces of pewter, platters, plates, mugs or bowls which she had brought with her to her new home and of which she was inordinately proud. A few of the wealthy women had pieces of silverware. For instance Lady Temperance Yeardley had a number of pieces willed her by her husband in 1627. Several of the inventories of Virginia settlers before 1650 include "2 dozen spoons and 2 small bowls"; "3 dozen large spoons"; "1 salt cellar, 1 bowl, 1 tankers, 1 wine cup and a dozen spoons." Lord Calvert in 1647 had one blue jug, five old pewter dishes, one "bason," five plates, twelve pewter spoons, one silver sack cup, three "small bitts of sylver plate." In New England six settlers listed silver pieces in their wills before 1650.

But silver plate was dear to the heart of the homemaker wherever she lived. In the next fifty years the colonial homemakers acquired a considerable amount of beautiful silver plates, spoons, salt cellars, tankards and bowls. Elizabeth Digges had 261 ounces of silver at the time of her death in 1699,[60] and Sarah Willoughby had "a large sugar basin, one large and three small salt cellars, twenty four spoons, two beer-bowls and one claret, a small tankard, a candle and a dram cup and a small porringer" (1690). Although Elizabeth and Sarah were exceptionally fortunate, many other homemakers acquired silver pieces during the latter part of the 18th century. Table silver consisted of spoons of all sizes and some knives. In general each person was expected to have his own knife which he used for many purposes, including spearing food from the family trencher at meal time. Governor Winthrop owned the first fork in New England in 1633,[61] and Rich Robbs the first in Virginia in 1677. Later tortoise shell, horn, iron and silver forks came into use, but they were still considered a luxury at the end of the Revolutionary War.

China pieces also appeared early in the 18th century. Lord Berkeley in 1718, left "2 china bowls, 2 sets of china tea cups and saucers, 11 chocolate cups and saucers, a tea pot, sugar dish, one glass and a china tea cannister." [62] A few of the women had earthenware plates. Toward the end of the century china came into common use and crowded out wooden and pewter dishes in most of the well established homes of the colonies.

Because most of the food was handled by the fingers, the colonial homemakers collected a surprising amount of table linen. Napkins were easier to care for than soiled

clothes. Since greasy or sticky fingers had to be wiped on
something, the wise homemaker supplied napkins of whatever material she could afford. The finest napkins were
made of linen damask, but in poorer homes cotton canvas,
lockraum, oznaburg, holland, dowlas, diaper, muckaback
or Virginia cloth was used.[63] Table cloths were also available, at least in the well-to-do homes since they were
pleasanter to use and more easily cared for than the table
tops which had to be scoured and polished. This was especially true when mahogany tables came into use. By the
end of the 18th cenutry, most of the colonial homemakers
were able to serve their families at pleasantly appointed
tables with enough dishes and table service to make each
meal a social event as well as appeasement of hunger.

5

She Laid Her Hand to the Distaff and Spindle

If you have had even a brief glimpse of the replicas of the ships—almost toy ships today—in which the early colonists crossed the Atlantic Ocean, you will understand at once why the women of the expeditions brought very few clothes with them. It wasn't religion alone that made them dress in the simplest bodice and skirt, but also the limited space for cargo of any kind.

The ships making up Menendez's armada ranged from the "San Pelayo," 900 tons with twenty-seven families aboard besides officers, seamen, soldiers and priests, to the smaller vessels of sixty to one hundred and fifty tons which were also crowded to the last foot of space with artizans and their families.[1] The first Jamestown settlers arrived in the "Sarah Constant," a one hundred-ton vessel carrying seventy-one persons, the "Goodspeed," a forty-ton vessel carrying fifty-two persons and the "Discovery," a twenty-ton craft carrying twenty persons. The "Mayflower" was a bit larger, having been, like most of the rest, a refurbished freighter. It was a 180-ton vessel and carried 102 persons. Compare the size of these colonizing vessels with the "Queen Elizabeth" of the 20th century. She is a 85,673-ton vessel carrying 2,200 persons on an average voyage, (or thirty-nine tons per person as compared with two tons per person on the "Mayflower.") No wonder Priscella Mullin had no room to bring extra clothing. There was literally no room for "dainties" or other excess baggage. Thus, clothing the family soon became a problem for the homemaker colonists along the Atlantic Seaboard and in Louisiana.

These struggling women not only had very few clothes in which to do their daily chores, but the clothes they had brought with them were ill adapted to pioneer conditions. They had not been made to survive hard work on rocky beaches or among bramble bushes and tough undergrowth. No matter how often they darned, patched, turned upside down and inside out, the clothing did not last long. Don Diego de Molina, writing in 1613 five years after Mrs. Forrest arrived, refers to the clothing of the Virginia coloists as being so ragged that the settlers were virtually naked, and William Bradford, writing about conditions during the third year after the Pilgrims landed at Plymouth, reported that "many wer ragged in aparell and some litle beter than halfe naked." [2]

Since the women in the early years did not have either the raw material or the tools with which to make cloth, they depended almost wholly upon the importation of materials from Spain, England, France and Holland. The Spanish women in Florida and the French women in Louisiana were almost completely dependent on their home lands for clothing during the entire colonial period. The Dutch women in New Amsterdam brought sheep with them and planted small "patches" of flax, but they did not seriously attempt to meet the clothing needs of their families, since they could obtain European cloth and clothing readily through their well-established trading facilities. It was not until after the British took over the colony in 1664 that they had need to produce cloth themselves.

To the English colonial homemakers, each vessel brought some "cloath, hose, shoes, leather, etc, . . . [but] they had need to be husbanded," since they were never adequate. In 1627, when Mr. Fels and his group of settlers came to Plymouth, Bradford reported, "the plantation had some benefits by them, in selling them corne and other provisions of food for clothing; for they had diverse kinds, as cloath, perpetuances, and other stuffs, besides hose, and shoes, and such commodities as the planters stood in need of." [3] Two years later twenty-five settlers from Leyden arrived with "125 yeards of Karsey, 127 ellons of linen cloath, shoes, 66 pr and many other perticulers." What a welcome they must have received from the women of the colony!

As the tide of emigration quickened, in spite of the harrassment by the French and Spanish pirates on the high seas, the population rose from 210 settlers in 1610 to over 27,000 settlers in 1640. The trickle of imported cloth and clothing which the emigrants brought with them, while never abundant, did meet the most pressing needs of the colonists. The problem for the homemaker was that of finding commodities with which to pay for the imported materials. Thus her clothing problem, while not as urgent as her problem of feeding her family, was nevertheless a very insistent one.

The Jamestown settlement tried exporting a number of commodities, but with none were they more successful than with tobacco, which grew readily in the area. Ten tons were sent to England in 1619, and it soon became the chief article of export from the colony. It was accepted in England in payment for British food, clothing and other commodities which were needed by the colonists, so that no concerted effort was made by the women of the colony to meet the clothing needs of their families through local production. For instance, the ships bound for Virginia were alowed to carry 150 dozen shoes and their full quota of passengers (1653), since so few were made by the colonists.

In contrast, the New England colonies had no such commodity as tobacco to pay for their much needed food and clothing. Their first exports were furs, lumber and later corn and fish to the West Indies. In 1627 the Plymouth colony made a trade agreement with their London financiers that among other essential articles, fifty pounds of shoes and hose should be sent to the colony at the rate of 6 shilings for a bushel of corn.[4]

The following year additional clothing was sent, but even more was needed by the increased population, so trade relations with the Dutch colony to the south were established by which "sugar, linen cloth, Holand finer and courser stufes" were exchanged for the precious corn of the colony. But, each such payment meant tightening belts against famine. Little wonder that they issued the edict (1634), "That no person man or woman, shall hereafter make or buy any Apparell, either Woolen, or Silk, or Linen, with any Lace on it, Silver, Gold, or Thread, under the penalty of forfeiture of said clothes. Also that no person either man or woman, shall make or buy any Slashed Clothes, other than one Slash in each Sleeve and another in the back. Also all Cut-works, embroideries, or Needle-word Caps, Bands or Rails, are forbidden hereafter to be made and worn under the aforesaid Penalty; also all gold or silver Girdles Hat band, Belts, Ruffs, Beaver hats are prohibited to be bought and worn hereafter." [5]

Such restrictive legislation was not wholly the result of Puritanic beliefs; it was, in fact, chiefly based on fear of destitution. So great were the pressures to obtain the basic elements of food and secure shelter that ornamental clothing appeared not only frivolous in the sight of God, but actually dangerous as diverting their efforts from the ever-present hazards that beset them. The importation of durable fabrics and clothing was encouraged, and small beginnings were made toward the meeting of their own clothing needs.

The cultivation of flax and the making of both linen and woolen cloth was well known to the colonial homemakers of New England, for such occupations were prevalent in the districts from which they came. Some of them were highly proficient in the arts of making linen, silk and woolen cloth, but they did not attempt to raise flax or make cloth until furs and other export articles became scarce, and the payment of imported goods cut into their supplies of corn and other vital products. Flax and wool had been available to them as early as 1629.[6] By 1640 there were nearly one thousand sheep in New England and enough cleared land to grow flax. In Virginia, flax grew wild in abundance, and by 1649 there were over 3,000 head of sheep in the colony.

Interestingly enough, clothing the family was considered a leisure-time activity by the colonial homemaker as knitting or embroidery is today. For instance, the well-dressed Dutch women used the products of their small flax fields for extra beautiful table linen or personal adornment and a few women produced and wove silk as a hobby. The average homemakers took up their spindles and shuttles in their idle moments between soap making, cooking and candle-dipping. It probably seemed a leisure-time activity in contrast to felling trees, plowing rocky fields, grinding gritty corn or fighting off Indians. But a closer look at the processes involved in tanning leather or making cloth suggest aching muscles, tired backs and throbbing feet.

Animal skins were the first clothing resource of the colonial homemaker.[7] Although even in the early years she had limited supplies of wool, flax, cotton, hemp, and silk, the hair from such animals as the deer and beaver, leather was the most readily available material for making shirts, breeches, etc. The Indians taught the colonists their tanning processes, which were comparatively simple and needed no elaborate equipment. The tanning was generally done by the men of the colony. Fashioning the fur and leather into clothing was done by the women.

Buffalo hides were used for robes, blankets, cloaks and moccasins. Cow hides and goat skins were used for shoes and shoepacks. Gloves and mittens were made from squirrel and beaver skins; caps were made from raccoon, rabbit, wolf, fox, woodchucks, wild cat and bear skins. Beds and bedding were also made of bear skins. But the most popular leather with the early colonial dressmaker was buck skin from which she made shirts, pantaloons, moccasins, breeches, petticoats, waistcoats, shoes and a dozen handy articles, such as bags, belts and bellows.

Although leather as clothing material was gradually replaced by woolen and linen cloth, the homemakers used it for breeches, waistcoats, caps, shirts and gloves through the 18th century. Advertisements and inventories of the time show that about a third of the servants and slaves wore leather clothes, and many of the well-furnished men's wardrobes included buck or sheep skin breeches and waistcoats. In the frontier settlements most of the clothing continued to be made of leather because it was often the only material available to the homemaker.

Linen was actually available to the women in the Jamestown settlement soon after their arrival as wild flax and water flag were found in abundance near the settlement and were pronounced to be of very excellent quality when samples were sent to England in 1622.[8] However, the products were not grown for local consumption. The bulk flax was sent to England to be processed into cloth and clothing for the colony. To this end Governor Yeardley was directed by the English Company to promote the cultivation of flax. Every family was ordered in 1619 to cultivate one hundred plants and the governor five thousand. But few colonists responded, and soon the order was forgotten as attention was focussed on the raising of tobacco, which was not only a more profitable product but one that could be far more easily prepared for the market.

To produce linen cloth took at least sixteen months of tedious care and processing from the planting of the flax seed to the finished cloth.[9] In the spring, when the plants were three or four inches tall, the young women and children weeded the beds barefoot since the tiny shoots were very delicate and died from the least bruises. The plants were considered mature by the first of July when the stalks turned yellow, at which time they were "pulled" up and "spread" on the ground to dry. It took several turnings on

each of the next two or three days to get the stalks dry
enough to be ready to be drawn through the coarse combs,
or "ripples," which removed the seed bolls. This was such
heavy, dusty work that it was usually done by the boys
or men of the family.

Next came the rotting or "retting" process to destroy the
gluey substances in the fibres. Two methods were used.
The quicker way was to pile "bates" of flax solidly in a
pool of running water. The slower method of "dew-ret-
ting," "a vile and naughty way," was used most frequently
by the colonial woman because pools of running water
were not often available. So she counted on dew and rain
and many washings to clean the stalks. When the plants
were thought to be cleaned of all the gluey substances, they
were spread out on the ground and turned over day after
day until they were dry. Then they were tied in handy
bundles for "braking." This process was done on a big
"flax-brake," which took strong backs and arms to separate
the fibres from the "shives," or waste.

Next the flax was moistened and drawn across the
"hackles," which were large combs of varying fineness.
This was done over and over again. The coarsest comb, or
"riffler," was used first and sometimes followed by six other
finer "hackles." The fibres were thus pulled free of dirt and
tow, and gradually formed into long filaments ready to be
spun into thread. (The tow was used in coarser threads.)

Spinning was done at first with a twirling distaff which
twisted the loose brown filaments together to form a single
continuous thread. Later spinning wheels were made or
imported, and weights were used to twist the filaments under tension to obtain finer, smoother threads. The threads
were then wound into "knots" or skeins. This tedious task

was often referred to in the literature of the day as the lovely recreation of the ladies which gave grace to their minds and bodies.

Not so the next step in the process, for it was obviously hard work. Since the natural color of the linen thread was a light brown, the skeins had to be bleached. This meant carrying and heating the water for thirty or forty separate washings in the "bucking tubs" and the use of carefully saved ashes or flaked lime and sometimes buttermilk. When the skeins were deemed white enough and were thoroughly dry, the thread was wound on bobbins or dyed to suit the taste of the homemaker and later wound on bobbins ready for use on the loom.

Making woolen cloth was also a laborious and irksome task.[10] After the shearing of the sheep, the fleeces had to be torn apart with care and all pitched or tarred locks, burrs, daglocks, or feltings had to be removed; some of the latter were saved to be used in coarser yarns. Next the fleeces were washed and dried, and rape oil or pork fat was worked into the wool either before or after the wool was dyed. This was a slow process, as about three pounds of grease had to be evenly worked into each ten pounds of wool.

Then the wool was carded. This process consisted of pulling a tuft of wool over a large coarse brush with wire teeth until a quantity of fibre had been caught in the teeth, at which time the carder pulled a second, heated "wool-card," or brush, across the first. This was repeated until the fibres lay in parallel rows between the teeth and could be lifted out and rolled into small, fleecy curbs, or "rov-ings." These were then spun into thread, or they were combed into more even thread. Six skeins of yarn was a good day's work and took twenty miles of walking back and forth in front of the wool spinning wheel. The finer and smoother the thread, the more beautiful the cloth that could be made from it. So the ambitious young women stretched the fibres until one of them, Mistress Mary Prigge, spun fifty hanks of yarn from one pound of wool, or 84,000 yards of thread, which measured nearly forty eight miles in length. It is to be wondered if Mary Prigge thought of the hanks of yarn as an achievement or as recreational activity.

Cotton was also available to the colonial homemakers along the Atlantic seaboard.[11] Seeds were purchased in the West Indies and planted at Jamestown in 1607. In 1622 a Mr. Gooken at Newport News reported excellent crops of cotton, but few if any of the other colonists in Virginia tried to raise cotton. Instead they imported small quantities of it from the West Indies as did the New England and other colonists. It was a difficult product to handle, since the seeds had to be picked out by hand. However, it was carded on the wool-cards and spun with linen and woolen threads. It was also used as stuffing in petticoats, warrior's armors and bed quilts.

Silk thread and cloth were far more highly prized by the colonial homemaker than by later generations of women. Who would dream today of the President's wife ravelling out old chair seat covers and old silk dresses to bleach and dye and form new cloth for dresses and seat covers. Yet that is what Martha Washington did in her spare time and thought it only decent economy.

Yet every effort to produce silk in the southern colonies eventually failed.[12] King James sent silk worms, seeds and plantings of mulberry trees in 1609 and 1613 to Virginia. By 1619 a little silk cloth had been produced, and the Assembly passed a law requiring each planter to plant six

mulberry trees each spring for seven years. The slight success was acclaimed in a poem:

> Where wormes and Food doe naturally abound;
> A gallant Silken Trade must there be found.
> Virginia excels the World in both—
> Envie nor malice can gaine say this troth!

Three years later Governor Wyatt brought more silk
worms and seed and a few skilled workers from Spain and
France, but the project failed in spite of repeated laws and
urgings by the governments in England and in the colony.
A few women raised the worms and wound the delicate
filaments, but only as an interesting side line. Perhaps the
extreme care and delicacy of the work proved too irksome
or confining for her pioneer outlook and active life. A
booklet written in London in 1620 indicates the conditions
that were necessary for the growth of the silk worms. It
was thought needful to "provide also faire and fit middle
lodgings for the Silkwormes: for this delicate creature,
which clothes princes . . . cannot indure to bee lodged in
bare and beggerly roomes, but in those that be large, sweet,
neat, wel ayred and lightsome. . . . No ill smels must come
neere them, they must be kept sweet, and oft perfumed;
therefore having such store of sweetwoods in Virginia as
you have there, you shall do well to make their rooms and
tables of those woods . . ." [13] Such provisions for the well-
being of silk worms was not possible for any but the
wealthiest women, and apparently weaving was more to
their liking and the results more evident and beneficial to
their families. The looms ranged from small table models
on which she wove tape, braid, belting, garters, ribbons,
shoe laces, suspenders and hat bands to the full-sized models, which were about the size of a large four-poster bed.

Often the loom took up half the room, whether it was the main living room of the house or an attic. On the large estates a "weaving house" was often built or a separate room set apart for this work.

Preparing the loom for the weaving process was slow and exacting. Each thread of "warp" had to be put in place and held at an even tension. When this was done the weaving itself consisted of three basic motions: the foot treadle was depressed to separate the warp threads, the shuttle was thrown across and the batten was swung to push each thread close to the preceding one. Three yards of broadcloth was a heavy day's work and meant that one weaver had pressed the treadle, thrown the thread, and swung the batten three thousand times—nine thousand coordinated movements. Yet this was leisure time work to be done in her free moments.

Perhaps she thought of it so because some of the weaving resembled art embroidery. Certainly she wove many beautiful bed covers and other articles for her home. She achieved a whole rainbow of colors in her dyes.[14] She had no neatly packaged aniline dyes from the corner drugstore. Rather, she went to her garden and deep into the forest to find most of her colors. Reds and pinks she brewed from sumac berries, the roots of madder, pokeberries and alum, cochineal and logwood. Her yellow dyes came from the leaves of horse's laurel, devil's bit, Jerusalem artichokes, St. John's worts, the roots of the barberry shrubs, the bark of sassafras and balsam and from fustle and copperas. Blue was her favorite dye and came from indigo leaves. Green was made from indigo, alum and goldenrod, brown from the bark of oak, walnut and maple, purple from the iris and combinations of dyes, and black from field-sorrel leaves, logwood and copperas.

Boiling, clearing the dyes of sediment, mixing, reboiling

Indigo processing in South Carolina, 1740, from the Mouzon Map of the Parish of St. Stephen. (Courtesy of the Charleston Library Society, Charleston, South Carolina)

and redying the yarn and woven cloth took more hours of labor than can be easily estimated because she tucked it in between her other duties and took little account of the time or effort. Mrs. John May of Boston gives us a glimpse in her diary of how she accomplished it. She wrote on one day: "A large kettle of yarn to attend upon. Lucretia and self rinse, scour through many waters, get out, dry, attend to, bring in, do up and sort 110 score of yarn; this with baking and ironing. Then went to hackling flax." [15]

Knitting came nearer to being a leisure-time activity. Girls were taught to knit as soon as they could hold the needles and often knit stockings and mittens by the time they were four years old. Dressmaking and tailoring were serious work, but tambouring, lace making, embroidering, and quilting were saved for relaxing-time hours, or for social occasions when neighbors shared in the work.

All this labor in making cloth was important not only because it was a significant element in the social structure of the community life. Lacking most of the Old World ways of expressing personal and family status in the community, clothing was of unusual importance. Both men and women dressed in silk, satins and velvets while still living in rude huts. Many European visitors traveling through the colonies remarked on the incongruity of the lavish dresses of the women and their primitive surroundings. As the "Simple Cobbler of Aggawam" stated in 1647, "I can make my selfe sick at any time with comparing the dazzeling spender wherwith our gentlewomen were embellished in some former habits, with goosdom, wherewith they are now surcingled and debauched. We have about five or six of them in our colony: if I see any of them accidentally, I cannot cleanse my phansie of them for a month after. I speak sadly; me thinkes it should break the hearts of English-men to see goodly English women imprisoned in French cages, peering out of their hood-holes for some men of mercy to help them with a little wit, and no body relieves them. It is no marvel they weare drailes, on the hinder part of their heads, having nothing as it sems in the fore-part, but a few squirrills braines, to help them frisk from one ill-favored fashion to another. . . . When I heare a nugiperous Gentledame inquire what is the newest fashion of the Court, with egge to be in it all hast, whatever it be, I look at her as a very gizzard of a trifle, the product of a quarter of a cyper, the epitome of nothing, fitter to be kickt, if she were kickable substance, than either honoured or humoured." [16]

As late as 1793 Rochefoucauld-Liancourt [17] remarked on the satin gowns of the ladies of Portland and Yarmouth, Maine, and the ankle-deep mud through which they waded on their way to church and their rude though hospitable homes. Madeleine Hachard wrote that though the ladies of New Orleans often were reduced to eating cracked corn, they dressed in the richest damasks and velvets.

Even the restrictive sumptuary laws regarding the clothing of the Puritans in Virginia and Massachusetts took account of the social standing and the wealth of the wearer.[18] Men and women alike were fined for wearing clothes above their station in life. It was all right for Judge Sewall's wife to wear her "new gown of sprig'd Persion" but her maid servant was permitted only homespun and calico. Mary Ring of Plymouth had seven smocks, one red, one violet and one of mingled colored petticoats, one white and two violet waist coats, four stomachers, one black, one murrey, two white and three blue aprons, white and blue stockings, two gowns and material for others at a time when many of the women were still wearing buckskin

**French Cartoon by Jacquemin, about 1776–1778. (From the Collections
of the Library of Congress)**

garments (1631). The contrast was even greater in the southern colonies where the governor's wife dressed in satin while she was served by servants or slaves dressed in "Indian cloth" or oznaburg.

But events in England during the century from 1640 to 1740 changed the "leisure-time" cloth-making activities of the colonial homemakers along the Atlantic seaboard into stark necessities. From 1640 to 1660 immigration almost ceased and with it the importation of essential commodities, especially clothing. The colonial men and women, as we have seen, had been forced to meet their housing and food problems but had made very little effort to meet their clothing needs. The turbulent events in England and the restrictive laws she enacted awakened the first real sparks of independence in the colonies during the last half of the 17th century. It was during these years that the men and women for the first time sought to meet all the basic needs of their families by their own endeavors. For the first time they became aware of the fact that they could survive in comfort in their new homes by their own ingenuity and hard work. What a bit of yeast that was! How it affected the homemakers is a tale of many happenings. For the women in each of the colonies met the challenge in different ways and at different times.

New England women, because of the urgency of their clothing problems were first to respond. They had the potentials necessary in materials and skills and, in time, acquired the spinning wheels, looms and other equipment to speed the production of cloth. The Plymouth colony set the pace by a law in 1633 "that no sheep could be sold [or taken] out of the colony under penalty of forfeiting due value," and in 1639 "that every householder sow one rodd of ground square at least with hemp or flax yearly." [19] This

was followed by a General Court order of the Massachusetts Bay Colony in 1640 which stated that, "whereas yt
is observed as experience hath made appeare, that much
growned within there libertyes may be well improved in
hempe & flaxe, and that we myght in tyme have supply of
lynnen cloathe amongst orselves, and for the more speedy
prcuring of hemseed. It is ordered that every prticuler
family within these Plantations, shall prcure & plant this
present yeare at lest one spoonefull of Englishe hempseed,
in some fruitful soyle at lest a foote distant betwixt eur
seed; and same so planted shall presearve and keepe in
husbandly manner for supply of seed for another yeare." [20]

In a second order in the same year the magistrates and
deputies were required to find out the amount of flax seed
available in the colony, the number of people that could
be trained to brake, spin and weave, the number of wheels
available, the best methods of speeding up the training of
workers, and to offer a bounty for the production of homespun cloth. The following year the men of five families
received the bounty and the General Court ordered that
the children work at flax and hemp with "dewe times for
foode and rest and other needful refreshings." Connecticut
also passed a law in 1640 which required every family to
raise a half pound of hemp or flax each year and two years
later forced each of its towns to buy and weave the cotton
brought in by the government from the West Indies. In
1644 inspectors were appointed, two in each town, to set
the wages of the weavers of linen and woolen cloth.

Meantime in Rowley, Massachusetts, by 1643 a rudimentary factory for weaving cloth was started and was producing "linens, fustians, dimities, and look immediately to
woolens from their sheep." The raising of sheep,[21] was
encouraged by permitting the flocks to graze on the Com-

mon, forbidding the sheep to be taken from the colonies
or the killing of any under two years old, and by earnest
appeals to the public as in the following one issued by the
Massachusetts Bay Colony in 1645:

"Forasmuch as woolen cloth is so usefull a commodity, without wch wee cannot so comfortably subsist in these pts by reason of could winters, it being also at psnt very scarce and deare
amongst us and likely shortly so to be, in all those pts from
whence we can expect it, by reason of ye warrs in Europe destroying, in great measure, ye flocks of sheepe amongst ym,
and also ye trade and meane's itselfe of making woolen cloth
and stuffs, by ye killing and otherwise hindring of such prsons
whose skill and labors tended to yt end; and wherease, through
ye want of woolen cloaths and stuffs, many pore people have
suffered much could and hardship, to ye impairing of some of
yir healths, and ye hazarding of some of yir lives, and such
who have bene able to pvide for yir childrn cloathing of cotton cloth (not being able to get other) have, by yt means, had
some of yir children much scorched with fire, yea, diverse burt
to death, the Govt yr fore doth hereby desire all ye towns
seriously to weigh yr pmises, and accordingly yt you will carefully endeavor ye pservation and increase of such sheepe as
they have already, as also to pcure more, with all convenient
speede, nts yir sevrall townes, by all such lawfull wayes and
meanes as God shall put into their hands."

Results came slowly. Besides the raising of sheep and
planting of flax, the necessary equipment had to be made,
much of its hand-hewn out of wood or fashioned from
wire, bits of metal and leather. The flax brakes, swingling
blocks, hackels, wheels, reels and looms took time to carve
and fit into place. The wool cards and combs and the
heavier, larger wheels and reels needed for working with
wool required sturdy, precise work which too often had to

be set aside for the more urgent tasks of survival. Yet the work went forward and accumulated a momentum during the century that not only met the clothing needs of the colonists and made exporting of goods possible but changed forever the functions of the homemaker in clothing her family.

The beginnings were small and simple.[22] In 1639 an inventory in Massachusetts included 4 yards of "homemade cloth." In 1642 the author of *New England's Fruits* stated that "In prospering hempe and flax so well it is frequently sowne, spun and woven into linnen cloath; and so with cotton wooll (which we have at very reasonable rates from the Islands) and our linnen yarne, we can make dimities and fustians for our summer cloathing; and having a matter of 1000 sheepe which prosper well to begin withal, in a competent time we hope to have wollen cloath there made."

Nine years after the Rowley fulling mill was started, Johnson reported another fulling mill which "caused their little ones to be very diligent in spinning cotton-woole, . . ." In 1655 John Hull related in his diary that twenty persons organized a "benevelance" "to improve children and youth in several manufacturers." [23] But voluntary efforts were not enough. In 1656 the Massachusetts General Court passed the first compulsory labor law affecting women.

It stated that "fearing that it will not be so easy to import clothes as it was in past years, thereby necessitating more home manufacture . . . all hands not necessarily employed on other occasions as women, girls and boyes shall . . . spin according to their skill and ability, and that the selectmen in every town, do consider the condition and capacity of every family, and accordingly do assess them at one or more spinners." [24] Each spinner was required to produce three pounds of linen, cotton or woolen yarn per week for thirty weeks in each year. Children and some homemakers were assessed at ¾, ½, or ¼ of the quantity produced by a full-time spinner according to their ability or available time. The spinners were formed into "squadrons" of ten persons with a supervisor to be sure that no "lazy bones" rested in any family from the governor's to the pauper's. Classes were arranged for learners and failure to obey the law drew a penalty of 12 pence for every pound short of the assessment, which was more than half a day's pay for a laborer.

The result of the aroused public sentiment was amazing and far reaching in its effect upon the work of the homemaker. By 1660 the New England colonists had more than 100,000 sheep, and by 1675 the production of woolen was their chief industry in spite of the restrictive Navigation Act of England. Home production of cloth, extensive as it was, proved inadequate to meet the pressing needs of the colonists. Capital was needed to build and equip worsted and fulling mills and pay spinners, weavers and other workers. Local governments supplied the needed capital in many instances, and thus drove the first wedge in the separation of women's work in the clothing industry from the home and into the cloth-making factories of the 19th century.

The first fulling and woolen mills were merely the extension or enlargement of the work at home. Women who had the wheels, reels and looms used them to add to the family economy, as in the case of Mary Avery of Boston who ran a thriving business (1685–1689) by making cloth, hats, and brooms and bartering her products for other necessities. First, the homemaker wove pieces of cloth for her neighbors who did not have looms. Later, merchants in the cities sent thread to the enterprising women with instruction for the kind of cloth they wanted.

In other instances where capital became available, as in the case of Gabriel Harris of New London, the whole family cooperated. In 1684 he had "four looms and tacklings" and a silk loom at which his six children and one Indian servant worked.[25] John Cornish (1695) had two furnaces for dyeing, 2 combs, four looms and a fulling mill. He did not card or spin but purchased or traded wool ready to be combed or yarn already spun. By 1740 there were several fulling mills and one worsted mill in New England, and every home was a beehive of activity; even the Indian women in the vineyards were set to work. Flax and wool were grown locally, and the trade in cotton and dye woods from the West Indies was booming.

Little wonder that the woolen merchants in London became alarmed and put through the Woolen Act of 1699, which prohibited any vessel or wagon to carry wool, woolfells, worsteds, yarn, cloath, serge, kersey, frizes, shalloons, etc., out of the colony where it was produced.[26] The effect of the law was to give added purpose to the colonists and stimulate the further growth of the industry.

In 1719 the purpose of the New England settlers was strengthened by the arrival of one-hundred disgruntled families of Scotch and Irish weavers from Londonderry, most of whom settled along the Merrimac River in New Hampshire.[27] Both the men and women were skilled weavers, and soon produced unusually fine linen cloth. Some of them became itinerant weavers going from settlement to settlement. They either lived with a family having one or more looms or set up their own loom in some unused building and did the weaving for the whole settlement. A few of these were women, and they, as itinerant weavers, became the first of a long line of women who were detached from their homes by their work in the clothing industry.

Between 1700 and 1740 the governments of New Hampshire, Massachusetts, Rhode Island and Connecticut repeatedly offered bounties on woolen, cotton and linen cloth, grants of land for the building of "weaving shops" and the money from taxes to support the infant factories.

In 1720 a town meeting was called in Boston to consider the establishment of a spinning school.[28] It was proposed that a suitable house he procured and a weaver and his wife hired. The wife was to instruct the children who were to be supplied by Daniel Oliver, chairman of the "Overseers of the Poor," in the art of spinning flax. The town was to pay the subsistence of the children for three months, after which time the master was to pay them wages for their work. The town also agreed to provide twenty spinning wheels and offered a premium of five pounds sterling (the price of a good cow) for the first piece of cloth finished. After getting no response, the town offered a year later a loan of 300 pounds to anyone who would start the school. It is thought that Daniel Oliver set up the spinning school at his own expense as he later willed the "Spinning School House" to the town. The school was opened in 1721, and a large gathering of women assembled with their spinning wheels on the Commons and made a gala day of the event. The school remained open for three of four years. Other attempts at teaching the children to spin were made, and in 1737 a tax was placed on carriages to support the spinning school at Boston. Several families also attempted to cultivate silk worms, and in 1734 Connecticut offered premiums for silk thread or cloth, but only a limited amount was made.

In the Middle Atlantic colonies the century between 1640 and 1740 saw no serious shortage of clothing. An early writer (1670) stated that in New York "everyone makes their own linen and a great part of their woolen cloth for their ordinary wearing." In 1701 Daniel Denton added to a similar statement that "had they more Tradesmen amongst them, they would in a little time live without the help of any other country for their clothing." [29] Seven years later Caleb Heath estimated that the colonists in New York made three fourths of all the linen and woollen cloth used in the colony. Lord Cornbury became concerned over the increase in the production of cloth and reported to London that "if they are suffered to goe on in the notions they have . . . the consequence will be, if once they can see they can cloathe themselves, not only comfortabaly, but handsomely too without the help of England, who are already not very fond of submitting to government, would soon think of putting in execution designs they had long harboured in their breasts. This will not seem strange, when you consider what sort of people this country is inhabited by." Lord Cornbury was quite right. The colonists did come to recognize their ability to meet their own needs and before long were seeking full independence. Toward that end in 1734 a society was formed to foster the production of linen cloth and a factory house was built in 1734 on the Common, equipped with spinning wheels and flax for the employment of the poor of the city.

In Delaware and New Jersey, Thomas Paschale tells us "Most of the Sweads and Fins are ingenious people . . . Their women make most of the Linnen cloath they wear, they Spin and Weave it and make fine Linnen." [30] They also made enough cloth to export to Sweden. The Quakers who settled in the area about 1663 were advised by one of their leaders (1685) that girls should be instructed in "the spinning of flax, sewing and making all sorts of useful needlework, knitting gloves, and stockings . . . or any other useful art or mystery." Wiliam Keith, reporting to the Lord's of Trade in London, wrote in 1728 that "The old women and children who could not work out of doors were given profitable employment in carrying on family manufacturers."

Many of the Quaker women who came to Pennsylvania between 1681 and 1700 were already trained in spinning and weaving, and the Germans who came in 1783 were expert spinners, weavers and stocking knitters. By 1692 Germantown was a thriving town famous for the linen cloth and durable stockings that the industrious workers produced.[31] William Penn offered a premium for the finest linen cloth in 1685 and encouraged the production of cloth by land grants to the immigrants. By 1740 the colony was able to meet its own needs and export a considerable amount to other colonies.

In the southern colonies an entirely different set of circumstances shaped the way the homemakers met their clothing problems in the century between 1640 and 1740.[32] Climate and soil were probably the roots of these circumstances. The kinds of women who emigrated to Virginia and most of all the craze for tobacco, were the evident causes of the lack of initiative on the part of most of the southern women in the production of clothing for their families. As early as 1627 Charles I had remarked that the Virginia Plantation was built on smoke alone, and before 1700 the colony exported more than fifteen million pounds of tobacco. Though the size of the crops of tobacco and the prices they brought fluctuated many times during the century, the southern planters always had direct markets for their tobacco at convenient landing places on the shores of the navigable rivers and harbors. At their very doorsteps they could exchange their tobacco for English manufactured cloth and clothing. Hugh Jones reported in 1723 that clothing and cloth and other commodities, made in London or Bristol, could be shipped to private landing places in Virginia with less trouble or expense than to the farthest shires in England.

With such a ready supply of cloth and clothing, it is little wonder that the southern colonial homemakers made very little effort to produce cloth themselves. It is doubtful if they could have produced the elaborate clothing they wore, for the wealthiest among the southern settlers followed the height of fashions in London. Mrs. Frances Pritchard's wardrobe included an "olive colored silk petticoat, petticoats of silver and flowered tabby and of velvet and white-striped dimity, a printed calico gown lined with blue silk, a white striped dimity jacket, a black silk waistcoat, a pair of scarlet sleeves, a pair of holland sleeves with ruffles, a Flanders lace band, one cambric and three holland aprons, five cambric handkerchiefs and several pairs of green stockings," and Sarah Willougby had, "a red, a blue and a black silk petticoat, a petticoat of India silk and of worsted prunella, a striped linen and a calico petticoat, a black silk gown, a scarlet waistcoat, with silver lace, a white knit waistcoat, a striped stuff jacket, a worsted prunella mantle, a sky colored satin bodice, a pair of red paragon bodices, three fine and three coarse holland aprons, seven handkerchiefs and two hoods." [33]

The ladies were not adverse, however, to having their servants and slaves produce the cloth for their own wearing. Many of the homes had spinning wheels and wool-cards, and a few had looms. Negresses were trained as spinners and weavers and became proficient enough to produce cloth for the local markets when trade in tobacco sank below the needs of the colony.

Governor Berkeley was deeply concerned over the lack of industry in the Virginia colony. He ordered the clothing for his family from London, but he also set up looms on his own estate and had a number of his servants and slaves trained to spin and weave. In 1646 he encouraged the Assembly to pass the following law:

For the better education of youth in honest and profitable trades and manufactures . . . the Commissioners of the several counties . . . at their discretion, make choice of two children in each county at the age of eight or seven years at the least, either male or female, which are to be set up to James City between this and June next to be employed in the public flax houses under such master and mistress as shall be there appointed in carding knitting and spinning. And that the said children be furnished from the said county with six barrels of corn, two coverlets or one rug and one blanket, one bed, one wooden bowl or tray, two pewter spoons, a sow shote of six months old, two laying hens, with convenient apparel both linen and woolen, with hose and shoes . . . that there be two houses built by the first of April next . . . 10,000 lbs. of tobacco set aside to build houses.[34]

After Berkeley was returned to office under Charles II, he again successfully urged the House of Burgess (1666) to pass a compulsory labor law using the poor women and children as the workers. The law reads:

Whereas the present Obstructions of Trade and the Nakedness of the Country so Sufficiently Evidence of what necessity it is to provide for a Supply by improving all Means of improving and Raising Manufacturers among our Selves and the Governor's Honour having by apparent demonstrations manifested that our poverty and necessity proceeds more for want of Industry than of Ability since five Women or Children of 12 or 13

Years Old may provide Sufficient Clothing for thirty persons with much Ease if they would betake themselves to Spinning which cannot be objected against if Weavers and Looms were provided. It is therefore proposed that within two Years at furthest the Commissioners of Each County Court may be Enjoyned to provide and Set up a Weaver and Loom in Each of the respective Counties of this Country. . . .[35]

A further law two years later was passed, "Empowering County Courts to build work-houses assisted by vestry . . . for the educating and instructing poor children in the knowledge of spinning, weaving and other useful occupations and trades and power granted to take poor children from indigent parents to place them to work in those houses."

To encourage the production of flax the assembly in 1673 required every county to buy one quart of flax seed and one quart of hemp seed for each tithable inhabitant, who was required to produce at least one pound of each, or two pounds of one. The Assembly also offered rewards to encourage the production of wool in 1682 and linen in 1693.[36] In 1694 Mrs. Sarah Emperor of Lower Norfolk received a reward for the "best linen cloth."

Mr. Durand wrote a pamphlet in 1686 in which he stated that the land of Virginia "is so rich and so fertile that when a man has fifty acres of ground, 2 men-servants, a maid and some cattle, neither he nor his wife do anything but visit among their neighbors, . . . when a man squanders his property he squanders his wife's also, and this is fair, for the women are foremost in drinking and smoking." [37]

But the acting governor in 1708 saw the situation in a different light; he wrote, "It was necessity that forced them at first upon this course, but the benefit they have found by it, in the late scarcity of goods, and ye Experience they have gained, therein serves to have confirmed in them too great an inclination to continue it in so much that this year, in some parts of the Country, the planting of tobacco has been laid aside and ye improvement of ye manufactures of Cotton, Woolen, and Linnen followed with an unusual Alacrity and Application." [38]

Governor Berkeley was also interested in the production of silk. In 1654 Edward Digges had imported Armenian silk weavers who were experts in handling the silk worms and cocoons and had procured an allowance of 4000 pounds of tobacco for them from the government. Premiums were offered, and in 1662 the House of Burgesses passed an act requiring all landowners to plant ten mulberry trees for every one hundred acres they owned. The results were gratifying, if not stupendous. Governor Berkeley was able in 1668 to send three hundred pounds of silk to Charles II who said it was of excellent quality. Mrs. Garrett and Mrs. Burbage became distinguished for both the quality and quantity of the delicate silk fibres they produced, but the industry remained largely in the hands of a few women who did it as a side line. [39]

Most of the women of Maryland also bought their clothing with tobacco, although they had cotton and flax of their own planting as early as 1634. It was not until the last quarter of the 17th century that any real effort at local production was made. Like Virginia after the restrictive Navigation Act of 1662, the government offered bounties on flax and hemp (1671–1695). In 1706 hemp and flax were permitted as legal tender, and between 1723–1740 the bounties were increased to one hundred pounds of tobacco for one hundred pounds of flax, but this did not greatly stimulate the production of cloth. Many home-makers speeded up the production of cloth on their planta-tions or smaller farms, but their efforts were not coordi-nated or made effective as in the case of the homemakers in New England. The wealthy women continued to order their clothing from England, and from the few inventories still extant, it is possible to catch a glimpse of the elegance of their dress. Madame Henrietta Maria Lloyd, for in-stance, had: "1 satin gown and petticoat; 1 silk gown and patticoat; 1 old silk gown and petticoat; 1 mourning gown and quilted petticoat; 1 silk mantle; 2 silk petticoats and scarf; 1 good warm gown; 2 smock coats and 2 waist-coats; 1 pr. of bodices; a gauze coat; 1 flowered satin party coat; 4 party coats; 4 pr. shoes and 1 pr. galoches; silk and worsted stockings; 2 headdresses; box of handkerchiefs; a flowered satin morning gown; a long scarf lyned with vel-vet; 2 prs. of stays; a black scarf; 1 gowne and party coat; 1 silk petticoat with silver fringe; 1 silk mourning gowne; 1 sable tippet and strings; 2 short aprons; a girdle and mask." [40]

The women who settled in the Carolinas seem to have been of a different temperament. John Lawson, writing in about 1700, describes the homemakers as "the most in-dustrious Sex in that Place and by their good Housewifery, make a great deal of Cloath of their own cotton, Wool and Flax; some of them keeping their families (though large) very decently apparel'd both with Linnens and Woolens so that they have no occasion to run into the Merchant's debt." [41] A quarter of a century later William Byrd made similar osbervations. He reported, "We saw no Drones there, which are but too Common, alas, in that Part of the World. Tho' in truth, the Distempers of Laziness seizes the Men oftener much than the Women. These last Spin, weave and knit, all with their own hands, while their husbands, depending on the Bounty of the Climate, are Sloathful in everything. . . . There is but little wool in that Province, tho' cotton grown very kindly, and so far south is Seldom nippt by the Frost. The Good Women mix this with their Wool for their outer Garments; for want of Fulling, that kind of manufacture is Open and Sleazy." [42]

The governments of both North and South Carolina provided substantial bounties on flax and hemp for export Gooch reported in 1739 that, "The common people in all parts of the colony and indeed many of the better sort are lately got into the use of looms, weaving coarse cloth for themselves and for the negroes. And our new inhabitants on the other side of the mountains make very good linen which they sell up and down the country."

The Carolinians were also interested in producing silk. Governor Nathaniel Johnson began the sericulture about 1702 on his plantation in St. Thomas which he called "Silk Hope." [43] His friends followed his example and the French Huguenot settlers produced several bales of silk in 1710 and 1716. Many women became proficient in winding the delicate fibres and were further encouraged by the bounties offered by both the governments. In 1731 a group of silk weavers from Switzerland settled in South Carolina and greatly increased the colony's output. Many of the wealthy women on the plantations took up sericulture as a hobby and met with considerable success.

Silk culture was planned as the prime project of the emigrants of Georgia. Slavery was forbidden by the Council because "silk and other products were such as women and children would be of as much use as negroes." [44] Professional silk reelers were brought from Europe but they were dissatisfied with their working conditions and sabotaged the machinery. In 1732 Mr. and Mrs. Camuse came from Italy and began training workers and producing silk in larger quantities. Two years later they sent eight pounds of lovely silk to England. After Mr. Camuse's death Mrs. Camuse continued the industry until her death in 1749, when Widow Barriky took over the work. Silk was also produced by the Salzburgers, who had settled along the Savannah River. Fourteen of the women of the colony were given awards by the trustees for their proficiency in reeling silk filaments.

Although cotton and flax grew abundantly in Louisiana as in the other southern colonies, the French homemakers of the area appear to have had very little interest in cultivating them for the production of cloth. Some spinning and weaving was done on the plantations, but it was mostly the work of the servants and slaves for household use. The ladies and their families dressed in the latest fashions from France, which came with each boat load of emigrants.

Sericulture was a fashionable hobby. The Ursuline nuns taught the girls in the orphanage how to handle a filature. Madame Hubert was an expert and carried on a number of experiments with the cocoons.[45] She was so successful that she was able to send two pounds of silk to France in 1718. By 1726 she was widely known for her accomplishments and had set the fashion for silk culture among her friends, but it remained an avocational hobby for a few wealthy women.

6

Clothing Became an Industry

In the years between 1740 and 1775, every aspect of the life of colonial homemakers took on a new, driving force, but none were more evident than the thrust they gave to the production of cloth. They saw the population of the colonies rise from about 900,000 to 2,200,000 people. They lived through the agonies of the French and Indian War (1754–1763), and they participated vigorously in the protests against the British restrictions on colonial production and trade. The Stamp Act (1765) and the Townsend Act (1767) infused them with a patriotic urge that found expression in a hundred ways and changed the whole way of life for many of them.

The effect on their clothing activities was to speed up the magnetic pull of the nascent factories. Because the factories were more efficient than production in the home, the factories were considered a boon to society. No thought was given to the fact that the new system of production would take a goodly portion of all of the women out of the homes of the land. These changes came earlier and were most evident in New England where climate and soil, as well as the Puritan spirit, tended to intensify the problems of survival. In 1748 the Society for Promoting Industry and Frugality was formed in Boston and its work of promoting home industries was soon evident. *The Boston Newsletter* of December 17, 1750, made the following announcement.

"Linnen Manufacture: Publick Notice is hereby given, that Sundry Looms for Weaving of Linnen, of all Sorts, are set up at the Linnen-Manufacturing House in the Common below Thomas Hancock's Esq.: where all Persons may have their Yarn wove in the best and Cheapest Manner, and with the utmost Dispatch. At the same Place, money will be given for all Sorts of Linnen Yarn. And whereas the setting up and establishing the Linnen Manufacture is undoubtedly at the utmost Importance in this Province: It is proposed by a number of Gentlemen, very soon to open several Spinning-Schools in this town, where children may be taught gratis. And children, that are suitable for such Schools, to learn the useful and necessary Art of Spinning: and that they will give all other proper Countenance and Encouragement to this Undertaking."

The building was completed in 1751, and on the day of its opening 300 "young female spinsters" brought their wheels and flax to the Common where they spent the day spinning thread for the factory. Two years later Rev. Samuel Cooper preached at a meeting of the Society and asked for funds.[1] Four hundred and fifty three pounds sterling was collected. The same year the General Court granted 15,000 pounds for the erecting of a spinning house and proposed that one person from each town should come to the school for instruction. In 1753 the Court assigned the luxury taxes of carriages for the support of the factory on the grounds that the "number of poor is greatly increased

. . . and many persons, especially women and children, are destitute of employment and in danger of becoming a public charge." The factory was built of brick fronting on Long Acre Street. On the front wall was portrayed the figure of a woman holding a distaff in her hand. But the subsidy was inadequate. The school was given new life in 1762 by John Brown, who offered to teach children gratis for four months, after which time they would be paid for their work. Five years later the school was closed on the repeal of the Stamp Act and used thereafter intermittently until 1780 when the building was sold for money to support the army.

Another factory was started in Boston by William Molineaux and other philanthropists. The "Manufacturing House" [2]was located on Tremont Street where expert English mistresses taught the children how to spin and weave. Molineaux himself boasted that they had "learned at least three hundred children and women to spin in the most compleat manner." The weaving of woolens, linens, duck and sail cloth was done on the twelve looms and bleached in the yards or placed in the fulling mill or dye works on the premises. Other factories were built by the local governments, and public support throughout New England. One small town, for instance, manufactured 30,000 yards of cloth in one year, mostly the work of the women.

Besides their cooperation with the local governments and philanthropic Societies, the homeowners of New England made three notable contributions to the development of the clothing industry. First, they formed societies of their own, such as the "Daughters of Liberty," to stimulate production through their celebrated spinning bees; secondly, they donated time, effort, and products to the well-being of the church or community, and they also stepped up their home production amazingly.

The first definite notice of a meeting of the "Daughters of Liberty" [3] was in Providence, Rhode Island, in March of 1776 when seventeen young ladies met at the house of Deacon Ephraim Bowen and spun all day long for the public benefit. At the next meeting their number had so increased that they had to move to the court house to accommodate all that came. The event was reported in the *Boston Chronicle,* April 7, 1766, in which the editor wrote, "There they exhibited a fine sample of industry, by spinning from sunrise until dark, and displayed a spirit for saving their sinking country, rarely to be found among persons of more age and experience." The editor of the *New York Journal* was even more enthusiastic over the event. He reported it as an inspiring event and indicated the prodigious output of cloth by several New York women. "What a glorious example Newport has set us. Rouse, O My Countrymen. We are well informed that one married lady and her daughter of about sixteen, have spun sixty yards of good fine linen cloth, nearly a yard wide, since the first of March, besides taking care of a large family. The linen manufacture is promoted and carried on, with so much spirit and assiduity, among all ranks that we are assued there is scarcely enough flax to be had in town, to supply the continued consumption of that Article."

Groups of patriotic women gathered in nearly every town in New England, and from sunrise to sunset spun and wove linen, cotton, and woolen thread, which they gave to worthy causes. This was not a new venture for them. As early as 1754, after the soldiers had been fighting in the French and Indian War for four months and needed new clothing, the women volunteered their services. They manufactured the homespun and made more garments than were requested to relieve the needs of the men who were fighting.

In August of 1767 [4] they gave the day's work to Rev. Webster. At Rowley thirty-three ladies gave their work to Rev. Jewell. At Ipswich seventy-seven ladies gave their work to Rev. Cleveland. At Beverly sixty ladies gave their work to Rev. Champney. At Yale College sixty ladies gave their work to President Ezra Stiles, and at Brookfield, Rhode Island, they gave to Rev. Forbes as reported in the Providence Gazette August 5, 1769:

On the 12 of July the good women of the second precinct in Brookfield—true daughters of liberty and industry, stimulated by their fair sisters, met at the house of Rev. Mr. Forbes to the number of fifty five, with 34 wheels; and from five o'clock in the morning to seven in the evening, picked, carded, and spun of cotton, wool and two 762 knots and a few threads; and of flax, hatcheled and spun 936 knots and 35 threads, all which they generously gave to Mr. Forbes. The young lady that excelled at the linen wheel, spun 70 knots. And among the matrons there was one who did the morning work of a large family, made her cheese etc., carried her own wheel, sad down to spin at nine in the morning, and by seven in the evening spun 53 knots, and went home to milking. As the cool of evening came on, about five o'clock they all descended from the chambers and rooms of the house into the front yard, on the green, where with their buzzing wheels, innocent chat, neat and decent apparel (chiefly homespun) friendly activity, and thr very perfection of female harmony, made a most agreeable appearance. The next day for severl suceeding days others as well affected to their minister, and the cause of liberty and industry, but could not leave their families to join their sisters on the said day, sent in their 40 knots each, spun out of their own materials.—A very striking example of generosity and public economy.

Evidences of the increased production of thread and cloth in New England by the colonial homemaker are found in most of the printed material of the period. The poem in the *Massachusetts Gazette* of November 9, 1767, expresses the growing sentiment of the times linking women's work in the clothing industry with the cause of freedom.

> Young ladies in town and those that live round
> Let a friend at this season advise you.
> Since money's so scarce and times growing worse,
> Strange things may soon hap and surprise you,
> First then throw aside your high top knots of pride
> Wear none but your own country linen.
> Of economy boast. Let your pride be the most
> To show cloaths of your own make and spinning.
> What if homespun they say is not quite so gay
> As brocades, yet be not in a passion,
> For when once it is known this is much wore in town,
> One and all will cry out 'Tis the fashion.
> And as one and all agree that you'll not married be
> to such as will wear London factory
> But at first sight refuse, till e'en such you do choose
> As encourage our own manufactory.

The women were encouraged to increase their production in many ways. Notices of their accomplishments appeared in the local newspapers and almanacs.[5] In Newport, Rhode Island, for instance, it was reported that a famly produced thirty stockings and 487 yards of cloth in nineteen months. At new Fairfield, Connecticut, Mrs. Hungerford spun 126 skeins of worsted yarn in about twelve hours. Another family, "manufactured 980 yards of woolen cloth besides two coverlids and two bed-ticks and all the stocking yarn of the family." Publicity was given to the fact that the president of Harvard University and the graduating class of 1768 all wore homespun clothes as did the president and first graduating class of Brown University in 1769.[6]

Sericulture was also attempted by a few New England women.[7] In 1747 Governor Law wore a coat and stockings made of New England silk, and three years later his daughter wore what was said to be the first silk dress produced locally. By 1758 a little silk was produced in Newport and Boston and silk lace in Ipswich. Dr. Stiles recorded in his journal of 1772 that a shipment of 455 pounds of exceedingly fine raw silk was sent to London from Charleston, Massachusetts, and the material for a gown for Mrs. Stiles of her own silk. What an accomplishment for "idle hours"!

In New York similar events were taking place.[8] The *New York Gazette* of February 18, 1762, carried the notice: "Spinners employed—St. Andrew's Society desirous to employ such poor scots women as are capable of working and for want of employ became the Objects of the Society's charity." Two years later a group of men set up a woolen manufacturing plant at Hempstead, Long Island, with fourteen looms for the avowed purpose of giving bread to poor families, although they were not adverse to pocketing the profits.

It was also in 1764 that the Society for the Promotion of Arts, Agriculture and Economy in New York City was organized and proceeded to offer premiums on linen and woolen cloth.[9] The following year the Society advertised for fifty spinning wheels to keep more women busy. In 1766 the Society offered ten pounds sterling (more than two weeks' wages for a laborer) for the first three stockings frames of iron to be set up in the colony, a medal for the first flax mill that was run by waterpower and thirty pounds sterling (over a month's pay) for the first good bleaching field. The next year the Society announced that it had given 600 pounds "to encourage linen manufacturing in

this city—to employ 300 poor for 18 months passed
—by relieving number of distressed women, now in the
Poor-House" from expense to the city. The same year Governor Moore of New Jersey reported that "The custom of
making these coarse cloths [woollen and linsey-woolen] in
private families prevails throughout the whole Province,
and in almost every house a sufficient quantity is manufactured for the use of the family. . . . Every home swarms
with children, who are set to work as soon as they are able
to spin and card; and as every family is furnished with a
loom, the Itinerant Weavers, who travel about the country,
put the finishing hand to the work." [10] Two years later a
letter urging the boycotting of English goods was published
in the *Pennsylvania Journal*. It stated that the writer, who
was traveling through New Jersey, saw many evidences of
the growing sentiment for self determination. He wrote,
"At another gentleman's house where I was, his lady was
spinning fast, and had five clever girls spinning along with
her ever since they heard that the Boston Parliament was
dissolved; it's expected that they will soon have a good
deal of cloth to sell." [11] In Salem County "associations of
ladies were formed, recommending to the patriotic females
throughout the union to enter immediately upon the business of domestic manufactures by plying the spinning wheel
and the loom." In Gloucester County it was resolved "that
our young women instead of trifling their time away, do
prudently employ it in learning the use of the spinning
wheel." [12] The state government added a further impetus
to the work of the women by offering bounties for cloth
produced locally.

The women of Pennsylvania were no less active. At
Bethlehem, Pennsylvania, the "Sister House" of the Moravian Community was set up (1749) to do the spinning

and weaving of blankets, coverlets and other bed and table linen, handkerchiefs, neck cloths, garters, stockings and gloves.[13] The state government offered bounties on cloth in 1684, 1701, 1722, and 1729. In Philadelphia an association was formed in 1764 to start a manufacturing plant. They bought a large building and a sufficient number of wheels, looms and other accessories to employ one hundred persons in the production of cloth.

A few women in Pennsylvania also made silk thread.[14] Through Benjamin Franklin's influence a filature for winding the fibre was set up in 1769, and two years later workers from Europe with 2,311 pounds of cocoons were set to work in the plant. Susannah Wright, a notable Quaker lady, made sixty yards of mantua silk which was sent to England where it was made into a court dress for Charlotte of Mechlenburg, Queen of England. Grace Fisher was also a distinguished Quakeress whose hobby was making beautiful silk cloth until the danger of war altered her use of her leisure time.

For the southern homemakers the years from 1740 to 1775 showed only a few changes in the ways they met their clothing problems. England still supplied them with all sorts of cloth from the finest broadcloth to the coarse cotton cloth worn by the slaves. But here and there one can note the quickening of interest in local production. In 1745 Eliza Lucas, at the suggestion of her father, set up a tiny factory on the estate she was managing for him in South Carolina.[15] He wrote, "I send by this Sloop two Irish servents, viz.: a Weaver and a Spinner. I am informed Mr. Cattle hath produced both Flax and Hemp. I pray you will purchase some, and order a loom and spinning-wheel to be made for them, and set them to work. I shall order Flax sent from Philadelphia with seed, that they may

not be idle. I pray you will also purchase Wool and sett
them to making Negroes clothing which may be sufficient
for my own People. As I am afraid one Spinner can't keep
a Loom at work, I pray you will order a Sensible Negroe
woman or two to learn to spin, and wheels to be made for
them; the man Servant will direct the Carpenter in making
the loom and the woman will direct the Wheel."

Twenty years later Governor Fauquier sent an official
report on Virginia that stated, "The Planters wives spin
the Cotton of this County and make a strong coarse cloth
with which they make Gowns, etc. for themselves and Children, and sometimes they come to this Town and offer
some for sale. Of this Cotton they make Coverlids for Beds
which are in pretty general Use through the Colony." [16]

By the middle of the 18th century most of the inventories of the plantations included wool cards, wheels and
looms. For instance the inventory (1767) of the three
estates of Philip Ludwell included one loom and harness,
three spinning wheels and several wool cards.[17]

George Washington had a weaving house at Mt. Vernon
where cloth was woven (1767) for at least twenty-five
families in the neighborhood.[18] For his own plantation it
has been estimated that about one thousand yards of cloth
was woven by the one white woman in charge and her five
Negro women helpers. Robert Carter had six Negro weavers on his estate at about the same time. However, it was
not until the English obstruction of trade immediately
preceeding the outbreak of the Revolutionary War that
many land owners like Colonel Daingerfield started to produce cloth. In the diary of John Harrower, an indentured
servant, appears the following (1775): "This morning 3
men went to work to break, swingle and heckle flax and
one woman to spin in order to make course linnen for

shirts to the Nigers. This being the first of the kind that was made on the Plantation. An before this year there has been little or no linnen made in the Colony." He also went "into the Forest" to engage spinners for cotton to be made into gowns and "Vest coats."

In South Carolina, the French and Swiss Huguenots exported a total of 651 pounds of silk between 1742 and 1755. In the latter year Eliza Pinckney took the silk cloth she had produced on her own estate with her to London where she had three dresses made from it.[19] One of these she gave to the Princess Dowager of Wales on whom it was greatly admired. In 1761 the estate legislature gave the workers in silk at Charleston one thousand pounds sterling to build a filature that would speed up their production. Most of the silk was exported to England, but enough was brought to New York for mention to be made of the industry in the *New York Gazette* on January 6, 1767, and in later issues of the newspaper.

As in Virginia the people of Georgia sought to train orphans and the children of the poor in the clothing industry. To this end Rev. George Whitefield built an "Orphan House" at Bethesda.[20] A visitor in the town left a record of the daily routine of the establishment which was not unusual for those years. The children rose at 5 a.m., prayed for fifteen minutes; went to church at 6 a.m. and to breakfast at 7 a.m. They went to their "employs" from 8 a.m. to 10 a.m. and attended classes from 10 a.m. to 12 noon, at which time they had an hour for dinner. They worked again from 1 p.m. to 2 p.m., went to classes between 2 p.m. and 4 p.m., then to work again from 4 p.m. to 6 p.m. and to study between 6 p.m. and 7 p.m.; after which they went to church. Supper was served at 9 p.m. and the children marched off to bed shortly thereafter.

Their "respective Employs" included "carding, spinning, picking cotton or wool, sewing, knitting. One serves the Apothecary who lives in the House, others serve in the Store or Kitchen; under the Taylor, who lives in the House; and we expect other Tradesmen, as a Shoemaker, Carpenter, etc. to which others are to be bound." The girls were taught reading and sometimes writing but mostly spinning, knitting and sewing.

During the period from 1755 to 1772, the people of Georgia, mostly women, produced about 500 pounds of silk per year and exported a total of 8,829 pounds of silk in a few years. De Brahm states that "they made much progress that the Filature, which is erected in City of Savannah could afford to send in 1768 to London 1,084 pounds of raw silk equal in goodness to that manufactured of Piedmont but the Counties to encourage that manufactory being taken off, they, discouraged, dropt their lands from the culture . . . [so that by] 1771 only 290 pounds was produced." [21]

The war years (1775–1781) found the New England homemakers well prepared to help the cause of independence through their efforts in the clothing industry. As Macy states in his History of Nantucket, "The suffering for clothing was inconsiderable throughout the war. For immediately, on being cut off from the use of English manufactures, the women engaged within their own families in manufacture of various kinds of cloth for domestic use. They kept their household decently clad, and the surplus of their labors they sold to such as chose to buy rather than make for themselves. In this way the female parts of families, by their industry and strict economy frequently supported the whole domestic circle; evincing the strength of their attachment and the value of their service to those on whom they themselves were wont to depend for protection and support." [22]

The work of the homemakers was greatly augmented by the influx of over 30,000 weavers from Ireland and Scotland. Together, their infant manufactories became the "sinews of the North" and were able to meet the needs of the newly formed army as well as the people who stayed at home. Soldiers volunteering for eight months' service in New England was given a home-spun, home-made, all-wool coat as a bounty.[23] These became known as "Bounty coats" and were highly prized as the name of the woman who made it and the town where she lived was sewn into each coat.

In 1777 when a Connecticut woman heard of the sufferings of the Continental troops in Pennsylvania, she sent all of her blankets to the Army and slept in her clothes to keep warm.[24] Another woman sheared, spun, dyed and wove the woolen cloth which she made into a new uniform to replace the ragged one her husband wore when he came home for a brief leave from the fighting. In Northboro, Massachusetts, forty-four women spun 2,223 knots of yarn and gave it to be made into uniforms for the soldiers.

The help the homemakers of New England gave to the problem of clothing the military and civilian population can never be wholly estimated or even completely told, for each year some deserted attic yields a diary or packet of letters that tells again the story of the tremendous effort the women made to meet the clothing needs of the war years.

In Philadelphia a Society was formed in 1775 to encourage domestic production of cloth in the colony. The Society set up "The American Manufactory" on the corner of Ninth and Market Streets with a jenny and twenty-four spindles. They made an appeal to the women of the colony in the *Pennsylvania Packet and General Advertizer* of December, 1775.

To the good women of this province. As the spinning of yarn is a great part of the business of cloth manifacture in those counties where they are carried on extensively and to the best advantage, the women of the whole country are employed as much as possible. The managers of the American Manufactory in this City being, desirous to extend the circle of this part of their business, wish to employ every good spinner that can apply, however remote from the factory, and as many women in the country may supply themselves with the materials there, and may have leisure to spin considerable quantities, they are hereby informed that ready money will be given at the factory up Market Street, for any parcel, either great or small, of hemp flax or woolen yarn. The managers return their thanks to all these industrious women who are now employed in spinning for the factory. The skill and deligence of many entitles them to the public acknowledgment. We hope that, as you have begun, so you will go on and never be weary in well doing.[25]

About 500 women were employed in making cloth. Most of their work, however, was in their homes with wool, flax, cotton and yarn being supplied them by the factory. The business was suspended during the British occupation of Philadelphia, but another company in the city was able to continue its business and successfully filled a large contract for uniforms for the Continental Army. Maryland opened two clothing factories during the war years at Baltimore and Carrolton, and a small factory was started at Georgetown, Virginia. Concerning the southern colonies, Thomas Jefferson stated that during the war years "we have manufactured within our families the most necessary articles of cloathing."[26]

English Cartoon on poverty in the Colonies during the Revolutionary
War. (From the Collections of the Library of Congress)

The emphasis on necessary clothing in many of the records both in New England and the more southerly colonies is in sharp contrast to the reports of at least one of the visiting travelers. George Grieve reported, "The rage for dress amongst the women in America, in the very height of the miseries of the war, was beyond all bounds; nor was it confined to the great towns, it prevailed equally on the sea-coasts, and in the woods and solitudes of the vast extent of country from Florida to New Hampshire. . . . In travelling into the interior parts of Virginia I spent a delicious day at an inn, at the ferry of the Shenandoah . . . with the most engaging, accomplished landlord, a native of Boston transplanted thither; who with all the gifts of nature possessed the arts of dress not unworthy of Parisian milliners, and went regularly three times a week . . . seven miles, to attend the lessons of one De Grace, a French dancing master, who was making a fortune in the country." [27]

The post-war years (1781–1800) made a profound difference in the lives of most of the homemakers in the newly formed states of the Union. It was during these years that two major events, long foreshadowed, took place. First, capital was consolidated and made available for the development of many industries, especially the clothing industry, which directly affected the lives of the women. Second, mechanical and improved power methods replaced hand work to an increasingly large extent, which again vitally affected the contributions of the homemakers to the clothing industry. As early as March, 1726, the *New York Gazette* [28] reported that a machine had been built at Derby, England, which made organize silk cloth at the rate of 318,504,960 yards every twenty-four hours and could be run by a girl of eleven years who thus replaced the work of thirty-three persons. Nothing further was heard of this particular machine but the report of it and the arrival of several notable inventors speeded up the building of factories in nearly every town from Maine to Georgia. The southern states were slower in accepting the factory system than the northern or central states.

As long as women and children could do most of the work of making cloth in the home, there was a gain because their labor would otherwise have been lost. With the coming of machinery, able-bodied men were no longer needed for even the heavy work which could be and was done by girls of six to twelve years of age. People were enthusiastic about the use of the idle. Such philanthropists as Mathew Carey pointed out that girls between the ages of ten and sixteen years had extra value to the factory since most of them "are too young or too delicate for agriculture" and needed work to protect them from the "vice and immorality to which children are exposed by a career of idleness." [29] George Washington saw the value of the work of women and young girls. In a letter to Lafayette he said, "Though I would not force the introduction of manufactures by extravagant encouragements, and to the prejudice of agriculture, yet I conceive much might be done in the way of women, children, and others, without taking one really necessary hand from tilling the earth." [30]

Hamilton pointed out the great advantage offered by machinery in that it made use of "The employment of persons who would otherwise be idel, and in many cases a burthen on the community, either from bias of temper, habit, infirmity of body, or some other cause indisposing or disqualifying them for the toils of the country. It is worthy of remark, that, in general, women and children are rendered more useful, and the latter more early useful, by manufacturing establishments, than they would otherwise be. . . . The husbandman himself experiences a new source of profit and support, from the increased industry of his wife and daughters, invited and stimulated by the demands of the neighboring manufactories." [31]

On the memorable occasion of the opening of a cotton mill in 1800 in South Carolina, Mr. Lloyd made a speech in which he stated, "Here will be found a never-failing asylum for the friendless orphans and the bereft widows, the distribution of labor and the improvements in machinery happily combining to call into profitable employment the tender services of those who have just sprung from the cradle as well as those who are tottering to the grave, thus training up the little innocents, to early and wholesome habits of honest industry, and smoothing the wrinkled front of descreptitude with the smile of competency and protection." [32]

A few years earlier New Hampshire passed an act which empowered the Overseers of the Poor to bind out all poor or idle to the factory owners. This made available an extensive supply of cheap labor, mostly of women and children. By the end of the 18th century the practice of child labor was so common that a French traveler wrote that "men congratulate themselves upon making early martyrs of these innocent creatures, for is it not a torment to these poor little beings . . . to be a whole day and almost every day of their lives employed at the same work, in an obscure and infected prison?" [33]

Some people in New England were bitterly opposed to the factories. They started a new social movement in which they sought "to convince the populace of the error by growing their own flax [and wool] having some one in the family to dress it, and all the females spin, several weave and bleach the linen." [34] There was a brief revival of spinning bees in Massachusetts, and on May Day of 1788 at Portland, Maine, more than one hundred women with sixty wheels spun twenty-three skeins of seven knots each of cotton and linen yarn. While the movement failed in its major effffort, it is of interest to note that Hamilton, after reporting on seventeen different industries, enumerates "a vast scene of household manufacturing" of cloth. [35] He concludes this portion of his report with the statement that "it is computed in some districts that two-thirds, three-fourhs, and even four-fifths of all the clothing of the inhabitants are made by themselves." One instance will suffice to show the worth of the home industry that was so soon to disappear. Mrs. Nott lived on a stony farm in Connecticut. [36] Her husband was very ill and so she did his work about the farm. In mid-winter one son, who was later to be the president of Union College, needed a new suit to get a job. Mrs. Nott sheared a half grown fleece and in a week had carded, spun, and woven the cloth from which she made a suit for him before the week was out.

Such skills could not be imprisoned in a factory where only a single activity was needed. This was the tragedy of progress for women. Beginning with the clothing industry, most of the household arts moved out of the home and into the ever-swelling factories. Women had no choice, really. They were forced by economic circumstances to leave their homes and follow their work into the clatter and whirring of many machines. A few women furthered the movement before the end of the century. [37] Mrs. Susannah Shepard of Wrentham, Massachusetts, invented a new kind of cloth from the yarn and waste at her husband's factory.

Hannah Wilkinson Slater invented cotton sewing thread and Sibylla Masters invented a method of weaving straw hats. But, all of the homemakers had to face the problem of how to make a "living home" out of a house that was ceasing to be the center of the productive life of the family—even as we, today, still face the problem.

7

Survival of Mind and Body

Running through the elemental cares of helping to provide food, clothing and shelter for their families was the cadaverous spectre of disease and pestilence, which the colonial homemakers had to face continuously. Some of the horror they brought with them; some of the disease were the results of poor diets, climatic conditions and insanitary habits of living. In the first twenty-five years of each settlement it was not the Indians who reduced their numbers by half but the diseases they did not know how to cure or control. William Wood drew a vivid picture of the conditions in Massachusetts. He wrote, "Whereas many died at the beginning of the plantations, it was not because the country was unhealthful, but because their bodies were corrupted with sea-diet which was naught, the Beefe and Pork being tainted, their butter and cheese corrupted, their Fish rotten, and voyage long by reason of crosse Winds, so that the winter approaching before they could get warme houses, and the searching sharpness of the purer Climate, creeping in at the crannies of their crazed bodies cause death and sicknesse." [1]

It will be remembered that the Plymouth settlers landed in a foot of snow and that Bradford wrote that "cold and wet lodging had so taynted our people for scarsely any of us were free from vehement coughs, as if they should continue long in this state it would endanger the lives of many and breed diseases and infections among us." [2] Tuberculosis, scurvy, rheumatism, diptheria, influenza, small-pox and many dietary diseases swept the settlements time after time. Little wonder the first house built by the Pilgrims became a hospital which was "full of beds as they could lie one by another."

At Jamestown, Lord Delaware had found the colony located in "a verie noysome and unholsome place" with the settlement seriously deplete not alone by starvation but by small-pox, yellow fever, dysentry and measles. Here, too, a hospital, "Mount Malady, a guest house for sicke people," was built before the settlement was five years old.[3]

William Penn had already lost a third of his company from small-pox when he landed in 1682.[4] He was greeted with the news of serious illnesses among the Swedish settlers to the north who had suffered from epidemics in 1642, 1657 and 1660. In fact, all of the colonies were visited by recurring epidemics of diseases throughout the entire 17th and 18th centuries. It was a pathetic struggle against unknown adversaries with death always at their elbows.

The women of the colonies had the additional problems of childbearing.[5] They married young and often suffered continuously thereafter from lack of proper care. The records of 323 New England families of eight or more children show that a very large percentage of the women died or became invalids by the time they were forty or fifty years old. The record of the deaths of their babies is shocking and must have added greatly to their mental anguish.

One woman lost nine of the ten children she bore before she died at 45 years of age. Another lost seven of the thirteen children she bore before she died at 47 years of age. Mrs. Laurens had twelve children in twenty years of whom only five survived her. Cotton Mather's three wives bore him fifteen children of whom only two survived him; Judge Sewall's first wife had fourteen children of whom only three survived him.[6]

That any children survived the frailities of infancy was due more to their high natural resistance to disease than to the care they were given. When the colonists emigrated to America, the study of medicine in Europe was just emerging from the necromancy and superstitious beliefs of the medieval world. By the end of the 17th century, only the groundwork for the scientific study of medicine had been laid. Women on the continent had shared in the existing knowledge and had been participating members of the professions of surgeons, physicians, midwives and nurses.

In England after Henry VIII had confiscated the Catholic hospitals in 1538, there was serious confusion in the practice of medicine. The king ordered that none should practice "physick or surgery" unless examined and approved by the Bishop of London or the Dean of St. Paul, but the law was not strictly enforced. Bishop Bonner licensed the first midwife in 1642 and in 1662 Mrs. Cellier got a Royal Charter to incorporate the midwives into a guild. She did not succeed, due in part to the fact that many of the midwives had not been licensed by the bishop.[7]

Women practicing medicine had learned their skills largely from necessity whenever sickness or accidents occurred in their homes, which was almost constantly. They had been their own apothecaries, nursed the sick and acted as physicians and surgeons in emergencies.

The women of quality considered it a duty "to have a competent knowledge in Physick and Chyrurgery, that they may be able to help their maimed, sick and indigent neighbors; for commonly all good and charitable Ladies make this a part of their housekeepers business." [8] Outstanding among the women of the 17th century were Lucy Apsley Hutchinson, Lady Anne Halkett, Elizabeth Lawrence Bury and Elizabeth Bedell, all of whom were famous for their medical knowledge and skill. It was Lady Worthley Montague in the next century who shocked the English medical men into recognizing the value of vaccination for small pox. It should be remembered that these women and the many others who attended the schools of England were taught the use of herbs, first aid, and the elementary care of the sick as part of the regular curriculum of the schools.

In France, Germany and Holland there were a number of distinguished women in medicine such as Louise Bourgeois and Madame Dupuis in France, Frau von Siebold and Frau von Heidenreich in Germany, and Anna Maria von Schurman and Catherine Cramier Hight in Holland.[9]

While the knowledge and skills of these women seem crude to us today, they had access to the best knowledge and skills of their times. Note, for instance, that Sir Theodore Mayerne, physician to Henry IV and Louis XIII of France and James I and Charles I of England, had as his favorite remedies raspings of human skulls and balsam of bats, which was composed of adders, bats, suckling whelps, earth worms and the marrow of the thigh bone of an ox.[10]

Besides the knowledge and skills, such as they were, that the colonial homemaker brought with her, she had access to two types of medical literature. The most commonly available medical data were in the handwritten "receipt" books in which women had collected recipes for meat pies and prescriptions for all kinds of medicine from their mothers, relatives, friends and physicians. For instance, Helen Sprat, a gracious old lady in England, sent her neice, Alice Ross, in Maryland several packages of seeds, and on January 15 of 1725 she wrote, "I have sent hear to in this my Great Book on Receipts and with all the Prescriptions that I have almost ever had from all the Dockters, so that if you or any Friend you have has a head that way they may Set up Great Praktes and do good that way. . . ." [11]

Hannah Penn had access to her mother-in-law's recipe book from which the following prescription for the inflamation of the eyes was taken. "Take of Hogs grease ye newest two ounces, of Tulia well preserved & fairly powered 1 ounce, of Harmatics well mashed and fairlt powered one scruple, of Aloes well washed & made into powder 12 grains, of pearle made into fine powder 3 grams, mix these altogether with a little fennel water and make ym up into an ointment, but first steepye hogs grease in rose water 6 hours and wash it after ye 12 several times in ye best white wine yt may be gotten, by ye space of 5 or 6 hours, & when ye party whose eyes are troubled with Rheume goath to bed, let ym put in ye corner of each eye of this oynment ye quanity of an ordinary pins head, and anoint all ye outside of ye Eye lides with a lick of ye same." [12]

Martha Washington's receipt book contained the following prescription for Capon Ale which "is good for any who are in consumption, & it is restorative for any other weakness." It reads, "Take an old Capon with yellow Leggs pull him and crush ye bones, but keep ye scin whole and then take an ounce of carraway seeds, and an ounce of anny seeds and two ounces of harts horne and one handful of rosemary tops, a piece or 2 of mace and a Leamon pill, Sow all these into ye bellie of your Capon & chop him into hot mash or hot water and put him into two gallons of strong ale when it is working, after let it stand for two or three dayes & put a lump of sugar into every bottle wh will make it drink brisker." [13]

Some of the colonial homemakers had access to the best medical books of the time. A few of these were written by women such as, Hannah Wooley's *Queen's Closet,* Ann Culpepper's *Directory for Midwives,* and Jane Sharp's *The Midwife's Book* and her *Compleat Midwife's Companion,* and J. Wolveridge's *Speculum Matrices,* or *The Expert Midwive's Handbook.* A few libraries in each of the colonies contained medical books of historic worth as well as current books containing data on local herbs and remedies of which John Josselyn's *New England Rareties* is a good example. It included "plants of the country with the physical and chyrurical remedies wherewith the natives constantly use to cure distempers, wounds and sores." Peter Kalm's three volumes on his voyage along the Atlantic Coast contains many bits of medical data and advice, and William Cole's *Adam in Eden* or *Nature's Paradise* included "A Table of Appropriations shewing for what part every plant is chiefly medicinable throughout the whole Body of Man." For the brain he recommended "wood, betomy, sage, rosemary, lavender, marjerome, primroses, cowslips, beares eares, lilly of the valley and misselto." In all, he listed 343 trees, herbs and fruits that should be used in prescriptions for ailments in the different parts of the body. One book on midwifery was printed in the colonies during the 17th century. It was a reprint of *A Present to be Given to Teeming Women by their Husbands or Friends. Containing Scripture Directions for Women with Child, how to prepare for the hour of Travel.*

While these and other medical books were available to a few women in each of the colonies, most of the women emigrating to America knew that they would have to depend on their own knowledge of pharmacy and medical care. Many of them brought seeds and young plants for their herb gardens. Sir Francis Drake reported that the Spanish had well kept gardens when he razed St. Augustine in 1585. The French in Louisiana brought quinine, ammoniac, antimony, diaphragmalic, rhubarb and spirits of wine with them, and by 1699 they were exporting eighty six species of medicinal plants to France.[14]

The first mention of a garden in Virginia was made in 1633 by a passing voyager.[15] He described it as a two-acre plot containing apple, pear and cherry trees and rosemary, sage, marjoram and thyme. In Connecticut Lady Alice Apsely Fenwick planted an herb garden at Saybrook from seeds she brought with her from England. Thomas Peel, the "chirurgeon" at the nearby Fort, became interested in her herbs and used them in the prescriptions they both developed. Her garden was typical of hundreds of others from Maine to Florida for herbs were as necessary as corn and eggs—so much so that Alice Morse Earle has been able to list 173 varieties of medicinal plants in her book, *Old Time Gardens.*

From the Indians, the colonial homemakers learned to use sassafras wood, which the Spanish thought would cure almost anything, and china-root, or nut grass, which they claimed cured their stomach aches. The Indians also taught the colonial women the medicinal properties of jimsonweed, smutwheat, golden rod, elderberry, catnip and strawberry-leaf tea and Seneca oil, or vaseline. Most of the colonial homemakers experimented with the herbs available to them such as Jane Colden Farquher of New York, who "discovered a great number of plants never before described and has given Properties and Virtues, many of which are found useful in medicine . . ." and Maria Drayton of Charleston, South Carolina, who was also a "scientific Botanist." [16] Elinor Laurens and her two daughters, Martha and Catherine, contributed to the growing knowledge of medicinal plants, and Catherine Laurens learned to manufacture opium of the highest quality.

In 1743 Anne Ferguson asked the Council of South Carolina for a patent on the medicinal oil she had extracted from cypress trees. Five years later Mary Johnson petitioned the Virginia Assembly for money to make public the cancer cure that she had concocted. The Assembly granted her one hundred pounds sterling, a noble sum in those days. Evidently the cure was not successful, for the Virginia House of Burgesses granted Constant Woodson one hundred pounds sterling for her cancer cure twenty-three years later.[17]

The colonial newspapers of the 18th century are filled with advertisements of "Cures" of all kinds.[18] Mrs. Hughes of Virginia offered to cure "Ringworms, Scald Heads, Sore Eyes, the Piles, Worms in children and several other disorders" promising "No cure no pay." Widow Read, mother-in-law of Benjamin Franklin, claimed her ointment would cure any "Itch." She advertised for several years in *The American Mercury* and *The Pennsylvania Gazette*. "Mother" Mary Bannister invented the "Spirits of Venice Treacle" about 1731. It rapidly gained a wide popularity as an antidote for snake bites and other poisons and had several imitations on the market. It was generally composed of sixty-four herbs, drugs and sweeteners and remained on the market until well into the 19th century. During the 18th century most of the cities had several regularly established apothecary shops and nearly all of the doctors dispensed their own drugs so that the homemakers in all of the larger settlements had access to most of the known drugs of the period.

The number of trained medical men available to the colonial homemakers in sickness and emergencies was very limited and their training of doubtful value. The Spanish women at St. Augustine had only the soldiers (nurses and medical men) of limited training to help care for the sick of their families. No physician came with the first settlers of Jamestown, Virginia, but William Wilkinson and Thomas Wooton, both members of the Royal College of Physicians of London, arrived later in 1607 but died soon thereafter.[19] In 1608 John Russell, "Chirurgeon," and two apothecaries arrived on the supply ship. Dr. Laurence Bohune came with Lord Delaware in 1610 and was made "Phisition generall" of the colony. For his services he was given "500 acres of land and twenty tenants to be placed thereupon att the Companies charge." Other physicians followed him in office but were never adequate to the needs of the growing colony.

The Pilgrims brought with them on the *Mayflower* Giles Heale, "Chirurgeon," who had been an apprentice in the Guild of Barber-Surgeons in London for one year.[20] However, he returned to England in 1621. Samuel Fuller became the physician for the colony in 1623. The planners for the Massachusetts Bay Colony chose Andrew Mathews, barber-surgeon, to serve the Company in New England for three years, but the homemakers in many of the other adventures had no physician as in the case of the settlers at Weymouth, Massachusetts, who did not have a physician until 1644 when Reverend Thomas Thacher came to be their pastor and physician. In 1646 Jasper Gunn came to a settlement in Connecticut which he made his headquarters as a dealer in metal ware, repairer of kettles and skillets and physician-surgeon. This was not an uncommon practice. Most of the early physicians had to supplement their income by running ferries, trading in furs, teaching, keeping a general store or becoming a farmer, which indicates the kind and extent of the medical assistance available to the homemakers of New England.

The Dutch West India Company sent no doctor with their first settlers but depended on the barber-surgeons that were on each of their trading vessels.[21] In 1631 Herman Meynderts Van den Boogaerdt, surgeon on the *Eindracht,* decided to settle in New Amsterdam. He was nineteen years old. Six years later Johnnes La Montagne, a learned Huguenot graduate of the University of Leyden, arrived, and others followed him so that in the seventy-five years between 1695 and 1770 seven physicians and thirty "chirurgeons, or barber-chirurgeons" were given "small burgher rights" in the growing colony. Of these medical men William Smith stated in 1757, "Few Physicians amongst us are eminent for their skill. Quacks about like locust in Egypt. ... This is less to be wondered at as the profession is under no kind of Regulation. Any man at his pleasure sets up for Physician, apothecary and Chirurgen". The colony had made an effort to regulate the practice of medicine in 1649 and in the Duke of York's Code of 1665, but to little effect. These laws were reenforced in 1753 and 1760 by requiring licenses of all practioners, but the medical services available to the homemakers of the colony remained meager and poorly trained.

The earliest mention of a medical man in the Swedish settlements of New Jersey concerned Jan Peterson from Alfendolft, who was employed by the colony as a "barber-chirurgeon" and paid ten guilders per month in 1638.[22] Other settlements along the Delaware River, Newton and Little Timber Creeks had no physician until 1731.

John Goodson, "Chirurgeon to the Society of Free Traders," came to Philadelphia just before William Penn arrived with three physicians, Thomas Lloyd, Thomas Wynne and Griffith Owen.[23] Henry Hooper, "Chirurgeon," began his practice of medicine in Maryland in 1637, and two years later Thomas Gerard was elected to the Assembly of the colony and given two hundred and thirty pounds of tobacco "for physick administered to Richard Lee." James Oglethorpe brought with him to the Georgia Colony in 1730 Noble Jones, physician and surgeon, and Patrick Graham, apothecary, to care for the medical needs of the whole scattered settlements.

Thus, although there was an awareness of the need for skilled medical services as shown by the inclusion of medical men in many of the major colonizing efforts, the physicians, surgeons and apothecaries brought to the settlements were never adequate to the needs of the homemakers, either in number or training. They were non-existent in most of the far-flung frontier settlements. As Winterbotham points out as late as 1796, "It is remarkable that in Cape May County [New Jersey] no regular physician has ever found support. Medicine has been administered by women, except in extraordinary cases." [24] It is apparent from the records of all of the colonies that most of the actual care of the sick was in the hands of the homemakers, many of whom were as well trained in medicine as the men of the period. Recognizing these facts, Cotton Mather defended the ability of women in the field of medicine and taught his own daughter from the very considerable library in the field of medicine which he acquired.

In Massacuhsetts the homemakers had several women physicians to help them. Ann Mounfort Eliot, besides bearing six children and caring for her home, "dispensed salutary medicines" and "availed herself of the best medical works that the could obtain." [25] She was deeply loved and honored for her medical services to the settlers. Patience Miller of Northampton, Massachusetts, "was a skilful physician and surgeon and was the only doctor at Northfield during the first two settlements." Sarah Alock and her husband were doctors at Roxbury, Massachusetts.[26] They collected a library of about one hundred books, over half of which were in the field of medicine. When Sarah died in 1665 she was proclaimed as a "vertuous woman of unstained life, very skilful in physick & chirurgery, exceeding active yea, unwearied in ministering to ye necessities of others."

In the records of the southern colonies are repeated references to such "doctoresses" as Katherine Hebden, Mary Vanderdonck O'Neal and Mary Bradnox of Maryland and Katherine Shrewsbury, Martha Stratton and Mary Seal of Virginia, each of whom seem to have had an extensive practice.[27] Regarding Mary Willing Byrd, Lord Chastellux wrote, "She takes great care of her negroes, makes them as happy as their situation will admit, and serves them herself as a doctor in time of sickness. She has even made some interesting discoveries on the disorders incident to them, and discovered a very salutary method of treating a sort of putrid fever which carried them off commonly in a few days, and against which the physicians of the country have exerted themselves without success." [28]

There were also a number of women who were faith-healers in most of the colonies, such as Mercy Wheeler of Plainfield, Connecticut, who seems to have been much be-

Mary Willing Byrd. (Courtesy of the Virginia State Library, Richmond, Virginia)

loved.[29] Some of the faith-healers became involved in a confusion of medical ideas and witchcraft which caused a great deal of suffering and discredit to the other women in medicine.

As indicated earlier, the colonial homemakers married while still in their teens and had many children. Hence, one of their recurrent pressing needs was for a competent midwife. This need was felt even before the settlers made harbor at Boston. John Winthrop on board the *Arabella* recorded in his journal June 1, 1630, that "a woman in our ship fell into travail and we sent and had a midwife out of the *Jewell*" come to attend her.[30] In each of the settlements there were one or more older women who acted as midwives. They were highly respected and often given a house or land, or other inducements to serve the women of the little communities. Whenever necessary these women traveled by canoe, horseback, or on snowshoes to the bedside of the women in travail.

Among the prosperous homemakers, their frequent childbirths were often turned into social events.[31] Most of them had handsome "child-bed linen" and "quilted satin Childbed Baskets and Pincushions." "Groaning cakes" were baked for the occasion and "groaning beer" obtained to cheer the men. Gifts of clothing, jewelry and money were brought to the new mother. Judge Sewall wrote of one such occasion in his famous journal, "my wife treated her Midwife and Women: Had a good dinner, Boil'd Pork, Beef, Fowle; very good Rost Beef, Turkey Pye, Tarts. Madam Usher carved, Mrs. Hannah Greenleaf; (midwife) Ellis, Cowell, Wheeler, Johnson, and her daughter Cole, Mrs. Hill our Nurse's Mother, Nurse Johnson, Hill . . ." and eight other persons were present to rejoice with Judith Hull Sewall on the birth of her thirteenth child.

Hannah Penn arrived in Philadelphia in December of 1699 and was taken to the home of Hannah Carpenter, wife of the richest merchant in town.[32] Here Hannah Penn bore her first child, assisted by midwife Ann Parsons, nurse Anna Harason, two Quaker women ministers, her step-daughter, Laetitia, and two women friends who made a memorable occasion of the event.

Women were the only midwives in the colonies until well into the 18th century. The first mention of a male midwife has been found in the Records of York County, Maine, for July 6, 1675. The record states, "We present Capt. Francis Rayns for presuming to act the part of a midwife, the delinquent examined by the court, fined fifty shillings for his offence and paying fees five shillings [the price of a bushel of wheat] is discharged." [33] However, it is evident from the personal journal of Zerobabel Endecott, who was a contemporary physician, that he acted as mid-wife on a number of occasions. "His Booke" contains the following: "For Sharp & difficult Travel in Women with Child by J.C. Take a Lock of Vergins haire on any Part of ye head, of half the Age of ye Woman in travill Cut it very small to fine powder then take twelve Ants Eggs dried in an oven after ye bread is drawne or other wise make them dry and make them to powder with the haire, give this to a quarter of a pint of Red Cows milk or for want of it in strong ale wort." The journal also contained ob-servations on obstetrical operations which he apparently performed.

Toward the middle of the eighteenth century the "ac-couchers," as the male midwives were called, became avail-able to the colonial homemakers.[34] Dr. John Dupuy was the first of these trained men, but he died very soon after his arrival in the new land. Other "acouchers" followed, bringing with them new knowledge and skills to the age-old problems of childbirth. Outstanding among these were James Lloyd of Boston, Attwood Tennent of New York, William Shippen of Philadelphia and John Moultrie of Charleston, South Carolina, each of whom rendered a significant contribution to the homemakers recurrent problems of childbirth.

But the general public of the 18th century was not ready for so violent a change in their cultural pattern. Many husbands and homemakers fought bitterly against men as "accouchers" and against their new fangled notions of cleanliness, the use of forceps and the caesarean operations. "Obstetrics" was a bad word used only in condemnation of those who dared to tamper with God and nature.

Nurses, though more frequently available to the colonial homemaker than either physicians or midwives, were also less well trained. They rarely advertised in the newspapers but were mentioned in many of the diaries, journals, memorials and epitaphs of the periods. Only the Dutch settlers gave the nurse any real professional status. Catelina de Trio, a nurse, was sent over with the first group of Dutch West India Company employees to Manahata.[35] The 1629 Charter of the Company stated that "Patroons and colonists . . . shall for the first procure a comforter of the sick there." The "Ziezkenstroosters," as they were called, were women trained to give physical nursing and spiritual consolation to the sick. These nurses were followed by the better trained midwives who were each given a house or a salary by the company. As the people in the towns of the colony grew more prosperous, the work of the company-paid nurse became more and more the care of the poor and indigent. The well-to-do expectant mother hired her own midwife or accoucher.

Similar provisions for the care of the poor and indigent were made in all of the other colonies. The Town Records are filled with orders to pay nurses for the care of the sick who could not care for themselves. The first real hospital in the colonies grew out of this need, particularly the need of poor women and orphans for proper care during illnesses. The hospital was set up by Dr. Jacob H. Varravanger in New York City "in a clean house" with Hilletje Wilbruch as matron.[36]

In New Orleans the homemakers had only ship surgeons and physicians to help their local medical women until 1727 when six nuns trained in nursing at Rouen, France, arrived and took over the care of the patients in the first regular hospital in the colony. Most of the patients were sick soldiers, but the nuns served all who came to them for help.[37]

In the latter half of the 18th century the colonial homemakers had additional medical facilities available to them in the care of their families. Some hired wet-nurses for their babies. Frances Tasker Carter, who had thirteen children, told the tutor of her older children, Philip Fithian, that she had used Negro "wenches" to suckle several of her children.[38] Occasionally, an advertisement appeared in one of the newspapers such as the following from the *New Jersey Gazette* of December 24, 1777:

Wanted, as soon as possible a Young Woman with a good breast of milk to take the nursing of a child. Such a person applying to the Printer hereof, having a good reputation, will meet with proper encouragement.

Advances in medical knowledge such as the practice of vaccination for small pox (about 1725) and improved operative procedures greatly assisted the homemakers in the care of their families, but hospital care as we know it today came a century later. Sickness of all kinds remained a home problem throughout the period with the homemakers the chief nurses, midwives, surgeons and physicians.

With death forever licking at her ruffled petticoats, the colonial homemaker must have found the task of keeping up the morale of her family very difficult. She generally had children of all ages to care for, assign tasks and teach the laws of survival in a wilderness. Besides her own children were the children of the previous marriages of her husband, orphaned relatives, bound-out or apprenticed children and slaves, all of whom needed care and supervision. She was, in fact, a veritable plant-manager, superintending a dozen activities at the same time with all the hazards of incompetent labor and inadequate, dangerous facilities.

While the men scouted for Indians and calculated the crops in terms of seasons, the homemaker struggled to synchronize fats and ashes for soap, oils and wax for candles, flax and cotton for summer clothes and wool for winter chill, each food in its season for preserving and overall to accomplish a joyful harmony of labor and love.

A glimpse of the confusing multiplicity of these activities is seen in such journals as that of Philip Fithian, written while he was at Nomini Hall in Virginia, or Christopher Marshall's memorandum of January, 1778, are illustrative. He states, "As I have in this Memorandum, taken scarcely any notice of my wife's employment, it might appear as if her engagements were very trifling, the justice which her services deserve by entering them minutely which is not the case but the reverse, and to do her that would take up most of my time, for this genuine reason how that from early in the morning till late at night, she is constantly employed in the affairs of the family, which for some months has been very large, for besides the addition to our family in the house [is] a constant resort of comers and goers who seldom go away with dry lips and hungry bellies. This calls for her constant attendance not only to provide, but also to attend at getting prepared in the kitchen, baking also on the table, Her cleanliness about the house, her attendance in the orchard, cutting and drying apples, of which several bushels have been procured, add to which her making cider without tools, for the constant drink of the family, her seeing all our washing done, and her fine clothes and my shirts, the which are all smoothed by her, add to this her making of twenty large cheeses, and that from one cow, and daily using milk and cream, besides her sewing, knitting, & . . . I think she has not been above four times . . . to visit her neighbors . . . but has at all times been ready in any affliction to me or my family, as a fathiful nurse and attendant, both day and night. . . . This is a great encouragement to me." [39]

Such a household needed a manager with great foresight, the wisdom of experience, the patience of a saint and the spirit of the noblest of women. Abigail Adams was such a woman. In a letter to Mrs. Shaw Quincy she wrote, "I consider it as an indispensable requisite that every American wife should herself know how to order and regulate her family; how to govern her domestics and train her children. For this purpose the all-wise Creator made woman an helpmeet for man and she who fails in these duties does not answer the end of her creation." [40] She might well have added that such "regulation" of her family was not only a duty but a matter of survival, for that family survived best in which the plant-manager was most knowledgeable and skilled in the arts of the home. Death by freezing or starvation was the price of ignorance, lack of foresight, or careless management of the available resources. This was the basic challenge to the colonial homemaker—not the processes themselves, important as they were, but the synchronization of many processes which were essential to life in the new nation.

While the precocity of colonial children has been well established by the numerous references to their ability to read, write, sew, knit and cook at a very early age, it must also have been true that many of the bound-out children were a care rather than a help to the homemaker. This would have been true in the cases where the children were bound-out when they were under ten years of age. Some of these children came in the several shiploads of young boys and girls that were collected from the streets and orphanages of England, Ireland, Scotland and Holland. Others were bastards or children of the poor, indigent or criminal parents who had become a financial burden to the communities.

For instance, in Virginia Timothy Ryan ran away, leaving three children, Mary eight years old, Martha five years old, and Jeremiah two years old, to be bound out by the court.[41] Moses Love of Massachusetts, "a minor aged two years and eight months . . . he being a poor child & his parents not being able to support it . . . sd apprentice . . . shall . . . serve at such Lawful employment . . . as he shall from time to time be capable of doing. . . ." Mary Kenmore was a nine months baby when she was similarly bound out, and in 1745 the records of Pennsylvania state that "Overseers of Poor bind Deborah Dobson, a poor child (2yrs. 9mos) to Fred'k Gyger (for) 15 yrs 3 mos to be taught to read & write Eng. lan. & to knit, sew and spin & at end 1 new suit besides old ones."

The care and training of these children must have been

a major problem for the homemaker since she was responsible for their care in sickness and their moral upbringing. Many indenture papers included such restrictions on the activities of the children as "Taverns or Ale-houses she shall not frequent, at cards, Dice or any other unlawful game she shall not play; Fornication she shall not commit." [42] Other indentures required that the child ". . . be brought and educated in civil and Christian manner," which referred not only to reading the Bible but to knowing how to act in a civilized society. As Alice Morse Earle puts it, "It is impossible to overestimate the value these laws of etiquette, these conventions of customs had at a time when neighborhood life was the whole outside world." [43]

The homemakers had a number of books on etiquette to help them, such as *The Boke of Curtayse* (1460), *The Boke of Nurture* (1577), *The Mirror of Compliments* (1635) and *The Schole of Vertue* (1557). The last contained chapters on "How to order thyself when thou rysest and in apparelynge thy body," "How to behave thyself in going to the streate and in the school . . . in the church . . . in taulkynge with any man . . . [and] syttynge at the table." The book also included chapters on "The fruites of gamynge, vertue and learynge, . . . charity, love and pacience, . . . Against anger, envie and malice, . . . the horrible vice of swearynge, . . . filthy talkynge, . . . [and] lyinge."   ;

The chapter on table manners is delightful and reflects more of the temper of the times than is at first apparent. It reads in part,

Saulte with thy knyfe than reach and take,
The bread cut fayre And do not it breake.
Thy spone with pottage to full do not fyll,
For fylynge the cloth, If thou fortune to spyll,

For rudness it is thy pottage to sup,
Or speake to any, his head in the cup.
Thy knyfe se be sharpe to cut fayre they meate;
Thy mouth not to full when thou dost eate;
Not smackynge thy lyppes as commonly do hogges,
Nor gnawynge the bones as it were dogges;
Such rudness abhorre, Suche beastlynes flie,
At table behave thy selfe mannerly.
Thy fyngers se cleane that thou ever kepe,
Hauynge a Napkyn theron them to wype;
Thy mouth therwith Cleane do thou make,
The cup to drynke in hande yf thou take,
Let not thy tongue at the table walke,
And of no matter Neyther reason nor talke.
Temper thy tongue and belly alway,

For silence kepynge thou shalt not be shent,
Where as thy speache May cause thee repent.
Bothe speache and silence are commendable,
But sylence is metest In a chyldeal the table.

Pyke not thy teethe at the table syttynge,
Nor vse at thy meate Ouer muche spytynge;
This rudness of youth Is to be abhorde;
Thy selfe manerly Behave at the borde.
If occasion of laughter at table thou se,
Beware that thou vse the same moderately.
Of good maners learne So much as thou can;
It wyll thee preferre when thou art a man.
Aristotle the Philosopher this worthy sayinge writ,
That "maners in a chylde are more resquisit
Then playnge on instrumentes and other vayne pleasure;
For vertuous maners Is a most precious treasure."

The number of indentured children in each home is difficult [44] to determine. Robert Turner brought seventeen in-

dentured servants with him when he came to Philadelphia in 1683. However, most of them were grown men and women who soon worked out their indentures. Elizabeth Drinker in the same city had three indentured children under eleven years of age in 1784. The indenture generally required that the children be taught to read, write, cypher and learn work or trade that would be profitable to themselves and the community. While the homemakers cared for the boys, the men of the family taught them the trade or occupation of the family. The women taught the girls the household tasks, which generally included cooking, cleaning, spinning, weaving, knitting, sewing and corollary activities. The indenture agreements occasionally included training in such fields as tailoring, glovemaking and mantue making.

If the homemaker knew her three R's, she often taught all the children of her household to read and write, since a limited amount of education was required for all children in New England and was included in most of the indenture agreements in the other colonies. The education of slaves and their children were less often provided for in the sale of their services. The homemakers frequently taught the Indian and Negro women slaves to perform the household tasks and very occasionally gave them further education as in the case of Phillis Wheatley and some of the slaves manumitted by their Quaker and other owners.

Only in the homes of the wealthy during the latter half of the 18th century were the homemakers relieved of their duties as managers and teachers in their homes. Martha Washington and a few others employed housekeepers who managed the household servants as the men overseers handled the field workers of the estates. An occasional widower advertised for a housekeeper, as in the following from the *Pennsylvania Packet* of September 23, 1780.

Wanted at a Seat about half a days journey from Philadelphia, on which are good improvements and domestics,
A single Woman of unsullied Reputation, an affable, cheerful, active and amiable Disposition; cleanly, industrious, perfectly qualified to direct and manage the female Concerns of country business, as raising small stock, dairying, marketing, combing, carding, spinning, knitting, sewing, pickling, preserving, etc., and occasionally to instruct two young Ladies in those Branches of Oeconomy, who, with their father, compose the Family. Such a person will be treated with respect and esteem, and meet with every encouragement due to such a character.

While indentured children were required to work long hours, it should be remembered that this was also true for the children of the family. All children had economic value in the eyes of the colonists who had no aversion to child labor. A widow with four or five children was far more desirable economically than a young woman without children. As Rev. Francis Higginson wrote in 1629, "Little children here by setting of corne may earne more than their owne maintenance." [45] As he had eight children of his own he did very well. Each child was computed to be worth about one hundred pounds sterling in terms of his work during his minority. At Rowley, Massachusetts, the settlers in 1639 built the first fulling mill in the colonies "and caused their little ones to be very diligent in spinning cotton wool." At Boston a work-house was built in 1682 to employ the children who were "shamefully spending their time in the streets." Playing unproductive games was anathema in all of the colonies for the children of the poor.

This point of view was held by most of the colonists throughout the periods, regardless of improved conditions. Idleness, which had been considered a sin in the early years largely because the work of every hand was essential to survival, remained a strong conviction in the minds of the people for many generations. The children themselves believed in their economic value. Read, for instance, of the daily work of Elizabeth Foote from her diary (February 3 to October 23, 1775).

Fix'd gown for Prude,–Mend Mother's Riding hood,–Spun shoe thread, Fix'd two Gowns for Welsh's girls,–Carded tow,– Spun linnen, Worked on cheese Basket,–Hatchel'd Flax with hannah, we did fifty-one pounds apiece,–pleated and ironed, read a sermon of Doddridge's,–Spooled a piece,–milked the cows,–Spun linnen, did fifty knots, help'd Nab Make a broom of Guinea Wheat straw,–Spun Thread to whitten, Spun Harness twine,–Set a red Dye,–Had two scholars from Mrs. Taylors,–one carded two pounds of whole wool and felt, Nationally . . ." [46]

In many instances the homemakers had also to assume the responsibilities generally carried by the men of the families such as the supervision of the land or business or the handling of family monies.[47] Judge Sewall records in his diary, "took 24 shillings [with which he could have bought four pounds of candy] in my picket and gave my wife [Judith] the rest of my cash £4,3sh-8d and tell her she shall now keep the Cash; if I want I will borrow of her. She has a better faculty than I at managing Affairs; . . ." Abigail Adams handled the very limited financial resources of the family during her husband's long absences on government business. Eliza Lucas and Elizabeth Haddon handled the financial aspects of their fathers' colonial estates, and

Deborah Read Franklin was noted for her "industry and frugality" in caring for the family enterprises while her husband was in France on diplomatic missions.

Many of the colonial wives had a working partnership with their husbands [48] in which each of them carried a share in the family project. Many like Margaret Backer of New York City acted as her husband's attorney. Margaret supervised the local aspects of her husband's importing business, particularly during his frequent absences in Europe. Ruth Richardson of Maryland kept the Talbot Company prosperous while her husband was away. Miriam Gratz acted as her husband's attorney and increased the family fortune. Hannah Penn, who had no known power of attorney, administered the affairs of the colony while her husband was ill and after his death. Mrs. Andrew Galbraith of Donegal, Pennsylvania, took an active part in her husband's political campaign, and Anna Zenger not only published the *New York Weekly Journal* while her husband was in jail, but was very influential in promoting his acquittal on the charge of printing libelous papers against the governor. The wives of tradesmen from Maine to Georgia assisted their husbands in their shops and crafts. Travelers of the period refer to the wives as managers, or chief assistants, in all sorts of enterprises, such as innkeeping, barbering, fishing expeditions, and merchandising and banking ventures.

The colonial homemakers also supplemented her husband's income by producing more commodities than the family needed, such as a great variety of foodstuffs, cloth, candles, soap, cosmetics, medicines and dyes. These were sold in the open market or traded for other needed articles. She also performed a number of different types of service for which she was paid, such as boarding children and adults, acting as legal representative, caring for indigent members of the community and, as in the case of Elizabeth Davenport, acting as representative and business agent of Governor Winthrop.

The colonial homemakers who assisted their husbands through their social accomplishments were legion. There were a galaxy of southern hostesses from Lady Temperance Flowerdew Yeardley, who came to Virginia in 1609, to Martha Washington, who made their homes the meeting places of the notable men and women of their days. George Washington, writing of his home, said, "for in truth it may be compared to a well resorted tavern as scarcely any strangers who are going from North to South or from South to North, do not spend a day or two at it."

Of the many superb hostesses of Philadelphia, Sarah Franklin Bache, Deborah Norris Logan, Susanna Wright and Dorothy Payne were outstanding. In New York City Mary Spratt Alexander, Catherine Van Renslaer Schuyler and Janet Livingston Montgomery were hostesses of distinction. In New England, Margaret Tyndal Winthrop and Dorothy Hancock of Boston, Mrs. John North of Gardiner, Maine, and Deborah Lothrop Putnam of Norwich, Connecticut, were notable for their support of their husbands through their gracious hospitality.

The social accomplishments of these brave women are not to be shrugged aside as inconsequential or easily attained. They were the product of a long struggle against the maddening loneliness of the isolation of the pioneer homes. When a bride visited her parents three miles away she had to get a horse from the pasture, improvise a halter, ride bareback and ford or swim the river that bounded the property. This took so much time that was needed at home that it could not be done often, or in winter. Some women became very dexterous travelers along the rivers in their handhewn canoes, and many became expert horse riders. But there were few roads in the early days, and these were impassable in rain and snow. Travel by carriage did not become common until well into the 18th century. Months went by without a homemaker seeing her neighbor a few miles away.

The isolation was felt even in the towns of New England.[49] It bred a kind of fear that made each town a closed corporation with the houses "set down close to each other." Strangers became ogres and could not be entertained in any home without permission of the town council. In 1650 Mr. Gedny was fined for "suffering several strangers in his house, being an ordinary, in time of lecture." The effect of this fear and isolation must have been very frustrating and morbidly stultifying for the homemakers who had few reasons to contact other members of the colony and so were more isolated than the men, who met frequently at the "Ordinary." In the southern colonies, where climate conspired to help them, the women over-rode the difficulties and found diversions in many kinds of social occasions.

The first diversions available to the colonial homemakers were the church meetings and official occasions such as weddings and funerals and executions. Necessity helped through the need for cooperative endeavors such as log rollings, house raisings, harvesting, corn huskings and country fairs when the whole countryside assembled to help one another, sell their surplus products and enjoy the sociability engendered by their cooperation. The homemakers also had quilting parties, candle dippings, spinning matches and other joint household tasks that relieved the monotony of her tasks.

Added to these were the holidays, which were at first condemned in New England, but were constantly increased in number in the southern colonies. There were eight principal holidays: Thanksgiving, Christmas, New Years, Easter, All Fool's Day, May Day, Valentine's Day and the Royal birthdays. Henry Spelman, visiting in Virginia in the very early days (1613), wrote of the settlers, "When they meet at feats or otherwise they use sprots much like ours heare in England as ther daunsinge, which is like our darbysher Hornepipe a man first and then a woman and so through them all, hanging all in a round, ther is one which stand in the midest with a pipe and a rattell with which when he begins to make a noyes all the rest gigetts about wriinge ther neckes and stampinge on ye ground." [50] In the 18th century social life became very gay, especially in such centers of culture as Savannah, Georgia, Charleston, South Carolina, Annapolis, Maryland, Williamsburg, Virginia, Philadelphia, Pennsylvania, and New York City, where dancing schools and theatrical and musical occasions greatly enriched the social life. Echoes of the laughter reached even the outposts of the land and gave prophetic courage to the women who had ventured farther west into the wilderness. Their family morale was based on the kind of courageous integrity that sustained them when they were "liable every hour of the day and of the night to be butchered in cold blood or taken . . . as hostages," and yet could say with Abigail Adams, "Difficult as the day is, cruel as this [war] has been, . . . I would not exchange my country for the wealth of the Indes, or be any other than an American, though I might be queen or empress of any nation upon the Globe." [51]

8

First She Learned the Techniques of Survival

If you seek the underlying motives of a people, look to the education of their youth, particularly the education of their girls. Much has been written on the colonial homemaker's education, or lack of it. Historians have pointed out that there were no schools for girls for nearly a hundred years after the first settlement, but they have forgotten that every tribe, or emerging nation, has taught its children first the arts and facts of physical and, later, spiritual survival. This is what each of the colonial groupings did with both their girls and boys.

Such education was concerned with the elemental facts and processes of physical survival and was, of necessity, limited in scope if you can call such knowledge limited that included the practical chemistry of preserving food stuffs, making soap and candles, brewing medicines and salves, the practical physics of the "lug pole" over the fire place, the flax "brake," the spinning wheel and the loom, the practical astronomy of weather predictions for sowing and harvesting crops, the manly arts of defense against Indians and trained soldiers, and the practical political

237

science of hammering out a democratic form of government. Only after the colonists had attained some degree of security and affluence was the curriculum expanded to include the noble subjects of Latin and Greek.

The first public recognition of the need for the formal education of the children in the New England colonies is to be found in the report of Governor Bradford four years after their arrival in which he stated that the colony desired to set up a common school but was prevented from doing so for "want of a fitt person, or hithertoo means to maintaine one." [1] Eleven years later Brother Philemon Portmort was employed and a small school started. In 1636 the first plan to educate spiritual leaders was implemented, and in 1642 (seventeen years after landing) the Massachusetts Bay Colony passed an ordinance that required that all children should be taught to read and write so as "to understand the principles of religion, the capital laws of the country" and be trained in employments that would be profitable to themselves and the community.

The law was carried out with surprising thoroughness, and so satisfactory were the results that they gave leadership to similar efforts in other New England colonies. Girls, as well as boys, were taught to read and write and, in some cases, to cypher. It is true that their reading was at first largely confined to the Bible, the catechism, and other religious writing because their major learnings remained in the field of physical survival, especially for girls who were concerned with the processes of homemaking. That they learned the processes eagerly and competently, in spite of dangers and disasters is shown in the remarkable way in growth and enrichment of an emerging nation.

They did not accomplish these wonders with empty hands, for they brought with them a rich legacy of knowledge and skills, not only in homemaking, but in intellectual and spiritual realms as well. Most of the women who emigrated to America brought with them memories of the profound religious struggle and aftermath of the reformation. The Bible had been translated into the venacular and become a basic text for the protestant religious groups. Education was necessary to understand the text and so became popular both for men and women during the sixteenth century. Girls and boys were taught together, separately, secretly, or in regularly organized schools of several kinds. The teachers were both men and women. Many of the Protestant teachers in England were refugees from France, Belgium and Holland, and many Catholic teachers fled from England to the continent and were followed by their students. The first of a series of documents on women's education in England appeared in 1524.[7] It was written by Richard Hyrde, commending the scholarship of Margaret More Roper. Thomas Becon, an ardent reformer, was followed by Nicholas Udall (1548), Roger Ascham (1571), Richard Mulcaster (1581) and others, all of whom treatises urging the education of women, chiefly for religious reasons.

In the tumultuous century that followed the death of Elizabeth I, there were several outstanding writers on women's education such as Thomas Fuller, Richard Brathwait, John Locke and Daniel Defoe. Their opinions were sharply criticized by Sir Matthew Hale, the celebrated Lord Chief Justice, and a number of other writers. Thomas Powell, who wrote *The Art of Thriving,* in 1635 stated concerning women, "Let them learne plaine workes of all kind, so they take heed of too open seeming. Instead of song and musick, let them learne cookery and laundry, and instead of reading Sir Philip Sidney's *Arcadia* let them read the grounds of huswifery. I like not a female poetesse at any hand: let greater personages glory their skill in musucke, the posture of their bodies, the greatnesse and freedome of their spirits, and their arts in arraigning of men's affections at their flattering faces: this is not the way to breed a private gentleman's daughter." [3]

Women themselves became concerned with the problem of their education and expressed their interest in several areas of literature. Carroll Camden recently stated that "between 1524 and 1640, over fifty women wrote eighty five compositions, fifty eight of which were printed separately and the rest in collections." [4] Dorothy Leigh's *Mothers Blessing* appeared in 1616 and was in its seventh edition in 1624. Lady Lettice Morison Falkland wrote a number of treatises. Margaret Cavendish, Duchess of New Castle, wrote thirteen volumes of biography, drama, poetry romance and science. Alphra Behn, her contemporary, wrote seventeen dramas, of which several were historical. Catherine Fowler Phillips wrote *The Matchless Orinda* and many letters and poems. Mary Ward, Bathsua Pell Makins, Hannah Wooley, Elizabeth Josceline and Mary Astell each championed women's education, again largely for religious reasons. However, Mary Browne Evelyn and a number of other "learned" women were afraid of arousing any interest in their sisters and daughters beyond the fireplace and the "bucking" tub. The controversy was heated and must have been well known to many of the women who chose to come to the new and barren land. For a real understanding of their problem it is necessary to take a cursory look at the education of women in England.

The girl's schools in England, after the closing of the convents, were of three general kinds; the dame schools, the private schools for the gentry and the charity schools. [5]

The dame schools were small, proprietory fee-paying town schools, taught by both men and women, and included little beyond the "three R's." The larger private schools such as Mary Ward's school at Hayworth, Ladies Hall at Depford, Mrs. Salmon's at Hackney, Mrs. Crosse's at Exeter and Mrs. Makins' at Putney were generally larger schools and catered to the nobility and those with social aspirations. Their curricula varied but in general included grammar, "rhetoric," "logick," "physick," "tongues," mathematics, geography, history, music, poetry and some natural philosophy. The less "learned" schools taught the girls to "dance, sing, play on the bass viol, virginals, spinet and guitar, make waxwork, japan, paint on glass, raise paste, make sweet meats, sauces and everything that was genteel and fashionable." In 1682 Hannah Wooley listed in *The Gentlewoman's Companion* the "Things I pretend greatest skill in," as "Works wrought with the needle, all transparent works, shellwork, mosswork, also cutting of prints, and adorning rooms and cabinets, or stands with them. All kinds of Beugle-works upon wyers, or otherwise. All manner of Pretty toys for closets. Rocks made with Shell or in Sweets. Frames for looking-glasses, pictures or the like. Feathers of Crewel for the corners of beds. Preserving all kind of sweet-meats wet and dry. Setting out for banquets. Making salves, oyntments, waters, cordials, healing any wounds not desperately dangerous. Knowledge in discerning the symptoms of most diseases and giving such remedies as are fit in such cases. All manner of cookery. Writing and arithmetic. Washing black or white sarsnets. Making Sweet Powders for the hair, or to lay among Linnen. All these and several things besides too tedius here to relate, I shall be ready to impart to those who are desirour to learn." [6] As Hannah Wooley was an outstanding educator of her time, the picture she gives of the kind of education women were receiving in England during the American colonial period is very revealing.

The first charity school in England was probably at Christ's Hospital in London in 1553, in which girls and boys were cared for and given a very limited education.[7] Similar orphanage-schools were set up in Bristol, Exeter, Plymouth and elsewhere and were supported by gifts largely collected through the churches. With the passage of the Poor Law of 1601 it became the responsibility of each locality to care for and train the children of poor and indigent parents and orphans in some kind of profitable work. Church wardens and Overseers were authorized to assess the inhabitants in order to build and maintain "poor-houses" in which to train the children for the trades. By the end of the century there were more than a thousand such charity schools established by the wardens of the Church of England or by one of the other religious groups, which vied with one another in the education of the children of the poor. The education was of the most elementary type, largely reading, and sometimes writing and numbers. Most of the time was spent in learning enough about a trade to be able to be apprenticed according to the rules of the guilds. The girls were apprenticed to pouchmakers, weavers, corders, lacemakers, drapers, silk throwsters, cardmakers and other handicrafts workers, or they were sent into domestic service. The conditions in the schools were incredible. The girls were bound out as young as possible, having been "taught nothing but to labor beyond her strength in the most menial occupations and to tremble at the frown of her tyrant." The masters or mistresses to whom the girls were bound out were very rarely investigated before the girls left the schools, and further interest in the girl's welfare was negligible. As one report in 1723 stated, " 'tis little better than murdering them."

It was from these centuries of intellectual, religious and political turmoil in England that the homemakers of the American colonies came to their new homes. Each of the three types of English schools with which they were familiar were influential in setting the pattern of education in the new land. The dame schools in the colonies were similar to the English schools in their coeducational aspects and in their elementary curricula. Private schools for girls in the colonies came later but had curricula similar to the English schools. Only in the traditional education of the children of the poor was there any distinct change in the pattern. As an outgrowth of the Massachusetts Bay Colony Ordinance of 1642, which required apprenticeship education for the poor, came the first universal compulsory educational law for all of the children of the colony. Thus was formed the basic tenant upon which the universal free school system of education in United States was developed.

The so-called "charity schools" in the colonies, which followed the English movement by more than a century, were also religious foundations. They derived their impetus from such societies as the Society for the Propogation of the Gospel in Foreign Parts, the Quakers and the Pietistic groups. They also resembled their English counterpart in organization and curricula.

How much the colonial homemakers were affected by the position of women on the continent of Europe is hard to determine.[8] Since the Pilgrims spent somewhat more than ten years in Holland, it is probable that many of the women had heard of or read some of the writings of the famous Anna van Schurman (1607–1678) of Utrecht, and since the Pilgrims were joined by Huguenot refugees from

France and Belgium, some of the women may have known and read the writings of Marie de Gournay (1565–1645), Madeleine de Scudery (1607–1701) and Anne Dacier (1651–1720) of Paris. Some of these writings appeared in the libraries of the colonies. The women may also have known of the Salons of Marguerite de Valois or Catherine Rambouillet and of Marie d'Medici, Queen and regent of France, Christina, Queen of Sweden, Anne of Austria, Marie Therese of Spain and Sophia, regent of Russia, all of whom reigned during the first century of the migration of the colonial homemakers.

With such a background of culture, it is doubtful if the majority of the early settlers in America were either illiterate or without intellectual interests. Historians have sought to determine the percentage of illiterates among the colonists by counting the signatures and marks on various legal documents, but the data are too fragmentary to be representative, especially those of the women colonists. However, historians have concluded from this that only twenty-five to forty percent of the women were literate.[8] They neglected to take into account the fact that most of the women were married, or *'feme covert,'* and their signatures not needed on the documents the historians consulted. For instance, Elizabeth Lawrence Carteret signed her name on the pre-marital agreement concerning her property when she married her second husband in 1681 and to a document freeing a slave the following year, but years later she signed her will with only a mark. Jemima Wilkinson also signed her will with a mark, although it is known that she could write.

Evidences that the colonial homemakers continued the intellectual interests of their mothers and grandmothers in England, France and Holland is evident in (1) the books they brought with them, or that were made available to them in the homes of friends, the public libraries and book-stores; (2) the education available to them through the compulsory education laws, the religious foundations and the private schools and tutors; (3) their literary accomplishments in their correspondence, diaries, receipt books, and journals, their ownership of printing presses and news-papers and their published works in the field of poetry, drama and narrative and historical writing; (4) their teach-ing experience on every level of education in the colonies; (5) their extensive medical experiences and (6) their at-titudes toward their children's education.

While it is true that the early colonists had little room for books in their luggage in the small sailing vessels, it is also true that books take up less space than high-boys and great woolen cloaks. The libraries of the colonists of the seventeenth century ranged from a "pcell of ould books" valued at a few shillings to collections of over four thou-sand volumes. In New England such libraries as those owned by Increase Mather of Boston, Samuel Lee of Rhode Island and Governor John Winthrop of Connecticut con-tained close to a thousand volumes. C. K. Shipton found that a surprisingly high percentage of the early settlers in New England brought books with them. Amcng the women who had libraries was Anna Palsgrave of Rox-bury, Massachusetts, who owned medical books and Pliny's Natural History. Madam Usher had a Bible, thirty-one books and several manuscripts. Rebecca Bacon of Salem, Massachusetts, left a will in which she listed three Bibles, a concordance, five religious books, "two of Dr. Sibs and one of Mr. Preston, Markam and ten smal bookes. Two pounds." Lady Deborah Moody brought with her to Gravesend, Long Island "The largest collection of books which had yet been brought into the colony." [10] It contained one Latin Bible, eighteen religious books, one on matters of state, another on the matters of the king, one Latin dictionary, sixteen Latin and Italian works, The Voyage of Mendoza, Sylva Sylvarum, Barta's works, a Conference book, the Knights of King James, and eleven other books—in all a total of fifty-seven volumes.

In Virginia Governor Yeardley and Temperance, his wife, had a library of twenty volumes as early as 1620.[11] Colonel William Byrd of Westover, Virginia, had a library of "near 4,000 volumes in all Languages and Faculties" (1667), and the library of Ralph and Margaret Wormeley had over 400 volumes. Sarah Willoughby of Lower Norfolk, Virginia, had about 110 volumes, several in Latin and Greek (1673). Martha Williamson had the largest library in the county in 1691. Jane Porge in 1651 left three Bibles, one piety and nine Latin books. Elizabeth Digges, said to have been the wealthiest woman in the colonies, left "a pcell of ould small Bookes, one large Bible and other ould large Bookes." John De Brahm, writing in 1748, said, "Almost every house in America has some choice authors, if not libraries of religious, philosophical, and political writers. Booksellers import the newest editions which soon find admirers and purchasers. The Province of Georgia was scarcely settled thirty years before there were three fine libraries in Savannah, the fourth at Ebenezer and fifth on the Savannah River. In these libraries were books written in the Caldaic, Hebrew, Arabic, Sirian, Coptic, Malabar, Greek, Latin, Dutch, French, German, Spanish and English."

Most of the private libraries were small at first, but the records show that there was a fairly continuous flow of books from England to the colonies.[12] In Boston, for instance, between 1645 and 1711 there were thirty bookstores in the downtown area besides five printing presses. Joanna Perry had a bookstore on King Street until she died in 1725, and Mary Butler had a "Library of Books for sale or let" for several years (1788–1791). Anne Smith had a similar bookstore in Philadelphia, and Mary Goddard had one in Baltimore in 1784.

That the books were circulated among neighbors and friends is evident in the correspondence and the diaries of men and women. One Boston woman advertised in the *Boston Newsletter,* July 7, 1712,

A certain Person have lent two Books viz; Ruchworth's & Fullers Holy War & forgotten unto whom; These are desiring the Borrower to be so kind as to return said Books unto the Owner.

Rev. Eric Biork, pastor of the Old Swede Church in New Jersey, wrote in 1697, "We hardly found here a Swedish book but they were so anxious for the improvement of their children that they lent them to one another, so that they can al read tolerably well." [13] Charles XII, of Sweden sent nearly two thousand books to the colony by 1770. In 1621 Thomas, a preacher in Virginia, bequeathed his library, valued at one hundred marks, to the proposed college. Between 1656 and 1732 five loan libraries were opened in Boston, Massachusetts (1656), Baltimore, Maryland (1698), Charleston, South Carolina (1698), New York (1729), and Philadelphia, Pennsylvania, (1732). It should be noted in passing that some of the books in these libraries were written by women such as Mlle. de Scudery's romances, Ann Bradstreet's poems, Hannah Wooley's *Queen-Like Closet* and Alphra Behn's dramas.

It must also be remembered that the education of girls

was indicated in all of the early plans for the education of youth. In New England and New York, girls attended the dame schools, and in the Middle Atlantic colonies they attended the schools of the religious organizations with the boys. Later they attended the private schools or had tutorial training in all of the colonies. Though limited both as to opportunity and curricula, education was available to the young women in all of the colonies, even in the early days of the settlements.

The literacy of the colonial homemakers is also evident in their literary accomplishments from the publication of Ann Bradstreet's *Poems* in 1650 to the published works of Hannah Adams and Mercy Warren at the end of the eighteenth century. Many of the two thousand diaries that have been preserved were written by women. The first printing press to be brought to the colonies was actually brought by Mrs. Glover in 1638. The first woman printer, and there were at least thirty before the end of the period, was Dinah Nuthead, who signed her name with a mark, yet was given a license to print and later became a government printer. Twenty of the women printers were also publishers.

If, as some historians have written, only twenty-five percent of the colonial homemakers were literate, how does it happen that all the teachers of the dame schools were women, and many of the teachers in the later elementary and secondary schools were also women? One woman even taught for a short time at Harvard University. Their literacy is less readily seen in their medical "receipt books," yet there are repeated references, as in the case of Sarah Alcock, to their having read the latest books in the field of medicine.

The attitudes of both the men and women concerning the education of the girls are significant and diverse.

Though the New England, Middle Atlantic and Southern colonies had common backgrounds, they had very different climatic conditions, religious convictions and economic problems. Each of these aspects of their colonial life affected their attitudes toward the education of women.

The New England Puritans believed in the inferiority of women's intellect and her subjugation to men, hence they did not believe in her extended education. However, since she was also a "Child of God," she needed to be able to read the Bible to save her soul, so the first compulsory education laws included girls. The climatic and economic conditions in New England lengthened the struggle for physical survival and the inherent necessity for competent training and work in the household industries on which their very life depended. There were not enough women or servants and slaves to release many women for intellectual pursuits for over a hundred years after the first settlement. Thus the fear of want and disaster reenforced the religious convictions of the men regarding the inferiority of women intellectually. As Governor Winthrop put it in 1645 when he was writing about Governor Edward Hopkin's wife, who was a "godly young woman of special parts who was fallen into a sad infirmity the loss of her understanding and reason, . . . by occasion of her giving herself wholly to reading and writing and had written many books . . . if she had attended her household affairs, and such things as belong to women, and not gone out of her way to meddle with such things as are proper for men, whose minds are stronger, etc., she had kept her wits, and might have improved them usefully and honorably in the place God had set her." [14]

That the same conviction was held more than a century later is shown in John Eliot's letter in 1782 to Jeremy

Belknap. He wrote, "We don't pretend to teach ye female part of ye town anything more than dancing or a little music perhaps, . . . except ye private schools for writing. . . ." [15] Even John Adams was a reluctant supporter of his daughter's intellectual interests. He wrote to her on April 18, 1776, "I learned in a letter from your Mamma, that you was learning the accidence. This will do you no hurt, my dear, though you must not tell many people of it, for it is scarcely reputable for young ladies to understand Latin and Greek—French, my dear, French is the language next to English—this I hope your Mamma will teach you." [16]

President Ezra Stiles of Yale College attested to the following statement on December 22, 1783: *"BE IT KNOWN* to you that I have examined Miss Lucinda Foote, twelve years old, and have found that in the learned languages, the Latin and the Greek, she has made commendable progress, giving the true meaning of passages in the *AEneid* of Virgil, the select orations of Cicero, and in the Greek testament, and that she is fully qualified, except in regard to sex, to be received as a pupil of the Freshman Class of Yale University." [17] Being denied admission to Yale, Lucinda pursued the full course of study under President Stiles' tutelage. Later she married and had ten children.

Regardless of their modes of justification for thinking that women should not be educated, the fact remains that in New England women's productive work never ceased to be essential to survival during the colonial period. Hardly had the colonists forced back the Indians and gathered in their harvests than there rose the harrowing experiences of four European wars into which they were drawn and their own war of independence—King William's War (1689–

1697), Queen Ann's War (1702–1713), King George's War (1744–1748), the French and Indian War (1754–1763), and the American Revolution (1775–1781). Each of these conflicts increased and lengthened the need for the products of women's hands.

Men in the southern colonies had much the same attitudes towards the education of women as the men of New England, but for different reasons. The drudgery of physical survival was soon taken over by servants and slaves, and homeowners were freed for other duties. While the religious convictions of the southern colonists were not a driving force, the men accepted the attitude of the Church of England regarding women in all matters outside the home. In general the attitude of the men agreed with Lord Berkeley's, who wanted no public schools for either sex.

Compulsory education at public expense was provided for the children of indigent parents, orphans and bastards through apprenticeship training. The education of the more fortunate children was left to the voluntary choice of parents through tutors, or Oldfield schools, and later, religious and adventure schools. Under these circumstances girls were rarely urged to obtain a liberal education. It was not until 1779 that Thomas Jefferson came out strongly for the "training of all free children, male and female, for three years in reading, writing and arithmetic." [18] It was still later that he wrote a friend, "I have sworn upon the altar of God, eternal hostility against every form of tyranny over the mind of man." It was then that he took time enough to list the books he thought young women should read "to enable them when become mothers, to educate their own daughters and even direct the course for their sons."

In the Middle Atlantic colonies the climatic and economic influences were neither as drastic in their effects on the people as in New England nor as readily acceptable as in the southern colonies. Also the Middle Atlantic colonies were settled somewhat later and benefited by the previous experiences of the earlier colonizing groups. Hence, while women's work was essential to physical survival, the sharp necessity for their work was not prolonged into the second half of the eighteenth century, except in the frontier settlements. Fear of the loss of their productive work was not a strong motivation. Further, their lack of fear was strongly reenforced by their educational traditions and religious convictions. It was to the middle Atlantic colonies that the English Quakers and German Pietistic groups came in large numbers. These were the religious groups that believed in the equality of woman in church affairs, so from these came earnest belief in the education of all women. The Quakers, under the leadership of George Fox, and the Moravians under John Comenius firmly believed in the equal education of boys and girls. The German Mennonites, Dunkers and Lutherans believed in the elementary education of women. Each of the sects based their educational aims on learning as a necessity for salvation.

With the preponderance of opinion in favor of the education of women, it is not surprising to find men of the middle Atlantic colonies expressing their views on the subject in a positive manner. Among these were Anthony Benezet, who had a girl's school in Philadelphia (1755), John Armstrong Neal, who wrote a moving *Essay on Education and the Genius of the Female Sex* (1773), John Bennett, who wrote four essays on *The Strictures of Female Education* (1788), and Benjamin Rush, who wrote and lectured in defense of the higher education of women. He based his argument on five factors in American colonial life, . . . "first, early marriage, which leave little time for it, and that little time must be spent on the more useful branches of literature; second, the state of property, which requires that everyone in America work to advance his fortune, makes it necessary that females be capable of assiting as stewards and guardians of their husband's property; third, as the husband is taken from home on business, it follows that the wife must be prepared to intelligently educate her children; fourth, political freedom and men's possibility of taking part in the conduct of government requires that women should be qualified to a certain degree by a peculiar and suitable education, to concur in instructing their sons in the principles of liberty and government; and fifth, the lack of a class of servants who know their duties, and do them, requires that female education be directed to domestic affairs." [19] This is the most advanced point of view held by any man writing during the colonial period.

It is of considerable interest to note that although there were women writers and publishers in the thirteen colonies, they wrote no public protests against their limited educational opportunities until the drastic need for the products of their hands had lessened. It was not until 1778 that Abigail Adams wrote, "I regret the trifling narrow, contracted education of the females of my own country," and to her husband wrote, "If you complain of education in sons what shall I say of daughters who every day experience the want of it? With regard to the education of my own children I feel myself soon out of my depth, destitute in every part of education. I most sincerely wish that some more liberal plan might be laid and executed for the benefit of the rising generation and that our new Constitution may be distinguished for encouraging learning and virtue. If we mean to have heroes, statesmen and philosophers, we should have learned women. The world perhaps would laugh at me, but you, I know, have a mind too enlarged and liberal to disregard sentiment." [20]

Eliza Southgate Bowne, recalling her childhood in the late eighteenth century wrote, "I found the mind of a female, if such a thing existed, was thought not worth cultivating." But Mercy Warren believed in the mental capacity of women. She wrote, "I believe it will be found that the deficiency lies not so much in the inferior contexture on Female Intellects as in the different Education bestow'd on the Sexes, for when the Cultivation of the mind is neglected in either, we see ignorance, stupidity and ferocity of manners equally conspicuous in both. . . . My dear, it may be necessary for you to *seem* inferior; but you need not be so. Let them have their little game, since it may have been so willed. It won't hurt you; it will amuse them." [21]

Though women did not write freely or extensively about their limited educational opportunities, they did support the education of girls in each of the colonies by giving land and money.[22] Mary Whaley gave ten acres of land in Virginia for a school in honor of her son Matthew who had recently died and left a legacy for the school in 1706. In 1753 Elizabeth Smith Stith donated 125 pounds to start a free school at Smithfield, Virginia, and left a legacy of 120 pounds for the education of six poor children. The boys were to attend the school for three years and learn reading, writing and arithmetic, and the girls were to attend two years and learn reading and writing. In South Carolina as early as 1711, Mrs. Edwards, Lady Moore, Sarah Baker, Mrs. Skine and Mrs. Haig encouraged the education of Negro children by gifts and personal assistance. In New England, Esther Coster gave the land upon which Yale

A Dame School in New England. (Courtesy of the Library of the United States Office of Education)

University later stood for the encouragement of religion and education. Another woman gave the land to start a school in Essex County, Massachusetts, where Mary Gill taught in 1773.

There is little doubt but that the dame schools of New England were a direct carry-over from England. Probably Bridget Fuller, who was the first dame school teacher to be mentioned (1635), had taught school in her home in England and so was asked to teach in her new home. William Shenstone's *Portrait of a Dame School* might describe the simple schools of either country. He wrote in part,

> Near to this dome is found a patch so green
> On which the tribe their gambols do display;
> And at the door th' imprisoning loard is seen.
> Lest weakly wights of smaller size should stray;
> Eager, perdie, to bask in sunny day!
>
> The noises intermixed which thence resound,
> Do learning's little tenement betray:
> Where sits the dame, disguised in look profound,
> And eyes her fairy throng, and turns her wheel around.
>
> Her cap, far whiter than the driven snow,
> Emblem right meet of decency does yield:
> Her apron dyed in grain, as blue, I throw
> As is the harebell that adorns the field
> And in her hand, for sceptre, she does wield
> Tway birshen sprays.[23]

In some instances the good dames were indeed little more than glorified baby-sitters who entertained the children by teaching them to sing or shout their ABCs, but this could not have been true of Bridget Fuller or the dame who taught the Winslow children at nearby Marshfield.[24] Dame Margery Hoar, who also taught in the early days at Braintree, Massachusetts, was described as "amiable and good. A gentle woman of piety, prudence and peculiarly accomplished for instructing young gentlewomen, many being sent to her from other towns, especially from Boston." Goodwife Wickham in the New Haven Colony was also a talented and beloved teacher. But perhaps the best proof of the educational ability of the teachers of the dame schools is that they were retained as teachers in many of the public schools of the growing communities, and continued to teach well into the nineteenth century. They taught a very limited curricula of reading, writing and numbers. Their schools were in their kitchens. Their equipment consisted of a few stools and benches drawn up near the fireplace for light and heat. A Horn-book or two, a Bible and a few religious tracts were the only books she had. From these the children learned to read and to recognize numbers. Writing presented a serious problem for quills and ink were scarce and precious. The dame had no black-board and chalk; no slate or slate pencil. The children learned amid the spicy smells of baking bread, stewing bear meat and roasting apples. On dark days the dame augmented the fire light with one or two of her precious candles and stirred the stew, or spun the yarn while she listened to the children recite their lessons.

The New Englanders soon found that even elementary education could not be left to the whims of the parents and masters, some of whom couldn't or wouldn't teach their children and apprentices or send them to a dame school. This was particularly true for the poor and indigent parents in the colonies. The Massachusetts Bay Colony after seventeen years of struggle recognized that the education of the children was very inadequate and promptly passed the Ordinance of 1642, which made elementary education compulsory and universal within the colony. It stated, "taking into consideration parents and masters in training up their children in learning and labor . . . especially of their ability to read and understand the principles of religion and the capital laws of the country, and to impose fines upon all those who refuse to render such accounts to them when required." [25]

Five years of intermittent enforcement of the ordinance, or lack of it, led to the passage of a new law in 1647 which stated, "It being one chief point of that old deluder, Satan, to keep men from the knowledge of the Scriptures, . . . that learning might not be buried in the grave of our fathers in church and commonwealth, the Lord assisting our endeavors, . . . It is therefore ordered that every township in this jurisdiction after the Lord hath increased them to the number of fifty householders, shall then forthwith appoint one within their town to teach all such children as shall resort to him to write and read, . . . that where any town shall increase to the number of one hundred families or householders, they shall set up a grammar school, the master thereof being able to instruct youth so far as they may be fitted for the University, provided, that if any town neglect that performance hereof above one year, that every such town shall pay five pounds to the next school till they shall perform this order." [26]

In the following years, laws were passed by Plymouth, Watertown and other communities implementing the Massachusetts Bay Colony laws and increasing the fines on delinquent towns.[27] The Selectmen of the towns were very conscientious about their duties as was indicated in the Day Book of Woburn, Massachusetts, which stated that

"The Selectmen mette the 5.day of Octob. 1674 and agreed on the 15 day of this instant mo. to goe throo the Towne, and ecsamin the familys about catichising." At the first Provincial Assembly of the colony in 1691, the members confirmed the previous laws regarding education which required that all children should be taught to read and write, sometimes to cypher, and "be brought up or employed in some honest calling which may be profitable to themselves and the publick." In 1768 the Assembly passed a law empowering each precinct to raise money for the improvement of their schools, thus setting the pattern for our present school system.

The Connecticut colonies followed the lead of the Massachusetts Bay Colony and passed a compulsory education law in 1650. The New Haven colonists clearly stated their educational aims in their Code of 1655, in which they stated: "Where as too many parents and masters, either through an overtender respect to their own occasions and business, or not duly considering the good of their children and apprentices, have too much neglected their duty in their education while they are young and capable of learning, it is ordered that the deputies . . . [keep a vigilant eye on parents and masters and fine them or they] may take such children or apprentices from such parents or masters and place them for years, boys till they come of age of one and twenty and girls till they come to age of eighteen years, with such others who shall better educate and govern them, both for public convenience, and for the particular good of the said children and apprentices." [28] A series of similar laws was passed to meet the changing conditions in the colony, but they were evidently still struggling with recalcitrant parents and masters in 1690 as, "This Court observing that notwithstanding the former orders, . . . there are many persons unable to read the Holy Word of God, or the good lawes of the Colony, which evill, that it grow no farther . . . it is hereby ordered that all parents and masters shall cause theire respective children and servants, as they are capable, to be taught to read distinctly the English tongue, and that the grand jury men in each towne doe once in a year at least, vissit each family they susspect to neglect this order, and sattisfy themselves wither all children under age and servants in such famalyes can read well the English tongue." [29]

The colonists in the Rhode Island and Providence plantations entrusted the education of the children to the town governments. The apprenticeship agreements and other documents of the colonies indicate that they practiced the same educational procedures as Massachusetts, though not as strictly. Thus the New England colonists took the responsibility for the education of the children out of the hands of the parents and secured it in the local governments, going so far as to give the local governments the power to enforce the education of all of the children, even if it meant breaking up the family and binding the children out to people who could afford to educate them.[30] The town "Elders" or Selectmen regularly inspected the children whom they had bound out, and if they were not being taught to read, they were removed from the foster home and placed elsewhere. The children also had the right to appeal to the "Elders" if they thought that they were not being educated, which they did on a number of occasions. England's answer to the problem had been compulsory work-houses for the poor and voluntary attendance at private schools for all other children. The New England colonies set a new precedent by applying the law regarding the education of the children of poor and indigent parents to all children, whatever their financial status.

The school "dams" were paid by the parents or by the town.[31] Patience Blake of Dorchester Neck, Massachusetts, in 1762, for instance, was paid by the town—"Recd of Noah Clap Treasurer of the Town of Dorchester, the sum of Four pounds by ye Hand of Constable Moseley, being what was granted the Inhabitants of Dorchester Neck in May last towards a school. I say recd by me. Patience Blake." In Lexington, Massachusetts, in 1716 the town "Elders" "Voted that all scollers that com to school, to pai two pens per week: for reading, and: 3: pens for righting and siphering and what that amounts to at the years End: so much of the fifteen pounds to be deducted and stopt in the Town Treasury whilst the next year."

Girls did not attend the public schools on equal terms with the boys. In some of the New England towns they were excluded from the public schools in the early years, but in the majority of cases they attended at times when the boys were busy with other duties such as during crop seasons, before and after the hours the boys were taught. In some of these day schools the girls were taught in separate rooms and in separate schools when the town could afford more than one school teacher. Only gradually was the public education made available to the girls. In the earliest schools just reading was required by law, but by 1771 the laws included writing as a requirement for the girls. A few schools extended their curricula to include arithmetic, fractions, grammar, spelling and composition.

The deep conviction of the New England settlers that every child, even the poorest, had a right to an education was well stated by Samuel Sewall in 1719—"The poorest Boys and Girls in this Province, such as are of the lowest condition, whether they be Indians or English or Ethiopians—they have the same Right to Religion and Life that the richest Heirs have." [32] To this end free education was offered to the children of the poor and indigent parents. Sewall notes in his Dairy of October 16, 1721, that "Mrs. Martha Cotes, Mistress of our Charity School was buried; . . . Had a great character as to devotion and piety." Little is known of this school or the extent of its influence. It was not until 1789 that the Massachusetts Charitable Society was organized to cope with the growing educational problems of the poor girls of Boston and environs.

Some of the dame schools continued as private schools, and among the more famous was that of Madam Sarah Knight, who opened a school soon after her celebrated trip to New York.[33] Hannah Mather Crocker wrote about her in 1706, saying that "She was famous in her day for teaching to write. Most of the letters on business and notes of hand, and letters on friendship were wrote by her. She was a smart, witty, sensible woman, and had considerable influence at that period." Both Dr. Samuel Mather and Benjamin Franklin attended her school.

Mrs. Todd advertised in the *Boston Gazette*, May 24, 1736, that she would "teach young women writing and cyphering." Rev. William Bentley in his diary covering 1759–1819 mentions eight school mistresses with whom his children studied. He admired the teaching of Mrs. Abigail Rogers and Mrs. Higginson and spoke highly of Mrs. Saunders. Of Mrs. Rogers he wrote, "She possesses the best education of our New England families, with a steady and firm temper, and has had the greatest applause in the education of our daughters, of which she has instructed 60 at one time." [34]

As the communities became more prosperous school masters and mistresses opened schools offering special subjects, such as Elizabeth Cain who taught spinning (1759), Margaret Mackewain of Boston and Mary Campbell of

Newport who taught pastry and cookery, and Peter Pelham of Boston and Mary Cowley of Newport who taught dancing and Psalmody (1743). In 1673 a dancing school had been proposed but promptly "put down." Schools of needlework were numerous during the eighteenth century and their curricula elaborate. The following advertisements will give some idea of their fields of training. *Boston Gazette*, May 26, 1755;

WAX WORK.—This is to give notice, That Mrs (Abigail) Hiller still continues to Keep School Hannover-Street, a little below the Orange-Tree, where young Ladies may be taught Waxwork, Transparent and Filligree, painting on Glass, Quillwork and Featherwork, Japanning, Embroidering with Silver and Gold, Tenstich, & Likewise the Royal Family to be seen in Waxwork. Also Board and Lodging to be had at cheapest Rate.

Twelve years later the following advertisement appeared in the same newspaper:

Embroidery School.—To the Young Ladies of Boston. Elizabeth Courtney, as several Ladies has signified of having a desire to learn that most ingenious art of Painting on Gauze & Catgut, proposes to open a School, and that her business may be a public good, designs to teach the making of all sorts of French Trimmings, Flowers, and Feather Muffs and Tippets, and as those arts above mentioned (the Flowers excepted) are entirely unknown on the Continent she flatters herself to meet with all due encouragement, and more, so as every Lady may have a power of serving herself of what she is now obliged to send to England for, as the whole process is attended with little or no expense. . . .[35]

Some of the schools were boarding schools such as the Boston school to which Elizabeth Saltonstall sent her daughter, reminding her that she should "carry yourself very respectively and dutifully to Mrs. Graves as though she were your mother." [36]

A few private schools for girls offered a combination of academic subjects with music and handiwork.[37] The academic subjects included besides the three Rs, grammar, spelling, French and, later, Latin and elocution. Some of the women teachers were honored for their unusual services such as, Sarah Osborn of Newport, Rhode Island who taught for thirty years. She died when she was eighty-three years old greatly revered by the community in which she had lived and worked.

Alice Morse Earle in her *Child Life* states that "The first school where they taught [the girls] branches [subjects] not learned in the lower schools was started in 1780 in Middletown, Connecticut, by a graduate of Yale College named William Woodbridge." [38] This is quite possible as two of the Yale students had held a school the previous summer, teaching the girls arithmetic, geography and composition. They also taught at a private school at Newburyport the following winter. There were at least ten academies, or schools of advanced learning for girls, by the end of the eighteenth century in New England. Most of these were boarding schools. Their curricula had advanced to include English, Latin, Greek, French, speaking, geometry, logic, geography, and music.

There were a number of distinguished teachers in these schools. Among them were Susannah Rowson and Sarah Pierce. Susannah Rowson was also the author of a best seller novel, *Charlotte Temple,* which was published in Philadelphia in 1794, Sarah Pierce was a remarkable teacher. One historian wrote of her school, "This school was for a long period the most celebrated in the U.S. and brought together the most gifted and beautiful women of the continent. They were certain to be methodically taught and tenderly cared for, and under her mild rule they could hardly fail to learn whatever was most necessary since adorned." Two such students were Catherine and Harriet Beecher, who studied directly under Sarah Pierce.[39]

Tutorial education in the New England Colonies was very limited. Cotton Mather tutored his own children and wrote in his diary in 1705, "As soon as tis possible I make the children learn to write. And when they can write I employ them in Writing out the most agreeable and profitable Things that I can invent for them." [40] Mercy Warren studied with her brother under Rev. J. Russell, and when her brother went off to college, she continued to study at home the subjects he was studying at college. She must have had a brilliant mind as John Adams wrote to her in 1774, "I have a feeling of inferiority whenever I approach or address you. I feel that your attainments dwarf those of most men." [41] Abigail Adams wrote of her early education, "My early education did not partake of the abundant opportunities which the present days offer, and which even our common county schools now afford.[42] I never was sent to any school. I was always sick. Female education in the best families, went no further than writing and arithmetic: in some few instances music and dancing." Jane Turrell also studied at home. Her husband wrote of her that "Before she was eighteen years she had read and in some measure digested all the English poetry and polite pieces of prose, printed and manuscript, in her father's well furnished library. . . . She had indeed such a thirst after knowledge that the leisure of the day did not suffice, but she spent whole nights in reading. . . . What greatly contributed to increase her knowledge, in divinity, history, physic, controversy, as well as, poetry, was her attentive hearing most that I read upon those heads through the long evenings of the winter as we sat together." [43]

To give one other illustration of the struggle that brilliant women made to satisfy their intellectual yearnings, Hannah Adams wrote in her memoirs, "I was very desirous of learning the rudiments of Latin, Greek, geography and logic. Some gentlemen who boarded at my father's offered to instruct me in these branches of learning gratis, and I pursued these studies with indescribable pleasure and avidity." [44]

Samuel Peters, writing in 1781, said of the New England women, "They are not permitted to read plays; cannot converse about whist, Quadrille, or operas; but will freely talk upon the subjects of history, geography and the mathematics. They are great casuists and polemic divines; and I have known not a few of them so well skilled in Greek and Latin, as often to put to the blush gentler learned men." [45] While Samuel Peters was expressing only one man's viewpoint, his statement is corroborated by many others, not only in New England, but in each of the colonies, and by the extensive evidence of the intellectual attainments of the women.

9

The Education for More Than Survival

The Dutch women colonists brought with them memories of bitter religious and political controversies in which
their parents and relatives had taken part in their homelands. They came chiefly from countries where the Dutch
Reform and Calvinistic churches held sway and where the
Synods of 1538 and 1586 had ordered that schools be set
up in all of the towns for the education of both boys and
girls. The West India Company Charter of 1629 reflected
the earlier laws in that it required that school masters be
included in the roster of colonists. For the first nine years
the colonists were absorbed in the problems of food, shelter
and trade with the Indians. Then in 1633 Domini Everar-
dus Bogardus, their first paster, and Adam Roelandsen,
their first teacher, arrived and started a school for the boys
and girls under the aegis of the Reformed Dutch Church.
Since the founders of the Reformed Church did not believe
in the equality of men and women, the schooling of the
girls was limited. However, Wickersham states that their
marriage contracts as early as 1642 included the promise
"To bring up their children decently, according to their

267

ability, to keep them at school, and to let them learn reading, writing and a good trade. . . ." [1]

In 1647 Peter Stuyvesant became concerned over the
lack of interest in the education of the children and suggested to the Council, "Whereas, by want of proper place,
no school has been kept in three months, by which the
youth is spoiled, so is proposed, where a convenient place
may be adapted to keep the youth from the street and
under a strict subordination." It is interesting to note that
Stuyvesant mentioned neither religion or learning, but only
the control of juvenile delinquency. Two years later it was
suggested that "There ought to be also a public school . . .
so that the youth, in so wild a country, where there are so
many dissolute people, may first of all be well instructed
and indoctrinated not only in reading and writing but also
in the knowledge and fear of the Lord." [2]

Peter Cornelius Plockhoy in 1659 made the following
suggestions regarding the education of the youth of New
Amsterdam. He wrote, "The children and youths shall be
taught in our common school, so that everywhere equality
be regarded. All receive the same instructions, all, whether
their parents be rich or poor . . . and the maidens in addition to the care of the housekeeping and the going about
with and looking after the children, shall learn some work
capable of supporting them, so that they, should they later
leave the community or be not married, may be in a situation to maintain themselves." [3] It was not, however, until
1658 that the Burgomaster petitioned for a school master
who could teach Latin, and 1661 before there is any clear
evidence of very serious concern for the extensive education of the youth of the colony.

The Duke of York took over the colony for England in
1664, and in the following year an apprenticeship law was

passed that concerned the education of the children. It stated that "The Constables and Overseers are strictly required frequently to Admonish the Inhabitants of Instructing their children and Servants in Matters of Religion and the Lawes of the Country, . . ." [4] Under this law hundreds of paupers and illegitimate girls were bound out and taught to read, sometimes to write, and always to knit, spin, weave, wash and cook. For instance, on June 30, 1719, the Court "Ordered that the Church Wardens put Susannah Marie Beyer a poor child without Parents or Relations in this City aged about nine years Apprentice unto Obadiah Hunt and Susannah his wife for the term of Nine Years. The master and mistress to Maintain with Apparell Meat Drink washing & lodging & teach her Housewifery." In the apprenticeship agreement no academic education is mentioned, and probably none was provided in spite of the Law of 1664. Later laws required that the poor children be "religiously educated and taught to read, write and cast accounts." [5]

The educational problems of the colony were difficult for the English conquerors, since most of the inhabitants spoke Dutch and very reluctantly learned to speak and write in English. [6] There were a few dame schools, especially on Long Island, which the girls attended. In 1676 Matthew Hillyer stated that he "hath kept school for children of both sexes for two years past to satisfaction." In 1700 John Shutte was commissioned to teach English, and there is some evidence that the girls attended the public elementary schools that were opened throughout the colony. Late in the eighteenth century Catherine Schuyler mentioned that wagon loads of spelling books were carried into the countryside to supply the farmers and frontier settlements with educational material.

The Swedish and Finnish settlers who came under Dutch leadership to the land that is now New Jersey and Delaware in 1638, may have had a few schools in the early years of the colony.[7] In 1642 Governor Printz was advised "before all, the Governor must labor and watch that . . . all men, and especially the youth, be well instructed in all parts of Christianity, and that a good ecclesiastical discipline be observed and maintained." In 1693 it was enacted "that the inhabitants of any town within this province shall and may by warrant . . . make a rate for the salary and maintaining of a school master within the said town for so long as they think fit."

Meanwhile the colonists who had settled along the Delaware River managed to engage an occasional Lutheran minister to teach their children in schools which were kept very irregularly in the early years. Both boys and girls were taught reading and writing. In 1693 the colonists requested a new supply of books from the homeland, and Charles XI replied by donating 400 primers, 500 catechisms, a number of Bibles and many religious tracts. A few permanent schools were started soon after, but the records are very scant. Israel Acrelius stated that the "people scarcely knew what a school was . . . which is the reason why the natives of the country can neither write nor cypher."[8] But he was over-pessimistic as schools were built so that by 1750 there were at least twenty permanent schools in the area.

In 1717 Governor William Keith wrote to the Society for the Propogation of the Gospel in Foreign Parts in London requesting missionary help in the education of the youth of the growing colony. Rev. George Ross came to New Castle in 1705, and in 1727 he wrote, "There are some private schools within my reputed district which are put very often into the hands of those who are brought into the country and sold for servants. Some schoolmasters are hired by the year, by a knot of families who, in their turn entertain him monthly and the poor man lives in their houses like one that begged an alms, more than like a person in credit and authority. When a ship arrives in the river it is common expression among them who stand in need of an instructor for their children, Let us go and buy a Schoolmaster. The truth is, the office and character of such a person is generally very mean and contemptible here, and it cannot be otherways 'til the public takes the education of children into their mature consideration." [9] The following year Rev. Beckett came and remained about two years, in which time he inspired the building of three churches and a number of schools. Regarding his experience he wrote, "There is no public school in all the country, the general custom being, for what they call a neighborhood (which lies sometimes four or five miles distant) to hire a person . . . to teach their children to read and write English, for whose accommodations they meet together at a place agreed upon cut down . . . trees and build a log house in a few hours . . . whither they send their children every day during the term for it ought to be observed by way of commendation of the American planters nowadays, that whatever pains or charge it may cost, they seldom omit to have their children instructed in reading and writing the English tongue." [10]

Mention of a few of the schools to which the girls went include the school taught by two widows, Mrs. Lewis and Mrs. Thompson, at Lewes, Delaware, to which Deputy Governor David Lloyd sent his daughters. [11] Debby and Polly Thelwell had a school in Wilmington, Delaware, during the days of the Revolution, and Mrs. Elizabeth Way was a celebrated teacher of needlework until her death in

1798. But education was not required as in New England so that Willard Hall, who was later Secretary of State, when he left his home in Massachusetts and settled in Dover, Delaware, in 1803 was duly shocked. He wrote, "There was then no provision by law in the state for schools. Neighbors or small circles united and hired a teacher for their children. . . . The teachers frequently were intemperate, whose qualifications seemed to be inability to earn anything in any other way. . . . Even in the best neighborhoods teachers of the young frequently were immoral and incapable."

William Penn and the colonists he brought with him were devout Friends, or Quakers, who believed in the equality of the "inner light" of men and women. Salvation rested on the ability of each individual to understand the principles of Christ and to live by them. Hence their spiritual leader, George Fox, urged the establishment of schools that were "civil and useful" for boys and girls. In William Penn's Frame of Government (1682) he included "a committee of manners, education and arts that all wicked and scandulous living may be prevented and that youth may be successively trained up in virtue and useful knowledge and arts." At the first meeting of the General Assembly of Penn's Province, the members agreed that "All children within the province of the age of twelve years shall be taught some useful trade or skill to the end none may be idle but the poor may work to live and the rich, if they become poor, may not want." The following year the Assembly ordered that "persons having charge of children should have them instructed in reading and writing before they were twelve years of age, or pay a fine of five pounds for every sound child." [12]

Other compulsory, universal educational laws were passed

to meet changing conditions in the colony, and in 1697 a plan was worked out by the Council for the establishment of public schools in Philadelphia. Enoch Flower had opened a private school in Philadelphia as early as 1683, and soon afterwards Samuel Carpenter started a grammar school. Thomas Budd, an enthusiastic colonist, believed that it would "be well if a law were made that all Persons . . . do put their children seven years to the publick School, or long if the parents please. That schools be provided in all towns and cities . . . to teach and instruct Boys and Girls in all the most useful Arts and Sciences . . . to read and write true English, Latine and other useful speeches and languages and fair writing, arithmetic and book-keeping and the boys to be taught and instructed in some mystery or trade . . . and the girls to be taught and instructed in spinning of flax and wool, and knitting gloves and stockings &." [13] By way of encouraging the education of the girls, he described a spinning school he had visited in Germany. He stated, "after a maid hath been three years in the Spinning School, that is, taken in at six, and then continues until nine years, she will get eight pence the day, and in these parts I speak of, a man that has most Children, lives best." As in New England, child labor was an accepted part of colonial life in the Middle Atlantic colonies, and training for work life, or vocational education, was an integral part of their educational aims for both boys and girls. Among the Quakers women were employed freely as teachers and were members of administrative committees governing the policy of the schools.

William Penn offered a haven to all religious faiths. Hundreds of persecuted people in Europe accepted his offer. A large group of German Pietists arrived in 1683 and settled in Germantown, establishing schools within ten

years. Daniel Falckner wrote in 1694, "We are now beginning to build a house here [on the banks of the Wis-
saerickson River] . . . for we are resolved, besides giving
public instruction to the little children of this country, to
take many of them to ourselves and have them night and
day with us; so as to lay in them the foundations of a stable
permanent character." [14] Another school was built in 1706
in Germantown. Christopher Dock had a school at Skip-
pack perhaps as early as 1714. In 1725 he wrote, "regarding new students, If it is a girl, I ask the girls who among
them will take care of this new child and teach it." By
1802 there were sixty Mennonite schools flourishing in the
colony.

The Reformed Church also extended their educational
endeavors in Pennsylvania, establishing a school in Lancaster County in 1747 and others by 1760. Under the
auspices of the Society for the Propagation of the Gospel
in Foreign Parts of the Church of England, several schools
were started early in the eighteenth century. Cleator started
a school of from forty-five to eighty pupils in New York
City. He moved about and finally settled in Rye with fifty-
one pupils, one third of whom were girls. Rowland Jones
came under the same auspices and established a coeducational school at Chester, Pennsylvania, in 1730. He recorded
that "one girl exceeds all. She had a great many parts in
the Bible by heart and had the whole Book of St. John
and hardly would miss a word." [15] The girls were given the
same lessons as the boys with needlework added. In 1766
these were in reading, writing and spelling.

The Moravian settlers were intensely interested in education. They established a coeducational school in Germantown in 1742 in the home of Anna Nitschmann, Countess

von Zingendorf, and a boarding school for girls at Bethlehem, Pennsylvania in 1749. Their leader, Comenius, believed in equal education for both sexes and the paramount
importance of early learning. In the first years of their
settlement the Moravian parents put their children in the
church nurseries at the age of one or two years. The church
members fed, clothed and cared for the children at the
common expense of the church treasury. When the children had learned sufficiently, they were sent on to the
boarding schools that were also maintained by the church
members. Comenius advocated a wide curriculum consisting of metaphysics, physics, optics, astronomy, geography,
chronology, arithmetic, history, geometry, statistics, mechanics, dialectic, grammar, rhetoric, economics, polity,
morality, piety and religion.[16]

The school soon became famous and was visited by John
Adams en route to Philadelphia in 1777. The letter he
wrote his daughter about the school has been preserved
and reads, in part, "I have been, in the progress of my last
journey, a remarkable Institution for the education of
young ladies. . . . About one hundred and twenty of them
live together, under the same roof; they sleep all together,
in the same garret, every night. I saw one hundred and
twenty beds, in two long rows in the same room, with a
ventilator, about the middle of the ceiling, to make a cir-
culation of air in order to purify it of the gross vapours,
with which the perspiration of so many persons would
otherwise fill it. The beds and bed clothes were all of them
of excellent quality and extremely neat. . . . I wish you had
an opportunity to see and learn the various needlework and
other manufactures in Flax, cotton, silk, silver and gold
which are carried on there." [17]

In 1785 the boarding school was thrown open to children of other faiths and became known as the Moravian Female Seminary. During the first century of the school's existence, it is estimated that more than seven thousand pupils were taught in its classrooms. They came from New York, Maryland, New Jersey, Rhode Island, Connecticut, South Carolina, Nova Scotia and the West Indies. In 1794 Linden Hall, a seminary for girls, was established at Lititz, Pennsylvania, and other schools were opened at Lancaster, York, Emaus and other towns in the state.

By the end of the first quarter of the eighteenth century, the middle Atlantic colonies had become prosperous enough to support a growing number of private, adventure schools. These were boarding or day schools and taught by men and women of considerable ability and versatility. They taught the young people the subjects for which they or their parents asked; not merely the three R's and religion. Their curricula included dancing, proper manners, domestic arts, writing as a speciality and "higher" subjects. The following advertisements give a picture of the educational advantages offered.

Philadelphia, 1738

This is to give notice that Theobold Hacket dancing master (lately come from England and Irelant) has opened a dancing school in this city at the house where Mr. Brownell lived in Second Street, where he will give due attendance and teach all sorts of fashionable English and French dances after the newest and politest manner practiced in London, Dublin and Paris and will give all ladies and gentlemen and children (that please to learn of him) the most graceful carriage in dancing and genteel behaviour in company on all occasions, that can possibly be given by any dancing master whatsoever ..." [18]

New York, 1763

Dunlap Adams, Writing Master, has lately open'd school, in Queen-Street, near the Fly, at half a guinea per month. Hours of teaching is from 10 to 12 in the forenoon. Those who can't spare time in the day time, may be taught at night.[19]

New York, 1767

Flowering.—I take the Method to inform the Publick, that I intend keeping a Sewing-School on Golden Hill, next door to the Sign of the Harp and Crown—and will teach young Ladies to flower on cambrick—and several Pieces of Needle Work too tedious to mention. Isabella Jones.[20]

After 1750 more advanced studies were offered in some of the adventure schools.[21] For instance, one Pennsylvania teacher advertised to teach young ladies "true spelling with the rules for pointing with propriety." He assured the young ladies that neither their age or education need discourage them from finding a husband as he had "The honour to give the finishing stroke in education to several of the reputed fine accomplished ladies in New York, some of which were married within two, three or four years afterwards." In 1771 Maria Gibbon opened a "School for French and English . . . where young Ladies may be taught to speak and read French and English. She likewise will teach fine and plain Work."

In New Jersey in 1778, Anne Davenport also started a school according to her advertisement in the *Pennsylvania Evening Post* of July 8th.

As the Subscriber is very pleasantly situated in a large and airy house in Burlington, she proposed to her friends, the keeping of a BOARDING SCHOOL for any number of young ladies under twelve.–As provisions are scarce and other articles at this time very high, she hopes a generous price will be given, in order to enable her to answer the expectations of those parents who choose to place their children under her care and tuition." [22]

An academy for girls was started in Philadelphia at the suggestion of Anthony Benezet in 1754, which came under the supervision of the City Board of Overseers and had an advanced curriculum. In 1765 Dr. William Shippen started his school for midwives which was the first of its kind in the colonies. John Poor started a "Female Academy" in 1780, which also had an advanced curriculum, and the Quakers started Westtown Boarding School in 1799 in Philadelphia. In Morristown, New Jersey, the Morris Academy for boys and girls was started in 1790 and Hill's Boarding School for both sexes was established at Wilmington, Delaware, in 1797. In New York City Jackson advertised his academy for both sexes as early as 1756, and Isabella Graham started her Young Ladies' Academy in 1789.

A few of the wealthier families in the Middle Atlantic colonies employed governesses or tutors to teach their children.[23] For instance, Elizabeth Cowperwaite of Flushing, Long Island, in 1683 received a scarlet petticoat for thirty weeks schooling of Martha Johanna. Dr. Cadwalader Colden tutored his second daughter, Jane, in Linnaeus' classification of plants at which she became highly proficient. The occasional advertisements about tutoring suggested a limited occupational field. For instance, in 1762 a subscriber in New York "Wants Employment, a single woman who can be well recommended for her honesty and fidelity, is well qualified to instruct children of both sexes in all that is necessary for their years and would go in a gentleman's family in Town or Country, on reasonable terms." In 1767 a subscriber "Wanted a decent middle aged Woman who has been used to the care of Children, she must be able to teach Young Ladies to read and the use of the needle." [24]

Not all women who advertised themselves as qualified school teachers could be trusted, according to Thomas Thomas, who put the following notice in the *Pennsylvania Gazette* in March of 1745.

Notice is hereby given to all good people not to take precents which some of a strolling woman who goes under the name of Elizabeth Castle, alias Morrey. She pretends to be a school mistress, tayloress and staymaker, embroiderer and doctoress. She is of middle stature, high schouldered, grey eyed, and very well qualified in lying, cheating, defrauding, cursing, swearing, drunkeness, talebearing, backbiting, mischief making among neighbors and is reported to be a thief. She carries with her a quantity of pieces that shine like gold by which she hath deceived several women and children, to their great prejudice. She squeaks when she speaks and hath one damage in Newtown, Chester County. This is but little of what might be said in the bonds of truth. Thomas Thomas.[25]

Some of the advertisements concerned indentured women teachers, as in the case of the American Mercury subscriber who had "a likely Young Woman's Time to be disposed of, that can write, do Plain-work, and Mark very well, fit to teach school; by George Brownell, School Master in Philadelphia." [26] Jane Hoskens, a Quaker preacher, has fortunately left us an account of her experience as an indentured teacher. She stated that "One Robert Davis a Welchman with his wife and two daughters, were going [from England] to settle in Philadelphia; a friend told me of their going, and went with me to them, we soon agreed that he should pay for my passage, and wait until I could earn money on the other side of the water, for which he accepted of my promise without note or bond or being bound by indenture in the usual manner." She arrived in Philadelphia in March of 1712 when she was nineteen years old. After she had been in the city three months, Robert Davis tried to make her sign indenture papers binding her to a stranger. She declined to do so and was confined by law. Her friends offered to pay her indebtedness, but she declined their help. Then "The Principals of four families living in Plymouth, Pennsylvania, who had several children, agreed to procure a sober young woman, as a school-mistress to instruct them in reading, &c., And on their applying to their friends in town, I was recommended for that service. When we saw each other I perceived it my place to go with them; wherefore on their paying Davis twelve pounds currency, being the whole of his demand against me, I bound myself to them by indenture for three years, and went cheerfully with them to the aforesaid place. . . . The children learned very fast, which afforded comfort to me and satisfaction to their parents." [27]

The children of indigent parents, orphans and bastards presented a serious problem in New York City by the beginning of the eighteenth century.[28] In 1710 a charity school was started by Mr. Huddleston and supported by The Society for the Propagation of the Gospel in Foreign Parts. Mrs. Sarah Huddleston, his mother, began teaching in the school in 1715 and continued to do so for a year after her son's death. She had about forty pupils, some of whom were girls. The mayor of the city wrote of her, "She discharged her duty with diligence and fidelity" and ordered the City Treasurer to pay her eight pounds for teaching the children of the poor. The Society for the Propagation of the Gospel gave her twenty pounds for her labor and continued their interest in the education of the poor children. In 1760 the Society advertised in the *New York Mercury*:

WANTED immediately, a sober Woman, of a fair Character and Qualifications, necessary to keep a school, for the instruction of Thirty Negro Children, in reading, sewing, etc., Such a Person by applying to any one of the Clergy of the Church of England in the City, may be informed of the Terms which are advantageous.

N.B. The intended school will be chiefly supported by a Charitable Society and well disposed Christians in England. It is, therefore hoped that such persons as have a regard for the Souls of their poor young souls, especially those born in their house, will be ready to assist in forwarding and promoting this laudable undertaking.[29]

Seven years later Mistress Justice Lowner had a catechising school in New York City.[30] Books were supplied by her associates in the Society for the Propagation of the Gospel. The Society recorded of her that she was "faithful and diligent. She takes great pains and employs her whole time to her business" and seemed to be "very happy with her employment." She died in 1774. Another charity school was started in New York City by Trinity Church in 1739. Data about the school is scant, but a Benefit Concert was given for it in 1756, and others later.

In Pennsylvania the problem of the education of poor children also attracted the attention of philanthropically

minded people. In 1722 *The American Mercury* of Philadelphia carried the following advertisement:

A person just arrived in Philadelphia who offered to give his
services to educate the poor Negroes, men and women, without expense to their masters and mistresses, whether they were
Roman Catholics, Episcopalians, Presbyterians, Independents,
Water-Baptists or the people called Quakers.[31]

In 1740 Mr. Hocker and Sister Petrona of the Cloisters
at Ephrata began a school for the poor children in the
nearby communities on Sabbath Day afternoons.[32] They
taught the children both secular and religious subjects. In
Providence, Pennsylvania, a society was formed to teach
English to the children of the poor German immigrants.[33]
In 1755 and in 1765 benefit concerts were given for the
support of a charity school in Philadelphia. In 1796 Anne
Parrish opened a school for poor girls in Pewter Platter
Alley and a few years later formed a "Society for the Free
Instruction of Female Children." In 1797 the school was
known to have had fifty children to whom they taught spelling, reading, writing, arithmetic and sewing. The following
year when the yellow fever orphaned many children a society was formed to establish a Catholic orphan's home and
school in the city. Although the efforts to educate the children of the indigent parents, orphans and bastards was de-
sultory and limited, the idea of the need for their education
was never wholly lost and came to its fruition in the nineteenth century.

Governor Berkeley was inaccurate in his famous reply
in 1671 to the question of the Commissioners of Foreign
Plantations in London: "What course is taken about the
instructing of people within your government in the Chris-

tian religion?" he was asked. He replied, "The same course that is taken in England out of towns; every man according to his ability instructing his children. . . . But, I thank God, there are no free schools or printing, and I hope we shall not have these hundred years; for learning has brought disobedience and heresy and sects into the world; printing has divulged them and libels against the best government. God keep us from both." [34] The Governor's reply, however inaccurate as to "free schools," reflected the majority opinion of the voting members of the southern colonies. All of the early education laws were concerned with the binding out of the children of indigent parents, orphans and bastards and apprenticeship education. The Maryland settlers were too involved in religious controversies to pass any general education laws until 1694. The settlers in the Carolinas and Georgia in the early years left the education of the children to parents and missionaries. The original grant of Charles II for a government in South Carolina was written by John Locke in England, who did not believe in public education so did not include provision for it in his frame of government. In Florida under Spanish rule, the children were educated in the schools of the Catholic Church, and under the brief English rule (1763–1783) no definite steps were taken to establish public schools.

Apprenticeship laws and practice, on the other hand, were direct and clear in Virginia.[35] One hundred orphans, "save such as dyed on the waie," were shipped to Virginia in 1620. In the next ten years there were, in all, over fifteen hundred children, orphans and luckless kidnapped children of England and Europe who were brought to Virginia to be bound out as servants to the settlers. In 1621 the Governor was instructed to require each town to "teach some children fit for college intended to be built . . . to put prentices to trades and not let them forsake their trades for planting, or any such useless commodity." Twenty years later conditions had become so difficult that a law was passed by the Assembly (1643) to the effect that, "Whereas there hath been the general suffering of the colony that the orphans of diverse deceased persons have been very much abused and prejudiced in their estates by the negligence of overseers and guardians of such orphans, Be it therefore, enacted and confirmed . . . And all overseers, guardians of such orphans are enjoined by the authority aforesaid to educate and instruct them according to their best endeavors in Christian religion and in rudiments of learning and to provide for them necessaries according to the competence of their estates . . ." [36]

Three years later the Assembly further enacted that, "to avoyd sloath and idleness wherewith such young children are easily corrupted, . . . But as for the most part, the parents either through fond indulgence or perverse obstinacy, are most averse and unwilling to part with their children, Be it therefore enacted by the authority of this Grand Assembly" that the commissioners choose two children of seven or eight years of age of poor parents, bastards or orphans and send them to James City to work in "public flax houses" to learn "carding, knitting and spinning." In 1668 the Assembly empowered the Vestries in the towns to build houses for the children, and the towns were required to furnish the children with a supply of food and clothing. The later laws of 1705 and 1769 further defined the status of the children and their exploitation in the "work houses." [37]

It was not until 114 years had passed that any serious objection to the situation was raised. In the Vestry Book of Bristol Parish appears the following entry dated February

29, 1757. "This committee having taken under serious consideration the unhappy and indeed miserable circumstances of the many poor Orphans and other poor children. . . . Have Resolved earnestly to recommend it to their respective Vestries that they should join in a Petition to the General Assembly to procure an Act to enable the said Respective Vestries to erect a Free School . . ." [38]

During the seventeenth century Virginia had a serious problem of bastardy due to the number of women who were imported as servants from England and bound out or sold for domestic and agricultural labor. [39] The problem of training these unfortunate children was turned over to the Vestries of the several parishes and consisted of "reading ye vulgar tongue," sewing, spinning and knitting.

Several attempts in Maryland to pass laws concerning the apprenticeship and education of children of indigent parents, bastards and orphans failed to pass the Assembly, but traditional indenture papers appear to have been effective, as in the case of Wadden Hanse, a Swedish girl who was bound out in 1682 until she was eighteen years old with the proviso that she be taught to read and sew. In 1715 the Maryland Assembly passed a law that left to the discretion of the county courts all indenture procedures. [40]

The North Carolina court records of 1695 indicate that an orphan boy was bound out, his master "to teach him to read." [41] In 1715 the Assembly of North Carolina passed a law authorizing the apprenticing of orphans and later passed more comprehensive laws similar to those in Virginia, but the educational provisions were rarely observed. South Carolina and Georgia also followed the traditional practice of indenturing orphans and bastards.

In Virginia land holdings were large, tending to average about one thousand acres per family. This dispersed the population over wide areas and encouraged family education rather than public school education as in New England. Wealthy families like that of Robert Carter of Nomini Hall built and maintained their own schools, hiring teachers as they could. In other instances several families with adjoining, or nearby, property chose a central spot and built and maintained a school jointly. These Old-Field schools rarely included girls among their students.

The first free school in Virginia was a missionary venture in behalf of the Indians. The first free school for the settlers was started by a donation from a group of friends in England in 1622, but the massacre of the settlement that year relegated the idea of a school to later consideration. Several free schools were mentioned in documents preceding the time of the governorship of Lord Berkeley (1671), but it is doubtful if many of them admitted girls. However, in 1657 a Mrs. Peacock was teaching in a small school in Rappahannock County, Mary Coar was teaching in a school in Northumberland County, and Mary Whaley had a school in 1708. Hugh Jones, writing in 1724, stated that in most of the parishes small schools were being built where English and writing were being taught by men and women teachers who were presumably paid by the parents.

In Maryland free schools were started by donations from both Catholics and Protestants, and in 1723 a law was enacted to authorize the building of free schools. But since it excluded the Catholics from participation, little was accomplished. In 1757 Mary Anne Marsh opened a school in Baltimore, Maryland, and in 1792 the Poor Clares started a school for girls in Georgetown but later returned to France. In 1798 Teresa Lalor and two other ladies started the first free school in the District of Columbia, which later became Visitation Academy.

In North Carolina, although schools had been erected

by private endeavor, Governor Gabriel Johnston in 1736 said, "The Legislature has never yet taken the least care to erect one school, which deserves the name in this wide extended country, must in the judgment of all thinking men, be reckoned one of our greatest misfortunes."[42] About ten years later a law was passed to establish a school at Edenton, North Carolina. Other schools were erected soon afterwards, and in 1766 a school, or seminary, "whereby the rising generation may be brought up and instructed in the principles of the Christian religion and fitted for the several offices and purposes of life" was opened.[43] The first academy for girls was opened at New Berne, North Carolina, in 1764, and five other schools were established before the end of the period.

South Carolina erected a free school for the "instruction of the youth of this province in grammar and other arts and sciences and useful learning and also in the principles of the Christian religion" in 1710,[44] and two years later an Act was passed "that a fit person shall be nominated . . . to teach writing, arithmetic, and merchants' accounts, and navigation, and surveying and other useful and practical parts of mathematics." About 1737 the South Carolina Society was formed, which paid the salaries of a school master and a school mistress. They taught the girls of from eight to twelve years of age and boys of from eight to fourteen years of age. In 1787 an endowment for the establishment of school of agriculture and industry was left by the will of a settler. Ten years later the school was opened in Abbeville County and called the Lethe Agricultural Seminary. It was coeducational; the boys were taught farming, and the girls were taught to sew, knit, spin, cook, make beds, clean house, make and mend clothes when cut out, milk cows and make butter and cheese.

In 1743 the Common Council of Georgia agreed to pay

a teacher twenty pounds a year to teach in a free school,[45] and in 1752 several schools of the colony were supported by direct grants from the House of Commons in London. In 1796 George White in his *Historical Collections of Georgia* tells us that the first school to be opened at Goose Pond, Georgia, was taught by a deserter from the British Army who had settled in the community in 1784.

Florida had schools connected with the Catholic churches in which the priests taught the children of the settlers and the Indian neophytes soon after 1594.[46] The subjects taught were reading and writing, Spanish, singing and the catechism. Burns states that "probably more than seventy schools were established by the Catholics on the soil of the United States during the colonial period."

There is no doubt of the extended interest and services of the Society for the Propagation of the Gospel in Foreign Parts of the Church of England. Their first missionary to the southern colonies came in 1702, and in 1711 the Society sent Rev.[47] William Guy to Charleston, South Carolina, to start a free school. Other schools were financed directly by the Society, or jointly with other religious groups. For instance, in 1737 a school named "Irene or Peace" was started near Savannah, Georgia, and supported jointly by the English Society and the Moravians who had recently settled nearby. Holtz estimated that by 1785 the English Society had sent at least three hundred and nine missionaries to the colonies, most of whom taught in schools as well as preached in the churches.

If public schools were few and far between in the southern colonies, the same cannot be said of the private and adventure schools with flourished in all of the southern colonies. More than fifty of them were advertised in the Charleston, South Carolina, newspapers alone during the last forty years before the Revolution. The schools for girls varied from simple dame schools where they were taught merely to sew, read and observe polite manners to pretentious or serious academies in the last quarter of the eighteenth century.

One of the earliest of the dame schools was that of Mary Whaley who opened a model school for grammar and mattey practice in 1706 in Virginia.[48] Jane Duthy (1759) of Charleston, South Carolina, assured her friends that she would teach their children with "utmost care and fidelity." In Georgia Madam Dugas, a refugee from a San Domingo massacre in 1791, opened the first boarding school for girls in the colony at Washington in Wilkes County. In each of the dame schools the curriculum consisted chiefly of reading and sewing, with writing and arithmetic offered occasionally, as in the following advertisement:

A Writing school will be opened on Monday next the first day of March at Mrs. Tondee's large house, for instructing the youth of both sexes in this most useful branch of education in the very best manner. I will also teach in the most correct method, the English Grammar Arithmetick and Book Keeping at a reasonable rate . . . Dalziel Hunter.[49]

In a second group of adventure schools, needlework was given as the central subject of the curricula as in the case of Mrs. John Walker's school at Williamsburg, Virginia in 1752. She gave the young ladies lessons in needlework while her husband taught the boys more serious subjects. An advertisement in the *Virginia Gazette* in 1772 stated:

A well bred Woman of Character, Capable of teaching young Ladies the Degrees of Needlework, together with Reading and

Writing, etc. Will meet with great Encouragement by applying to the Ladies of the Burrough of Norfolk.[50]

In Augusta, Georgia in 1795:

Mrs. Sandwich observing the difficulty attending the education of young ladies and that, when their parents submit to the impropriety of sending them to a boy's school for reading and writing the useful and ornamental needleworks are wholly neglected; has therefore opened a school....[51]

A third group of adventure schools in the southern colonies were interested in teaching the arts. Dancing, horseback riding, music, elocution, drawing and painting were included in the curricula offered. Sarah Hallam, the well-known actress, on her retirement from the stage, advertised in the *Virginia Gazette* in 1775 that she was opening a dancing school in Williamsburg, Virginia, and promised "entire satisfaction." Mrs. Sarah Mansell advertised in the *Maryland Journal* of December 1, 1786, that at the Mansell Academy and Boarding School for Young Ladies, dancing, painting, drawing and many other subjects were taught. Elizabeth Smith taught singing at Annapolis, Maryland, in 1764. Mrs. Neill taught strumming the guitar in Williamsburg, Virginia, in 1734. Mrs. Gardiner had an Elocution school in Georgia in 1788. Mrs. Sully taught "forte-piano" in South Carolina in 1794, and Ann Winsor taught the harpsichord in Virginia during the same year.

Another group of adventure schools in the southern colonies were distinguished by their emphasis on the study of the French language.[52] One of the first of these was advertised in the *South Carolina Gazette,* May 11, 1734, in which Widow Varnod stated that she had "set up a French School for Young ladies" where she would also teach them embroidery. Elizabeth Duneau from England, "who had brought up many Ladies of rank and distinction" and has "kept one of the genteelest Boarding schools about London," proposed in 1770 to open boarding school for young ladies in which she taught "grammatically the French and English Languages, geography, history and many instructing amusements to improve the mind," besides all kinds of fashionable needlework and dancing, music, drawing, writing and arithmetic. A few schools offered the study of Spanish, Latin and Greek in their curricula.

After the middle of the eighteenth century, more attention was given to women's education and more serious studies offered in the adventure schools of the southern colonies. In Georgia James Cosgrove advertised in 1768:

The subscriber having acquired a competent skill and communicative faculty in the following Sciences by the laborious study and experience of a busy course of years in the most noted Seminaries Academies and Schools in Ireland, England and America, is desirous to serve the Publick in any literary capacity, and takes this method to request the sanction and encouragement of the Patrons or Science to open a school for the education of Young Gentlemen and Ladies in reading English with propriety and emphasis; writing accurately all the different hand in use; Arithmetick, Vulgar and Decimal, Mathematicks—the use of Globes, etc., also in the Latin and Greek Classicks—and he would teach the English and French tongues Grammatically! [53]   ;

In Charleston, South Carolina, an academy for both sexes was opened in 1774 "under the patronage of several respectable gentlemen of this province where English grammar, Latin, Greek, French, writing arithmetic bookkeeping, grography, algebra, geometry and natural philosophy" were offered.[54] In 1790 in the same city, a lady "capable of superintending the education of her sex" proposed opening an academy in "a large room in Bereford's Alley where the young ladies would be taught "the grammatical knowledge of the English language, reading, writing, needlework (useful and ornamental), French, Geography, music, Dancing and Drawing." The following year Mrs. O'Connor started a French and English Academy at 100 Tradd Street and "a governess" started a similar academy at 66 Meeting Street. Numerous other academies were advertised in the newspapers of the Carolinas, Virginia and Maryland.

As indicated earlier, productive life in the southern colonies tended to encourage education within the home.[55] Eliza Lucas Pinckney and many of the other brilliant women of the southern colonies started the education of their children before the end of their first year. Eliza wrote to Mrs. Bartlett in England on May 20, 1745, "Shall I give you the trouble my dear Madam to buy him [her son] the new toy (a description of which I enclosed) to teach him according to Mr. Lock's method (wch I have carefully studied) to play himself into learning. Mr. Pinckney himself has been contriving a sett of toys to teach him his letters by the time he can speak, you perceive we begin by by times for he is not yet four months old." Martha Ramsay is reported to have been able to read at three years of age and later to have studied French and learned treatises while she was still a child. Bessy Pratt wrote to her brother who was studying in England in 1732, "I find you have got the start of me in learning very much, for you write better already than I expect to do as long as I live; and you are got as far as the rule in Arithmetic, but I can't cast up a sum in addition cleverly but I am striving to do better everyday. I can perform a great many dances and am learning the Sibell, but cannot speak a word of French." [56]

When she was fifteen years old, Mary Ball, mother of George Washington, wrote to a friend, "We have not had a schoolmaster in our neighborhood till now in early four years. We have now a young minister living with us who was educated at Oxford, took orders and came over as assistant to Rev. Kemp. The parish is too poor to keep both and he teaches school for his board. He teaches Sister Susie, and me and Madam Carter's boy and two girls. I am now learning pretty fast." [57]

It is evident that tutoring was more common in the southern colonies than in those to the north. Lawson, writing in 1709, said there were many tutors in the area of whom some were women, who advertised in the local newspapers. For instance, in 1772 "A Middle aged Woman, who can be well recommended, and understands Musick, dancing, and all sorts of Needlework, and can speak Four different Languages," stated in her advertisement that she would "be glad to engage as a Tutoress to Children, or if encouraged would keep a School." Another, "A Young lady well acquainted with the French language–having resided several years in France–wishes a place in a genteel family to instruct young ladies in French and other useful and ornamental work" (1776).[58]

While the education of women was less passionately or aggressively motivated in the southern than in the New England and the Middle Atlantic colonies, there is plenty of evidence of educational opportunity for girls after the first years of the survival struggle.[59] Julia C. Spruill mentions several instances where men have provided for the education of their daughters in their wills. For instance, Clement Thrash (1657) directed that his entire estate be responsible for the schooling for his thirteen-year-old stepdaughter for three years, the instruction to be given by a Mrs. Peacock. John Russell provided that his daughter's education should be continued, "so long as she keeps herself without a husband." Peter Hopegood left instructions that his daughter should be taught in her home in Virginia until 1680 when she was to be taken to England to continue her education under the guardianship of an uncle. A few of the wealth settlers sent their daughters to England, as in the case of William Byrd, who sent his two daughters, Susan and Ursula, to a school in England, and John Baylor who sent his four daughters to a boarding school at Croyden, England.

In the early days in Louisiana and in the vast areas to the west, the education of the children was in the hands of religious orders of the Catholic Church under the French and Spanish monarchs. In New Orleans ten Ursuline nuns and two servants under the leadership of Mere Marie Tranchepain of Rouen, France, established the first girls' boarding school in United States in 1727 at the request of the governor of the colony. The school was partially supported by the French government. It took seven years to build a new convent and school, but when it was completed in 1734 its opening was a matter of civic splendor. "Accordingly, toward 5 o'clock, P.M. our Convent bells rang forth a merry peal to announce our decision [to move]. Immediately the troops ranged themselves on each side of the abode we were about to leave forever. Governor Bienville, Mr. Salmon, Intendant, together with the most distinguished citizens, and almost the entire population, came to form our escort. . . . All left the chapel in processional order; the citizens opening the march, followed by the children of our Orphanage and Day School and over forty of the most respectable ladies of the city, all bearing lighted tapers and singing pious hymns. Next came twenty young girls dressed in white who were followed by twelve others representing St. Ursula and her eleven thousand companion martyrs, and some little girls dressed as angels.

"The young lady who personated St. Ursula wore a costly robe and mantle, and a crown glitering with diamonds and pearls, from which a rich veil hung in graceful folds. . . . Last of all came the Religious and Clergy; the former bearing lighted tapers and the latter a rich canopy. . . . The soldiers marched on each side. . . . The military music, which accompanied the singing of pious hymns, contributed not a little to the beauty and impressiveness of the ceremony." [60]

The nuns started with twenty-four boarders and forty day students, all of whom were more than six years of age.[61] The nuns had been instructed to "make the pupils content and gay . . . allow them to play games, sharing in their youthful pleasures, but they must not permit anything indecent or improper such as comedies, cards, dances, or any loose or vulgar songs. The girls may play battledore and shuttlecock at bowls and a quiet game of chess." The Ursuline nuns offered the first organized practice training in teaching in the United States. They selected the brightest and best behaved among the older students and made them teaching assistants, or "dizainieres." The duties of these students were to assist in the classroom work and in the maintenance of discipline for two or three months at a time. Each "dizainiere" was responsible for ten children and could scold them when naughty, but was not to tell the teacher in charge unless the situation required serious correction. The student-teacher was to keep a record of the children's "disputes, or any tearing of clothes, or playing naughty games, or with boys, striking one another or running in the streets as they came along to school, or being noisy in the school hall, or disorderly in rank." The curriculum consisted of religion, French, and writing, arithmetic, sewing, knitting, fine needlework and the making of artificial flowers.

There were no schools for girls outside of New Orleans for some years after the first settlement.[62] The families on the plantations hired roving tutors, who occasionally settled in the area. When the Spanish took over the colony in 1769, they encouraged the education of all of the children so that in 1788 Governor Miro reported that there were eight schools in New Orleans. Late in the period a number of adventure schools advertised in the newspaper in New Orleans. Some of these were boarding schools run by very capable women. The curricula included French, grammer, spelling, writing, elocution, arithmetic, geography, English, Italian, history, mythology, chronology, dessein, piano-forte playing, singing, dancing, sewing and embroidery.

Far to the west the Franciscans who accompanied or followed Onata to New Mexico had established schools as early as 1629.[63] When Fray Alonso de Benavides in 1630 surveyed the schools of the Spanish colonies in America, he reported that schools and hospitals had been erected in each of the pueblo-settlements in New Mexico and Arizona. He stated that "After having made the house and the entire pueblo . . . they bring [the neophytes] to live . . . where they teach them to pray, . . . to read and write and sing . . . and even so in all the crafts and trades for human use as tailors, shoemakers, carpenters, blacksmiths, and the rest in which they are already very dexterous." The crafts that were taught to the girls included spinning, weaving, sewing and cooking.

From Teoas, Benavides reported that the friars taught reading, writing, singing and playing all instruments, and the pupils well taught in "Doctrine and with much care in polite life." At Tanos, Tompiras, Peccos and other missions he reported similar schools where the children of the settlers and the Indian neophytes learned to read and write and sing together. The Franciscan missionaries established the same kind of schools in the El Paso region of Texas by 1659. Later (1785–1789) they established schools for the Spanish settlers separate from the mission schools for the Indians and by 1795 the schools for the settlers became secularized with more formal curricula. Another group of Franciscans arrived in California in 1769 and erected schools with the same type of curriculum as in the early schools in New Mexico.[64] More formal schools were established about 1784 and regular academic schools by 1793. Some girls attended these schools so that it may actually be stated that women were given educational opportunities, however meager, in some instances in all of the colonial settlements from the Atlantic to the Pacific Ocean.

10

The Rights With Which They Wrought

Though we repeat it a hundred times, we will never know fully how much we owe, as women, to the Christian concept of equal rights for all individuals. Even if it is still only a vague concept in the minds of our lawmakers, it is a living concept and molds our lives with the force of a basic truth. The colonial lawmakers caught only occasional glimpses of this truth, but these were enough to keep faith alive in men and women, bond and slave.

Each major group of settlers brought with them a heritage of laws, customs and religious convictions which largely determined the rights and privileges they awarded the individual members of their society. The English settlers, for instance, were accustomed to certain women having the rights of feme sole, whether married or single, but their religious beliefs in most instances were opposed to such independent rights for women. The results were determined by the exigencies of each situation. Simply put, where women's contribution was greatly needed to survive, they were granted the right to contribute through one legal device or another. This adaptation of laws, customs and religious convictions to the more elemental requirements of survival in a wilderness was made by all the colonial groups in one manner or another.

Women's rights in England derived from the Anglo-Saxon and feudal days. Noble women, whether married or single, could be knights of the Kingdom, hold courts, vote for members of parliament, be held liable for military service and carry on any type of business in their own name and at their own risk as femes soles. In the *Liber Albus* of London, 1419, their rights to mercantile ventures were clearly stated and were similar to the laws of other cities such as Sandwich, Rye and Carlisle.[1] Two instances of the carry-over of most of these privileges are found in the grants to the Brent sisters in Maryland and Lady Deborah Moody on Long Island, New York. Women of lesser estate had been members of nearly all of the guilds in England since the fourteenth century and, as such, had carried on their trade or other occupation without regard to their marital status. In short, as British free women they had the rights of *feme sole* whether married or single throughout the centuries of their migration. It was during the eighteenth century with the invention of complicated machinery and amassed capital which replaced home industries that the English women, both married and single, lost most of their rights as individuals.

In the English colonies in America, women were recognized as femes soles if they were spinsters or widows, but they were considered femes couvertes if they had been married and their husbands had not been proven dead. Under Puritan law they had practically no rights as *femes couvertes*. The husband was head of the household and all that was within was his property, including any women. The English Quakers took the opposite point of view, but they did not implement their belief in the equal rights of women through laws in the colonies in which they settled.

The Dutch, German, Swedish and French groups differed widely in their beliefs. The strongly Calvanistic Lutherans and Huguenots believed in no rights for married women and so developed patriarchial communities. The Pietistic groups believed in complete equality in religious and civil rights and thus developed the only thoroughly democratic communities in the colonies.

The colonial homemaker's right to her own person can be seen only dimly through a murky fog of inconsistencies in the laws and customs of the period. In Virginia it was determined by law that "All children born in this country be bond or free according to the condition of their mother," [2] thus harking back to the ancient Egyptian laws of maternal blood lines. The action was due in large part to the irregularities in the status and morals of many of the women who had been imported for wives, bondswomen and slaves. Many of these women bore children indiscriminately, thus presenting problems of inheritance to the colonial courts. In New England and the Middle Atlantic colonies the imported women were few by comparison and presented no serious problem. The paternal blood lines were accepted wherever known.

Woman's right to choose her own husband was implicit in the civil marriage contract, but the right was abrogated by the practice of "purchase brides," the occasional sale of wives and the patriarchial form of government. As early as 1619 the need for women in the Virginia colony was so great that the directors of the Virginia Company in London decided "That a fitt hundreth might be sent of woemen, maids young and uncorrupt to make wives to the inhabitants and by that means to make the men there more settled and lesse moveable. . . . These women if they marry to the pub-liq farmers, to be transported at the charges of the company; if otherwise, then those that takes them to wife to pay the said company their charges of transportacon, and it was never fitter time to send them than nowe." [3]

In 1621 when a shipload of women was to be sent from London to Virginia, the settlers were advised, "In case they [the brides to be] cannot be presently married, we desire that they may be put with several householders, that have wives, until they can be provided with husbands . . . every man that marries them give 120 pounds of best leaf tobacco for each of them, we desire that the marriage be free, according to nature. . . . We pray you therefore, to be fathers of them in this business, not enforcing them to marry against their wills." [4]

Freedom of choice was virtually impossible under these conditions. The women sent thus to the colonies were thousands of miles from their homes, in a strange, new land, with no familiar resources, no friends, and in most cases sick from the journey and in mortal terror. These were scarcely conditions under which "free" choice could be made about anything, least of all a husband. No accurate accounting has been made of the number of women sent to the colonies to be sold as wives during the seventeenth and eighteenth centuries. Inducements were offered by all of the southern colonies. In some cases the women were parties to the contract; that is, they freely sold themselves for their passage money, depending on fate to give them a husband to repay the passage money on landing. Sixty forward maidens from the Bahamas came to Charlestown, South Carolina, in 1736, and themselves advertised for husbands. [5] The "casket girls" who were brought to Louisiana were probably better chaperoned but the pressure of cir-

Purchase brides for the Adventurers in Virginia, about 1621. (From the Collections of the Library of Congress)

cumstances must have been similar and made any free, or intelligent choice of a husband virtually impossible.

The trading or selling of wives appears to have been an "under the counter" kind of practice and not indulged in very frequently, although the sale of wives was practiced in England throughout much of the eighteenth century. In 1663 a New York man was sentenced by a Dutch court to be flogged and have his right ear cut off for selling his wife, and in Hartford, Connecticut, in 1645 a man was fined "for bequething his wyfe" to another man. As late as 1736 a Boston newspaper carried the following item:

The beginning of last week a pretty odd and uncommon adventure happened in this town, between two men about a certain woman, each one claiming her as his wife, but so it was, that one of them had actually disposed of his right in her to the other for fifteen shillings this currency, who had only paid ten of it in part, and refused to pay the other five, inclining rather to quit the woman and lose his earnest; but two gentlemen happening to be present, who were friends to peace, charitably gave him half crown apiece to enable him to fulfil his agreement, which the creditor readily took, and gave the woman a modest salute, wishing her well and his Brother Stirling much joy of his bargain.[6]

Fifteen shillings was the usual price for a buxom wife in those days. For the same money he could have bought five pounds of sugar or one half pound of tea or two bushels of wheat. Wives bring more in the 20th century, but then one finds inflation in all commodities for sale in the open markets of the world today.

Once married the woman's rights over her own person were partially defined by law. In *The Body of Liberties* drawn up by the Massachusetts Bay Colony in 1641 it states: "Everie marryed woeman shall be free from bodilie correction or stripes by her husband, unless it be in his owne defence upon her assault. If there be any just cause for correction, complaint shall be made to Authorie assembled in some Court, from which only she shall receive it." [7] By 1671 the law was modified to read: "and that no man shall strike his wife or any woman her husband, on penalty of such fine, not exceeding ten pounds for one offence, or such corporal punishment as the Court shall determine." In Virginia the common law "allowed a man to whip his wife providing provocation justified it and provided the stick was no larger than his thumb." The law, it is said, has never been revoked. [8]

The newspapers occasionally carried evidence of wife abuse, as in the case of Mrs. Alpine who advertised in the *Boston Evening Post* of November 7, 1763:

William McAlpine has no servants that have deserted their business, or run him into debt. But his wife, whom he has repeatedly beaten and abused, and finally kick'd out of doors, has (to shun his further abuses) removed from him. She has not run him in debt or taken anything out of his house, but her own property, which no man of humanity could refuse.

Sarah, who advertised in the *Pennsylvania Gazette* of December 27, 1775, stated:

Sarah S———— schoolmistress . . . take this method to inform the public not to trust S———— (her husband) on my account, for I shall never pay any more of his contractions . . . he abused me and turned me out of doors: . . . for his wicked doings I never more can him abide, nor he never more shall lie by my side.

The colonial woman's right to divorce was seriously curtailed by the general attitude of the courts regarding divorce and by the fact that her dower rights (⅓ to ½ of her husband's estate) were terminated by such action even she was the innocent party. The first divorce in the colonies (1660) was granted to a Finnish woman in Delaware on the grounds that "the wife receives daily a severe drubbing, and is expelled from the house as a dog. This treatment she suffered a number of years; not a word is said in blame of the wife, whereas he, on the contrary is an adulterer . . . . [they] appeal . . . that a divorce might take place, and the small property and stock be divided between them." [9]

The records give a number of instances in both the northern and southern colonies of county and other courts awarding a wife separate maintenance for herself and children where excessively cruel treatment had aroused the sympathy of the townspeople.

Adultery was a frequent cause for complaint on the part of both men and women. In Massachusetts Governor Hutchinson stated that "Female adultery was never doubted to have been sufficient cause, but male adultery after some debate and consultation with the elders was judged not sufficient" cause for divorce. [10] In 1686 Dorothy Clarke of Plymouth sought a divorce on grounds of the impotence of her husband and received a separation agreement instead of a clear divorce. This was common practice in the colonies, since such post-nuptiial contracts sustained the property rights of the wife. [11]

In a number of cases in the records of the southern colonies, agreements of separation, signed by the husband and wife, had all rights of legal divorce. The parties divided the property owned by them and remarried as they wished. While these agreements were not strictly legal, they were accepted as such in the Carolinas, Virginia and Maryland.

In Massachusetts in 1685 a statute had been passed

which entitled a widow to her dower rights only provided she had "not demerited the contrary by willful absence or Departure from her Husband or other notorious fact without reconciliation to him in his lifetime."[12] This meant that she lost her dower rights if she left her husband regardless of what he might have done to her. Thus women frequently accepted separation agreements in which the courts sustained their dower rights and separate maintenance for themselves and their children. In Massachusetts, for instance, less than a dozen divorces were granted before 1780, and in the south there was "no tribunal empowered to decree an absolute divorce." [13]

For a goodly number of women, the legal actions were too slow and difficult, as evidenced by the numerous advertisements for runaway wives in the newspapers of the period. Generally the advertisements contained accusations by the husbands of "extravagant conduct," "drinking strong drink," "continually running in debt," or "absented herself from his embraces—without the least provocation whatsoever." A few of the advertisers went so far as to threaten to prosecute to the full extent of the law anyone who befriended their errant wives. Legally, such wives lost all of their rights to their person and property (such as dower and inherited rights) whether real or personal, which must have made living very difficult indeed in any of the colonial settlements. They became virtual outcasts and prey to any marauding males.

Under the common law of England, the married woman as feme couverte was not only relieved of all responsibility for her own actions, but she was also unable to defend herself or her honor.[14] For any harm that came to a woman from defamation to rape it was her father's or her husband's responsibility to bring charges against the offender if he so desired and was at home when action was needed. For any illegal action of the daughter or wife, the father or husband was held responsible, since the law assumed that a woman acted always with the knowledge and consent of her father or husband. So strong was this belief that a court in Virginia recorded that Robert Brace had "degenerated so much from a man as neither to bear rule over his woman servant nor govern his house, but made one in that scolding society." Hence the court ordered him to be ducked and pay the court charges but later allowed him to pay a fine of one hundred pounds of tobacco.[15]

So read the law, but the court records of the colonies show endless inconsistencies in the application of the law to actual life situations. Under the common law a wife could not sue her husband for mistreatment, but cases of her doing so are numerous. Nor was the wife legally permitted to testify against her husband, yet she testified both against and in behalf of her husband very frequently, according to the court records. Married women sued for harm done to their persons occasionally and were frequently directly accused, as feme sole, of such illegal actions as swearing, drunkenness, immorality, larceny and of being a witch—with no husband in court to hide behind. The courts were equipped with branding irons, stocks, pillories, whipping posts, ducking stools and gallows to carry out their sentences against law breakers. Punishment of women was generally more severe than that meted out to men, especially in cases of immorality, and tended not only to be more brutal physically but also to be more destructive to personal integrity.

At Plymouth (1707) a woman was accused of immorality and was taken to the gallows to receive thirty stripes on her naked back and was required to wear a capital "A" for adultress forever. The man in the case was acquitted. In Maine, George Burdette was indicted "by the whole Bench for Deflowering Ruth, the wife of John Gouch of Agamenticus." George was fined twenty pounds sterling, the price of a pair of horses, and Ruth was ordered to stand publicly in a white sheet on two Sabbath Days and one General Court Day for all to see and condemn her.[16] In Pennsylvania in a similar case, the man was fined fifty shillings and the woman, in addition, was ordered to "stand at the whipping post for a quarter of an hour with a paper upon her breast bearing the inscription: "I heare stand for an Example to all others for committing the most wicked and notorious Sin of Fornication." [17] In West Salem, New Jersey, the records show an indictment for petty larceny in 1732 with the following outcome: " 'Tis ordered by the court that Eliza Crook receive twenty lashes well laid on her bare back, at the common whipping post, and that she stands committed until she pays fees. The said Eliza Crook prays delay of the said whipping, because she sayeth she is quick with child. And now a jury of matrons were summoned to wit: Susannah Goodwin, Sarah Hunt, Ann Grant, Mary Grey, Eliza Hackett, Sarah Test, Elizabeth Hall, Phoebe Saterthwait, Ann Woodnut, Eliza Huddy, Eliza Axford and Sarah Fithian being duly qualified according to law, do say that Eliza Crook is quick with a living child. On motion of the attorney general, the said Eliza Crook is committed into the sheriff's custody, till she be delivered of the said child, and then to receive her punishment." [18]

In cases of slanderous statements made by wives, the husbands appear to have assumed their legal responsibility under the law in something less than half of the cases on record in Virginia. In many of the cases the women were accused and punished directly by from ten to thirty-five lashes or "until ye blood come" upon their bare backs. Even so, the responsibility of the men for this misdemeanor was considered so onerous that In Virginia in 1662 a statute provided, "Whereas oftentimes many brabling women often slander and scandalize their neighbors for which their poore husbands are often brought into chargeable and vexatious suits, and cast in greate damages; Bee it therefore enacted . . . that in actions of slander occasioned by the wife as aforesaid after judgment passed for the damages the woman shalbe punished by ducking; and if the slander be soe enormous as to be abjudged at a greater damage than five hundred pounds of tobacco then the women to suffer a ducking for each five hundred pounds of tobacco adjudged against the husband if he refuse to pay the tobacco." [19]

In Maine they were more direct. In December of 1665 the record states: "We present Joane Forde the wife of Stephen Ford for calling the Constable Hornheaded Rogue and Cowhead Rogue, Joane Ford punished for this offence, by nine Stripes given her at the post at a Court holden at York." [20]

As noted earlier, the offer of free land was one of the chief inducements to emigrate to the new land. All of the colonies offered grants of land to women to attract them to the New World but rarely without limitations. The grants were made to the women as wives of the settlers, in which case the title was held by the husbands, to widows as heads of families, and to single women. In Salem, Massachusetts, "maid-lotts" had been given to the unmarried women settlers, but Governor Endicott pointed out that the town soon realized its error and sought to avoid 'all presedents & evill of graunting lotts unto single maidens not disposed of," so Deborah Holmes was refused a parcel of land but given a bushel of corn as it "would be a bad president to keep hous alone." [21] However, Elizabeth Poole must have escaped his supervision, for she was unmarried and not only owned land but founded the town of Taunton, Massachusetts. Also Abigail Bromfield is recorded as one of the three owners of the undivided land in Maine. The New England town records list women (widows and heads of families) as among those participating in the drawings for land such as for swamp land at Wenham, wood and meadow land at Rehobeth, planting lots at Salem and a house lot in Watertown.

In 1640 in Dedham, Massachusetts, the town meetng decided that, "Whereas Mris Smith and Mst Bacon being lately arived heer from Ireland have ben in our towne & not only well approved of, but also generally desired yet they might inhabitte with us, and howesoeur their husbands are not yet come, yet liberty is granted unto them to purchase in our towne for an habitacon: and such other accomodacons both upland and medowes to be given unto them as their stocks and estates shall Requier as appeth by a former order concrning ye same." [22]

It should be remembered that in New England the recording of land in a woman's name did not mean that she had unlimited rights in the land. In *The Body of Liberties* it states: "Any conveyance or alienation of land or other estaite what so ever, made by any woman that is married, any child underage, Ideott or distracted person, shall be good if it be passed and ratified by the consent of a general Court." In short, married women with the court's consent could own land in New England but not sell it. The wife's property was "the proper and sole estate of their husbands, and might be by him alienated, or disposed of without the knowledge or consent of such wives." [23]

However, in most cases in New England the wife could act with the approval of her husband in a joint action, and in 1646, and again in 1658, the laws were modified to require the wife's full consent for any legal transaction involving her property. In cases of established desertion the wife was sometimes awarded the right to act, and always where the pre-nuptial contracts were carefully written as in the case of Faith Dotey of Plymouth. Her contract states that "the said Faith Dotey is to enjoy all her house and land, goods and cattles, that shee is now possessed of, to her owne proper use, to dispose of them att her owne free will from time to time, and att any time, as shee shall see cause." [24]

In New Amsterdam the common law of England never had a chance to limit seriously the colonial homemaker's proprietary rights. The Dutch women of Long Island, Manhattan or the upper banks of the Hudson River had few problems of property ownership due to their sex. They were equal to their husbands in the eyes of the law, which recognized a community of possessions where there was no pre-nuptial contract. By the time the Duke of York took over the colony in 1655 the Dutch customs of land ownership by women had been well established so that such women as Cornelia De Peyster, Mary Spratt Alexander, Catherine Philipse and Cornelia Schuyler had few serious problems concerning their proprietary rights as married women. The court ruling concerning Mrs. Fabricus in 1670 is of interest. After spending one whole winter in the garret of her home, suffering all the while from fever and ague, she finally complained to the government about her husband, Rev. Jacobus, "and petitioned, that since the house belonged to herself, that her husband should be ordered to give up the keys and not presumed to enter it any more. After a careful investigation, through which they found that the husband was deserving of great blame, the court granted her request." [25]

In 1655 women over fourteen years of age were offered seventy-five acres of land if they would settle in Pennsylvania, and many responded, some as single women or widows and some as married women in which case the titles to the property were vested in their husbands.[26] In 1711 Madame Ferree, a widow, took out a patent for two thousand acres of land in Lancaster County. Mary Tewee, also a wealthy Huguenot widow, took up a similar tract of land in the same county. The lists of assesment rolls of the township included the names of such women as Martha Bizallen, Elizabeth Cartlidge and Rebecca Shaw.

Lord Baltimore offered the strongest inducements to women settlers of any of the great proprietors or companies.[27] He offered one hundred acres of land to the wives, between fourteen and forty years of age, the titles to which were given to the husbands, and large estates to the single women and widows of quality. The first land grants to women in Maryland were given in July, 1638, to Mistress Winifred Seaborne, one hundred acres, Mistress Mary and Mistress Margaret Brent large manorial grants. The Brent sisters brought over nine colonists and soon sent to England for more. They held the rights of "court-baron" and controlled several thousands of acres of rich land.

Four years prior to their arrival a bill had been passed by the Assembly limiting the proprietory rights of unmarried women. It read: "That it may be prevented that noe women here vow chastity in the world, unlesse she marry within seven years after land shall fall to hir, she must either dispose away of hir land, or else she shall forfeite it to the nexte of kinne, and if she have but one Mannor, whereas she canne not alienate it, it is gonne unlesse she git a husband." A letter of complaint brought forth the proprietors' vetoe to the Bill, and the Brent sisters as well as other unmarried women continued to develop the land along the Chesapeake Bay. They appear to have had full rights to convey or alienate their lands as the records show numerous such cases.[28]

In Virginia the members of the House of Burgesses in 1619 petitioned that lots of land allowed them for their wives as well as for themselves.[29] The petition was granted, and in some cases the additional land was recorded in the name of the wife as subject to her husband. The deeds and patents held by the single women and widows ranged in size from the twelve acres of Mary Holland (first recorded deed to a woman, August 14, 1624) to the 3000-acre plantation owned by Lady Dale as a widow and the 5000-acre estate of Ann Toft, a single woman, on the eastern shore, which grew to 19,250 acres by 1668.

While it was necessary to obtain her husband's consent for the sale of a wife's property, it was also required that the wife's consent be had by the husband for the sale of land in which she had any proprietory rights in Virginia. In 1742 the House of Burgesses and the Council granted Frances Greenhill, whose husband had deserted her twenty years previously, the right to sell or otherwise dispose of her land. When the decision was reviewed with the other records of the colony in England (1745), the right was disallowed lest it set a precedent. The decision concludes, "This is the first Instance wherein the Legislature in any of the Colonys abroad have taken upon them to alter the Law in so Settled and known a point as giving a power to a Feme Covert to sell or dispose of her Real and Personal Estate in the Supposed lifetime of her Husband and as it may not be advisable to countenance any attempts of this kind." [30] The incident shows how independently the colonial governments had been acting and how wide the gap had grown between the common law rights of women in England and the actual practice of those rights by the colonial homemakers by the middle of the eighteenth century.

In the Carolinas land was also granted homemakers as single women or widows on the same terms as men. Such women as Sarah Blakeway, Martha and Catherine Ramsay, Martha Logan and Eliza Lucas Pinckney were outstanding land owners of the period. The newspapers of the period contained frequent advertisements of the sale of land by women such as that of Anne Partridge (1739), which offered eighty-one acres for sale in South Carolina, and that of Margaret Haslein (1797), which offered twenty-five thousand acres for sale in North Carolina. In Georgia, as indicated earlier, women's proprietory rights varied. At first women had no proprietory rights. In 1740 limited rights were granted to inherit, hold any convey property. In 1750, when the King of England took over the colonial government from the trustees of the colony, all property rights came under the common law, and the wife's property was vested in the husband. However, women who were already land owners could not be dispossessed without serious loss to the colony, so the law was frequently ignored in actual practice.

In Florida both the daughters of Menendez, Dona Catalina and Dona Maria, owned and administered property. In New Mexico many women owned property. For instance, Magdalena de OGama in 1711 sold a piece of "land on the west side of the principal plaza at Santa Fe," and at the Pueblo of Santa Ana, Quieteria Contreras, wife of Jose de Jesus Montano, sold some land west of the Rio Grande to a tribe of Indians. The land was valued at 3,000 pesos but was paid for in bulls, cows, oxen, sheep, goats, and horses. In 1747 Juanatilla, a half breed woman, died, leaving a large estate at Pueblo San Buenaventura de Cochiti which she willed to her heirs.[31]

In Louisiana under both the French and Spanish regimes, the homemakers came under the community property system of the civil laws of the colony. These laws recognized the wife's share in all property acquired or improved during the marriage and protected her pre-marriage property rights.

The colonial homemakers' rights to personal or moveable property were under almost constant change.[32] Under the common law of England the husband was liable for his wife's upkeep, that is for food, shelter, clothing and doctor bills. He could be, and was, sued for these provisions in many instances, even when the wife was a feme sole trader or worked at an occupation. For instance, Katherine Ellenwood in 1682 complained in court that her husband Ralph gave her insufficient clothing and that she would not live with him anymore. She was granted clothing and an annulment of her marriage. Thus, theoretically, everything the wife had was provided by her husband. This was emphasized by the "shift" or "smock" marriages wherein the bride came to the wedding ceremony with almost nothing on. The husband was responsible for the previous debts of his bride, but if he married her in a "shift or chemise" on the King's highway, no creditor of hers could hold a claim against him. In such cases, the bride stood shivering in a closet and put her hand through the partly opened door, or she stood behind a screen draped in a sheet from the bridegroom's house. Thus, Thomas Elton was within his rights when he claimed that Margaret, his runaway wife, was a thief because she was wearing the clothes he had bought for her.

Neverthless, women both married and single owned personal as well as real property, as is attested to in the numerous wills and inventories of the women. This right could be hers through premarriage contracts, her husband's written consent, when she had the power vested in her by an agreement, and when the courts declared her feme sole. Actually, in the first census of the United States in 1790 there were two hundred and ten free white females, single or widowed, who were included as heads of families though they were not given the rights of such persons.

As to her rights of inheritance, a widow could demand her dower rights in her late husband's estate within two months after his death if he died intestate and if she did nothing to "demerit" her right.[33] In most of the colonies the dower rights consisted of the use of one-third to one-half of the husband's estate during her lifetime. Mrs. Waterman of Rhode Island in 1671 was allotted by the town council the enjoyment of house and lot and other lands and meadows with the cattle for her "maintenance and bringing up of the orphans, five small children." In Philadelphia, Pennsylvania, Mary Keys, a widow, petitioned to sell a brick house in Second Street "to meet bills and educate her two children." Thus, the dower rights generally meant the use of one-third of her husband's property, but not ownership of it.

In cases where the income thus derived was plainly inadequate for the support of the widow and children, a greater portion, generally one half, of the estate was awarded the widow. A Pennsylvania law of 1683 increased the dower rights of the widow to one-half of the husband's estate, both real and personal. And in Plymouth (1636) the dower rights were protected from seizures of property by creditors of the former husband. In Georgia at first the men settlers restricted all inheritance to male heirs, but later modified their laws to give the same dower rights to widows as in the other colonies. In Louisiana the dower rights of the Indian widows of the French settlers were placed above those of any French heirs and generally consisted of one-half of the husband's estate. In New Mexico the widows had full dower rights in their husband's estates, not merely the use of the property during their lifetime.

The inheritance of widows through wills left by their husbands was evidently very meager in the Massachusetts Bay Colony since in drawing up *The Body of Liberties* in 1647 the writers thought it necessary to include "if a man at his death shall not leave his wife a competent portion of his estate, upon just complaint made by the general court she shall be relieved." [34] Many of the wills specified that the widow was to be cared for during her lifetime or until she remarried, as in the case of John Potter who stipulated that his widow should have "a good riding horse saddle and bridle and cow [given] to son with whom she chose to live. Firewood to be brought to her room and she was to have everything to make her happy, until she married, then it was all to go to the daughters."

In Virginia the dower rights of the widows were confused with the husband's right to will any amount of property to his widow.[35] In 1673 a law was passed indicating that a husband could "devise more to his wife . . . but not lesse" than one-third of his estate. Actually, the records are full of wills in which the widows have been devised the entire estate of their husbands in all of the thirteen colonies and Florida, Louisiana and New Mexico.

The colonial wife's right to her husband's personal or moveable property was generally the use of one-third of his property after the debtors were satisfied if he died intestate and there were no children or after all debts and legacies were paid under a will. In Connecticut (1696) the widow received that part of her husband's personal estate which was equal to the amount given the oldest child, provided it was not more than one-third of the estate. In Pennsylvania (1683) the widow was allowed one-half of her late husband's personal estate.

In contrast, the husband had unlimited rights over his wife's personal property, his rights taking precedence over all others after her death, except in cases where there were antenuptial agreements which were honored in all of the colonial courts.

In most of the colonies, daughters could inherit on the same basis as sons. In Georgia the restrictions on the daughters' right to inherit were complete at first.[36] Later they were modified to permit a daughter to inherit 500 acres of land, and in 1740 this right was extended to two thousand acres of land. In Louisiana and New Mexico daughters generally had equal rights with the sons in questions of inheritance.

The colonial woman's right to devise her own property, both real and personal, seems to have been without restrictions where she had established clear ownership as feme sole or through antenuptial or postnuptial agreements. If she had not been thus foresighted, she might, like one Connecticut widow, be allowed by the court to devise only her clothes and bedding.

Married women's contractual rights were also nil under the common law, but many married women carried on business enterprises as feme sole traders in all the colonies nonetheless,[37] sometimes simply because their work or service was needed and no one complained, as in the case of shopkeepers and tavern owners. Sometimes the wives had their husbands' consent or acted as his agent, as did Mistress Pakes of Maryland who had a letter of attorney from her husband "to doe any business whatsoever." Other women had been bequeathed "the sole and seperate use" of the property indicated or had the right to act according to an anti-nuptial agreement that her husband had signed. The courts could and did grant married women the rights of feme sole. In some cases the reason for the action was given, as in the case of desertion by the husband. In other cases need for her work was implied rather than stated, as when Elizabeth Sharret was licensed to run a public house at Haverhill, Massachusetts (1666), although married. In New Amsterdam the married women had full burgher rights and owned many types of commercial ventures as will be seen in the subsequent chapters.[38] In Pennsylvania a law was passed in 1718 that indicated the same bending of the law to meet the needs of the settlers. "Be it enacted, That where any mariners or others are gone, or hereafter shall go, to sea, leaving their wives at shop-keeping or to work for their livelihood at any other trade in this province, all such wives shall be deemed, adjudged and taken, and are hereby declared to be, as feme sole traders, and shall have ability and are by this act enabled to sue and be sued, plead and be impleaded at law in any court or courts of this province, during their husbands' natural lives, without naming their husbands in such suits, pleas or actions."

The limitation of the contractual rights of married women was most evident where the wife worked for wages, as in the case of school teachers. Her earnings were frequently paid to her husband instead of to her. At Chelsea,

Massachusetts, "Mr. Abijah Hastings (was paid) for the sum of £3,12,2 being in part for his Wife's keeping school ..." (1763), and in 1765 the town "Gave an order in favor of Mr. Andrew Tucksbury for the sum of £2.6 lawful money for his wife's schooling twelve scholars, each 17 weeks and three days, at three shillings and two pence one farthing per week." The husband could and did claim ownership of his wife' earnings under the common law of England as is virtualy true today in England.

In the administration of community life, women's position was no less ambiguous. Not only was there confusion in the laws, but there is also considerable disagreement among the scholars as to the meaning of the historical data available. Richard Morris states that women were everywhere in the colonies denied the franchise, and Earl Barnes states that under the Old Providence Charter of Massachusetts women voted for all elective offices for nearly a hundred years. It is certain, however, that no woman signed the Mayflower Compact and that Bradford very early (1623) refuted the libel of woman's participation in the government of the Plymouth Colony. He wrote: "Touching our governements, you are quite mistaken if you think we admite weomen ... to have to do in the same, for they are excluded, as both reason and nature teacheth they should be." Nevertheless the names of single women and widows as landowners have been found in the early poll lists of such towns as Scituate, Cambridge, Weston and Worcester in Massachusetts, Burlington in Vermont, and Wethersfield, Hartfield and Windsor in Connecticut. Their names also appeared on tax roles, formal petitions of the colony as property owners. They voted on the use and distribution of the land held in common, on roads and town improvements and on local officials as the right to vote rested on property ownership. Voting itself was simple. The voter merely dropped a kernel of corn, a grain of wheat or a dry bean into a box designated as "yes" or "no." Or they raised their hands to be counted, or they joined a group with similar ideas in a corner of the room.

Married women's names also appeared in the incorporation of towns such as Newton in New Jersey, Princeton, the Second Parish of Worcester and North Hampton in Massachusetts and Hennicker in New Hampshire. The covenants of incorporation included those "called of God into the Church State of the Gospel," so women perforce were included as individuals and probably voted on matters pertaining to the church community.

In New Amsterdam the Governor wrote to Deborah Moody in 1655, urging her to get every person in Gravesend to vote, which she did, signing her name along with John Tilton as clerk of the elections. In New Amsterdam a few women were enrolled as great or small burghers. They took the special oath of allegiance to "Keep fire and light" inside the city, had the right to engage in trade or other pursuits and to vote in municipal elections. But the extent to which they actually participated in the administration of the colony is not clear.

Margaret Brent, who had come to Maryland in 1638 and taken a very active part in the colony, was appointed by Governor Leonard Calvert as sole executor of his estate in 1647. Shortly thereafter she apeared before the Assembly and requested the right to vote. On January 21, 1648, the record states: 'Came Mrs. Margaret Brent and requested to have vote in the House for herself and voyce allsoe for that on the last Court 3rk Jan. it was ordered that the said Mrs. Brent was to be looked upon and received as his Ldp's Attorney. The Governor deny'd that the s'd Mrs. Brent should have any vote in the house. And the s'd Mrs. Brent protested against all proceedings in this Assembly unlesse she may be present and have vote as afores'd." [39] But her protests were in vain, for it was many years before a woman's voice was again heard in the Assembly of Maryland.

In Virginia in 1699 the House of Burgesses limited the voting rights of women regarding the election of Burgesses, "Provided always and it is the true intent of this act that no woman, sole or covert, infants under the age of 21 or recusant convict being free holders shall be entitled to give a vote or have a voice in the election of burgesses." [40] The law suggests that women property owners had been voting on local problems that affected their estates and may even have been influencing the election of burgesses for the same reason.

As the colonies grew, the right to vote shifted from simple property ownership to include persons in mercantile and other pursuits. In 1733 under the English control, the "widdows of the city protested their limitations" in the *New York Journal* of January 21, 1733, as follows:

Mr. Zenger,
We, the widows of this city, have had a Meeting, and as our case is something Deporable, we beg you will give it Place in Your Weekly *Journal,* that we may be relieved, it is as follows. We are House keepers, Pay our Taxes, carry on Trade and most of us are she Merchants, and as we in some measure contribute to the Support of Government, we ought to be intituled to some of the Sweets of it; but we find ourselves entirely neglected, while the Husbands that live in our Neighborhood are daily invited to Dine at Court; we have the vanity to think we can be full as Entertaining, and make as brave a Defence in Case of an Invasion and perhaps not turn Taile so soon as some of them.

Public opinion, generally, sided with Thomas Jefferson's view regarding women's participation in any governmental affairs. He wrote, "But our good ladies, I trust, have been too wise to wrinkle their foreheads with politics. They are contented to soothe and calm the minds of their husbands returning ruffled from political debate. They have the good sense to value domestic happiness above all others." [41] Or, as the *Virginia Gazette* stated it, a good wife was "Humble and modest from reason and conviction, submissive from choice and obedient from inclination." In the *North Carolina Journal* of September 4, 1797, appeared this poem:

> Woman's a book of tiny size
> Suited to catch the coxcomb's eyes;
> In silks and muslins neatly bound,
> And sometimes richly gilt around.
> But what is strange in readers sight
> This book oft' stands unlettered quite!
> The frontispiece is gayly drest
> Blank paper fills up all the rest!!!

In the *Boston Evening Post* of December 10, 1744, in a dialogue between a husband and wife concerning the education of their daughter, the father concludes the poem by saying:

> Prithee, good madam, let her first be able
> To read a chapter truly in the Bible,
> Make her expert and ready at her prayer
> That God may keep her from the devil's snares;
> Teach her what's useful, how to shun deluding
> To roast, to toast, to boil and mix a pudding
> To knit, to spin, to sew, to make or mend,
> To scrub, to rub, to earn and not to spend,

I tell thee wife, once more, I'll have her bred
To book'ry, cookr'y, thimble, needle, thread
First teach her these, and then the pritty fool,
Shall fig her crupper at a dancing school.

These opinions held by the men of the colonies did not make for the improvement of the homemaker's position. But there were some writers of the period who, while not admitting women's equality, had a keen respect for certain of her abilities. Benjamin Franklin in his letters often showed a high respect for his wife's capabilities in the management of his affairs while he was abroad. John Adams in his *Sketches of the History, Genius, Disposition, Accomplishments, Employment, Customs and Importance of the Fair Sex* traced his defence of women with so delicate a hand as to suggest a soft and supple caterpillar, many hued and ticklish to the touch. The Reverend Charles Stearns enumerated women's moral qualities, which rendered her amiable to the other sex with such finesse that his seventy-six paged poem, "The Ladies' Philosophy of Love," was ordered to be printed by Act of Congress in 1797. Another voiced his opinion in the *Virginia Gazette* Oct, 15, 1736, in which he said, "Then Equal Laws let Custom find, And neither sex oppress; More freedom to Womankind Or give to Mankind less." [42]

The first strong plea on behalf of women was written by Thomas Paine in *An Occasional Letter on the Female Sex* which appeared in August, 1775. He pointed out that, "Even in countries where they may be esteemed most happy, constrained in their desires in the disposal of their goods, robbed of freedom of will by the laws, the slaves of opinion, which rules them with absolute sway, and construes the slightest appearance into guilt, surrounded on all sides by judges who are at once their tyrants and seducers, . . . who does not feel for the tender sex?" [43]

In 1794 J. Armstrong Neal gave a commencement address at the Young Ladies Academy in Philadelphia in which he urged the education of women because he thought they had some ability to think. Three years later Brockden Brown published his dialogues in which he plead for the natural rights of women to share in the political and economic life of the nation. At the close of the 18th century Thomas Branagan was also writing his book, *"Excellency of the Female Character Vindicated,—Being an investigation relative to the cause and effect of the encroachment of men upon women's rights and the too frequent degradation and consequent misfortunes of the fair sex."* He believed women's mental capacity equal to that of men but that the poor educational opportunities open to women and the general public opinion of their lack of ability tended to degrade women. He thought that the "contempt for the mental capacity of the sex expressed by many learned authors proceeds more from envy than ignorance."[44]

Mercy Warren was the first woman writer in the colonies to actively defend her sex. She wrote: "I believe it will be found that the Deficiency lies not so much in the Inferior Contexture of Female Intellects as in the different Education bestow'd on the Sexes, for when the Cultivation of the Mind is neglected in Either, we see Ignorance, Stupidity & Ferocity of Manners equally Conspicuous in both. . . . let us by no Means Acknowledged such an Inferiority as would Check the Ardour of our Endeavors to equal in all Accomplishments the most Masculine Heights that when these temporary Distinctions subside we may be equally qualified to taste the full Draughts of Knowledge & Happiness prepared for the Upright of every Nation & Sex; when Virtue alone will be the Test of Rank, & the grand Oeconomy for the Eternal Duration will be properly Adjusted." [45]

In 1777 Hannah Lee wrote to her brother Richard, sometime president of the Continental Congress, urging him to endorse the enfranchisement of women. His answer was evasive. He stated, "You complain that widows are not represented and that being temporary possessors of their estates ought not to be liable to the tax . . . Perhaps 'twas thought rather out of character for women to press into those tumultuous assemblages of men where the business of choosing representatives is conducted . . . for both [widows and single land owners] of whom I have the highest respect and would at any time give my consent to establish their right of voting. . . . Commissioners are annually chosen by the freeholders and housekeepers, and in the choice of whom you have as legal a right to vote as any other person." [46] And there the matter stood.

The constitution of the United States, when adopted left the determination of the eligibility of voters to the several states. While it was being written, Abigail Adams wrote to her husband, John Adams, "I cannot say, that I think you are very generous to the ladies; for, whilst you are proclaiming peace and goodwill to men emancipating all nations, you insist upon an absolute power over your wives." [47]

The first state constitutions were somewhat hastily drawn and did not definitely exclude the female sex from voting. The first state to actually disenfranchise women was New York in 1778. In New Jersey all inhabitants of full age who were worth fifty pounds were alowed to vote according to the state constitution of 1776.[48] The women who were property owners took advantage of the right to vote, but since married women were not property owners, they were excluded. The property requirement was abolished in 1807 when a new constitution was drawn up which limited the voting rights to men only. The women, still too busy fighting for the survival of their children, made no protest for half a century.

There are many evidences that women participated in local affairs with or without the right to vote.[49] Mary Starbuck of Nantucket, for instance, was very influential in civic affairs and spoke her mind freely in the town meetings. Mrs. Susanna Luke of Northhampton County, Virginia, did not hesitate to protest the actions of the Justice of the Peace, Thomas Harmanson, as a "false, forsworn judge" who kept "poor people from their rights" and for "such unjust judges as he . . . the land mourned," and this she "would declare . . . before the Court, the Governor and the King." Mary Dodge Woodbery, a widow of Beverly, Massachusetts, not only voted in church affairs but was very influential in civic affairs as well, and Nancy Rumsay of Goshen and Elberton, Georgia, a restauranteur and later an innkeeper was the political boss of Elbert County for nearly half a century.[50]

In spite of their limitations under the law, women participated in the official life of each of the communities. They acted on juries in cases involving women. Seven women were appointed state or public printers: Ann Franklin of Rhode Island, Margaret Draper of Boston, Elizabeth Holt of New York, Dinah Nuthead of Maryland, Elizabeth Timothy of South Carolina, Ann Green of Maryland, and Clementine Rind of Virginia. Three women were official diplomats and interpreters for the colonists: Sarah Kierstesde for New Amsterdam, Mary Musgrove for the

Georgia settlers, and Catherine Montour for the Pennsylvania settlers. Anne Wood acted as treasurer of Lancaster County, Pennsylvania, during her husband's illness and after his death, and Maria Van Renselaer was treasurer of Rennsselaerswyck on the upper Hudson River. Women also held office as postmistress, tax collector, prothonotary, bellringer, poundkeeper, official wharfinger and director of the almshouse. They were also jailers appointed by the county courts in Virginia and elsewhere. While these were minor or brief positions in the political life of the communities, they were prophetic of the place women have come to take in the life of the community and the nation.

11

Rights of Women in Economic Servitude

Women in economic servitude in the colonial days also had prophetic glimpses of their future. They found them in the strange adventures of a new world and in the sweeping opportunities of a new land where almost anything could happen. Why else would hundreds of women have voluntarily entered servitude as "free-willers" or "redemptioners" and risked their lives in filthy, leaky boats to come to an unknown land and subject themselves to be sold at the first landing place? Alsop wrote in 1666 that "the women that go over into this Province [Maryland] as Servants, have the best luck here as in any place of the world besides; for they are no sooner on shoar but they are courted into a copulative matrimony . . ." [1] That few of the women ever realized the fruition of their dreams only makes the picture of their situation the more heart rending.

Redemptioners were those immigrants who worked as servants for a given number of years to repay the amount of their passage money to America. Some came with their mistresses and soon found husbands. Van Rensselaer reports an amusing circumstance in this connection.[2] In 1653

Hans Fromer demanded the release of comely Maryken Huybertsen, who had not completed her term of service with Mistress Anna Van der Donck. The colony Burghers granted his request, whereupon many other swains demanded the release of their sweethearts. These pleas also were granted, and the mistresses had to send to Holland for another boat-load of servants with whom they made more rigid contracts for service.

A few of the redemptioner-women were well educated and became teachers; others were skilled in one or more of the many household industries and were therefore greatly in demand. Most of them came voluntarily, believing that they could improve their situation on the completion of their period of servitude. They were adventurers along with their mistresses.

Others were enticed or shanghaied and came unwillingly.[3] During the 17th and 18th centuries the demand for women workers in the colonies was so great that avaricious men and women in Bristol, London, and other seaports made a living by coercing young people onto the ships sailing west. The practice became so frequent that in 1670 a law was passed forbidding anyone to steal and transport women and children to New England. Bruce points out that "It was no uncommon thing at this period to find men and women in the seaport towns, but especially London and Bristol, who earned a livelihood by alluring very young persons to their houses by gifts of sweetmeats, and who cropped the hair of the victims thus secured, so as to alter their appearance beyond recognition, and then disposed of them to persons engaged in sending out laborers to the plantations." In another place he cites the case of "Mary Cooper, a young woman in search of employment, [who] had been told that by going on board she would find a place in Virginia, which was represented to her as a town situated only a few miles below Gravesend on the Thames."

In the British Museum there is a collection, *Black Letter Ballads,* one of which is named "The Trappaned Maiden, Distressed Damsel" and describes a case in point. It consists of seventeen verses from which the following is taken:[4]

> The Girl was cunningly trapan'd
> Sent to Virginny from England;
> Where she doth Hardship undergo,
> There is no cure, it must be so;
> But if she lives to cross the main,
> She vows she'll ne'er go there again.
>
> Five years I served I
> Under Master Guy,
> In the land of Virginny O
> Which made me for to know
> Sorrow, grief and woe.
> When that I was weary, O.
>
> When she sits at meat
> Then I have none to eat.
>
> The cloathes that I brought in
> They are worn very thin.
>
> Instead of Beds of Ease
> To lye down when I please
>
> Upon a bed of straw
> I lay down ful of woe

So soon as it is day,
To work I must away,
In the land of Virginny, O;
Then my Dame she knocks
With her tinder box
When that I ways weary, O.

I have played my part
Both to Plow and Cart,
In the land of Virginny, O
Billats from the wood,
Upon my back they load,
When that I was weary, O.

The water from the spring
Upon my head I bring.

I'm ready at command

The mortar for to make
Which made my heart to ake.

No rest that I can have
Whilst I am here a slave.

In misery I spend
My time that hath no end.

Like the purchase-brides, the redemptioners were generally sold at the first convenient port of debarkation. Their arrival was advertised, and the sale proceeded as of any other desirable commodity. One such advertisement read:

Just imported . . . a parcel of likely English and Irish Servants, men and women; and are to be disposed of, by William Hartly,

Thomas Robinson or Lawrence Anderson, on board the said Snow now lying off opposite to Market Street Wharff.[5]

One such girl was sold to a family in Maryland and in 1756 wrote the folowing letter to her father, John Sprigs, in White Cross Street near Cripple Gate, London:

Honred Father

My being forever banished from your sight, will I hope pardon thr Boldness I now take of troubling you with these, my long silence has been purely owing to my undutifullness to you, and well knowing I had offended in the highest Degree, put a tie to my tongue and pen, for fear I should be extinct from your good Graces and add a further Trouble to you, but too well knowing your care and tenderness for me so long as I retained my Duty to you, induced me once again to endeavour if possible, to kindle up that flame again. O Dear Father, be- live what I am going to relate the words of truth and sin- cerity, and Ballance my former bad Conduct [to] my sufferings here, and then I am sure you'll pitty your Destress Daughter, What we unfortunat English People suffer here is beyond the probibility of you in England to Conceive, let it suffice that I one of the unhappy Number, am toiling almost Day and Night, and very often in the Horses druggery, with only this comfort that you Bitch you do not halfe enough, and then tied up and whipp'd to that Degree that you'd not serve an Annimal, scarce any thing but Indian Corn and Salt to eat and that even begrudged nay many Neagroes are better used, almost naked no shoes nor stockings to wear, and the comfort after slaving dureing Masters pleasure, what rest can get is to rap ourselves up in a Blanket and ly upon the Ground, this is the deplorable Conditions you poor Betty endures, and now I beg if you have any Bowels of Compassion left show it by sending me some Relief, Cothing is the principal thing wanting, which if you should condiscend to, may easely send them to me by any of

the ships bound to Baltimore Town, Potaosco River, Maryland, and give me leave to conclude in Duty to you and Uncles and Aunts, and Respect to all Friends
Honred Father your undutifull and Disobedient Child
Elizabeth Sprigs.[6]

Binding oneself out as a "free-willer" was not uncommon in all the colonies and brought little social condemnation as in the case of Mary Vander Ripe of New York and Mary Wood of Virginia.

This Indenture Witnesseth that Mary Vander Ripe of the City of N. Y. Spinster in consideration of her being Justly indebted unto Just Sory of the same place, Cooper in the sume of fifteen pounds lawfull money of N. Y. and having no other way to pay or Satisfy the same than by Servitude hath put herself & by these presents doth put herself a servant . . . during the full end and term of four years."
"Mary Wood spinster bound herself to serve William Wale of Accomack, planter for three years to receive her diet, clothing, lodging and at the expiration of the time, three barrels of Indian corn and a suit of clothes.[7]

The girls who were bound out by their parents, directly or by wills, were generally indentured to learn a trade or because of the poverty of the parents.[8] One mother bound out her daughter until she should be twenty-two years of age to pay a heavy medical bill. Elizabeth Thorn, a widow "Because of very great poverty and want . . . do bind my daughter Ann Thorn for seven years and four months to William Young to be brought up and educated in civil and Chirstian manner . . . as a servant ought to be." Mercy Estance of Providence, Rhode Island, made the following agreement for her daughter to learn a trade:

Mercy Estance hath put ... her Daughter Jerusa Sugars ... to
be an Apprentice ... untill the said Child doe attaine to the full
and just age of Eighteene yeares ... said Master ... to learn
the said Jerusa Sugars the art and mistry of a Tailor ... and
to learn her to Read Well.[9]

The indenture of children by the Courts was usually occasioned (1) by the death of parents and near relatives of
a child, which was not uncommon in the pioneer days,
(2) by the proven incompetence of parents due to indi-
gency or a criminal record, or (3) by the arrival of a shipload of children without parents from across the ocean.
These children rarely had an opportunity for normal,
healthy living.

Orphans according to common law were the responsibility of the community; hence the courts of the colonies
arranged for the care of the orphan girls if they inherited
estates or bound them out to matrons to earn their board
and keep as in the following instance recorded in the New
York records of 1719.

Ordered that the Church Wardens put Susannah Maria Beyer
a poor child without any parents, or Relations in this City
Aged about Nine years Apprentice unto Obadiah Hunt & Su-
sannah his wife for the Term of Nine Years the Master &
Mistress to Maintain with Apparell Meat Drink Washing &
Lodging & teach her Housewifery.[10]

The colonial laws that required indigent and criminal
parents to release their children to the town to be bound
out were based on the English Poor Law of 1601, modifi-
cations of which were early enacted by the colonies. At
New Plymouth in 1641 it was enacted "That those that
have reliefe from the townes and have children, and doe

not ymploy them, That then it shall be lawfull for the Towneship to take order that those children shall be put to worke in fitting ymployment according to their strength and abilities or placed out by the Townes." [11]

The following year the records show: "Concerning the placeing and disposing of Ffrancis Billingtons children according to the Act and order of the Court, it is ordered and agreed upon . . . that Gyles Rickett shall take . . . a girl .. . . untill she shall accomplish the age of twenty years or be married . . . That Gabriell Ffallowell shall have another . . . a girle . . . untill . . . age of twenty years or be marryed." [12]

In 1735 the law in Massachusetts was broadened to include the parents who failed to educate their children: "Be it further enacted that where persons bring up their children in such gross ignorance that they do not know or are notable to distinguish the alphabet or twenty four letters, at the age of six years, in such case, the overseers of the poor are hereby empowered and directed to put or bind out into good families such children, for a decent and Christian education, as when parents are indigent and rated nothing to the public taxes, unless the children are judged incapable through some inevitable infirmity." [13]

In New York the following year it was ordered "That such parish children as may be hereafter sent to the poorhouse for Maintenance, that Care be taken by the Masters there of (by Directions of the Church Wardens and Overseers of the Poor) that they be religiously educated and taught . . . to qualify them to be put out apprentices." [14]

The children of parents with criminal records were also bound out. In the following instance in New York the father petitioned that arrangements be made for the care of his family. "Pursuant to an Order of ye Govr. and Council . . . upon Petition of John L. Roux now a Prisoner in this Citty and referring the Same to the Mayor and Aldermen of the Said Citty that they Consider to Supply the Necessities of ye Prisoner's wife and children . . . Ordered that the Overseers of the Poor doe put the Children of the Said Petitioner in some Good Reputable Families for their Subsistence during his Imprisonment." [15]

In Virginia an apprenticeship law was passed in 1646 which provided "That the justices of the peace should at their discretion, bind out children to tradesmen or husbandmen to be brought up in some good and lawfull calling" and that two children were to be taken from each such poor family and brought to James City to work in the "public flax houses." [16]

The first group of immigrant children to be shipped to the colonies was sent to Virginia in 1619. There were one hundred children on the boat that brought eight hundred and eleven servants to the Jamestown settlement. It was in the agreement that the children should be bound out to settlers who would teach them the knowledge and skills of a trade and to read and write. The plan appears to have worked very well for the settlers. In 1628 it is estimated that between fourteen and fifteen hundred children were sent to Virginia, some legally from the orphanages and alms houses of England and others lured aboard the ships by many illegal methods. These children were in fact little better than slaves.

New Amsterdam received several cargoes of children from the almshouses of Holland during Governor Stuyvesant's regime, and others followed under the English government. The New England colonies were less in need of young workers and were averse to having large numbers of children landed in their ports. However, four hundred Irish children were brought over, and most of them were absorbed by the northern colonies. The children were generally from ten to fifteen years of age and served from three to ten years, or in the case of the girls, until they were married.

The convict women who were bound out were generally immigrants, since servitude was not generally used as a means of punishment in the colonies. When the women arrived they were sold into service at the point of debarkation to the highest bidder. Some of the colonies seriously objected to this practice, particularly in New England. In 1697 when Massachusetts, Virginia and Maryland objected to having convict women landed in their colonies, the agent for the Carolinas replied to the Council of Trade and Plantations in London: "You may be assured that the Proprietors will acquiesce to the Lords Justices' pleasure if they transport them [convict women] to Carolina. What reception they will find there I cannot say, though it will be better than elsewhere, for the most of the West Indian settlements (if not all, to my certain knowledge) will not receive women convicts. If you resolve to send them to Carolina I have a ship bound thither that will carry them at the usual rate."[17] Maryland had passed a law in 1676 requiring all masters of the vessels to swear "whether any servants on board this shippe be felons convict," but it is estimated that at least 20,000 convicts were sent to Maryland before 1775.[18] Although some of the convicts, both men and women, were political prisoners and became valuable citizens in the colonies, many others were derelicts and presented very serious problems to the colonists. Their position in colonial society was just above that of the slaves with whom they had two situations in common: their masters could sell any of their unexpired time and they could punish them personally.

The slave women in the colonies were either captive Indians or imported Negroes. In 1637 the women of the Pequot Indian Tribe were used as slaves in New England, and in 1676 the Virginia Assembly Passed a law permitting the liftime enslavement of Indians taken in war. Indian children were sometimes treated as servants rather than slaves and were taught religion and a vocation. In 1662 a law was passed requiring that Indian children could be held as slaves no longer than English servants, but workers were in such great demand that the law offered little or no protection for the Indians who were taken in battle. In 1667 Ann Toft had four Indian slaves, and two years later she bought eight more, all of whom served until they were twenty-four years old. She gave each one clothing, a cow and some corn as a "going-away" present when she freed them. But not all the owners of Indian slaves were as generous as Ann Toft. In 1751 Anne Williams, an Indian slave, sued her master for her freedom, but her petition was denied by the Court.[19] In general, Indians did not make good servants and so were gradually replaced by the Negroes who were shipped in from Africa and the Barbadoes.

The first Negroes were sold in Jamestown, Virginia, in 1619, in New York in 1625, and in New England about 1650. The slave women had no rights to person or property, and although a few gained freedom through manumission and were given an education, the great majority remained without rights or privileges. They were the property of their owner to be used in any way the owner desired and as such were in the lowest social status in the community.

All of the women servants in the colonies suffered from some discriminating practices. In general the women servants came from the lowest classes of society in their homeland and did not always find husbands in the colonies. They were thrown in intimate contact with men of their own class and very frequently used for licentious purposes. Also they had no security even of home and job, for their services could be sold as any other commodity at the pleasure of their masters, as can be noted in the following advertisements chosen from many in the newspapers of the time.

American Weekly, June 3–10, 1731:
A likely young Dutch servant woman's time for three years to be disposed of, she is a very good seamstress at Extraordinary or plain work, and pretty handy at house work; those inclined to purchase her time may agree with Anthony Furnas in Philadelphia.

New York Weekly Post Boy, March 7, 1747–8:
To be sold An Irish Servant girl's time, being 4 years and 3 months; she is fit for either town or country and is a very good spinster. Enquire of the printer hereof.

The servant girl's life was incredibly difficult. She worked long hours at very heavy tasks and was permitted very few recreations. In some colonies she worked in the fields, but generally she was assigned to the productive work of the household under the supervision of her mistress. Her position in colonial society is epitomized in the following advertisement from the *New York Gazette,* February 20, 1748–1749.

To be sold "A Young Wench about 29 Years old that drinks no strong Drink, and gets no children; a very good drudge. Enquire of the printer hereof."

Some attempts were made by the colonial governments to alleviate the harshness of the life of the women in servitude and indicate, perhaps, more clearly than anything else their pathetic position in the life of the colonies. The laws concerning the treatment of servants in *The Body of Liberties* of the Massachusetts Bay Colony and in the Laws of the Duke of York were based directly on the ancient laws of the Jews as recorded in Exodus 21:2–11,23:12 and Leviticus 25:39–46. Primitive and harsh by our standards, the laws suggest kindly treatment of the slaves and recognize that all of the women of the household were saleable property of the husband.

Based on English custom, the New England laws required that all indentured agreements be registered in the colony records and have the approval of the Magistrates. If either party failed to keep the agreement, a complaint could be brought to court as the authorities were empowered to act in accordance with the evidence submitted. In general, mistresses agreed to give the servant adequate food, clothing and shelter and teach her the rudiments of learning, religion and household crafts.[20] In 1642 and again in 1703 and 1758, the selectmen of the Massachusetts Bay Colony were instructed to investigate how the apprentices were being treated and to report any failure on the part of the masters and mistresses to abide by the laws and customs of the colony. Similar laws were enacted by the New Plymouth colony in 1671 and in Connecticut in 1650, and reenacted later.

Servants, but not slaves, could complain directly to the

Court's regarding any inadequacy of lodging or clothing, insufficient food, neglect of their training, cruel punishment or denial of their freedom at the end of their contractual time, but only the very courageous dared to bring such complaints to court.

Excessive cruelty on the part of the master or mistress was considered just cause for the removal of the bond servant as shown in the New York law of 1665: "If any Masters or Dames shall Tyrannically and Cruelly abuse their Servants, upon complaint made by the Servant to the Constable and Overseers, they shall take Speedy redress therein, by Admonishing the Master or Dame not to provoke their Servants . . . and in Case any master or Dame by such Tyranny and Cruelty, and not Casually, shall smite out the Eye or Tooth of Any such Servant after due proof made shall be sett free from their Service, And have a further allowance and recompense as the Court of Sessions shall Judge Meet." [21]

In Virginia in 1640 Anne Belson, "a servant unto Theodore Moyses for the term of eight years hath complained to the board against said master for his illusage of her, by putting her to beat the mortar for all his household." He had promised to treat her as a child and have "paternal care over her" and to invest her legacy of 500 pounds of tobacco in a cow and to give her a sow and a calf. "The court taking into consideration the grievious and tyranical usage" of Anne gave her her freedom and required that "said Moyses shall within one month deliver unto her, or her assigns, the said sow and cow calf with such apparel and corn as shall be . . . adjudged and pay court costs." Forty years later a cruel mistress was "prvented from having servants," [22] but these were isolated instances. The many cases of runaway servants suggests that few had the knowledge or courage to seek a legal solution to their problems.

Illegal extension of the time of the indenture agreement was also a serious problem for the servants. In 1686 Elizabeth Day of Philadelphia, "having served her Mr. Griffith Jones 4 years according to Indentures is denied not onlie her freedom money accdg to ye Law of ye province, & yr for requests both." [23] The Court ordered her to be released from bondage and given the customary monies.

Since the good behavior of the servant was the responsibility of the master or mistress under the common law, they were permitted to give unruly servants "due correction and that in the presence of some officier, if any Magistrate shall so appoint." Magistrates were empowered "to summon offenders and have them punished by whipping or otherwise." [24] In Maryland and other southern colonies the master was allowed to give any servant ten lashes without court approval.

Servants were expected to be obedient, amiable, hard working and incorruptible. In New Plymouth Colony in 1655 it was enacted that "servants or children that shall play att Cards or dice for the first offence to bee corrected att the discretion of theire parents or Masters and for 2cnd offence to bee publickly whipt." [25] In all of the colonies the binding agreements contained restrictions on the dress and conduct of the servants. They were forbidden to go to the taverns or other places of amusement, play any of the popular games such as cards or checkers, or participate in any of the out of doors sports. Nor were they permitted to marry without the consent of their master or mistress. Generally when a clandestine marriage was discovered the woman servant was required to serve at least an extra year for legalizing her relationship with the man she loved.

Insubordination on the part of a servant woman in Connecticut was severely punished. "Forasmuch as incorrigiblness is also adjudged to be a sin of death" the Court granted that "any two magistrates have liberty and power fro this court to commit such prson or prsns to the house of correction, and there to remayne under hard labor and severe punishment, so long as the court or the major part of the magistrates shal judge meet." [26] Similarly in New York (1655): "And if any children or servants become rude, stubborn or unruly... the constable or overseers ... have power ... to inflct such corporal punishment as the merit of their fact in their judgement shall deserve, not exceeding ten stripes, provided that such children and servants be of 16 years of age." [27] However, full-grown servants, both men and women, were given many more stripes for single offences, as in the case of Elizabeth Leveret who was working on a plantation in Virginia in 1663. She was given thirty stripes for stealing a pig and another thirty for insolence to her mistress and was ducked in the river several times for her "incorrigible, impudent conduct," which the southern colonists did not quite believe was a "sin of death." [28]

By far the most frequent offense committed by the servants was that of running away from a life that they found unendurable. Scarcely a newspaper was issued without an advertisement of a runaway slave, servant or apprentice, more than half of whom were men. The following are typical of the advertisements regarding female fugitives. The *Pennsylvania Gazette* of April 20–27, 1738, carried an advertisement to the effect that Elizabeth Perry, servant, ran away with James Yates, servant teacher. Elizabeth, English woman, was "about twenty years, middle siz'd, fresh-colour'd and squint ey'd. She had on a striped stuff Gown, a cloak without a cape, two striped Petticoats, a white Apron and a red and white speckled one, strong low leather-heel'd Shoes." [29] Corneilius Van Horne, their master, offered five pounds sterling for the return of the two servants or fifty for either one. The *Pennsylvania Journal* of November 25, 1762, included the following:

Run-away from James Whitall, of Red-Bank, Gloucester County, An Irish Servant Girl, named Mary Heany, short and thick: Had on when she went away, A lightish coloured Jacket, an old black Quilt, brownish striped Petticoat, blue Yarn Stockings, and Neat Leather Shoes, with Buckles in them.

Rewards for the return of the runaways varied greatly but the highest reward found in the present search was found in the *New Jersey Gazette* of July 10, 1780:

ONE THOUSAND DOLLARS REWARD

Ran away this morning from the subscriber, a Negro Wench named Maria, alias Amoritta; She is about 34 years of age: tall and well made, her face long and features more regular than are common with her colour; She had on, or took with her, a pale blue and white short short linsey gown and petticoat almost new, a petticoat of green baize, a pair of new high-heel'd leather shoes, good shifts of brown homespun linen, and aprons of the same. It is supposed she will endeavor to get into the Jersies, as she came from thence . . . She also took her female child with her, named Jane, about 4 years old, well made, fat, round faced and lively; had on or took with her a brown homespun frock, also a blue and white linsey frock; . . . John Duffield.

If caught the fugitives were given twenty-five lashes on the naked back, or they were ducked in the river, or they were made to pay any cost involved in their recovery, or they were required to serve twice the time lost, or they were given any combination of the punishments. Though the punishments were severe no amount of them stopped the under privileged men and women from trying to escape the intolerable conditions under which they had to live. One ghastly example is that of Mary Pain who was found dead of starvation in the woods near the plantation of her master, William Williams, for whom a slow death was preferable to the life she had been forced to live.[30]

In Virginia runaway servants were pursued at public expense.[31] Anyone harboring a runaway was fined sixty pounds of tobacco for each day and night they sheltered the fugitive. In 1669 anyone returning a runaway was given 1,000 pounds of tobacco, but this was later reduced to 200 pounds. In a few years nineteen of the Virginia counties had paid for 466 runaway slaves and servants, which is perhaps the strongest evidence needed to indicate the degradation of the colonial women in economic servitude.

The rewards of their labor would cause an immediate "walk-out" today. In the early days several of the colonies offered as much as fifty acres of land to women servants to emigrate. The land was to be theirs after ten years of labor, but even this advantage did not last long in any colony. Generally at the end of the indenture period, the woman servant was given some clothing and an animal such as a goat or a cow. In 1638 in Maryland each maid servant was entitled to food for one year and also "one new pettycoat and wast coat one new smock one pair of new Shoes one pair of new Stockings and the Cloths formerly belonging to the Servant." [32]

In Virginia "Mary Wood spinster bound herself to serve

William Wale of Accomack, planter, for three years to receive her diet, clothing lodging and at the expiration of the time, three barrels of Indian corn and a suit of clothes." In New York Elizabeth Burger was bound out for nine years and nine months, for which she was to receive "one week and one Sabbath days suit of cloaths of all sorts & 6 shifts and one years board to learn a trade, washing and scrubbing excepted . . . ," and Mary Batman, after five years of service in Charlestown (Massachusetts), was to receive a she-goat to help her start a new life.[33]

Even these meager rewards were sometimes refused or evaded so that the servant women had nothing with which to start their new "free" life, as in the case of Rebecka Hammon who appealed to a New Jersey court on August 7, 1686. The record states that "Upon ye Complaynt of Rebecka Hammon against her late Master Robert Zane for want of nesesary apparel as allsoe his failure in some covenants that he was obliged by Indenture to perform. It was ordered yt ye said said Rob: Zane before ye first day of month next should finde and give ye said Rebecka Hammon apparell to the value of three pounds, seaven shillings and six pence and allsoe 50 acres of Land to her and her heirs forever and case ye sd Rob: shall dislicke this order then to stand to and abide by ye Act of Assembly in the like case provided. Whereupon ye said Rob: Zane did at last declare that he would comply with ye aforesaid order and answer ye same." [34] However, he did not do so as Rebecka appealed to the court twice later in the same year, declaring that Robert Zane had complied with none of the court orders.

With the meager information we have it is impossible to say who failed Rebecka Hammon and a hundred others like her. It is only clear that women in economic servitude in the colonies suffered greatly even when the laws were on their side, for they were made vulnerable by their inferior position in society. That so many of them survived and became valuable citizens of the new nation is a tribute to their courage and the tenacity with which they clung to their dreams and to life itself.

12

She Struggled with God and the Devil

One cannot fully understand the heart-breaking religious experiences of American colonial women without remembering that they brought with them from the seventeen countries of their origins every brand of religion from ancient Hebrew to glorified Millennium. All the love and hate, learning and wisdom, superstition and terror, necromancy and exorcism of three thousand years were in their heritage. Yet they dared to start anew in an unknown land, believing in spite of persecution and bloodshed in their gift of faith in themselves and their destiny. It was this Christian belief in themselves as individuals, equal workers and inheritors in the Kingdom of God that sustained them and gave them the strength to endure and achieve.

This "inner light," as the Quakers called it, flamed up in the darkness of Puritan theocracy and was dimmed by Purital superstition only to flare more hotly in the persons of Anne Hutchinson, Mary English, Mary Dwyer and a hundred others who broke the dominating power of the preachers in New England and led the way to religious tolerance. It sustained the starving, frightened Catholic

349

homemakers in Florida, Louisiana and the distant western settlements. It gave strength to the Lutheran, Pietist, Baptist, Methodist and Quaker women and inspired at least two women who founded new churches of their own designs.

The colonists also brought with them the belief in witchcraft born in time beyond our knowledge, for witches are older than written language, but they did not make the headlines until about 630 years ago when Pope John XXII in an effort to rid Christendom of the pagan worship of the devil, recognized their existence and ordained their punishment. About a hundred years later Pope Innocent VIII further defiined the powers of the inquisitors who were seeking to ferret out the worshippers of black magic all over Europe and England. That hundreds of innocent people were caught in the gross superstition only aggravated the horror and spread the fear. In the following century the Reformation added fury by imbricating the designs of a host of splinter churches, each accusing the other of consorting with the Prince of Demons with his forked tail. Extremists appeared in every country in Europe and in many instances became the focal point for political uprisings. There was the case of Thomas Munzer and the German Anabaptists who were held responsible for the peasant uprising at Mulhausen and were executed in 1525.

In England in 1656 Evelyn wrote regarding the extremists in London, "the parish churches are filled with sectaries of all sorts blasphemous and ignorant mechanics usurping the pulpits everywhere." [1] The superstition of witchcraft was prevalent throughout the 17th century in England.[2] James I permitted forty executions in his ten year reign; Charles I permitted only one in the first seven years of his reign; during the reign of Charles II, Sir Matthew Hale, then presiding Justice at Bury, St. Edmunds in Suffolk, in

1664 ordered the execution of two pathetic old widows, Amy Duny and Rose Cullender, on the basis of the most grotesque evidence. The last case of witchcraft in England was that of Jane Wenham who was convicted of being a witch in 1712. She was later given a royal pardon.

Women have been deeply involved in witchcraft from most ancient times. They brewed the magic potions and appeased the demons with many varied devices. There can be no doubt but that they greatly heightened the ferocity of the witch hunts with their dramatic seizures and howlings, their erratic behavior and their malicious lies until every poor, bemused neighbor was suspect. The Reformation in many cases released women from ancient strictures and gave them a voice in church affairs. Bathsua Makins in her famous "Essay to Revive Antient Education of Gentle-women" (1673) points out "our very Reformation of Religion seems to be begun and carried on by women. Mrs. Ann Askin (Askew) a person famous for Learning and piety so seasoned the Queen (Catherin Parr, sixth wife of Henry VIII) and Ladies at Court, by her precepts and Examples and after sealed her Profession with her blood, that the Seed of Reformation seemed to be sowed by her hand." [3] While Ann Askew was only one of many martyrs during the struggle of the Church of England to become established, her example undoubtedly inspired among the early Baptists such women as Mrs. Allaway, the lace woman of Bell Alley, to become a widely known "She-preacher" and Katherine Chidley who was also well known among the Brownists of the period.

To disentangle the many elements, the women of each church or religious group will be discussed chronologically as they appeared upon the American scene. Thus the Catholic women will be discussed first.

Dona Catalina Menendez worshipped in one of the first rude Christian chapels ever to be built in North America. It was located on one side of the town square of St. Augustine, Florida. She probably cared for the sanctuary and helped the priests who taught the catechism to her children and the Indian neophytes of the settlement. Far to the west her Spanish-Mexican sisters performed similar chores in the tawny adobe chapels of New Mexico, Arizona and California.

When later missionaries visited these areas they heard a story of an earlier missionary woman. At first they discredited the authenticity of the story because they knew of no such missionary woman who had visited the southwest territory previously. But when they heard the same story from men in widely different tribal villages, they began to wonder and so recorded the story of the "Woman in Blue" who was presumed to be Maria de Jesus de Agreda. The old men said "that when they were boys [about 1630] a beautiful white woman carrying a cross came to their lands, dressed in white, gray and blue, clear to her feet, her head covered with a cloth, or veil. She spoke to them, shouted and harangued them in a language which they did not understand. The tribes of the Rio Colorado shot her with arrows and twice left her for dead. But, coming to life, she left by the air. . . . A few days later, she returned many times to harangue them." While there is evidence that a nun by the name of Marie de Jesus lived at Agreda, Spain in 1630 and is reported to have preached to the Indians along the New Mexican border, no record of her journey to America has been found.[4]

In Maryland the Catholic women who came to Lord Baltimore's province also helped in the care of the altar, in providing funds for the church and in maintaining the rights of the Catholics during the years of political strife. No nuns came to the Maryland colony until 1792, so most of the religious education of the children had to be carried on by the homemakers under the leadership of the few priests of the colony.

Margaret Brent, a leading woman of the colony, legally adopted the daughter of an Indian Chief, named her Mary and later saw her married to Giles Brent, her nephew. It was perhaps this same spirit of tolerance and understanding of people that kept the colonists of Maryland from writing a law condemning witches. In June, 1654, Captain John Boseworth of the ship *Charity of London* was hailed into court at St. Mary's City for the hanging of Mary Lee as a witch while on the high seas three weeks before landing. The Captain was condemned for his action, but no penalty was indicated. In the same year Mrs. Manship was accused of witchcraft, but was not condemned. Eleven years later Elizabeth Bennett was accused of "burglary, felony, murther and other trespasses" through witchcraft, but she was cleared on all charges, and no further cases were brought to the court.[5]

In Louisiana the Ursuline nuns became the leaders of the homemakers in religious activities of the French colony. Their hospital, orphanage and school did more than heal the body and teach the minds of the children. They were an active religious force in the colony and set the example for all of the women who followed them, whether they were professed nuns or homemakers, in the turbulent years of colonial growth.

Far to the north in 1755, the English with the help of troops from Massachusetts took over the control of Nova Scotia and deported about seven thousand Catholic settlers from their homes, intending to disperse them among the southern English colonies. Something over 1200 refugees were dumped ashore in Boston Harbor and scattered among the nearby towns. The grown men and women were placed at any kind of labor available, and the children were bound out to any free-holder who would accept them. Since Catholics had been forbidden to settle in the New England colonies from their establishment and were looked upon as agents of Anti-Christ, their welcome was bitter and grudging. How many heroines survived the ordeal is unknown, but their unfaltering faith found fruition in the tolerance of later generations.

The newly established Church of England was the second religious organization to appear in the new land. When Mrs. Forest and Ann Burras arrived at Jamestown, Virginia, in the fall of 1608, there was a squalid little chapel in which they thanked God for their safe journey. By the next spring the thatched roof had so rotted away that it had to be replaced, and soon the church itself had to be repaired. In 1610 Lord Delaware found the church "ruined and unfrequented." He ordered it rebuilt of better material and craftsmanship. His royal instructions had been explicit. They instructed the governors to see to it that the "Word and service of God were preached, planted and used." [6]

The colonists followed the instructions in so far as the maintenance of the church was concerned.[7] John Smith reported that Mary Robinson gave two hundred pounds of a better built church, and other women in 1617 gave "one communion silver guilt cup and two little chalices in a black leather cover and one yellow and blew damaske communion claoth and one surpliss." But the Virginia adventurers gave little evidence of a driving religious purpose. They were protesting against nothing, either religious or political in the early days of the colony. Rather they were paid adventurers who had set out to better their fortunes in the new land. As the colony grew, new churches were built and the parish became the local unit for the administration of many community affairs. Each landowner was tithed for the support of the minister and expected to attend church with his or her family and servants on the sabbath. The first General Assembly in 1619 passed a law requiring every citizen to attend Divine Service on the Sabbath Day or pay a fine for each absence. But such a law was impossible to administer in a land where the parishioners were scattered over hundreds of acres and where many were of undetermined or different faiths. A number of Dutch and Polish workers who had emigrated to start the production of soap ashes and glass, could notbe forced to attend. Similarly, the French Huguenots who came to start the silk industry were disinclined to worship in the state church, as were the Swedish and German Lutherans, the Jewish settlers, and later the large groups of Scotch and Irish Covenanters, English Quakers and Welsh Baptists. The protests of these emigrants and the passage of the Tolerance Act in England in 1688 tempered the handling of the early puritannic laws. A few scattered indictments appear in the Virginia records such as Sarah Purdy's indictment for shelling corn on Sunday and, three years later, Elizabeth Cook's indictment for getting drunk on the Sabbath.[8]

At least six women were accused of witchcraft in Virginia, but only one suffered death as a result.[9] In 1655 Ann Godby accused Mrs. Robinson of being a witch and was indicted for slandering her erstwhile friend. Mr. Godby had to pay the fine for her indiscretion. Four years later an old woman, Katherine Grady, was held responsible for a violent storm at sea and hung at yard's arm by Captain

Bennett. When his ship reached Virginia the Court refused to uphold his action. In 1665 Alice Stephens accused a neighbor of being a witch and was denounced for her temerity. Fourteen years later Alice Cartwrite was accused of being a witch. She was searched for witches marks or "teats" and declared innocent by Mary Chichester who was forewoman of the jury who acquitted her. Another twelve years passed and then Jon Byrd and his wife Anne sued Charles Kinsey for slander because he had accused Anne of being a witch. She was thoroughly examined by a jury of women and the case dismissed. Jane Jennings was similarly accused in the same year and her case was also dismissed. Five years later Elizabeth Dunkin and Eleanor Morris were accused of practicing witchcraft, but in both cases the evidence was considered unconvincing and the cases dismissed.

Only in the case of Grace Sherwood did the situation become grave enough to warrant serious consideration.[10] Grace Sherwood was the daughter of a small landowner who was a respected mechanic. She married James Sherwood, who had been allotted fifty acres of land in 1680 and was a modestly successful farmer. Evidently, Grace was an independent soul given to ignoring conventional customs. In 1698 the gossip about her became loud enough for her to hear it. She and her husband promptly sued Richard Capps for defamation of character and demanded fifty pounds sterling (the price of a good male slave) as damages. The case was dismissed.

Later in the same year, Grace and her husband sued John and Jane Gisburner for slander and asked one hundred pounds sterling in damages. John and Jane gave evidence that Grace had bewitched their hogs to their death and withered their cotton plants. Before such evidence the suit for slander was dismissed. But the Sherwoods were not satisfied for they returned to court to sue Anthony and Elizabeth Barnes for slander, again demanding one hundred pounds sterling in damages. Elizabeth's defence was that Grace came to her house one night and jumped over her bed, drove her and whipped her and "went out of the key hole, or crack of the door like a black catt." In the face of such "conclusive" evidence, Grace's case of slander was dismissed.

Seven years passed during which James Sherwood died and Grace grubbed and scrubbed to keep alive. In 1705 she sued Luke and Uxor Hill for assault, having been "brused, maimed & barbarously beaten." She was awarded twenty shillings damages with which she could buy six bushels of wheat. Luke Hill retaliated by accusing Grace of being a witch. In March Grace was ordered to be searched by a jury of women, and Elizabeth Barnes, the forewoman, reported finding "Two things like titts with several other spotts." In May Grace was again hailed into Court and her house searched for signs of voodoo. In June a formal trial was ordered and she was searched again. On the tenth of July she was tried by water, which consisted of carrying her out on the river where the water was "above a man's depth," binding her hands together and dumping her overboard. If she sank she was innocent, but probably dead. If she swam, she had occult help and thus was guilty. Grace preferred to live; she swam ashore and was condemned to a common jail for several years. In 1714 she was issued a land grant and her name disappeared from the records.

Another Anglican Church woman suffered from the witch hysteria. She was Mary English, who lived with her husband in Boston. He was a very successful businessman.[11] They were both accused of consorting with the Devil and were imprisoned in 1692. They had been critical of the "Covenanters" and he had resented having to pay toward the support of the local church merely because he lived in Boston, when the wished to worship in an Anglican Church. Such heretical ideas were bitterly resented, since they must have come directly from the Devil himself.

The prison to which Mary was taken was very unhealthy, and she, who had never been robust and had born seven children, contracted tuberculosis, despite the fact that she was given special privileges due to her husband's wealth and social standing. Friends finally prevailed upon her husband, Philip, to escape with her to New York. Arrangements were made quietly and they were soon safe among friends in New York City. About a year later they returned to Boston. All of their property had been confiscated and they were in dire circumstances. Mary died soon after, but Philip lived to help build a church of his own faith.

In most of the colonies the women members of the Church of England cooperated with the ministers by giving money ,time and effort toward the maintenance if the church nearest their home, thus foreshadowing the revival of the work of the deaconesses in the Church of England by two centuries. Mary Taney, wife of Sheriff of Calvert County, Maryland, wrote in 1685 to the Archbishop of Canterbury, calling attention to "sad condition" of his "stray flock," requesting 600 pounds for church and minister. When her petition reached the King's ears, he granted the full sum from his private purse to establish the Church of England in Maryland.[12]

In the Carolinas and Georgia where the Church of England was strong the women were very active. Affra Coming, for instance, gave seventeen acres for a church in

Charlestown, South Carolina, in 1698, and Lady Berkeley Blake contributed heavily to St. Phillip's Church of which she was not even a member. In the eighteenth century when the Society for the Propagation of the Gospel in Foreign Parts sent missionaries to the colonies the women cooperated, especially in the development of religious schools.

The first settlers in New England were a unique group. The Pilgrims constituted a group of intensely religious "Separatists" who escaped from England in 1608 during the heat of the religious persecution. Their leaders were men educated at Cambridge University and able to express their convictions in clear, strong language. For twelve years the ministers knit their followers into a deeply religious oligarchy. When they found that their young people were being weaned away from their harsh tenants, they broke with the more liberal Se-Baptists in Holland and came to the wilderness of Massachusetts. For kindly Governor Bradford there was no alternative. He wrote, "As necessitie was a taskmaster over them, so they were forced to be such, not only to their servants but in a sorte, to their dearest children; the which, as it did not a little wound ye tender harts of many a loving father and mother, so it produced likewise sundrie sad and sorrowful effects. For many of their children, that were of best dispositions and gracious inclinations, haveing lernde to bear ye yoake in their youth, and willing to bear parte of their parents burden, were, often times so oppressed with their hevie labours, that though their minds were free and willing, yet their bodies bowed under ye weight of ye same and become decreped in their early youth, the vigor of nature being consumed in ye budd as it were. But that which was more lamentable and of all sorrowes most heavie to be borne, was, that many of their children, by these occasions, and ye great licentiousness of youth in ye countrie, and ye manifold temptations of the place were drawn away by evill examples into extravagante and dangerous courses, getting ye raines off their neks and departing from their parents. Soon became souldiers, others took upon them for viages by sea, and others some worse courses, tending to disoluteness and the danger of their soules, to ye great grief of their parents and dishonor of God. So that they was their posteritie would be in danger to degenerate and be corrupted." [13]

The same "necessitie" was taskmaster in shaping the attitudes of the Pilgrims and Puritans toward the women of their church. The excessive breaches in religious conformity in England had driven them back to the Old Testament concept of no rights for women except those of passive acceptance. As Milton expressed it in *Paradise Lost,*

> Whence true authoritie in men, though both
> Not equal, as their sex not equal seem'd
> For contemplation hee and valour form'd
> For softness shee, and sweet attractive grace.
> Hee for God only, shee for God in him.
>
> To whom thus Eve with perfect beauty adorn'd
> My Author and Disposer, what thou bidst
> Unargu'd I obey; So God ordains,
> God is thy Law, thou mine; to know no more
> Woman's happiest knowledge and her praise.[14]

But times had changed since Eve's day, and even the face of "necessitie" changed when confronted with wilderness problems and women's will to share in their solution. When they arrived in the new land, each group of New England colonists was, in fact, an enlarged patriarchal family with all the advantages of a cohesive group of people working together under strong leadership. Their weakness lay deep in their consciousness, which had become fixed like concrete through persecution and hardship under layers of religious convictions. It took village-shaking convulsions of abnormal behavior and death to penetrate and bend the will of the ministerial leaders to a tolerance of individual rights for every member of their society to think and act on his or her own convictions.

The repressive attitudes of the leaders took effect early in the lives of the children who were conditioned to fear nearly everything. Governor Winthrop pointed out that during their long journey across the sea, no child "had shown fear or dismayedness." [15] Certainly drowning was to be preferred to eternal flames of hell. Ann Dudley, who was later to become our first American poet, was one of the company. At six years of age she had been taught to grieve over her "neglect of Private Duteys" rather than a broken doll, and at sixteen years to accept the small-pox which "smott" her as a proper rebuke to her pride and vanity "because she was carnell and sitting loose from God." [16] Her father, Thomas Dudley, governor of the colony and one of the chief witch-hunters, believed in no tolerance whatsoever. As he put it:

> Let men of God in courts and churches watch
> O'er such as do a Tolerance hatch,
> Lest that ill egg bring forth a cocktrice
> To poison all with heresy and vice.[17]

Samuel Sewall in his diary has left us brief glimpses of how his sensitive daughter Elizabeth reacted to the morbid teachings. In 1689 when she was still seven years old he wrote, "It falls to my Daughter Elizabeth's share to read the 24 Isaiah which she doth with many Tears not being very well, and the Contents of the Chapter and Sympathy with her draw Tears from me also." Seven years later he wrote: "When I came in past 7 at night, my wife met me in the entry and told me Betty had surprised them. I was surprised with the abruptness of the Relation. It seems Betty Sewall had given some signs of dejection and sorrow; but a little while after dinner she burst out into an amazing cry, which caus'd all the family to cry too; Her Mother ask'd the reason, she gave none; at last she said she was afraid she should goe to Hell, her Sins were not pardon'd, She was first wounded by my reading a Sermon of Mr. Norton's about the 5th of Jan. Text Jno. 7:34 Ye shall seek me and shall not find me. And those words in the Sermon Jno. 8.21 Ye shall seek me and die in your sins ran in her mind and terrified her greatly." Later in the month she was terrified by Cotton Mather's Sermon on "Why hath Satan filled thy Heart." In the month following, "Betsy comes in to me almost as soon as I was up and tells me the disquiet she had when waked: told me she was afraid should go to Hell ,was like Spira, not elected . . . I answered her Fears as well as I could and pray'd with many Tears on either part; hope God heard us. I gave her solemnly to God."

Two months later Betty was near hysteria. He wrote: "Betty can hardly read her chapter for weepink; tells me she is afraid she is gon back, does not taste that sweetness in reading the Word which once she did; fears that what was once upon her is worn off. I said what I could to her and in the evening pray'd with her alone."

At seventeen years Betty was so timid that she fled in terror from her first two suitors but was finally induced to marry a year later. When she died at thirty-five, having borne eight children in great spiritual and physical travail, her father wrote: "God has delivered her now from all her fears." [18]

Cotton Mather's daughter had a similar indoctrination. When she was four years old her father wrote: "I took my little daughter Katy into my Study and there I told my child That I am to Dy Shortly and Shee must, when I am Dead, Remember every-thing, that I now said to her. I set before her the sinful condition of her Nature and I charged her to pray in secret places everyday. That God for the sake of Jesus Christ would give her a New Heart. I gave her to understand that when I am taken from her she must look to meet with more Humbling Afflictions than she does now she has a Tender Father to provide for her." [19]

However, Cotton Mather continued to live for thirty more years, but frail little Katy soon succumbed to the rigors of colonial life.

Family discipline was so merged in that of the church and community that children had no escape for their joyful energy. At home the rule was stern, arbitrary, relentless. Complete subjugation of the young was expected and the rod used freely to break the will of any daring boy or girl who presumed to differ with their parents. If the youth persisted it became a matter for the community court. A Connecticut law of 1650 reads: "If any Childe or children above sixteene years old and of sufficient understanding, shall Curse or smite theire naturall father or mother, hee or they shall bee put to death, unless it can bee sufficiently testified that the Parents have been very unchristianly negligent in the education of such Children, or so provoake them by extreame and cruell correction that they have beene forced thereunto to preserve themselves from death (or) maiming. Exo.xxi:17; Levit: xx.(9); Exo:xxi.15." [20]

Even as late as 1788 when the Northwest Territory Code was written it was ordained that "Children that disobeyed their parents might, on the approval of a justice of peace, be sent to jail till they were humbled. For a child who struck a parent the law prescribed ten stripes." [21]

It is a dark picture, indeed, that the Puritans left us of their daily lives with funerals, executions and religious services as their chief or only entertainment. Their religious services were an epitome of their whole lives—cold, harsh and repressive of every normal emotion. They were called to their Meeting Houses by drum, horn, bell or gunfire, there to sit shivering more from the blasts of hell than from the wintry chill. Sometimes they had to sit thus rigid for from two to three hours, but when the ministers was inspired, his prayers alone lasted one or two hours and the service was extended to four or five hours. No escape was possible, at least in Salem, where selectmen were ordered to lock the doors during the services. Tithingmen were appointed to watch over the youths "and use such raps and blows as in his discretion meet." [22]

For the youths who sinned by profaning "Ye Lord's Day" in the time of "Publick Divine Service" by "rude and Indecent Behaviour in Laughing and playing" there was a fine of from three to five shillings. [23] In the case of Jona and Susan Smith the court added court costs because "they did smile" during Divine Service. This amounted to more than a week's pay for a laborer. Of course the girls ought to have known better, for all Puritan children were taught to pay special reverence to ministers by never laughing in their presence or within their hearing.

The picture of the lives of the Puritans would not have been so bleak and barren if they could have allowed themselves occasional holidays as the more festive cavaliers did in Virginia. Judge Sewall stated their case well when he wrote "men came hither to avoid anniversary days, the keeping of them such as 25 of Dec." [24] On the first Christmas in the new land they had erected "ye first house for commone use to receive them and their goods." Sixty-three years later Sewall wrote, "carts come to town and shops open as usual. Some, somehow observe the day [Christmas]." But not with his approval, for holy days were to be determined only by the ministers. Each Sabbath Day was so determined. While the sun shone on that day "No one shall travel, cook victuals, make beds, sweep house, cut hair or shave. . . . No woman shall kiss her child on the Sabbath or fasting day. No one shall ride . . . or walk in his garden or elsewhere except reverently to and from meeting." [25]

The people took the Sabbath Day laws so seriously that the records of every town are full of cases of lawlessness such as that of John and Sarah who dared to sit under an apple tree in Goodman Chapman's orchard and talk together;[26] or that of Jonathan who impulsively kissed his wife on his own door step after three years absence. For such "lewd and unseemly behavior" he spent two hours in the Boston public stocks.

For "repeaters" there was no hope. Anne Walker, for instance, in February of 1638 "having before this day beene often privately Admonished of sundry Scandalls, as Drunkenish, Intemperate, & Uncleane or wantonish behavior, & likewise of Cruelty towards her children & also of manifold lyes & still to this day psisting impenitently therein, was therefore now wth Joynt Consent of ye Congregation Cast out of ye Church" into the utter darkness of social ostracism in a society where life itself depended on cooperative endeavor.[27]

Governor Bradford was deeply concerned with what he

considered the evil record of the early colonists and came
to the conclusion that their wickedness was due to three
potent factors;[28] first, the Devil carried greater spite against
the holiness of the Puritans; second, the meanness of mankind stopped, or damned up, sought a place to flow like
water; and third, that the colony made evil acts more evident by their constant snooping into each other's lives and
publicising each detail. No one who has read deeply into
the lives of the Puritans can doubt the wisdom of at least
the last two of his conclusions. Modern psychologists would
use different words, but the meaning would be the same.
Normal instincts or drives if "stopped or damned up" from
natural expression often will seek hateful, anti-social out-
lets. Some of these expressions are found in the lewd and
vicious snoopings of the sanctimonious and the interpreta-
tions they put upon normal behavior; some in the defeat
of drunkenness and wanton behavior; others in overt,
brutal, anti-social conduct and still others in direct attacks
on religion itself. The last was, in fact, the most deadly expression of all and was the one most fiercely fought, as we
shall see through nearly a century of torture.

The homemaker's share in the struggle for religious
tolerance was implicit in her right as a Covenanter. In
many instances the single women and widows signed the
written document of the Covenant with the men, as in the
case of Northampton and Worcester, Massachusetts, and
Henniker, New Hampshire. At Princeton, Massachusetts,
on August 12, 1764, twenty-three men and nineteen women
signed the following covenant which one needs to read
verbatim to get any real awareness of the depth of their
religious fervor.

We whose Names are hereunto Subscribed apprending our
Selves called of God in to the Church State of the Gospel:

Do first of all confess ourselves unworthy . . . we do thankfully lay hold on His Covenant, and Solemnly enter into Covenant with God, and with one another according to God.

We declare our Serious belief of the Christian Religion. . . .

We acknowledge our everlasting & indispensable Obligations to glorify God in all the Duties of a Godly, Sober, & Righteous Life; & particularly in the Duties of a Chh State and a Body of People associated for an obedience to Him, in all the Ordinances of the Gospel . . .

We engage . . . to walk together as a Church of the Lord Jesus Christ, go to church . . .

And all this we do, fleeing the blood of the Everlasting Covenant, for the pardon of our many Errors, and praying that the glorious Lord Jesus, who is the Sheperd would prepare & strengthen us for every Good work, to do his will; working in us that which shall be well pleasing in his Sight: to whom be Glory forever & ever, Amen.[29]

As regular Covenanters in good standing, the homemakers who were heads of households (widows with families) were assessed as the men for the minister's salaries. In some towns the homemakers signed petitions regarding church matters and voted on issues brought before the congregation. But there was considerable variation in these practices. The Brattle Street Church in Boston, for example, liberalized their admission to communion and allowed women to vote on all church matters. Increase Mather and other ministers of nearby churches thought these practices had a direct tendency "to subvert the order and liberty of the churches." [30]

Women were, in general, severely dealth with in any cases of so-called wickedness, such as being absent from church when they were not demonstrably ill, or admitting that they did not like the preaching. Governor Winthrop reports the case of Mrs. Oliver at some length.[31] She evidently interested him enough to record her protest against the imprisoning leadership of the ministers. Her courage was magnificent. Even he admits it. In the face of a council of sour-lipped ministers she maintained (1) that magistrates should be represented at the ordaining of ministers, (2) that all who live in the same town and confess to the same faith should receive communion together, and (3) that excommunication should be very sparingly administered. For such "radical" ideas she was sent to jail. Five years later she was "adjudged to be whipped for reproaching the magistrates. She stood without tying, and bore her punishment with a masculine spirit, glorying in her suffering. But after (when she came to consider the reproach which would stick by her, etc.) she was much dejected about it." And who wouldn't be in such a mentally blind society where there was not even the desire to understand! Nevertheless, three years later she again protested vigorously against the narrowness of the thoughts of the elders. This time she had a cleft-stick placed on her tongue for half an hour. Winthrop does not mention her again, but William Hutchinson in his *History of New England* mentions that in 1650 "a poor Wretch, Mary Oliver, probably weary of her Life from the General Reputation of being a Witch, after long Examination was brought to Confession of her Guilt, but I do not find that she was executed." [32] It is possible that both men were writing about the same woman. In any case, both Winthrop and Hutchinson treated the case of Oliver with smug self righteousness which kept them from seeing that her protests struck at the very foundation of the theocracy. She made visible the weakness in the structure that was, in the end, to crumble the overweening power of the ministerial leaders. The men saw only a tongue-wagging woman who ought to be silenced, but they both lived to see the weakness widen and deepen in spite of the efforts that were made to shut out all such "errors."

It was Anne Marbury Hutchinson who turned the search light of their weakness and in so doing turned the colony into two opposing camps, one under the banner of the Covenant of Grace and the other under the Covenant of Works.[33] The woman who set off the fireworks was born in Lincolnshire, England, about 1600. She was the daughter of a learned preacher, Francis Marbury, who saw to it that Anne was well educated. She is said to have been a cousin of John Dryden. She married William Hutchinson and had fourteen children. She and her husband had been members of John Cotton's church in England, and a year after her eldest son migrated with Rev. John Cotton to Boston they followed in company with Rev. John Wheelright, a brother-in-law of Anne's. They arrived in Boston in September of 1634. Anne and her husband joined the church in Boston and soon made many friends, as she was not only highly intelligent but a warm-hearted, generous woman who understood the problems of women and was very helpful in times of illness, especially childbirth, as she was an excellent midwife.

Soon she gathered a group of women in her home to discuss religious problems as the men were doing in similar group meetings. The women met frequently, and because Anne was a woman of "ready wit and bold spirit" as well as one "beloved," "all the faithful embraced her conference and blessed God for her fruitful discourses." Husbands began to attend, then elders and ministers, until as Governor Winthrop reported, "In time she had more resort to her for counsel about matters of conscience than any minister, I might say than all the elders in the country."[34] This was a major crime in a religious patriarchal society, and Anne was soon made aware of the fact.

Of the many moot questions that were discussed in her meetings, none brought forth more asperity than the question of the "indwelling of the Holy Ghost." Anne was convinced of the efficacy of the Covenant of Grace. Love, good works and kindness were the result of the indwelling of the Holy Spirit, thus there was no need for infant baptism. She pointed out that too many of the ministers were teaching the Covenant of Works which concerned only frail human conduct, which in itself could not bring salvation. Thus Anne struck at the basic authority of the ministers, the very heart of the theocracy. The entire colony was enjoined in the subsequent battle. Even the children imitated their parents and fought lustily for the Covenant of Grace or the Covenant of Works.

Anne was supported by Governor Sir Henry Vane, Rev. John Cotton, Rev. John Wheelright and most of the people of Boston who had come under the spell of her eloquence and dynamic personality. She was opposed by grim Deputy Governor John Winthrop (who wanted to be governor), Rev. John Wilson, both hell-fire eaters, and the country magistrates who reacted more to the confusion her voice raised in the community than to any clear-cut difference in religious beliefs.

The strength of the two groups of people was tested in the general election of May, 1637, in which Winthrop won the governorship over Sir Henry Vane. In the fall when the dust of battle had settled a little, Rev. John Cotton recanted, Sir Henry Vane left for England in disgust, and Rev. John Wheelright and Anne were brought into Court. Rev. Wheelright was promptly banished from the colony, and Anne was accused of several outrages and questioned daily by the ministers and elders for three months. Her trial in the General Court lasted two days. Her responses to their questions were so well grounded in the Bible with which she proved herself more familiar than they that her questioners were often lamentably confused.

Four main charges emerge from the melee.[35] First, she was accused of holding two public lectures a week in her home to which sixty to eighty people came. Concerning this the General Court ruled "That though women might meet (some few together) to pray and edify one another, yet such a set assembly (as was then in practice at Boston) where sixty or more did meet every week, and one woman (in a prophetical way, by resolving questions of doctrine, and expounding Scripture) took upon her the whole exercise, was agreed to be disorderly and without rule." Second, she did not preach infant baptism or their kind of free Grace. Third, she accused the ministers of being poorly grounded in the New Testament, and fourth, she traduced the clergy for their attitudes and actions. This was rank treason. The judgment of the General Court was that she was guilty on all counts and hence was ordered banished from the colony.[36] But out of their great mercy, because it was early in November and bitterly cold and she already showed that she was well advanced in her latest pregnancy, "they committed her to a private house," the home of Joseph Welde, deputy of the General Court, and well removed from her own home and children. Here, the elders and her own friends were permitted to see her, "but none else." Only a few friends dared to come to her, but the elders came often and continually bated her with forked questions. By spring they had enough damning evidence to satisfy them.

On March 15 and 22 of 1638, she was brought before

the august body of the church to hear the reading of her excommunication. The wording of it is so savage that it must have taken all of her magnificent faith and courage to stand erect and face that body of former friends and supplicants of her care. The document reads, "Forasmuch as yow, Mrs. Huchinson, have highly trangressed & offended, & forasmuch as yo whave soe many ways *troubled the Church with yor Erors* & have drawen away many a poor rule, & have *upheld yor Revelations*: & forasmuch as *yow have made a Lye,* &c. Therfor in the name of our Lord Je: Ch: & in the name of the Church I doe not only pronownce yow worthy to be cast owt, but I *doe cast yow out* & in the name of Ch. I *doe deliver you up to Sathan,* that yow may learne no more to blaspheme, to seduce & to lye, & I doe account yow from this time forth to be a Hethen & a Publican & soe to be held of all the Bretheren & Sisters, of this congregation, & of others: therfor *I command yow* in the name of Ch: Je: of this Church *as a Leper to withdraw yor selfe owt of the Congregation;* that as formerly yow has dispised & contemned the Holy Ordinances of God, & turned yor Backe one them, soe yow may now have no part in them nor benefit by them." [37]

But she was not dismayed; in fact, her spirits were now free and greatly revived. She moved down the aisle with dignity and was joined by Mary Dwyer, who accompanied her out of the church. Later in the week she gathered her family and a few followers and went to Rhode Island where they established a settlement at a point that is now Newport. Here her last baby was born, a poor little misfit who died soon after birth. Her husband's death followed four years later. After this series of tradgedies she went to a new settlement near New Rochelle, New York, where she and her family were killed during an Indian raid of the village. It is doubtful if she had any idea of how great her gift was, not only to New England and to all colonial women, but to us who live in the light she dared to kindle.

A year after Anne Hutchinson left Boston, Lady Deborah Dunch Moody arrived.[38] She was also a free-thinker, born in Wilshire, England. Her father had been a member of Parliament under Queen Elizabeth and a vigorous champion of liberty and constitutional rights. Her husband, Sir Henry Moody, had been made a baronet in 1622. Deborah had one son before her husband died in 1632. After his death she became restless and went to London. She was a highly educated woman and deeply interested in religious matters.

In 1639 she came to Salem, Massachusetts, hoping to find religious freedom. She found only the bitter aftermath of Anne Hutchinson's trial, but still hoping, she moved to Lynn, Massachusetts, where she was warmly greeted. Four hundred acres of land were granted her, and she bought a farm at Swampscott valued at 1,100 pounds sterling. It was a very handsome piece of property. She attended church regularly and was amazed at what she heard. Being honest and accustomed to expressing her ideas, she soon found herself at odds with the elders. She believed, as Anne Hutchinson did, in the "indwelling of the Holy Spirit," which made infant baptism unnecessary. This was heresy, so she and two other women were excommunicated in 1642. But she was not accused of being a witch or banished from the colony. She owned enough property to make her taxes of serious value to the community. She promptly bought a boat and with her son and a few friends sailed around Cape Cod to the colony of New Netherlands. It is interesting to note that she did not sell her property in Massachusetts but continued to received money on her investments. Governor William Kieft of New Netherlands gave her patent to a pie-shaped piece of land at Gravesend, Long Island, just above Coney Island. She and the men she brought with her built a house in 1645 and laid out a town in 1646 with a representative form of government and complete religious freedom. No church was founded in the early years because the settlers, Lady Deborah included, rejected the office of a preacher, the keeping of the Sabbath and infant baptism. Whenever they met, they read the Bible aloud to one another and commented on it if they so desired.

Lady Deborah's colony prospered.[39] She appears to have governed the community with a gentle, steady hand so that it became the haven for visitors of all sorts, who marveled at her ability to live in peace with Anabaptists, Quakers, Jews, Lutherans and other dissenting groups. Until she died in 1659 she continued to use her influence and resources in the cause of religious freedom and tolerance.

In Massachusetts the struggle for existence had been intensified by the drop in immigration and the flow of English commodities on which the colonists had depended. Food and clothing were scarce, and tremendous efforts were needed to survive and become self sustaining. It was in the midst of this struggle that the Quakers came to New England and reopened the fearsome question of salvation. Their first missionaries were women—homemakers who left their children to preach their Gospel. They constituted a singularly impudent frontal attack upon the Puritans. Ann Austen, a mother of five children and "already stricken in years," came with young Mary Fisher, twenty-two years old, to Boston in July, 1656, more than twenty-five years before William Penn received the charter for his "Holy Experiment."[40] When the two Quaker women arrived in

Boston Harbor on *The Swallow,* Deputy Governor Richard Bellingham ordered that they be kept aboard ship until their baggage could be searched for books containing "corrupt, heretical and blasphemous doctrines." One hundred books were seized and burned in the market place. Then the women were taken to the town prison, although there was no law concerning Quakers at the time. In prison they were deprived of light and writing materials. Anyone speaking to them was fined five pounds sterling (the price of a good ox). The women were stripped naked and searched for "tokens" of witchcraft. None was found, but they were held in prison for five weeks and then ordered back on board ship with neither their bedding nor their Bibles to be landed somewhere in the Barbadoes Islands.

Two days later eight more Quakers arrived, four of whom were women. This group was kept in prison for eleven weeks without material comforts, including sufficient food for health. Anyone caught giving them food was fined. The following year the General Court ordered that the penalty for entertaining Quakers would be forty shillings, which was the equivalent of ten bushels of peas and rye. This was later increased to forty shillings for every hour that a Quaker was aided in any way, a monstrous fine for those days.

Mary Clark, hearing of the persecutions, left her children in London with her husband and came to Boston in 1657 to warn the Magistrates to desist from their persecution of the innocent Quakers.[41] She was given twenty stripes on her bare back with a cord whip that took both a man's arms to wield. The same year Ann Hutchinson's sister, Katherine Scott, "a grave and sober ancient woman of good breeding, education and circumstances of unblameable conversation," left her children in Providence, Rhode Is-

land, and came to help the suffering Quaker women in
Boston. She was given ten stripes and threatened with
hanging if she appeared in Boston again. Among those
who came the following year was Horred Gardiner, mother
of many children. She came from Newport with her servant girl to carry her nursing baby. They were both imprisoned in Boston and received ten lashes each on their
bared backs. Dorothy Waugh and Sarah Gibbon came in
April, 1658, and were able to speak at one meeting before
they were imprisoned and beaten.

In October of the same year the General Court of Massachusetts ordered the death penalty for any Quaker who
returned to the colony after being banished. The law
changed nothing, and it was a woman who proved it. Mary
Dwyer, who had come to Boston in 1635, became a Quaker
while in England on a visit.[42] She and Anne Burden arrived
from London in 1658 and were promptly imprisoned. Ann
Burden was transshipped back to England. Mary Dwyer
was the wife of the Secretary of the Rhode Island settlement, so she was delivered to her husband after he had
promised not to let her lodge in the colony even for one
night or to speak to anyone.

In October of the following year Mary Dwyer returned
to Boston with two fellow Quakers who were men. The
three were condemned to death by hanging by the General
Court under Governor Endicott. The men were promptly
hung. In the dim light of her dark cell Mary Dwyer wrote
the deathless words of her justification. On the 26th day of
the 8th month of 1659 she wrote, "Whereas I am by many
charged with the guiltiness of my own Blood; if you mean
in my coming to Boston, I am therein clear and justified
by the Lord, in whose Will I came, who will require my
blood of you be sure; who have made a Law to take away

the Lives of the Innocent Servants of God, if they come among you, who are called by you, Cursed Quakers. . . . I am a living Witnesse for them and the Lord. . . . It lyeth upon me, in love of your Souls, thus to perswade you. I have no self-ends, . . . In Love and in the Spirit of Meekness I again beseech you, for I have no Enmity to the Persons of any, but you shall know, That God will not be mocked, but what you sow, that shall ye reap from him, that will render to every one according to the deeds done in the body, whether good or evil; Even so be it saith. Mary Dwyer." [43]

The day following, the executioners came for Mary. At the gallows, they tied her feet together, placed the halter around her neck and covered her face with a handkerchief. At the very moment of releasing the support, an order came to stop the hanging and to take Mary back to the prison. Two things had happened; Mary's son had pleaded her cause with great courage and the townspeople had let it be known that they did not approve of the hanging of the two good Quaker men. Mary was put on a horse and accompanied by four men, taken fifteen miles south in the direction of the Rhode Island settlement. She reached home exhausted in body and spirit and was refreshed by the love of her family and friends. On March 21 of the following year, she returned again to Boston, this time in company with William Leddra, another Quaker. On March 31, 1660, both were condemned to be hung. On April 1 Mary was marched a mile to the gallows between rows of soldiers who had been ordered to beat their drums continuously so that no one could hear anything Mary might say. And so she went to her death accompanied by the throb of dissonant drums.

As her lifeless body hung from the gallows, Humphrey

Atherton of Boston pointed to it in jest and said, "She hangs there as a flag!" [44] He little knew how truly he spoke, for her death galvinized into action many who had taken little interest in the course of events. One of these was Edward Burrough, who wrote "A Declaration of the Sad and Great Persecution and Martyrdom of the . . . Quakers in New England!" The document was published in London in 1660.[45] He mentioned twelve strangers who received twenty-three whippings, eighteen free born who received twenty-three whippings, sixty-four who were imprisoned, two who were beaten to jelly with pitched ropes, twenty-five who were banished, two who were kept fifteen days without food, one who was laid neck and heels in irons for sixteen hours, one whose right hand was deeply burnt, three whose right ears were cut off, eighteen who were banished on pain of death, many who were bound out to pay their heavy fines and three who were put to death.

When Charles II heard of the persecutions, he ordered them stopped. All Quakers were to be given full citizenship privileges in the colonies.[46] The order was read to the General Court in Boston on November 27, 1661, but it made no impression on the Puritans. The King reiterated his order again on June 28, 1662, but the King was too far away for his voice to carry any weight. The Puritan "Church-State" was fighting for its life and was not to be deterred by a King 3000 miles away.

The persecutions went on—too many to include here, yet the experience of Elizabeth Hooton may serve to illustrate the temper of the people, both Quaker and Puritan, and the times in which they lived.[47] Elizabeth Hooton was among the first followers of George Fox in England and the first woman to preach his doctrine (1647). She was already a martyr when she came to New England at sixty years of age. She had landed in Virginia and travelled north to Boston, enduring incredible hardships in 1661. She was promptly put in prison and after some months taken to the border of the wilderness and left to find her way south. She struggled through the forests until she reached a settlement in Rhode Island. From here she shipped to the Barbadoes and back to Boston, this time with her daughter to accompany her. They were immediately transshipped to Virginia and back to England.

Elizabeth then appealed to the King and procured a special license from him to build a house in which to live and hold meetings in New England. Later in the year, she arrived in Boston and requested permission to build a house under the King's license. She was refused and sent to Piscataqua. From here she was sent to Hampton where she was imprisoned and put in the public stocks for four days; from thence to Cambridge where she was locked in "a close foul dungeon" and kept for two days without food or drink. The man who succeeded in bringing her some milk was fined five pounds sterling, which was more than the price of a cow. She was taken from the prison, tied to a post and given ten lashes with a three-cord knotted whip, then taken to Watertown where she was given ten lashes with a willow rod that cut deeply into her back. By the time she was taken to Dedham it was bitterly cold, but she was tied to a cart and given ten lashes. They put her on a horse and carried her "into ye wilderness many miles, where was many wild beasts both beares & wolves & many deep waters where I waded . . . though I ware in ye night to goe 20 miles, . . ."[48]

She traveled slowly, and, staggering painfully, she groped her way to Newport, Rhode Island, step by step, mile by mile until her friends found her and brought her to their home and cared for her wounds. Before long her strength revived. She then returned to Boston for her clothes and was whipped again and three times more before she got back to Rhode Island. Again and again she returned to Boston. Each time she was whipped, left in the woods, threatened with death. Yet she lived on to trudge seventy miles on foot on one of her journeys. Her indomitable spirit survived seventy years, the last ten of which she gave largely to freeing New England from its intolerance.

The tenants and practices of the Quakers were diametrically opposed to those held by the Godly Covenanters, who deeply and passionately believed in a Judaistic theocracy whose very existence rested on intolerance as a deadly sin. Whereas the Quakers, freed from Judaism, followed the precepts of Jesus of Nazareth in love and tolerance for all and even supported the separation of church and state. Little wonder the Puritans of Massachusetts hounded the Quakers as in no other colony and in so doing forced the Quakers to excesses enacted in no other colony.

Not all of the enthusiastic workers helped the cause of the Quakers, for as in every movement there was a fringe element that complicated the situation. As late as 1677 Judge Sewall recorded in his diary that "A female Quaker (Margaret Brewster) in sermon time came in a canvass frock, her hair dishevelled, loose like a periwigg her face black as ink, led by two other quakers, and two other Quakers followed. It occasioned the greatest and most amazing uproar that I ever saw." [49] However, the martrys so greatly outnumbered the fanatics among the Quakers that the fringe element made no lasting impression. The crack in the theocracy that Mrs. Oliver had opened by her criticisms of the ministerial leaders and magistrates and that Anne Hutchinson had pried open with her defiance was torn assunder by the Quaker women and men who bled and died in the cause of religious tolerance.

Whether the persecutions of the Quaker women precipitated the witchcraft hysteria in New England or were only overlapping influences and events is impossible to say. Certainly the leaders of the church-state were extremely sensitive to any action or event that might be a threat to their vested interests. They had long known of witchcraft and legislated against it in Massachusetts as early as 1636. The law was reenacted in 1642 and 1646. In 1692 the law was elaborated upon with a plethora of meaningless words. In essence, all the laws of the New England colonies concerning witchcraft read, "If any Christian, soe called, be a witch, yt is, hath, or consulted with a familiar spirit, he or they shall be put to death." [50]

The first case under these laws, according to Governor Winthrop, was heard in 1645 at Springfield, Massachusetts; the first hanging for witchcraft was perpetrated in 1648 at Charlestown, Massachusetts, and the last in Boston in 1692. In all, there were at least thirty-four deaths due to witchcraft accusations and probably ten times that number of cases brought to court and eventually dismissed. Of the known executions for witchcraft, twenty-eight occured in Massachusetts and three in other colonies. No one apparently has totaled the number of men and women that were accused, but Samuel Drake has estimated that in Massachusetts between March, 1692, and May, 1693, over two hundred persons were dragged into prison on charges of witchcraft.[51] Fifty of these died before Governor Phips listed the prisoners in May of 1693. Most of the accused had lain in prison all winter under conditions that only the most hardy could survive. Twenty persons were executed by hanging, in 1692—thirteen women and seven men—and ten more were condemned and excommunicated, but not hung. New Hampshire tried two cases, but both of the accused parties sued for slander and won their cases. The Pilgrims at Plymouth tried two cases, but both of the accused were acquitted. Although nearly all of the towns in Massachusetts and Connecticut suffered from the hysteria of witchcraft, Boston and Salem became the centers of the malady.

A review of the court records brings several factors into sharp relief. First, and most evident, is the fact that while the laws against witchcraft were made and carried out by the men of the colonies, it was the women who were both the accusers and the accused in well over seventy-five per cent of the cases brought to court. The reasons for the predominance of witches over wizards are legion, but certainly one of them was the greater repression of the emotional life of the colonial women than of the men under the religious patriarchal form of government.

The second factor that stands out in bold relief is even more appalling, for it relates women's medical services to the art of witchcraft. Margaret Jones, the first witch to be hung in Massachusetts, was a generous physician who brewed many of her own medicines and often dispensed them without charge.[52] She was so simple and successful in her treatments of the sick that she was accused of using witchcraft. Her very wisdom and generosity were suspect and led not only to her death by hanging but to the suspicion for half a century of every other warm-hearted woman who sought to save the life of friend.

The testimony brought against the accused ranged from sheer village gossip, often vindicative accusations based on hearsay, to spectral evidence which was pure fantasy and by its very nature could present no factual data. Against gossip the accused had a defense in the right to bring a suit for slander, and this was done successfully in a number of cases. But who can prove her "Shape" was not consorting with the Devil? Of course, no one could. The so-called objective tests were tried but proved nothing to the unbelieving, though they were conclusive proof to those who wanted to believe. The water test was practised in Connecticut (as described earlier), but was disapproved in Massachusetts. The snow test was tried on Mary Webster of Hadley, Massachusetts, in 1683.[53] She was buried in a snow drift and left to survive if she could. She dug herself out of her snow prison in the bitter cold of a winter night and lived to be seventy years old. A thorough search of the home of the accused for evidences of witchcraft was current practice, and a careful examination of the body of the accused was scrupulously carried out. Any physical abnormality such as a birthmark, a wart, or other slight blemish was considered damning evidence. Any nervous habit such as twitching, stuttering or an unconscious movement was considered clear proof of familiarity with the Devil.

The touch test was quite as damning as other tests, but more elusive since it rested not so much on the reaction of the accused as on the histrionic ability of the accuser. At Salem in the spring of 1692, Mrs. Cary was accused of being a witch.[54] She was forced to stand with her arms held cruciform while John Indian roared and tumbled about on the floor "like a hog." When she was forced to touch him he instantly recovered. John Indian was a slave of Rev. Parrish who did the heavy outdoor work. He was also the husband of Tituba, a confessed witch. When there was danger of his being accused of witchcraft, he wisely began throwing violent fits to show that the witches were persecuting him. Thus, he threw a fit before the gentle Mrs. Carey

Trial for witchcraft at Salem, 1692, from a painting by T. H. Matteson.
(Essex Institute, Salem, Massachusetts)

who could only stand bewildered before such defensive cunning. Later she was "cried out upon" by the group of adolescent girls who soon became infamous for their histrionic ability and wiley tricks. More than one intelligent man was completely hood-winked by their antics.

The group included nine Salem girls from nine to twenty years of age who performed their "crying out upon" people with such shocking success that they were invited to Andover to ferret out the local witches.[55] They were brought into a house, and one by one blindfolded men and women were brought before them to be touched. If the girls relaxed from their contortions, the one touched was proved to be a witch. The girls were in good form: they alternately capered and relaxed all day. By evening Justice Bradstreet made out forty warrants for arrest and then "declared himself done with signing any more warrants on such evidence." Though his decision did not stop the practice of accepting such evidence in court, his opinion was upheld by a meeting of twelve ministers in Boston who stated that the touch test was not "infallible evidence" and "frequently liable to be abused by the deevil's legerdemain." The ministers also suggested that spectral evidence might be fallible for a "daemon may assume the Shape of the innocent" as Mary Esty had claimed in her petition "that no more Innocent Blood be shed . . . by my own Innocency I know you are in the Wrong way."[56]

In the summer of 1692 Governor Phips requested the twelve ministers in the Boston area to investigate the legality of the cases of witchcraft which were now bursting out of the prisons.[57] The question as to whether it was lawful for the judges to try such cases at all had been raised by Mary English and had disturbed the Governor as it did many other serious minded people in the colony. The opinion of the twelve ministers supported the courts which were under their leadership, but indicated that the trials should be "managed with exceeding tenderness towards those that may be complained of, especially if they have been persons formally of unblemished reputation." However, the document containing these opinions was not made public, and no one noticed any change in the behavior of the judges.

Cotton Mather was the amanuensis of the meeting of ministers and with William Stoughton, the presiding Justice, largely determined the outcome. William Stoughton had no doubts. He believed to the end in the infallibility of the "teats" on the body, the touch tests and especially in spectral evidence. Cotton Mather was strangely curious about the whole question of witchcraft. In February of 1692 he wrote in his diary, "about his Time I had many wonderful Entertainments, from the *Invisible World* in the Circumstances of a Young Woman, horribly *possessed* with *Divels*. The Damsel was cast into *my* cares, by the singular Providence of God; and accordingly besides my Cares to releeve her, the *advise* her, to *observe* the prodigious things that befel her, I procured some of my devout Neighbors, to join me in *Praying* for her. Wee kept *Three* Successive Dayes, of Prayer with Fasting on her behalf; and then wee saw her Delivered; for which, wee kept a Time of solemn *Thanksgiving*. [What an actress she must have been!] But after a while, her *Tormentors* returned, and her *Miseries* renewed; and my Neighbors being now either too *weary* or too *busy* to do as afore, tho' they made much *Prayer* daily *with* her as well as *for* her, I did alone in my Study, *fast* and *pray* for her Deliverance. And, unto my Amazement, when I had kept my *third Day* for her, shee was finally and forever delivered from the hands of *evil Angels*." [58]

In August of the same year he wrote to John Cotton, Our Good God is working of Miracles. Five witches were Lately Executed, impudently demanding of God, a Miraculous Vindication of their Innocency. Immediately upon this, Our God Miraculously sent in Five Andover-Witches who made a most ample, suprising, amazing, Confession of all their Villainies and declared the Five newly executed to have been of their Company; discovering many more; but all agreeing in Burroughs being their Ringleader, who, I suppose, this day receives his Trial at Salem, whither a Vast Concourse of people is gone; . . . About this prodigious matter my Soul has been Refreshed with some Little short of Miraculous Answers of prayer; which are not to be written; but they comfort mee with a prospect of an hopeful Issue." [59]

So curious was he that he offered to take six of the accusing group of girls at Salem into his home to study them at close hand. His offer was declined so he interested himself in the manifestations of the Devil nearer home, not believing that he who plays with fire will surely get burned. In January of 1694 he recorded, "And one memorable Providence, I must not forgett. A Young Woman being arrested, possessed, afflicted by *evil Angels,* her Tormentors made *my* Image or picture to appear before her, and then made themselves Masters of her Tongue so far, that shee beg in her Fits to complain that I threatened her and molested her, tho' when she came out of them, shee own'd that *they* could not so much as make my *dead Shape* do her any Harm, and that they putt a *Force* upon her Tongue in her Exclamations. Her greatest Out-cries when shee was *herself,* were, for *my* poor *Prayers* to bee concerned on her behalf.

"Being hereupon extremely sensible how much a malicious Town and Land, would insult over mee; if such a lying *Piece of a Story* should fly abroad, that the Divels in *my Shape* tormented the Neighborhood, I was putt upon some Agonies, and singular Salleys and Efforts of Soul, in the *Resignation* of my Name unto the Lord; . . ." [60]

Little wonder he was frightened, for he was not the only prominent person "cried out upon." Several men and even Lady Phips, wife of the Governor who had signed a release for one of the prisoners during her husband's absence had been accused. Such cases were so patently false that they threw doubt on the whole procedure.

In October of 1692 Governor Phips, in response to a petition inspected the evidence against many of the prisoners that had been brought to Boston.[61] Where the conviction had been made only on spectral evidence, he ordered the release of the prisoners. The remainder of the cases he referred to a special court. Of the fifty-two cases sent from Salem in January, 1693, forty-nine rested solely on spectral evidence and were dismissed. Stoughton, however, signed five new death warrants. The Governor, when he heard of it, was highly indignant and investigated each of the cases and released all of the prisoners.

There were no more hangings for witchcraft, for, as Dr. Bentley put it, "as soon as the judges ceased to condemn, the people ceased to accuse." [62] But the travesty, the grotesque parody of the courts of justice, hung over the people for more than a generation. The prisoners, released by court order, could not leave their cells until they had paid the jailor for their room and board, and even the iron shackles that they had worn on their wrists and ankles. One cannot help wondering what would have been the situation if the people accusing had had to pay the bill for the prisoners as we do today. Even the formerly well-to-do people had no ready cash for all their property had been confiscated. Relatives and friends did what they could, but some of the prisoners without such resources had to stay on in the prison until their services could be sold or they could be bound out as servants for their prison debts.

Nor were they free from suspicion when they returned to their home towns, barren with neglect. So long as they or their accusers lived, the "Shape" of their sufferings remained. It is impossible to know which were the more tormented, the innocent, or the accusers. A number of the magistrates, including Judge Sewall, finally admitted their fallacy and expressed regret for their part in the procedures. But of the accusers, few could ever again face the real truth of their actions. This was particularly true of the nine Salem girls. Ann Putnam had testified in nineteen cases, Elizabeth Hubbard in twenty, Mary Walcott in sixteen, and the others in fewer cases. The effect on them was more tragic than death. Marion Starkey has described their situation as they stood on Gallows Hill after the hanging of their last eight victims in September of 1692 with keen understanding.[63] She states that "Seven months of carefully cultivated hysteria had not improved these flowers of Puritan maidenhood. They had coarsened and toughened and become nearly as insensible to normal feeling as so many automats. People who shrank from the cruelty of their jests at the dying misjudged them, for they were no more capable of conscious cruelty than of any other really human feeling. The very violence of their apparent emotion disguised a sick inner apathy. Given over so long to a world of dark fantasy, they were no longer capable of response to the electric shock of reality. Almost any of those who hung on the gallows had been happier than they...."

Eight years later Ann Putnam, pathetically aged, made

a confession of her fallacy and desired "to lie in the dust and earnestly beg forgiveness of all those unto whom I have given just cause of sorrow and offense whose relations were taken and accused." [64] It speaks volumes for the congregation before which she stood, that they forgave her and welcomed her back into their fellowship.

The Puritans who settled in the middle Atlantic colonies were never a dominating force. [65] Without their repressive influence witchcraft did not thrive. In the settlement of Puritans at Easthampton, Long Island, Goody Garlicke was accused of being a witch in 1657, but the case was dropped. Across the Island at Oyster Bay, Mary Wright, a pathetic little old woman, was accused of being a witch in 1660. The local court became so confused over her answers that they referred the case to the General Court of Massachusetts. No evidence could be found on which to convict her, so she was acquitted, only to be excommunicated later for joining the Quakers. Five years later Mary Hall and her husband were accused of using witchcraft to cause a death in the village. The case was taken to New York City, and for three years Mary was held in prison before she was finally acquitted on the grounds of inadequate evidence.

13

The Coming of Tolerance

The tragedy of the Puritan "Church-State" was hastened
by the tolerance of its Lutheran neighbor to the south. The
settlers in New Netherlands, it will be remembered, were
self-respecting Lutherans whose first minister arrived very
soon after their first landing in 1624. While the early
burghers and patroons were not intensely religious, they
were stanch supporters of their faith and somewhat reluctant to accept emigrants of other faiths. The Dutch
women warmly supported their churches. Catherine Phillipse built and endowed a church near her manor house,
and other women supplied beautifully embroidered religious vestments and altar pieces, but they seem to have
taken no part in the administration of the church.

When the English took over the colony in 1665, the
Church of England became the official church of the colony,
but most of the Dutch women clung to their faith and
passed on a deep reverence for it to their children's children. This was a real achievement amid the clamour of
many voices that were shouting for attention and advocacy
in the rapidly growing colony. Freedom of religious belief

acted like a magnet and drew colonists of many faiths so that twenty-two years after the English took over the colony Governor Thomas Dongan wrote, "New York has first a chaplain belonging to the Fort of the Church of England; secondly, a Dutch Calvinist, Thirdly, a French Calvinist, Fourthly, a Dutch Lutheran, . . . Here bee not many of the Church of England; few Roman Catholicks; abundance of Quakers preachers men and women especially; Singing Quakers, Ranting Quakers; Sabbatarians; Antisababtarians; Some Anabaptists some Independents; some Jews; in short, of all sorts of opinions there are some."[1]

The first group of Jews consisting of two men and one woman arrived in Virginia in 1624, and in the following years small groups of Jews settled in most of the colonies along the eastern seaboard. One of the first Jewish synagogues was built in New Amsterdam in 1654, and others were built as the groups of Jews grew large enough to support a synagogue. The homemakers were in the middle of each endeavor. To illustrate, Bilhah Abigail Franks, who was the "spiritual mother of the women's auxiliaries" in New York, organized a committee to raise funds for the completion of a synagogue.[2] She mobilized every woman of her faith to give what she could. Some gave money, but many others gave bits of jewelry and even dearly cherished heirlooms that they and their families might have a fitting place to worship Jaweh in their new homeland.

It is little wonder that Governor Dongan of New York referred to the members of the Friend's Church as "singing" and "ranting" Quakers, for their entrance upon the American scene was undoubtedly the most dramatic and outspoken of all the religious groups who sought refuge in the new world. Their founding was baptised in blood and tears, and their benevolence was known throughout the land.

In Rhode Island where many sought asylum, the government took the position that they had "No law amongst us whereby to punish any for only declaring by words their minds and understandings concerning the things and ways of God as to salvation and our eternal condition." [3] On Nantucket Island the Quakers formed a strong church in which Mary Starbuck was a gifted member. On Long Island Lady Deborah Moody permitted them to have their first meeting on her land in 1657 and may have helped them with the building of their first meeting-house two years later. [4] In 1662 when several Quakers were arrested by the Puritan element on the Island, she was able to have the prisoners remanded to her care. In the rest of New York there was slight objection to the Quakers who soon gave evidence of being worthy citizens.

Elizabeth Harris was the first Quaker missionary to the southern colonies. [5] She visited a number of settlements in Virginia and Maryland and made many converts. When she returned to England a year later she kept the interest of the faithful alive through her letters and the books she sent until other Quakers came the following year. Four women came in 1658 and were so successful that they were ordered to leave the colony. In 1659–1660 the General Assembly passed a more stringent law against the Quakers "as an unreasonable and turbulent sort of people." The Assembly was not concerned with the Quakers' way of salvation as with the social and political problems that there presence aggravated. For instance, the Quakers did not and still do not believe in physical combat, so they would not join with the other colonists to defend the settlements. They refused also to pay the tithing tax for the support of the Church of England and in general aroused the suspicions of the magistrates concerning their vested interests.

These were disturbing elements but in no way comparable to the danger that the Quakers presented to the "Church-State" in New England. The persecutions therefore never were as severe as in the northern colonies.[6] Mary Thompkins and Alice Ambrose were said to have been unusually bold in their missionary endeavors and were sentenced to thirty-two lashes each and to be drawn to the pillory with a noose having a running knot tied about their necks. Theirs was an exceptional case and not repeated.

The Quakers had had serious problems in England also, and when William Penn worked out his "Holy Experiment," the new colony in America was like an oasis in a desert of persecution.[7] Four boat loads of Quakers arrived in Philadelphia in 1681–1682, and over fifty boat loads of emigrants arrived in 1683. By 1700 Philadelphia alone had one thousand houses and five thousand inhabitants. Many of the immigrants were of other religious faiths and from other countries than England, but the English outnumbered all the other nationalities and the Quaker church remained the dominant religious influence until Revolutionary War days.

Of all the religious groups who came to the new land, none offered women the opportunity to serve as did the Quakers, and no group of homemakers, however religious, made the breadth of contribution that was made by the Quaker women. Besides being missionaries and preachers, they attended the annual meetings of the Society of Friends and took active part in the decisions made. They agreed or disagreed with current practices without the fear of twenty lashes on their bared backs or a cleft stick on their tongues.

Hannah Lloyd was one such homemaker.[8] She was the daughter of William Penn's first magistrate and arrived in Philadelphia in 1683. She married twice, converting both husbands to her religious faith, and became the first woman representative appointed to the General Meeting of ministers of the Society of Friends. She was also a well-known preacher and traveled through New England and other sections of the new land. It is said of her that, "Though not large in appearance, yet with great modesty and soundness of expression, 'her doctrine dropped as the dew, and distilled as the small rain.'"

She had a hundred counterparts, homemakers who believed so deeply in their religion that they pushed their soap pots back of the house and trudged the long, lone trails in the heat of summer and the biting cold of winter to tell others of the love of God. Some were highly educated and could quote the classics as well as the Bible; others, like Rebecca Hubbs, had little or no formal education yet stirred the hearts and minds of their listeners and left an indelible impression on the life of the colonies.

Hannah Penn, second wife of William Penn, served in a different way.[9] She administered the Proprietorship of the Colony of Pennsylvania for many years during her husband's illness and after his death. Notably, she contributed to the friendship maintained with the Indian tribes, the peaceful negotiations of the boundary lines of the colony and the sound rules of self government that were established.

Elizabeth Haddon came to New Jersey in 1700 with a housekeeper and two men servants to occupy the land owned by her father.[10] She married John Estaugh and acted as clerk of the women's meetings of the church for fifty years. Unofficially, she was a tower of strength in the struggling community. Elizabeth Evans was another such homemaker. She sat as elder of the church for many years, though she lived in a cave near Mount Laurel. She was long remembered for her understanding and her wisdom. We learn of the worth of Martha Awbrey Thomas through an elegaic poem written in 1726 to her memory as a "worthy Elder in the Church." The incident is not unusual, for in the Society of Friends both men and women appreciated the work of women as well as that of men. They frequently expressed the lasting depth of their appreciation in poems and other writings about the women of their church, so that we know today far more about the early Quaker homemakers than those of any other faith. Thus, we can more accurately estimate the vastness of their contributions to the growth of religious tolerance that has made our nation strong, or perhaps possible.

William Penn's treatment of the one case of witchcraft that came before him is a good illustration of Quaker tolerance.[11] The case concerned the loss of certain livestock, presumably bewitched to their death. William Penn found a technical error and dismissed the case without rendering any accusative judgment. Fifty years later there appeared in the *Pennsylvania Gazette* a waggish report of a witch hunt at Burlington, New Jersey. It is probable that Benjamin Franklin wrote the story and the whole colony laughed. According to his story, four people agreed to take certain infallible tests to determine whether they had occult powers—two, a man and a woman who were accusers, and two a man and a woman who had been accused of witchcraft. "It seems the Accused had been charged with making their Neighbors Sheep dance in an uncommon Manner, and with causing Hogs to Speak, and sing Psalms, and to the great Terror and Amazement of the King's good and peaceable Subjects in this Province." A crowd of nearly three hundred gathered to watch the spectacle. Scales were fixed on the gallows that had been built on front of the Judge's house so that the ladies could see without mingling with the hoi-polloi. A huge Bible was placed on one side of the scales and the participants placed on the other side, one by one. All were proven guilty, for each weighed more than the Bible, for all its weighty words. Then the participants were taken to the mill-pond. The men were stripped for skin diving, but the women retained their "shifts" (chemises). All four were dumped overboard and all four swam safely to shore. But the crowd was not satisfied. They thought that the women's "shifts and garters" had held them up, which was most unfair. Therefore another try should be made in warm weather when all the participants could be equally naked.[12]

Contrast these two occasions, one an event, the other an article in a newspaper, with the happenings in New England in 1682 and the later date and you will get some idea of the benevolence of women working on equal terms with men in the field of religious endeavor. This is not to imply that women were solely responsible for the chasm of difference, but rather to suggest that the excessive repressions of women (over one half of the population) on the one hand the freedom of women on the other had profound effects on the outcome in each case. If you hold women down in one area they will come popping out in another like old-fashioned down pillows, sometimes to your embarrassment. Undoubtedly, the demonstration of their freedom under God was the greatest gift the Quaker women gave to our Dear-bought Heritage.

Among the refugees who accepted William Penn's offer of sanctuary were a group of Pietists known as Moravians who were members of the Church of the United Brethren.[13]

In their group were a number of women of great strength and ability who left a heritage chiefly in the field of religious education. Anna Caritas Nitschman and Johanna Molther (Baroness von Seidewitz) came to the Barony of Nazareth in the wilderness of Pennsylvania in December of 1740. Ten years earlier, when Anna was fifteen years old, she had been made an elder of the church and had formed a choir of seventeen young women at Herrnhut in Saxony, Germany. She named the group the "Covenant of the Single Sisters." When she came to Nazareth, she set out to build a series of choirs in the new religious adventure. Before long there were seven choirs, each with its own house and clearly defined duties to the total church group. They consisted of choirs for the children, the older girls, the single sisters, the married couples, the widows and widowers, the older boys and the single men.

In December of 1741 Count Zinzendorf came with his daughter Beningna who assisted in developing a school during her two year stay in the colony. Anna Nitschman married Count Zinzendorf in 1757 after the death of his first wife in Germany. She continued to work for the improvement of the growing religious colony. Juliana Nitschman, a deaconess in the church, was the wife of Bishop Nitschman who was a cousin of Anna's. Juliana had been one of the original members of the Choir of the Single Sisters, and with her husband and four sons came to America in 1749 to work for the church. She was called by many "the Mother of Pennsylvania" when she died at thirty-nine years of age.

The women of the settlement dressed uniformly in a tight basque waist and a very full skirt of gray or brown cloth, changing to white on festival days.[14] They wore cornered white caps made of very fine linen, which they had produced on their land. The caps were tied under their chins with distinctive ribbons. The children wore red ribbons, the older girls light red, the single sisters pink, the married women blue, and the widows white.

The regime of the settlement was rigorous. They appeared dressed for prayers at 5:00 a.m. and had breakfast at 6:00 a.m. Then they worked until 11:30 a.m., though they had a brief break at 9:00 a.m. for plain bread. The dinner at 11:30 a.m. consisted of broth, meat and a vegetable in season but no desert, after which they went back to work until 3 p.m. vespers. After vesper prayers they might have a bit of bread and applesauce or sugar cake and a smidge of dried beef. At 5:00 p.m. supper was served in the great dining hall where all the announcements were made. Evening prayers were said at 8:00 p.m. often with a string quartet to accompany their singing. At 9:00 p.m. the warden locked the doors of each house, inspected the leather water buckets and installed the night watchmen or sisters for their all-night vigil.

The first group of United Brethern had joined Oglethorpe's colony in Georgia in 1734 where they also made a contribution to the religious and educational life of the colony.[15] In 1753 Anna Catherine Kalberlahm went with a group of missionaries to Wachovia in the Carolinas where they established schools and greatly influenced the religious life of the colonies.

Another group of Pietists broke away from the Mennonite settlement in Germantown, Pennsylvania, and in 1732 folowed Conrad Beissel to Cocalica Crick where they built the Ephrata Community, consisting of two houses— one for the men and one for the women.[16] All of the members swore themselves to celibacy, and community property. Sister Maria and Sister Naemi Eicher were the first two women to follow Conrad Beissel into the wilderness. These women with Barbara Mayer and Maria Hildebrand formed the nucleus of the Ephrata Sisterhood. Sister Maria Eicher, who had come to America in 1726, was made prioress and was the first to adopt a distinctive dress. By 1740 there were about thirty-five women in the settlement. Besides producing most of their food, clothing and shelter, the colony made paper, printed books and pamphlets and developed a remarkable school of church music. Some of the sisters wrote both the words and the music to many of the hymns and choral numbers. The sisters remained semi-cloistered. They taught in the village religious school and did considerable charity work, especially in sharing their foodstuffs and cloth with the needy in the nearby area.

The settlement grew slowly and never had more than three hundred members at any time. Though it survived until 1900 when it consisted of seventeen elderly persons, it could not sustain itself and so was disbanded. Fortunately, the depth and richness of their religious life has been preserved in the exquisite beauty of their chorals so that we who pause to hear can know the heritage they left us.

New York, like Pennsylvania, was a mecca of many religious groups. Among these was a small group of Wesleyan Methodists who settled in New York City in 1755. They consisted of about fifty German families who had escaped from the persecutions of Turenne in the Palatinate and lived for ten years in Ireland. In the liberality of New York they lived peaceably and gradually took on the habits of the sophisticated city.

One day Barbara Ruckle Heck came home from market to find her brother playing a game of cards with some of his friends.[17] Horrified, she threw the cards into the fireplace and lectured the men on the hell fire that awaited them if they continued in such sinful activity. Greatly agitated by what she thought was the beginning of the falling away of the members of the church, she hurried to the home of her cousin, Philip Embury. He was the best equipped by education to become their minister and so she charged in upon him and forcefully exclaimed, "Brother Embury, you must preach to us, or we shall go to hell and God will require our blood at your hands!"

Philip Embury looked about him. The group had been living in New York for eleven years and were only now getting on their feet financially. He answered her question with another: "How can I preach? For I have neither house or a congregation?"

If Barbara was non-plussed by his answer she did not show it. She promptly promised him to raise a congregation and bring them to his own house for their first meeting. They arrived shortly—four neighbors who sat piously while he preached. Thus was started the Methodist Church in America.

It grew so rapidly that in two years the idea of a church building was projected. Barbara Heck drew the architectural plans that were accepted and white-washed the walls when it was built. When missionaries from England came the following year, Barbara, her husband and family moved to Salem, New York, where she started another Methodist Society. A few years later she moved to Canada and again started a Methodist Church so that she may justly be called the progenitor of the Methodist Church in United States and Canada. She died at seventy still filled with deep religious enthusiasm. What a superb legacy to leave to her children's children!

Anne Lee Standerin also had the fire of a religious conviction.[18] She, too, was determined to save the "lost souls of Israel," but by quite a different theology. Anne Lee was born in Toad Lane in Manchester, England, in 1738. Her father was a blacksmith and poor even in the best of times. She was the second of eight children and went to work as a small child in a cotton factory. Later she worked at a hatter's and was cook in a public infirmary. She never went to school but learned whole books of the Bible by heart. She is said to have been a pious child and to have had heavenly visions frequently. When she was twenty-two she joined a group of radicals known as "Shakers" due to their ritualistic, shaking dance. Anne became an enthusiastic member and championed their cause with feverish teachings and preachings in the street sof Manchester. In 1762 she married Abraham Standerin, a blacksmith, and had four children, all of whom died in infancy. Her grief and frustration only added to her deep-steated belief in the depravity of mankind, particularly in the area of sex. Though she continued to live with Abraham (her last child was born in New York City after he had left her in 1776) she continued to preach fanatically against marriage and concupiscence as a deadly sin.

She was imprisoned a number of times in Manchester and once was stoned by a mob. In 1770 while she was imprisoned for disturbing the peace, she had a profoundly inspiring vision. In it she found herself the "visible leader of the Church of God on earth." God was revealed to her as a dual personality. Christ had been the masculine manifestation of God. She was the female manifestation whose mission it was to establish the government of the "United Society of Believers in the Second Appearing of God." Thus she was to usher in the Millennium. Once convinced of her mission she worked harder than ever, frequently disturbing the peace of Manchester. Once she was imprisoned for fourteen days without food but was fed by her flock. They poured milk through a tube pushed through the keyhole of her prison door. To the amazement of her warden, she came forth more determined than ever. But life in Manchester was becoming very difficult, so in 1774 with eight followers including her husband, brother and niece, she came to New York. She stayed in New York City and did laundry work until her husband left her for another woman in 1775. Then she joined the rest of the group at Watervliet, just north of Albany, New York. She helped in clearing the land and building the houses.

Between 1780 and 1784 she made a number of successful trips through New England to raise money and recruit new members. She died in 1784 utterly worn out by her work. She was completely fearless, wholly dedicated to her mission, and remarkably selfless in her interests and conduct. While she had dignity of bearing, she spoke simply and was neither proud nor avaricious. She taught and lived frugally, honestly and industriously. She was warmly charitable and had great personal humility in spite of the awesomeness of her mission. By the time of her death she had made disciples in Massachusetts, Connecticut and New York. These followers carried on her church. A century later they had twenty settlements in seven states and about six thousand members. In the late nineteenth century the membership dropped steadily. Celibacy and community property had become unpopular, and Anne Lee's Millenium ceased to be more than a memory of a woman, dedicated to a cause that could not stand in the face of modern scientific exploration.

But before scientific sophistication had weakened the hold of Anne Lee's followers, they had to compete with a rival religious group that settled a scant twenty-five miles to the west. Four years after Anne Lee's death, Jemima Wilkinson settled her flock of believers in her "New Jerusalem" near Schnectady, New York.[19] Jemima differed from Anne in many ways. Where Anne had suffered real poverty, pain and persecution, Jemima had to invent the appearance of suffering. For Jemima was born at Cumberline, Rhode Island, in 1752 to a prosperous farmer. She was the eighth of twelve well-fed children and taught to read and write at an early age. She was allowed to gratify her aversion for any kind of work, her interest in reading and in embellishing her natural beauty.

About 1774 the "New Light Baptists," or "Separaters," formed a church in nearby Providence, Rhode Island, and Jemima Wilkinson became deeply interested. She retired from all social life; then from even her family. She stayed in bed claiming she was ill. The doctor finally admitted her ailment was mental. In the spring of 1776 she fell into a thirty-six hour trance. She was pronounced dead and carried in a coffin to the church. In the middle of the service she arose and spoke feebly to the people.

Soon after she explained to all who would listen that her body had been dead and that her soul had gone to heaven. She had looked about her in awe when she heard a cry, "Who will go and preach to a dying world?" She had then answered, "Here am I, send me."[20] Whereupon she had immediately left the heavenly hosts who were praising God and reanimated her body with the Spirit of Jesus Christ. For she was in her new person to enact the second coming of Christ, to reign on earth a thousand years and then be translated to join the heavenly hosts in their eternal worship of God.

Her audience was fascinated, even if some were unbelieving. She went on to explain that she must pass through many trials and sufferings, for it was already the "eleventh hour," the last call of mercy that would ever be made to a sinful, earth-bound people. This was strong medicine, and religious persecution by this time was hard to come by. Nearly everyone was agitated about freedom and national defence, for a war was going on. The people of Rhode Island had always been tolerant of religious vagaries and now had other things to think about. Even in this confusion Jemima held her own. She went to the Quaker meetings and loudly proclaimed her "Calling from God to be the Universal Friend."

She was tall, graceful, beautiful with deep eyes that were hypnotic in their hold upon people. Her manners were gracious and a little condescending, as could be expected from one with a mission like hers. But the Quakers did not like what she said and told her so. This was the persecution she planned. The more they reproved, the more she aggravated them. Slowly, she drew about her a few dissenters from various churches who came to believe in her miraculous power. Later, when she taught celibacy and the subordination of all family responsibility to the needs of her church, which had taken on at least the aspects of communal property, she found herself in real difficulty and had to move.

However, she was believed by many and helped by a number of very prominent people such as Governor Hopkins of Rhode Island, William Potter, Chief Justice in whose household she lived for six years and many of her "miracles" were performed, John Babcock and James Parker who financed much of her work in the early years of her ministry. She was invited to speak first in the nearby towns and later in many of the large cities where she attracted large crowds, as much by her pageantry as by her hell-fire orations. Marquis Chastellux went to see her but found the crowd too great to get near the building. He saw her later and wrote, "a very comely young woman, is, or pretends to be, impressed with the belief that she is in her own person the Saviour of the world revived, and travels from place to place attended by twelve young men, whom she calls her apostles; and who, if the general assertion be credited, have literally followed the precept of 'making eunuchs of themselves for Christ's sake!" [21] Other distinguished visitors to the country went to hear her and had the same general reaction.

She dressed in the finest silks, linens and broadcloth and kept herself well above her followers with the possible exception of a very few who handled the funds and other details of her personal life. Rachel Miller was one of these. She was Jemima's personal notary as well as her *confidente*. When the situation of Jemima's church in New England became difficult due to a confusion in the financial reports, Jemima had another vision. This time, to go west and convert the Indians. She sent twenty-five of her disciples to northern New York to build "The New Jerusalem" for her and her followers in 1788. She joined them two years later when her comfort was assured. But trouble followed her. James Parker and William Potter sued her for their share in the communal property, but all the land had been purchased in the name of Rachel Miller and so could not be attached for Jemima's church's debts.

Francois La Rochefoucauld-Liancourt visited her here and described her evening meeting as follows: "Jemima stood at the door of her bed-chamber on a carpet, with an armchair behind her. She had on a white morning gown and waistcoat, such as men wear, and a petticoat of the same colour. Her black hair was cut short, carefully

combed and divided behind into three ringlets; She wore a
stock and white silk cravat, which was tied about her neck
with affected negligence. In point of delivery she preached
with more ease than any other Quaker I have yet heard;
but . . . an eternal repetition of the same topics. . . . She is
said to be about forty years of age, but she did not appear
more than thirty. She is of middle stature, well made, of a
florid countenance, and has fine teeth and beautiful eyes
. . ." [22]

He was invited into her bedroom and found it more of
an elegant French boudoir than the cell of a saint. He did
not believe in her sincerity and reported a number of gos-
sipy stories about her financial and moral indiscretions.
Whether the rumors were true or not, there remains the
fact that Jemima did not build for the future. Did she think
she would live for a thousand years? No one knows for
certain, but she did not have her followers develop any
self-sustaining industries as did Anne Lee. She depended
solely on gifts to herself and her church. This, with Jemima's tastes for elegant living, was difficult. She was able
to hold together a small group of seventy-five men and
their families and about a hundred celibates until her death
in 1819. Then the settlement fell apart, but not without
rancour over the division of the spoils she left.

She was mentioned by Hannah Adams, the first of the
women scholars, in her volume, *Views on Religions,* published in 1801, as of doubtful sincerity.[23] It is not surprising that a woman of Hannah Adam's caliber would find
Jemima Wilkinson insincere. No women could have been
more diametrically opposite in nature and appearance.
They were both called eccentric, but Jemima was forward,
self assured and aggresive while Hannah was timid and
retiring. Jemima was strong physically and very beautiful

while Hannah was sickly all of her life and homely in appearance. Jemima preached repetitious, emotional sermons that have long since been forgotten while Hannah was a scholar who worked with infinite patience to add to the world's knowledge of religion. Lastly, Jemima probably believed only in the gullibility of mankind while Hannah weighed each religious idea carefully and admitted, "I never arrived to that degree of decision that some have attained. In this as in every other debatable subject, I would adopt the following lines:

If I am right, thy grace impart still in the right to stay;
If I am wrong, O teach my heart to find the better way." [24]

In essence this was the contribution of Hannah Adams to the long line of women who fought for religious freedom. Here, in Medfield, Massachusetts, where she was born and in Boston where she traced the history of many religious concepts could still be heard the echoes of bitter religious persecution. Yet she was able to sweep the horizons of the human knowledge of her day—sift out the truths and weigh them with great impartiality. During her long, productive life she wrote six volumes on religion, which were at once recognized as authoritive in the field. She was as truly a New England devotee of religion as Ann Hutchinson or Mary Dwyer. She lived in a day of tolerance which they had helped to make possible and added her contribution to theirs as the last gift of colonial women to the religious life of the colonies, for while she was still writing, a new nation was evolving out of thirteen transigent colonies.

14

Above and Beyond Their Duties
as Housewives and Mothers

In the earlier chapters of this variegated portrait of colonial homemakers there has been an attempt to show what the immigrating women brought with them, what they found in the new land, and what they did with their resources to help build homes in the wilderness. But such a portrait would be incomplete and inaccurate if it did not also include the women's share in the building of the economic, social and political life of the communities and the nation.

It has been presumed by a host of writers of the period that the homes—the houses and adjacent lands—were the circumferences of the colonial homemakers' lives. The women have been pictured as heroine-homebodies, completely surrounded and engrossed by babies, looms and cook pots. These they had in abundance, but they were only a fraction of the total picture of the homemakers' lives and work. Evidence has already been shown of their production of surplus commodities in their home industries such as food, clothing and household necessities to meet community needs, as well as their participation in the educational and religious life of the colonies. The remaining chapters will be concerned with the colonial homemakers' share in meeting the financial needs of her family and the economic, cultural and political needs of the communities that were "above and beyond" her usual duties as wife and mother.

The women did not come empty headed or empty handed. They brought with them a multitude of talents and learned techniques which they put to work almost at once. A goodly number of these activities they accomplished within the boundaries of their homes, as extensions of their usual functions, or as a base from which they transacted various types of economic enterprises. A second group of activities required separate rooms, which were often leantos or buildings adjacent to their living quarters, and a third group of extra-housewifely duties took them away from their homes.

Always underlying these extra-housewifely and nursery duties has been the problem of the legal, or social, sanctions for their work; always the question, age old yet new to every generation: What is the rightful sphere of women outside the bedroom, kitchen, and nursery? No one questions the homemaker's right to bear children, care for her children, or cook for her husband, but let her venture ever so slightly beyond these elemental duties and the question is raised again, fresh as a daisy, as though it had not been asked and answered a thousand times in the course of the rise and fall of many nations. The colonial homemakers, like their foremothers, answered the question in their own way, and in the answer lies the challenge to all later generations of American women to succor, sustain and enrich the life of their day with all of the talents and resources at their command.

The surplus commodities produced by the colonial home-makers were multituinous and represented every phase of colonial activity. Margaret Oliver and her mother of South Carolina were excellent butchers (1765). Jane Mooreland of Philadelphia made succulent sausages and pickled tongue (1761). Susannah Harrwood, Elizabeth Phillips and Mary Jeffes were noted for their savory sturgeon. Sister Bradish was commended for her excellent brewing of beer by President Dunster of Harvard College. Phila-delphia had four famous women bakers and three women caterers. Margaret Cresswell of South Carolina was noted for her pastry as was Elizabeth Anderson of Georgia and Sarah Sells of New York City. Duchess Quamino of New-port, Rhode Island, a manumitted Negress, was highly suc-cessful as a cateress. Mistress Stagg of Williamsburg, Vir-ginia, charmed all of her customers with her delectable confections, conserves and jellies. Martha Logan raised seeds, plants and shrub-roots for sale and even wrote a gardener's calendar to help her buyers. Mary Crathorne of Philadelphia processed mustard and chocolate to de-light the taste of everyone. And a long, long list of other colonial homemakers produced surplus vegetables, milk, butter, cheese, eggs, fruits, grains, seeds, herbs, ointments and medicines, all of which were produced to meet the families' financial crises and the communities' needs.

The colonial homemakers' efforts to meet the communi-ties' needs for cloth of many kinds has been explored earlier. Besides meeting these basic needs for cloth, the homemakers knit all sorts of garments and mended them. In New York in 1751 Elizabeth Boyd gave notice "that she will as usual graft Pieces of knit Jackets and Breeches

Betsy Ross's contribution. (From the Collections of the Library of Congress)

not to be discern'd, also graft and foot Stockings, and Gentlemens Gloves, mittens or Muffatoees made out of old Stockings, or runs them in the Heels. She likewise makes Childrens Stockings out of Old Ones." [1] She also did tailoring, dressmaking, dress designing and mantua making. Betsy Ross Ward used her ability in this field to make the national flag for George Washington. Mary Wallace and Clementine Ferguson were famed couturiers in New York in 1751, designing dresses after the latest fashions on the continent, while Mary Morcomb excelled in making beautiful, diaphanous mantuas and covered umbrellas as a sideline. Other women devoted themselves to the millinery art, creating headgear ranging from simple bonnets to towering creations of straw, crinoline, felt and silk.

Another group of homemakers did fine laundering, clear starching, "wet scowering," "dry scowering," glazing and dying .Their advertisements appear in many of the newspapers of the later period.[2] Mrs. McClellan stated in the *South Carolina Gazette* of December 15, 1737, that "she had lately filled up a calender and would glaze all silks, linens, damasks, calicoes, bed and window curtains, women's gowns and petticoats, men's night gowns and thread stockings." Still another group of homemakers made stays to underpin the elegant gowns of the day.

The surplus production of leather goods by the colonial homemakers included most of the articles made of buckskin, cow hide and the softer leathers.[3] Mary Wilson of Norfolk, Virgina (1772), and Mary Ogden of New York City (1769) were shoemakers by trade. Elizabeth Kelly of Maryland (1747), Widow Zacharias (1754) and Rebecca Leech (1741) of Philadelphia, and Catherine Park (1781) of Richmond, Virginia, were tanners, while Mary Robinson (1738) of South Carolina and Mary Cowley

"Bunkers Hill or America's Head Dress," and English cartoon. (From the Collections of the Library of Congress)

(1741) of Pennsylvania specialized in dressing buckskin and making breeches and many other articles from it, and Martha Linton specialized in making harnesses, whips and other leather goods of calf and cow hide.

Elizabeth Franklin of Boston was famous for her "Crown Soap" and wax and tallow candles which she produced for the wholesale and retail trade in competition with such other producers as Elizabeth Paris of Philadelphia who was also a chandler of note.[4] Many other homemakers were adept at peeling, slicing and weaving willow baskets of all shapes and sizes, as well as making brooms and brushes, all of which appeared in the peddler's packs from Maine to Georgia.

In a number of occupational ventures the colonial women used their homes as their offices where they transacted the business aspects of their enterprises. The activities included in this grouping were work as attorneys-in-fact, trade in ship cargoes and shipping enterprises, and ownership and management of ferries and fishing and whaling ventures.

The outstanding colonial woman attorney was Margaret Brent of Maryland.[5] In the eight years 1642 to 1650 her name appears as attorney in the Maryland court records one hundred and twenty-four times. She acted as attorney for her sister Mary, her brother Fulke and many of her neighbors. In 1647 she was named as executrix and residuary legatee for the estate of Governor Leonard Calvert. She was highly successful, partly because she never married and so could act freely in behalf of her clients as feme sole.

Many women acted as attorneys for their fathers or husbands, having been given the right to act under the power of attorney they had been given. Elizabeth Haddon brought with her the power of attorney from her father to buy land and negotiate a settlement in New Jersey. Lady Mary Craven Andros was given the power of attorney to settle Governor Edmund Andros' estate after his departure from New York, regarding which she was highly commended. Rachel Miller, it will be recalled, had the power of attorney for Jemima Wilkinson and handled the financial affairs of her church as well. In 1693 Mrs. Susanna Hartley appeared with Major Lillington as attorneys to Captain George Clark in the first recorded case in North Carolina, and in 1777 Lord Stirling stated, "I have appointed my wife Sarah, Countess of Baskenridge, to be my attorney during my absence." [6]

The court records contain numerous references to women acting as attorneys for their husbands, relatives and friends. For example, in the Massachusetts records of 1691 appear these items: "Mary Peacoke wife & Atturney to Sam Peacock no present . . . Margaret Hundlock, wife & Atturney to Edward. . . ." "Bethy Archer wife & Atturney to hir husband Jno Archer, Plaintiff, . . ." [7]

In most instances the colonial courts granted the widow the right to be executrix and administrator of her late husband's estate if he died intestate. Such a law was included in the *Body of Liberties* drawn up in 1636 in Massachusetts. To illustrate, David De Frees left no will when he died in 1721 in Connecticut. The court appointed "Mrs. Martha Defrees widow relict of said deceased" to make out an inventory of David's estate and to administer same. The court records also show that many men in each of the colonies designated their wives as sole executors of their estates in their wills. [8] The will of John Todd is quoted because of its brevity and clarity. It reads, "I give and devise all my estate, real and personal to the Dear Wife of my

Bosom, the first and only Woman upon whom my all and only affections were placed, Dolly Payne Todd, . . . I appoint my dear Wife executrix of this my will . . ." (Dolly later became the wife of President James Madison.) [9]

Frances Culpepper, who married three colonial governors, handled many of the problems of the proprietorship of the Carolinas after the death of her first husband, Governor Samuel Stevens; [10] later she married Sir William Berkeley, Governor of Virginia, and assisted in the handling of his estate after his death; still later, she married Philip Ludwell, Governor of North Carolina, and again assisted in the disposal of her late husband's estate. Elizabeth Smith of Long Island, New York, had a similar experience.[11] She handled the estate of her first husband, William Lawrence, who died in 1680, and also that of her second husband Governor Philip Carteret of New Jersey who died in 1682. Two years later she married Colonel Richard Townley whose estate she handled after his death in 1711.

While colonial women were not professional lawyers, with the possible exception of Margaret Brent, they did go into court frequently as attorneys-in-fact to fight for the family property and honor.[12] Generally, they clearly established their power of attorney by written statements, but many times the courts supplied the necessary papers when life and necessity were involved.

Other home-based occupations of the colonial homemakers were concerned with the ships and their cargoes. It will be remembered that Eliza Knight was among the merchant adventurers who financed the Mayflower expedition, and a number of colonial women followed her example. Temperance Grant of Rhode Island took over the family shipping business when her husband died in 1744

and was very successful for twenty-two years, owning a
number of privateer vessels that traded along the Atlantic
seaboard and with the Barbadoes.[13] Anne Hack had a similar business in Virginia in 1665.[14] But perhaps the most
notable of the women ship owners was the enterprising
Margaret Hardenbroeck de Vries Phillipse of New Amsterdam.[15] She owned what was probably the first regularly
maintained fleet of packet ships in the colonies. Though
married twice, she handled her own affairs, bought and
traded in her own name and frequently went to Holland
as super cargo on her own ships. She is reported to have
had unusually fine financial acumen and amassed a considerable fortune before she died in 1690. Another New
York matron did a thriving business in ship cargoes. She
was Polly Spratt Provoost Alexander who became not only
the leading social light in New York City and owner of
the "smartest" shop in town, but also a very able financier,
especially in the buying and selling of cargoes at the
wharves.[16] Many New England women also indulged in
shipping ventures but of a more limited nature. "The Pepperell women (of Boston) saved their pin money and sent
little ventures in the argosies which floated the baronial
treasures of the family into foreign ports." [17] Mary Anne
Faneuil of Boston as well as a number of women in Rhode
Island made similar ventures.[18] Mary Anne Faneuil, it is
said, packed her discarded "snuff-boxes, buckles, & glove
strings" in small boxes for her brother to give to the Captains in port who were charged with the selling of the articles at ports en route.

Some colonial homemakers lived on the wharves that
they owned; others transacted the business of their wharves
in an office in their homes nearby. The New England newspaper advertisements for the sale of ship cargoes mention

Mrs. Hodge's wharf, where a one hundred and twenty-ton schooner was for sale.[19] Mary Dudley built a wharf at Saybrook, Connecticut, to accommodate the passengers on her ferries. In Pennsylvania three women are mentioned as owners of wharves;[20] Widow Allen (1725), Widow Hun and Widow Church, but little is known of their activities concerning the wharves. In Savannah, Georgia, Widow Fitzwalter was appointed (1742) to the county office of "Wharfinger" on the death of her husband who had held the office.[21]

A number of colonial women also owned and operated ferry boats.[22] Mary Dudley's boats have already been mentioned in connection with the wharf that she and her son built in 1720. Ruth Haskins ran three boats as ferries between Salem and Beverly in Massachusetts in 1701. Abigail Smith Grimes operated a ferry boat between Rocky Hill Landing and South Glastonberry that was started in 1650 and continued by herself, occasionally assisted by her daughter and granddaughter and at times by some of the men of the family. Widow Johnson had a ferry at Perth Amboy in New Jersey in 1764 and Widow Austin had ferries that crossed the Delaware in 1772.[23] The Maryland Assembly gave Mrs. Fenwick five hundred pounds of tobacco in 1657 and a monopoly to run a ferry boat across the river.[24] Widow Beasely was similarly paid for "setting people over the river." In 1760 Elizabeth Skinner was given 4900 pounds of tobacco to "keep a good boat fit for such use and transport the inhabitants of the Country, their horses and carriages, over Oxford ferry . . . as often as they shall have occasion." Deborah Nichols, who had ferry boats running from Baker's Landing to Hog Island, was also given an allowance by the county government.

In the following century at least a dozen colonial homemakers of Maryland were running ferries across the rivers, bays and other waterways in Maryland.[25] Mrs. Hughes had a tavern three miles from Baltimore and a ferry across the Patapcoe River in 1744; Elizabeth Wilson had a ferry at Annapolis, (1746) and Anne Conner had ferries from Pig Point on the Patuxent River to Annapolis in 1762. Sarah Raymer ran ferries between her tavern at Broad Creek on Kent Island and Annapolis in 1763 and Sarah Flynn had "good boats and skillful hands" to carry people from Annapolis to her "well furnished" tavern. Mary Anne Noble kept a ferry "over to Virginia to John Shurden's Landing" and across the mouth of Piscataway Creek to William Digge's Landing in 1764. Anne Middleton had a tavern on Kent Island in 1770 and ran a ferry for her guests to and from Annapolis; in 1773 Flora Dorsey was given an allowance by Anne Arundel County to keep a ferry across the Patapsco River, for twenty-five years.

In Virginia Sara Clayborne was paid "for ferrying in the Countries Service" in 1684, and about forty years later Elizabeth Kennon was given a fifteen year contract by the Bristol Parish Vestry to run a ferry.[26] In 1774 Janet Mitchell and Mary Gibbons kept a ferry at Yorktown to meet the town's needs. In North Carolina, Annie Wilson and Elizabeth Hill ran ferries across the Perquimans River in 1715 and 1756 and Jemimah Cannon had a ferry across the Chowan River about fifteen miles from Edenton in 1795. In South Carolina Madam Parker, Elizabeth Hazelwood and Katherine Welshuysen owned and ran ferries between 1741 and 1754, and Mrs. Timrod had a ferry at Charleston in 1795. The ownership of ferries appears to have been a highly profitable occupation for the women as many of the continued in the field for a number of years.

The colonial homemakers of Nantucket Island and a number of other seacoast towns were successful in the use of their fishing and whaling vessels.[27] Experience Coffin of Nantucket Island was willed (1725) one half of her husband's estate, which consisted chiefly of fishing and whaling equipment. She sent her ships to sea and continued to manage the business with real success. Dinah Starbuck was bequeathed a number of fishing and whaling vessels and continued the business of her late husband with equal success. Judith Barnard in 1734 listed her estate as "a whole boat, oars, craft to boat, an outfit for shore whaling, one share in the Old Wharf, 5/12 share in the Sloop Ranger and ¼ share in the mill."

The colonial women apparently did not man the fishing and whaling vessels but kept the accounts, sold the fish and helped sight the schools of whales and fish.[28] For instance, Abigail Baker was riding horse back along the eastern shore of Long Island in 1700 when she sighted thirteen whales in her six-mile ride. She gave the alarm to the men and was given a share of the plunder when the accounts were cleared. The only colonial homemaker who was in the whaling industry, about whom we have first-hand evidence, was Martha Turnstall Smith who came to Long Island in 1683. In 1705 her husband died, but she proceeded to manage the family whaling business with remarkable skill. Her accounts for 1707 contain the following:

Jan. ye 16, 1707, my company killed a yearling whale, made 27 barrels.

Feb. ye 4, Indian Harry, with his boat, struck a stunt whale and could not kill it,—called my boat to help him. I had but a third, which was 4 barrels.

Feb. 22, my two boats, and my son's, and Floyd's boats, killed a yearling whale of which I had half,—made 36, my share 18 barrels.

Feb. 24, my company killed a small yearling, made 30 barrels.[29]

By June fifth her catch had amounted to about 315 pounds worth of oil, which made a handsome profit for a season's work in any field.

There is no way of knowing how many women went to sea as pirates or members of the crews on privateer vessels, which were working for personal or governmental gain during the 18th century. Generally the women took men's names and did not disclose their sex to anyone until forced to do so by circumstances beyond their control. Edgar Maclay mentions a woman on the privateer *Revenge* who was discovered when the vessel was captured and the crew imprisoned, but we can find no corroborating evidence. However, Louisa Baker, alias Lucy Brewer, of Massachusetts left a record of her exploits. She was born in 1792 in Plymouth County, Massachusetts, and enlisted in the United States Navy when she was about twenty years old. She served for three years as a sailor on the frigate *Constitution,* took part in three military engagements and was given her due share of the prize money. When she returned to Boston she bought herself some beautiful dresses and sat down to write the story of her life, which was published in 1815 and in two subsequent editions.

Anne Bonny was a true pirate. She was the illegitimate daughter of an Irish lawyer who settled in Charleston, South Carolina, where he practiced law and became wealthy. Anne grew up a beautiful pampered heiress, but she had a violent temper and was accuesd of killing her

U.S.S. Constitution, by Muller. (Courtesy of the United States Navy)

Anne Bonny, pirate. (From the Collections of the Library of Congress)

English maid with a case knife. While still very young she eloped with James Bonny and fled from the wrath of her father to the stronghold of pirateers at New Providence in the Bahamas. Here she met and fell in love with "Calico" Jack Rackam. She dressed as a man, and together they engineered the theft of the fastest vessel in the harbor and plundered the coast successfully for several years. At one time she was set ashore in Cuba to have her first child unbeknownst to anyone but Rackam. Finally, there vessel was captured and they and their crew brought before the Court of the Vice Admiral at St. Jago de la Vega, Jamaica, on November 28, 1720. Of the crew that stood arraigned and condemned to death there were two who spoke up. They said, "Milord, we plead our bellies." A roar of incredulous laughter and jeers greeted their claims, but the court surgeon reported, after his examination of them (Anne Bonny and her friend, Mary Read) that they were indeed women and well along in their pregnancies. The rest of the crew were hung. Mary Read died in childbirth in the fetid prison, but Anne Bonny, who was still in her teens survived and was finally pardoned, it is thought, through friends of her father in Jamaica. But to this day no one knows what became of her or even her maiden name—only that it was a highly respected name in Charleston, South Carolina.

Perhaps the activity that was most clearly an extension of the colonial woman's household tasks was that of keeping of an inn or coffee house.[30] Very early in the colonial period the settlers felt the need for central meeting places other than their churches. The "publick house" as it was called at first was intended not only for the entertainment of wayfarers but for the comfort and advantage of the local population as well. The Connecticut settlers ruled in 1644 that "one sufficient inhabitant" in each town should

operate an inn or "ordinary" since "strangers were straitened," and the General Court of Massachusetts Bay Colony
in 1656 ordered a fine levied on every town that did not
have some kind of "publick house." However, many of
the settlers were reluctant to undertake the enterprise as
the local magistrates continually snooped and restricted the
sale of liquor and the reception of strangers without references. Inducements were offered to prospective inn-keepers
by a number of the towns in the form of land, pasturage
and exemption from school taxes and church rates. Many
colonial homemakers became inn keepers in a desperate
effort to feed and clothe their families.

Earle states that by 1714, when Boston had a population
of nearly ten thousand, "It had thirty-four ordinary or inn
holders of whom twelve were woman; four common victual-
lers, of whom one was a woman; forty-one retailers of
liquor, of whom seventeen were women, and a few cider
sellers." [31] John Melish at the end of the century noted
that even in the outpost town of Johnstown, New York,
nine of the sixty houses were taverns.[32] Some of these were
owned and operated by women as was true for the hundreds of other taverns throughout the colonies along the
eastern seaboard.

Ownership of a "publick house" in New England was
the right, or duty, of "one sufficient inhabitant" in each
town. Just what the term meant is not clear, but in Boston
in 1638 a license to own a tavern was given Katherine Bar-
riton along with several men, and in 1647 Mrs. Clark of
Salem, Massachusetts, was licensed to keep such a house
if she could find a man to manage it, probably a bartender,
which she did and ran the inn successfully for a number
of years.[33] The settlers at Plymouth decided in 1663 that
"James Leonard of Taunton, having buried his wife and

in that respect not being so capable of keeping a publicke house, there being alsoe another ordinary in the town," cancelled his license. Twenty years later Mrs. Nicholas Howard was licensed "to entertain Lodgers in the absence of her husband," but in many other instances married woman innkeepers were not permitted to entertain men guests while their husbands were away, regardless of their worthy reputations or their straitened circumstances.

During the period, the "publicke house" grew from a simple clapboard shack and lean-to to a variety of rooming houses, boarding houses, taverns, restaurants, hotels, coffee houses and resorts similar to our motels today. The early clapboard shack generally had one public room simply furnished with tables and chairs and a lean-to room where the travelers slept. Sarah Knight described a number of taverns at which she stayed during her journey from Boston to New York City in 1704. At one stop she records in her journal, "I pray'd her to show me where I must lodge. Shee conducted mee to a parlour in a little back Lento [lean-to], which was almost filled with the bestead, which was so high that I was forced to climb on a chair to gitt up to ye wretched bed that lay on it, on which having Strecht my tired Limbs and lay'd my Head on a sad-coloured pillow, I began to think on the transactions of ye past day." At Rye, Connecticut, she wrote, "But arriving at my Apartment found it to be a little Lento Chamber furnisht among other Rubbish with a High Bedd and a low one, a long table, a Bench and a Bottomless Chair. Little Miss went to scratch up my Kennell which Russelled as if shee'd bin in the Barn among the Husks and supose such was the contents of the Tickin—nevertheless being exceedingly weary down I laid my poor Carkes never more tired and found my Covering as scanty as my bed was hard.

Anon I heard another Russelling noise in the room—called to know the matter—Little Miss said she was making a bed for the men; who when they were in Bed complain'd their Leggs lay out of it by reason of its shortness—my poor bones complained bitterly not being used to such Lodgings and so did the man who was with us; and poor I made but one Grone which was from the time I went to bed to the time I riss which was about three in the morning, Setting up by fire till light." [34] Sarah Knight complained about the food also. On one night she wrote, "We would have eat a morsell, but the Pumpkin and Indian-mixt Bread had such as aspect, and the Bare-legg'd Punch so awkerd or rather a sound that we left both," and went supperless to bed.

However, many of the taverns were very well run. Lord Ley in 1637 declined to stay with Governor Winthrop in Boston because the inn where he was staying was so well ordered that he was as well accommodated there as anywhere else.[35] As transportation improved, the number of taverns increased and their accomodations became more gracious. When George Washington made his New England tour in 1789 he commented favorably in his diary on several inns that were run by women.[36] At "the Tavern of Mrs. Haviland, who keeps a very neat and decent inn" he was well pleased. In Boston "at a Widow Ingersoll's (which is a very decent and good house)" he really enjoyed himself.

A few years later John Melish noted that even in Little Falls, which was two hundred miles northwest of New York City, he found the breakfast table set with "table-cloth, tea tray, tea-pots, milk-pot, bowls, cups, sugartongs, casters, plates, knives, forks, tea, sugar, cream, bread, butter, steak, eggs, cheese, potatoes, beets, salt, vinegar, pepper and all for twenty five cents." [37] In Pennsylvania fifty women advertised their taverns in the newspapers and 745 licenses (twenty per cent of the total) were granted to women tavern keepers for from one to fourteen years duration between 1762–1776.[38] Many more women kept inns without licenses, as is evinced by oblique references to their establishments in correspondence and other documents.

Among the more famous inns in Pennsylvania before 1750 were Mariner's Compass and Four Horseshoes, owned by Elizabeth Walton; the Hen and Chickens, owned by Widow Brientnall; The West India Coffee House, owned by Margaret Ingram; and The Crooked Billet, owned by Barbara Lewis.[39] Later in the century Sarah Mackinet's Sadler's Arms became famous for its food and entertainment. Her inn was set on a lot 79 feet by 636 feet and had an orchard for a back yard.

In the southern colonies there were fewer inns during the seventeenth century than in the northern colonies, largely due to the dispersed population, poor means of transportation and the warm hospitality of the estate owners.[40] However, Ann Moore in Northumberland County, Virginia, was granted a license "to keepe an Ordinary at the house where shee now liveth; Wine, Drames, & Beer to sell according to Act of Assembly" (1652–1655). As the roads improved the number of taverns increased rapidly. Among the more well known was the tavern at Williamsburg owned by Mary Luke in 1710 and The King's Tavern (1752–1784) owned by Jane Vobe "where all the best people resorted," according to one French traveler. George Washington frequently stopped there, but Martha Washington preferred the quieter inn kept by Elizabeth Churchill Dawson, widow of a former president of William and Mary College.

Mary Davis' advertisement from *The Virginia Gazette*

of March 22, 1779, gives a typical picture of an inn of the day.

The subscriber begs leave to inform the publick, in general, and her friends in particular, that she has removed from Lester's ferry, and rented Dr. Carter's large brick house, on the main street of Williamsburg, where she proposes to accomodate Ladies and Gentlemen with private lodgings. She has 12 or 14 very good lodging rooms, with fireplaces to most of them, which will hold two or three beds each. She is willing to rent out some of them yearly, to such as may incline to find their own beds and furniture. The rooms above are convenient for Gentlemen, those below for Ladies; the house consisting of two parts, and divided length-wise by a brick partition. She has also another house on the lot, separate from the first, with two rooms and fireplaces below, very suitable for a family. Her terms will be entirely regulated by her friends. She is now tolerably prepared for the reception of lodgers and horses, but hopes to be more completed so by the ensuing April court.

Mary Davis

N.B. Any Ladies that may choose to spend a few weeks in private times whether for pleasure of education, may do it here both reasonably and with convenience.

Marquise de Chastellux mentioned several southern taverns. The worst one was Mrs. Teaze's Tavern where "a solitary tin vessel was the only bowl for the family, the servants and ourselves." Later he wrote of stopping at a tavern in Petersburg, Virginia, in 1780–1782 where the landlady and her daughter were elegant in dress and charming and easy in conversation. They were such delightful company that at first he was afraid their conversation was a ruse to cover the poor food they would serve, but the dinner was as excellent as their conversation. "Scarcely had we had time to admire the neatness and beauty of the cloth before it was covered with plenty good dishes." [41]

In Maryland the most renowned hostess of a tavern was probably Elizabeth Marriott at The Sign of the Ship in Annapolis where she is said to have amassed a fortune of 3000 pounds by 1755.[42] Her daughter, Anne Howard, inherited the tavern and entertained George Washington at her inn in 1774. Sarah Chilton had an excellent tavern in Baltimore in 1772, and Sarah Flynn advertised in the *Maryland Gazette* as early as 1759 that "all Gentlemen Ladies and Others, that have Occasion to travel the Road from the Southward, on the Eastern Shore of Maryland" were notified that she had opened her house in Frederick-Town at Sassafras Ferry and offered her customers "Genteel Entertainment and good usage."

North and South Carolina had many taverns by the middle of the 18th century.[43] Elizabeth Sinclair had a tavern in Hyde County, North Carolina, and Elizabeth Slaughter in Chowan County. The little town of Edentown had eight taverns owned by women between 1741–1753. Jane Eldridge's tavern on the "Green" was a center of business and social life of "Charles-Town," South Carolina as was Mrs. Peach's "New Tavern in Church Street" and Mrs. Ramsay's "on the Bay." In Savannah, Georgia, Lucy Tondee's Tavern was the famous meeting place of the Council of Safety during the Revolution. Many simpler boarding houses were maintained for transients such as Ann Imer's House "being convenient to the provincial free school" or Esther Coop's House on Broad Street in "Charles-Town."

The first license to sell chocolate and coffee was given to a woman in Boston in 1670, but it was not until 1745 that the first coffee house in Philadelphia was opened by

Widow Roberts.[44] Ten years later Mary Ballard advertised in the *Boston Evening Post,* December 8, 1775:

For the Entertainment of Gentlemen, Benefit of Commerce, and Dispatch of Business, a Coffee House is this day opened in King Street. All the Newspapers upon the Continent are regularly taken in, an several English Prints and Magazines are ordered. Gentlemen who are pleased to use the House, may at any Time of Day, after the manner of those in London, have Tea, Coffee, or Chocolate, and constant Attendance given by their humble Servant Mary Ballard.

Also in Boston, Mrs. Fennecy gave notice to the public that she would entertain "select companies, Fire Clubs and Fishing parties" and Mary Burke assured the public that she could entertain sleighing parties very agreeably.[45] Abigail Williams had a sure sense of advertising appeal as evidenced in her notice in the *Providence Gazette,* March 9, 1765:

For the Convenient Reception and Entertainment of Gentlemen and Ladies, whenever they are disposed to recreate themslves by and excursion into the Country, whether at Morning or Evening,

On Monday next will be open'd by
Abigail Williams,

At the Sign of the White House, The House of Jeremiah Williams Cranston)

The rural Tea and Coffee House

Very pleasantly situated about three miles from the Town of Providence, on one of the most delightful Rooads in New England.

Those who are pleased to favor her with their Company may depend on the best of Entertainment, and the civilest Usage, as it will be her Constant Endeavor to deserve a continuance of their Favour.

N.B. Travellers may be genteely accommodated at the same Place.

Andrew Burnaby, a traveling clergyman of 1759, has left us a delightful description of the resort taverns near New York City. He stated that "There are several taverns pleasantly situated upon East River, near New York where it is common to have these turtle-feasts. These happen once or twice a week. Thirty or forty gentlemen and ladies meet and dine together drink tea in the afternoon, fish and amuse themselves till evening and then return home in Italian chaises, a gentleman and a lady in each chaise. On the way there is a bridge, about three miles distant from New York, which you always pass over as you return, called the Kissing Bridge where it is part of the etiquette to salute the lady who has put herself under your protection." [46]

Farther south on the Ashley River in Maryland, Martha Wallis offered to entertain ladies and gentlemen with tea and coffee at her delightful house about four miles "up the path"; [47] Mrs. MacGregor who ran "a Genteel Coffee-House" offered her well-kept garden as an inducement to amuse the ladies and gentlemen while she served them tea or dinner; and Mrs. Campbell's "Coffee House" in Williamsburg, Virginia, became a very popular rendezvous for many of the gentry of Virginia.

Many of the larger taverns were located in the cities for the accomodation of travelers and transients such as Mrs. Leather's House at Newbury, Massachusetts, where lawyer William Pynchon of Salem used to stay whenever court convened in the neighborhood.[48] Other taverns were located on or adjacent to the docks where "Publick Vendues" of cargoes from the nearby ships were frequently held. Widow Davenport owned such a house known as The King's Head Tavern at Boston, and Widow Lawrence owned a similar establishment in New York City "on the New Dock" where not only cargoes but prize ships of the privateers were sold at public auction (1747).

A goodly number of inns were located at ferry stations such as Madam Van Borsum's Ferry Tavern at Breucklen (Brooklyn), New York, and Mrs. Hughes' Tavern at Baltimore, which stood near the Patapscoe River over which she also ran a ferry (1744).[49] Taverns were also a part of each new out-post village, as in the case of Mrs. Cota's House in North Yarmouth, Maine.

It is evident that the function of these "Publicke Houses" was not merely to house and feed tourists. Actually, the taverns served many important functions in the colonial communities.[50] For instance, many of the town and proprietors' meetings were held in such inns as at Margaret Pratt's The Ship Tavern in Salem, Massachusetts, or Goodwife Woodward's House in Wenham, Massachusetts. The inns were neutral ground where the business of the community could be argued and settled. Occasionally, the taverns were turned into courtrooms or jails and even used as schools in emergencies. But they were probably used more consistently for business purposes than for any other, for they were the original exchanges in the colonies. Real estate was often sold at auction in them; lotteries had their drawings in the taverns; nearly all of the first insurance offices were located in them, and in New York City Margaret Todd's Sign of the Black Horse was the headquarters of the Boston Post. Taverns were also the meeting places for pirates, plotters, politicians, and patriots, as well as the headquarters for both armies during the Revolution.

Garnett Andrews in the delightful reminiscenses of a Georgia lawyer tells of Nancy Rumsey who, when he knew her, was "fat, square, and forty." [51] She had started her tavern-keeping with a "traveling restaurant." She had an oxcart which she drove to the town square and from which she removed the hind door, exposing a large cider barrel. She set up her table with cups, pint and quart pots, a box of ginger bread and a small bag of chestnuts. Every court day she appeared and sold her simple wares. Soon she had money enough to build a house at Goshen near Elberton. It became a tavern and she the most important politician of them all. Each candidate for office sought her support, and, what is more, subsidized her, for he knew that his opposition was doing the same thing and he hoped to outbid the rascal. Every young lawyer looked to her to mention his name, and even the judges paid her homage. Thus for half a century Nancy Rumsey ran Elbert County with her tavern more of a county seat than the courthouse.

Perhaps the most comforting function of the taverns to the modern reader was their use as places of entertainment, especially in New England.[52] Amid the bleakness of its landscape in winter and its puritanic rules, the "Publicke House" must have appeared as a beacon of joyous light to the Puritan wife. Here she could sit and talk whilst her order for liquor was being collected and perhaps have a nip with her hostess. In the Plymouth Colony in 1663 "Mistris Lydia Garrett" was allowed to sell liquors "alwaies provided . . . shee sell none but to housekeepers, and not lesse than a gallon at a time." How the "housekeepers" must have enjoyed that errand!

Here also were held the first dramatic performances.[53]

Little plays called drolls were given, and many a ruse was resorted to in New England by the "starveling" actors to circumvent the Puritan prejudices. They billed concerts of music and "monstrous sights" of moose, walrus, camels, lions, leopards, deformed animals and people, bull baiting, moving puppets, elaborate clocks, mechanical devices, electrical machines, balloons and the first lightning rods.

In Philadelphia the Free Masons disported themselves at Peg Mullen's Beefsteak House, and in Savannah, Georgia, Mary O'Neal and Abigail Minis had a monopoly on such entertainment as skittle alley, shuffle board, billiards and other games.[54] As truly as their churches were the embodiment of their religious aspirations, the taverns were the embodiment of their pulsing vibrant life. Commerce flowed through them; laughter filled their rooms, and patriotism found substance in their atmosphere. For the colonial women the inn was an enlargement of her home, the work an extension of her usual duties, and best of all she could have her children with her helping with the work as a family project and still be an active participant in community affairs. No wonder so many of them decided on this method of earning a living for themselves and their families.

15

She Expanded Her Home to
House Her Financial Enterprises

In the struggle to support their families the colonial
homemakers carried on a number of fascinating occupations in the lean-tos that were adjacent to their living
quarters. These included their work as barbers, morticians,
merchants and workers in glass, wood and metal. Women
acted as barbers in nearly all of the colonies, largely as re-
placements for their absent or sick fathers and husbands.
However, Elizabeth Butler advertised herself as a capable
barber as early as 1765 in Charleston, South Carolina.[1]
Judge Bentley of Boston repeatedly mentions women barbers in his diary, and Christopher Marshall noted that he
was "shaved by the barber's wife" several times in his
travel notes, as did a number of other tourists of the period.

The barber chairs and other equipment were generally
located in a corner of the main room of the house or in a
lean-to room, which made it easy for the homemaker to
maintain the work as a side-line to housekeeping and innkeeping. A few advertised as beauticians or dressers of

Lydia Barrington Darrach. (Courtesy of Sophie Drinker and the Frick
Art Reference Library, Philadelphia, Pa.)

women's hair and makers of powders and wigs. Most of this work was done in their homes, but some of the women went to the homes of wealthy socialites to dress, powder and ornament the hair of their patronesses in the latest European fashion.

Two colonial homemakers in Philadelphia were morticians;[2] the more famous was Lydia Darrach, a heroine of the Revolutionary War, but Rebecca Seaton also gave evident satisfaction to her clients. Women were frequently pall-bearers as indicated in the diaries of the day. Sarah Eve of Philadelphia wrote in 1772–1773, "B. Rush, P. Dunn, K. Vaughan and myself carried Mr. Ash's child to be buried; foolish custom for Girls to prance it through the streets without hats or bonnets."[3] Other girl pall-bearers mentioned in the diaries were dressed in white and wore long veils with no mention of their "prancing" through the streets. In New York City Blanche White advertised her services as a mortician in 1767, and in Virginia Sarah Overstreet performed these services as a sideline to her medical services.[4]

Colonial homemakers entered the field of merchandising almost as soon as they unpacked their clothes after landing for merchandising was a familiar field to them. Many of their mothers and grandmothers had been members of the Merchants' Guilds in England and on the continent. They sold so many different kinds of goods that it has been necessary to group them under the major commodity that they had for sale: imported goods, food stuffs, bakeries and delicatessens, hardware, books, real estate and human cargo.

It is not surprising to find that Catelyn Trico was among the first women traders. She came to Albany in 1623 in the ship *Unity* and lived there three years, "all of which time ye Indians were all as quiet as Lambs and came and Traded with all ye Freedom Imaginable, . . ." [5] In 1626 she moved to New York City and later to Long Island. Following her were four remarkable Dutch business women who became the leading importers in the colony.[6] Cornelia Lubbetse de Peyster came to New Amsterdam to be married in 1651. She imported the first salt to the colony and became an ingenious importer of much needed goods. Margaret Hadenbrook de Vries Philipse became not only a leading ship owner but also merchant princess through her extensive importing trade. Maria de Peyster, who married Paulus Schrick, John Spratt and David Provoost, carried on an expansive trade with Europe, the Barbadoes and other American colonies to support herself and her three children. Mary (Polly) Spratt Provoost Alexander was an outstanding merchant as well as a notable importer.[7] She was barely twenty-six years old when Samuel Provoost, her first husband, died, and she took over his extensive business to support her three children. She had a row of offices built in front of her house and directly on the street, with a large store on one side. Thus she could manage her home and still keep a sharp eye out for the business.

The road or street in front of her offices had been paved with small round stones in 1657 by Madam Van Cortland to reduce the mud and dust. Polly added the first side walk in the colonies. She had large flat stones laid in front of her buildings and on up the street on either side. The effect was clean and delightful street for the ladies with their long ruffles and flounces and became the talk of the whole colony. Her store "was acknowledged to be one of the best appointed in the city, and her social position was in no way affected by her business pursuits."

In 1721 Polly married James Alexander by whom she had seven children. She continued her business life with scarcely a break. In a letter to her brother, her husband James wrote in 1721, "Two nights agoe at eleven o'clock my wife was Brought to bed of a Daoughter and is in good health as can be Expected, and does more than can be Expected of any woman, for till within a few hours of her being brought to bed She was in her Shop and ever Since has given the price of Goods to her prentice, who comes to her and asks it when Customers come in. The very next day after She was brought to bed she Sold goods to above thirty pounds value. And here the business matters of her Shop which is Generally esteemed the best in New York, she without the Least help from me, you may guess a little of her success." [8]

In New England besides the ventures of the Faneuil and Pepperell ladies were a number of homemakers whose careers included the importation of saleable commodities.[9] Among these was Madame Le Mercier who had a store on Back Street, Boston. She advertised that she had "every sort of Beauties, just received from France" in 1779, which was quite an accomplishment considering that there was a fierce war going on. After the Revolution (1784) Margaret Phillips advised the Bostonian homemakers that she had "a large and beautiful assortment of Picked Goods, Suitable to the Season" and just imported from London. Mrs. Greely and Miss Love had similar stocks of beautiful imported goods from London.

In Pennsylvania forty women advertised their shops in the newspapers, and at least fifty-four others had merchandise for sale, most of which had been imported. Mrs. Redmond evidently had a luxury shop as early as 1724, as she advertised diamond rings, earrings, watches, silver tweezers, snuff boxes and "a variety of other goods too tedius to mention." [10]

Southern newspapers also carried advertisements of

women importers.[11] Sarah Packe of Williamsburg, Virginia, advertised mourning clothes in 1737 after the death of Queen Wilhelmina Dorothea Caroline in England. Her advertisement offered "Bombazeens, Crapes and other Sorts of Mourning for Ladies; also Hatbands, and Gloves for Gentlemen." Hannah Lade had imported goods in her shop in 1741, and Elizabeth Carne offered the public a long list of hats, cloth, ribbons and sundry other articles" recently imported in 1748. In Charleston, South Carolina, Lucy Weaver offered a wide assortment of goods in 1735 including glass, tea, sugar, lace hoop petticoats, stays and "other sorts of European Goods at reasonable rates." Catherine Seurlock and Margaret Warden advertised the sale of imported food commodities such as flour, butter, milk, vinegar and seeds from New York and Philadelphia. After the middle of the eighteenth century, Charleston had an increase in the number of women importers.[12] Frances Swallow went to London in 1766 to pick out her stock personally, and Anne Waller, Mary Cooper and Anne Matthews also were successful importers who delighted the tastes of the southern ladies with the beauty and variety of their stocks.

Local produce as well as imported commodities were also sold at the public markets and fairs that were held periodically in most of the colonies.[13] Boston had an established market for the sale of local produce and other goods as early as 1633. Salem maintained a similar market in 1634 and Hartford, Connecticut, and Providence, Rhode Island, in 1643. To these markets and fairs flocked not only the farmer's wives and families but also the city people to buy and sell their excess produce from carrots to cloth.

In 1656 the Dutch homemakers on Manhattan petitioned and received the authority to have every Saturday reserved as "Market-day" and that the "Sale" should be held "on the strand, near the house of Master Hans Kierstede." [14] Here the town wives, the farmers' wives and the "Wilden women" brought their produce and wares for sale. Sarah Kiersteade, wife of Hans, had a large shed built in her back yard adjacent to the Market where the "Wilden Women" could come to sell their wares such as wild fruit, baskets, brooms and blankets. The market days were so successful that in 1659 the Dutch settlers decided to hold a semi-annual "Kermis," or six-weeks open air market, which included exhibits, contests, sports and amusements. Philadelphia had a similar fair with carefully drawn up rules to regulate the trade and the amusements in 1693.

In the southern colonies the fairs were gala occasions.[15] The farm women traveled from great distance to attend, for it was about their only chance not only to exhibit their poultry, preserves and pickles, but also to see the latest fashions and attend the games, matches, music and dancing. A number of itinerant dealers brought their wares to the fairs. Ann Dalrymple advertised that she would attend the Ashley Ferry and Strawberry Fairs and bring with her an assortment of millinery, "cambricks, hollands, farlix, edgings ribbons, fans, powder" in 1737. Three years later Judith Miller advertised that she would bring an extensive colection of goods to the Ashley Fair, which she would raffle off. Far to the west in New Mexico and Arizona, animal fairs were being held at Santa Fe and Taos where corn, wheat, beans, and cloth of cotton and wool were sold by the Spanish settlers, and buffalo hides and deer skins were sold by the Indians.

General stores with diversified stock were owned and run by numerous homemakers in each of the colonies.[16]

Many of the stores were arranged in the front portion of their homes as was true of the three women who had stores in Manchester, Massachusetts. They were Abby Trask who kept a store for forty years and employed "a large number of young women . . . from time to time," Mrs. Hooper Allen who was a "person of great business capacity," and Mary Baker who kept "a fancy goods store for many years." Mary Starbuck, known in Nantucket Island lore as the "Great Woman," kept a careful account of her business transactions in connection with her general supply store.

Some of the homemakers on Manhattan and the upper Hudson River settlements continued in the traditions of their distinguished forebears.[17] Earle tells us that "Lysbet, the widow of Merchant Reinier, became the wife of Domine Drisius of New York. She carried on for many years a thriving trade on what is now Pearl Street, near Whitehall Street, and was known to everyone as Mother Drisius. The wife of Domine Van Varick also kept a small store, and thus helped out her husband's salary." Elizabeth Van Es Vancker owned and operated a very successful store until her death in 1694. The inventory of her effects included a large quantity of goods and peltries, silver-clasped Bibles, gold and stone rings, and silver tankards and beakers. Mrs. Murray and her husband had a large store on Manhattan, and it was here that she detained General Howe so that General Washington was able to retreat and regroup his forces during the Revolution.

In Philadelphia, Margaret Duncan was the first woman merchant on record.[18] She had a store at "No. 1 S. Water Street" from 1721 to 1802, but what she sold is not given in the record. Probably, her stock consisted of a little of every kind of surplus goods or imported items that were available to her. Later, when the newspapers were published, the shopkeepers used them to advertise their goods in great detail. Anne Hume of Burlington, West Jersey, had an advertisement in the *Pennsylvania Journal* of September 20, 1764, that listed over one hundred and sixty-seven items from beans to jewels.

In the southern colonies the majority of the women shopkeepers kept general stores, or at least a varied stock.[19] Anne Waller in Charleston, South Carolina, carried dry goods, guns, pistols and gold watches among other things. Susannah Crockett, also of Charleston, sold Italian chairs, silk shoes, medicines, stationary, draperies, wine, tea and sugars, while Anne Matthews carried gunpowder and gunflint, loaf sugar, fiddles, spices, teapots, chafing dishes, pudding pans and a line of fashionable millinery. Abigail Minis, the Savannah, Georgia, tavernkeeper, kept a thriving general store as a side line to her tavern.

Janet Schaw, a Scotchwoman who was visiting in Wilmington, North Carolina, in 1775, kept a journal in which she described what was in all probability the first "Ten Cent Store" in the colonies. She noted "that the Mrs. of this place is a pattern of industry, . . . She has (it seems) a garden, from which she supplies the town· with what vegetables they use, also with mellons and other fruits. She even descends to make minced pies, tarts, and cheese-cakes and little biskets, which she sends down to town once or twice a day, besides her eggs, poultry, and butter, and she is the only one who continues to have Milk . . . all her little commodities are contrived so as not to exceed one penny a piece, and her customers know she will not run tick, which were they to run by the length of sixpence must be the case, as that is a sum not in everybody's power, and she must be paid by some other articles, whereas the two coppers, (that is, half pence) are ready money. I am sure I would be happy in such an acquaintance." [20]

A few homemakers specialized in selling seeds such as

Hannah Dubre who sold them either wholesale or retail in 1753 and Mrs. Fillion who sold "very good fresh cabbage seed" in 1738.[21]

The bakery and delicatessen stores of colonial days offered an alluring array of tempting foods.[22] Here the homemakers were at their most seductive tasks; no wonder they were very successful. Jane Bennet offered to bake "the best pound cake, an order, one shilling a pound," if the purchaser furnished the ingredients. Mistress Stagg of Williamsburg, Virginia, in 1738 offered "Hartshorn and Calvesfoot jellies fresh every Tuesday" and "mackaroons, Savoy biscuits and Barbadoes sweetmeats" any day. Margaret Nelson of Charleston in 1769 offered rich "plumb" cake, biscuits, "syllybubs and jelleys," custards, blomage, rice cups, four kinds of pudding, "orange and mince pye, snow cheese, apple tarts, three kinds of cheese cakes, preserved oranges, marmalade, collard and potted beef" and many articles to tedious to enumerate." Mrs. Bell had "good anchovies to be sold at reasonable rates" in 1732, and somewhat later Ann Forrester had pickled herrings and coffee for sale in Bedon's Alley.

Most of the woman shopkeepers carried cosmetics and drugs as a sideline, but a few specialized.[23] Sarah Watson in Virginia offered the public "an excellent eye water" that would "take of specks, cataracts, and strengthen weak eyes," lip salve, tooth powder, almond paste for hands and face, and perfumed wash balls. Widow Mankin in Philadelphia offered the public "a select Parcel from London, consisting chiefly of such things as are principally used in the Modern Practice of Physick, being a great variety of Masteria Medica, both simple and compound, Chymical and Gallenical." Jane Tytler was a pharmacist. She came from Scotland with her husband who was a chemist. Judge

Bentley, noting her death, called her a very worthy woman but reported that she died in the poor house in 1824 at the age of eighty four years.

At least eight colonial homemakers were tobacconists. Mary Pelham of Boston advertised in 1748:

Mrs. Mary Pelham formerly Widow Copley on the Long Wharf, tobacconist,) is removed into Lindell's Row against the Quaker's Meeting House, near the upper end of King Street, Boston, where she continues to sell the best Virginia Tobacco, Cut, Pigtail, and spun of all sorts, by wholesale or Retail at the cheapest Rates.[24]

Mary Pell was a tobacconist in New York City in 1771. Widow Gordon (1726), Margaret Allen (1720), Elizabeth Evans (1753), and Katherine Wadle (1762) were tobacconists in Philadelphia between 1720 and 1762. Grace Vaughan raised and sold tobacco in Northampton County, Virginia, as did many other southern women. Agnes Lind, a milliner in Charleston, South Carolina, sold tobacco as a side line along with other shopkeepers.

Nearly all of the general stores mentioned earlier carried some items of clothing or clothing accessories, but a few women owned ladies' or gentlemen's specialty shops and catered to the elite of the cities. In Boston Mrs. Nutmaker sold every conceivable article of clothing for women and children from hats and bonnets to buttons and buckles (1717–1742), all in the most elegant manner.[25] In Philadelphia Mary Cahell sold "all sorts of gentlemen's caps. Also ladies and childrens caps, mantilets, pillareens, hoods, bonnets, long and short cloaks, mantles and scarfs, with black bags and roses for gentlemens hair or wigs; all which she makes after the newest and neatest fashions, very cheap.

N. B. She makes turbans for Negroes." Mrs. Hannah
Moses sold such accessories as Jewelry snuff boxes, brass
and enamel pens, and children's rings.

In the southern colonies about sixty homemakers advertised their stock of cloth or clothing in the newspapers of
the period, and they were only a small percentage of the
total number of women who took this means to support
themselves and their children.[26] The variety of goods included "sundry calicoes and chintz," brocades, English
Persians "a-lamode," lustering, paduasoy, flowered lawns,
fashionable ribands, gold and silver lace, Italian egrets,
leghorn hats, hoop petticoats, imported serges, Irish linens,
"stomachers with Bows," feathers of white and color, satin
and callimanco shoes, white silk and colored stockings,
French silk gloves and Barcelona handkerchiefs.

Hardware stores that were owned and run by colonial
women were less numerous but quite as important to the
women and their communities they served.[27] Mary Jackson of Boston advertised in 1748 that she had for sale "at
the Braziery, cutlery also Pewter and lead by the hundred
weight and Nails of all sorts by the cask or smaller quantity, at reasonable rates." Later she offered a wider range
of stock, which included "mourning goods," a handsome
new chaise and "Tea-Kettles and Coffee Pots, copper
Drinking-Pots, brass and copper Sauce-Pans, Stew pans,
Kettle-pots, Fish-Kettles, new fashioned tureens," butter,
Pork and "Florence Oil."

Toward the end of the eighteenth century Sally Salter
of Boston advertised iron skewers, spoons and other
kitchen utensils that had been made in Lynn,[28] and Mrs.
Tucker of Charleston advertised a fresh consignment from
London of Handirons, "coffee Beggins," roasting ovens of
various sizes, spits and skewers, wire Parrot cage, copper

stills, pewter worms, saucepans, ladles, moulds, and boxes. In Philadelphia Mary Eddy had a hardware store that sold iron-mongery, cutlery, hard goods, and joiner's, shoe-maker's and watch maker's tools. In 1771 her advertise-ment contained a list of items that filled over two columns of eighty-four lines each. In allied fields, Anne Vander-spugel sold glass in New York City in 1737; Mary Emer-son of Philadelphia sold second-hand furniture in 1764; in Charleston Anne Milner and Madam Farmer dealt in lime stone and Mary Frost sold "very good Hay and corn Blades" in 1750; and Marie Warwell sold cement and jelly pots in 1767.

Bookstores were also owned and operated by struggling homemakers.[29] Joanna Perry, widow of Michael Perry who owned a bookstore on King Street in Boston, carried on the business until her death in 1725. Later in the century Mary Butler had a "Library of Books for sale or let." In New York City Catherine Zenger had a bookstore in con-nection with her husband's printing shop. Elizabeth Bass of Burlington, New Jersey, advertised her bookstore in the *American Weekly Mercury* in 1726. In Philadelphia Mary Grafton had a bookstore in 1745, and Cornelia Bradford managed a bookstore along with her printing business. Anna Maria Ott specialized in selling German books in 1770, and Mrs. Dickson of Lancaster, Pennsylvania, had a "choice collection of books" for sale. In 1773 when Anne Smith returned from an extended trip to Lodon she an-nounced "a handsome assortment of books" for sale. In Baltimore Mary Goddard had a bookstore in connection with her printing and publishing business, and Elizabeth Timothy had a similar book shop in Charleston. Elizabeth Wicking had a bookshop in the same city in 1740, which she kept stocked with imported books. A number of these enterprising women added stationary and musical instruments to their store of books.

For "under-privileged" women the colonial homemakers seemed to have acquired an amazingly prominent place in the field of merchandising, even in the area of the sale of land and houses.[30] Sarah Boylston ran advertisements for the sale or rental of houses and other property in the Boston newspapers for twenty years (1745–1765). Sarah Dow offered houses to rent in the *New York Evening Post* in 1746. Mary Beadels of Trenton, New Jersey, and Annie Clothier also of New Jersey offered homes and land for rental or sale.

Most of the newspapers in the southern colonies carried notices signed by women advertising land and houses for rental or sale.[31] Some of these advertisements offered the sale of personally owned property, others were notices by women who were acting as executives of estates left in their charge. Other advertisements indicated that the signator was acting as an agent in the sale of property. For instance, Henrietta Dulaney of Maryland offered 2,750 acres for sale in 1755, and in Maryland Justina Moore offered 1,000 acres for sale in 1734. Sarah Blakeway's advertisements were prominent in the *South Carolina Gazette* from 1736 to 1741 when she gave notice to the public that she was leaving the Province. Bartlett reports three real estate agents who were women in Georgia between 1765–1783.

Most of the colonial homemakers owned slaves and indentured servants in each of the colonies. Elizabeth Diggs is said to have owned 108 slaves, or more than any other person in Virginia in 1699. Merchandising human cargo was not uncommon. Both Negro slaves and indentured white woman were sold on the open market, as in the case of Rachel White who advertised in 1780:

To be Solde, By subscriber. . . . A Likely healthy Negro Wench, about 24 years of age; She has had the measles and smallpox and can do all kinds of housework, at which she is very handy, and will be sold for no fault.[32]

Susannah Marsh advertised Negroes for sale in New York City in 1747, and Mrs. Stapleford offered Negroes for sale along with groceries and gunpowder in Philadelphia in 1742. Sarah Blakeway offered slaves for sale or for hire repeatedly in her advertisements which appeared between 1736 and 1741 in *The South Carolina Gazette*. Many advertisements offered for sale the unexpired time of indentured servants. Mrs. Knox at Bull Wharf in Boston offered seven indentured maids to be disposed of in 1763. Other such advertisements have been given in Chapter XV.

While most of the stores that were owned and operated by colonial homemakers were housed in their homes, some of the store owners who had extensive or bulky commodities for sale, such as hardware and furniture, built lean-to sales rooms or separate buildings nearby, as did Polly Alexander. The homemakers who worked with glass, wood and metal generally used buildings adjacent to or near their living quarters because of the size of the commodities to be sold and the nature of the work they performed.[33] This was probably true for Mary Stevenson of Charleston who advertised herself as a competent glazier and painter in 1753, and Marie Warwell of the same city who advertised that she could mend all kinds of china, glass, plaster, bronze or marble in 1767. Mary Emerson of Philadelphia also probably did her silvering of mirrors and Ann Hawes her "painting and Glazing business . . . in all its branches" in separate buildings near their homes. However, Mrs. Decamps, glass engraver from Paris, may have lived in rooms back of her shop. She advertised in the *Pennsylvania Packet* in 1795 that she had "just opened her store, North Third Street, No. 95, where she engraves with borders, flowers, garlands, cyphers, figures, escutcheons, and in the most elegant, fashionable, neat and new style, all sorts of glasses, and glass wares, on the most reasonable terms."

In New York City Anne Vanderspiegel also was a glazier and sold glass in 1737,[34] and Mrs. Sommer ground glass for spectacles in 1753. Boston also had its homemakers who worked with glass. Elizabeth Flagg and her daughters advertised in the *Columbian Centinel* in 1795 "that they carry on the business of Rivetting and mending China and Glass, and needlework of all kinds, at their house, near the Boston Stone." The advertisement is suggestive of the frantic struggle that many Revolutionary War widows made to sustain themselves and their children through work of any kind that they could do in their homes and with their children.

Work with wood needed space.[35] Probably the colonial homemakers' work in this field started with the twenty-two Danish women who were brought to the Portsmouth settlement to saw lumber and make potash in 1731. In the next century Mary Smith advertised in the *American Weekly Mercury* of New York in 1735 that she wished to sell one half of a saw mill and six hundred acres of land, but gave no information as to whether she ever ran the saw mill. In Philadelphia Ann Page and Mary Emerson did joiners' work among other things, and Mary Butler of Baltimore made blocks of any size for ships in 1773. In allied work

Sarah Goodwin of Boston (1745–1756) and Widow Gale (1754) of Philadelphia did chair caning to support their families.

A number of colonial homemakers advertised themselves as workers in several trades.[36] Ann Page, for instance, advertised that she intended to continue her late husband's "business in its various branches, viz., for carpenters, joiners, chairmakers, etc., lignum vitae mortars and pesils, molds for wagon, cart and cheese-boxes, bench screws. Also iron turning for the West Indies, and mill spindles. N. B. Spinning wheels are also made, mended and sold at reasonable rates." Elizabeth Lawrence and Widow Gale were upholsterers; Ann King was an upholsterer and tassel maker in the same city, and Amelia Taylor made tassels, trimmings and rope hoops. In New York City Elizabeth Evans and Blanche White advertised as competent upholsterers in 1767–1777. In Charleston, South Carolina, Rebecca Weyman and Anne Fowler assured the public of the excellence of their work as upholsterers in 1762 and 1775. Most daring of all, Elizabeth Russell in 1754 advertised herself as a coachmaker. How much of the work she did herself is not clear, but it is doubtful if she was proficient in all of the different crafts involved in the making of even a simple coach.

However, colonial homemakers were amazingly diversified in their vocational interests.[37] In the handling of metals their work included silver, pewter, tin, brass, copper, bronze, iron and steel. Some of the work could be done in lean-to rooms, but most of their work with metals required separate buildings. Jane Kind of Boston, Jane Inch of Maryland, and Marguerite Hastier of New York City were silversmiths, and Mary Willett of Maryland and Charlotte Hera of Philadelphia were pewterers. Anna Hoyland was a brazier, tinner and sometime school teacher in South Carolina.[38] About the same time Mary Jackson, who had a store in Boston, advertised that she could make "Tea-Kettles and coffee pots, copper Drinking Pots, Brass and copper Sauce-Pans, stew-pans, Baking-pans, Kettle-pots and Fish Kettles." While in Virginia Hannah Daylies and her husband ran away from their master to whom they were indentured for several years more service. They were tinkers at which work Hannah was said to have been extremely good.

In Philadelphia Sarah Lancaster advertised in 1739 that she was moving her business of "sive weaver" from Market to Arch Street; Sarah Orr announced in 1752 that she was continuing to carry on her braziery and foundry business; and Margaret Paschal notified the public of her fine cutlery work in 1755. Hannah Donaldson advertised her foundry work in 1767.[39] In New York City one woman worked in metal and made combs in 1794; in Charleston, South Carolina Jane Massey advertised her work as a gunsmith from 1739 to 1741.

Three homemakers advertised as competent blacksmiths.[40] Heilke Pieterse carried on her business in New York City; Jane Burgess had her forge in Maryland; and Mary Salmon in Boston continued "to carry on the business of horse-shoeing, as heretofore, where all gentlemen may have their Horses shod in the best Manner, as also all sorts of Blacksmith's Work done with Fidelity and Dispatch" in 1754.

There were also three colonial homemakers who owned and operated iron mines, forges and furnaces. Anna Rutter Nutt was left a widow in 1737 and fell heir to one half of her late husband's estate along the French Creek in Pennsylvania.[41] She proceeded to operate the iron works with skill and efficiency, producing about twenty-five tons of iron per week. In Baltimore, Mary Butler appears to have had a forge since she advertised that she could make pumps for ships at her "Works." [42] The third owner of an iron works was mentioned by the French traveler Marquise de Chastellux.[43] He stated that Mrs. Erskine of Ringwood, New Jersey, had a lovely manor and a forge that was very profitable to her. She was a widow of forty years and apparently a very delightful hostess as well as owner of a successful iron forge.

In all likelihood each woman in the colonies faced with the problem of supporting herself and her family, whether wholly or in part, chose the occupation most readily open to her. Often this was the occupation or enterprise in which her husband had worked and in which the whole family had been involved. She found it most profitable to the family to continue the business or service after his death or disappearance. There is little or no evidence of personal choice on the woman's part. She simply did the expedient thing in view of a family crisis. To illustrate, she became a barber because her husband had been a barber, she had been his assistant and she had the barber's chair and other necessary equipment in her home. Customers were used to coming so it was quite natural for her to serve them and so hold her family together. Thus, barbering could not be called her chosen career, but rather the work she did to support her family whether she liked it or not. This is quite a different situation from that of the present-day career woman who may choose her occupation on the basis of her known abilities and preferences. The colonial homemaker rarely had the advantage of preferential choice of occupation, particularly where the occupation was an extension of her work in the home, be it pickling herring, selling "pillareens" or running an iron forge. She generally had only one advantage, and that was a knowledge of the occupation or enterprise because it had been carried on in her home and with her help. That she made this advantage count is evidenced by her successes.

16

From Home to Factory and Work Situation

The progress of the colonial homemakers from their fire-side tasks to the sweat-shop labor in the nascent factories was slow, irregular and incomplete. Some of their financial activities allowed them to remain in their homes near their children and firesides for another seventy-five years; other activities drove them relentlessly out of their homes by the end of the eighteenth century.

Of the occupations that required separate working quarters, although often adjacent to their living rooms, none was more demanding than that of printing and publishing. As stated earlier, there were at least thirty homemakers who were involved in the industry as owners, publishers and typesetters, not counting the wives and daughters who helped in the shops but about whom we know little or nothing. The number is not surprising, for women were well established in the industry in most of the countries from which the colonists emigrated:[1] France, Germany, Holland and England. Elizabeth Pickering was the first known English woman printer (1539), and between 1600–1800 sixty women became noted for their printing establishments in

England. In Mexico City Dona Maria de Benavides was a well-known printer in 1689, and seven years later Dinah Nuthead of St. Mary's, Maryland, became the first woman printer in the English colonies.

Of the thirty colonial women directly involved in the printing business, six became printers for the colonial governments and one for a city government. Sixteen of the printers were also publishers of newspapers and tracts, and nearly half (13) of the group started or continued to work in the southern colonies. Dinah Nuthead went to Annapolis, Maryland, in 1696 after her husband's death and petitioned the Assembly for a license to "print blanks bills, bonds, writs, warrants of attorney, letters of administration and other necessary blanks useful for the public offices of this province." [2] She promised to forfeit her license and go out of business if she should print anything other than specified. The Assembly granted her request but required that she give them a bond for one hundred pounds sterling as security. Two neighbors acted as her sureties. She signed the bond with a mark. Why she did not autograph the document is not known. While it may have been due to ignorance, it also may have been due to a number of other factors, as indicated in the case of Jemima Wilkinson or Elizabeth Carteret, mentioned earlier.

Four other Maryland homemakers became distinguished printers. Anne Catherine Hoof Green, a Dutch woman by birth, was the public printer for the city of Annapolis for eight years (1767–1775) and publisher of the *Maryland Gazette* at Annapolis.[3] When she undertook the printing business, she was about forty-five years old and had already given birth to six sons and eight daughters, only six of whom reached maturity. On the death of her husband in 1767, she stated in her paper, "I presume to address You for your Countenance to Myself and numerous Family, left, without your Favour, almost destitute of Support, by the Decease of my Husband, who, long abed, I have the satisfaction to say, faithfully served You in the Business of Provincial Printer; and I flater myself, that, with your kind Indulgence and encouragement, MYSELF AND SON, will be enabled to continue it on the same Footing. On this expectation I shall venture to supply my late Husband's Customers with News-Papers, on the same Terms he did, until I receive Orders to the Contrary, and shall be ready to publish from Time to Time, the Advertisements that shall be sent to the Printing-Office." [4] In 1768 she was given "nine hundred and forty-eight dollars and one half dollar" by the Assembly and thereafter was awarded forty-eight thousand pounds of tobacco annually when the Assembly was in session and thirty-six thousand pounds for the other years. Besides the newspaper and the work for the Assembly, she printed almanacs, pamphlets and tracts.

Earle tell us of "another energetic business woman," the widow of Nicholas Hasselbaugh of Baltimore whom William Goddard found carrying on the printing business bequeathed her by her late husband.[5] Goddard bought her out in 1773 and started the *Maryland Journal and Baltimore Advertiser,* which his sister, Mary Katherine Goddard, made famous through the years of the Revolution.[6] Mary Katherine was the daughter of the no less famous Sarah Updike Goddard, publisher of the *Providence Gazette,* who taught Mary Katherine the printing and publishing business so well that she was authorized by Congress to print the official copy of The Declaration of Independence on January 18, 1777, for distribution to the state legislatures. Only one of these imprints is still known to exist and is carefully treasured among the archives of our country in

Washington. Later Mary Katherine became postmistress of Baltimore until 1789 and operated a thriving bookstore on the side. Also in Maryland, Phoebe Herbert published the *Washington Spy* from 1795–1797 at Elizabethtown.[7]

In Virginia Sarah Packe was a partner of William Parks in a print shop in Williamsburg in 1749.[8] He died the following year and directed in his will that his wife Eleanore Parks and his son-in-law complete the printing of the laws of Virginia. Little else is known of the two women who were briefly involved as owners of the print shop.

Clementine Bird Rind published the *Virginia Gazette* between 1773 and 1775 and became state printer in 1774.[9] She stated in her newspaper that "she was unhappily forced to enter business on her own account" and appealed to the public to support her undertaking as she had numerous children to support. Clementine was a woman of remarkable strength and perception. One day "An Attentive Observer" sent in an anonymous article to her newspaper accusing "the guilty great" of misconduct and saying they were above the law and "amenable to the Publick" only through publicity in a newspaper. Clementine refused to publish the article and was threatened with legal action. Her reply was terse and clear. The affair, she said, "was cognizable in a court of law, where it must be more fully determined in the injured party's favoure than by publication in a newspaper,"[10] but if the author wished to sign the article and take full responsibility for possible libel suits, she would print the article. Her death in 1775 was deeply mourned.

By 1774 sentiments regarding the actions of the British government concerning the colonies were becoming sharp and out-spoken. Mrs. H. Boyle attempted to publish a loyalist newspaper in Williamsburg, but it survived only a few issues.[11]

In South Carolina Elizabeth Timothy published the *South Carolina Gazette* from 1739, shortly after her husband's death, until 1741 when her son Peter came of age and gradually took over the business.[12] He died in 1782 and Anne Timothy, his widow, took over the work as her mother-in-law had before her. She not only published the newspaper successfully twice weekly until her death in 1792, but became state printer as well. Her large printing house stood on the corner of Broad and King Streets in Charleston as a monument to her accomplishments. Mary Timothy Crouch maintained a printing press in Charleston after her husband's death in 1775.[13] However, in 1780, shortly before the surrender of the city to the British, she moved her printing press and other equipment to Salem, Massachusetts, where she printed *The Salem Gazette* for some time. After the British left Charleston, Elizabeth Boden published the *South Carolina Weekly Advertiser* for a number of years.[14]

Colonial women in New England were also active in the field of printing and publishing. Elizabeth Harris Glover was on the high seas en route to Massachusetts when her husband, the Reverend Jose Glover, died.[15] She thereby became owner (1638) of the first printing press to be brought to the colony. She had the printing press set up in Boston and took off the first imprint the following year. Two years later she married Henry Dunster, president of Harvard College, and retired from active participation in the business. Margaret Green Draper published the *Boston Newsletter* from 1774 until the British left Boston.[16] Then, as she was a loyalist, she left the colonies and eventually settled in England. Besides publishing the newspaper, she was printer for the governor and the Council. When Boston was beseiged, the other newspapers ceased publication, but

she continued to publish the *Newsletter* on "varityped, vari-
colored and vari-sized" paper under conditions that were
often next to impossible.

Penelope Russell was the publisher of the *Boston Censor*
in 1771.[17] She is said to have composed while working with
the type and sometimes set type without a written copy.
She also wrote ballads which she printed with a border of
wood cuts of coffins and death's heads, which were very
popular. Hannah Watson published the *Connecticut Courant* at Hartford during 1778 and 1779.[18]

Anne Smith Franklin, widow of James Franklin and
sister-in-law of Benjamin Franklin, was actually the first
New England woman printer.[19] She took over her late husband's printing and publishing business in Newport, Rhode
Island, shortly after his death in 1735. In 1736 she was
named state printer and became publisher of the *Newport
Mercury* when her son died in 1762. She also carried on
the business of printing "linens, calicoes, silks etc." She
was for a time aided by her son James and her two daughters, who were excellent type setters. She died in 1763, and
her epitaph appearing in the *Mercury* reads in part: "She
was a widow about 29 Years. . . . And though she had little to depend upon for a living yet by her Economy and
Industry in carrying on the Printing Business, supported
herself and Family, and brought up her Children in a
a genteel manner; . . . all of whom she bur'd before her
Death. . . . She was a Woman of great Integrity and Up-
rightness in Her Station Conversation, and was well beloved in the Town. She was a faithful Friend, and a com-
passionate Benefactor to the Poor, (beyond many of great
Estates) and often reliev'd them in the Extremity of Winter. . . ."[20]

Providence, Rhode Island, had another famous woman

publisher in the person of Sarah Updike Goddard.[21] After her husband's death she loaned her son William 300 pounds to start the *Providence Gazette* in 1765 and later became his partner. After he and his sister Mary Katherine went to Baltimore, she ran the printing plant until she sold it to John Carter in 1768.

New York City had three notable women printers during the colonial period. Anne Catherine Maul married Peter Zenger in 1722.[22] Twenty-four years later he died, leaving her with six children. He had been an excellent printer and publisher of the *New York Weekly Journal,* and she had assisted him in his work. After his death she published the newspaper but later resigned in favor of her stepson. Elizabeth Holt, originally from Virginia, came to New York City in 1754 with her printer husband.[23] He died in 1784, and she continued his publication of the *Independent Gazette,* later becoming printer for the state. Her Daughter, Elizabeth Holt, married Eleazer Oswald who died in 1795.[24] She continued the publication of his newspaper, the *Independent Gazeteer or Chronicle of Freedom* of Philadelphia and printed a number of German pamphlets. The third woman printer in New York City was Anne Greenleaf who published *The Argus* from 1798 to 1800.[25]

In 1740 Cornelia Smith of New York City became the second wife of Andrew Bradford, the famous printer of Philadelphia.[26] When he died two years later she took over the publication of the *American Weekly Mercury* and became a very successful publisher and bookseller in her own right for more than ten years. It is said that "she was remarkable for her Beauty and talents, but not so much for the amenities which give to female charm their crowning grace," a remark that must have made many a Philadelphia business woman raise her fan to hide her smile.

Margaret H. Bache published *The Aurora* in Philadelphia in 1798, and several other women were associated with the printing business in one capacity or another.[27] Deborah Read Franklin managed the print shop of her husband, Benjamin Franklin, while he was abroad. The two Humphrey sisters assisted in their father's shop in 1775 and Mary Biddle is named with Matthew Clarkson as editor of the *Pennsylvania Journal* in 1762.

In allied fields Elizabeth Short, the bookbinder, has been mentioned earlier.[28] Mary Katherine Goddard owned and perhaps operated a paper mill besides her other interests, and Anne Dickenson advertised her paper hanging manufactory in Philadelphia in 1788.

Colonial homemakers also owned and operated mills of several kinds. It will be recalled that the earliest settlers used primitive Indian quernes for grinding corn and other grains until a sufficient number of wind and water mills could be built. Widow Tuthill had a windmill in Massachusetts in 1642, and many homemakers built simple bolting mills, which sifted the flour from the quernes and early mills through several yards of sleasy cloth.[29] Often one such bolting mill served a neighborhood or a whole settlement, the women exchanging services for the work done. Hannah Chester of Wethersfield, Connecticut, owned two thirds of a grist mill in 1711, which she leased in 1716.

Catheryna Rombout Brett inherited a large tract of land between Albany and Tarrytown, New York, on which she built a grist mill near her home in 1708.[30] She was widowed at thirty-nine years but continued operating the mill with the aid of her three sons. Ann West Gibson of Cumberland County, Pennsylvania, had a similar experience.[31] She was widowed at forty-seven years and sought to support and educate her four sons from the proceeds of her grist mill and small farm. She soon found herself in debt, so she built a school house near her home and proceeded to teach the children of the vicinity as well as her own children.

In New Jersey Elizabeth Hoffmire decided to sell her three hundred acres of land, dwelling house, barn and grist mill "on a constant stream" in 1763, and Grace Reynolds and Elizabeth Hatkinson sold their grist mills in New Jersey in 1770 and 1771.[32] Near Philadelphia Thomas Masters built a water mill in which to process corn by a method invented by his wife, Sybilla, who went to England to procure a patent for her process.[33] The patent was granted in 1715 to Thomas Masters for "the sole use and Benefit of a new Invencion found out by Sybilla, his wife, for cleaning and curing the Indian corn." She called her product "Tuscarora rice" but later it became known as "hominy." The patent is said to be the first granted to any person living in the colonies.

Mrs. Drummond had a cider mill in 1734 on her estate on the eastern shore of Virginia,[34] and at Petersburg Mrs. Bowling, besides owning large warehouses of tobacco, had a grist mill, a bolting machine and a "cribble" in 1780. A number of other mills owned by women are mentioned in wills and litigation papers of Virginia. For instance, Dorothy Jordan willed her granddaughter a horse mill and a hand mill in 1690 and Ann Michael brought suit concerning her horse mill in 1682. It is probable that every large estate in the southern colonies had some sort of grist mill on it by 1700 as a basic necessity, but no mention was made of them unless they were involved in some sort of legal procedure.

Cassandra Ducker owned a fulling mill in Virginia in 1776 where "those who favored her with their custom might depend upon having their cloth done in the neatest and best manner," [35] and in 1779 James Throckmorton hired a fulling mill belonging to Widow Schuerman about three miles from Brunswick, New Jersey.

The two colonial homemakers who worked with hemp also had to have buildings separate from their living quarters in which to make the bulky rope and nets. Hemp was a native product as Lord Delaware indicated as early as 1609 when he pointed out the existence of "Hempe, better than English growing wilde in abundance" in Virginia. The same was true for the other colonies. Sarah Jewel advertised in the *Pennsylvania Packet* as a competent rope maker in 1748–1749,[36] and Hannah Beals in the same newspaper offered in 1767 "to supply any Person with seines, horsenets, pigeon-nets, minny-nets, casting nets, billiard table pockets and nets of every sort."

Two colonial homemakers are also known to have been shipwrights.[37] Anne Penrose of Philadelphia is so listed in the records "she being a widow in that shipbuilding family," and Elizabeth Russell advertised as a shipwright in the *South Carolina Gazette* in 1771.

Livery stables were another side-line business of the colonial homemakers. Generally they managed the stables in addition to their ownership of taverns for the convenience of their patrons.[38] Mrs. Hammerton, a Charleston, South Carolina, innkeeper, advertised a sedan for hire in 1757. Elizabeth Kelly and Martha Clifford in 1766 also kept stables in the same city, and in 1770 Anne Hawes advertised in the *South Carolina Gazette* that she had "at the Sign of Bacchus good stabling for Horses and Lodging for their Grooms" and "the best Liquors and relishes."

In Savannah, Georgia, in 1775 Jane Stutz advertised that she had a stable convenient for the patrons of her tavern.[39] In Maryland Sarah Flynn advertised in the *Mary-*

land Gazette in 1757 that she had a "chaise and pair and saddle horses for the convenience of persons stopping at her inn in Frederick-Town." In Philadelphia Sarah Mackinet advertised for more than ten years that she could stable more than forty horses at her tavern, Sadler's Arms. She also had a stage wagon to rent for any type of journey in 1763. In upper New York Hester Hudson not only ran a famous coffee house with a dry goods and grocery store attached, but also managed a stage coach line between Schenectady and Albany.[40] She advertised in the *Mohawk Mercury* of May 19, 1795:

The public is informed that the Widow Hudson's four horse stage leaves her Inn in Schenectady, every morning precisely at 5 o'clock (Sundays excepted) for the city of Albany; and starts from the city tavern in Albany at 3 o'clock in the afternoon and returns to Schenectady:—That her 2-horse stage sets off from the city tavern in Albany every morning (except Sunday) at 6 o'clock for Schenectady; and leaves Schenectady at 3 o'clock every afternoon for Albany.
Stage Terms—5 shillings for a passage to or from Albany 9 shillings going and returning the same trip, in either of the stages; 4 pence per mile for a passenger taken upon the road: 14 pounds baggage gratis, 150 pound rated the same as a passenger.

As church or college sextons the colonial homemakers may have had to live out side of their homes.[41] The records are not clear on this point. In the southern colonies, where a number of women are mentioned in the records as doing the work of sextons, the only references to them concern the wages paid them—Susanna Woodlief was paid four hundred pounds of tobacco in 1757 by Bristol Parish Vestry, and Sarah Williams was paid 250 pounds of tobacco

by the Sappony Church in Virginia. In Maryland Mary
Munroe was paid five pounds annually by St. Ann's Parish,
and Hanna Ingram received the same rate from St. John's
Parish. At Harvard College "Mrs. Landman began her
business as college sexton" on April 22, 1762, but no further reference to her, or her work, was made by President
Edward Holyoke who made the brief notation in his diary.

The few homemakers who hired themselves as housekeepers generally lived where they worked, hence single
women were in demand for the jobs.[42] One advertisement
of 1769 read, "A Single elderly woman experienced in the
business" desired a place to look after a dairy and attend
to poultry raising. A South Carolina planter offered the
equivalent of one hundred pounds sterling a year to a single woman who could act as housekeeper on his farm. A
few widows such as Mrs. Forbes at Mount Vernon were
employed by the wealthy planters, or as Isabella Cocke,
Mrs. Maria Digges and others at William and Mary College, but the field of employment was very limited.

A number of women worked as day helpers in the homes.
These women washed, sewed, and cared for the children
much as similar workers do today, only much more drudgery was expected of them. Mahala Douglas in Narragansett worked for a dollar and a half a week.[43] She made
butter and cheese and milked seven cows on week days and
nine on Sundays. A few women appear to have taken the
washing or sewing home with them and returned the completed work. Other day workers, including clerks in the
stores and other mercentile establishments, appeared early
in community life. These women did all of their work away
from their homes but not in an eight-hour, five-day week
as today. They generally worked at the pleasure of their
employer, from sun up to dark and six days a week with

no nursery school care for their children if they were widows wtih children to support.

Teaching, which started as a hearthside occupation for the homemakers, became one of the chief occupations that took them out of their homes. Women who supervised or taught in the private schools generally lived on the premises and treated the students as members of an enlarged family group. While these women may not have had much personal or family privacy, they at least had their children living with them. The women who taught in the town or publicly supported schools went out of their homes to teach as is true today. Many of them were wives and mothers, others were widows, but it would appear that all of them needed the work to meet the needs of their families. The work was irregular as schools were closed during the very bad weather in winter and at sowing and harvesting times when the work of the children was needed for the bare necessities of living. The pay was very low and in most of the colonies not the property of the woman if she was married, but of her husband. In spite of these drawbacks many colonial homemakers entered this field of professional work and carried it forward with distinction.

The colonial homemakers' production of surplus cloth should also be mentioned as a field of work that took them inevitably out of their homes. In the first two hundred years of immigration (roughly 1550–1750) the colonial homemakers produced surplus cloth to augment the family income, or widows did so to support themselves and their children. The work, however gruelling, was done in their homes with the men and children sharing in the heavy labor and neighbors with special equipment helping each other.

All of this changed with the coming of machinery and the factory. Only the woman's need to support herself and her children remained the same. First the fulling and finishing of the cloth, then the weaving, and lastly the production of thread necessitated leaving the home to meet the over-riding demand for more and more cloth for more and more people. The pace was too fast for clumsy hand methods in homes, so the homemakers turned to other occupations or were caught in the drag of necessity and followed their spindles and looms into the sweat shops of an emerging industrial nation.

Earlier in this study the women in medicine were discussed as a resource of the homemakers, now we would like to consider the field of medicine as an occupational opportunity for the colonial homemakers whereby they could support themselves and their families. Most of the work in the field of medicine also took the homemakers out of their homes. The women doctors treated a few of their patients in their homes and some of the nurses were paid to care for sick and indigent people in their homes, but generally the doctors as well as the midwives and nurses had to leave their homes to serve their patients.

Perhaps the immigrant women were as well or better prepared to work in this field than in any other in which they engaged. European and English women of the 17th and 18th centuries were expected "to have a competent knowledge of Physick and Chyrurgery, that they may be able to help their maimed, sick and indigent Neighbors; for commonly, all good and charitable Ladies make this a part of their housekeepers business." [44] The last entry in the apprenticeship Roles of the City of Bristol states, "Margaret Page, alias Woolfe, convenanted to teach and instruct Sarah Sanders, a yeoman's child, for five years, according to her best skill and knowledge in the art and business of Doctress and Chirurgery, which she now useth, and to find and provide for her all necessaries except clothing." [45]

No similar apprenticeship agreements were found in any of the colonial records. Undoubtedly the women who had been trained in England and on the continent passed on their knowledge and skills to their daughters and servants, but there was no guild of physicians and surgeons in the colonies to oversee the work or the training. The women in medicine had to work alone and under extremely difficult circumstances. They often had to travel through rain, sleet and snow, by canoes, horseback or no snow shoes. Mrs. Holmes Edmunds, for instance, was so in demand during the great snow storm of 1749 in Connecticut that she had to be taken out of a chamber window and carried through the deep snowdrifts to distressed patients several miles away.[46] While the men in medicine also had to endure hardships, they had a status in the communities that was rarely, if ever, accorded to the women.

No comprehensive account of the colonial women in the field of medicine has ever been made, but a cursory survey indicated that there were at least thirty-five women who were respected as physicians and surgeons, sixty-seven women who were given recognition as midwives, and numberless women nurses of one kind or another who were mentioned gratefully in diaries and other records. Seventeen of the women physicians and surgeons are mentioned in the official records of the New England colonies. The records start with Anne Mountfort Eliot of Roxbury, Massachusetts, who has been mentioned earlier.[47] When she died in 1687 the town voted to give her a "ministerial" tomb for "the great service she hath done this town." Sarah Alcock also of Roxbury and Patience Miller of Northampton also distinguished themselves in the field of medicine and philanthropy, for much of their work was done gratuitously. In Essex County, Massachusetts, Goodwife Bradstreet was paid ten "li" in 1656 for "twelve wekes sorgary

and taking payns in changing lining" for her patient. Anne
Edmonds was known as a skilled surgeon in 1660, while
Mary Folshamer (1675) and Goodwife Harris (1677)
appeared to have been general practitioners in medicine. It
will be remembered that Jane Hawkins, an able physician
in Boston, was ordered to leave the city in 1741 because
she was thought to have used witchcraft on Mary Dyer's
deformed baby, and Margaret Jones was found guilty of
witchcraft and hung seven years later on no substantial
evidence.

At Saybrook, Connecticut, Lady Apsley Fenwick assisted Dr. Thomas Peel who was "Chirurgeon" at the fort.
She grew the herbs he needed and cared for the sick of
the little settlement. Mary Hazard of Newport, Rhode Island (1739), was "accounted a very useful gentlewoman,
both to poor and rich, on many accounts, and particularly
amongst sick persons for her skill and judgment, which she
did gratis." [48] In Windham County, Connecticut, besides
Mrs. Holmes Edmunds was Hannah Bradford, who was
always ready to care for the sick with skill and tenderness,
and Anne Woodstock Eaton of Ashford who was a widely
known physician, midwife and nurse and who took care of
the whole village during an epidemic of "spotted fever."

In the settlements of Maine "Granny Winslow" (Anna
Huston Winslow) was "the only physician in whom the
early settlers believed," perhaps because she was, for many
years, the only person with any considerable konwledge of
medicine between Augusta and Bath.[49] Sarah Sands had a
similar rcord on Block Island where she practiced for a
number of years.

No clear distinction can be drawn between the colonial
physicians and midwives, as most of the physicians were
midwives as well as surgeons and general practitioners,

and many midwives acted as physicians or surgeons in emergencies. No attempt is made here to make the groups mutually exclusive, or to sharply differentiate their work.

Bridget Lee of Leyden came to Massachusetts in the *Anne* in 1623.[50] She became the third wife of Samuel Fuller, the first physician of Plymouth. In 1663 the settlers at Rehobeth requested her "to come and dwell amongst us, to attend on the office of midwife, to answer the town's necessity, which at present is great," but she did not accept. In 1626 Goodwife Wright was accused of using witchery in her work as midwife,[51] and in 1639 Anne Hutchinson and Mary Dyer were forced to leave Boston though they were known "to be very helpful in times of childbirth." Ruth Barnaby was born at Marblehead in 1664 and lived to be 101 years old, having served the community as midwife for forty years. Elinnor Baily and Judith March were midwives in Newbury in 1670, and Elizabeth Weeden was a midwife in Boston in 1677, while Mrs. Smith practiced in Essex County in the same year. Goodwife Osgood, Ruth Williams and Mrs. Gatchell also served in Essex County in the 1680s, as did Hannah Greenleaf in Boston and Isabel Babson in Salem in 1637. Later Isabel Babson moved to Gloucester where she received several grants of land as inducements to serve the settlement. Rachel Bunker came to Nantucket Island early in its settlement and is said to have officiated at the birth of 2,994 children. "Old Widow Wiat" who died at the age of ninety-four years in 1705 is reported to have officiated at the birth of 1,100 children, and Elizabeth Phillips of Charlestown, Massachusetts was awarded the following epitaph:

Here Lye Interred Ye
Body of

Mrs. Elizabeth Phillips,
Who
was born in Westminster,
in Great Britain &
commision'd
by John
Lord Bishop of London,
in Ye Year
1718 to ye office of
a Midwife:—
to this country, in
Ye Year 1719, & by
Ye Blessing of God
has brought into
this world above 3,000 children.[52]

She died in 1761 at the age of seventy-six.

In nearby Salem Anne Moore was given a grant of land in 1637 to settle in the town and serve as midwife.[53] In 1772 Mary Bass came from Boston at "the Request of Several Ladies" and pursued "the Business of Midwifery" in the growing town. Twenty years later Mary Wardilloe is reported to have attended at the births of twelve hundred babies very successfully. Thomas Pemberton in his manuscript history of the settlement mentions a midwife in 1787 who had attended at the birth of two thousand children in the village, but he neglected to mention her name. Judge Bentley failed to mention the name of "an antiquated Irish midwife who left all her property to a friend," which indicates perhaps better than anything else the degree of respect accorded the colonial women in medicine.

In Connecticut, Goodwife Beecher and Goodwife Potter came to the colonies in 1630.[54] Both settled among the New Haven colonists and practiced midwifery. In 1655 the town council stated that "It was ordered by the whole town that while the Widow Bradley continueth in the town, and is employed as a midwife, wherein she hath been very helpful, specially to the farms, and doth not refuse when called to it, she shall have a house and home lot, which may be convenient for her rent free." Lydia Robinson of New London is credited with twelve hundred deliveries with not a single case lost in her thirty-five years of practice. "Granny Griswold," the earliest midwife at Wethersfield, had nearly as good a record when she died at eighty years of age. Mary Turner of Newport, Rhode Island, had thirteen children of her own and lived to be eighty-seven years old. The *Newport Mercury* of February 26, 1760, said of her, "an experienced midwife, and otherwise useful in the community of assisting those who labored under the disorders incident to the Human body, with her advice and remedies."

The early Dutch settlers along the Hudson River had no woman physicians, and although Winterbotham reports that medicine was administered only by women in Cape May County in New Jersey, no records of their work are available.[55] De Kalm in his *Travels* (1748) mentions that "an old Swede remembered that his mother cured many people of dropsy by a decoction of the root of sassafras in water, but she used at the same time to cup the patient on the feet." Some patients were brought to this woman "Wrapped in sheets." In 1754 Margaret Powell advertised in the *New York Gazette* that she could cure "all Rheumatic Pains, sore legs and cataracts of the Eyes; but above all the canker, either in nose, mouth or throat" but she did not claim to be a physician.

On Long Island the records of 1780 mention the death of Mrs. Elizabeth King who had served the colonists as physician for thirty-odd years and assisted at over one thousand births.[56] Mrs. Peck had been a worthy midwife of Southold, Long Island, from 1760 to her death in 1775; Mrs. Lucretia Lester took over Mrs. King's practice and was "respected as nurse and doctress" for another thirty years, and Susannah Brown who had also been a doctor for twenty-six years, attended at 1,400 births and lived to be eighty-nine years old.

Elizabeth Ellet in her *Domestic History of the American Revolution* states that "A Lady in Ulster County, New York, studied medicine to aid homemakers while the doctors were with the army and to attend to the poor families in the country around her," [57] but unfortunately does not give us any facts about the woman herself. Margaret Hill Morris did the same kind of work in Philadelphia. She had a "very considerable knowledge of medicine and really practiced medicine. At one time she was treating thirty patients with small pox."

As will be recalled, the Dutch settlers along the Hudson River greatly prized their midwives.[58] Maryje Jans came in 1626 and was the first of a distinguished line of women in this field of medicine. She was followed by Eva Pietersen Evertsen who was the first of the midwives to be paid by the Dutch West India Company. Tryntae Jonas of Rotterdam sought employment with the Company, arrived in New Amsterdam in 1630 and was given a house on Pearl Street in 1635. Lysbet Dircksen became the town midwife in 1638 and a house was built for her by the colony. In 1655 Hellezord Joris became the town midwife and in 1660 was paid one hundred guilders to attend the poor of the settlement.

In 1670, six years after the British took over the colony, the Governor licensed Tryntje Meljers as an approved midwife for the settlement at Albany, New York, "in which Imployment she hath Continued for y span of fourteen years past in good reputation not refusing her assistance bot on y contrary affording her best help to y poorer sorte of people out of Christian Charity, as well as to ye richer sorte for reward, and there being severall other less skilfull women who upon occasion will pretend to be midwives where they can gain by it but refuse their helpe to y poore. These presents Certifye That I doe allow of y said Tryntje Meljers to be one of y profest sworn midwives at Albany, and that she and one more skilfull woman be only admitted to Undertake ye same there except upon Extraordinary occasions. They continuing their Charitable assistance to y poore and a diligent attendance on their calling." [59]

The custom of the Dutch women being attended by mid-wives of their own nationality seems to have survived well into the eighteenth century. It is not until after the middle of the century that we find English women advertising in the newspapers. Among the first such advertisements is that of Mrs. Ridgely, "Midwife, from London." She stated that, "Having practised for many years in that opulent city, with great success . . . she intends during her stay to resume that Practice, on a proper Recommendation, from Gentle-men of the Faculty; and will most carefully, tenderly, and punctually attend those Ladies who may please to favour her with their commands. . . ." [60] While other English women undoubtedly practiced midwifery in the colony, we found no reference to them.

Anne Parsons was mentioned earlier as the midwife who attended Hannah Penn in January, 1700, in Philadelphia. [61] She was an able midwife as was Mary Brodwell who served the settlement until 1730 when she died at the age of one

hundred years. Eunice Sprague was well known for her
work in Wyoming Valley, Pennsylvania. Mary East came
to Trenton, New Jersey, in 1780 from Albany, New York,
where she had practiced midwifery for thirty years. She assured the public that "She will with alacrity attend the calls
of those who will please to favour her with their custom,
and is to be met with at the Brewery, next door below Mr.
Pott's." Jemima Crane of the same city had some difficulty
but assured the public that "her unwearied study and endeavors to render her knowledge in the art of midwifery,
as compleat as the nature of it will admit, will prove pow-
erful inducements to engage the good opinion of the public in general. . . ." What her difficulty was is not explained.
She refers to it as "her past unfortunate history" and begs
the public "to look upon her with an eye of favor and humanity." Let us hope that they did, for she, along with the
other women in this field of medicine, was fighting a losing
battle against the invicible odds of professionally trained
personnel.

About Susannah Rohrer Muller we know a little more because she kept a journal, which has been preserved.[62] She
was born in Pennsylvania in 1756, left an orphan at an early
age, and married to her guardian when she was seventeen
years old. She had ten children of her own, but after her
sixth child she decided to help other women with their
childbearing problems, and two of her daughters followed
in her footsteps. She kept a record of her work which includes attendance at about 1,749 births. Besides her work
as a midwife she was consulted on many other medical
problems and was one of the first to use the new vaccination for smallpox.

There is a delightful letter in the archives of the College

of Physicians of Philadelphia dated June 2, 1774, from John Fothergill of London to William Logan of Philadelphia, recommending Mary Wesley who was coming to the colony. It reads in part:

Dear Friend,

The Bearer Mary Wesley, is the person I have engaged, to come over as a Midwife, a station that I think her very well qualified for both by nature and instruction. She has spared neither application nor expence to acquire a thorough knowledge of her business, and I think I may safely say, without depreciating any one, that she comes over as well qualified both to practice and instruct as any of her own sex, (and perhaps most of the other) as ever came to America. . . . I must desire thee to lend her what assistance she may want, till she gets into business, and draw upon me for what thou advances. Help her to a proper situation, which should be near the center of Friends, in a reputable part of the city, in a place easy to find and not difficult of access." [63]

The records of the Maryland courts mention at least four women doctors between 1643 and 1663.[64] Katherine Hebden and her carpenter husband Thomas entered several complaints for payment for her "chirurgery" and "physick"; Mary Bradnox sued William Cos for a calf as payment for her services, and Oliver Spry's wife sued Hambleton for a fortnight's work in the care of his wife, whom Mrs. Spry cured of "some Distemper." She was awarded 600 pounds of tobacco. Mary Vanderdonck O'Neal was a highly successful "doctoress" in Charles County where she did not hesitate to arraign her debtors into court when they did not pay their bills promptly. Among the midwives of Maryland were Mary Clocker (1651) Mrs. Johnson, Rose Smith and Mary Callahan about whom the *Maryland Gazette* stated in 1761 that "she was for many years an eminent midwife."

In Virginia Sarah Overstreet, who was the widow of a physician, filed a bill for her services in 1670 for her "trouble and pains" and for "funeral charges," but she does not appear to have claimed to be physician.[65] Mary Seal, Mrs. Edward Good, and Martha Stratton appear to have practiced medicine between 1680 and 1690. Katherine Shrewsbury is mentioned in 1693 as a school dame and female practitioner and is credited with saving the life of a man who was bitten by a poisonous snake. William Byrd referred to Mrs. Flemming as a "notable quack" and to Mrs. Levistone as a woman "who acts her in the double Capacity of a Doctress and Coffee Woman."

William Byrd's remarks and the limited number of references to women in the field of medicine in Virginia suggest that the inhabitants were more reluctant to accept women as physicians and surgeons than the New England settlers. This was apparently not so true for women as midwives.[66] As early as 1634 Widow Hollis is mentioned as being paid twelve hens for her services as a midwife. Fifty years later Mauldin Mayor was paid the same fee for the same service. Mrs. Haywood delivered the twentieth child of Rachel Thurston in 1652 with skill and care. Dorothy Bullock, Susannah Evans, Elizabeth Tindall and Goodwife Thorpe are mentioned in the records as serving the women of Virginia as midwives during the last half of the 17th century.

In the following century, as newspapers became available, several of the progressive midwives advertised themselves or were mentioned in the news columns.[67] Catherine Blaikley of Williamsburg, who died in her seventy-sixth year (1771), was mentioned as "an eminent midwife, . . .

who in the course of her practice brought upwards of three thousand Children into the World." In the same year Mary Rose put an advertisement in the *Virginia Gazette* stating that she had "studied and practised Midwifery for some Time past, with Success, . . . Ladies and others, are therefore desired to take Notice that they will be waited upon on the Shortest Warning, by their humble Servant." Two years later Mrs. Hughes, who had practiced midwifery for a number of years in the West Indies, came to Virginia and advertised that she could cure "ringworms, scald heads, sore eyes, the piles, worms in children and several other disorders," and she added, "No cure, no pay." However, her practice must not have been adequate to her needs as she also advertised her women's wear shop in which she carried dresses, cloaks, bonnets and calashes for sale. Julia Wheatley also advertised in the *Virginia Gazette* in 1776, but little is known of her practice.

At Charleston Mary Harris advertised her services as a midwife in 1738, and four years later Rebecca Pollard advised the public that she was "ready to wait on any sick Persons or Lying-in Women." [68] Twenty years later she assured the public that she was successful in handling cases of smallpox. Jane Creighton offered her services as midwife in 1745, and Elizabeth Hunt in 1766 is said to have delivered nearly four thousand children during her long years as a midwife. In 1771 Mary Kelsey advertised her liquor and dry goods store and assured the public that she was "ready to attend all such as shall be pleased to employ her as midwife." In 1768 Mrs. Grant advertised in the *South Carolina Gazette* that she had "studied that art regularly and practised it afterwards, with success at Edinburgh." Mrs. Brown in Charleston (1791) and Mrs. Munroe in New York City (1796) made similar claims for their medical education and previous practice and hoped the ladies of those cities would call upon them when needed.

Nurses who cared for bed patients in their homes were mentioned frequently in diaries, court records and correspondence, but often even their names are not included.[69] In New Amsterdam a nurse, Catelina de Trico, was included in the first group of traders, and the Dutch West India Company Charter of 1629 required that "Patroons and colonists . . . shall for the first procure a Comforter of the Sick there." Three of these *ziezkenstroosters* came with the first boat-loads of settlers, but further mention of nurses in the colony is very slight.

Homemakers who were paid by the local governments to care for the sick and indigent inhabitants are often named in the records, their services mentioned and generally the payment given them.[70] The Essex County, Massachusetts records of 1645 states that the county paid "to Goodwife Bullocke for fyve day attendance in sickness 7 [shillings] 6 [pence]" and to Ruth Williams four shillings for her nursing service in 1681. Topsfield, Massachusetts, paid Hanna Averill regularly for eight years (1722–1730) to care for Widow Averill who was an indigent invalid. At Buzzards Bay, Massachusetts, the town paid twenty-one pounds for the care and keep of James Bump in 1747. By 1770 the town set a uniform price of three pounds per year for the care of an indigent inhabitant. At Worcester (1778) Eleanor Walker was paid five pounds, 2 shillings for caring for Mary Hamilton and Martha Wiley was paid thirty-six pounds, eight shillings for board and nursing of Margaret Miles for one year.

In Maryland the provincial court ordered Calvert County to pay Mary Gilford for caring for a sick boy in 1659.[71] In North Carolina Mary Blount was paid forty shillings for caring for an indigent man and burying him in 1708, and Mrs. Robinson was paid a monthly stipend of one hundred pounds of tobacco for the care of a "poor decrepid man." In Virginia Elizabeth Morgan was given three hundred pounds for her care of Susannah Middleton for three months and the cure of her "sore legge," and at William and Mary College a nurse was hired in 1761 to care for the sick students in the dormitory.

The homemakers who nursed the indigent sick of the communities appear to have had no special training for their work. Occasionally they are referred to as nurses or "goodwives," but generally merely as women who were willing to add the care of a sick or indigent person to their household tasks for a specified sum of money. In one town in Massachusetts the plan of farming out the indigent proved so profitable that no "poor house" was needed. It is evident that the women found the work and pay acceptable for the practice continued and in time became one of the bases for our present public health programs.

Very few colonial homemakers worked in hospitals in the early years of colonization. When the first hospital was built at Jamestown, Virginia, in 1612 there were "keepers to attend" the sick "for their comfort and recoverie," but whether they were men or women, paid workers or volunteers, is not clear in the records.[72]

Some of the nuns who came to New Orleans in 1727 worked in the semi-military hospital of the colony.[73] The Ursuline Order of nuns continued to serve in the hospital until 1763 when they decided to confine their work to the field of teaching. Hilletje Wilbruch was matron of the first hospital in New York in 1658 and was paid one hundred florins a year.[74] Elizabeth Gardner was matron of the first hospital in Philadelphia in 1755. About twenty years later Alice

Redman, who was a nurse in a state hospital in Maryland, found the conditions so difficult after a year of service that she formally petitioned the Governor and Council. She stated in part, "Your petitioner humbly beg for an augmentation to her pay as she only is allowed two dollars a month. She has at this present time sixteen men for to cook and take care off she your petitioner as since she has been a nurse had a great deal of trouble she is oblige to be up day and night with some of the patients and never has been allowed so much as a little Tea, or Coffee which she your petitioner hopes your honors will take this petition into your consideration and your Petitioner in duty Bound will Ever Pray. P.S. She your Petitioner out of that two dollars pr month is oblige to buy brooms and soap we wash with if your honors will please to relieve your petitioner your petitioner will ever be bound to pray." [75] It is hoped that some action was taken in her behalf, but her petition came during the years of the Revolution when Maryland was intensely involved in the war.

The women also nursed in military hospitals and served the armies during field maneuvers.[76] Mrs. Allyn had been paid twenty pounds for her medical services to the soldiers during King Philip's War by the Council of Connecticut, and Sargent David Holden mentioned a number of women who served the army during the French and Indian War in New England. In Maryland Elizabeth Black and Eleanor Felton were among those who were known to have served the armed forces during the same war. These women baked bread, cooked food, washed clothes and cared for the wounded and sick soldiers.

Charlotte Browne, who traveled as Matron of the nursing service with General Edward Braddock's Army in the colonies in 1754–1757, left fragmentary diary, which gives us fleeting glimpses of the life and work of a nurse in the military service of the period. She wrote, "June 2, Very busy making Bread and Ginger Bread and boiling hams for one March. . . . The Roads are so Bad that I am almost disjointed. . . . June 5. We halted this Day, all the Nurses Baking Bread and Boiling Beef for the March to Morrow. . . . June 7. Having no Room to lodge in I lay'd in the Chimney, so wanted no calling in the Morning having no sleep all Night. At 4 we began to March. . . . Great Gusts of Rain, My Wagon and every thing in it wet and all the Sick allmost drown'd."[77]

By 1776 the need for nurses to serve the armed forces both in the field and in the hospitals greatly increased. Notices like the following appeared in the newspapers.

Wanted for the Continental Hospital in Williamsburg, some Nurses to attend the sick. Any such coming well recommended, will have good encouragement by applying to the Director of the hospital.[78]

The shortage of nurses became more serious as the war progressed. For instance, on May 31, 1778, Brigadier General Waine ordered that "The Commanding Officers of Regim'ts will assist the Regimental Surgeons in procuring as many Women of the Army as Can be prevailed on to serve as nurses to them who will be paid the usual price."

Similar orders were issued by other generals, and many patriotic women responded, but references to them are too fragmentary to draw any conclusions regarding their contribution as nurses to the war effort.

The colonial homemakers who entered the field of medicine did so almost incidentally, largely out of their desire to serve their neighbors or those less fortunate than themselves, as was said of Anne Eliot, who served "especially among the poor, to whom with a large charity she dispensed salutary medicine"; of Mary Hazard, who succored the poor without recompense, or of Susannah Miller, who entered the field of medicine as a dedicated midwife in direct opposition to her husband's wishes. He wanted her to earn money by doing fine needlework, but Susannah had heard the call of women in pain and was not deterred from her mission of helping them. The medical women in general were the "goodwives" of the settlements who helped those in pain and for which they were sometimes paid. It is quite evident that the practice of medicine, even midwifery, which was the most demandng, was more or less of a side-line activity for which no other training was needed than that afforded by experience under the tutelage of an older woman in the field and the reading of the medical books that were available to them.

That many of them desired greater knowledge is evident in the records. As early as 1633 Anne Eliot "earnestly availed herself of the best medical works that she could obtain, to increase her knowledge and confidence in its application." Sarah Alcock assisted her husband in collecting nearly fifty books in the field of medicine. Lady Apsley Fenwick sought medical information from Dr. Thomas Pell at the Fort near her home. Mary Turner, who had thirteen children of her own and lived to be 87 years old, between cases "employed all her leisure hours in reading," and Jemima Crane, who gave "unwearied study and endeavors to render her knowledge in the Art of Midwifery as compleat as the nature of it will admit," are good examples of the intellectual interests of the medical women.

Another evidence of their desire for more knowledge in th field is shown by their continual experimentation, much of which was fruitless or even dangerous.[79] However, Anne

Ferguson developed a medicine oil from cypress trees, Catherine Ramsay extracted opium from her flower bed, and Mary Johnson and Constant Woodson sought a cure for cancer and were successful enough to gain financial support from the Virginia Assembly. Hundreds of homemakers experimented with herbs and oils to find remedies to relieve the sufferings of their patients. While their experiments sound weird to us today, they were in general a sincere expression of the colonial medical women's desire to better understand their field of work and alleviate human suffering.

It should be remembered that the whole field of scientific medicine was just beginning to emerge in the centers of learning in England and on the continent where women were admitted to the Guilds and to most of the advanced medical training. When men and women trained in these centers of medical education began to emigrate to the colonies, the whole field of medical practice began to change for the better. Medical education took on a new significance. In 1772, for instance, Mary Bass not only offered her experience as a guarantee of her worth, but also advertised that she had been "instructed and recommended by the First Practioners in Midwifery in Boston."

Medical women emigrating to the colonies began to advertise their medical training, notably Mrs. Ridgely in 1765, who was trained in London, and Mrs. Grant (1768), Mary Rose (1771), Mrs. Brown (1791) and Mrs. Monroe (1796), who inserted advertisements in the newspapers similar to the following, which was sent in by Mrs. Malcolm to the *Independent Journal* in New York City September 30, 1785.

Mrs. Malcolm, Begs leave to inform the Public, that she has lately arrived from Edinburgh, where she studied and practiced Midwifery for a considerable number of years, and had the honour of attending several ladies of the first rank in that City. She has recommendations from most of the principal Professors of that art in Scotland, with a Diploma from the late Dr. Thomas Young, Professor of Midwifery in the University of Edinburgh. Any ladies chusing to employ her will be immediately waited upon by sending to her lodgings at Mr. Vanantwerp's, no. 61 Maiden Lane, and they may depend upon the utmost care and attention being paid them in the way of her business.

The number of women trained in medicine who immigrated to the colonies during the last half of the eighteenth century was very limited, while the number of men so trained was numerous. Also a considerable number of colonial medical men went to England or the continent for more training than they had received in the colonies, but no instance of a colonial medical woman going abroad for further training was found. It is one thing for a modern young woman to step over to the university in her town and take a course in biology, but it was quite another matter for a colonial woman with half a dozen children to cross the ocean and study medicine for a year or two as the men did. The situation illustrate a basic difference between men and women in any vocation. Men have little or no hesitation in placing their vocation, whether scientific, literary or mechanical, above home ties for extended lengths of time. Few women in any generation achieve a similar detachment from their homes. Only the Quaker women preachers appear to have achieved it in colonial times.

This does not mean that the colonial women in medicine did not want further training or did not try to get it. A number of women studied under individual doctors in their own locale. In Philadelphia in 1765 Dr. William

Shippen the younger, recognizing the seriousness of the situation, offered to give a course of lectures to the midwives of the vicinity. His announcement of the course brings the whole problem into stark relief. He stated in part:

Having been lately called to the assistance of a number of women in the country, in difficult labours, most of which were made so by the unskilful old women about them; the poor women have suffered extremely, and their innocent little ones were entirely destroyed, whose lives might have been easily saved by proper management; And being informed of several desperate cases in the different neighborhoods which have proved fatal to the mothers as well as to their infants, and were attended with the most painful circumstances, too dismal to be related, he thought it his duty immediately to begin his intended course of lectures on midwifery and has prepared a proper apparatus for that purpose, in order to instruct women who have had virtue enough to own their ignorance and apply for instruction, as well as all those young gentlemen now engaged in the study of that useful and necessary branch of surgery who are taking pains to qualify themselves to practice in different parts of the country, with safety and advantage to their fellow creatures.

The doctor proposes to begin his first course as soon as a number of pupils sufficient to defray the necessary expense shall apply. A course will consist of about 20 lectures, in which he will treat of that part of the anatomy which is necessary to that branch, explain all cases of midwifery, etc.

The female pupils to be taught privately, and assisted at any of their private labours when necessary.[80]

We find no record as to how many women attended the course or how many times Dr. Shippen gave the course. It was so soon over-ridden by the interest taken in the successful medical school, which was started the same year and attended only by men students. Three years later a medical school was started at King's College in New York City, and in 1783 Harvard College opened its medical school in Boston. Others followed, all open to men only. It was more than half a century before twelve dedicated, if "indelicate," women enrolled in the Boston Female Medical School and others two years later in the Woman's Medical College at Philadelphia.

17

Blossoms of the Heart and Scions of the Mind

Out of the blood, sweat and tremendous effort of a transplanted people to transform a dark wilderness into a semblance of the civilization they had left, there rose a few voices that transcended the sounds of the travail. Some of these were the voices of women. How they found time and energy to write poetry, or novels, or histories, or essays amid the confusion of large families, crowded quarters and continual danger is still a mystery. That only a few were able to do so is understandable. During the century of the first migrations only the poems of Anne Bradstreet, the slight historical essay of Anne Cotton, and the narrative of Mary Rowlandson have come down to us.

We do not even know when or where Anne Dudley Bradstreet, our first poet, was born or where she was buried.[1] We only know that she was born somewhere in England, probably in 1612, before her father became steward to the Earl of Lincoln at Sempringham and Tattershall Castle. Anne was, in her person, the epitome of the intelligent colonial woman who came to New England. She had their enduring toughness of courage that survived Indian raids, fires, droughts, tornadoes and many illnesses. She is remembered and honored because her escape from unbearable hardships found expression in poetry, while others found it in religious fanaticism, gruelling work, or insanity. From all accounts she was a woman of high integrity who sought answers to the ultimate questions of life and found solace in her religious faith.

Until she was about sixteen years old she lived with her parents in an atmosphere of intellectual stimulation, material comfort and religious and political unrest. Her father was very well educated and continued his intellectual interests in spite of his intensely Puritanic beliefs. He is said to have brought fifty or sixty books with him on the tiny ship *Arabella* and to have deeply influenced Anne's thinking.

At sixteen years of age Anne married Simon Bradstreet, sometime fellow at Emanuel College, protegé of her father and a puritan of slightly less intensity of belief than her father. He also was widely read and had a library of 800 books at the time their house was burned to the ground in 1666. Anne apparently took full advantage of the cultural life of her home and family. She was a great admirer of the French poet Du Bartas and was familiar with Shakespeare, Spencer and half a dozen other poets of her day. But, in none of these was she as consistent a student as in her study of the Bible and its historical background.

Her extensive reading may in part have been due to her frail constitution, for she was ill intermittently throughout her life and a helpless invalid the last five years. During her many periods of convalescence she read widely and "prayed without ceasing," for her home was ruled by an intense religious fervor that believed a person was "never too little to go to hell." In her "Religious Experiences,"

which are in prose and were included in the second edition
of her poems, she relates that, "In my young years, about
6 or 7 as I take it, I began to make conscience of my
wayes, and what I knew was sinfull, as lying and disobedience to Parents, &c I avoided it. If at any time I was
overtaken with the like evills, it was great Trouble. . . . I
also found much comfort in reading the Scriptures, especially those places I thought most concerned my Condition,
and as I grew to have more understanding, so the more
solace I took in them. . . . But as I grew to bee about 14 or
15 I found my heart more carnall and sitting loose from
God, vanity and the folleys of youth take hold of me.
About 16, the Lord layd his hand fore upon me and smott
mee with the small pox. When I was in my affliction, I
besought the Lord and confessed my Pride and Vanity and
he was entreated of me, and again restored me. . . . After
a short time I changed my condition and was marryed and
came into the Country, where I found a new world and
new manners, at which my heart rose. But after I was convinced it was the way of God, I submitted to it and joined
to the church at Boston." This was the same church in
which Ann Hutchinson and Mary Dyer were condemned
a few years later.

Anne goes on to say, "I have had great experiences of
God's hearing my prayers, and returning comfortable Answers to me, either in granting ye Thing I prayed for, or
else in satisfying my mind without it." But she continued
to be dissatisfied with the narrow doctrines of the Puritans,
as she stated, "I have often been perplexed that I have
not found the constant Joy in my Pilgrimage and refreshing which I supposed most of the servants of God hath.
. . . Many times hath Satan troubled me concerning the
verity of the Scriptures, Many times by Atheisme how I

could know whether there was a God; I never saw any
miracles to confirm me and those which I read of how did
I know but they were feigned. . . . When I have gott over
this Block, then have I another putt in my way, That ad-
mitt this bee the true God whom wee worship, and that
bee his word, yet why may not the Popish Religion be the
right? They have the same God, the same Christ, the same
word: they only interpret it one way, wee another. . . . But
some new Troubles I have had since the world has been
filled with Blasphemy, and Sectaries, and some who have
been accounted sincere Christians have been carried away
with them, that sometimes I have said, Is there ffaith upon
the earth? and I have not known what to think." [2]

We do not know when she wrote this quotation, but it
is obvious that her questioning mind kept her from joining
either side of the vicious religious controversies that splin-
tered the unity of the colony. Yet it is remarkable that the
daughter of Thomas Dudley and wife of Simon Bradstreet
did not at anytime express herself directly on such violent
questions as those raised by Anne Hutchinson and Mary
Dyer. Anne Bradstreet lived in the midst of these controversies, for her father was governor, or deputy governor of the
colony and her husband was a public official throughout
the period. She must have known of the death penalty in
the 1636 law against witches and the first hanging of a
witch in 1648 at Cambridge. She could hardly have escaped hearing the heated antinomian fight and the excommunication of Anne Hutchinson and Deborah Moody, nor
of the treatment of the Quakers including the hanging of
Mary Dyer in 1658. These events were part of her daily
life. She may have known these women personally, or attended their trials with her father or husband who sat in

judgment upon them, yet except for the vague reference to "Blasphemy, and Sectaries" quoted above, she made no statement about the events.

On only one current question did Anne express herself in poetry. This was in her "Dialogue between Old England and New England." [3] The poem was written in 1642 at a time when Charles I was beginning to regret the liberal charter he had given the Massachusetts Bay Company and was threatening to alter the charter. While it is evident that Anne was a monarchist at heart, she clearly sympathized with the independent spirit of the colonists. Her summary of the political situation was highly praised by her family and friends.

In spite of her frail health, about which she wrote at least nine poems between 1632 and 1669, she wrote a number of lengthy poems, most of them before she was thirty years old. These had been passed around among her friends, and when her brother-in-law, Rev. John Woodbridge, pastor of the Andover church, went to England in 1647, he took with him what was probably the best maunscript copy of her poems.[4] He registered these in a book named *The Tenth Muse lately Sprung up in America, written by Anne Bradstreet* on July 1, 1650, at The Company of Stationers in London, for which he paid the six pence rate. The book contained two hundred and seven pages which were 5½ by 3¾ inches in size. Besides her poems the book contained a preface by her brother-in-law, eight introductory poems of commendation and two anagrams. The second edition was published in Boston in 1678, six years after her death, largely due to her son Simon's efforts. It included her later poems and prose writings. The third edition was also published in Boston, but no printer or publisher was indicated; the fourth and definitive edition by John H. Ellis was published in Boston in 1758.

Her poems fall into four natural groupings: [5] her four by four allegorical personages, which are the longest and most pretentous of her poems, her miscellaneous poems of which "Contemplations" is the most gracious, her poems about her family and home, and her poems about herself and her poetry. Of her allegorical poems the "Four Monarchies," which she never finished, takes up one hundred and fourteen pages in *The Tenth Muse*. In it she sought to compare the degradation of ancient times with the enlightenment of her Christian world. Hardly a line is more than a rhymed paraphrasing of Raleigh's and other current histories with tyrants rampant and kingdoms like Sodom reeking in blood and sin. She worked on it for seventeen years, and beyond giving her gymnastic-like exercise in rhetoric, it probably was the outlet for her deeper fears and frustrations. In the lurid allegories she could safely express her hates and resentments without the danger of censure from family and friends.

In her shorter poems she wrote of Sir Philip Sidney and Du Bartas, whom she greatly admired, and of Queen Elizabeth. After praising the Queen's wisdom, she puts the question:

> Now say, have women worth? Or have they none?
> Or had they some, but with our Queen is't gone?
> Nay Masculines, you have thus taxt us long,
> But she, though dead, will vindicate our wrong.
> Let such as say our Sex is void of Reason,
> Know tis a Slander now, but once was Treason.[6]

In "Contemplations" Anne expresses her most serene mood.

Some time now past in the Autumnal Tide,
When Phoebus wanted but one hour to bed,
The trees all richly clad, yet void of pride,
Were gilded o'er by his rich golden head.
Their leaves and fruits see'd painted, but was true
Of green, of red, of yellow, mixed hew,
Rapt were my senses at this delectable view.

I wist not what to wish, yet sure though I,
If so much excellence abide below;
How excellent is He that dwells on high?
Whose power and beauty by His works we know.
Sure He is goodness, wisdome, glory, light,
That hath this under world so richly dight:
More Heaven than Earth was here no winter and no night.

I heard the merry grasshopper then sing,
The black-clad cricket, bear a second part,
They kept one tune, and played on the same string,
Seeming to glory in their little Art.
Shall creatures abject, thus their voices raise?
And in their kind resound their Maker's praise:
Whilst I as mute, can warble forth no higher layes?

Under the cooling shadow of a stately elm
Close sat I by a goodly rivers side,
Where gliding streams the rocks did overwhelm;
A lonely place, with pleasures dignified.
I once that lov'd the shady woods so well,
Now thought the rivers did the trees excell,
And if the sun would ever shine, there would I dwell.[7]

She composed two dozen or more short poems on occasions of importance to her family, on the burning of her home and of her deep love of her husband, as seen in the following excerpts:

VERSES UPON THE BURNING OF OUR HOUSE

When by the ruines oft I passed,
My sorrowing eyes aside did cast,
And here and there the places spy,
Where oft I sat, and long did lie.

Here stood that trunk, and there that chest;
There lay that store I counted best:
My pleasant things in ashes lie,
And them behold no morè shall I.
Under thy roof no guest shall sit,
Not at thy table eat a bit;

No pleasant tale shall e'er be told,
Nor things recounted of old;
No candle e'er shall shine in thee,
Nor bridegroom's voice e'er heard shall be.
In silence shalt thou ever lie.
Adieu, adieu; all's vanity.[8]

TO MY DEAR LOVING HUSBAND

If ever two were one, then surely we.
If ever man were lov'd by wife, then thee;
If ever wife was happy in a man,
Compare with me ye women if you can.
I prize thy love more than whole mines of gold.
Or all the riches that the East doth hold.
My love is such that rivers cannot quench,
Nor aught but love from thee, give recompence.
Thy love is such I can no way repay,
The heavens reward thee manifold, I pray!
Then while we live, in love lets go persever,
That when we live no longer, we may live ever.[9]

About herself and her work she wrote in her "Prologue to the Four Elements":

I am obnoxious to each carping tongue
Who says my hand a needle better fits,
A Poets pen all scorn I should thus wrong,
For such despite they cast on Female wits:
If what I do prove well, it won't advance,
They'll say it's stol'n, or else it was by chance.

But when my wondring eyes and envious heart
Great Barta's sugar'd lines do but read o're
Fool I do grudg the muses did not part
'Twixt him and me that overfluent store;
A Bartas can, do what Bartas will
   But simple I according to my skill.

Let Greeks be Greeks, and women what they Are
Men has precedency and still excell,
It is but vain unjustly to wage warre;
Men can do best, and women know it well
Preheminence in all and each is yours;
Yet grant some small acknowledgement of ours.

And Oh ye high flown quills that soar the Skies,
And ever with your prey still catch your praise,
If e're you daigne these lowly lines your eyes
Give Thyme or Parsley wreath, I ask no bayes,
This mean and unrefined ure of mine
Will make you glistring gold, but more to shine.[30]

After she received copies of the first edition of her poems
she set to work and revise and improve them. She wrote:

Thou ill-formed offspring of my feeble brain,
Who after birth did'st by my side remain,
Till snatched from thence by friends, less wise than true
Who thee abroad, expos'd to publick view,

Made thee in raggs, halting to th' press to trudg,
Where errors were not lessened (all may judg)
At thy return my blushing was not small,
My rambling brat (in print) should mother call,
I cast thee by as one unfit for light,
Thy visage was so irksome in my sight;
Yet being mine own, at length affection would
Thy blemishes amend, if so I could:
I wash'd thy face, but more defects I saw, . . .[13]

She was still at the revisions when her home and all of her papers were burned. Her last poem was written in the summer of 1669, three years before her death from tuberculosis. In it she expresses her great weariness of soul.

As weary pilgrim now at rest,
Hugs with delight his silent nest
His wasted limbs now lye full soft
That myrie steps have trodden oft.
Blesses himself to think upon
His dangers past and travails done.

Oh how I long to be at rest
And soar on high among the blesst.[12]

It is little wonder she was weary, for she had struggled all her life. Though she was financially well-to-do, she had to endure all of the hardships of primitive living. She moved to three new settlements, each time deeper into the wilderness, and bore eight children, all but one of whom survived her. Nor little wonder that the pious Rev. John Norton declared her a "peerless gentlewoman, the mirror of her age and glory of her sex." Today we can only marvel at her intrepid courage and accomplishment.

During the eighteenth century there were at least fifteen colonial homemakers who wrote poetry that was published, some posthumously. Eight of these were New Englanders, two of whom were Negroes. Elizabeth Foster Vergoose (1665–1757) of Boston was probably the author of the first edition of *Songs for the Nursery or Mother Goose's Melodies for Children,* which was printed by "T. Fleet at his printing House, Pudding Lane, 1719, Price two coppers," in Boston.[13] It is thought that Mrs. Vergoose read, or sang, folklore verses and rhymes of her own invention to her children and the children of the neighborhood, to whom she became "Mother Goose" through a corruption of her name. Finally she wrote the verses down for possible publication. No copy of the Fleet edition is extant. The earliest American edition, of which there are existing copies, was printed by Isaiah Thomas in Worcester, Massachusetts, in 1785. "Mother Goose" was buried in Boston near the Commons where children today still go to pay her homage.

Jane Colman Turell (1708–1735) was the daughter of Rev. Benjamin Colman of Boston who took a strange delight in his precocious daughter.[14] He taught her the catechism and may psalms and poems so that she could recite them at four years of age while sitting on the dinner table to entertain his guests. She became one of the best educated persons in the colony, having read practically every available book. She married Rev. Ebenezer Turell of Medford, Massachusetts, on August 11, 1726, and had three children, all of whom died early. Her first child was stillborn, and on the death of her second child who lived only eleven days she wrote:

> Ten days I hold him in my joyful arms,
> And feast my eyes upon his youthful charms;

But when the king of terrors does advance
To pierce its bosom with his iron lance.
Its soul released, upward takes its flight,
Oh, nevermore below to bless my sight!
Farewell, sweet babe! I hope to meet above,
And there with you sing our Redeemer's love.[15]

Jane Turell's poems and prose writings were collected by
her husband after her death at twenty-seven years of age,
and published under the title *Memoirs of the Life and
Death of that Pious and Ingenious Gentlewoman, Mrs.
Jane Turrell* in 1735.

Elizabeth Whitman (1751–1788), who is known under
the pseudonym of Eliza Wharton, was also the daughter of
a minister, living in Hartford, Connecticut.[16] She is thought
to have been the paramour of Judge Pierpont Edwards,
but this was denied by his family. She came to the Bell
Tavern in Danvers, Connecticut, in the spring of 1788 and
had a still-born child. She died September 20 of the same
year. Her poems found among her papers were mournful
and without great poetic quality. She would probably have
been forgotten if Hannah Foster had not used her tragedy
as the basis for her famous novel.

Judith Sargent (1751–1820) was born in Gloucester,
Massachusetts, into a prosperous mercantile family.[17] She
was tutored with her brother by Rev. John Rogers, a graduate of Harvard College, and married John Stevens when
she was eighteen years old. The young couple were apparently very happy. He was at first very successful in his
business. Her first published work appeared two years before his death. The article, "Encouraging a Degree of Self-
Complacency, Especially in Female Bosoms," appeared in
The Gentleman and Lady's Town and Country Magazine

in Boston in October, 1784, and was signed "Constantia."

Two years after the death of John Stevens, Judith married Rev. John Murray in whom she had become interested due to his religious convictions and work. He was one of the chief founders of the Independent Christian Universalist's Church, and she joined him in his vigorous work for the establishment of the sect in New England.

Between 1789 and 1794 sixteen of her poems were published in *The Massachusetts Magazine* often signed with her pseudonym. The *Boston Weekly Magazine* published seven other of her poems. Besides her shorter poems she wrote three plays, mostly in verse, and *The Gleaners,* which was a three volume collection of essays. Her plays, *The Medium, or Virtue Triumphant* and *The Traveller Returned,* were performed on March 2, 1795, and March 9, 1796, at the Federal Street Theatre in Boston, which had been opened in 1794. Thus, she is probably the first American woman to have her plays performed professionally, if briefly.

Her plays and much of her poetry were seriously criticized by Thomas Paine and other writers but continued to attract attention. In her introduction to a discussion of Charles I she wrote:

> Soft tears of pity trickling from the eye
> The cheeks of youth, with added charms supply;
> The pearly dew the yielding heart refine
> While every thought benevolence entwines.[18]

While in the 14th number of *The Gleaner* on the ingratitude of mankind she wrote:

> Why dwell forever on the gloomy side?
> Say, doth not God unerring preside?

> Why then ungratfully presume to scan
> With impious cavils marking every plan?
> Though truth and justice both surround his throne,
> And mercy gems the glories of his crown.[19]

Her contribution lies in her pioneering efforts to establish the fact that women could be devoted wives and mothers and still have time and energy to produce intellectual works of significant value. Her last work was the completion of her husband's autobiography on which he had been working for several years. After his death in 1815 she went to live with her daughter in Natchez, Louisiana, where she died in 1820.

Two of the eight New England poets of the last half of the eighteenth century were Negroes. Lucy Terry was a slave of Ensign Ebenezer Wells of Deerfield, Massachusetts, and was probably the first Negro in America to write poetry.[20] In 1746 she wrote a poem describing the Indian raid on Deerfield which was accurate, forceful and highly commended. Phillis Wheatley was born about 1755 in Africa.[21] She was brought to Boston and sold to Mrs. John Wheatley in 1761. She learned English very rapidly and was encouraged to study Latin and to read extensively. Before she was eighteen years old she had written a number of poems and had astonished the enlightened of Boston with her intellectual abilities. In her poem, "Being Brought from Africa to America" she stated:

> Twas mercy brought me from my Pagan land,
> Taught my benighted soul to understand
> That there's a God, that there's a Saviour too;
> Once I redemption neither sought nor knew,
> Some view our sable race with scornful eye,

Phillis Wheatley, Published according to Act of Parliament, September 1, 1773, by Arch'd Bell, Bookseller, No. 8, near the Saracens Head, Aldgate, London now in the Harris Collection of American Poetry and Plays Brown University, Providence, Rhode Island

"Their color is a diabolic die."
Remember, Christians, Negroes, black as Cain,
May be refined, and join the angelic train.[22]

As her health was not good, Mrs. Wheatley arranged for
her to go to England with her son who was settling there.
Phillis was warmly received in England, and a collection
of her poems dedicated to the Countess of Huntington was
published while she was in London in 1773. Shortly after
her return to America, her sponsors, the Wheatleys, died,
and she was left without any means of support. As she was
free, she married Peters who unfortunately was unable to
support her adequately. She had three children and died in
1784 in dire poverty.

Sarah Wentworth Apthorp Morton (1759–1846) was
born in Braintree, Massachusetts, of a wealthy family.[23]
She married Perez Morton in 1781 and had six children.
He was educated as a lawyer and distinguished himself as
Speaker of the Lower House of the General Court of Mass-
achusetts and as attorney general of the state in 1811.
Sarah is credited with writing the second (or first, depend-
ing on what source one is reading) American novel, *The
Power of Sympathy,* which was published in 1789, although there is still doubt concerning her authorship of it.
Her poems began to appear in the current magazines of the
same year. She had almost immediate success and contributed to *The Columbian, The Massachusetts Magazine, The
New York Magazine, The Boston Tablet* and *The Boston
Review and Monthly Anthology.* She frequently used the
pseudonym "Philemia." Her poem "Beacon Hill," which
appeared in 1797, was widely acclaimed. It was an historical poem and opens with:

Far from this spot, ye light delusions, fly,
While fix'd Attention lifts her boundless eye,
O'er Bunkers' field each hallow'd view explores,
Sees the twin-rivers lave the purple shores,
Where the high soil disdain'd the trembling flood,
And stained the white wave with Britannia's blood.[24]

William Bentley was stirred to write in his diary on November 1, 1797, "The talk now about Mrs. Morton's poem, Beacon Hill, and it is said to exceed any poetic composition from a female pen. She is called the American Sappho. Mr. Paine calls her so. . . . These poems are reduced to no class. The American genius refuses restraint. Posterity will wonder at the present age when they find what we admire." [25] (One cannot help wondering what he would have written after reading some of the poems of Gertrude Stein.)Mrs. Morton was undisturbed by his comments and continued to write until about 1823, mostly of her disappointments. Her husband retired from public life in 1823 and died five years later but Mrs. Morton lived until 1846.

Towering over the other talented New England women of the second half of the eighteenth century was Mercy Otis Warren who has quite justly been called "The first lady of the American Revolution." [26] She was born on September 14, 1728, at West Barnstable on Cape Cod and was the third of thirteen children. Being the first girl born into the family she soon learned to care for her younger brothers and sisters. Her father, James Otis, was a self-made, very successful lawyer who believed in the education of his children. Mercy was tutored with her older brother James by Rev. Jonathan Russell. When James went away

Mercy Otis Warren, from a painting by John Singleton Copely. (Courtesy of the Museum of Fine Arts, Boston)

to college, Mercy continued to study the same subjects he was studying and was particularly interested in history and public affairs.

On November 14, 1754, at the age of twenty-six years she married James Warren, a successful business man of Plymouth, who later became very influential in colonial politics. He was for some time president of the Provincial Congress and deeply involved in the growing spirit of independence. He encouraged his wife in her literary efforts and is said to have taken "as much pride in his wife's literary talent as in her housewifely competence." They had five sons between 1757 and 1766, two of whom survived her. Her husband lived until 1808 and she survived him by seven years, living until she was eighty-seven years old.

Although Mercy Warren associated with the intellectually elite of her day, including such travellers as Comte d'Estaing, one of the brilliant French admirals, and Duc de la Rochefoucauld-Liancourt, she never lost touch with her women friends such as Mrs. John Winthrop and Abigail Adams with whom she continued to discuss jellies, "fine linnen, satten, and muslin" and exchanged books, recipes and "scains of sewing silk." She started writing plays as an educative device to warn the people of the colonies of their serious political situation. Although the theatre was still frowned upon by many New Englanders, Mercy Warren hailed it as a speedy, valuable agency for the propagandizing of the public. Her plays lack plot, love interest, or women characters. They were in fact "rabid conversation pieces," written to be read rather than enacted. Her first play, *The Adulateur,* was a biting political satire which appeared in the March and April editions of the 1772 *Massachusetts Spy* and was followed by *The Defeat* in the *Boston Gazette* in 1773. She eulogized the famous "Tea

Party" in Boston in her poem, "The Squabble of the Sea
Nymphs: or The Sacrifice of the Tuscaroroes," from which
the following is taken:

> Bright Phoebus drove his rapid car amain,
> And plung'd his steeds beyond the western plain,
> Behind a golden skirted cloud to rest.
> Ere ebon night had spread her sable vest,
> And drawn her curtain o'er the fragrant vale,
> Or Cynthia's shadows dress'd the lonely dale,
> The heroes of the Tucararo tribe,
> Who scorn'd alike a fetter or a bribe,
> In order ran'd and waited freedom's nod,
> To make an offering to the Wat'ry God.

> Grey Neptune rose, and from his sea green bed,
> He wav'd his trident o'er his oozy head;
> He stretched, from shore to shore, his regal wand,
> And bade the river deities attend;
> Triton's hoarse clarion summon'd them by name
> And from old ocean call'd each wat'ry dame.

> The fair Salacia, victory, victory, sings,
> In spite of heroes, demigods, or kings;
> She bids defiance to the servile train,
> The pimps and syncophants of George's reign.[27]

The following she wrote, in part, "To the Hon. J. Winthrop, Esq. Who, on the American Determination, in 1774
to Suspend all Commerce with Britain (except for the real
Necessaries of Life) requested a poetical List of the Articles the Ladies might comprise under that Head."

> But what's the anguish of whole towns in tears,
> Or trembling cities groaning out their fears?
> The state may totter on proud ruin's brink,

The sword be brandish'd or the bark may sink;
Yet shall Clarissa check her wanton pride,
And lay her female ornaments aside?

And Heaven looks down, and sanctified the deed,
They'll fight for freedom, and for virtue bleed.[28]

In 1775 appeared her burlesque on good government, "The Group." It was printed in the *Boston Gazette* and the *Massachusetts Spy,* and was advertised for sale at nine coppers a copy. It had wide publicity not only in New England but in all of the colonies and in England as well. In her Introduction to the Prologue she states, "as the great business of the polite world is the eager pursuit of Amusement, and as the Public diversions of the season have been interrupted by the hostile parade in the capital; the exhibition of a new farce may not be un-entertaining."

Prologue to The Group
What! arm'd for virtue, and not point the pen,
Brand the bold front of shameless guilty men,
Dash the proud Gamester from his guilded car,
Bare the mean heart which lurks beneath a star,

Shall I not strip the gilding off a knave,
Unplac'd, unpension'd, no man's heir or slave?
I will or perish in the gen'rous cause;
Hear this and tremble, ye who 'scape the laws;
Yes, while I live, no rich or noble knave,
Shall walk the world in credit to his grave;
To virtue only, and her friends, a friend,
The world beside may murmur, or commend.[29]

In later years after the ebb of the tide of many battles, Mercy Warren wrote two tragedies in verse, "The Ladies of Castile" and "The Sack of Rome," which were published in 1790 but added no luster to her fame. However, her *History of the Rise, Progress and Termination of the American Revolution, Interspersed with Biographical, Political and Moral Observations* had remained a classic in its field. It was not published until 1805 after nearly twenty-five years of earnest study and revision. It was contained in three volumes of 400 pages each, including the appendices and spanned the thirty-five years of the struggle for independence that followed the Stamp Act in 1765. Although two other histories of the American Revolution had already been published, Mercy Warren's book was widely read and her anti-federalist leanings discussed throughout the newly formed nation. Thomas Jefferson particularly admired her. In 1801 he wrote her husband, "I pray you to present the homage of my great respect to Mrs. Warren. I have long possessed evidences of her high station in the ranks of genius." [30]

New York produced two women poets of distinction during the last half of the eighteenth century. Anne Eliza Schuyler (1752–1783) was born in New York City of a wealthy and distinguished family.[31] She was very well educated and married John J. Bleecker of New Rochelle, New York, when she was seventeen years old. About two years after their marriage they moved to Tomhanick, eighteen miles from Albany, when she gave birth to two daughters, the younger of whom died shortly after their flight from home before the advancing army of General Burgoyne in 1777. Her older daughter Margaretta became Mrs. Faugeres and also wrote poetry. Anne Eliza Bleecker was frail in health and of a despondent disposition, but was tenderly cared for by her devoted husband. Her poems show an appreciation of nature as in the following poem addressed to Mr. Bleecker while on a voyage down the Hudson River:

Methinks I see the broad, majestic sheet
Swell to the wind; the flying shore retreat:
I see the banks, with varied foliage gay,
Inhale the misty sun's reluctant ray;
The lofty groves, stripped of their verdure rise
To the inclemence of the autumnal skies.
Rough mountains now appear, while pendant woods
Hang o'er the gloomy steep and shade the floods;
Slow moves the vessel, while each distant sound
The caverned echoes doubly loud rebound.[32]

She died in the autumn of 1783 and her daughter arranged for the publication of her poems, with some of her
own, ten years later.

Margaretta Bleecker Faugeres (1771–1801), born at
Tomhanick, New York, was beautiful, talented and very
well educated.[33] She made her social debut in New York
City and became very popular. She married Dr. Peter
Faugeres, a ne'er-do-well who squandered her father's estate after his death in 1795, and treated her with shocking
cruelty until his own death in 1798. Left penniless, she
took a position as teacher in an academy in New Brunswick, but her mental and physical health had been seriously
injured by her unfortunate marriage, and she died at
twenty-nine years of age. Besides her shorter poems she
wrote a tragedy in five acts called *Belisarius,* which was
published in 1795 and highly praised. Her style is clear,
forceful and dignified. The following from a poem about
the Hudson River, which she and her mother loved so
dearly, is illustrative of her work.

Through many a blooming wild and woodland green
The Hudson's sleeping waters winding stray;
Now mongst the hills its silvery waves are seen,

Through arching willows now they steal away:
Now more magestic rolls the ample tide,
Tall waving elms its clovery borders shade,
And many a stately dome, in ancient pride
And hoary grandeur, their exalts its head.
There trace the marks of Culture's sunburnt hand,
The honeyed buckwheat's clustering blossoms view—
Dripping rich odors, mark the beard-grain bland,
The loaded orchard, and the flax-field blue;
The grassy hill, the quivering poplar grove,
The copse of hazel, and the tufted bank,
The long green valley where the white flocks rove,
The jutting rock, o'erhung with ivy dank;
The tall pines waving on the mountain's brow,
Whose lofty spires catch day's last lingering beam;
The bending willow weeping o'er the stream,
The brook's soft gurglings, and the garden's glow.[34]

Among the Pennsylvania and New Jersey colonists there were at least five homemakers who wrote poetry before 1800. Though none of them became first ranking poets, their accomplishments indicate the high intellectual level of the colonial women of the area. Susanna Wright (1697–1784) the earliest of the colonial women poets of Pennsylvania was born in Lancashire, England, in 1697.[35] Her father, a learned Quaker, brought his family to Chester, Pennsylvania, in 1714. After his wife died in 1722, Mr. Wright moved his family further up the Susquehanna River where Susanna took over the care of the household. Between "whangs" and silk reeling she learned to read and speak French fluently, became adept in Latin and Italian and wrote short poems which were published in the Philadelphia magazines. She never married but took an active part in community life and carried on a lively correspondence with the prominent men and women of the day. She championed the cause of the Indians in a day when fear of them left little or no room for the understanding of their problems. She died on December 1, 1784, in her eighty-eighth year full of wisdom and compassion and greatly honored by her co-colonists.

Annis Boudinot Stockton (1736–1801) was born into a distinguished and wealthy family in Darby, Pennsylvania.[36] She married Richard Stockton, probably in 1775, and went to live at Morven House in Princeton, New Jersey, where she gave birth to six children, all of whom she lived to see happily married. Her husband to whom she was deeply devoted became a very successful lawyer, noted patriot and signer of the Declaration of Independence.

Annis wrote a number of poems, mostly patriotic, and addressed them to members of her family rather than for publication. The following "Epistle to Mr. Stockton" is typical:

> But if the powers of genius ever heard
> A votary's prayer, and e'er that prayer prefer'd,
> On me may wit and elegance bestow
> Some emanation bright, some softer glow,
> Some sweet attractive that my heart may twine,
> Stronger than beauty, with each nerve of mine.
> For, Oh, I find on earth no charms for me
> But what's connected with the thought of thee.[37]

Her best known poems are "Peace," "The Surrender of Cornwallis," and "A Triumphal Ode to the Commander in Chief, Washington." Washington acknowledged her poem to him in one of his most gracious letters. Richard Stockton died in 1780, but Annis lived on for twenty years and died in her daughter's home on February 6, 1801.

Hannah Griffeths (1726–1817) was a Quaker of Philadelphia who "wrote only fugitive pieces of poetry," according to J. F. Watson who saw manuscript copies of some of her poems.[38] He wrote of her, "The goodness of her heart was very great, her wit lively and ever ready, and her talents of a high order; but her modesty and aversion to display always caused her to seek the shade." She lived to be ninety years old.

Elizabeth Graeme Ferguson (1739–1801) was the youngest of several children born in luxury and educated in an atmosphere of intellectual brilliance at Graeme Park near Philadelphia.[39] She made her social debut at sixteen years and was courted and beloved for her beauty and intelligence. She had an unhappy love affair with Benjamin Franklin's son, and since her health had never been vigorous, her father sent her to England where she met many distinguished men and women. Shortly after her return her mother died, and she married Henry High Ferguson secretly in 1772. He was a Scotsman ten years her junior and had strong Tory affiliations. In 1777 he became Commissar of Prisoners in the British Army. Elizabeth separated from him in 1778, but because she was suspected of treason to the colonies, her home at Graeme Park was confiscated by the government. Some of her estate was returned to her later through the influence of George Washington and other friends who had been frequent visitors in her home in earlier days and had remained staunch believers in her innocence and patriotism. Having no children, she adopted a nephew and niece on the death of their mother. Her chief literary accomplishment was the translation of Fenelon's "Techemachus," about which Griswold wrote after careful study of the manuscript, "She had command of a fine diction . . . and it appears to me that Fenelon has not been presented in a more correct and pleasing English dress." [40] She filled in her later days with a full transcription of the Bible, large sections of which she memorized. She died February 23, 1801, in her sixty-second year.

Deborah Norris Logan (1761–1839) was born October 19, 1761, in Philadelphia. Her parents were wealthy and well educated.[41] She attended Anthony Benezet's school for girls and married Dr. George Logan on September 6, 1781. She had three sons, one of whom survived her. Her home at Stenton in Germantown, Pennsylvania, was very beautiful and became a center where cultured men such as Benjamin Franklin and Thomas Jefferson were frequent guests. Dr. Logan died in 1821 but Deborah lived to be seventy-eight years old and died on February 2, 1839.

Her poetic efforts were trifling but her interest in history was most unusual. She neither wrote of current events, as did Mercy Warren, nor delved into ancient times, as did Hannah Adams. Rather, she collected, deciphered, copied and annotated an amazing number of documents concerning the founding and development of the colony of Pennsylvania and the newly formed nation. These composed a thousand pages of data gathered into eleven quarto manuscript volumes which have been of inestimable value to all historians of the period. After her husband's death she prepared a Memoir to him which was published by her great granddaughter in 1899.

18

More Treasures of the Mind

In the field of historical writing there were three women of literary significance besides Mercy Warren. They were Anne Cotton, Mary White Rowlandson and Hannah Adams. About Ann Cotton, our first woman historical writer, we know very little.[1] She may have been the Anne Graves who married Rev. Cotton, Rev. Eaton, and Rev. Doughty, all of Hangar's Parish in Virginia. She supported Nathaniel Bacon in 1675–1676 in his revolt against Governor Berkeley's lax measures in defense of the frontier settlements that were being attacked by marauding Indians. Th eleven paged pamphlet which she wrote as a newsletter to "Mr. C. H. Yardley, Northamptonshire" was entitled *"An Account of Our Late Troubles in Virginia,* by Mrs. Ann Cotton of Q (Queen's) Creeke." The original manuscript is preserved and gives the reader a clear, vivid account of each step in the series of events leading eventually to Bacon's death and the return of Governor Berkeley in Jamestown.

Mary White Rowlandson was born in England about 1635[2] Her father, John White, was the wealthiest of the

518

original proprietors of Lancaster, Massachusetts, and apparently well educated. Mary White married Reverend Joseph Rowlandson, the first minister to Lancaster, in 1656 and had four children one of whom died in infancy. During King Philip's War, the Indians threatened the settlement and Rev. Rowlandson went with others to Boston for help. The Indians attacked the village on August 22, 1675, while he was away. The Rowlandson home being large and fortified on three sides, was the gathering place for the forty-two persons left in the village. They endeavored to repulse the Indians but were overcome. Eleven men were killed; only one escaped. The women and children were taken captives and marched north into the forests of what are now Vermont and New Hampshire. Mary Rowlandson was separated from her son who was sixteen years old and her daughter who was eleven years old. The baby in her arms was shot during the struggle and died a few days later. Mary was held captive for about eleven weeks, and while she was not personally molested, she suffered from anxiety, exposure, starvation and the drudgery to which she was subjected. She was released by the Indians on May 2, 1675, on payment of twenty pounds sterling, which is said to have been collected by her women friends in Boston. Her son was released soon after on the payment of seven pounds sterling and her daughter escaped to a settlement in Rhode Island where she was tenderly cared for. Mary's husband died in 1678 and the town granted her an annual pension of thirty pounds sterling during her widowhood but the date of her death is not known.

Her narrative account of her capture and captivity was published in Boston in 1682 and was an immediate success. Its clear, forceful language initiated a new form of prose, that of personal narrative, which has been copied by many writers, but none with greater success. There have been at least thirty editions of the narrative, including the second edition which appeared in London in 1682. It is still as exciting reading as "The Third Reich" and not nearly as lengthy.

Hannah Adams (1755–1831) was born on October second, nearly a century after the capture of Mary Rowlandson.[3] Her father's home was in the now peaceful town of Medfield, Massachusetts, where he was a farmer and later owned a store. He was more interested in books than in money and had to struggle continually to keep a roof over the heads of his family of five children. To augment his slender earnings he boarded several divinity students from whom Hannah learned Latin, Greek, Geography and logic. Among the books that interested her most was Broughton's *Dictionary of Religions* published in England in 1742. She was very critical of the author's evasive definitions and stimulated to study to correct his numerous errors. The result, after years of study, was the publication of her first book, *Alphabetical Compendium of Various Sects*, in 1784, the first edition of which was sold out in less than a year.

Earlier reference (chapter 13) has been made to the contribution of Hannah Adams to religious thought in the colonial period. Each of her five books on religious subjects added to the understanding and tolerance of her readers, but her most notable literary accomplishment was her scholarly *History of the Jews,* which was one of her three historical treatises.

Her father's financial difficulties led to the necessity of Hannah's earning her own living while she was still in her teens. She tried teaching school, which was too strenuous for her frail constitution; then she tried sewing, knitting, making lace, spinning and weaving wool and plaiting straw for hats. None of these were very profitable, since she spent as little time as possible on them in order to do more studying. She did not marry but moved to Boston where she was permitted to study in the famous Athenaeum, a library usually forbidden to women, through the influence of Mr. and Mrs. William S. Shaw. Later these friends, with others, arranged for an annuity to be given to her, which freed her from the necessity of earning money. She spent the rest of her life in intensive study of history and religion until her death in 1831.

Hannah Adams is frequently referred to as the first American woman to make writing her profession. Although she cannot be said to have maintained herself on her royalties, she did seek to do so, whereas all of the other literary women of the colonial period did their writing of prose or poetry as an avocation to homemaking. Her *History of New England* published in 1799 was especially written for use in the schools and was well received as were her other works, but none of them were as financially successful as the sentimental novels of the period. All of her works, as Mrs. Hale pointed out, showed "great candor and liberality of mind and profound research." In contrast to Mercy Warren, who wrote about what she saw, heard and thought, Hannah Adams delved into the history of ideas and peoples through the centuries. She was so fascinated by these ideas that she drew about her a group of interested friends who formed what was perhaps the first women's literary club in America. In spite of ill health her optimistic view of life gave zest to every new day. As she herself expressed it in a letter a few days before her death, "how can anyone be tired of such a beautiful world?"

Besides her *Compendium of Religious Sects,* her most popular religious writing was her treatise on the *Truth and Excellence of the Christian Religion* published in 1801 and 1804 in which she brought together the writings of outstanding men in defence of Christianity and expressed some of her own deeply religious views.

Writing religious pamphlets was very popular throughout the eighteenth century. Each religious sect seeking to hold its members or acquire converts encouraged the practice. Mary Lloyd's "Mediations on Divine Subjects" is an illustration of such writings in Puritan New England.[4] Sophia Hume's "An Exhortation to the Inhabitants of the Province of South Carolina to Bring their Deeds to the Light of Christ in their own Consciences" is an illustration of the writings of women Quakers.[5] Most of the writings, while sincerely religious, had little literary value.

The sentimental novels of the last decade of the eighteenth century in America were concerned with moral issues which were closely linked to the religious life of the New England colonies. It is not an accident of history that Susanna Rowson's novel, *Charlotte,* and Hannah Foster's novel, *The Coquette,* which were published in Boston were so widely read. The key events of both novels were based on facts concerning the seduction of beautiful young girls and the sorrows of sin. Susanna Rowson's novel, published in Boston in 1790, was the best selling novel in America before *Uncle Tom's Cabin. The Coquette,* published in 1797, rocked the city of Boston and quickly went through numerous editions, second only to *Charlotte* in number of sales. It is interesting to note that these and other sentimental novels of the day were written with special appeal to women and had more than a casual feministic slant. They were the precursors of the "'bloomer girls" of half a century later. Garbed as they were in acceptable moral issues, dripping with tear-stained sentimentality, they managed to propagandize women on their place in the newly formed nation and suggest that their lowly position would not be improved by men but by their own efforts.

Susanna Haswell Rowson (1762–1824) was born in Portsmouth, England, and was brought to Massachusetts by her newly widowed father in 1762.[6] He was in the British Navy Revenue Service and stationed at Nantasket. Here Susanna met James Otis, brother of Mercy Warren, who was charmed by the little girl's knowledge of Virgil, Homer, Spencer and Shakespeare. In 1775 her father was ordered back to England, and his property in Massachusetts was confiscated by the colony. Susanna, then a young woman, returned to England where she became a governess in the home of the Duchess of Devonshire. In her spare time she wrote her first novel, *Victoria*, which was published in 1786 and dedicated to the duchess who had befriended her. The following year she married William Rowson, a musician and actor of limited ability. *Charlotte* was published in England in 1789. About twenty years later Matthew Carey, the famous publisher, wrote to her, "it may afford you great gratification to know that the sale of Charlotte Temple exceeds those of any of the most celebrated novels that ever appeared in England. I think the number disposed of must far exceed 50,000 copies; and the sale still continues." In the United States it ran through two hundred editions in a century.

She returned to America with her husband in 1793 and joined the Hallam theatrical company in Philadelphia and performed in Annapolis and Philadelphia for about three years. In 1796 Susanna and her family, for her husband appears only as a shadowy background, went to Boston where her now famous novel had been published. The following year the family left the stage, and Susanna opened a fashionable finishing school for girls. Susanna was childless, but she cared for her husband's young sister and adopted his illegitimate son and the orphan daughter of a relative. For the most part, she supported the family but never ceased to write in her spare time.

Her works include nine novels, a very considerable number of short poems and songs, an opera, "The Slaves of Algiers," a comedy and a farce. While she was teaching and administering the girls' school she was also editor of the *Boston Weekly* (1802–1805) and continued to contribute articles to the magazine until her death in 1824. Her free and easy style as well as her ability in wry witticisms is to be seen in the following selection from *The Slaves of Algiers or a Struggle for Freedom*.

> Well, ladies tell me—how d'ye like my play?
> "The creature has some sense," methinks you say;
> She says that we should have supreme dominion,
> And in good truth, we're all of her opinion.
> Women were born for universal sway,
> Men to adore, be silent and obey.

Hannah Webster Foster (1759–1840) was the daughter of a well-to-do Boston merchant who arranged for his daughter to be very well educated.[7] She took a lively interest in the political life of the day and wrote a series of articles that appeared in the Boston newspapers. These attracted the attention of Rev. John Foster, a Unitarian minister in Brighton, Massachusetts, who soon made her acquaintaince. In April of 1785 they were married and settled in Brighton where she became a prominent worker in the church and community. She had two daughters, both of whom became writers.

Hannah Foster based her novel *Coquette*, on the tragic life of Elizabeth Whitman whose suspected paramour was the eleventh son of the famous Puritan preacher Jonathan Edwards, and a cousin of her husband. It is written in the form of correspondence, which is often labored and surfeited with over-wrought emotions. These did not detract from its popularity, though they make it sorry reading today. However, her moral purpose is clear. The following year she published *The Boarding School, or Lessons of a Preceptress,* which was intended to help young people with their behavior problems but had scant success. After her husband's death in 1824, she went to live with one of her daughters in Montreal where she died in 1840.

Besides the outstanding women in American literature before 1800, there were a host of other homemakers who contributed to the literary level of the period but without notoriety.[8] They were women like Abigail Adams whose literary efforts were confined to her correspondence; the women journalists such as Elizabeth Kearney and the editors of the several newspapers mentioned earlier, and the writers of diaries and journals who were legion. Typical examples of these include Sarah Knight's journal of her trip to New York City, the diaries of Elizabeth Drinker, Hannah Callender, Ann Manigault and Friedericka Riesdesel and the memoirs of Mary Jeminson and Rebecca Hubbs. These were not best sellers, but each in its own way added to the color and richness of the cultural life of the period.

The artistic ability of the American colonial homemaker is to be found most often in her needlecraft, her decoration of her walls and furniture and the paintings on her gowns, hangings and glassware. These were not professional works of art, but no one can look at the exquisite lace, the intricate patterns of their embroidery or the ingenuity of their "Liberty Quilts" without recognizing the artistic ability of their makers. Our first professional American woman artist is generally thought to have been Henrietta Johnson who lived in Charleston, South Carolina, between 1709 and 1728.[9] She was the wife of Rev. Gideon Johnson, rector of St. Philip's Church and, for a time, commisary for the colony. He was drowned in 1716, and Henrietta, faced with supporting her three sons and two daughters, used her artistic talent in drawing pictures in pastel for sale. Fifteen of her pastel portraits have been identified.

In 1739, 1740 and 1743 Mary Roberts, widow of Bishop Roberts, advertised in the South Carolina Gazette that she could do "face painting," or portraits, and Miss Reid placed a similar advertisement in the same paper in 1772.[10] A year later Laeitia Sage of Philadelphia, who married Henry Benbridge, advertised as a portrait painter and miniature "paintress" in Charleston. She had studied painting with Charles Peale in Philadelphia and knew Polly Wrench who also studied painted miniatures in Philadelphia about 1750. Little is known about these women or the early women teachers of art. Painting and other art forms appeared in the curricula of the private schools about the middle of the eighteenth century. It was the natural outgrowth of the need for patterns and designs for the leisure time activities of the ladies, such as embroidery, and the embellishment of glass ware and furniture. It became as stylish to paint as to sing or "sit on a cushion and sew a fine seam."

Patience Lovell Wright (1725–1786) is generally accorded the honor of being America's first sculptor.[11] She was born in Bordentown, New Jersey, in a home of sub-

MᴿˢWRIGHT.

Publish'd as the Act directs Dec⁺1775.

Patience Lovell Wright, from a contemporary drawing published in the November 1775 issue of *The London Magazine*. (From the Collections of the Library of Congress)

stantial prosperity. Mr. Wright died in 1769, leaving her with the necessity of supporting her three children. As she had been very adept at modeling toy cats and dogs out of scraps of bread dough for her children, a friend suggested that she model portraits in wax. This was a popular form of art, several cities having wax museums. Patience Wright was successful from the start and soon was able to open a studio in New York City where she continued to prosper. In 1771 she went to England and later to Paris. Her best known work is the statue of William Pitt, Earl of Chatham, which, in 1779, was installed in Islip Chapel of Westminster Abbey. She did portraits of King George II and Queen Charlotte and a goodly number of celebrities including several of Benjamin Franklin, who was aboard at the time. Her bust of Thomas Penn was preserved in Independence Hall in Philadelphia.

Music was also considered an appropriate accomplishment for the southern colonial ladies of the eighteenth century.[12] It was taught in most of the private schools for girls by the middle of the century. Mary Hext, Elizabeth Anderson and Anna Maria Hoyland were among those who taught music in South Carolina. Mrs. Neill taught the guitar in Williamsburg, Virginia, and Elizabeth Smith taught singing in Annapolis, Maryland. Frances Carter had a harpsichord, harmonica, pianoforte, guitar, German flutes and other musical instruments in her home at Nomini Hall and an organ in her house at Williamsburg.[13] Most of her children were taught music on one of the instruments, as was true in most of the homes of the wealthy planters by the end of the century.

But in early New England music was considered a dangerous invitation to the Devil.[14] Calvin had bitterly opposed all music in the church except unaccompanied metri-

cal psalms sung by rote. In 1637 Anne Hutchinson per-
suaded Rev. John Cotton to permit women to join in the
congregational singing for which she and her pastor were
severely censured. Change came very slowly. It was not
until 1720, a century after their founding, that the colonists permitted the formation of singing schools to teach
the young people how to sing hymns from musical scores
rather than by rote. The first notice of a concert in the
colonies appeared in the *Boston Weekly News Letter* in
1731, but no further notice appeared until the winter of
1774 when a benefit concert was given for Mrs. Stamper
who was a member of the American Theatrical Company
and who had recently come from the Royal Theatre of
Edinburgh.

In the southern colonies where music flourished the first
concert, advertised in the *South Carolina Gazette* of April
8–15, 1732, was given for the benefit of Mr. John Salter
whose wife ran a boarding school where he taught music
occasionally.[15] Other concerts followed during the year. In
1762 the St. Cecilia Society was formed to foster the appreciation of music and a variety of concerts were given.
Miss Hallam and Miss Wainwright appeared on one of the
musical programs of 1765.

After the Revolutionary War The Uranian Society was
formed in 1791 and the Philharmonic Society in 1799, and
in New Orleans the first opera house was built, known as
The Theatre de St. Pierre, in 1791. The societies gave
great impetus to musical endeavors in the last decade of
the century. Sonneck mentions more than forty women
singers who appeared in concerts during the ten years appearing in towns from Savannah, Georgia, to Boston. Most
of the women were included in the musical programs only
once, but at least ten of them appeared on the programs in

more than one city. A number of these women were members of the Hallam-Douglas theatrical group who sang in concerts between theatrical engagements. Mrs. Pownall and Mrs. Henry, for instance, sang in concerts in Charleston, New York City, Boston and Philadelphia. Mrs. Grattan appeared mostly in Philadelphia and became the first woman musical manager, or impresario in the country.[17] George Washington attended a number of her concerts even when the weather was very bad, according to the notes in his diary.

Marianne D'Hemard, whose mother was a harpist, was probably our first musical prodigy.[18] She is reported to have given concerts at the age of six years in Philadelphia, Baltimore, Fredericksburg, Alexandria and Richmond, Virginia, in 1797–1798, "which excited the admiration of her hearers, so much so that she was looked upon as a phenomenon."

Much of the music performed before 1800 was religious in nature.[19] Many of the religious sects devised their own hymnals adapting new words to old tunes or creating new tunes to express their devotion. Noteworthy among these groups were the Moravians to whom music was almost like the breath of life and the Pietists at Ephrata, Pennsylvania, for whom Conrad Beissel is said to have composed two hundred and seventy-five hymns. The members of the two cloisters at Ephrata printed their first hymnal in 1747 which contained ninety-six hymns by lay members of the sect. Of these fifty-two were composed by twenty-three of the women members. Maria, their prioress, is known to have composed five of the hymns. They had five choirs singing together, three of which consisted of women singers who sang the soprano, alto, and tenor parts.

Performances on the stage preceded musical "exhibitions" by only a few years, due largely to the fact that the promoters were limited to the presentation of religious programs. In 1760 William Livingston erected a playhouse in Williamsburg, Virginia, with Mr. and Mrs. Stagg as leading actors, but Mr. Stagg died shortly thereafter, and Mrs. Stagg was forced to support herself by holding dancing assemblies in the building.[20] Thirty-three years later the Philadelphia Theatrical Company was formed with Nancy George as leading lady. They did benefit performances, one of which was to buy off the time, or indenture, of a Mrs. Davis. They went to New York City in 1751 where they did several performances and reorganized as the Virginia Company of Comedians. As such they toured the southern colonies until 1769 with Mrs. Osborne as the leading lady and Mrs. Parker, Miss Yapp and Mr. and Miss Douthwaite as supporting cast.

In 1750 the Hallam Company of London arrived in America and on September 5, 1752 began their nine-months engagement of "The Merchant of Venice" at Williamsburg, Virginia to "universal applause." [21] Mrs. Hallam was the star, supported by Mrs. Beccely, Mrs. Adcock, Mrs. Love, Mrs. Rigby, Mrs. Clarkson and Miss Nancy Hallam who also sang. In the next two years the company presented twenty-four full plays and eleven shorter pieces appearing in Williamsburg, New York City and Philadelphia. In 1754 they went to Jamaica where Mr. Hallam died. They returned to New York City in 1758. Mrs. Hallam married Mr. Douglas and the company was reorganized under the name of Comedians from London. Mrs. Hallam-Douglas continued to star with her son. Lewis Hallam, as her leading man. She was an actress of unusual ability and continued to fill the leading roles for the next eight to ten years.

Nancy Hallam as Imogene in *Cymbeline,* from a painting by Charles Willson Peale. (Courtesy of Colonial Williamsburg, Williamsburg, Virginia)

In 1766 the company was renamed The American Theatrical Company in deference to the rising sentiment
against England.[22] Mrs. Hallam-Douglas, who was getting
old, retired in favor of Margaret Cheer who appeared first
in Charleston on April 25, 1764, in *A Wonder: A Woman
Keeps a'Secret.* In the five years in which she was a star
she played forty-five to fifty different characters. She retired from the stage after her marriage to a man who
claimed to be Lord Rosehill in 1768 and appeared only
occasionally thereafter. Although Lord Rosehill returned
to England, she did not accompany him.

Miss Wainwright and Anne and Maria Storer were also
given occasional leading parts in the company productions
and were very well received, but the outstanding actress of
the later company was Nancy Hallam, neice of Mrs. Hallam-Douglas. She made her American debut in Charleston
in 1765 and married John Raynard, organist of the Kings-
ton Parish Church in Jamaica, on May 10, 1775. She is
said to have received the most extravagant praise of any
actress of the time. In the *Maryland Gazette,* September 6,
1770, appeared the following, signed simply "Y.Z." "She
exceeded my utmost idea! Such delicacy of manner! Such
classical strictness of expression! . . . The music of her
tongue—the vox liquida, now melting! . . . methought I
heard once more the warbling of Cibber in my ear. . . . The
characteristical propriety of Mrs. Douglass cannot but be
too striking to pass unnoticed. The fine genius of that
young creature, Miss Storer, unquestionably affords the
most pleasing prospect of an accomplished actress."

In 1774 and again in 1778 the Continental Congress
called for the immediate closing of all "shows, plays and
other expensive diversions and entertainments." [23] The
American Company gave its last performances before the

war in New York City in 1773 and in Charleston the following year, after which they went to the West Indies until 1784.

In the meantime the people of New England had been fortifying themselves against all such frivolities.[24] In 1750 two English strollers gave performances of *Otway's Orphans* in a Boston coffee house. The church fathers raised such stern objections that a law was passed prohibiting theatrical performances in the colony. The result was a plethora of ruses such as "Histronic academies," exhibitions and elocution recitals. The following advertisement is typical:

June 10, 1762 Newport, Rhode Island at King's Arms Tavern will be given "Moral Dialogues" in Five Parts. Depicting the evil effects of jealousy and other bad passions and Proving that happiness can only spring from the pursuit of Virtue. Mr. Douglas will represent a noble magnanimous Moor called Othello, who loves a young lady named Desdemona, and after he marries her, harbours, (as in many cases) the dreadful passion of jealousy. . . . Mrs. Morris—will represent a young and virtuous wife, who being wrongfully suspected, gets smothered (in an adjoining room) by her husband. . . . Mrs. Douglas—will be her faithful attendant who will hold out a good example to all servants male and female, and to all people in subjection. . . . Tickets, six shillings each to be had within . . . conclusion at half-past ten: in order that every Spectator may go home at a sober hour and reflect upon what he has seen, before he retired to rest.[25]

In 1790 a petition for the erection of a theatre in Boston was signed by many of the leading citizens, including Perez Morton.[26] A new Exhibition Hall was opened in August of 1792, which greatly angered Governor John Hancock.

However, public opinion was so strongly behind Perez Morton and the other supporters of the theatre that the old law was repealed the following year, and the New Federal Street Theatre where many noteworthy productions were given was built in 1794.

It was several years after the Revolutionary War was over before the American Theatrical Company returned to Philadelphia.[27] In 1784–1785 young Lewis Hallam and John Henry formed a company starring Mrs. Allen, but the group quarrelled and split into two companies in 1792. The New York group included Mrs. Henry Hallam, who had made her debut as Miss Sarah Tuke in small parts and later married Henry Hallam, and Mrs. Melmouth, who had already won high laurels in England for her performances in Macbeth and The Earl of Essex. Later she retired to run a diary farm in New York. The Philadelphia group included Mrs. Morris, who had made her debut in 1770 under Mrs. Hallam-Douglas, and Miss George, then the wife of Sir John Oldmixon. Susanna Rowson with her husband and sister-in-law joined the Philadelphia group on her return to America in 1793. While she was with the group Susanna adapted plays, composed music and songs and acted in eighty-eight parts, most of which were secondary roles. Later, she retired and opened a girl's school in Boston.

In many ways Susanna Rowson represented as truly the women of the last quarter of the eighteenth century as Anne Bradstreet did of the women of the first migrations.[28]

Between the two women lay nearly two centuries of violent, chaotic change. A new nation had been born; religious beliefs had been torn asunder; industries had mushroomed into prosperity, and great cities had come into being. Would Susanna Rowson have understood the struggles of Anne Bradstreet? Probably. She certainly would have loved the warm, tender lines in which Anne spelled out her love for her family. And, by the same token, Anne Bradstreet would have understood Susanna's care for her husband's stray child, for mothers are akin to life itself.

19

Ferments at Work

We have come at long last to the essence of our thesis, for however good and great were the contributions of the colonial homemakers to the well-being of their families and villages, these contributions were at best only the visible symbols of their inmost aspirations. Above and beyond these gifts of food, clothing and comfort were their gifts of the spirit—gifts that could only be made by women who believed in themselves as co-workers in the "Kingdom of God." It was this belief in themselves that made them stand straight and firm beside their husbands, sharing, in spite of legal disabilities, in the groping efforts of the colonists toward a new concept of government "by the people" and "for the people." It was not by chance that the movement started, not in the church of courthouse, but in the homes where the women dwelt.

The root of all later achievements was their desire to survive. Each man and woman when they touched the new soil sought first to live, and all life centered in the family groups. It was "the power of carrying the home outward, the working it into institutions common to other homes and other individuals" that built our nation.[1] As Weeden pointed out regarding the New England settlements, "this social tendency, deeper than their politics and deeper than their religion, this invetitable necessity binding the settlers together, issued in a better regulated community than the world had ever seen. The settlers instituted well ordered methods to possess and enjoy property; as far as possible, they carried the system of household and family into the religious meeting and into the town meeting."[2] Their settlements did not fail because each "plantation" was a "community in the egg," and all of the elements of their future institutions were "enfolded in the families and persons of these English men and women."[3] They were not concerned with lonely individual independence from all authority but in a power of people whose free will and action could determine the public good and become their law. So positive was their organization that before the middle of the eighteenth century it had extended to other colonies and set a pattern of social living.

At the side of each free man stood a homemaker who was neither slave nor concubine. In every joint effort of the several families, her help was needed. Meetings were held in her parlor, not in a downtown office or a smoke-filled room that excluded women. She was a contributing part of every house-raising or community endeavor. She knew that she was needed. Her courage was respected as that of men. She was bought back from captivity and honored for her bravery, as was Mrs. Nuice at the massacre of Jamestown in 1622,[4] or Mrs. Hendee of Vermont who rescued her own and fifteen of her neighbors' children from the Indians.[5] Jane McCrea's scalping and murder in 1777 aroused the colonists as no other killing of the period.

Women suffered and survived as did the strong men of

The Scalping and Murder of Jane McCrea, August 27, 1777. (From the Collections of the Library of Congress)

the colonies. Penelope Stout survived.[6] The ship on which she emigrated became stuck in shallow water, and the would-be settlers were attacked by Indians (1620). Her husband was killed. She was stripped, her skull fractured, her left shoulder so hacked she was never to regain full use of her arm, and her abdomen slashed across "so that her bowels appeared; these she kept in her hands" while she crawled to a hollow tree for shelter. She lived for six days on the juice of twigs. Then other Indians found her, and after a quarrel between young and old, she was taken to an Indian encampment and nursed back to health. Eventually she was given to the colony at New Amsterdam, married and bore ten children.

Penelope Stout's experience was not unique but rather illustrates the complexity of the relationship between the colonists and the Indians, some of whom killed without hesitation for the preservation of their land, and others who believed that coexistence was possible. In the effort of the colonists to strengthen the concept of coexistence among the Indians, several women took an active part. In the Dutch colonies Sarah Janses Kierstede (1664) was of inestimable value to the colonists as an interpreter not only of the language used at the meetings, but of the problems of the Indians of the area as well as those of the colonists.[7] Similarly, James Oglethorpe found the knowledge and understanding of Mary Musgrave Matthews Bosomworth of value for twenty-seven years.[8] By virtue of her French and Indian background she was able to understand the problems of colonization from both sides and render services of lasting value. Later Catherine Montour, rendered similar services to the colonists in Pennsylvania in their struggles with the "Six Nations" Indians.[9]

These were not so much isolated cases of women helping in the problems of colonization as notorious instances. In every settlement women dealt with the problem of co-existence with the Indians. They traded with the Indians at their hearthside; they employed Indians as servants; they fed and clothed many in times of drought and disaster and sought to teach them the ways of Christian living. These constituted one of the homemakers' positive gifts of the spirit toward coexistance, tolerance and understanding, which are the bases and strengths of our freedoms.

To pass their beliefs on to new generations we have seen how freely the women gave to the building of schools; they taught the young themselves and helped in the building of libraries. We have seen how they endured persecution from religious intolerance, signed as equal "covenanters" with the men and helped to develop diverse religious sects.[19] They were also responsible for the building of churches. Hardly had the Virginia settlement become secure before Mary Robinson gave two hundred pounds sterling to build a church. Margaret Duncan's "Vow Church" in Philadelphia was a thanksgiving offering to God for her life saved in a shipwreck. Mrs. Cursette in 1740 left an estate of three hundred pounds sterling to build a church at Hebron, Connecticut. Her executors, not wanting a new church, kept her gift a secret for twenty-five years, but in the end the church was built. Catherine Philipse built a church for the Indians on her estate along the Hudson River and in Wallingford, Massachusetts, the women and girls raised onions for money to build a church. These were also gifts of the spirit—gifts to embody the basic freedom of religious choice.

As communities grew there was need for central meeting places for the settlement of colony problems, and women helped to build them. In Essex, Massachusetts, in 1679 the women raised the first meeting-house with the aid of neighboring towns.[11] Their sluggard husbands were chagrined and convicted them of treachery, but the meeting-house stood. On Nantucket the Quaker women gave thirty-four pounds sterling toward a meeting-house, and at Watertown, Massachusetts, Elizabeth Beares, Elizabeth Faning and Mistress Loueran gave more than their allotment to the building fund.[12] In Lancaster, Alice Whiting sold her house and land for sixty pounds sterling and gave it to the town, and in New Amsterdam (New York City), Hanover Square still preserves the open space given by Tryntje Jansen and her husband. These were gifts of the spirit to house and institutionalize the freedoms of democracy in which the colonial women believed so deeply.

With the development of central governments in the several colonies, specific needs were expressed in petitions of many kinds which were signed by women as well as men. Lysbet Tysen of "Old Bergen" signed a petition with seven men in 1658 for exemption from taxation.[13] Sarah Fonteyn made her mark as did six of the fifteen men who signed a petition for a new road at Boswyck in 1662. Mary Ryder signed a petition with nine men at Newton. Long Island, to "Lord Stuyvesant" to use the minister's house and glebe for a school in 1661. Widow Jackson signed a petition with fifty-one men to create a separate town on the south side of the Charles River which became "New Town" in 1678, and in 1705 Elizabeth Bacon and six other heads of families petitioned to move the meeting house to a more central location near West Roxbury, Massachusetts, as they had to walk five miles to meetings.

In Philadelphia in 1695 Hannah Emlen and Elizabeth Ranstead along with seventeen Quaker men signed a petition to curb juvenile entertainment. The petition, except for the quaint language used, sounds strangely like a P.T.A. request today. It stated "That the great rudeness & wildness of ye youth & children of this Towne of Philadelphia is of very Evill & Dangerous Consequence, tending Onelly to Corrupt them in their Youth & Childhood, and to raise & strengthen that wicked spirit in them wch if not prevented will Increase to more ungodliness and Bring Ruine & Destitution upon Body & soule. . . . And that Parrents & Masters of Youth . . . leave off those wild, wicked practices. . . ." [14] The following year Ruth Van Hooren, Arie Bennit, Mardia Gibbins, Benia Hull and Joan des Marest signed their names, and Jane Raleman made her mark on a petition of two hundred and forty East Jersey inhabitants to King William III for a competent governor to care for the colony's needs.[15] (Fourteen of the men signed with a mark). Thus, women shared actively in the colonial efforts to solve the governmental problems.

Elizabeth Pott was not content to merely sign her petition.[16] Her husband, John Pott, "Doctor of Physicke" and late Governor of Virginia, had been unjustly accused of "Markinge other men's cattell for his owne. . . ." She went to London and petitioned Charles I directly. Her petition of September 30, 1630, "Humbly Sheweth that whereas your suppliant having taken a long & dangerous voyage to her excessive charge & the great hassarding of her Life, to appeale unto yr Matie., touching the wronge done unto her said husband. . . ." The lengthy appeal closes with the assurance that she ". . . now in great distres and misserie will daylie pray for yr Matie's long & happie raigne, royall Confort, & Princelie issue." King Charles read her petition, believed in her cause and referred the matter to the Virginia Commissioners who restored her husband "unto his lands and Libertie." [17]

In Maryland Governor William Stone was wounded, captured and imprisoned by the Puritan Party in 1655 in its struggle for power. Virlinda Stone, the governor's wife, wrote a clear report of the whole political situation to Lord Baltimore in England to refute the report that was sent by the Puritans to Lord Cromwell.[18] In the later struggle in 1689, Barbara Smith went to England to personally present her husband's case to their Majesties William and Mary.[19]

In Virginia the conflict between Governor William Berkeley and Nathaniel Bacon in 1676 was crucial to the colony and the wives of the men took an active part in the struggle.[20] Among the women were Mrs. Haviland, who acted as emissary for Bacon, Sarah Grendon and Lydia Cheesman, who assisted the insurgents in a number of ways, and Sarah Drummond who was Bacon's fiery advisor and chief defender. When her husband was condemned to death Lydia Cheesman offered herself in his stead, but the Governor refused her plea. Lady Frances Berkeley went to England to present her husband's case to King Charles II, but the reports of the cruelty of the governor to Bacon and his adherents was so great that he was recalled to England where he died. Among Bacon's adherents who had been killed was William Drummond. Sarah, his widow, petitioned Charles II for the restoration of her husband's estate, which had been confiscated to the governor. Her petition read in part, "So great was the said Governor's inveteracy against Your Petitioner's husband that he not only took away his life, but caused his small Plantation to be seized and given to himself by the Council, his goods to be removed and imbezled, and forced Your Petitioner with her five poor children to fly from their habitation, and wander in the Deserts and Woods, till they were ready to starve . . . For asmuch therefore, and for that Your Peti-

Lydia Cheesman at the trial of her husband, 1676. (From the Collections of the Library of Congress

tioner's said husband was sentenced, condemned and executed, as aforesaid, contrary to and against the Known Laws of His Maties Kingdom. . . ." [21] She begged that restoration of her husband's estate be made to her and her children, and her Petition was granted. While recent research has thrown some doubt on her accusations of Berkeley, there can be no doubt of her courage and devotion.

Margaret Brent did not bother with a petition.[22] In an hour of crisis, acting for Leonard Calvert, she saved the colony from further conflict in 1647 by selling his lordship's cattle and paying the disgruntled soldiers. Her actions, like the petitions, was an expression of the interest of the colonial homemakers in the political life of the colonies. The petitions, whether for family or community betterment, were joint efforts of men and women to express freely their desires for the improvement in the methods of governing.

It is impossible to say when the quilting bees and other social gatherings of the homemakers in the several colonies took on a deeper, more purposeful meaning than coverlets and gossip. The women of Burlington, New Jersey, held regular business meetings as early as 1681, but we do not know their purpose.[23] In Charleston the women formed a club in 1707, and "What is most singular," wrote Dr. Le Jau, "the women of the town are turned politicians also and have a club where they meet weekly among themselves. . . ." [24] It was, however, not until "taxation without representation" became a burning issue that women's actions in behalf of liberty became belligerent enough to be newsworthy. In Kinderhook, New York, a daring young dandy went to a "quilting frolic" and began making aspersions against the meetings of the Continental Congress.[25] The young women protested, but he persisted, whereupon the

A Quilting Bee. (From the Collections of the Library of Congress)

women laid hold of him, stripped him to the waist and covered him with molasses and the downy tops of the flags that grew in the garden. Then they sent him forth to face the village. He fought for his dignity in the courts, but the giggles of the girls had won a victory.

In 1748–1749 "The Boston Society for the Promoting of Industry and Frugality" was formed,[26] and three hundred "young female spinsters" declared their politics by bringing their spinning wheels and flax into the middle of the Boston Commons and treadling there a whole day for the cause of liberty. What a political rally that must have been with the whistling wheels and thrilling trebles of the young in heart! No wonder it made headlines all along the Atlantic coast and even echoed in the halls of Parliament. There is no telling how many brave men stood up and were counted for liberty because of the "Young female spinsters" on the Boston Commons.

Then came the Stamp Act in 1765 and the year following the birth of the "Sons of Liberty" and the "Daughters of Liberty." The "Sons" began to build the pattern of the War on Independence, and the "Daughters" clothed and fed the men both in body and spirit. The first of many meetings of the "Daughters of Liberty" was held in Deacon Ephraim Bowen's house in Providence, Rhode Island.[27] There followed other societies of "Daughters" in a dozen villages and towns in New England where fabulous quantities of yarn was spun and cloth woven. At Ipswich Reverend Cleaveland concluded his sermon to the spinners by observing "how the women might recover to the Country the full free Enjoyment of all our rights, Properties & Priveleges (which is more than the Men have been able to do) and so have the Honor of building not only their own but the houses of many thousands. . . ."[28]

In Philadelphia a non-importation agreement was written

in October of 1765, and six business women joined the men in signing an agreement.[29] Three years later *The Georgia Gazette,* January 6, 1768, published news of the "Daughters of Liberty" and praised the women for their spinning, frugality and the wearing of homespun as a stimulus to the Georgia women to do the same. *The Virginia Gazette* of July 27, 1769, expressed "greatest pleasure" at being able to inform their readers that the "Association of Ladies . . . meets with the greatest encouragement in every county that we have yet heard from." At the December State Ball the ladies wore homespun according to the Virginia Gazette December 14, 1769.

On January 31, 1770, a group of men in Boston met and agreed not to drink any tea until the revenue act concerning it was repealed. Five hundred and thirty-eight women of the area signed a similar agreement "in which number the Ladies of the highest rank and influence that could be waited upon in so short a time are concluded." [30] Tea as well as imported finery became a symbol of subservience to tyranny and word of the patriots' action spread to every colony. *The Virginia Gazette* of January 27, 1774, carried the following lead stories.

Newport, Dec. 20
We can assure the Publick, that a Lady in this Town, of affluent Circumstances, and equal to any One in it for good Sense, Politeness and Consequence, last Week came to the Resolution to have no India Tea drank in her Family until the Duty upon that Article is taken off; an Example well worthy the Imitation of every Individual in the Colony, and throughout the Continent.
It is a Matter of Fact, that the People in Boston are leaving off drinking India Tea very fast.
Williamsburg
By Letters from Boston, we hear that the Ladies of that Place,

to their Immortal Honour, have entered into an Association against the Use of East India Tea; and they intend selling their Compliments soon to all other Ladies on the Continent to refrain from that Baneful Practice, at least till America is freed from Parliamentary Taxation."

Their salute of farewell to the tea table which appeared in *The Virginia Gazette* on January 20, 1774 is delightful because of its effervescent spirit.

> A Lady's Adieu to her Tea Table
> Farewell the Tea Board, with its gaudy Equipage,
> Of Cups and Saucers, Cream Bucket, Sugar Tongs,
> The pretty Tea Chest also, lately stor'd
> With Hysen, Congo, and best Double Fine.
> Full many a joyous Moment have I sat by ye,
> Hearing the Girls' Tattle, the Old Maids talk Scandal,
> And the spruce Coxcomb laught at—maybe Nothing.
> No more shall I dish out the once lov'd Liquor,
> Though now detestable,
> Because I'm taught (and I believe it true)
> Its use will soften slavish Chains upon my Country,
> And Liberty's the Goddess I would choose
> To reign triumphant in AMERICA.

In the fall of the same year *The Virginia Gazette* carried notices of urgency and encouragement from their "sisters and countrywomen" in South Carolina and appeals to the "Dear Ladies" of Pennsylvania to join them in abstention of "all luxuries, especially Tea."

At Edenton, North Carolina, fifty-one women met at the home of Elizabeth King on October 25, 1774, and made a momentous decision: "As we cannot be indifferent on any occasion that appears to affect the peace and happiness of

English Cartoon of the meeting of the patriotic ladies of Edenton, North Carolina, October 25, 1774, from a mezzotint by Philip Dawe, 1775. (From the Collections of the Library of Congress)

our country, and as it has been thought necessary for the publick good to enter into several particular resolves, by meeting of the Members of Deputies from the whole Province, it is a duty that we owe not only to our near and dear relations and connections, but to ourselves who are essentially interested in their welfare, to do everything as far as lies in our power to testify our sincere adherence to the same, and we do therefore accordingly subscribe this paper as a witness to our fixed intentions and solemn determination to do so." They commended the Provincial Congress and agreed that they would stop "that Pernicious Custom of Drinking Tea" and ". . . would not promote ye wear of any manufacture from England" [31] until the taxes were removed.

News of their action reached England, and the following January James Iredell received a letter from his brother in London in which he stated: "I see by the newspapers the Edenton ladies have signalized themselves by their protest against tea-drinking. . . . Is there a female Congress at Edenton too? I hope not, for we Englishmen are afraid of the Male Congress, but if the ladies . . . should attack us, the most fatal consequence is to be dreaded . . . the only security on our side to prevent the impending ruin that I can perceive is the probability that there are few places in America that possess so much female artillery as in Edenton." [32] We cannot help wondering if he lived to know how many bands of "female artillery" swept the horizons from Maine to Georgia. He enclosed a copy of a caricature of the women's meeting which had been printed in London and thus unwittingly enhanced the fame of the women. News came in steadily from Meckenburg and Rowan Counties and elsewhere that similar associations were being formed, for as one correspondent soberly stated, "much, very much depends on the public virtue the ladies will exert at this critical juncture." [33]

And what did the "female artillery" do without imported tea? They made "Liberty Tea" out of loose-strife, sage, strawberry, currant, and ribwort leaves and "Labrador or Hyperion Tea" from raspberry leaves. Strange flavors, but definitely political. Every cup they drank was a political act in favor of independence, just as the homespun garments they made and wore. When Mary Slate of Mansfield, Connecticut, married Luke Flint just before he went off to do battle, the wedding party included most of the town.[34] Every dish at the wedding feast, every glass of wine was home grown and processed and all of the men's suits and the ladies' gowns, even to the silk handkerchiefs they carried so daintily, were homespun. Liberty was not an idle word but an incendiary idea, which they translated into daily actions.

The intensity of the purpose of these women was expressed by one woman in a letter to a British officer (1775). She stated, "I will tell you what I have done. My only brother, I have sent to the camp with my prayers . . . and had I twenty sons and brothers they should go. I have retrenched every superfluous expense in my table and family; tea, I have not drunk since last Christmas, nor bought a new cap or gown since your defeat at Lexington; and what I never did before, have learned to knit, and am now making stockings of American wool for my servants; . . . I know this—that as free, I can die but once: . . . these are the sentiments of all my sister Americans. . . ." [35] Ann Terrell of Bedford County, Virginia, sent her plea, "The Ladies whose Husbands are in the Continental Army," to *The Virginia Gazette,* which published it September 21, 1776, to be read by many. Anne Stockton wrote her poems on liberty in Pennsylvania, and Mercy Warren aroused all New England with her fiery and caustic poems on liberty. In New Jersey on May 6, 1778, "Belinda" penned a letter to Mr. Collins, editor of *The New Jersey Gazette* that held more than one stinging taunt. She wrote, "I do not remember whether your *Gazette* has hitherto given us the production of any woman correspondent—Indeed nothing but the most pressing call of my country could have induced me to appear in print. But rather than suffer your sex to be caught by the bait of that arch foe to American Liberty, Lord North, I think ours ought, to a woman, to draw their pens, and enter our solemn protest against it. Nay, the fair ones in our neighborhood have already entered into a resolve for every mother to disown her son, and refuse the caresses of her husband, and every maiden to reject the addresses of her gallant, where such husband, son or gallant, shews the least symptoms of being imposed upon by this flimsey subterfuge, which I call the dying speech, and last groans of Great Britain, pronounced and grunted out by her great oracle, and little politician who now appears ready to hang himself, for having brought the nation to the brink of that ruin from which he cannot deliver her."

While "Belinda" wrote, other women acted. *The Connecticut Courant* of September 10, 1775, carried a story of "a corps of female infantry," twenty in number, who "sallied from the Lyon Tavern" with a "flank guard of three chosen spirits of the male line" and marched one mile to Mr. Pitkin's Store where they commandeered 280 pounds of sugar "without opposition from powder, law or conscience." [36] Abigail Adams tells of a similar raid on Stephen Cabot's warehouse in Beverly, Massachusetts. On a cold November of 1770, about sixty women wearing lambskin cloaks and riding hoods marched down to the wharves accompanied by two oxcarts. At the warehouse the women overcame the watchman and rolled out two hogsheads of sugar, which they placed in the carts and drove away, after giving the watchman a reasonable sum for the sugar.[37]

Another group of women nearly tarred and feathered a mother of a new born son because she named him after Thomas Gage, the local representative of the British Government.[38] Baroness Riedesel, who was traveling with the English forces, reported that she thought "Boston was inhabited by violent patriots. . . . The women especially were shameless, that they regarded [her] with repugnance and even spat at [her] when [she] passed them." The Baroness did not understand that women could wage war as well as men when the rights of their homes and families were at stake.

During the years of the war the women did just that—they fought on every front. Many of the wives of the soldiers received no allotments before 1780 and very little then. The soldiers were so poorly and infrequently paid that they had nothing to send their families, so that many families suffered destitution. One wife wrote to her husband in December of 1778, "I am without bread and cannot get any, the Committee will not supply me, my Children will starve or if they do not, they must freeze, we have no wood, neither can we get any—Pray come home!" [39] Her plight was not uncommon. Many of the women were burdened with illness and despair.

Others with greater strength fought to save their crops and cattle to feed themselves and the army.[40] Creusa Wallace hid her crop and many family articles in the woods of New Hampshire. Madam Andrews drove her children and cattle up into the hills of Connecticut. Mrs. Horrys saved her potato crop by covering the celler in which they were stored with a slab of marble from the family vault. Hannah Hawk Brown saved her wine cellar by standing against the door and daring the Hessian soldier to cut her down. Betsy Vail of Oysterponds pulled the bungs out of her barrels of wine and let the liquor flow away before the angry soldiers could prevent her. Deborah Townsend saved her granary by beating the cavalryman who came to take the grain with her large bread shovel. He retreated and remarked, "if this woman is a sample of the wives of our opponents, it is useless to think of subdueing them." These instances are only illustrative of what happened in every colony. They could be duplicated a hundred times, for the homemakers as well as their soldier-husbands were involved in the fight for liberty to the death.

One way in which many of the women were able to help was in getting supplies for the Continental Army. The homemakers of New England made uniforms for the men. Mrs. Samples Craft slipped through the British guards and procured an essential supply of pins and needles.[41] Sarah Bache and her committee in Philadelphia made shirts for the soldiers, and Abigail Conduit and her group of women in New Jersey knitted garments for the men. Rebecca Motte sent her male slaves to work on the Fort at Charleston, and on May 8, 1781, fired the roof of her home which the British were using as headquarters. She used the combustible arrows that had been brought years before from the East Indies. They were shot from the barrel of a ponderous rifle and burst into flames on contact. Later she used the case in which the arrows had been kept for her assortment of knitting needles. Martha Bratton, left in charge of army supplies in North Carolina, blew up an ammunition dump to prevent the British from using it.

A Soldier's wife at Fort Niagara. (From the Collections of the Library of Congress)

Ammunition was in short supply in all of the colonies. Lead was very precious. Homemakers gave up their pewter plates and pots and even the lead from their window casings. Mrs. Nathan Sargent melted down her table furnishings and clock weights, and then removed the pewter inscription plates from the family tombs.[42] Mrs. Eliot Winship Craft made bullets at Worcester, at one time working for three days and nights without stopping to meet pressing army need. Other women supplied the army at Niagara and other battle fronts. Mrs. Proctor, who owned a tool factory at Salem, helped in collecting an arsenal for the army.

Money was also in short supply.[43] Many of the towns and colonies borrowed money to outfit and pay their fighting men. Women's names appear on many of the lists of lenders. For instance, at Haverhill, Massachusetts, Rachel Duston and Mary Baker each loaned twelve pounds sterling, Mehitable Carleton thirty-six pounds, Abigail Smiley forty-eight pounds, Anna Cushing fifty-seven pounds and Widow Phebe Hatch 626 pounds sterling. Women also gave money outright. In Philadelphia Esther Reed and Sarah Bache headed up a group of women who eventually raised 300,000 dollars in Continental money which was equal to about 7,500 dollars in gold.[44] A broadside of about two thousand words was circulated to encourage the women's campaign for money. It read in part: "Who amongst us will not renounce with highest pleasure, those vain ornaments, when she shall consider that the valiant defender of America will be able to draw some advantage for the money which she may have laid out in these. . . . This is the offering of the Ladies. The time has arrived to display the same sentiments which animated us at the beginning of the Revolution . . . when we renounced the use of teas . . . when our liberty was interested; when our republican and laborious hands spun flax" for the soldiers.[45]

One thousand, six hundred, forty five women were contributors. They included women of all classes from the Negro maid who gave seven shillings, six pence, to the Countess de Luzeren who gave one hundred dollars in specie and the Marquis de Lafayette who gave one hundred guineas in the name of his wife.

Not to be outdone by their neighbors the "Ladies of Trenton, New Jersey" in July of 1780, were "emulating the noble example of their Patriotic Sisters in Pennsylvania and being desirous of manifesting their zeal in the glorious cause of American Liberty, having this day assembled for the purpose of promoting a subscription for the relief and encouragement of those brave men in the Continental Army." [46] The assembled women appointed a chairwoman for each county of the state to collect the much needed funds. Later in the year an open letter of about one thousand words was circulated urging the women of New Jersey to increase their contributions.

Other women gave food and such care as was possible to the soldiers.[47] While the British occupied New York City, the scarcity of food was very great and the prisoners of war held by the British suffered acutely. Mrs. William Whetten, Mrs. Adam Todd and Mrs. Sarah Whaley brought food from their kitchens and rendered so many other services to the imprisoned soldiers that George Washington heard of their work and commended them.

Many women filled the powder horns of their soldier-husbands as they fought side by side or took their husband's place when they fell in battle as did Molly Pitcher and Margaret Corbin, who were honored for her deed by an act of Congress in July, 1779. The resolution read, "re-

Molly Pitcher, Mrs. Molly Ludwig Hays McCauley, at the Battle of Monmouth, June 28, 1778. (From the Collections of the Library of Congress)

Nancy Hart of Georgia. (From the Collections of the Library of Congress)

Mrs. Murray's Strategy on Manhattan. (From the Collections of the Library of Congress)

solved, That Margaret Corbin, wounded and disabled at the battle of Fort Washington while she heroically filled the post of her husband who was killed by her side, serving a piece of artillery, do receive during her natural life, or continuance of said disability, one half of the monthly pay drawn by a soldier in the service of these States; and that she now receive out of public store one suit of clothes, or value thereof in money." [48]

Women were also spies, couriers and active participants in the wartime activities. Elizabeth Ellet has collected the heroic acts of 168 women in her three volumes of *Women in the American Revolution,* and many more have been found since her volumes were published. The following have been chosen to show the range of the women's activities. Lydia Darrah overheard plans being made by some British officers while she was supposed to have been asleep and carried the details to the American forces. [49] Susannah Livingston saved the state papers of New Jersey when the British arrived by appearing to comply with their commands. Mrs. Mary Murray detained General Howe and his officers with food, wine and song until she was sure that Major General Putnam could make an orderly retreat and join General Washington. Behethland Moore, when only fifteen years old, carried a message in the night to Captain Wallace in South Carolina. Grace and Rachel Martin held up at gun point a British courier and two officers, took the documents they carried and sent them to General Greene. Emily Geiger was intercepted by British soldiers when she was carrying a message from General Greene to General Sumter. She promptly ate the document and when released continued her journey and delivered the message orally. Nancy Hart captured five English soldiers and at another time tied some logs together with grape vines and on this makeshift raft crossed the river to the British encampment, gathered the needed information and returned to the American headquarters in Georgia. Another time she dressed and acted as an insane man and was able to gather important information for Colonel Clarke.

Dame Trefethen's house was at the head of a high bluff overlooking the mouth of the Piscataqua River in New Hampshire.[50] A British boat anchored nearby and the men came ashore to fill their barrels with fresh water from her well. She said nothing, but while the men were in town quenching their thirst with more than water, she rolled the barrels over the edge of the cliff and discreetly returned to her fireside, where the soldiers found her knitting and looking as innocent and helpless as her white hair suggested.

Sally St. Claire, a beautiful Creole girl of South Carolina, and Deborah Sampson, a former school teacher of Massachusetts, were bolder. They dressed as men and joined the army. Sally was killed, but Deborah served as Robert Shirtliffe for many months. She was wounded twice but was able to preserve the secret of her sex until she developed brain fever in Philadelphia. When she recovered, she was secretly discharged with honor by General Washington who kept her secret. Later she was happily married. The women of Groton, Massachusetts, were no less bold. When Mrs. Wright and Mrs. Shattuck heard that the British were coming, they rounded up all the women of the town, had them dress in men's clothes and arm themselves with whatever guns, pitchforks and sling-shots they could find. They formed ranks at Jewetts Bridge, caught and made prisoner a British spy, sent the message he carried to the American headquarters, and dispersed the detachment of British soldiers that came their way.

Do you doubt that such women believed in themselves?

Not just in the idea of liberty for which they fought so nobly, but in themselves as co-workers in establishing liberty in the new land? Their bravery, great as it was, incidental to their objective of standing shoulder to shoulder with their husbands so that they could together make a new and better world for their children. They were no less women for all their bravery. It never occurred to them to be "ersatz" women—they were women of dignity and feminity. This is the essence of their gift to us. This is "the dear-bought heritage."

Because of it we women, the homemakers of today, are still restless and searching, for we have not yet garnered the full measure of our aspirations. We have still to outlaw war, do away with poverty and disease and find the paths of joy and righteousness for our children. Let no future generation say of us that we failed in bestowing our full measure of gifts toward the solution of our problems today.

Notes

References given are not inclusive of all known sources but have been chosen for their availability, interpretation of events and original sources, and breadth of activity. For further study, reference is made to *The American Woman in Colonial and Revolutionary Times, 1565–1800, Syllabus with Bibliography,* by Leonard, E.A., Drinker, S.H., and Holden, M.Y., hereinafter referred to as Leonard, E.A., *Syllabus.* (For specialized bibliography, see *104 Outstanding Colonial Women,* pp. 111–125.)

CHAPTER 1

1. Choate, C.A.: *Gulf States Hist. Mag.* Vol. 1: 342 ff.
   Robertson, J.A.: *Fla. State Hist. Soc. Publ.*: No. 11.
   Shipp, B.: *Hist. De Soto.*
   Smith, B.: *Narrative De Soto.*
   U.S.: *De Soto Expedition.*
2. Brevard, C.M.: 63–65.
   Shea, J. Vol. 1: 127.
3. Connor, J.T.: *Fla. State Hist. Soc. Bull.*: No. 5, Vol. 2.
   Dewhurst, W.: 52–113.
   Fairbanks, G.R.: *Spaniards in Fla.* 22–23.
   Gray–Thompson: Vol. 1: 10–12.
   Lowery, W.: 142–225.
   Shea, J.: Vol. 1: 100–182.
4. Hammond, G.P.: 69–89.
   Shea, J. Vol. 1: 186 ff.

Twitchell, R.E.: *Leading Facts N.M. Hist.*: Vol. 1; see Index.
    Archives N.M. Vol. 1; see Index.
Villarga, G.P.: 91–103, 224–227.

5. Ashe, S.A.: Vol. 1: 11–12.
    Hume, M.A.: 52–53.
    Stanard, M.: *Va. 1st Cent.*: 18 ff.
6. Beverly, R.: 24–44.
    Kercheval, S.: 1–15.
    Spruill, J.: *Women's Life.* 9–20.
    Stanard, M.: *Va. 1st Cent.*: 35–111.
7. Ames, A.: *Mayflower and Her Log.*
    Bradford, W.: 106 ff.
    Marble, A.R.: *Women in Mayflower.*
8. Baird, C.W.: *Hist. Huguenot Emigration. Vol. 1*
    Leonard, E.A.: *Syllabus*: 21.
9. Felt, J.B.: 411–414.
    Lord, *et al.*: Vol. 1: 203–209.
10. Arthur, S.C.: *Old New Orleans.*
    Chambers, H.E.: Vol. 1: 50–68.
    Gayarre, C.: Vol.: 57–80.
    Kendall, J.S.: Vol. 1: 7 ff.
11. Colton, J.M.: *Annals.*
    Leonard, E.A.: *Syllabus.*
    Van Rensselaer, Mrs. J.K.
    Van Rensselaer, M.G.: Vol. 1.
12. Bernheim, G.O.
    De Brahm, J.G.: 20 ff.
    Faust, A.B.: Vol. 1.
13. Lebenson, A.L.
    Marcus, J.R.: Vol. 1.
    Pool, D.
14. Dogget, C.
    Panagopoulos, E.P.: *Fla. Hist. Quart.* 35: 95–115.
15. Spruill, J.: *Women's Life*: 9.
    Woody, T.: ed. *Women*: Vol. 1: 239.
16. *Loc. cit.*
17. Hart, A. *Commonwealth Hist. Mass.*: Vol. 2: 372.
18. de Crevecoeur, J.H.: 43–44.

CHAPTER 2

1. Bradford, W.: *Hist. Plymouth*: 148.
   Arber, E.: 136.
2. Gray–Thompson,: Vol. 1: 10 ff.
   Lowery, W.: 142, 152–159.
   Shea, J.: Vol. 1: 134–136.
3. Lowery, W.: 430.
4. Dewhurst, W.: 52–53.
   Gray–Thompson,: Vol. 1: 10–11.
   Lowery, W,: 224–225.
5. Dewhurst, W.: 69.
   Gray–Thompson: 11.
6. Connor, J.T.: *Fla. State Hist. Soc. Bull.*: No. 5, Vol. 2: 283.
   Dewhurst, W.: 73,
   Gray–Thompson: Vol. 1: 12.
7. Bancroft, H.: *Hist. Ariz. and N.M.*: 145 ff.
   Bolton, H.E.: *Spanish Exploration*: 202–211.
   Villagra, G.P.: 103.
8. Twitchell R.E. *Archives, N.M.*: Vol. 1: 44.
   Chavez, A.: *N.M. Families*: 19, 54.
9. Priestly, H.: 35.
   Rey, A.: *N.M. Hist. Rev.*: Vol. 23: 22–32.
10. Chavez, A.: *N.M. Families*: Intro.
    Shea, J.: Vol. 1: 205–208.
11. Leonard, E.A.: *Syllabus*: 18.
    Spruill, J.: *Women's Life*: 20 ff.
    Stanard, M.: *Vol. Va.*: 15–54, *Va. First Cent.*: 97.
12. Stanard, M.: *Col. Va.*: 34.
13. Stanard, M.: *Va. First Cent.*: 96.
14. Force, P.: Vol. 3: 9–17.
    Spruill, J.: *Women's Life*: 6.
15. Stanard, M.: *Va. First Cent.*: 35, 110.
16. Brown, A.: *Genesis U.S.*: Vol. 1: 492.
    Nugent, N.: Vol. 1: xxi: 163–181.
17. Andrews, M.P.: *Va. Old Dominion*: 105–106.
    Spruill, J.: *Women's Life*: 232–233.
    Stanard, M.: *Col. Va.*: 56.
    Stith, W.: *Hist. Va.*: 235–236.
    Tyler, L.G.: *Narratives*: 378.
18. Nugent, N.: Vol. 1: 163–181.
19. Bradford, W.: *Hist. Plymouth*: 96, 121, 124.

20. *Ibid*: 105–108, 124.
21. Bemis–Burchard: Vol. 1: 261.
    Holliday, C.: 78.
22. Bradford, W.: *History Plymouth*: 110–128.
23. *Ibid.*: 128–149.
24. *Ibid.*: 146, 175, 217.
25. *Ibid.*: 156–157.
26. Calhoun, A.: Vol. 1: 68.
    Emery, S.: 28.
    Essex Institute Hist. Colls.: Vol. 1: 28–32. Vol. 19: 167–175.
    Morison, S.: *Builders Bay Colony*: 26.
    Morris, R.: 131.
    Winthrop, J.: Vol. 1: 252–303.
27. Bailey, R.F.: 20.
    Bruce, D.H.: Vol. 1: 26–30.
    Leonard, E.A.: *Syllabus*: 20.
28. Jones, F.R.: *Middle States*: 15–16.
    Wright, L.B.: *Atlantic Frontier*: 161–211.
29. Shurtleff, H.R.: 113.
30. Van Rensselaer, Mrs. J.K.: 8 ff.
31. Green, H.C. and M.W.: Vol. 1: 412–420.
    Van Rensselaer, Mrs. J.K.: 22–26, 109–110.
    Van Wyck: 136.
32. Leonard, E.A.: *Syllabus*: 20.
33. Chambers, H.E.: *Hist. La.*: Vol. 1: 58–68.
    French, B.F.: *Hist. Colls.*: 99–104.
    Hamilton, P.J.: *Gulf States Hist. Mag.*: Vol. 1: 1–12.
    King, G.E., and Ficklen, J.R.: 30–31.
    Leonard, E.A.: *Syllabus*: 21.
34. Chambers, H.E.: *Hist. La.*: Vol. 1: 70–71.
    French, B.F.: *Hist. Colls.*: 95.
35. French, B.F.: *Hist. Colls.*: 157–180.
    Kendall, J.S.: Vol. 1: 9.
36. Connor, R.D.: Vol. 1: 25–77.
    McCrady, E.: *Hist. So. Car. Proprietary.*
    Newsome, A.R.: *Records Emigrants N.C.H. Rev.*:
        Vol. 11: 39–54, 129–142.
    Spruill, J.: *Women, Founding So. Colls., N.C.H. Rev.*:
        Vol. 13: 202–218.
37. Burrage, H.S.: 19–21.
    Hatch, L.C.: Vol. 1.
    Sylvester, H.M.: Vol. 1.

38. Beedy, H.C.: 33–35.
    Md. Hist. Mag.: Vol. 2: 216.
    Williamson, W.D.: Vol. 1: 209–210.
39. Caulkins, F.M.
    Cogswell, E.C.
    Whiton, J.M.
40. Baird, C.W.: Vol. 1: 136–137.
    Beedy, H.C.: 34–36.
    Bouton, N.: *N.H. Papers*: Vol. 1: 114.
    Whiton, J.M.: 50.
    Williamson, W.D.: Vol. 1: 308–325.
41. Thompson, Z.: 16–29.
42. Adams, C.F.: *Antinomanism*.
    Adams, C.F.: *Three Episodes*.
43. Andrews, M.P.: *Fouding Md.*: Vol. 1: 59–60, 85, 199–200.
    Bozman, J.L.: Vol. 2: 30 ff.
    Browne, W.H.: *Hist. Palalinate*: 64 ff.
    Hall, C.C.: *Narratives*.
    Shea, J.: Vol. 1: 40–86 ff.
    Wright, L.B.: *Atlantic Frontier*: 258–301.
44. Ives, J.M.: 223 ff.
    Md. Hist. Mag.: Vol. 5: *Records*.
    Ramey, Mary E. W.: *Margaret Brent*.
45. Barker, J.N.: *Sketches*.
    Fiske, J. *Dutch and Quaker Colonies*: Vol. 2.
    Hazard, S.: *Annals Pa.*: 510 ff.
    Watson, J.F.: *Annals Phila.*: Vol. 1: 44 ff.
46. Wharton, A.H.: *Col. Days*: 67–69.
47. Hazard, S.: *Annals Pa.*: 647.
48. Ellis–Evans, S.: 926.
    Faust, A.B.: *German Element*: Vol. 1.
    Sachse, J.F.: *German Sectaries*: Vol. 1.
    Watson, J.F.: *Annals Phila.*: Vol. 2: 43.
49. Drinker, S.H.: *Hannah Penn*.
50. Bartlett, H.R.: *18th Cent. Ga. Women*.
    Coulter, E.M.: *Hist. Ga.*
    McCain, J.R.: *Ga. Proprietory*.
51. Dogget, C.: 17 ff.
52. Bancroft, H.H.: *Works*: Vol. 34: 306–393.
    Leonard, E.A.: *Syllabus*: 17.

CHAPTER 3

1. Andrews, C.M.: *Col. Folkways*: 86–90.
   Bancroft, H.H.: *Works*: Vol. 34: 307–310.
   Bricknell, J.: 31.
   Bruce, P.A.: *Social Life Va.*: 223–238.
   Dunton, J.: 137.
   Spruill, J.: *Women's Life*: 48, 140.
   Stanard, M.: *Col. Va.*: 166–185.
2. Morgan, E.S.: *Puritan Family*: 39–44.
   Newhall, J.R.: 222–225.
   Powell, C.L.: *New Engl. Quart.*: Vol. 1: 323–334.
   Weeden, W.B.: Vol. 1: 217–220, 293–295, 412.
3. Ansbury, T.: Vol. 2: 25, 95, 739.
   Burnaby, A.: 145.
   Peters, S.: 325–333.
   Stiles, H.R.: *Bundling*.
   Weeden, W.B.: Vol. 2: 864.
4. Bradford, W.: *Hist. Plymouth*: 116–117.
   Calhoun, A.: Vol. 1: 54–64.
   Powell, C.L.: *New Engl. Quart*: Vol. 1: 323–334.
5. Botkin, B.A.: 726–728.
   Calhoun, A.: Vol. 1: 61–63.
   Van Rensselaer, Mrs. J.K. 68.
   Watson, J.F.: *Annals Phila.*: Vol. 2: 418.
   Weeden, W.B.: Vol. 2: 538.
6. *Va. Gazette*: Mar. 15, 1771.
   Archives, N.J.: Ser. 2, Vol. 2: 137.
7. Calhoun, A.: Vol. 1: 61–63.
8. Bruce, P.A.: *Social Life*: 223.
   Calhoun, A.: Vol. 1: 70.
   Spruill, J.: *Women's Life*: 159.
   Watson, J.F.: *Annals Phila*: Vol. 2: 418.
              London Daily Advertiser: July 13, 1765.
9. Bruce, P.A.: *Social Life*: 225.
   Spruill, J.: *Women's Life*: 151.
   Stanard, M.: *Va. 1st. Cent.*: 180–181.
   V.M.H.B.: Vol. 50: 74–80; Vol. 51: 384.
10. *Archives, N.J.*: Ser. 1, Vol. 27: 541–542.
    Beedy, H.C.: 73.
    Calhoun, A.: Vol. 1: 88–89.
    Holliday, C.: 115.

Mather, C.: Vol. 1: 11.
Spruill, J.: *Women's Life*: 46–48, 140.
Va. Gazette: June 7, 1770.
Weeden, W.B.: Vol. 1: 284.
11. *Archives, N.J.*: Ser. 1, Vol. 27: 270.
12. *Ibid.*: Ser. 1, Vol. 2: 10–11, 19–20, 33–34.
13. *Ibid.*: Ser. 1, Vol. 27: 455–456, 462–463, 561–562.
14. *Ibid.*: Ser. 2, Vol. 3: 230.
15. *Ibid.*: Ser. 1, Vol. 24: 74.
16. *Maine Hist. Soc. Coll.*: Vol. 1: 280.
    Newhall, J.R.: 276.
    Weeden, W. B.: Vol. 1: 294.
17. *Archives, N.J.*: Ser. 1, Vol. 24: 104.
18. Ellis, J.H.: *Works of Anne Bradstreet*: 391–394.
    Griswold, R.W.: 19.
    Leonard, E.A.: *Syllabus*: 103.
19. Brown, A.: 78–80; 96–97.
    Holliday, C.: 100–101.
20. Adams, A: Letters: 10, 89, 93.
21. Holliday, C.: 102.
    Ravenel, H.H.: *Eliza Pinckney*: 90–175.
22. Leonard, E.A.: *Syllabus*: 70–71.
23. Fowler, W.: 44–45.
24. Clement, J.: 93–94.
    Fowler, W.: 69–70.
    Hanaford, P.: 33–34.
25. Fowler, W.: 196.
26. Bemis–Burchard: Vol. 1: 270, 289.
    Briggs, M.S.: 3–15.
    Eberlein, H.D.: 42; 63.
    Perley, S.: *Essex Antiq.*: Vol. 1: 183–186.
    Rawson, M.N.: 175.
    Weeden, W.B.: Vol. 1: 192, 213–214, 283; Vol. 2: 528, 531.
27. Bemis–Burchard: Vol. 1: 290.
    Bruce, P.A.: *Econ. Hist. Va.*: Vol. 2: 184.
    Earle, A.: *Home Life*: 32–43.
    Rawson, M.N.: 172–174.
    Surrey, N.M.: *Commerce, La.*: 260.
    Tryon, R.M.: 221–225; 232–235.
28. Bemis–Burchard,: Vol. 1: 290.
    Earle, A.: *Home Life*: 417.
    Langdon, W.: 108–109.

29. Earle, A.: *Home Life*: 254–255.
    Felt, J.B.: 174.
    Smith, H.: 115–117.
    Tryon, R.M.: 235–236.
30. Earle: A.: *Home Life*: 256–257.
    Holliday, C.: 116.
    Tryon, R.M.: 221–225.
31. Marshe, Withman: *Journ. Mass. H.S. Colls.*:
    Ser. 1, Vol. 7: 177.
32. Bemis–Burchard,: Vol. 1: 260–291.
    Briggs, M.S.: 169–175.
    Felt, J.B.: 407, 173.
    Rawson, M.N.: 140–150.
    Spruill, J.: *N.C.H. Rev.*: Vol. 12: 322–329.
    Weeden, W.B.: Vol. 1: 284; Vol. 2: 531, 804–805.
33. Bemis–Burchard: Vol. 1: 268–270.
    Briggs, M.S.: *Homes Pilgrims*s 172–175.
    Weeden, W.B.: Vol. 2: 531.
34. Earle: *China Collecting*.
    Force, Peter: Vol. 3: 9–17.
    Tryon, R.M., 221–225.
35. Spruill, J.: *Women's Life*: 41.
    Stanard, M.: *Col. Va.*: 58–59.
36. Bruce, P.A.: *Econ. Hist. Va.*: Vol. 2: 177.
    Chastellux: Vol. 2: 201–202.
37. Earle, A.: *Home Life*: 257–259.
    Spruill, J.: *Women's Life*: 23–24; 37.
    Stanard, M.: *Col. Va.*: 56; 78.
    Weeden, W.B.: Vol. 1: 216.
38. Stanard, M.: *Col. Va.*: 80–81.
39. Force, Peter: Vol. 3: 9–17.
40. Ibid: Vol. 4: 19.
    Hall, C.C.: *Palatinate*: 123–124.
41. Acrelius: 156–159.
    Bruce, P.A.: *Econ. Hist. Va.*: Vol. 2: 167, 172–173, 176–178,
    183–184.
    Van Rensselaer, Mrs. J.K.: 147.
    Weeden, W.B.: Vol. 1: 106–107, 215–217, 229, 414–417;
    Vol. 2: 804–806.
    Williams, R.J.: *Fithian's Journ*: 251–268.
42. Langdon, W.C.: 82.
    Manges, F.M.: 110.

Spruill, J.: *Women's Life*: 286–288.
43. Andrews, M.P.: *Va. Old Dominion*: 105–106.
    Bruce, P.A.: *Institutional Hist. Va.*: Vol. 2: 71.
    Tyler, L.G.: *Narratives*: 378.
44. Vets. Foreign Wars: *America*: Vol. 2: 116.
45. Fowler, W.: 56–68.
46. *Ibid.*: 22–23.
47. Chase, G.W.: 210–212.
    Earle, A.: *Col. Dames*: 21.
48. Lord, *et al.*: 44–45.
49. Biddle-Lowrie: 56.
    Seaver, J., ed.: *Mary Jemison.*
50. Van Rensselaer, Mrs. J.K.: 24–26; 79.
51. Fowler: 101–104.
52. Freeze, J.G.: *Hist. Columbia Co., Pa.*: 35.
53. Fowler,: 337–339.
54. Cobb, S.H.: 241.
    Reid, W.M.: 82.
    Simms, J.R.: Vol. 1: 106–111, 149–151.
55. *Dorchester Town Records*: Vol. 4: 236.
    Weeden, W.B.: Vol. 1: 273.

CHAPTER 4

1. Connor, J.T.: *Fla. State Hist. Soc. Bull*: Vol. 2: No. 5, 326.
2. Gray–Thompson,: Vol. 1: 12.
3. Connor, J.T.: *Fla. State Hist. Soc. Bull*: Vol. 2: No. 5, 19; 21.
4. *Ibid.*: 85, 227.
5. *Ibid.*: 235, 295, 317, 335.
6. Gray–Thompson: Vol. 1: 104–105.
7. *Ibid.*: Vol. 1: 105.
    Dickenson, J.: *Journ. Pa. Hist. Soc.*: MSS No. AM0512;
        No. AM0531.
8. Gray–Thompson: Vol. 1: 11, 105.
9. Brown: *Genesis U.S.*: Vol. 1: 648.
10. Ames, S.: *Eastern Shore*: 53.
    Smith, J.: *Gen. Histoire (1624 ed.)*: 86.
11. Bruce, P.A.: *Hist. Econ. Va.*: Vol. 2: 291.
    Gray-Thompson: Vol. 1: 29.
    Spruill, J.: *Women's Life*: 67.
12. Brayley, A.W.: 19–20.

13. *Ibid.*: 19.
14. *Ibid.*: 40.
15. *Ibid.*: 58–59.
16. *Ibid.*: 41–44.
17. Trumbull, J., ed.: *Records, Conn.*: Vol. 3: 301.
18. Brayley, A.W.: 81.
19. Bidwell-Falconer: 40.
20. *Ibid.*: 41; 45–47.
21. Earle, A.: *Home Life*: 128.
    Gray–Thompson: Vol. 1: 63.
    Surrey, N.M.: *Commerce, La.*: 155–156, 250 ff.
22. Josselyn, J.: *New England Rarities.*
23. Gray–Thompson: Vol. 1: 78–79.
24. Bidwell–Falconer: 19–20.
    Langdon, W.C.: 280–283.
    Rawson, M.N.: 58.
25. Gray–hompson: Vol. 1: 19–20.
26. Bidwell–Falconer: 18.
    Bradford, W.: *Hist. Plymouth*: 117, 166.
27. Bidwell–Falconer: 18, 28.
28. Gray–Thompson: Vol. 1: 17.
29. Bradford, W.: 99, 116.
30. Andrews, M.P.: *Founding Md.*: 59–60.
    Hall, C.C.: *Narratives.*: 40.
31. Earle, A. *Home Life*: 143–145.
    Van Rensselaer, Mrs. J.K.: 157–158, 266.
32. Connor, J.T.: *Fla. State. Hist. Soc. Bull.*: No. 5, Vol. 2: 225.
    Gray–Thompson: Vol. 1: 105.
    Robertson, J.A.: *Notes on Transfer from Spain*: 7–21.
33. Bradford, W.: *Hist. Plymouth*: 146.
    Giles, D.: 67.
    Gray–Thompson: Vol. 1: 327–328.
34. Bruce, P.A.: *Econ. Hist. Va.*: Vol. 1: 328, 469, 496.
    Gray–Thompson: Vol. 1: 25–26.
    Spruill, J.: *Women's Life*: 81, 306.
    Va. Hist. Mag.: Vol. 5: 10.
35. Bemis–Burchard: Vol. 1: 270.
    Bruce, P.A.: *Econ. Hist. Va.*: Vol. 2: 175–176; 183–184.
    Earle, A.: *Home Life*: 146, 151–153.
    Langdon, W.C.: 21.
    Rawson, M.N.: 59.
36. Brayley, A.W.: 21.

37. *Ibid.*: 23–24.
    Earle,: *Child Life*: 29–31.
        Home Life: 131–133.
    Gray–Thompson: Vol. 1: 172.
    Rawson, M.N.: 64.
38. Earle.: *Home Life*: 133.
    Gray–Thompson: Vol.: 47, 161.
    No. Car. Colonial Records: Vol. 1: 905.
    Todd, V.: 52.
39. Tolles, F.B.: 98.
40. Brayley, A.W.: 32–34; 49.
41. *Ibid.*: 68.
42. *Ibid.*: 22–23; 91.
    Giles, D.: 69.
43. Brayley, A.W.: 76 ff.
    Felt, J.: 152.
    Weeden, W.B.: Vol. 1: 195.
44. Bartlett, H.R.: 72.
    Langdon, W.C.: 82.
    Surrey, N.M.: *Commerce, La.*: 266–267.
45. Earle, A.: *Home Life*: 150.
    Rawson, M.N.: 71–73.
46. Bemis-Burchard: Vol. 1: 276.
    Smith, H.E.: 82.
47. Kimball, M.: 2.
48. Bemis–Burchard: Vol. 1: 268–270; 275–277.
    Earle, A.: *Child Life*: 31.
        Home Life: 10; 134; 152–153.
    Rawson, M.N.: 77.
    Smith, H.E.: 111.
    Van Rensselaer, Mrs. J.K.: 161.
    Weeden, W.Б.: Vol. 1: 216.
49. Earle, A.: *Colonial Dames*: 85–86.
50. Earle, A.: *Home Life*: 111, 155.
51. Gray–Thompson: Vol. 1: 76.
    La Memoirs, La.: 25.
52. Bradley, R.: 23.
53. Spruill, J.: *Women's Life*: 67.
54. Earle, A.: *Home Life*: 146.
    Rawson, M.N.: 83.
    Weeden, W.B.: Vol. 2: 540–541.
55. Earle, A.: *Home Life*: 158–159.

56. Gray–Thompson: Vol. 1: 454.
57. Spruill, J.: *Women's Life*: 65–66.
    Williams, R.J.: *Fithian's Journ.*: 121.
58. Wylie, J.C.: P.M.H.B.: Vol. 27: 436–440.
59. Smith, H.: *Col. Days*: 293
60. Bruce, P.A.: *Econ. Hist. Va.*: Vol. 2: 172–173.
    Spruill, J.: *Women's Life*: 27–29.
    Standard, M.: *Col. Va.*: 97–98.
    Williams, R.J.: *Fithian's Journ.*: 251–268.
61. Bruce, P.A.: *Econ. Hist. Va.*: Vol. 2: 169.
    Earle, A.: *Home Life*: 76–78.
    Weeden, W.B.: Vol. 2: 541.
62. Bruce, P.A.: *Econ. Hist. Va.*: Vol. 1: 339.
    Stanard, M.: *Col. Va.*: 94–96.
63. Bruce, P.A.: *Econ. Hist. Va.*: Vol. 2: 167–168.
    Earle, A.: *Home Life*: 76–77.

CHAPTER 5

1. Andrews, M.P.: *Founding Md.*: 55.
   Banks, C.E.: 9, 47.
2. Bradford, W.: *Hist. Plymouth*: 156.
3. *Ibid.*: 222; 247.
4. *Ibid.*: 228.
5. *Ibid.*: 234.
   Earle, A.: *Home Life*:282–286.
   Myers, G.: 28–46.
   Smith, E.: *Hist. Newburyport*: 20.
6. Earle, A.: *Home Life*:188.
   Leonard, E.A.: *Syllabus*: 80–82.
   Tryon, R.M.: 192.
   Weeden, W.B.: Vol. 1: 193.
7. Earle, A.: *Home Life*: 109.
   Tryon, R.M.: 68–69; 91; 188–189; 196–197.
   Weeden, W.B.: Vol. 1: 228, 308; Vol. 2: 534; 681.
8. Bruce P.A.: *Econ. Hist. Va.*: Vol. 1: 239.
9. Earle, A.: *Home Life*: 167–186; 234.
   Little, F.: 156–166.
   Tryon, R.M.: 207–209; 213.
10. Earle, A.: *Home Life*: 187–206; 237.
    Langdon, W.C.: 294.

Little, F.: 166–168.
Rawson, M.N.: 250–255.
Tryon, R.M.: 209–210.
11. Bruce, P.A.: *Econ. Hist. Va.*: Vol. 1: 246.
Earle, A.: *Home Life*: 206–209.
Gray–Thompson: Vol. 1: 15, 26, 182–183; Vol. 2: 673–674.
12. Bruce, P.A.: *Econ. Hist. Va.*: Vol. 1: 366–368.
Leonard, E.A.: *Syllabus*: 82.
13. Univ. Chicago: *Encyclopedia Britannica*: quote,
          Vol. 20: 660–661.
Gray–Thompson: Vol. 1: 184–185.
Kercheval, S.: 13–14.
Stanard, M.: *Va. 1st Cent*: 124, 190, 232–244.
14. Earle, A.: *Home Life*: 193–194.
Little, F.: 166.
Rawson, M.N.: 40–43.
Weeden, W.B.: Vol. 1: 393.
15. Earle, A.: *Home Life*: 202.
16. Ward, N.: *Simple Cobbler Aggawan.*
Woody, T.: *Ed. Women*: Vol. 1: 171.
17. Rochefoucauld: Vol. 2: 212.
18. Bruce, P.A.: *Econ. Hist. Va.*: Vol. 1: 187.
Chase, G.W.: 122.
Leonard, E.A.: *Syllabus*: 86.
19. Earle, A.: *Two Cents. Costume.*: Vol. 1: 61–69.
Felt: 158.
Little, F.: 38.
Tryon, R.M.: 29–30.
Weeden, W.B.: Vol. 1: 170–171.
20. Bagnall, W.R.: Vol. 1: 4–6.
Bidwell–Falconer: 14.
Clark, V.S.: 32.
Little, F.: 32–33, 38–39.
Weeden, W.B.: Vol. 1: 170–171.
21. Earle, A.: *Home Life*: 188.
Little, F.: 3, 35–36.
Tryon, R.M.: 31–32.
Weeden, W.B.: Vol. 1: 173; 176–177.
22. Earle, A.: *Home Life*: 188.
Weeden, W.B.: Vol. 1: 107.
23. Earle, A.: *Home Life*: 188.
Little, F.: 34.
Weeden, W.B.: Vol. 1: 196.

24. Calhoun, A.: Vol. 1: 125.
    Coman, K.: 64.
    Earle, A.: *Home Life*: 189.
    Leonard, E.A.: *Syllabus*: 83–85.
    Little, F.: 36–37.
    Weeden, W.B.: Vol. 1: 197–198.
25. Weeden, W.B.: Vol. 1: 201, 304–306, 389; Vol. 2: 496.
26. Earle, A.: *Home Life*: 192.
    Weeden, W.B.: Vol. 1: 388.
27. Bolton, C.K.: 49–55, 100.
    Earle, A.: *Home Life*: 180.
                Narragansett: 45–46.
    Little, F.: 34, 56, 58.
    Sheldon, G.: *Hist. Deerfield*: Vol. 1: 606.
    Weeden, W.B.: Vol. 1: 305; 494–495.
    Wright, R.: *Hawkers and Walkers*: 105.
28. Bagnall, W.R.: 19–20.
    Little, F.: 60–61.
    Tryon, R.M.: 86.
    Weeden, W.B.: Vol. 2: 495, 527, 910.
    Wharton, A.H.: *Col. Days*: 93.
29. Bagnall, W.R.: 8, 12.
    Bidwell–Falconer: 15.
    Little, F.: 43–44; 53–54.
30. Little, F.: 45.
    Tryon, R.M.: 47–48.
31. Bagnall, W.R.: 9, 52–54.
    Bidwell-Falconer: 15.
    Earle, A.: *Home Life*: 181, 190.
    Little, F.: 47, 255.
    Pennypacker, S.: *Settlement Germantown*.
32. Little, F.: 13.
    Spruill, J.: *Women's Life*: 74–75, 80.
33. Bruce, P.A.: *Econ. Hist. Va.*: Vol. 2: 194.
    Spruill, J.: *Women's Life*: 75.
34. Bruce, P.A.: *Econ. Hist. Va.*: Vol. 2: 455.
    Clews, E.W.: 355.
    Little, F.: 14, 17.
    Stanard, M.: *Col. Va.*: 202.
    Tryon, R.M.: 37–38.
35. Bruce, P.A.: *Econ. Hist. Va.*: Vol. 2: 445–446.
    Clark, V.S.: 32.
    Clews, E.W.: 357.

Tryon, R.M.: 39–41.
V.M.H.B.: Vol. 17: 227–228.
Woody, T.: *Ed. Women*s Vol. 1: 269.

36. Bruce, P.A.: *Econ. Hist. Va.*: Vol. 2: 458–470.
    V.M.H.B.: Vol. 3: 708.
37. Durand, M.: pamphlet, 1686.
38. Little, F.: 66.
39. Bruce, P.A.: *Econ. Hist. Va.*: Vol. 1: 366.
    Gray–Thompson: Vol. 1: 24, 184.
    Hamilton, P.J.: *Colonization, South*: 128–219.
40. Gray–Thompson: Vol. 1: 180.
    Hirsch, A.H.: 247–250.
    Little, F.: 23, 70.
    Richardson, H.D.: 14.
    Spruill, J.: *Women's Life*: 115.
    Tryon, R.M.: 40–42.
41. Gray–Thompson: Vol. 1: 46.
    Lawson, J.: 86.
    Spruill, J.: *Women's Life*: 82.
    Tryon, R.M.: 97.
42. Gray–Thompson: Vol. 1: 181–182.
43. *Ibid.*: 185–186.
    Little, F.: 24–25.
    McCrady, E.: *Hist. So. Car. Proprietory*: 350.
44. Gray–Thompson: Vol. 1: 186–188.
    Leonard, E.A.: *Syllabus*: 82.
45. Gray–Thompson: Vol. 1: 75.
    La. Memoirs: 25.
    Surrey, N.: *Commerce, La.*: 164.

CHAPTER 6

1. Bagnall, W.R.: 29, 35–36.
   Dow, G.F.: *Arts and Crafts*: 281.
   Little, F.: 61–62.
   Tryon, R.M.: 36–37.
   Weeden, W.B.: Vol. 2: 732–733.
2. Coman, K.: 117.
   Little, F.: 80.
3. Earle, A.: *Col. Dames*: 241–242.
   Mason, G.: *Newport*: 358.
   Tryon, R.M.: 55; 106.

4. Bagnall, W.R.: 56–59.
   Earle, A.: *Col. Dames*: 242.
            Home Life: 184.
            Stage Coach: 173.
   Little, F.: 78.
   Tryon, R.M.: 106–107; 129–130.
   Waters, T.F.: Vol. 2: 299.
   Weeden, W.B.: Vol. 2: 732–733.
5. Gottesman, R.S.: *Arts and Crafts, 1726–1776*: 260, 263.
6. *Archives, N.J.*: Ser. 1, Vol. 27: 209.
   Bagnall, W.R.: 56.
   Earle, A: *Home Life*: 183.
7. Bagnall, W.R.: 23, 42–44.
   Felt, J.: 145.
   Little, F.: 142–143, 148–150.
   Mitchel, E.V.: 245.
   Weeden, W.B.: Vol. 2: 689.
8. Bagnall, W.R.: 51–53.
9. Coman, K.: 114–117.
   Gottesman, R.: *Arts and Crafts, 1726–1776*: 254, 258–259.
   Little, F.: 76.
10. Tryon, R.M.: 77–79, 90–101.
    Wright, R.: *Hawkers and Walkers*: 105.
11. Tryon, R.M.: 54.
12. *Ibid.*: 102, 135–136.
13. Bagnall, W.R.: 5–18, 27, 51–54, 70–71.
    Gottesman, W.R.: *Arts and Crafts, 1726–1776*: 258.
    Little, F.: 76.
14. *Archives, N.J.*: Ser. 1, Vol. 27: 176–177, 352–354, 588–589;
                            Vol. 29: 331.
    Biddle–Lowrie: 24.
    Little, F.: 148.
    Reninger, M.: *Journ. Lancaster Co. Hist. Soc.*:
                            Vol. 63: 183–190.
15. Dexter, E.A.: *Col. Women*: 119–125.
    Earle, A.: *Home Life*: 182–183.
    Ravenel, H.H.: *Eliza Lucas Pinckney*: 182–183.
16. Spruill, J.: *Women's Life*: 80.
    W.W. Quart: Vol. 21: 170.
17. V.M.H.B.: Vol. 21: 395–416.
18. Little, F.: 14, 67, 73.
    Spruill, J.: *Women's Life*: 76.
19. Ravenel, H.H.: *Eliza Lucas Pinckney*: 128–130.

20. Bartlett, H.: 102.
    Spruill, J.: *Women's Life*: 191–193.
21. Bartlett, H.: 56.
22. Tryon, R.M.: 60.
23. Coman, K.: 114.
    Earle, A.: *Home Life*: 247–248.
    Olin, W.: *Mass. Soldiers and Sailors of the Rev.*: Vol. 2: 105.
    Weeden, W.B.: Vol. 2: 848.
24. Earle, A.: *Home Life*: 184–185.
    Little, F.: 83.
    Weeden, W.B.: Vol. 2: 789.
25. Bagnall, W.R.: 63; 70.
    Coman, K.: 115–118.
26. Tryon, R.M.: 60.
27. Chastellux: Vol. 2: 115.
28. *New York Gazette*: Mar. 21, 1726.
29. Calhoun, A.: Vol. 2: 172.
    Leonard, E.A.: *Syllabus*: 83–84.
30. Calhoun, A.: Vol. 2: 172.
31. Bidwell-Falconer: 128.
    Calhoun, A.: Vol. 2: 172–174.
    Coman, K.: 147.
32. Calhoun, A.: Vol. 2: 172–174.
    Kohn, A.: 1–20.
    Woody, T.: *Women's Ed*: Vol. 2: 7.
33. Calhoun, A.: Vol. 2: 173–174.
34. Earle, A.: *Home Life*: 185.
    Weeden, W.B.: Vol. 2: 855.
35. Woody, T.: *Women's Ed*: Vol. 2: 6.
36. Earle, A.: *Home Life*: 202–203.
    Weeden, W.B.: Vol. 2: 862.
37. Bagnall, W.R.: 161, 173–174.
    Dexter, E.A.: *Career Women*: 201.
    Earle, A.: *Home Life*: 207.
    Little, F.: 117.
    Weeden, W.B.: Vol. 2: 912–913.

CHAPTER 7

1. Green, S.A.: *Hist. Medicine Mass.*: 4.
2. Bradford, W.: *Hist. Plymouth*: 105–107.
   Holliday, C.: 6; 113.

3. Stanard, M.: *Va. 1st Cent.*: 95.
4. Jones, F.R.: *Col. Middle States*: 270.
5. Earle, A.: *Customs*: 23.
   Hall–Smith: *Pedigogical Sem.*: Vol. 10: 275–314.
   Holliday, C.: 114–116.
   Spruill, J.: *Women's Life*: 48, 140.
6. Wallace, D.D.: *Life Henry Laurens*: 58.
7. Clark, A.: 259, 263, 273–275.
   Findley, P.: *Lucinda*: 339–340.
8. Anderson, J.: *Women Puritan Times*: Vol. 2: 54–107.
   Chadwick, J.R.: 445–446.
   Clark, A.: 254–265.
   Gardiner, D.: 263–264.
   Hurd–Mead, K.: 403.
9. Chadwick, J.R.: 445.
   Findley: *Lucinda*: 330–333.
   Hurd–Mead, K.: 430–506.
10. Bosworth, F.H.: 281.
11. McHenry, H.: *Md. Hist. Mag.*: Vol. 9: 107–156.
    Spruill, J.: *Women's Life*: 74.
12. Penn, Hannah: *Recipe Book: Hist. Soc. Pa. MSS. Misc. MSS.*
    William Penn: Vol. 6: 53–79.
13. Wylie, J.C.: *P.M.H.B.*: Vol. 27: 436–440.
14. Gray–Thompson: Vol. 1: 334.
    La. Memoirs: 17–19.
    Surrey, N.: *Commerce, La.*: 281.
15. Holman, M.C.: *Conn. Mag.*: Vol. 11: 251–254.
    Stanard, M.: *Col. Va.*: 69.
16. Dexter, E.A.: *Col. Women*: 118–119.
    Earle, A.: *Col. Dames*: 85, 281.
    Ramsay, D.: *Memoirs*: Vol. 2: 221. ff.
    Spruill, J.: *Women's Life*: 47–48, 230.
    Wallace, D.: *Henry Laurens*: 440–442.
17. *Journ.* House Burgesses, Va.: Vol. 7: 303–329;
    Vol. 11: 42, 124–125.
    Spruill, J.: *Women's Life*: 268–269.
    Va. Gazette: June 16, 1768.
18. Dexter, E.A.: *Col. Women*: 68.
    Spruill, J.: *Women's Life*: 74, 269, 278.
    Wallace, D.: *Hist. So. Car.*: Vol. 1: 389.
19. Blanton, W.B.: 5, 11.
    Packard, F.R.: 5–7.
    Tandy, E.: *N.Y. State H.A. Quart.*: Vol. 4: 51.

20. Alden, E.: *Boston Med. and Surg. Journ.*: Vol. 49: 152.
    Bradford, W.: *Hist. Plymouth*: 260.
    Chase,: *Haverhill*: 97, 179, 275.
    Gordon, M.B.: 116, 189.
    Steiner, W.R.: *Conn. Mag.*: Vol. 11: 35.
    Tandy, E.: *N.Y. State H.A. Quart.*: Vol. 4: 50.
21. Gordon, M.B.: 152–153.
    Jacobson, A.C.: *Med. Times N.Y.*: Vol. 44: 167–169.
    Shryocks, R.: *Medicine and Soc. Amer.*: 12.
    Walsh, J.J.: Vol. 1: 18–21.
22. Norris, G.W.: 9.
    Prowell, G.R.: 237.
23. Campbell, J.L.: *Journ. Med. Assoc. Ga.*: Vol. 14: 271–276.
    Gordon, M.B.: 231.
    Norris, G.W.: 10.
24. Prowell, G.R.: 237.
25. Gregory, S.: 27.
    Hurd–Mead, K.: *Med. Rev. Rev.*: Vol. 39: 105.
    Sigourney, L.H.: 156–180.
26. Cobbledick, M.R.: 81.
    Green, S.A.: 54.
    Morison, S.E.: *Intellectual Life*: 136–138.
27. *Archives, Md.*: Vol. 4: 268, 446; Vol. 10: 97, 122, 415;
        Vol. 23: 161, 357, 361.
    Spruill, J.: *Women's Life*: 267–268.
28. Chastellux: 279–282.
    Spruill, J.: *Women's Life*: 308.
29. Larned, E.: *Windham Co.*: Vol. 1: 428–431, 453.
30. Winthrop, J.: *Journ.*: Vol. 1: 45.
31. Dexter, E.A.: *Col. Women*: 64–65.
    Earle, A.: *Customs*: 8–9.
    Sewall, S.: *Diary: Mass. Hist. Colls.*: Ser. 5, Vol. 6: 51.
    Spruill, J.: *Women's Life*: 50.
    Weeden, W.B.: Vol. 1: 420.
32. Drinker, S.H.: Hannah Penn: 8–9.
33. *Maine Hist. Soc. Colls.*: Vol. 1: 285.
    Endicott, Z.: *Synopsis of Med.*: Essex Tracts, No. 5.
34. Dexter, E.A.: *Col. Women*: 66.
    Spruill, J.: *Women's Life*: 275.
    Thoms, H.: 8–9.
    Toner, J.M.: 58.
35. Thoms, H.: 6–7.
    Van Rensselaer, Mrs. J.K.: 6.

36. Bosworth, F.H.: 285–302.
    Earle, A.: *New York*: 90–91.
    Tandy, E.: 50.
    Van Rensselaer, Mrs. J.K.: 82.
37. Lowery, W.: *Spanish Settlement*: 378–380.
38. *Archives, N.J.*: Ser. 2, Vol. 1: 530.
    N.J. Gazette: Dec. 24, 1777.
    Williams J.K.: *Fithians Journ.*: Vol. 1: 70.
39. Calhoun, A.: Vol. 1: 200–201.
    Duane, W., ed.: 157–158; 167; 171.
40. Adams, A.: *Letters*: 401.
    Holliday, C.: 84.
41. P.M.H.B.: Vol. 30: 348–353, 427.
    Seybolt, R.F.: *Apprenticeship Ed.*: 34.
    Spruill, J.: *Women's Life*: 58.
42. Seybolt, R.F.: *Apprenticeship Ed.*: 29–30, 51.
43. Holliday, C.: 89.
44. Earle, A.: *Child Life*: 211–226.
    Furnivall, F.J., ed: *English Manners*: 231 ff.
    Spruill, J.: *Women's Life*: 70.
45. Calhoun, A.: Vol. 1: 123–124.
    Force, P.: Vol. 1: *New England's Plantation*.
46. MSS. copy in Conn. Hist. Soc.
47. Holliday: 133.
    Sewall, S.: *Diary. Mass. H.S. Colls*: Vol. 6: 93.
48. Andrews, C.M.: *Col. Folkways*: 85–90.
    Biddle-Lowrie: 40–41 (Mrs. Galbraith).
    Dexter, E.: *Col. Women*: 169–170 (Mrs. Zenger).
    Drinker, S.H.: *Hannah Penn*.
    Earle, A.: *N.Y.*: 160 (Margaret Backer).
    Lebeson,: 178–182 (Miriam Gratz).
49. Ellis, A.B.: *First Church*: 20.
    Kelso, R.W.: 39–40.
    Waters, T.F.: *Ipswich*: Vol. 2: 386.
    Weeden, W.B.: Vol. 1: 20, 56, 73, 406.
50. Tittle, W.: 3.
51. Adams, C.F.: *Letters*: 93.

CHAPTER 8

1. Bradford, W.: *Hist. Plymouth*: 170.
   Clews, E.W.: 58–61.

Martin, G.H.: 1–6.
Winsor, J.: *Memorial Hist. Boston*: Vol. 4: 237.
2. Camden, C.: 37–58.
Gardiner, D.: 143–202 (also see Index)
Leonard, E.A.: *Syllabus*: 15–16.
3. Ashton, J.: 18.
James, B.B.: 259.
4. Camden, C.: 58.
5. Ashton, J.: 18.
6. Gardiner, D.: 225, 241, 261–262.
Wallas, A.: 22.
7. Clark, A.: 132–133, 200.
Gardiner, D.: 276–299, 301–307, 314–315, 321–322.
Kemp, W.: 20–23.
8. Hale, S.J.: *Distinguished Women*: see Index.
Leonard, E.A.: *Syllabus*: 15–16.
9. Bruce, P.A.: *Institutional Hist. Va.*: Vol. 1: 402–441, 452–457
James, E.: *W.M. Quart.*: Ser. 1, Vol. 3: 98.
Kilpatrick, W.: *Dutch Schools*: 229.
Martin, G.H.: 75.
10. *Colonial Soc. Mass. Publ.*: No. 28: 108, 111, 113–136.
Herrick, C.A.: *The Library, London*: Ser. 3, Vol. 9: 1–6.
Lamb, M.J.: Vol. 1: 172.
Morison, S.S.: *Intellectual Life*: 140–144.
Wright, T.G.: 115–116, 219–224.
11. Bartlett, H.R.: 101.
Bruce, P.A.: *Institutional Hist. Va.*: Vol. 1: 411–421.
Stanard, M.: *Col. Va.*: 295–307.
W.M. Quart.: Ser. 1, Vol. 2: 169 ff; Vol. 3: 246–248;
Vol. 8: 18 ff.
12. Dexter, E.A.: *Career Women*: 103–104.
Col. Women: 30.
Ford, W.C.: 94.
Herrick, C.A.: *The Library*: Ser. 3, Vol. 9: 7–17.
Littlefield, G.E.: *Boston Book Sellers*.
Woody, T.: *Ed. Women*: Vol. 1: 230–234.
13. Calhoun, A.: Vol. 1: 192–193.
Powell, L.P.: 13–16.
14. Dexter, E.A.: *Col. Women*: xxi.
Leonard, E.A.: *Syllabus*: 47–48.
15. Woody, T.: *Ed. Women*: Vol. 1: 145–146.
16. De Windt, C.A.: Vol. 2: 4–5.
17. Yale Memorabilia Colls., Yale Univ. Library.

18. Woody, T.: *Ed. Women*: Vol. 1: 275.
19. Good, H.: 226–234.
    Rush, B.: *Essays*: 19–20, 75–92.
    Woody, T.: Ed. *Women*: Vol. 1: 302–303.
20. Adams, C.F.: *Letters*: 98–99.
    Earle, A.: *Child Life*: 93.
21. Bowne, E.S.: 56–59: 60–61.
    Brown, A.: *Mercy Warren*: 241–242.
22. Calhoun, A.: Vol. 1: 83–84.
    Dexter, F.B.: *New Haven Col. Hist. Soc. Colls*: Vol. 9: 80.
    Hurd, D.H.: Vol. 131–132.
    McCrady: *Royal Govt.*: 49–50; 485; 486.
    Stanard, M.: *Col. Va.*: 268–269.
    W.M. Quart: Ser. 1, Vol. 5: 115; Vol. 6: 1–6, 77–78;
         Vol. 7: 266–267.
23. Shenton, W.: 262 ff.
24. Calder, I.M.: *New Haven*: 131: (Goodwife Wickham).
    Updegraff, H.: 137: (Mrs. Hoar).
25. Clews, E.W.: 58–59.
    Seybolt, R.: *Apprenticeship Ed.*: 37–38.
26. Clews, E.W.: 60–62.
27. Bentley, W.: *Diary*: Vol. 2: 29–32.
    Mason, Sr. M.P.: 8–41.
    Sewall, S.: *Hist. Woburn*: 66–68.
28. Clews, E.W.: 78–80.
29. Mason, Sr. M.P.: 12.
30. Earle, A.: *Child Life*: 64.
    Seybolt, R.: *Apprenticeship Ed.*: 60.
31. Blake, F.E.: *Dorchester Neck*: 45.
    Dexter, E.A.: *Col Women*: 80.
32. Dexter, E.A.: *Career Women*: 17.
    Sewall, S.: *Mass. Hist. Soc. Colls.*: Ser. 5, Vol. 7: 293.
33. Bentley, W.: *Diary*: Vol. 2: 79–403.
    Brooks, G.: 75–102.
    Dexter, E.A.: *Col. Women*: 82–94.
    Greene, H.C. and M.W.: Vol. 1: 442–455.
    Wharton, A.H.: *Col. Days*: 41.
34. Dexter, E.A.: *Career Women*: 9.
35. Dow, G.F.: *Arts and Crafts New Engl.*: 275.
36. Earle, E.A.: *Child Life*: 100.
37. Hopkins, S.: *Life of Sarah Osborn*.
38. Earle, A.: *Child Life*: 95–96.
39. Vanderpoel, E.N.: 1–9.

White, A.C.: 110–120.
Woody, T.: *Ed. Women*: Vol. 1: 340.
40. Mather, C.: *Diary*: Vol. 1: 535–537.
41. Violette, A.G.: 31.
42. Earle, A.: *Child Life*: 93.
43. *Ibid.*: *Child Life*: 176–190.
44. Holliday, C.: 93.
45. Peters, S.: 325.

CHAPTER 9

1. Leonard, E.A.: *Syllabus*: 52–53.
   Powell, L.P.: 24.
2. Clews, E.W.: 200–201.
   Pratt, D.J.: 7.
3. Pennypacker,: *Germantown*: 189–202.
4. Calhoun, A.: Vol. 1: 193.
   Clews, E.W.: 222–223.
   Seybolt, R.: *Apprenticeship Ed.*: 66.
5. *Ibid.*: 68.
6. Earle, A.: *N.Y.*: 35, 40.
   Humphreys, M.G.: *Catherine Schuyler*: 74.
7. Clews, E.W.: 318.
   Holtz, A.A.: 21.
8. Woody, T.: *Ed. Women*: Vol. 1: 209–210.
9. Calhoun, A.: Vol. 1: 194.
10. *Loc. cit.*
    Powell, L.P.: 38.
11. Calhoun, A.: Vol. 2: 59.
    Powell, L.P.: 42–43, 60–61.
12. Calhoun, A.: Vol. 1: 201.
    Leonard, E.A.: *Origins of Personnel Service*: 5–14.
    Staughton, G., *et al.*: 95–96.
13. Budd, T.: 43–47.
    Clews, E.W.: 281–282.
    Wharton, A.H.: *Col. Days*: 46.
14. Brumbaugh, M.G.: 167 ff.
    Woody, T.: *Ed. Women*: Vol. 1: 210–213.
15. Kemp, W.: 126, 267, 271.
16. Haller, M: *Moravian Hist. Soc. Trans.*: Vol. 15: 1–397.
    Reichel, W.C.: *Hist. Bethlehem Female Seminary*.
    Wickersham, J.P.: 151–158.
    Woody, T.: *Ed. Women*: Vol. 1: 216, 235, 330–331.

17. De Windt, C.A.: Vol. 2: 6.
18. Woody, T.: Ed. Women: Vol. 1: 218.
19. Gottesman, R.: *Arts and Crafts, 1726–1776*: 8.
20. *Ibid.*: 277.
21. *Ibid.*: 311.
    Wharton, A.H.: *Col. Days*: 126.
22. *Archives, N.J.*: Ser. 2, Vol. 2: 294.
23. Earle, A.: N.Y.: 35.
24. Dexter, E.A.: *Col. Women*: 96.
    Woody, T.: *Ed. Women*: Vol. 1: 194.
25. *Ibid.*: 189–190.
26. Dexter, E.A.: *Col. Women*: 96.
27. Evans, W. and T.: *Friends Library*: Vol. 1: 460–473.
28. Kemp, W.: 83: 95–96.
29. *Ibid.*: 256.
    Woody, T.: *Ed. Women*: Vol. 1: 229.
30. Kemp, W.: 259.
31. Woody, T.: *Ed. Women*: Vol. 1:218.
32. *Ibid.*: 211.
33. Burns, J.A.: 135.
    Dexter, E.A.: *Career Women*: 17.
    Sonneck, O.G.: 67–68, 161–163.
    Weber, S.: 23–64.
    Woody, T.: *Ed. Women*: Vol. 1: 202, 211–212.
34. Clews, E.W.: 359.
    Leonard, E.A.: *Syllabus*: 53–55.
    Wertenbaker, T.J.: *First Amer.*: 252–253.
35. Clews, E.W.: 351.
36. *Ibid.*: 354.
37. *Ibid.*: 355–356.
38. Holtz, A.A.: 22–23.
39. Bruce, P.A.: *Institutional Hist. Va.*: Vol. 1: 145.
    Tyler, L.G.: *W.M. Quart*: Ser. 1, Vol. 5: 219–223.
40. Clews, E.W.: 409.
41. *Ibid.*: 479.
42. *Ibid.*: 480.
43. *Ibid.*: 489–490.
    Blandin, I.M.: 217–222.
44. Clews, E.W.: 448; 463–465.
    Knight, E.W.: *Doc. Hist. Ed.*: Vol. 4: 63–68.
45. White, G.: 21–31.
46. Burns, J.A.: 146.
    Goebel, E.J.: 26.
47. Dalcho, F.: 93–99.

McCrady, E.: *Hist. So. Car. Proprietory*: 701–703.
Waring, M.: *Ga. Hist. Quart.*: Vol. 14: 324–334.
48. Blandin, J.M.: 129–131.
Tyler, L.G.: *W.M. Quart*: Ser. 1, Vol. 4: 1–14; Vol. 6: 71–85.
Woody, T.: *Ed. Women*: Vol. 1: 282.
49. Bartlett, H.: 109.
50. Knight, E.W.: *Doc. Hist. Ed.*: Vol. 1: 659.
Spruill, J.: *Women's Life*: 199–200.
51. Dexter, E.A.: *Career Women*: 14–16. ;
52. McCrady, E.S.C.: *Royal Govt.*: 490–491.
Spruill, J.: *Women's Life*: 197.
Woody, T.: *Ed. Women*: Vol. 1: 292.
53. Waring, M.: *Ga. Hist. Quart*: Vol. 14: 327.
54. Woody, T.: *Ed. Women*: Vol. 1: 296–297.
55. Ravenel, H.H.: *Eliza Pinckney*: 113.
Spruill, J.: *Women's Life*: 55.
56. Stanard, M.: *Col. Va.*: 112–113, 272–273.
Woody, T.: *Ed. Women*: Vol. 1: 273.
57. Earle, A.: *Child Life*: 94.
58. McCrady: *Proprietory Govt.*: 70–73.
Spruill, J.: *Women's Life*: 256.
59. *Ibid.*: 185–187, 193–194, 255.
60. King, G.: *New Orleans*: 69.
Leonard, E.A.: *Syllabus*: 56.
Ursulines: *New Orleans. MSS Record*: 16–17.
61. Burns, J.A.: 71–79.
Burns-Kohlbrenner: 29–33.
Goebels: 45–48.
Semple, H.C.: *Ursulines in N.O.*
62. Burns, J.A.: 80.
63. Ayer, E.E.: 66–67.
64. *Ibid.*: 18–65.
Burns, J.A.: 55–62.
Goebel: 27–29.

CHAPTER 10

1. Camden, C.: 144–149.
Clark, A.: 35–38, 152–154, 236–238.
Leonard, E.A.: *Syllabus*: 25–36.
Riley, H.T.: 181–182.
Stopes, C.C.: 36 ff.

2. Hening, W.W.: Vol. 3: 140.
3. Calhoun, A.: Vol. 1: 216.
4. Early, R.: 152–153.
   Woody, T.: *Ed. Women*: Vol. 1: 240.
5. Carruth, G., *et al.*: 59.
6. Calhoun, A.: Vol. 1: 86–87.
   Earle, A.: *Col. Dames*: 26–29.
7. Brigham, W.: 273.
   Gray, F.C.: *Mass. Hist. Soc. Colls.* Ser. 3, Vol. 8: 216–237.
8. Campbell, T.B.: 63.
9. Calhoun, A.: Vol. 1: 195.
10. Hart, A.B.: *Commonwealth Hist. Mass.*: Vol. 2: 364–366.
11. Morris, R.: 139–142.
12. *Ibid.*: 173 ff.
13. Hart, A.B.: *Commonwealth Hist. Mass.*: Vol. 2: 364–366.
14. Gray, F.C.: *Mass. Hist. Coll.*s Ser. 3, Vol. 8: 216–237.
    Morris, R.B.: 185–197.
    Reeve, T.: 37–78.
15. Ames, S.: *Eastern Shore*: 191.
16. *Maine Hist. Soc. Colls.*: Vol. 1: 271–272.
17. Pennypacker, S.W.: *Pa. Cases*: 54.
18. Johnson, R.G.: *Hist. Salem*: 111.
19. Ames, S.: *Eastern Shore*: 194.
    Hening, W.W.: Vol. 2: 163–167.
    Morris, R.B.: 193.
    Neill, E.D.: 294, 406.
20. *Maine Hist. Soc. Colls.*: Vol. 1: 281.
21. Earle, A.: *Col. Dames*: 50.
    Essex Instit. Hist. Colls.: Ser. 2, Vol. 1: 28–32.
    Morris, R.B.: 131.
22. Hill, D.G.: 69.
23. Gray, F.C.: *Mass. Hist. Soc. Colls.*: Ser. 3, Vol. 8: 191–237.
24. Morris, R.B.: 135–137.
25. Fernow, B.: *Records New Amsterdam*: Vol. 6: 252; Vol. 7: 44–94.
    Lamb, M.J.: Vol. 1: 250.
26. Dexter, E.A.: *Col. Women*: 101–102.
    Earle, A.: *Col. Dames.*: 50–51.
27. Andrews, M.P.: *Founding Md.*: Vol. 1: 85.
28. Calhoun, A.: Vol. 1: 247.
    Calvert Papers: Ser. 1, Vol. 1: 165.
    Spruill, J.: *Women's Life*: 11.
29. Nugent, N.M.: 3 ff.

30. Morris, R.B.: 154.
31. Twitchell, R.E.: *Archives, N.W.*: Vol. 1: 146.
32. *Essex ounty Records.*: Vol. 8: 356.
33. Calhoun, A.: Vol. 1: 96.
    Pennypacker, S.W.: *Pa. Cases*: 56.
34. Brigham, W.W.: 281.
    Calhoun, A.: Vol. 1: 97.
35. Hening, W.W.: Vol. 3: 335, 371–374.
    Woody, T.: *Ed. Women*: Vol. 1: 253.
36. Manges, F.: 46.
37. Small, W.H.: 173.
    Woody, T.: *Ed. Women*: Vol. 1: 164.
38. Bradford, W.: *Amer. Hist. Rev.*: Vol. 8: 299.
39. *Archives, Md.*: Vol. 1: 215.
40. Hening, W.W.: Vol. 8: 307.
    McKinley, A.: 35.
41. Holliday, C.: 143.
42. *Va. Gazette*: Oct., 15–22, 1736.
    Woody, T.: *Ed. Women*: Vol. 1: 254.
43. Conway, M.D.: Vol. 1: 45–46.
44. Branagan, T.: 118–119.
45. Brown, A.: *Mercy Warren*: 241–242.
46. Lee, R.H.: *Letters*: Vol. 1: 392–393.
47. Adams, A.: *Letters*: 75.
48. Whitehead, W.A.: *N.J. Hist. Soc. Proc.*: Ser. 1, Vol. 8: 101–105.
49. Ames, S.: *Eastern Shore*: 158.
50. Andrews, G.: *Reminiscences*: 36–38.
    Boatwright, E.M.: *Ga. Hist. Quart.*: Vol. 25: 301–305.

CHAPTER 11

1. Hall, C.C.: *Narratives*: 354–361.
   Leonard, E.A.: *Syllabus*: 37–38.
2. Van Rensselaer, Mrs. J.K.: 16–17.
3. Bruce, P.: *Econ. Hist. Va.*: Vol. 1: 612–614.
   Great, Britain. *Public Record Col.*: Vol. 13: No. 29, I.
4. V.M.H.B.: Vol. 4: 218–220.
5. *Pa. Gazette*: July 6, 1737.
   Woody, T.: *Ed. Women*: Vol. 1: 191.
6. Calder, I.M.: *Col. Captivities*: 151 ff.

7. N.Y. Hist. Soc. Colls.: *Apprenticeships; 1694–1708*: Ser. 2, Vol. 18: 179.
   Ames, S.: *Eastern Shore*: 80–81.
8. *Ibid.*: 79.
9. Seybolt, R.: *Apprenticeship Ed.*: 61.
10. *Ibid.*: 68.
11. *Ibid.*: 36.
12. *Loc. cit.*
13. Clews, E.: 68.
14. Seybolt, R.: *Apprenticeship Ed.*: 72.
15. *Ibid.*: 70.
16. Clews, E.: 355–357.
17. Calhoun, A.: Vol. 1: 251.
18. Woody, T.: *Ed. Women*: Vol. 1: 265.
19. Ames, S. *Eastern Shore*: 72–76; other cases: see Index.
20. Seybolt, R.: *Apprenticeship Ed.*: 36–65.
21. *Ibid.*: 80.
22. *V.M.H.B.*: Vol. 5: 234.
23. Pennypacker, S.W.: *Pa. Cases*: 110.
24. Clews, E.: 223.
    Seybolt, R.: *Apprenticeship Ed.*: 30.
25. *Ibid.*: 31;51.
26. Calhoun, A.: Vol. 1: 120.
27. Clews, E.: 223.
28. Ames, S.: *Eastern Shore*: 187–191.
29. *Archives, N.J.*: Ser. 1, Vol. 11: 531–532.
30. *Accomack Wills and Deeds, 1676–1690*: Vol. 6, 134.
    Ames, S.: *Eastern Shore*: 92.
31. *Ibid.*: 89–92.
32. Gray-Thompson.: Vol. 1: 365.
33. *N.Y. Hist. Soc. Colls.*: *Apprenticeships*: Ser. 2, Vol. 18: 196.
    Weeden, W.B.: Vol. 1: 85–86.
34. *Gloucester Co. Hist. Soc. Bull.*: 9, 21, 31.

CHAPTER 12

1. Brailsford, M.R.: 218.
   Leonard, E.A.: *Syllabus*: 38–46.
2. Fiske, J.: *New France and N.E.*: 141–196.
   Lower Norfolk Co. (Va.) Autiquary: Vol. 3: 53.
3. Gardiner, D.: 227, 270.

Makin, B.: *Essay*: 28.
Masson, D.: Vol. 3: 49, 189–191.
4. Bolton, H.E.: *Rim of Christendom*: 418.
Shea, J.J.: *Hist. Cath. Church*: Vol. 1: 197–198.
5. Parke, F.N.: *Md. H. Mag.*: Vol. 31: 271–298.
Richardson, H.D.: *Sidelights Md. Hist.*: Vol. 1: 141–143.
6. .Stanard, M.M.: *Va. 1st Cent.*: 37–96.
7. Bean, Mrs. R. B.: *V.M.H.B.*: Vol. 55: 78–84.
Tyler, L.G.: *Narratives; Va.*: 339.
8. Bruce, P.A.: *Instit. Hist. Va.*: Vol. 1: 34.
9. *Ibid.*: Vol. 1: 278–289. .
James, E.W.: *W.M. Quart.*: Ser. 1, Vol. 1: 127–129; Vol. 2: 58–60.
Lower Norfolk Co. (Va.) Antiquary: Vol. 1: 20–21, 56.
10. *Ibid.*: Vol. 3: 34–38, 52–57.
James, E.W.: *W.M. Quart*: Ser. 1, Vol. 3: 96–101, 163–164, 190–192, 242–245; Vol. 4: 18–23.
11. Chever, G.F.: *Essex Institute Hist. Colls.*: Vols. 1, 2, 3.
Harris, R. B.: *Essex Institute Hist. Colls.*: Vol. 66: 282–284.
12. *Md. Archives*: Vol. 8: 114–118.
Spruill, J.: *Col. Women*: 246.
Strickland, A.: 51–52.
13. Bradford, W.: *Hist. Plymouth*: 45–46.
Earle, A.: *Customs*: 16–17.
14. Masson, D.: Vol. 3: 49.
15. Earle, A.: *Child Life*: 2.
16. Bradstreet, A.: *Poems*.
Ellis, J.H.: *Intro.*: xiv ff.
17. Univ. Chicago: *Encyclopaedia Britannica*s (1944 ed.): Vol. 7: 710.
18. Earle, A.: *Customs*: 9–12.
Sewall, S.: *Mass. Hist. Colls.*: Ser. 5, Vol. 5: 308; 419–423.
19. Earle, A.: *Customs*: 12–15.
20. Trumbull, J.H.: *Public Records Conn.*: Vol. 1: 515.
21. Calhoun, A.: Vol. 2: 57–58.
22. Earle, A.: *Sabbath*: 56, 82.
23. Calhoun, A.: Vol. 1: 117.
Earle, A.: *Sabbath*: 57.
24. Earle, A.: *Customs*: 17, 214–215.
Tittle, W.: 2.
Wharton, A.H.: *Col. Days*: 55–57.
25. Earle, A.: *Sabbath*: 245.

26. *Ibid.*: 246–247.
27. Ellis, A.B.: *First Church, Boston*: 19.
28. Bradford, W.: *Hist. Plymouth*: 363–365.
29. Blake, F.E.: *Princeton, Mass.*: Vol. 1: 137–145.
    Cogswell, L.W.: *Hennicker*: 107.
    Trumbull, J.H.: *Hist. North Hampton*: Vol. 1: 106–107.
30. Cooke, G.W.: 29–31.
    Dexter, E.A.: *Col. Women*: 209.
31. Earle, A.: *Sabbath*: 259.
    Winthrop, J.: *Hist. New England*: Vol. 1: 338–340.
32. Drake, S.G.: *Annals Witchcraft*: 64.
33. For life of Anne Hutchinson, see Leonard, E.A.: *Syllabus*:
    42, 117.
34. Anderson, J.: *Memorable Women*: 185.
    Winthrop, J.: *Hist. New England*: Vol. 1: 294.
35. *Ibid.*: Vol. 1: 240, 249.
36. *Ibid.*: Vol. 1: 295.
37. *Mass. Hist. Soc. Proc.*: Ser. 2, Vol. 4: 190–191.
38. For life of Deborah Moody, see Leonard, E.A.: *Syllabus*:
    43, 119.
39. Winthrop, J.: for his account, see *Hist. New England*: Vol. 2:
    148–150, 164, 339–340, 430.
40. Jones, R.M.: *Quakers*: 26–36.
    Leonard, E.A.: *Syllabus*: 44–46.
41. Ellis, G.E.: *Puritan Age*: 442.
    Jones, R.M.: *Quakers*: 75, 84–89.
    Sewel, W.: Vol. 1: 311.
42. Jones, R.M.: Quakers: 53, 84–89.
    Sewel, W.: Vol. 1: 403–415.
43. Hart-A.B.: *Amer. Hist. Contemporaries*: Vol. 1: 479–481.
44. Jones, R.M.: *Quakers*: 53.
45 Hart-A.B.: *Amer. Hist. Contemporaries*: Vol. 1: 484–486.
46. Currier, J.J.: 144–151, 252, 383–390, 677.
47. Jones, R.M.: *Quakers*: 105–108.
    Manners, E.: *Elizabeth Hooton*.
    Sewel, W.: Vol. 1: see Index.
48. Manners, E.: 41.
49. Coffin, J.: 120.
50. Bouton, N.: N.H. *Papers*: Vol. 1: 384, 415–419.
    Leonard, E.A.: *Syllabus*: 40–41.
    For Salem Witchraft, see Starkey, M.L.
51. Drake, S.G.: *Annals Witchraft*: 190.

52. Robbins, F.G.: *Essex Institute Hist. Colls.*: Vol. 65: 220.
    Winsor, J.: *Memorial Hist. Boston*: Vol. 2: 133.
53. Trumbull, J.R.: Vol. 1: 235.
54. Starkey, M.L.: 139–142, 178.
55. *Ibid.*: 182–183.
56. Sheahan (Beston), H.B.: 73–74.
    Starkey, M.L.: 111–113, 202–204, 210–211.
57. *Ibid.*: 157–158.
58. Mather, C.: *Mass. Hist. Colls.*: Ser. 7, Vol. 7: 160–161.
59. *Ibid.*: 142.
60 *Ibid.*: 178.
61. Starkey, M.L.: 219–221, 228, 230.
62. Upham, C.W.: Vol. 2: 469.
63. Starkey, M.L.: 208. Quote courtesy of Marion Starkey and
    Dolphin Books, Doubleday & Co.
64. *Ibid.*: 258–259.
65. Ross, P.: Vol. 1: 173–175.

CHAPTER 13

1. Fernow, B.: *Doc. Hist. N.Y.*: Vol. 1: 116–117.
   Kemp, W.W.: 63.
2. Lebeson, A.L.: *Jewish Pioneers*: 111, 118.
3. James, B.: 166.
4. Ross, P.: Vol. 1: 163–169, 357, 362.
5. Bowden, J.: 339.
   Bruce, P.A.: *Institutional Hist. Va.*: Vol. 1: 226–236.
6. Spruill, J.: *Women's Life*: 249–250.
7. Burt, M.S.: *Phila.*
8. Biddle-Lowrie: 11–12.
9. Drinker, S.H.: *Hannah Penn.*
10. Clement, J.: *N.J.H.S. Proc.*: Ser. 3, Vol. 7: 103–105.
11. Pennypacker, S.W.: *Pa. Cases*: 35–36.
    Robbins, F.G.: *Essex Inst. Hist. Colls.*: Vol. 65: 223.
12. *Archives, N.J.*: Ser. 1, Vol. 11: 220–223.
13. Leonard, E.A.: *Syllabus*: 43.
14. Myers, E.L.: 19, 35, 44–46.
15. Fries, A.L.: *Road, Salem.*
16. Leonard, E.A.: *Syllabus*: 41.
17. Buog, C.W.: 243 ff.
    Dexter, E.: *Col. Women*: 148–150.
18. Leonard, E.A.: *Syllabus*: 46.

19. Hudson, D.: *Memoirs.*
    Tyler, A.F.: *Freedom's Ferment*: 115–121.
    Updike, W.: 266–272, 574–577.
20. Hudson, D.: *Memoirs*: 23–24.
21. Wright, R.: *Hawkers and Walkers*: 223–224.
22. Adams, J.Q.: *Journ. Amer. Hist.*: Vol. 9: 257.
    Rochefoucauld, L.: *Travels*: Vol. 1: 201–215.
23. Tilden, O.M.: *Dedham Hist. Soc. Reg.*: Vol. 7: 83–100.
24. *Loc. cit.*
    Leonard, E.A.: *Syllabus*: 107.

CHAPTER 14

1. Gottesman, R.: *Arts and Crafts, 1726–1776*: 275, 325, 327,
   332.
   Leonard, E.A.: *Syllabus*: 87.
2. Gottesman, R.: *Arts and Crafts, 1726–1776*: 282, 285, 297,
   298.
   Spruill, J.: *Women's Life*: 286–287.
3. *Archives, N.J.*: Ser. 1, Vol. 26: 346.
   Leonard, E.A.: *Syllabus*: 96.
   Manges, F.M.: 104–105.
   Spruill, J.: *Women's Life*: 288–289.
4. Dexter, E.: *Col. Women*: 2.
   Leonard, E.A.: *Syllabus*: 98.
   Manges, F.M.: 112.
5. Drinker, S.H.: *Md. H. Mag.*: Vol. 56: 335–351.
   Leonard, E.A.: *Syllabus*: 94–95.
6. *Archives, N.J.*: Ser. 2, Vol. 1: 467.
7. *Mass. Bay Col. Records Court Assistants*: Vol. 1: 237, 275,
   330.
   Worcester Soc. Antiq. Colls.: Vol. 3: 23, 48.
8. De Forest, E.J.: Vol. 1: 171–173.
9. Holliday, C.: 297–298.
10. McCrady, E.: *Hist. So. Car. Proprietory*: see Index.
11. Drinker, S.H.: *N.J. Hist. Soc. Proc.*: Vol. 79: 95–110.
12. Andrews, M.P.: *Founding Md.*: 202.
    Hist. Md.: Vol. 1: see Index.
    Semmes, R.: see Index.
13. Leonard, E.A.: *Syllabus*: 98.
    Mason, G.: *Reminiscences*: 358–361.
14. Ames, S.: *Eastern Shore*: 142–144.
    Leonard, E.A.: *Syllabus*: 97–98.

15. Earle, A.: *N.Y.*: 162–163.
    Van Rensselaer, Mrs. J.K.: 33.
16. James-Jameson: see Index.
    Lamb, M.J.: Vol. 1: 271.
    Van Renseslaer, Mrs. J.K.: 234–236.
17. Earle, A.: *Col. Dames*: 56.
    Weeden, W.B.: Vol. 2: 621, 628.
18. Weeden, W.B.: Vol. 1: 366.
19. Dexter, E.: *Col. Women*: 114.
    Hoadley, C.H.: *Col. Records Conn.*: Vol. 6: 212, 284, 323.
    Manges, F.M.: 114.
    Woody, T.: *Ed. Women*: Vol. 1: 164–165.
20. Dexter, E.: *Col. Dames*: 114.
21. Spruill, J.: *Women's Life*: 304.
22. Adams-Stiles: Vol. 1: 909–911.
    Felt, J.: *Annals, Salem*: 301.
    Leonard, E.A.: *Syllabus*: 97–98.
23. *Archives, N.J.*: Ser. 1, Vol. 28: 34, 81.
24. Spruill, J.: *Women's Life*: 32, 241, 303–304.
    Tilghman, O.: Vol. 2: 11 (Deborah Nichols).
25. *Mass. Hist. Soc. Colls*: Ser. 1, Vol. 7: 172 (Mrs. Hughes).
    Spruill, J.: *Women's Life*: 302–304 (Elizabeth Wilson, Anne
        Conner, Sarah Raymer, Anne Middleton, and Flora Dorsey).
    Woody, T.: *Ed. Women*: Vol. 1: 206. (Sarah Flynn and
        Mary Noble).
26. Dexter, E.: *Career Women*: 121–122 (Elizabeth Hill).
    Spruill, J.: *Women's Life*: 303–304.
    Woody, T.: *Ed. Women*: Vol. 1: 260 (Jemimah Cannon and
        Anne Wilson).
27. Worth, H.B.: *Nantucket H.A. Bulls*: Vol. 2: 206, 308–319.
28. Halsey, A.F.: 108.
    Leonard, E.A.: *Syllabus*: 98.
29. Baker, Louisa: *An Affecting Narrative—as a Marine*.
    Dexter, E.: *Col. Women*: 55–56.
    Earle, A.: *Col. Dames*: 74–75.
    Edwards-Rattray: 231–234.
    Gosse, P.: *Hist. of Piracy*: 202–204.
    Weeden, W.B.: Vol. 1: 436.
    Maclay, E.S.: *Hist. of Amer. Privateers*: 8.
    Woodbury, G.: *Great Days of Piracy*: 188–194.
30. Earle, A.: *Stage Coach*: 2, 3.
    Leonard, E.A.: *Syllabus*: 78–80.
31. Earle, A.: *Stage Coach*: 25.

32. *Ibid.*: 85.
33. Dexter, E.: *Col. Women*: 3, 205 (Mrs. Black, and James Leonard).
    Earle, A.: *Stage Coach*: 20 (Mrs. Howard).
    Weeden, W.B.: Vol. 1: 14, 207 (Katherine Barriton).
34. Earle, A.: *Stage Coach*: 76–78.
    Knight, S.J.: *Journal*.
35. Earle, A.: *Stage Coach*: 6.
36. Dexter, E.: *Career Women*: 127.
37. Earle, A.: *Stage Coach*: 85.
38. Manges, F.M.: 81.
39. *Ibid.*: 71–96.
40. Spruill, J.: *Women's Life*: 295–301.
41. Chastellux: *Travels*: Vol. 2: 25, 76, 129, 345.
42. Spruill, J.: *Women's Life*: 297–298.
43. *Ibid.*: 293–300.
44. Dexter, E.: *Col. Women*: 12.
45. Dexter, E.: *Career Women*: 117–118.
46. Burnaby, A.: 90.
47. Spruill, J.: *Women's Life*: 297.
    Macaulay, A.: *W.M. Quart*: Ser. 1, Vol. 11: 183–191.
48. Dexter, E.: *Career Women*: 121 (Mrs. Leathers).
    Col. Women: 10–11 (Mrs. Lawrence, and Mrs. Davenport).
49. *Mass. Hist. Soc. Colls.*: Ser. 1, Vol. 7: 172 (Mrs. Hughes).
    Earle, A.: *N.Y.*: 162, 207 (Mrs. Van Borsum).
    Rochefoucauld: *Travels*: Vol. 2: 212 (Mrs. Cota).
50. Dexter, E.: *Col. Women*: 8. (Mrs. Pratt.)
    Earle, A.: *Stage Coach* (Mrs. Todd) 48–49, 198.
    Wenham Hist. Soc.: *Town Records*: 145, 150 (Goodwife Woodward).
51. Andrews, G.: *Reminiscences*: 36–38.
    Boatwright, E. M.; *Ga. Hist. Quart*: Vol. 25: 301–305.
52. Dexter, E.: *Col. Women*: 205–206.
53. Earle, A.: *Stage Coach*: 198–203.
54. Spruill, J.: *Women's Life*: 300.

CHAPTER 15

 1. Duane, W.: 176–177.
    Spruill, J.: *Women's Life*: 289.
 2. Dexter, E.: *Col. Women*: 73–78.
    Leonard, E.A.: *Syllabus*: 97.

Manges, F.M.: 111.
3. Wharton, A.H.: *Col. Days*: 147–148.
4. Blanton, W.B.: 163.
   Gottesman, R.: *Arts and Crafts (1726–1776)*: 141.
5. Colton, J.M.: 23.
   Leonard, E. A.: *Syllabus*: 90–93.
6. Van Rensselaer, Mrs. J.K.: see Index.
7. *Ibid.*: 233–236.
8. Earle, A.: *N.Y.*: 162.
   Van Rensselaer, Mrs. J.K.: 262.
9. Dexter, E.: *Career Women*: 140–141.
10. Dexter, E.: *Col. Women*: 22–24.
11. Spruill, J.: *Women's Life*: 276–279.
12. *Ibid.*: 280–284.
13. Bidwell-Falconer: 45–47.
    Weeden, W.B.: Vol. 1: 111.
14. O'Callaghan, E.B.: *New Netherlands*: 239.
    Van Rensselaer, Mrs. J.K.: 25–26.
15. Spruill, J.: *Women's Life*: 110, 279.
    Twitchell: *Leading Facts N.M.*: Vol. 1: 453.
16. Dexter E,: *Col. Women*: 209–210 (Mrs. Starbuck).
    Lamson, D.F.: 286–287, 337–338.
17. Earle, A.: *N.Y.*: 159–161.
18. *Archives, N.J.*: Ser. 1, Vol. 24: 424–426 (Mrs. Hume).
    Wharton, A.H.: *Col. Days*: 76 (Mrs. Duncan).
19. McCrady, E.: *Royal Govt.*: 670–676.
    Marcus, J.R.: Vol. 2: 13–14, 358.
    Spruill, J.: *Women's Life*: 280.
20. Andrews, C.M.: *Journ. Lady*: 178–179.
    Dexter, E.: *Col. Women*: 116–117.
21. *Ibid.*: 114–117.
    Spruill, J.: *Women's Life*: 278 (Mrs. Fillion).
22. Dexter, E.: *Col. Women's*: 46 (Jane Bennett).
    Spruill, J.: *Women's Life*: 276, 287–288.
23. Dexter, E.: *Career Women*: 38–39 (Mrs. Tylter).
        Col. Women: 29–30 (Mrs. Mankin).
    Spruill, J.: *Women's Life*: 283 (Mrs. Watson).
24. Ames, S.: *Eastern Shore*: 66 (Mrs. Vaughan).
    Dexter, E.: *Col. Women*: 20–21 (Mrs. Pellham, and
        Mrs. Gordon).
    Gottesman, R.: *Arts and Crafts (1726–1776)*: 318.
    Manges, F.M.: 68 (Mrs. Allen), 42 (Mrs. Evans), 112
        Mrs. Waddle).

Spruill, J.: *Women's Life*: 283 (Mrs. Lind).
25. Dexter, E.: *Col. Women*: 41 (Mrs. Cahill).
  Marcus, J.R.: Vol. 2: 13–14 (Mrs. Moses).
  Woody, T.: *Ed. Women*: Vol. 1: 163(Mrs. Nutmaker).
26. Dexter, E.: *Career Women*: 142–143.
  Spruill, J.: *Women's Life*: 278–284.
27. Dexter, E.: *Col. Women*: 30–33.
  Dow, G.F.: *Arts and Crafts*: 228–231.
  Everyday Life: 126.
28. Dexter, E.: *Career Women*: 145 (Mrs. Saltonstall, and Mrs. Tucker). *Col. Women*: 51 (Mrs. Emerson).
  Gottesman, R.: *Arts and Crafts* (*1726–1776*): 352 (Anne Vanderspiegel).
  Manges, F.M.: 58 (Mary Eddy).
  Myers, A.C.: *Narratives Pa.*: 288–290 (Madame Farmar).
  Prime, A.C.: *Arts and Crafts*: Vol. 2: 149 (Marie Warwell).
  Spruill, J.: *Women's Life*: 278 (Mary Frost, and Anne Milner).
29. *Archives, N.J.*: Ser. 1, Vol. 11: 108–109 (Elizabeth Bass).
  Dexter, E.: *Career Women*: 145 (Mary Butler, Mrs. Dickson, and Katherine Goddard).
  Col. Women: 30 (Joanna Perry).
  Manges, F.M.: 49 (Mary Grafton), 54–55 (Anna Ott).
  Spruill, J.: *Women's Life*: 278 (Elizabeth Timothy, and Elizabeth Wicking).
  Thomas, I.: Vol. 2: 444 (Mrs. Zenger), 447 (Cornelia Bradford), 449 (Anne Smith).
30. *Archives, N.J.*: Ser. 1, Vol. 12: 245 (Mrs. Clothier), 324 (Mrs. Dow); Vol. 24: 142 (Mrs. Beadels).
  Dexter, E.: *Col. Women*: 109–110 (Mrs. Boylston).
31. Bartlett, H.R.: 65–66.
  Spruill, J.: *Women's Life*: 306–307 (Henrietta Dulany, Justina Moore, and Sarah Blakeway).
32. *Archives, N.J.*: Ser. 1, Vol. 12: 339 (Susannah Marsh); Ser. 2, Vol. 4: 320 (Rachel White).
  Dexter, E.: *Col. Women*: 114 (Mrs. Knox).
  Manges, F.M.: 48 (Mrs. Stapleford).
  So. Car. Gazette: Feb. 1, 1736; Oct. 30, 1736; Jan. 1, 1741 (Mrs. Blakeway).
33. Dexter, E.: *Career Women*: 149 (Mrs. Harves, and Mrs. Decamp).
  Col. Women: 51 (Mrs. Emerson).
  Prime, A.C. *Arts & Crafts*: Vol. 2: 149 (Mrs. Warwell).
  Spruill, J.: *Women's Life*: 228 (Mrs. Stevenson).

34. Dexter, E.: *Career Women*: 149 (Mrs. Flagg).
     Gottesman, R.: *Arts and Crafts (1726–1776)*: 96, 352 (Mrs. Sonner and Ann Vanderspiegel).
35. *Archives, N.J.*: Ser. 1, Vol. 1: 256, 430 (Mrs. Smith).
     Dexter, E.: *Col. Women*: 51 (Mrs. Goodwin).
     Manges, F.M.: 103 (Mrs. Page, and Mrs. Emerson): 113 (Mrs. Gale).
     Spruill, J.: *Women's Life*: 289 (Mrs. Butler).
     Weeden, W.B.: Vol. 1: 168 (Danish Women).
36. Gottesman, R.: *Arts and Crafts (1726–1776)*: 137 (Elizabeth Evans); 141–142 (Blanche White).
     Manges, F.M.: 103–105 (Ann Page, Elizabeth Lawrence, Elizabeth Russell, Widow Gale, and Amelia Taylor).
     Prime, A.C.: *Arts and Crafts*: Vol. 1: 205 (Ann King).
     Spruill, J.: *Women's Life*: 288 (Rebecca Weyman, and Ann Fowler).
37. Eberlein: *Pract. Bk. Amer. Antiq*: 181, 350–357.
     Kerfoot, J.B.: see Index.
     Spruill, J.: *Women's Life*: 288.
38. Dexter, E.: *Col. Women*: 54–55 (Mary Jackson).
     Phillips, U.P.: *Plantation and Frontier*: Vol. 1: 352–353 (Hanna Daylies).
     Spruill, J.: *Women's Life*: 199, 257–288 (Anna Hoyland).
39. Dexter, E.: *Col. Women*: 53–54 (Mrs. Paschal, and Sarah Lancaster).
     Gottesman, R.: *Arts and Crafts (1777–1799)*: 237.
     Manges, F.M.: 103 (Sarah Orr, and Hannah Donaldson).
     Spruill, J.: *Women's Life*: 289 (Jane Massy).
40. Dexter, E.: *Col. Women*: 53 (Mary Salmon).
     Earle, A.: *N.Y.*: 159 (Heilke Pieterse).
     Spruill, J.: *Women's Life*: 289 (Jane Burgess).
41. Bining, A.C.: *Pa. Iron and Manuf. 18th Cent.*
     James, Mrs. T.P.: *Memorial*.
     Pa. Soc. Col. Dames: *Forges and Furnaces in Pa.*
42. Spruill, J.: *Women's Life*: 289.
43. Chastellux: Vol. 2: 160.
     Gottesman, R.: *Arts and Crafts (1726–1776)*: 216.

CHAPTER 16

1. Hamill, F.: *Biblio. Soc. Papers*: Vol. 49: 304–312.
2. Bibbins, R.M.: 76–77.

Dexter, E.: *Col. Women*: 166–167.
Richardson, H.D.: *Sidelights Md.*: Vol. 1: 147.
Spruill, J.: *Women's Life*: 263.
Wroth, L.C.: 13–14.
3. Dexter, E.: *Col. Women*: 174–176.
Dunton, J.: 139–143.
Wroth, L.C.: 84–93.
4. Sprupill, J.: *Women's Life*: 264.
5. Earle, A.: *Col. Dames*: 58.
6. Bishop, J.L.: Vol. 1: 176–177.
Dexter, E.: *Career Women*: 103–104.
Hamill, F.: *Biblio. Soc. Papers*: Vol. 49: 314.
Spruill, J.: *Women's Life*: 266.
Wroth, L.C.: 119–146.
7. Hamill, F.: *Biblio. Soc. Papers*: Vol. 49: 314.
8. Spruill, J.: *Women's Life*: 263.
Wroth, L.C.: 12–15.
9. Dexter, E.: *Col. Women*: 174–175.
Earle, A.: *Col. Dames*: 63.
Hamill, F.: *Biblio. Soc. Papers*: Vol. 49: 314.
Spruill, J.: *Women's Life*: 265.
Wroth, L. C.: 87.
10. *Va. Gazette*: Dec. 30, 1773.
11. Hamill, F.: *Biblio. Soc. Papers*: Vol. 49: 314.
12. Cohen, H.: 4–10, 133, 164, 233–241.
Dexter, E.: *Career Women*: 102.
Earle, A.: *Col. Dames*: 64.
Salley, A.S.: *Biblio, Soc. Amer. Proc.*: Vol. 2: 28–69.
Spruill, J.: *Women's Life*: 263–264.
Thomas, I.: Vol. 2: 156–158.
13. Dexter, E.: *Career Women*: 108–109.
Earle, A.: *Col. Dames*: 64.
Salley, A.S.: *Biblio, Soc. Amer. Proc.*: Vol. 2: 66.
Tapley, H.S.: 56–59.
Thomas, I.: Vol. 1: 398; Vol. 2: 168.
14. Dexter, E.: *Career Women*: 103.
15. Hamill, F.: *Biblo. Soc. Papers*: Vol. 49: 311–312.
Winship, G.P.: 1–3.
Winterich, J.T.: 25–26.
16. Dexter, E.: *Col. Women*: 176–177.
Hamill, F.: *Biblio. Soc. Papers*: Vol. 49: 314.
Thomas, I.: Vol. 1: 393–394.
17. Hamill, F.: *Biblio. Soc. Papers*: Vol. 49: 314.

Thomas, I.: Vol. 1: 338, 348, 397; Vol. 2: 263, 283.
18. Brigham, C.: 72–73.
    Thomas, I.: Vol. 2: 277.
19. Dexter, E.: *Col. Women*: 168–169.
    Earle, A.: *Col. Dames*: 65–66.
    Mason, G.L.: *Newport*: 84.
    Sanborn, A.H.: *Newport Hist. Soc. Bull.*: No. 65: 1–11.
20. Dexter, E.: *Col. Women*: 212–213.
21. *Ibid.*: 171.
    Earle, A.: *Col. Dames*: 57.
    Woody, T.: *Ed Women*: Vol. 1: 262–263.
22. Dexter, E.; *Col. Women*: 169–170.
    Van Rensselaer, Mrs. J.K.: 300–306.
    Winterich, J.T.: 98.
23. Dexter, E.: *Career Women*: 107.
    Hildeburn, C.R.: 96–98.
24. Dexter, E.: *Career Women*: 105.
    Seidensticker, O.: 168; 253.
    Winterich, J.T.: 165.
25. Brigham, C.: 73.
26. Dexter, E.: *Col. Women*: 169.
    Hamill, F.: *Biblio. Soc. Papers*: Vol. 49: 313.
    Manages, F.M.: 113–114.
27. *Archives N.J.*: Ser. 1, Vol. 24: 90, 100 (Mrs. Biddle, and
    Mrs. Clarkson).
    Brigham, C.: 73 (Margaret Bache).
    Dexter, E.: *Career Women*: 106 (Deborah Franklin, and
    Misses Humphrey).
28. *Ibid.*: 103–104.
    Prime, A.C.: *Arts and Crafts*: Vol. 2: 279.
    Woody, T.: *Ed. Women*: Vol. 1: 164–165.
29. Adams-Stiles: Vol. 1: 638.
    Brayley: 25–28, 46.
30. Green, H.C., and M.W.: Vol. 1: 410–420.
31. Biddle-Lowrie: 60–62.
32. *Archives, N.J.*: Ser. 1, Vol. 24: 206 (Elizabeth Hoffmire);
    Vol. 27: 40; 289–290 (Grace Reynolds); Vol. 27: 478–479,
    505, 609–610 (Elizabeth Hatkinson).
33. Barker, C.R.: *P.M.H.B.*: Vol. 53. 168–174.
    Needles, S.H.: *P.M.H.B.*: Vol. 8: 285–293.
34. Ames, S.: *Eastern Shore*: 117–125.
35. *Archives, N.J.*: Ser. 2, Vol. 3: 366.
    Md. Gazette: Sept. 12, 1776.
36. Dexter, E.: *Col. Women*: 54. (Hannah Beale).

Little, F.: 14 (Lord Delaware).
Manges, F.M.: 102 (Sarah Jewel).
37. Spruill, J.: *Women's Life*: 288–289.
Whitton, M.O.: *These Were the Women*: 14.
38. Spruill, J.: *Women's Life*: 289, 297, 302.
39. Manges, F.M.: 71; 114 (Sarah Mackinet).
Spruill, J.: *Women's Life*: 298; 300.
40. Dexter, E.: *Career Women*: 122.
41. Dow, G.F.: *Holyoke Diaries*: 26 (Mrs. Landman).
Moore, J.S.: Part 2: 8, 107, 143, 144.
Spruill, J.: *Women's Life*: 304–305.
42. Spruill, J.: *Women's Life*: 77, 311–313.
43. Earle, A.: *Old Narragansett*: 36.
44. Clark, A.: 255.
Leonard, E.A.: *Syllabus*: 76–78.
45. Gardiner, D.: 299.
46. Larned, E.D.: 66–67.
47. Drake, F.S.: *Hist. Roxbury*: 189 (Ann Eliot).
Essex Co. Records: Vol. 1: 419 (Mrs. Bradstreet); Vol. 2: 227–228 (Mrs. Edmonds); Vol. 6: 21 (Mary Folshamer); Vol. 6: 351. (Mrs. Harris).
Green, S.A.: *Hist. Med. Mass.*: 55 (Sarah Alcock).
Packard, F.R.: 48 (Jane Hawkins).
Temple-Sheldon: 68, 164, 363 (Patience Miller).
Winthrop, J.: *Hist.*s Vol. 2: 345–346 (Margaret Jomes).
48. Dexter, E.: *Col. Women*: 59 (Mary Hazard).
Holman, M.C.: *Conn. Mag.*: Vol. 11: 251–254 (Lady Fenwick).
Larned, W.C.: 66–67 (Hannah Bradford, and Ann Eaton).
49. Earle, A.: *Customs*: 357 (Sarah Sands).
Hanson, J.W.: 65 (Ann Huston Winslow).
50. Bliss, W.R.: *Old Colony*: 53.
Green, S.A.: *Hist. Med. Mass.*: 54.
Gregory, S.: *Letter*: 26.
51. Blanton, W.: 167 (Goodwife Wright).
Dexter, E.: *Col. Women*: 64–65 (Hannah Greenleaf).
Essex Co. Records: Vol. 4: 243 (Mrs. Bailey, and Mrs. March); Vol. 6: 351 (Mrs. Smith); Vol. 8: 15 (Mrs. Osgood); Vol. 8: 60 (Ruth Williams); Vol. 8: 145 (Mrs. Gatchell); Vol. 8: 345 (Mrs.. Williams).
Findley, P.: *Lucina*: 345 (Anne Hutchinson).
Hurd-Mead: *Med. Rev.*: 105 (Mrs. Wiatt).
Macy, W.F.: Nantucket: 93–94 (Rachel Bunker).
Packard, F.R.: 49 (Ruth Barnaby).

Pringle: R.: 39–40 (Isabel Babson).
Sewall, S.: *Mass. H.S. Coll.*: Ser. 5, Vol. 5: 40 (Elizabeth Weeden).
Winthrop, J.: *Hist.*: Vol. 1: 313–316 (Mary Dyer).
52. Green, S.A.: *Hist. Med. Mass.*: 55.
Thoms, H.: 3.
53. Bentley, W.: *Diary*: Vol. 2: 308.
Dexter, E.: *Col. Women*: 67 (Mary Bass).
Felt, J.: *Annals*: 438.
54. Adams-Stiles: Vol. 1: 941–942 (Granny Griswold).
Osterweis, R.G.: 36–37 (Widows Beecher and Potter).
Thoms, H.: 2; 9 (Mrs. Bradley).
Woody, T.: *Ed. Women*: Vol. 1: 63 (Mrs. Turner).
55. Wicks, S.: 16 (quote De Kahm).
Winterbotham, W.: Vol. 2: 385.
56. Griffin, A.: 180–181.
57. Ellet, E.F.: *Domestic Hist. Rev.*: 43.
Friends Hist. Soc. Bull.: Vol. 9: 2–14.
58. Bosworth, F.H.: 285 (Lysbert Dirckson).
Thoms, H.: 6 (Hellezo d Joris, and Eva Evertson).
Van Rensselaer, Mrs. J.K.: 8 (Maryje Jans).
Walsh, J.J.: 21–22 (Tryntae Jonas).
59. Earle, A.: *N.Y.*: 91.
60. Dexter, E.: *Col. Women*: 66.
Gottesman, R.: *Arts and Crafts (1727–1777)*: 308.
61. *Archives, N.J.*: Ser. 2, Vol. 4: 398, 508 (Jemima Crane).
Drinker, S.H.: 8.
Johnson, F.C.: *Wyoming Hist. Geneo. Soc.*: May 11, 1888: 55–58.
Thomas, H.: 6.
62. *German Amer. Annals*: Feb., 1903: 73 ff.
Wiles, A.M.: *Lancaster Co. Hist. Soc. Publi.*: Vol. 14: 168–172.
63. Philadelphia, College Physicians, Libr. Gilbert Coll: *MSS Letters*: (Z 10–18,, 2: 145).
64. *Archives Md.*: Vol. 4: 268 (Katherine Hebden), 446 (Mary Bradnox); Vol. 23: 161, 357–361 (Mary O'Neal).
Md. H. Mag.: Vol. 8: 23 (Mrs. Spry).
Spruill, J.: *Women's Life*: 273 (Mrs. Callahan).
Steiner, W.K.: *Bull Johns Hopkins Hosp.*: Vol. 13, Nos. 137–138: 197.
65. Blanton, W.B.: 173–174.

Spruill, J.: *Women's Life*: 268–269.
66. Blanton, W.B.: 165–166.
    Thoms, H.: 11.
    Spruill, J.: *Women's Life*: 271–272.
67. Spruill, J.: *Women's Life*: 273–274 (Catherine Blaikley, and Julia Wheatley).
    Woody, T.: *Ed. Women*: Vol. 1: 263–264 (Mary Rose, and Mrs. Hughes).
68. Spruill, J.: *Women's Life*: 273–274.
    Woody, T.: *Ed. Women*: Vol. 1: 263.
69. Jelliffe, S.E.: *Med. Libr. and Hist. Journ.*: Vol. 4: 145–161.
    Van Rensselaer, Mrs. J.K.: 6
70. Bliss, W.R.: *Buzzard's Bay*: 2–65.
    Essex Co. Records: Vol. 8: 219, 317, 340 (Mrs. Bullocke, and Mrs. Williams).
    Topsfield Town Records: 270–271 (Mrs. Averill).
    Worcester Soc. Antiq. Colls.: Vol. 4: 324–325; 335 (Mrs. Walker and Mrs. Wiley).
71. Spruill, J.: *Women's Life*: 270.
    W.M. Quart: Ser. 1, Vol. 3: 131 (College Nurse).
72. Blanton, W.B.: 149–155.
73. Baudier, R.: *Cath. Church La.*: 107, 138, 183.
74. Bosworth: 287–302 (Hilletje Wilbruch).
    Morton, T.: *Hist. Pa. Hosp.*: 32, 544 (Elizabeth Gardner).
75. Spruill, J.: *Women's Life*: 271.
76. Spruill, J.: *Women's Life*: 270–271.
    Steiner, W.R.: *Johns Hopkins Hosp. Bull.*: Vol. 16: 244.
77. Harrison, F.: *V.M.H.B.*: Vol. 32: 305–320.
78. Dexter, E.: *Career Women*: 29–30.
    V.M.H.B.: Vol. 14: 186–187; Vol. 32: 305–320.
79. Earle, A.: *Col. Dames*: 85–86.
    House Burgesses Va. Journ.: Vol. 7: 303; 329; Vol. 11: 42; 124–125.
    Spruill, J.: *Women's Life*: 268–269.
80. *Pa. Gazette*: Jan. 31, 1765.
    Woody, T.: *Ed. Women*: Vol. 1: 227–228.

CHAPTER 17

1. Leonard, E.A.: *Syllabus*: 103, 112.
2. Ellis, J.H.: *Intro.*
   White, E.W.: *W.M.Q.*: Ser. 3, Vol. 8: 355–377.

3. Campbell, H.: 82.
   Ellis, J.H.: *Intro.*
4. White, E.W.: *W.M. Quart*: Ser. 3, Vol. 8: 355–358.
5. *Ibid.*: 360–364.
6. *Ibid.*: 365.
7. Ellis, J.H.: *Intro.*: lxviii.
   Griswold, R.W.: 20.
8. Bradstreet, A.: *Norton Ed.*: 344.
9. *Ibid.*: 270.
10. Ellis, J.H.: *Intro.*: lxii: 101–107.
11. White, E.W.: *W.M. Quart*: Ser. 3, Vol. 8: 369.
12. Caldwell, L.: 55.
13. *Mother Goose's Melodies.* 1870 ed. xi-xix.
    New Engl. Hist. and Geneo. Reg.: Vol. 27: 144, 311.
    Starrett, V.: *Mother Goose.*
14. Dexter, E.: *Col. Women*: 137.
    Earle, A.: *Customs*: 13.
    Leonard, E.A.: *Syllabus*: 104–105.
    May, C.: 21–25.
    Turrel, E.: *Memoirs.*
    Winsor, J.: *Mem. Hist. Boston*: Vol. 2: 429–430.
15. Brooks, C.: *Hist. Medford*: 319–324.
16. Hanson, J.W.: *Hist. Danvers*: 206–208.
17. Field, V.B.: *Univ. Maine Studies*: Ser. 2, No. 17: 1–90.
18. *Ibid.*: 93.
19. *Ibid.*: 92.
20. Greene, L.: 242–248.
    Sheldon, G.: *Slavery, Old Deerfield.*
21. Leonard, E.A.: *Syllabus*: 104.
22. Wheatley: *Poems.*
    Woody, T.: *Ed. Women*: Vol. 1: 132.
23. Cairnes, W.B.: 205.
    Dexter, E.: *Career Women*: 97.
    Pendleton-Milton: *Univ. Maine Studies*: Ser. 2, No. 20.
24. *Ibid.*: 64.
25. Bentley, W.: *Diaries*: Vol. 2: 246.
26. Leonard, E.A.: *Syllabus*: 104; 123.
27. Griswold, R.: 22.
28. *Ibid.*: 23.
29. Warren, M.: *Poems.*, 1775 ed.
30. Hutcheson, M.M.: *W.M. Quart*: Ser. 3, Vol. 10: 378.
31. Ellet, E.: *Women Rev.*: Vol. 2: 141–246.
    Griswold, R.: 28–29.

May, C.: 26–33.
32. Griswold, R.: 28.
33. Ellet, E.: *Women Rev.*: Vol. 2: 241–246.
   Griswold, R.: 35–37.
   May, C.: 34–38.
34. Griswold, R.: 37.
   Leonard, E.A.: *Syllabus*: 125.
35. Reninger, M.: *Lancaster Co. H.S. Journ.*: 6 Vol.: No. 63:
   183–189.
   Watson, J.F.: *Annals Phila.*: Vol. 1: 559–561.
36. Bill, A.: 21–33.
   Boudinet, J.J.: *Life of Elias Boudinet*: Vol. 1: 28–32, 179.
   Leonard, E.A.: *Syllabus*: 122.
   Wharton, A.H.: *Col. Days*: 113.
37. Bill, A.: 21–33.
38. Watson, F.J.: *Annals Phila.*: Vol. 1: 559–561.
39. Biddle and Lowrie: 46, 80.
   Bridenbaugh, C. and J.: *Rebels*: 107, 113, 152, 285.
   Ellet, E.: *Women Rev.*: Vol. 1: 189–201.
   Gratz, S.: *P.M.H.B.*: Vol. 39: 257–321, 385–409; Vol. 41:
   385–398.
   Hale, S.J.: 312.
   Leonard, E.A.: *Syllabus*: 115.
40. Griswold, R.: 25.
41. Ashmead, H.G.: 47–75.
   Biddle-Lowrie: 80.
   Leonard, E.A.: *Syllabus*: 117.
   Smith, T.: *P.M.H.B.*: Vol. 68: 243–268.

CHAPTER 18

1. Force, P.: *Tracts*: Vol. 1.
   Harrison, F.B.: *V.M.H.B.*: Vol. 50: 289–299.
   Hubbell, J.B.: *Amer. Lit. Mag.*: Vol. 10: 179–201.
2. Cairns, W.B.: 190–198.
   Dexter, E.: *Col. Women*: 130–134.
   Leonard, E.A.: *Syllabus*: 100.
   Marvin, A.P.: 10; 95; 98–114.
   Peckham, H.H.: *Captured by Indians*.
   Trent and Wells: Part 2: 193–204.
3. Adams, Hannah: *Memoirs*.
   Hale, S.J.: 159.

Leonard, E.A.: *Syllabus*: 106–107.
Tilden, O.M.: *Dedham Hist. Soc. Reg.*: Vol. 7: 83–100.
Woods, H.F.: *Brookline*: 157–163.
4. Dexter, E.: *Col. Women*: 134–137.
Leonard, E.A.: *Syllabus*: 106.
5. *Ibid.*: 117.
Salley, A.S.: *So. Hist. Asso. Publs.*: Vol. 6: 143.
Wallace, D.D.: Vol. 1: 411.
6. Dunlap, W.: Vol. 2: 381–387.
Leonard, E.A.: *Syllabus*: 105–106, 121.
Pancoast, H.S.: 349.
Smith, T.: *P.M.H.B.*: Vol. 68: 263–268.
Vail, R.W.: *Susanna Rowson*.
Wegelin, O.: 30–31.
7. Brown, H.: *Sentimental Novel*: 4 ff.
Dexter, E.: *Career Women*: 99–100.
Mott, F.L.: 39–40.
Winsor, J.: Vol. 3: 637 ff.
8. Adams, C.F.: *Letters*.
Familiar Letters.
Callender, H.: *P.M.H.B.*: Vol. 12: 432–456.
Drinker, E.: *P.M.H.B.*: Vol. 13: 298–308
Hubbs, R.: *Memoirs*.
Knight, S.: *Journal*.
Leonard, E.A.: *Syllabus*: 100–102.
Manigault, Anna: S.C.H.G. Mag.: Vols. 20, 21.
Mills, W.: *Hist. Houses* (E. Kearney).
Seaver, J.: *M. Jemison, Life*.
Stone, W.L.: *F. Riesdesel, Letters and Journ.*
9. Flexner, J. T.: 91–93.
Keys, H.E.: *Antiques*: Vol. 16: 490–494.
Morgan, J.H.: 8–9.
Rutledge, A.W.: *Amer. Phil. Soc. Trans.*: Vol. 39, Pt. 2: 122–123, 157, 178.
Wallace, D.D.: Vol. 1: 409.
Willis, E.: *Antiquarian*: Vol. 11: 46–48.
10. Bridenbaugh, C. and J.: *Rebels*: 166–168.
Leonard, E.A.: *Syllabus*: 121.
Morgan, J.H.: 12.
Prime, A.C.: *Arts and Crafts*: Ser. 1: 8, 38.
Rutledge, A.W.: *Amer. Phil. Soc. Trans.*: Vol. 39, Pt. 2.
Spruill, J.: *Women's Life*: 259.
11. Bridenbaugh, C. and J.: *Rebels*: 174.

Gottesman, R.: *Arts and Crafts (1726–1776)*: 391–393.
Long, J.C.: *N.J. Hist. Soc. Proc.*: Vol. 79: 118–123.
Morgan, J.H.: 12, 21.
Scudder, H.E.: 80–84.
12. Leonard, E.A.: *Syllabus*: 109.
    Spruill, J.: *Women's Life*: 198–201, 259.
13. Spruill, J.: *Women's Life*: 102.
14. Bentley, W.: *Dairy*: Vol. 1: see Index; Vol. 2: see Index.
    Bliss, W.R.: *Sidelights Meeting Houses*: 221–233.
    Drinker, S.H.: *Music and Women*: 268.
    Earle, A.: *Customs*: 250.
    Hood, G.: *Hist. Music N.E.*
15. Sonneck, O.G.: 10 ff.
    Spruill, J.: *Women's Life*: 100–101.
16. Sonneck, O.G.: 117 ff., 208 ff.
17. Fitzpatrick, J.: *Wash. Diary*: Vol. 4: 253.
    Sonneck, O.G.: 33, 85.
18. *Ibid.*: 54.
19. Ellis-Evans: 480.
    Miller, E.K.: *Antiques*: Vol. 51–52: 260–262.
    Sachse, J.F.: *German Sectaries*: Vol. 2: 128–160.
20. Dexter, E.: *Col. Women*: 157.
    Leonard, E.A.: *Syllabus*: 108–109.
    Spruill, J.L.: *Women's Life*: 259.
    Standard, M.: *Col. Va.*: 229–251.
21. Dexter, E.: *Col. Women*: 157–166.
    Dunlap, W.: Vol. 1: see Index.
    Hornblow, A.H.: 69 ff.: see Index.
    Leonard, E.A.: *Syllabus*: 114.
    Seilhamer, G.O.: Vol. 1: see Index.
    Spruill, J.: *Women's Life*: 259–261.
22. Dunlap, W.: Vol. 1: see Index.
    Hornblow, A.H.: see Index.
    Leonard, E.A.: *Syllabus*: 121.
    Odell, G.C.: see Index.
    Seilhamer, G.O.: see Index.
23. Dexter, E.: *Career Women*: 78.
24. *Ibid.*: 79.
    Earle, A.: *Stage Coach*: 200–203.
25. Dexter, E.: *Col. Women*: 159.
    Earle, A.: *Stage Coach*: 200–203.
26. Dexter, E.: *Career Women*: 79.
    Dunlap, W.: Vol. 1: 242–259.

27. Dexter, E.: *Career Women*: 78–83.
28. *Ibid.*: 10–11, 82–83, 90, 97–99.
   Hornblow, A.H.: Vol. 1: 209–212.
   Leonard, E.A.: *Syllabus*: 121.
   Mott, F.L.: 39.
   Seilhamer, G.O.: 155, 171, 351.

CHAPTER 19

1. Weeden, W.B.: Vol. 1: 19.
2. *Ibid.*: 50.
3. *Ibid.*: 19.
4. Spruill, J.: *Women's Life*: 232–233.
5. Fowler, W.: 22–23.
   Lovejoy, E.M.: 131.
6. Raum, J.O.: Vol. 1: 76–78.
   Stockton, F.R.: 59–68.
7. Lamb, M.J.: Vol. 1: 207.
   Van Rensselaer, M.G.: Vol. 1: 479.
8. Bartlett, H.R.: 10–31.
   White, G.: *Hist. Colls. Ga.*: 21–30.
9. Biddle-Lowrie: 16.
   Freeze, J.G.: *P.M.H.B.*: Vol. 3: 79–87.
10. Blake, F.E.: *Princeton*: Vol. 1: 137 ff (Covenanters).
   Dexter, E.: *Col. Women*: 106 (Mrs. Philipse).
   Earle, A.: *Col. Dames*: 75 (Mrs. Duncan).
   Holliday, C.: 298 (Mrs. Cursette).
   Spruill, J.: *Women's Life*: 247 (Mrs. Robinson).
11. Crowell, R.: 78–81.
12. Nourse, H.S.: 138 (Alice Whiting).
   Starbuck, A.: 533 (Nantucket Women).
   Van Rensselaer, Mrs. J.K.: 199 (Tryntje Jansen).
   Watertown Records: Vol. 2: 69, 74.
13. Fernow, B.: *Docs., N.Y.*: Vol. 14: 511 (Sarah Fonteyn);
      496 (Mary Ryder).
   Jackson, F.: 50–51 (Widow Jackson); 126 (Elizabeth Bacon).
   Van Winkle, D.: 49 (Lysbet Tysen).
14. Bronner, E. B.: *Friend's Hist. Asso. Bull.*: Vol. 43: 29–32.
15. *Archives, N.J.*: Ser. 1, Vol. 2: 326.
16. Stith, W.: 235–236.
   W.M. Quart: Ser. 1, Vol. 14: 96–100.

17. Great Britain Public Record Office Ref. C.O. 1/5 No. 85 f. 234r. London.
18. Hall, C.C.: *Narratives*: 265–267.
    Spruill, J.: *Women's Life*: 236.
19. *Archives, Md.*: Vol. 8: 153–155.
    Md. H. Mag.: Vol. 2: 373–374.
    Spruill, J.: *Women's Life*: 236.
20. *Ibid.*: 233–235.
21. *V.M.H.B.*: Vol. 22: 234–235.
22. Spruill, J.: *Women's Life*: 238–240.
23. Johnson, R.G.: *Salem West Jersey*: 127.
24. Wallace, D.D.: *Hist. So. Car.*: Vol. 1: 177.
25. Cometti, E.: *N.E. Quart*: Vol. 20: 338.
    Conn. Courant: Oct. 2, 1775.
    Moore, F.: *Diary Rev.*: Vol. 1: 141.
26. *Boston Common*: 63.
    Weeden, W.B.: Vol. 2: 679–680.
27. Mason, G.C.: 358
28. Waters, T. F.: Vol. 2: 299.
29. Bishop, J.L.: Vol. 1: 379.
    Manges, F.M.: 46.
30. Earle, A.: *Col. Dames*: 245–246.
    Felt, J.B.: 196.
    Waters, T.F.: Vol. 2: 298.
31. Earle, A.: *Col. Dames*: 252–254.
    Wharton, A.H.: *Col. Days*: 127.
32. *Loc. cit.*
33. Spruiil, J.: *Women's Life*: 245.
    Va. Gazette: Sept. 15, 1774.
34. Moore, F.: *Dairy Rev.*: Vol. 1: 267.
35. Bishop, J.L.: Vol. 1: 394.
36. *Conn. Courant*: Sept. 10, 1775.
    Moore, F.: *Diary Rev.*: Vol. 1: 128.
37. Earle, A.: *Col. Dames*: 249.
    Hurd, D.H.: Vol. 1: 704.
    Stone, E.: 83–84.
38. Cometti, E.: *N.E. Quart*: Vol. 20: 338–339.
39. *Ibid.*: 330.
40. Griffin, A.: 135–142 (Mrs. Brown, Mrs. Vail, and Mrs. Townsend).
    Jennings, G.P.: 42–43 (Mrs. Andrews).
    Powers, G.: 148–151 (Mrs. Wallace).

Ravenel, H.H.: *Charleston*: 308.

41. Ellet. E.F.: *Women Amer. Rev.*: Vol. 1: 236 (Mrs. Bratton).
Lamson, D.F.: 285–326 (Mrs. Craft).
Mills, W.J.: 227–228 (Mrs. Conduit).
Moschzisker, A. (Mrs. Bache).
Wallace, D.D.: *Hist. So. Car.*: Vol. 2: 272 (Mrs. Mott).

42. Beard, M.: *Through Women's Eyes*: 55 (Mrs. Proctor).
Worcester Soc. Antiq. Colls. Bull.: No. 16: 391–396 (Mrs.
Sargent, and Mrs. Eliot Crafts).

43. Chase, G.W.: 407.

44. Moschzisker, A.
Scharf-Wescott: Vol. 2: 1689.

45. *P.M.H.B.*: Vol. 18: 361.

46. *Archives, N.J.*: Ser. 2, Vol. 4: 486–488.
Lee, F.B.: *N.J. Col. and State*: Vol. 2: 259–262.

47. Lyman, S.E.: *N.Y. Hist. Soc. Quart. Bull.*: Vol. 29: 77–82.

48. Biddle and Lowrie: 67.
Hall, E.H.: *Margaret Corbin*.

49. Bartlett, H.R.: 79–81 (Nancy Hart).
Bunce, O.B.: 162 (Behethland Moore).
Ellet, E.F.: *Women Amer. Rev.*: Vol. 1: 171 (Lydia Darrah);
Vol. 2: 115 (Susan Livingston).
Johnson, J.: *Traditions*: 311–312 (Grace and Rachel Martin).
Wallace, D.D.: *Hist. So. Car.*: Vol. 2: 278 (Emily Geiger).

50. Bunce, O.B.: 110–117 (Deborah Sampson); 323–326 (Sally
St. Clare).
Butler, C.: 336 (Women of Groton).
Meloon, E.S.: *Granite Monthly*: Vol. 66: 22–25 (Dame
Trefethen).

Bibliography

Accomack Co., Va. *Wills and Deeds, 1676–1690.* State Library, Richmond, Va.

Acrelius, Israel. *The History of New Sweden and the Settlements on the Delaware River.* Stockholm, Sweden, 1759.

Adams, Charles F., ed. *Antinomianism in the Colony of Massachusetts Bay.* Boston, Mass., 1894.

——, ed. *Familiar Letters of John Adams and His Wife, Abigail Adams during the Revolution.* New York, 1876.

——, ed. *Letters of Mrs. Adams, Wife of John Adams.* Boston, Mass., 1840.

——. *Three Episodes of Massachusetts History.* 2 vols. Boston, Mass., 1892.

Adams, Hannah. *Memoirs of Miss Hannah Adams, Written by Herself.* Boston, Mass., 1832.

Adams, J. Q. "Jemima Wilkinson," *Journ. Amer. Hist.* Vol. 9: 249–257 (1915).

Adams, Sherman W. & Stiles, Henry B. *History of Ancient Wethersfield, Connecticut.* 2 vols. New York, 1904.

Alden, Ebenezer. "Early History of the Medical Profession in Norfolk County." *Boston Med. & Surgical Journ.* Vol. 49 (1854).

Ames, Azel. *The Mayflower and her Log.* Boston, Mass., 1901.

Ames, Susie. "Law in Action: Court Records of Virginia's Eastern Shore." *W. & W. Quart.* Ser. 3, 4: 177–191 (1947).

——. *Studies of the Virginia Eastern Shore in the 17th Century.* Richmond, Va. 1940.

Anbury, Thomas. *Travels.* 2 vols. New York. 1789, reprinted 1923.

Anderson, James. *Memorable Women of the Puritan Times.* London, England, 1862.

Andrews, Charles M. *Colonial Folkways: A Chronicle of American Life in the Reign of the Georgies.* New Haven, Conn., 1919.

———. *A Journal of a Lady of Quality, Janet Schaw.* New Haven, Conn., 1921.

Andrews, Garnett. *Reminiscences of an Old Georgia Lawyer.* Atlanta, Ga., 1870.

Andrews, Matthew P. *Founding Maryland.* New York, 1933.

———. *Tercentenary History of Maryland.* 4 vols. Chicago, 1925.

———. *Virginia, Old Dominion.* Garden City, N.Y., 1937.

Apprenticeship Indentures, 1694–1708. N.Y. Hist. Soc. Colls., Publ. Fund. Vol. 18 (1885).

Arber, Edward, ed. *The First Three English Books on America: 1511–1555.* Westminister, England, 1895.

Arthur, Stanley C. *Old New Orleans.* New Orleans, La., 1931.

Ashe, Samuel A. *History of North Carolina.* 2 vols. Raleigh, N.C., 1925.

Ashmead, Henry G. *Historical Sketch of Chester on the Delaware.* Chester, Pa., 1883.

Ashton, John. *Social Life in the Reign of Queen Anne.* New York, 1883.

Ayers (Mrs.), Edward E. (trans.). *Benavides.* Los Angeles, Calif., 1900.

Bagnall, William R. *The Textile Industry of the United States: 1639–1810.* Cambridge, Mass., 1893.

Bailey, Rosalie F. *Pre-Revolutionary Dutch Houses and Families.* New York, 1936.

Baird, Charles W. *History of the Huguenot Emigration to America.* 2 vols. New York, 1885.

Baker, Louisa. *An Affecting Narrative . . . as a Marine.* Boston, 1815, 1816, 1817.

Bancroft, Hubert H. *The Works of Hubert H. Bancroft.* Vol. 34. San Francisco, Calif., 1884–1888.

———. *History of Arizona and New Mexico.* San Francisco, Calif., 1889.

Banks, Charles E. *Planters of the Commonwealth: 1620–1640,* Boston, Mass., 1930.

Barker, C.R. "The Gulp Mill." *P.M.H.B.* 53: 168–174 (1929).

Barker, James N. *Sketches of the Settlements on the Delaware River.* Philadelphia, Penna., 1827.

Bartlett, Helen R. *Eighteenth Century Georgia Women.* University of Maryland, Ph.D. typed thesis., 1939.

Baudier, Roger. *The Catholic Church in Louisiana.* New Orleans, La., 1939.

Bean (Mrs.), Robert B. "The Colonial Church in Virginia." *V.M.H.B.* 55: 78–84 (1948).

Beard, Mary R., ed. *Through Women's Eyes.* New York, 1933.

Beedy, Helen C. *Mothers of Maine.* Portland, Me., 1895.

Bemis, Albert F. and Burchard, John. *The Evolving House.* 3 vols. Cambridge, Mass., 1933–1936.

Bentley, William. *Diary: 1759–1819.* 4 vols. Salem Mass., 1905–1914.

Bernheim, G.D. *The History of the German Settlements and of the Lutheran Church in North Carolina.* Philadelphia, Pa., 1872.

Beverly, Robert. *History and Present State of Virginia in Four Parts.* Richmond, Va., 1855.

Bibbins, Ruth M. *The Beginnings of Maryland in England and America.* Baltimore, Md., 1934.

Biddle, Gertrude B. & Lowrie, Sarah D., eds. *Notable Women of Pennsylvania.* Philadelphia, Pa., 1942.

Biddle, Henry D., ed. *Extracts of the Journal of Elizabeth Sandwith Drinker: 1759–1807.* Philadelphia, Pa., 1889.

Bidwell, Percy W. & Falconer, John I. *History of Agriculture in Northern United States: 1620–1860.* Wash., D.C., 1925.

Bill, Alfred. *A House Called Morven.* Princeton, N.J., 1954.

Bining, Arthur C. *Pennsylvania Iron Manufacturing in the 18th Century.* Penna. Hist. Commission Publ. Vol. 4. Harrisburg, Penna., 1938.

Bishop, Cortlandt F. *History of Elections in the American Colonies.* New York, 1893.

Bishop, John. *History of American Manufactures: 1608–1860.* 2 vols. Philadelphia, Pa., 1864.

Blake, Francis E. *Annals of Dorchester Neck, Massachusetts.* Boston, Mass., 1899.

———. *History of the Town of Princeton, Massachusetts.* 2 vols. Princeton, Mass., 1915.

Blandin, Isabella M. *History of Higher Education of Women in the South Prior to 1860.* New York, 1909.

Blanton, Wyndham B. *Medicine in Virginia in the 17th Century.* Richmond, Va., 1930.

Bliss, William R. *Colonial Times in Buzzard's Bay.* Boston, 1900.

———. *The Old Colony Town.* New York, 1893.

———. *Side-Lights from the Colonial Meeting-House.* New York, 1894.

Boatwright, E.M. "Status of Women in Georgia." *Ga. Hist. Quart.* 25: 301–324 (1941).

Bolton, Charles K. *Scotch-Irish Pioneers.* Boston, 1910.

Bolton, Herbert E. *Rim of Christendom.* New York, 1936.

————. *Spanish Exploration in the Southwest: 1542–1706.* New York, 1916.

Boston Common. Boston, 1916.

Bosworth, F.H. *The Doctor in Old New York.* New York, 1898.

Botkin, Benjamin A. *Treasury of New England Folklore.* New York, 1947.

Boudinot, Jane J. *Life of Elias Boudinot.* 2 vols. Boston, 1896.

Bouton, Nathaniel, ed. *Provincial Papers of New Hampshire.* Vol. 1, 1623–1686, Concord, N.H., 1867.

Bowden, James. *History of the Society of Friends in America.* London, England, 1850.

Bowne, Eliza S. *A Girl's Life Eighty Years Ago.* 1783–1809. New York, 1887.

Bozman, John L. *The History of Maryland from its first Settlement in 1633 to the Restoration in 1660.* 2 vols. Baltimore, Maryland, 1837.

Bradford, William. *The History of the Plymouth Plantation: 1606–1646.* New York, 1908.

————. "A Letter," *Amer. Hist. Rev.* 8: 295–301 (1902–1903).

Bradley, Richard. *The Virtue and Use of Coffee with Regard to the Plague and other Infectious Distempers.* London, England, 1721.

Bradstreet, Anne (Norton ed.). *Poems.* New York, 1897.

Brailsford, Mabel R. *Quaker Women: 1650–1690.* London, England, 1915.

Branagan, Thomas. *Excellency of the Female Character Vindicated.* Harrisburg, Pa., 1807.

Brayley, Arthur W. *Bakers and Baking in Massachusetts.* Boston, 1909.

Brevard, Carolina M. *The History of Florida.* New York, 1904.

Bricknell, John. *The Natural History of North Carolina.* Dublin, Ireland, 1737.

Bridenbaugh, Carl and Jessica. *Rebels and Gentlemen.* New York, 1942.

Briggs, Martin S. *Homes of the Pilgrim Fathers in England and America.* New York, 1932.

Brigham, Clarence. *Journals and Journeymen.* Philadelphia, 1950.

Brigham, William. *The Compact with the Charter and Laws of the Colony of New Plymouth.* Boston, 1836.

Bronner, E.B. "An Early Example of Political Action by Women." Bull. Friend's Hist., Assoc. 43: 29–32 (1954).

Brooks, Charles. *History of the Town of Bedford, Massachusetts: 1630–1855.* Boston, 1855.

Brooks, Geraldine. *Dames and Daughters of Colonial Days.* New York, 1900.

Brown, Alexander, ed. *The Genesis of the United States.* 2 vols. Boston, 1890.

Brown, Alice. *Mercy Warren.* New York, 1896.

Brown, Herbert R. *The Sentimental Novel in America: 1789–1860.* Durham, N.C., 1940.

Browne, William H. *Maryland, History of the Palatinate.* New York, 1884.

—— and Hall, C.C., eds. *Maryland Archives.* 51 vols. Baltimore, 1883–1916.

Bruce, Dwight H., ed. *The Empire State in Three Centuries.* 3 vols. New York, 1898.

Bruce, Philip A. *An Economic History of Virginia in the 17th Century.* 2 vols. New York, 1895.

——. *The Institutional History of Virginia in the 17th Century.* 2 vols. New York, 1910.

——. *Social Life in Viriginia in the 17th Century.* Richmond, Va., 1907.

Brumbaugh, Martin G. *Life and Works of Christopher Dock.* Philadelphia, 1908.

Budd, Thomas. *Good Order Established in Pennsylvania and New Jersey, 1685.* Reprint, Cleveland, O., 1902.

Bunce, Oliver B. *The Romance of the Revolution.* New York, 1854.

Buog, Charles W. *Representative Women in Methodism.* New York, 1893.

Burnaby, Andrew. *Travel through the Middle Settlements in North America: 1759–1760.* London, England, 1775.

Burns, James A. *The Catholic School System.* New York, 1908.

Burns, James A. & Kohnbrenner, B.J. *The History of Catholic Education in the United States.* New York, 1937.

Burrage, Henry S. *The Beginnings of Colonial Maine.* Portland, Me., 1914.

Burt, Maxwell Struthers. *Philadelphia.* New York, 1945.

Butler, Caleb. *The History of the Town of Groton, Massachusetts.* Boston, 1848.

Cairns, William B. *Selections from Early Writers: 1607–1800.* New York, 1909.

Calder, Isabel Macbeath. *Colonial Captivities, Marches and Journeys.* New York, 1935.

————. *The New Haven Colony.* New Haven, Conn., 1934.

Caldwell, Luther. *An Account of Anne Bradstreet.* Boston, 1898.

Calhoun, Arthur W. *The Social History of the American Family.* 3 vols. New York, 1945.

Callender, H. *P.M.H.B.* Vol. 12: 432–456 (1888).

Calvert Papers. First Selection, vol. 27. Baltimore, Md., 1889–1899.

Camden, Carroll. *The Elizabethan Woman.* Houston, Texas, 1952.

Campbell, Helen. *Anne Bradstreet and Her Time.* Boston, 1891.

Campbell, J.L. "A Sketch of the Early History of Medicine and Surgery in Georgia." *Journ. Med. Assoc. Ga.* Vol. 14: 271–276 (1925).

Campbell, T.B. *Virginia Oddities.* Richmond, Va., 1933.

Carruth, Gordon, *et al. Encyclopedia of America Facts and Dates.* New York, 1956.

Caulkins, Frances M. *History of New London, Connecticut.* New London, Conn., 1852.

Chadwick, James R. *The Study and Practice of Medicine by Women.* New York, 1878.

Chambers, Henry E. *The History of Louisiana.* 3 vols. New York, 1925.

Chase, George W. *The History of Haverhill.* Haverhill, Mass., 1861.

Chastellux, Marquis de. *Travels in North America in the Years 1780–1782.* Trans. George Grieve. New York, 1828.

Chavez, Fray Angelico. *Origins of New Mexico Families.* Santa Fe, N.M., 1954.

Chever, George F. "The Prosecution of Philip English and His Wife for Witchcraft." *Essex Institute Hist. Colls.* Vols. 1, 2, 3 (1868–1870).

Choate, Chaerls A. "De Soto in Florida." *Gulf States Hist. Mag.* Vol. 1: 342 (1902).

Clark, Alice. *Working Life of Women in the 17th Century.* London, England, 1919.

Clark, Victor S. *The History of Manufactures in the United States.* 3 vols. Wash., D.C., 1916–1928.

Clement, JoJhn "Elizabeth Estaugh and Some of Her Contemporaries." *N.J. Hist. Soc. Proc.* Ser. 3, 7: 103–105 (1912).

————. *Noble Deeds of America Women.* Buffalo, N.Y., 1851.

Clews, Elsie W. (Mrs. Parsons). *Educational Legislation and Administration of the Colonial Governments.* New York, 1899.

Cobb, Sanford H. *The Story of the Palatines.* New York, 1897.

Cobbledick, Melville R. *Property Rights of Women in Primitive New England.* New Haven, Conn., 1937.

Coffin, Joshua. *The History of Newbury, Newburyport & West Newbury*. Boston, 1845.

Cogswell, Elliott C. *The History of Nottingham, Deerfield & Northwood, New Hampshire*. Manchester, N.H., 1878.

Cogswell, Leander W. *The History of the Town of Hennicker, New Hampshire*. Concord, N.H., 1880.

Cohen, Hennig. *The South Carolina Gazette*. Columbia, S.C., 1953.

Colton, Julia M. *Annals of Old Manhattan: 1609–1664*. New York, 1901.

Coman, Katherine. *The Industrial History of the United States*. New York, 1905.

Cometti, Elizabeth. "Women in the American Revolution" *New Engl. Quart.* 20: 329–346 (1947).

Connor, Jeanette Thurber, trans. and ed. "Colonial Records of Spanish Florida." *Fla. State Hist. Soc. Bull.* No. 5, vols. 1 & 2 (1925–1930).

———, ed. "Pedro Menendez de Aviles." *Fla. State Hist. Soc. Publ.* No. 3 (1923).

Connor, Robert D. *The History of North Carolina*. 6 vols. New York, 1919.

Conway, Moncure D. *The Life of Thomas Paine*. 2 vols. New York, 1892.

Cooke, G.W. *Unitarianism*. Boston, 1902.

Coulter, Ellis M.A. *Short History of Georgia*. Chapel Hill, N.C., 1933.

Covey, Cyclone "Puritanism and Music in Colonial America." *W.M. Quart.* Ser. 3, vol. 8: 378–388 (1951).

Crevecoeur, J. Hector de. *Letters from an American Farmer*. London, England, 1782.

Crowell, Robert. *The History of the Town of Essex: 1634–1700*. Boston, 1853.

Currier, John J. *The History of Newbury: 1635–1902*. Boston, 1902.

Dalcho, Frederick. *Historical Account of the Protestant Church of South Carolina*. Charleston, S.C., 1820.

De Brahm, John G. *The History of Three Provinces; South Carolina, Georgia & East Florida*. Cambridge, Mass., 1849.

De Forest, Emily J. *A Walloon Family in America*. 2 vols. Boston, 1914.

De Windt, Carolina A., ed. *Journal and Correspondence of Miss Adams*. 2 vols. 1842.

Dexter, Elizabeth A. *Career Women of America: 1776–1840.* Francestown, N.H., 1950.

———. *Colonial Women of Affairs.* Boston, 1924.

Dexter, Franklin B. "The Removal of Yale College of New Haven." *New Haven Colonial Hist. Soc. Colls.* 9: 80 (1918).

Dewhurst, William W. *The History of St. Augustine, Florida.* New York, 1881.

Dickenson, J. "Journal." Pa. Hist. Soc., Phila., Pa. Manuscript Collection. A.M. 05 12; mss. no. A.M. 053.

Dogget, Carita. *Dr. Andrew Turnbull and the Smyrna Colony.* 1919.

Dorchester Town Records: 1632–1692. Boston, 1883.

Dow, George F. *Arts and Crafts in New England; 1704–1775.* Topsfield, Mass., 1927.

———. *Essex County Quarterly Records.* 7 vols. Salem, Mass., 1911.

———, ed. *The Holyoke Diaries: 1709–1856.* Salem, Mass., 1903.

———. *Everyday Life in Massachusetts Bay Colony.* Boston, 1935.

———, ed. *Topsfield Town Records.* Topsfield, Mass., 1917.

Drake, Francis S. *The Town of Roxbury.* Roxbury, Mass., 1878.

Drake Samuel G. *The Annal sof Witchcraft.* Boston, 1869.

Drinker, Cecil K. *Not So Long Ago: A Chronicle of Medicine and Doctors in Colonial Philadelphia.* New York, 1937.

Drinker, Elizabeth. "Journal: 1777–1778." *P.M.H.B.* 13: 298–308 (1889).

Drinker, Sophie H. *Music and Women.* New York, 1948.

Drinker, Sophie H. *Hannah Penn and the Proprietorship of Pennsylvania.* Philadelphia, 1958.

Drinker, Sophie H. "The Two Elizabeth Carterets" *N.J.H. Soc. Proc.* 79, No. 2: 95–110 (1961).

Drinker, Sophie H. "Votes for Women in the 18 Century New Jersey." *N.J.H. Soc. Proc.* 80: 31–45 (1962).

Drinker, Sophie H. "Women Attorneys of Colonial Times." *Md. H. Mag.* 56: 335–351 (1961).

Drummond, Sarah. "Petition for Land Confiscated after Bacon's Rebellion." *V.M.H.B.* 22: 234–235 (1914).

Duane, William, ed. *Passages from the Diary of Christopher Marshall.* Philadelphia, 1849.

Dunlap, William *History of the American Theatre.* 2 vols. New York, 1832.

Dunton, John. *Life and Errors.* London, England, 1705.

Durand of Dauphine. *Memoir of a French Refugee, 1686.* Trans. Fairfax Harrison, privately printed 1923.

Earle, Alice M. *Child Life in Colonial Days.* New York, 1899.

―――. *China Collecting in America.* New York, 1892.

―――. *Colonial Dames and Goodwives.* Boston, 1895.

―――. *Customs and Fashions in Old New England.* London, England, 1893.

―――. *Home Life in Colonial Days.* New York, 1899.

―――. *In Old Narragansett.* New York, 1898.

―――. *Old Time Gardens.* New York, 1901.

―――. *The Sabbath in Puritan New England.* New York, 1893.

―――. *Stagecoach and Tavern Days.* New York, 1900.

―――. *Two Centuries of Costumes in America.* 2 vols. New York, 1903.

Early, Ruth H. *By-Ways of Virginia History.* Richmond, Va., 1907.

Eberlein, Harold and McClives, Abbot. *A Practical Book of Early American Antiques.* Garden City, New York, 1936.

Edwards, Everett J. and Rattray, Jeanette E. *Whale Off: The Story of American Shore Whaling.* New York, 1932.

Ellet, Elizabeth F. *Domestic History of the American Revolution.* New York, 1850.

―――. *Women of the American Revolution.* 3 vols. New York, 1948–1950.

Ellis, Arthur B. *History of the First Church of Boston: 1632–1880.* Boston, 1881.

Ellis, Franklin & Evans, Samuel. *History of Lancaster County, Pennsylvania.* Philadelphia, 1883.

Ellis, George E. *The Puritan Age and Rule in Massachusetts: 1629–1685.* Boston, 1888.

Ellis, George E. *Works of Anne Bradstreet.* Gloucester, Mass., 1962.

Emery, Samuel H. *History of Taunton, Massachusetts.* Syracuse, N.Y., 1893.

Endicott, Zerobabel. *His Book, Synopsis of Medicine.* Ed. G. F. Dow. Essex Institute Tract No. 5. Salem, Mass., 1914.

Evans, William and Thomas, eds. *Friends Library.* 14 vols. Philadelphia, 1837–1850.

Fairbanks, George R. *Spaniards in Florida.* Jacksonville, Fla., 1868.

Faust, Albert B. *The German Element in the United States.* 2 vols. Boston, 1909.

Felt, Joseph B. *Annals of Salem*. Salem, Mass. 1827.

Fernow, Berthold, ed. *Documents Relating to Colonial History of the State of New York*. 14 vols. Albany, New York, 1883.

Fernow, Berthold. ed. *Records of New Amsterdam*. 7 vols. New York, 1897.

Field, Vena B. *Constantia: A Study of the Life and Works of Judith Sargent Murray*. University of Maine Studies. Ser. 2, No. 17, 1931.

Findley, Palmer. *Priests of Lucina: The Story of Obstretics*. Boston, 1939.

Fiske, John. *Dutch and Quaker Colonies in America*. 2 vols. Boston, 1899.

Fiske, John. *New France and New England*. New York, 1902.

Fitzpatrick, John C., ed. *Diaries of George Washington*. 4 vols. Boston, 1925.

Flexner, James T. *American Painting: First Flowers of Our Wilderness*. Boston, 1947.

Foote, Elizabeth. *Diary*. Mss. Conn. Hist. Society. Hartford, Conn.

Force, Peter, ed. *Tracts and Other Papers Relating to Colonies in North America*. 3 vols. Wash., D.C., 1836.

Ford, Worthington C. *Boston Book Market*. Boston, 1917.

Fortier Alcee. *The History of Louisiana*. 4 vols. New York, 1904.

Fortier, Alcee. *Louisiana Studies: Literature, Customs and Dialects, History and Education*. New Orleans, La., 1894.

Fowler, W.W. *Woman on the American Frontier*. Hartford, Conn., 1883.

French, Benjamin F. *Historical Collections of Louisiana and Florida*. 3 vols. New York, 1869.

Freeze, John G. *History of Columbia County, Pennsylvania*. Bloomsburg, Pa., 1883.

———. "Madame Montour." *P.M.H.B.* 3:79–87 (1879).

Fries, Adelaide L. *The Road to Salem*. Chapel Hill, N.C., 1944.

Furnivall, Frederick J., ed. *Early English Meals and Manners*. London, England, 1868.

Gardiner, Dorothy. *English Girlhood at School*. London, England, 1929.

Gayerre, Charles. *The History of Louisiana*. 2 vols. New York, 1854.

German American Annals. 21 vols. New York, 1903–1919.

Giles, Dorothy. *Singing Valleys*. New York, 1940.

Gloucester County Historical Society. *Organization and Minutes of the Gloucester County Court: 1686–1687*. Woodbury, N.J., 1930.

Goebel, Edmund J. *A Study of Catholic Secondary Education during the Colonial Period.* Wash., D.C., 1936.

Good, Harry G. *Benjamin Rush and His Services to America.* Education. Berne, Ind., 1918.

Gordon, M.B. *Aescuplapius Comes to the Colonies.* Ventor, N.J., 1949.

Goss, Philip. *History of Piracy.* New York, 1932.

Gottesman, Rita S. *The Arts and Crafts in New York: 1726–1776.* New York, 1938.

———. *The Arts and Crafts in New York: 1777–1799.* New York, 1954.

Gratz, Simon. "Material for a Biography of Mrs. Elizabeth (Graeme) Fergusson." *P.M.H.B.* 39:257–321, 385–409 (1915); 41: 385–398 (1917).

Gray, Francis C. "Early Laws of Massachusetts." *Mass. H.S. Colls.* Ser. 3, 8:191–237 (1843).

Gray, Lewis C. and Thompson, Esther K. *The History of Agriculture in Southern United States to 1860.* 2 vols. Wash, D.C., 1933.

Great Britain Public Record Office. *Calendar of State Papers.* Vol. 13, no. 29 I., Reference C. O. ⅕ no. 85f 234r. London, England.

Green, S.A. *History of Medicine in Massachusetts.* Boston, 1881.

Green, Harry and Mary W. *Pioneers Mothers of America.* 3 vols. New York, 1912.

Greene, Lorenzo J. *The Negro in Colonial New England: 1620–1776.* New York, 1942.

Gregory, Samuel. *A Letter to the Ladies in Favor of Female Physicians for Their own Sex.* Boston, 1850.

Griffin, Augustus *Griffin's Journal: First Settlers of Southhold.* Orient, N.Y., 1857.

Griswold, Rufus W. *The Poets and Poetry of America.* Philadelphia, Pa., 1847.

Hale, Sarah J. *Distinguished Women.* New York, 1853.

Hall, Clayton C. *The Lords Baltimore and the Maryland Palatinate.* Baltimore, Md., 1902.

———. *Narratives of Early Maryland: 1653–1684.* New York, 1910.

Hall, Edward H. *Margaret Corbin.* New York, 1932.

Hall, G.S. & Smith, T.L. "Marriage and Fecundity of College Men and Women." *Pedigogical Seminary.* 10:275–314 (1903).

Haller, Mabel. "Early Moravian Education in Pennsylvania." *Moravian H.S. Trans.* 15:1–397. (1953).

Halsey, A.F. *In Old Southhampton.* New York, 1940.

Hamill, Frances "Some Unconventional Women before 1800: Printers, Booksellers and Collectors." *Biblio. Soc. Papers.* 49: 300–314 (4th Quart., 1955).

Hamilton P.J. "Beginnings." *Gulf States Hist. Mag.* 1:1–12 (1902).

——. *Colonization of the South.* Philadelphia, 1904.

Hammond, George P. *Don Juan de Onate and the Founding of New Mexico.* Santa Fe, N.M., 1927.

Hanaford, Phebe. *Daughters of America.* Augusta, Me., 1882.

Hanson, John W. *History of Danvers.* Danvers, Mass., 1848.

Hanson, John W. *History of Gardiner, Pittstown and West Gardiner,* Maine. Gardiner, Me., 1852.

Harris, Ralph B. "Philip English." *Essex Inst. Hist. Colls.* 66: 282–284 (1930).

Harrison, Francis B. "Footnotes upon some 17th Century Virginians." *V.M.H.B.* 50:289–299 (1942).

——. "Mrs. Charlotte Browne with Braddock's Army, Diary." *V.M.H.B.* 32:305–320 (1924).

Hart, Albert B., ed. *American History as Told by Contemporaries.* 5 vols. New York, 1897–1929.

Hart, Albert B. *Commonwealth History of Massachusetts.* 5 vols. New York, 1928.

Hatch, Louis C. *The History of Maine.* 5 vols. New York, 1919.

Hazard, Samuel. *Annals of Pennsylvania: 1609–1682.* Philadelphia, Pa., 1850.

Heartman, Charles F. ed. *Letters and Poems by Phillis Wheatley.* New York, 1915.

Hening, William W., ed. *Statutes at Large—Laws of Virginia.* 13 vols. New York, 1823.

Herrick, Cyril A. "The Early New Englanders—What Did They Read?" *The Library.* Ser. 3, vol. 9., London, England (1918).

Hildeburn, Charles R. *Sketches of Printers and Printing in Colonial New York.* New York, 1895.

Hill, Don Gleason. *Early Records of the Town of Dedham, Massachusetts: 1636–1659.* 5 vols. Dedham, Mass., 1894.

Hirsch, Arthur H. *Hugenots of the Colony of South Carolina.* Durham, N.C., 1928.

Hoadley, Charles H., ed. *Colonial Record of Connecticut: 1636–1776.* 15 vols. Hartford, Conn., 1850–1890.

Hoadley, Charles H., ed. *Records of the Colony of New Haven: 1638–1649.* Hartford, Conn., 1857.

Holliday, Carl. *Women's Life in Colonial Days*. Boston, 1922.

Holman, Mabel C. "A Story of Early American Womanhood." *Conn. Mag.* 11:251–254 (1907).

Holtz, Adrian A. *A Study of the Moral and Religious Elements in American Secondary Education up to 1800*. Chicago, 1917.

Hood, George. *History of Music in New England*. Boston, 1846.

Hopkins, Samuel. *Memoirs of the Life of Sarah Osborn*. Worcester, Mass., 1799.

Hornblow, Arthur H. *The History of the Theatre in America*. 2 vols. Philadelphia, 1919.

Hubbell, Jay B. "John and Ann Cotton of Queen's Creek, Virginia." *Amer. Lit.* 10:179–201 (1938).

Hubbs, Rebecca. *A Memoir—A Minister of the Gospel in the Society of Friends*. Philadelphia, n.d.

Hudson, Daniel. *Memoirs of Jemima Wilkinson*. Bath, N.Y., 1844.

Hume, Martin A. *Sir Walter Raleigh*. New York, 1926.

Humphreys, Mary G. *Catherine Schuyler*. New York, 1897.

Hunter, William, ed. *Virginia Almanac*. Williamsburg, Va., 1754.

Hurd, D.H. *The History of Essex County, Massachusetts*. 2 vols. Philadelphia, 1888.

Hurd-Mead, Kate C. *The History of Women in Medicine*. 2 vols. Haddam, Conn., 1938.

Hutcheson, Maud M. "Mercy Warren." *W.M. Quart.* Ser. 3, 10:-378–402 (1953).

Ives, Joseph M. *The Ark and the Dove*. New York, 1936.

Jackson, Francis. *The History of the Early Settlement of Newton: 1639–1800*. Boston, 1854.

Jackson, John W., ed. *Margaret Morris, Her Journal with Biographical Sketch and Notes*. Philadelphia, 1949.

Jacobson, A.C. "Earliest Manhattan Practioners." *Medical Times N.Y.* 44;167–169 (1916).

James, Bartlett B. and Jameson, J.F., eds. *Journal of Jasper Danckaerts: 1679–1680*. New York, 1913.

James, Bartlett B. *Women of England*. Philadelphia, 1908.

James, Edward. "Grace Sherwood." *W.M.Quart.* Ser.1, 3:96–245 (1894), 4:18–23 (1895).

———. "Notes on Illiteracy." *W.M.Quart.* Ser. 1, 3:98 (1894).

———. "Witchcraft in Virginia." *W.M.Quart.* Ser. 1, 1:127–129 (1891), 2:58–60 (1893).

James, (Mrs.) Thomas Potts (Isabella Batchelder). *Memorial of Thomas Potts jr.* Cambridge, Mass. 1874.

Jelliffe S.E. "The Dutch Physician in New Amsterdam and His Colleagues at Home." *Medical Library & Hist. Journ.* 4:145–161 (1906).

Jennings, George P. *Greens Farms.* Greens Farms, Conn., 1933.

Johnson, Fred, C. "Pioneer Physicians of Wyoming Valley (Pa.)." *Wyoming H.G.S. Mag.* 55–58 (May 11, 1888).

Johnson, Joseph. *Traditions and Reminicences, Chiefly of the American Revolution in the South.* Charleston, S.C., 1851.

Johnson, Robert G. *An Historical Account of the First Settlement of Salem in West Jersey by John Fenwick, Esq, Chief Proprietor of Same.* Philadelphia, 1839.

Jones, F.R. *Colonization of the Middle States and Maryland.* Philadelphia, 1904.

Jones, Rufus. *The Quakers in the American Colonies.* New York, 1911.

Josselyn, J, *New England Rarities Discovered.* London, 1672.

Kelso, Robert W. *The History of Public Poor Relief in Massachusetts: 1620–1920.* Boston, 1922.

Kemp, W.W. *The Support of the Schools in Colonial New York by the Society for the Propagation of the Gospel.* New York, 1913.

Kendall, John S. *The History of New Orleans.* 3 vols. New York, 1922.

Kercheval, Samuel. *The History of the Valley of Virginia.* Strasburg, Va., 1925.

Kerfoot, J.B. *American Pewter.* Boston, 1924.

Keys, Homer E. "Coincidence and Henrietta Johnston." *Antiques.* 16:490–494 (1929).

Kilpatrick, William H. *The Dutch Schools of New Netherlands and Colonial New York.* Wash, D.C., 1912.

Kimball, Marie. *Thomas Jefferson's Cook Book.* Richmond, Va., 1941.

King, Grace E. *New Orleans: The Place and the People.* New York, 1895.

King, Grace E. and Ficklen, John R. *The History of Louisiana.* New Orleans, La., 1905.

Knight, Edgar W. *Documentary History of Education in the South.* 5 vols. Chapel Hill, N.C., 1949–1953.

Knight, Sarah K. *Journal: 1666–1727.* New York, 1935.

Kohn, Augustus. *Cotton Mills of South Carolina.* Charleston, S.C., 1907.

Lamb, Martha J. *The History of the City of New York.* 2 vols. New York, 1877.

La Memoirs, Biographical and Historical Memoirs of Louisiana. 2 vols. Chicago, 1892.

Lamson, D.F. *The History of the Town of Manchester, Massachusetts.* Manchester, Mass., 1895.

Langdon, William C. *Everyday Things in American Life: 1776–1876.* New York, 1941.

Larned, Ellen D. *Historic Gleanings of Windom County, Connecticut.* Providence, R.I., 1899.

Lawson, John. *The History of Carolina.* London, 1718.

Lebeson, Anita L. *Jewish Pioneers in America; 1492–1847.* New York, 1931.

Lee, Francis B. *New Jersey as a Colony and as a State.* 3 vols. New York, 1902.

Lee, Richard H. *Letters.* J.C. Ballagh, ed. 2 vols. New York, 1911–1914.

Leonard, Eugenie A. *Origins of Personnel Services in American Higher Education.* Minneapolis, Minn., 1956.

Leonard, E.A., Drinker, S.H. and Holden M.Y. *The American Woman in Colonial and Revolutionary Times: 1565–1800, A Syllabus with Bibliography.* Philadelphia, 1962.

Little, Frances. *Early American Textiles.* New York, 1931.

Littlefield, G.E. *Early Boston Booksellers.* Boston, 1900.

Long, J.C. "Patience Wright of Bordentown." *N.J.H. Soc. Proc.* 79:118–123 (1961).

Lord, Robert H., Sexton, John E. and Harrington, Edward T. *The History of the Archdiocese of Boston: 1604–1943.* 3 vols. New York, 1944.

Lovejoy, Evelyn M. *The History of Royalton, Vermont.* Burlington, Vt., 1911.

Lowery, Woodbury. *Spanish Settlements within the Present Limits of the United States: 1562–1574.* 2 vols. New York, 1959.

Lyman, Susan E. "Three New York Women of the Revolution." *N.Y.H.S.Quart. Bull.* 29:77–82. (1945).

McCain J.R; *Georgia as a Proprietory Province.* Boston, 1917.

McCrady, Edward. *The History of South Carolina Under the Proprietory Government.* New York 1897.

———. *The History of South Carolina Under the Royal Government.* New York, 1899.

McHenry, Howard. "Some Old English Letters." *Md. Hist. Mag.* 9:107–156. (1914).

McKinley, Albert E. *The Suffrage Franchise in the Thirteen English Colonies in America.* Philadelphia, 1905.

Macaulay, A. "Journal." *W.M.Quart.* Ser.1, 11:183–190 (1902–1903).

Maclay, Edgars. *History of American Privateers.* New York, 1899.

Macy, Obed. *The History of Nantucket.* Boston. 1835.

Macy, William F. *The Nantucket Scrap Basket.* New York, 1930.

Makin, Bathusda. *An Essay to Revive the Antient Education of Gentlewomen.* London, 1673.

Manges, Frances M. *Women Shopkeepers, Tavern Keepers and Artisans in Colonial Philadelphia.* University of Pennsylvania Ph.D. Thesis, 1958 (typed).

Manigault, A. *S.C.H.G. Mag.* Vols. 20, 21.

Manner, Emily. *Elizabeth Hooten: 1660–1672* London, England, 1914.

Marble, Anne R. *The Women Who Came in the Mayflower.* Boston, 1920.

Marcus, Jacob R. *Early American Jewry: 1649–1794.* 2 vols. Philadelphia, 1951–1955.

Marshe, Witham. "Journal." *Mass. Hist. Soc. Colls.* Ser.1, 7:177–179 (reprint 1846).

Martin, G.H. *The Evolution of Massachusetts Public Schools.* New York, 1894.

Marvin, A.P. *The History of the Town of Lancaster, Massachusetts.* Boston, 1859.

Massachusetts Bay Colony Record Court Assistants. 3 vols. Boston, 1901.

Mason, Sister Mary Paul. *Church–State Relationships in Education in Connecticut: 1633–1953.* Wash., D.C., 1953.

Mason, George C. *Reminiscences of Newport.* Newport, R.I., 1884.

Masson, David. *Life of Milton.* 7 vols. New York, 1873.

Mather, Cotton. "Diary: 1687–1708." *Mass. H.S. Coll.* Ser. 7 & 8 (1911–1912).

May, Caroline, ed. *America Female Poets.* Philadelphia, 1848.

Meloon, Everett S. "A New Hampshire Heroine." *Granite Monthly.* 60: 22–25 (1928).

Miller, Elizabeth K. "An Ephrata Hymnal." *Antiques.* 51: 260–262 (1947).

Mills, Weymer J. *Historic Houses in New Jersey.* Philadelphia, 1902.

Mitchell, Edwin V. *The American Village.* New York, 1938.

Morgan, Edmund S. *The Puritan Family: Essays on Religion and Domestic Relations in the 17th Century, New England.* Boston, 1944.

Morgan, John Hill. *Early American Painters.* New York, 1921.

Moore, Frank. *Diary of the Revolution.* 2 vols. New York, 1860.

Moore, Josiah S. *Annals of Henrico Parrish, Virginia.* Richmond, Va., 1914.

Morison, Samuel E. *Builders of the Bay Colony.* New York, 1930.

————. *The Intellectual Life of Colonial New England.* New York, 1956.

Morris, Margaret. "Revolutionary Journal," *Bull. Friend's Hist. Soc.* 9: 2–14, 65–76, 103–114 (1919).

Morris, Richard B. *Studies in the History of American Law.* New York, 1930.

Morton, Thomas. *History of Pennsylvania Hospital: 1751–1895.* Philadelphia, 1895.

Moschzisker, Ann von. *The Emergency Aid of 1776.* Philadelphia, 1917.

Mother Goose's Melodies, 1870 ed. New York, 1879.

Mott, Frank L. *Golden Multitudes.* New York, 1947.

Myers, Albert C. *Narratives of Early Pennsylvania, New Jersey and Delaware.* New York, 1912.

Myers, Elizabeth L. *A Century of Moravian Sisters.* New York, 1918.

Myers, Gustavus. *Ye Olden Blue Laws.* New York, 1921.

Needles, S.H. "The Governor's Mill and the Globe Mills." *P.M.H.B.* 8: 285–293 (1884).

Neill, E.D. *Virginia Carolorum: The Colony: 1625–1685.* Albany, New York, 1886.

Nelson, William, Whitehead, William and Stryker, William, eds. *New Jersey Archives.* Ser. 1, 2, 3. 1880–1914.

Newhall, James R. *The Annals of Lynn.* Lynn, Mass., 1890.

Newsome, A., ed. "Records of Emigrants." *N.C.H. Rev.* 11: 39–54, 129–142 (1934).

Norris, G.W. *Early History of Medicine in Philadelphia.* Philadelphia, 1886.

Nourse, Henry S., ed. *Early Records of Lancaster, Massachusetts 1643–1725.* Lancaster, Mass., 1884.

Nugent, Nell M. *Cavaliers and Pioneers: Abstracts of Virginia Land Patents and Grants: 1623–1800.* 5 vols. Richmond, Va., 1934.

O'Callaghan, E.B. *Documentary History of New York.* 15 vols. Albany, N.Y., 1853–1887.

————. *The History of New Netherlands.* New York, 1845.

Odell, G.C. *Annals of the New York Stage*. 2 vols. New York, 1927.

Olin, W.M. compiler. *Massachusetts Soldiers and Sailors of the Revolution*. 17 vols. Boston, 1896.

Osterweis, Rollin G. *Three Centuries of New Haven: 1638–1938*. New Haven, Conn., 1953.

Packard, Francis R. *The History of Medicine in the United States*. New York, 1931.

Panagopoulos, E.P. "The Background of the Greek Settlers in the New Smyrna Colony." *Fla. H.Q. Rev.* 35: 95–115 (1956).

Pancoast, H.S. *Introduction to American Literature*. New York, 1898.

Parke, Francis N. "Witchcraft in Maryland." *Md. H. Mag.* 31: 271–298 (1936).

Peckham, Howard H. *Captured by the Indians*. New Brunswick, N.J., 1954.

Pendleton, Emily and Ellis, Milton. "Philemia: Life and Works of Sarah Wentworth Morton." *University of Maine Bull*. Vol. 34, No. 4, 1931.

Penn, Hannah. "Recipe Book." *Historical Society of Pennsylvania, Misc. Mss., of William Penn: 1674–1716*. Vol. 6: 53–79.

Pennsylvania Society of Colonial Dames. *Forges and Furnaces in the Province of Pennsylvania*. Philadelphia, 1914.

Pennypacker, Samuel W. *Settlement of Germantown*. Philadelphia, 1899.

———. *Pennsylvania Colonial Cases*. Philadelphia, 1892.

Perley, Sidney. "Methods of Heating in Olden Times." *Essex Antiq.* 1: 57–58, 183–186 (1897).

Peters, Samuel. *The History of Connecticut*. Boston, 1781.

Philadelphia, College of Physicians. *Library, Gilbert Coll., Mss. Letters*. (Z10–18, v. 2, p. 145)

Phillips, Ulrich B. *Plantation and Frontier*. 2 vols. Cleveland, O., 1910.

Pool, David de Sola. *Portraits Etched in Stone*. New York, 1952.

Powell, Chilton L. "Marriage in Early New England." *New Engl. Quart.* 1: 323–334 (1928).

Powell, L.P. *The History of Education in Delaware*. Wash., D.C., 1893.

Powers, Grant. *Historical Sketches of the Discovery, Settlement and Progress of Events in Coos County and Vicinity: 1754–1785*. Haverhill, N.H., 1841.

Pratt, Daniel J. *Annals of Public Education in the State of New York: 1626–1746.* Albany, N.Y., 1872.

Priestly, Herbert I. *The Coming of the White Man.* New York, 1929.

Prime, Alfred C. *The Arts and Crafts in Philadelphia, Maryland and South Carolina: 1721–1785.* Ser. 1, 2. Philadelphia, 1929–1932.

Pringle, James P. *The History of the Town of Gloucester, Massachusetts.* Gloucester, Mass., 1892.

Prowell, G.R. *The History of Camden County, New Jersey.* Philadelphia, 1886.

Ramey, Mary E. *The Chronicles of Mistress Margaret Brent.* 1915.

Ramsay, David. *Memoirs of the Life of Martha Laurens Ramsay.* London, 1815.

Raum, John O. *The History of New Jersey.* 2 vols. Philadelphia,, 1877.

Ravenel, H.H. *Charleston, the Place and the People.* New York, 1906.

Ravenel, H.H. *Eliza Lucas Pinckney.* New York, 1896.

Rawson, Marion N. *Candle Days.* New York, 1934.

Redman, Alice. "The Petition of a Nurse." *Md. H. Mag.* 17: 379 (1922).

Reeve, Tapping. *The Law of Baron and Feme.* Albany, N.Y. 1888.

Reichel, William C. *The History of Bethlehem Female Seminary: 1785–1858.* Philadelphia, 1858.

Reid, W.M. *The Mohawk Valley.* New York, 1901.

Reninger, Marion. "Susanna Wright." *Lancaster H.S. Journ.* 63: 183–189 (1959).

Rey, Agapeto. "The Missionary Aspects of the Founding of New Mexico." *N.M. Hist. Rev.* 23: 22–32 (1948).

Richardson, Hester D. *Sidelights on Maryland History.* 2 vols. Baltimore, Md., 1913.

Riley, Henry T. (trans.). *Liber Albus.* London, 1861.

Robbins, Fred G. "Witchcraft." *Essex Inst. Hist. Colls.* 65: 209–239 (1929).

Robertson, J.A. "Narratives of the Fidalgo of Elvas." *Fla. State Hist. Soc. Publs.* No. 11. 2 vols. (1933).

———. "Some Notes on the Transfer by Spain of Plants and Animals to Its Colonies Overseas." *James Sprunt Hist. Studies.* Vol. 19, No. 2. Univ. of N.C., 1927.

Rochefoucault-Liancourt, Francois de la. *Travels through the United States of North America.* 2 vols. London, 1800.

Ross, Peter. *The History of Long Island.* 3 vols. New York, 1905.

Rush, Benjamin. *Essays, Literary, Moral and Philosophical.* Philadelphia, 1806.

Rutledge, Anna W. "Artists in the Life of Charleston." *Amer. Phil. Soc. Trans.* New ser. Vol. 39, pt. 2 (1949).

Sachse, Julius F. *German Sectaries of Pennsylvania.* 2 vols. Philadelphia, 1899–1900.

Salley, Alexander S. "First Presses." *Biblio. Soc. Proc.* Vol. 2: 86–69 (1908).

———. *Narratives of Early Carolina.* New York, 1911.

Salley, Alexander S. "Biblio. of Women Writers." *S.H.A. Publ.* Vol. 6: 143 (1902).

Sanborn (Mrs.) A.H. "The Newport Mercury." *Newport H.S.Bull.* No. 65:1–11 (1929).

Saunders. W.M., ed. *North Carolina Colonial Records of 1662–1776.* 10 vols. Raleigh, N.C., 1886.

Scharf, John T. and Westcott, Thomson. *The History of Philadelphia.* 3 vols. Philadelphia, 1884.

Scudder, Horace E., ed. *Men and Manners in America One Hundred Years Ago.* New York, 1876.

Seaver, James E., ed. *Narrative of the Life of Mary Jemison.* Batavia, N.Y., 1842.

Seidensticker, Oswald. *The First Century of German Printing in America: 1728–1830.* Philadelphia, 1893.

Seilhamer, G.O. *The History of the American Theatre.* 2 vols. Philadelphia, 1888.

Semmes, Raphael. *Captains and Mariners of Early Maryland.* Baltimore, Md., 1937.

Semple, Henry C., ed. *Ursulines in New Orleans.* New York, 1925.

Sewall, Samuel. Diary. 3 vols. *Mass. H.S. Colls. 5, 6, 7* (1878–1882).

Sewall, Samuel. *History of Woburn.* Boston, 1868.

Sewel, Willem. *The History of the Quakers.* 2 vols. Philadelphia, 1832.

Seybolt, Robert F. *Apprenticeship and Apprenticeship Education.* New York, 1917.

Seybolt, Robert F. *The Town Officials of Colonial Boston: 1634–1775.* Cambrridge, Mass., 1939.

Shea, John G. *History of the Catholic Church in the United States.* 4 vols. New York, 1886–1892.

Sheahan, Henry (Beston). *American Memory.* New York, 1937.

Sheldon, George. *A History of Deerfield, Massachusetts.* 2 vols. Greenfield, Mass., 1895.

————. *Negro Slavery in Old Deerfield.* Privately printed. n.d.

Shenton, William. *Poems.* London, 1854.

Shipp, Barnard. *History of De Soto in Florida, 1512–1568.* Philadelphia, 1881.

Shryock, Richard H. *Medicine and Society in America: 1660–1860.* New York, 1960.

Shurtleff, Harold R. *The Log Cabin Myth.* Cambridge, Mass., 1939.

Sigourney, Lydia H. *Examples of Life and Death.* New York, 1852.

Simms, Jeptha R. *Frontiersmen of New York.* 2 vols. Albany, N.Y., 1882–1883.

Sioussott, Anna. "Colônial Women of Maryland." *Md. H. Mag.* 2: 214–226 (1901).

Small, Walter H. *Early New England Schools.* Boston, 1914.

Smith, Buckingham. *Narratives of De Soto.* New York, 1904.

Smith, Thelma. "Feminism in Philadelphia." *P.M.H.B.* 68: 243–268 (1944).

Smith, Euphemia V. *The History of Newburyport.* Boston, 1854.

Smith, Helen E. *Colonial Days and Ways.* New York, 1900.

Smith, John. *Works of John Smith.* See L.G. Tyler Narratives.

Sonneck, Oscar G. *Early Concert Life in America: 1731–1800.* New York, 1949.

Spruill, Julia C. *Women's Life and Work.* Chapel Hill, N.C., 1938.

Stanard, Mary M. *Colonial Virginia.* Philadelphia, 1917.

Stanard, Mary M. *The Story of Virginia's First Century.* Philadelphia, 1928.

Starbuck, Alexander. *History of Nantucket.* Bostotn, 1924.

Starkey, Marion L. *The Devil in Massachusetts.* New York, 1961.

Starrett, Vincent. *All About Mother Goose.* Boston, 1930.

Staughton, George, Nead, Benjamin and McCamant, Thomas, eds. *The Duke of Yorke's Book of Laws: 1676–1682; Charter and Laws of the Province of Pennsylvania: 1682–1700.* Harrisburgh, Pa., 1879.

Steiner, Walter R. "Governor John Winthrop Jr. of Connecticut as a Physician." *Conn. Mag.* 11: 35–37 (1907).

Stiles, Ezra. "Report on Ann Hutchinson's Trial" *Mass. Hist. Soc. Proc.* Ser. 2, 4: 159–191 (1887–1889).

Stiles, H.R. *Bundling, Its Origin, Progress and Decline in America.* Albany, N.Y., 1869.

Stith, William. *The History of Virginia.* New York, 1865.

Stockton, Frank R. *New Jersey from Discovery to Recent Times.* New York, 1896.

Stone, Edwin M. *The History of Beverly, Massachusetts.* Boston, 1843.

Stone, William L. trans. and ed. *Letters and Journals of Baroness Friederika Riedesel.* Albany, N.Y., 1867.

Stopes, Charlotte C. *British Free Woman.* London, 1894.

Strickland, A. *The Lives of Seven Bishops.* London, 1866.

Surrey (Mrs.), Nancy M. (trans.). *Calendar of Manuscripts in Paris, Archives de Colonies.* Wash., D.C., 1926.

Surrey (Mrs.), Nancy M. *The Commerce of Louisiana during the French Regine: 1699–1763.* New York, 1916.

Sylvester, H.M. *Maine Pioneer Settlements.* 5 vols. Boston, 1909.

Tandy, Elizabeth. "Our Colonial Heritage of Community Medicine." *N.Y. State Hist. Assoc. Quart.* 4: 49–54 (1923).

Tapley, Harriet S. *Salem Imprints: 1768–1825.* Salem, Mass., 1927.

Temple, Josiah H. and Sheldon, George. *History of the Town of Northfield, Massachusetts.* Salem, N.Y., 1875.

Thomas, Isaiah. *History of Printing in America with a Biography of Printers and an Account of Newspapers.* 2 vols. Worcester, Mass., 1810.

Thompson, Zadock. *History of Vermont.* Burlington, Vt., 1833.

Thoms, Herbert. *Chapters on American Obstetrics.* Springfield, 1933.

Tilden, Olive M. "Hannah Adams." *Dedham Hist. Soc. Reg.* 7: 83–100 (1896).

Tilghman, Oswald. *History of Talbot County.* 2 vols. Baltimore, Md., 1915.

Tittle, Walter E. *Colonial Holidays.* New York, 1910.

Titus, Anson., ed. *Madame Knight, Her Diary and Times.* Bostonian Soc. Publ. 9: 99–126 (1912).

Todd, Vincent H. *Baron Christopher von Graffenried's Account of Founding New Bern Adventures.* Raleigh, N.C.. 1920.

Tolles, F.B. *Meeting House and Counting House.* Chapel Hill, N.C., 1948.

Toner, Joseph M. *Toner Contributions to the Annals of Medical Progress in United States.* Wash., D.C., 1874.

Trent, William P. and Wells, Berry W., eds. *Readings from Colonial Prose and Poetry.* New York, 1903.

Trumbull, J.H., *History of Northampton, Massachusetts*. 2 vols. 1898.

Trumbull, J. H., ed. *Public Records of Connecticut: 1636–1776*. 15 vols. Hartford, Conn., 1850–1890.

Tryon, Rolla M. *Household Manufactures in United States: 1640–1860*. Chicago, 1917.

Turrell, Ebenezer. *Memoirs of Jane Turrell*. Boston, 1735.

Twitchell, Ralph E. *Leading Facts of New Mexican History*. 5 vols. Cedar Rapids, Iowa, 1911–1917.

Twitchell, Ralph E. *The Spanish Archives of New Mexico*. 2 vols. Cedar Rapids, Iowa, 1914.

Tyler, Alice F. *Freedom's Ferment*. Minneapolis, Minn., 1944.

Tyler, L.G. "Education in Colonial Virginia." *W.M. Quart.* Ser. 1, vols. 5, 6 (1897–1898).

Tyler, L.G. "Grammer and Mattey Practice." *W.M. Quart.* Ser. 1, 4: 1–14 (1895).

Tyler, L.G. *Narratives of Early Virginians:1606–1625*. New York, 1907.

Tyler, L.G. "Will of Elizabeth Stith." *W.M. Quart.* Ser. 1, 5: 115.

United States De Soto Expedition Commission, 76th Congress, 1st Session, House Document No. 71, Final Report. Wash., D.C., 1939.

University of Chicago. *Encyclopaedia Britannica*. Chicago, 1944.

Updegraff, Harlan. *Origin of the Moving School in Massachusetts*. New York, 1907.

Updike, Wilkins. *History of the Episcopal Church in Narragansett, Rhode Island*. Boston, 1907.

Upham, Charles W. *Salem Witchcraft*. New York, 1959.

Ursuline Sister. *The Ursulines in Louisiana: 1727–1824*. New Orleans, 1886.

Vail, Robert W. "Susanna Rowson." *Amer. Antiquarian Soc. 1933*. Worcester, Mass.

Vanderpoel, Emily N. *Litchfield School: 1792–1833*. Cambridge, Mass., 1903.

Van Rensselaer (Mrs.), John K. *The Goede Vrouw of Mana-ha-ta*. New York, 1898.

Van Rennselaer, Mariana G. *History of the City of New York in the 17th Century*. 2 vols. New York, 1909.

Vaux, G. "Diary of Hannah Callendar." *P.M.H.B.* 12: 432–456 (1888).

Van Winkle, Daniel. *Old Bergen*. Jersey City, N.J., 1902.

Van Wyck, Frederick. *Keskachauge, or the First White Settlement on Long Island*. New York, 1924.

Varner, John, G. and Jeanette J. *Garcilaso de la Vega's Florida of the Inca*. Austin, Texas, 1951.

Veterans of Foreign Wars. *America-Original Sources*. 12 vols. Chicago, 1925.

Villagra, Gasper Perez de. *Expedition*. Los Angeles, Calif., 1933.

Violette, Augusta G. *Economic Feminism in American Literature Prior to 1848*. Orono, Me., 1925.

Virginia, Journal of the House of Burgesses: 1619–1776. 13 vols. Richmond, Va., 1905–1915.

Wallace, David D. *History of South Carolina*. 4 vols. New York, 1934.

Wallace, David, D. *Life of Henry Laurens*. New York, 1915.

Wallas, Ada. *Before Blue Stockings*. New York, 1930.

Walsh, J.J. *History of Medicine in New York*. 5 vols. New York, 1919.

Ward, Nathaniel. *Simple Cobbler of Aggawan in America*. Boston, 1713.

Waring, Martha G. "Savannah's Earliest Private Schools." *Ga. Hist. Quart*. 14: 324–334 (1930).

Warren, Mercy. *Poems, Dramatic and Miscellaneous*. Boston, 1790.

Waters, Thomas F. *Ipswich in the Massachusetts Bay Colony: 1700–1917*. 2 vols. Ipswich, Mass., 1917.

Watertown Records. 5 vols. Watertown, Mass. 1894.

Watson, John F. *Annals of Philadelphia and Pennsylvania in the Olden Times*. 2 vols. Philadelphia, Pa., 1844.

Webber, Mabel L. "Extracts from the Journal of Mrs. Ann Manigault: 1754–1781." *S.C.H.G. Mag*. Vols. 20, 21 (1919–1920).

Weber, Samuel. *The Charity School Movement in Colonial Pennsylvania: 1754–1763*. Philadelphia, 1905.

Weeden, William B. *Economic and Social History of New England: 1620–1789*. 2 vols. Boston, 1890.

Wegelin, Oscar. *Early American Fiction: 1774–1830*. New York, 1929.

Wenham Town Records. Wenham, Mass., 1930.

Wertenbaker, Thomas J. *First Americans*. New York, 1929.

Wharton, Anne H. *Colonial Days and Dames*. Philadelphia, 1908.

White, Alain C. *The History of the Town of Litchfield, Connecticut: 1720–1920*. Litchfield, Conn., 1920.

White, E.W. "Anne Bradstreet." *W.M. Quart*. Ser. 2, 8: 355–377 (1951).

White, George. *Historical Collections of Georgia*. New York, 1854.

Whitehead, W.A. "Female Suffrage in New Jersey." *N.J. Hist Soc. Proc.* Ser. 1, 8: 101–105 (1856).

Whiton, John M. *Sketches of the History of New Hampshire from Its Settlement 1623– to 1833*. Concord, N.H., 1834.

Whitton, Mary O. *These Were the Women:1776–1860*. New York, 1954.

Wickersham, James P. *History of Education in Pennsylvania*. Lancaster, Pa., 1886.

Wickes, Stephen. *History of Maryland and New Jersey*. Newark, N.J., 1879.

Wiles, Alice M. "Susannah Rohrer Muller and Her Ancestry." *Lancaster County (Pa.) Hist. Soc. Publs*. Vol. 14, No. 5 (1937).

Williams, John R. *Philip Vickers Fithian, Journal and Letters: 1767–1774*. Princeton, N.J., 1900.

Williamson, W.D. *History of Maine*. 2 vols. 1839.

Willis, Eola. "Henrietta Johnston" *Antiquarian*. 11: 46–48 (1929).

Winship, George P. *The Cambridge Press*. Philadelphia, 1945.

Winsor, Justin, ed. *Memorial History of Boston*. 4 vols. Boston, 1881.

Winterbotham, William. *An Historical, Geographical, Commercial and Philosophical View of American United States*. London, 1795.

Winterich, John T. *Early American Books*. Boston, 1935.

Winthrop, John. *History of New England: 1630–1649*. 2 vols. Boston, 1853.

Woodbury, George. *The Great Days of Piracy*. New York, 1951.

Woods, H.E. *History of Brookline*. Boston, 1874.

Woody, Thomas. *A History of Women's Education in the United States*. 2 vols. New York, 1929.

Worth, Henry B. "Nantucket Lands and Landowners." *Nantucket Hist. Assoc. Bull.* 2: 75–76, 306 (1901).

Wright, Louis B. *The Atlantic Frontier, Colonial American Civilization: 1607–1763*. New York, 1947.

Wright, Richardson. *Hawkers and Walkers*. Philadelphia, 1927.

Wright, T.G. *Literary Culture in Early New England*. New Haven, Conn., 1920.

Wroth, Lawrence C. *History of Printing in Colonial Maryland*. Baltimore, Md., 1922.

Wylie, J.C. "Mrs. Washington's Book of Cookery." *P.M.H.B.* 27: 436–440 (1903).

Yale Memorabilia Colls. Yale University Library, Hartford, Conn.

NEWSPAPERS, MAGAZINES AND HISTORICAL COLLECTIONS.

Connecticut Courant.
Essex Institute Historical Collections.
Johns Hopkins Hospital Bulletin.
Lower Norfolk County (Va.) Antiquary.
Maine Historical Society Collections.
Maryland Historical Magazine.
Massachusetts Historical Society Collections and Proceedings.
New England Historical and Genealogical Register.
New York Gazette.
New York Historical Society Collections.
Pennsylvania Gazette.
Pennsylvania Magazine of History and Biography.
South Carolina Gazette.
South Carolina Historical Magazine.
Virginia Gazette.
Virginia Magazine of History and Biography.
William and Mary Quarterly.
Worcester Society of Antiquity Bulletin.

Index

641

DATE DUE